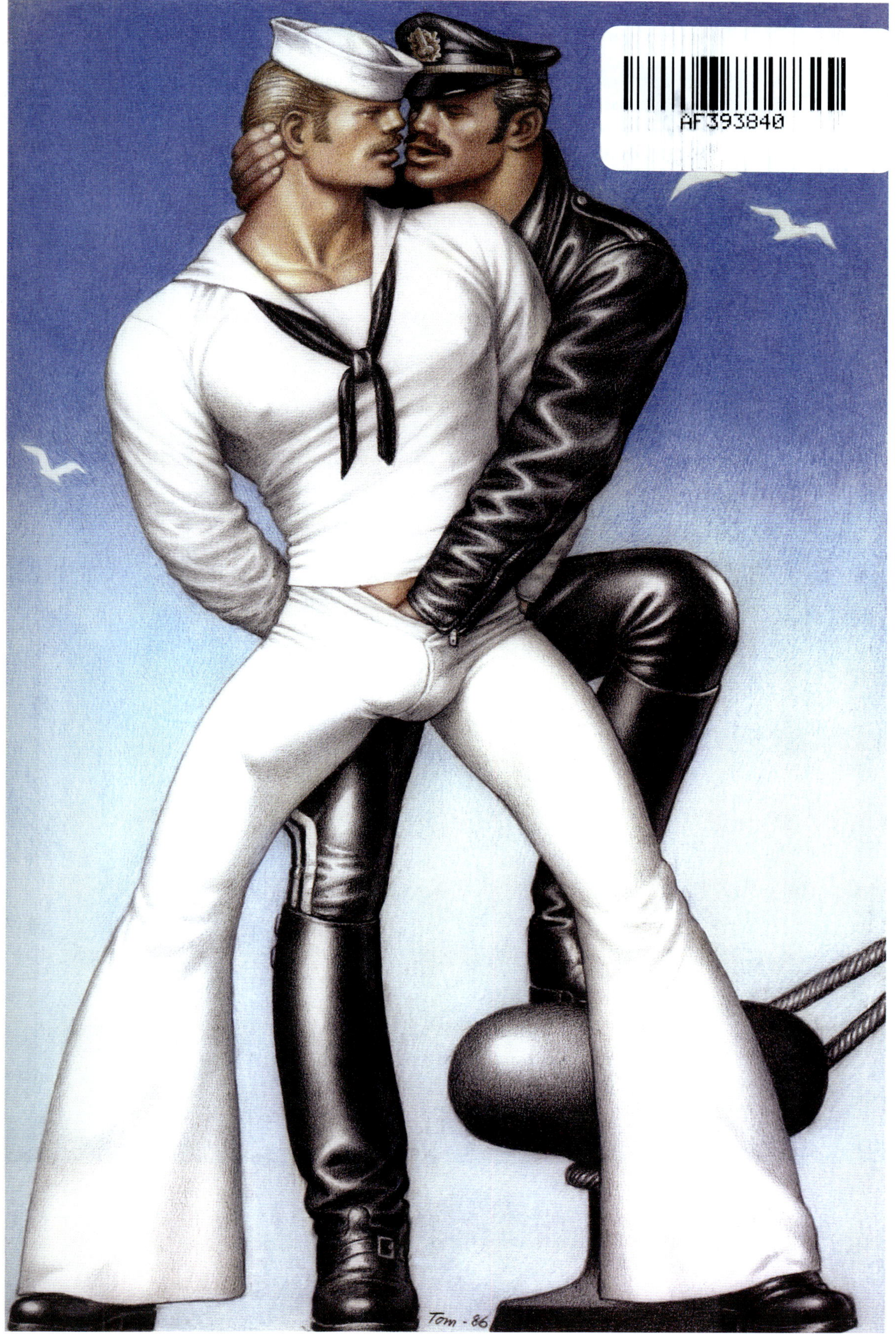
Tom -86

Mein schwules Auge • My Gay Eye 14/15.   mygayeye.com • info@mygayeye.com

Die Herausgeber danken allen, die mit Text oder Bild zu diesem Buch beigetragen haben.
The editors wish to thank all the artists and writers who contributed to this book.
Cover: Josh Paul Thomas   p. 1: Tom of Finland   p. 2: Carr Galen   Frontispiz: Marc DeBauch   p. 400: Rick Castro
Für die Unterstützung bei den Übersetzungen danken wir • *We wish to thank the translators for their support:* Jim
Baker, Florian Hetz, Grant Nichols, Florian Rogge, Sunita Sukhana, Maja Überle Pfaff and Simon Williams.

Tom of Finland®
F O U N D A T I O N

TomOfFinlandFoundation.org   Gallery representation for the work of Tom of Finland
Post Office Box 26658   David Kordansky Gallery
Los Angeles, California 90026   5130 West Egdewood Place
USA   Los Angeles, California 90019
+1 213 250 1685   USA

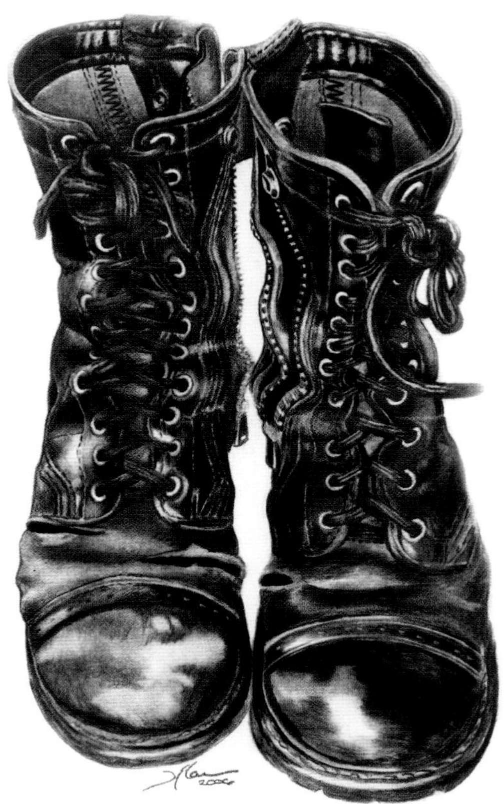

2. Auflage 2022
© Konkursbuch Verlag Claudia Gehrke 2018. All rights reserved
Images © the artists. Tom of Finland images © Tom of Finland Foundation. Texts © the authors
PF 1621 – D-72006 Tübingen , Tel. +49 (0) 7071-66551 und +49 (0) 172-7233958
E-Mail: gehrke@konkursbuch.com – konkursbuch.de – facebook: konkursbuch.verlag
· Gestaltung / *design*: Die Herausgeber / *the editors*. Grafische Konzeption: Sven Barletta

ISBN 978-3-88769-944-4

Rinaldo Hopf & Axel Schock

Mein schwules Auge
My Gay Eye

Tom of Finland Foundation Special

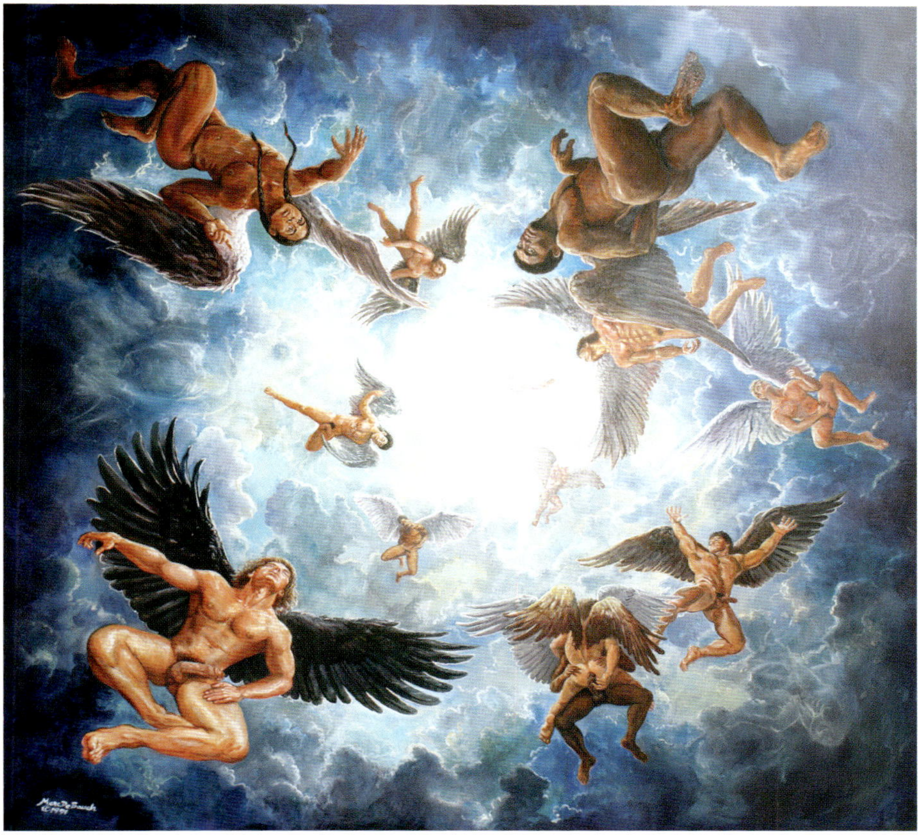

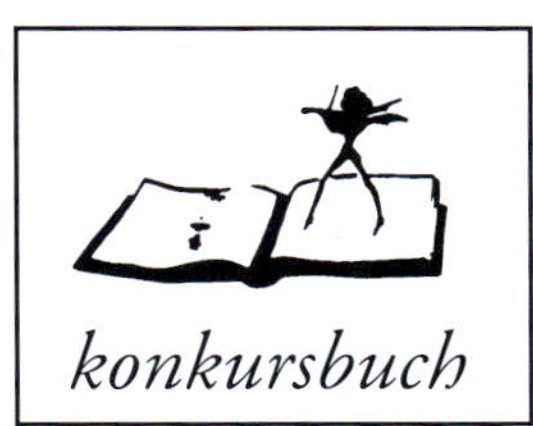

MARC DeBAUCH
Ceiling Mural / Deckengemälde in TOM House

konkursbuch

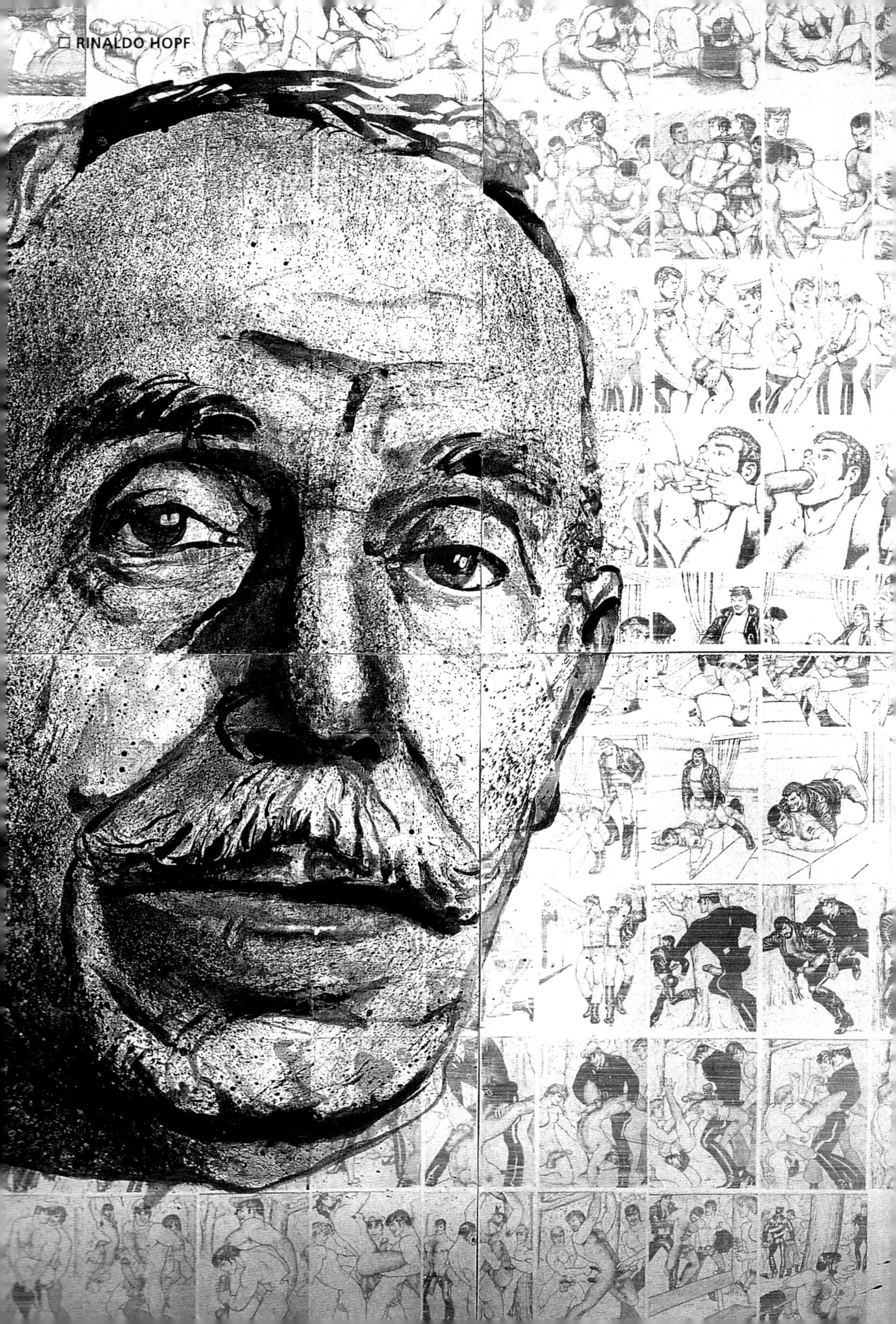
RINALDO HOPF

Vorwort • Foreword

Ganz gleich, ob sie in Polizei- und Matrosen-
uniformen, in Lederkluft oder im Bikerdress
stecken, diese Männer sind allesamt so gut
bestückt und ihre Hintern so kugelrund, dass
sich die Hosen überdeutlich wölben.
Alles an diesen Männern ist übergroß – die
Schwänze, die Muskeln, ihre Potenz und
sexuelle Lust, ja selbst das Grinsen in ihren
zufriedenen Gesichtern.
Vielleicht gerade deshalb haben diese Zeichnungen mittlerweile
Generationen schwuler
Männer auf der ganzen
Welt nicht nur in jeder
Hinsicht angeregt,
sondern sind auch bild-
hafter Ausdruck ihrer
sexuellen Befreiung
geworden.
Welche weit darüber-
hinausgehende Bedeu-
tung diese ungehemmt
von Tom of Finland aufs
Papier gebrachten por-
nografischen Phantasien
über die Jahrzehnte er-
langt haben, zeigte sich
2014, als die Finnische
Post auf Anregung der
Foundation Briefmarken
mit Motiven des 1991
verstorbenen Künstlers
herausbrachte. Jene
Bilder, die früher auf
versteckten Wegen vervielfältigt, vertrieben
und unter Pseudonym veröffentlicht werden
mussten, können nun unbekümmert auf
Briefumschläge geklebt werden.
Keine anderen Postwertzeichen des Heimat-
landes von Touko Laaksonen alias Tom of
Finland hatte ein solches internationales Echo
ausgelöst. Noch vor der Veröffentlichung
lagen Bestellungen aus circa 180 Ländern vor.

Das Werk Tom of Finlands hat längst nicht nur
Kultstatus innerhalb der weltumspannenden
schwulen Community, sondern ist Teil der
Popkultur und Kunstgeschichte geworden.
Entscheidend dazu beigetragen hat Tom of

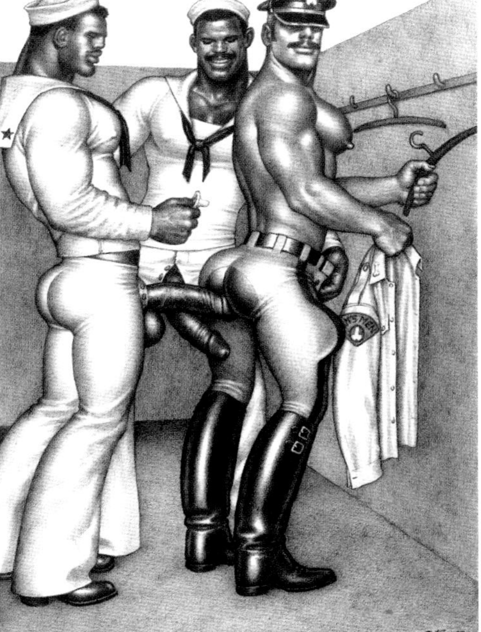

No matter whether they are in police and
sailor uniforms, in leather or in biker gear,
these men are all so well equipped and their
butts are so round that their trousers bulge
suggestively.
Everything about these men is oversized –
the muscles, their potency and their sexual
desire, even the grin on their contented
faces.
Perhaps that is why these drawings have not
only inspired gene-
rations of queer folk
around the world in
every way, but have
also become a pictori-
al expression of their
sexual liberation.
The far-reaching signi-
ficance of these unres-
trained pornographic
fantasies put on paper
by Tom of Finland
over the decades was
demonstrated in 2014,
when the Finnish Post,
initiated by Tom of
Finland Foundation
released stamps with
images of artwork by
the artist, who died in
1991. Those drawings,
which used to be
reproduced in secret,
distributed and pu-
blished under a pseudonym, are now being
affixed to envelopes.
No other postage stamps from Tom of
Finland's homeland had caused such an
international echo. Even before the publication, orders from around 180 countries were
made.

The work of Tom of Finland has not only
cult status within the global gay community,
but has become part of pop culture and art
history.
Tom's last partner, Durk Dehner, also his
manager, estate administrator and cofounder of Tom of Finland Foundation in Los

Finlands letzter Lebensgefährte Durk Dehner, zugleich auch sein Manager, Nachlassverwalter und gemeinsam mit ihm Gründer der Tom of Finland Foundation in Los Angeles.

Tom of Finland und seine Kunst, aber auch deren Einfluss auf schwule Künstler nachfolgender Generationen sowie die Arbeit der Stiftung stehen im Mittelpunkt dieses Sonderbandes des Jahrbuchs *Mein schwules Auge*, das erstmals zweisprachig erscheint.

Die Tom of Finland Foundation ermöglichte uns, aus ihren umfangreichen Beständen bislang unveröffentlichte Arbeiten Toms vorzustellen; darunter auch einige Vorlagen und Skizzen, anhand derer sich beispielhaft sein Arbeitsverfahren nachvollziehen lässt. (S. 33). Wenig bekannt ist zudem, wie viele verschiedene Techniken Tom of Finland beherrschte (S. 19).

Die Foundation bewahrt allerdings nicht nur Tom of Finlands eigenes Werk, sondern auch die wahrscheinlich größte Sammlung schwuler Kunst des 20. und 21. Jahrhunderts. Wir sind stolz darauf, in diesem Band erstmals einen Querschnitt daraus präsentieren zu können (S. 91).

Zu den selbstgesetzten Aufgaben der Foundation zählt nicht zuletzt auch die Förderung zeitgenössischer schwuler Künstler. Ab Seite 203 zeigen wir deshalb einen kleinen Einblick in deren vielfältige Aktivitäten und stellen Arbeiten von Fotografen, Malern und Zeichnern vor, die im ehemaligen Wohnhaus von Tom of Finland in Los Angeles als Artists in Residence zu Gast waren oder durch Ausstellungen und andere Stiftungsprogramme gefördert wurden.

Viele Künstler haben sich vom Werk Tom of Finlands inspirieren lassen, wie die Arbeiten u.a. von G.B. Jones und Josh Paul Thomas zeigen, der unser Cover-Motiv fotografiert hat. Und auch Literaten huldigen dem Großmeister der schwulen Kunst. Für diesen Band haben wir vier Schriftsteller gebeten, sich von einer seiner Zeichnungen zu einer Kurzgeschichte anregen zu lassen (S. 36).

Wir danken allen Autoren und Künstlern, die durch ihre Text- und Bildbeiträge diesen Sonderband von *Mein schwules Auge* bereichert haben – und insbesondere der Tom of Finland Foundation, ohne die das Buch in dieser Form nicht möglich gewesen wäre.

Rinaldo Hopf & Axel Schock
Berlin, im Februar 2018

Angeles, has made a decisive contribution to setting the legacy of Tom of Finland into motion.

Tom of Finland, his art and his influence on gay artists of subsequent generations, as well as the work purpose of Tom of Finland Foundation, are the focus of this special volume of *My Gay Eye*, which appears for the first time in both German and English.

Tom of Finland Foundation enabled us in presenting some of Tom's previously unpublished works from his extensive archive; including preliminaries and sketches to illustrate his work process (p. 33) and examples of the many techniques he mastered. (p. 19)

Twentyseven years since Tom's passing the Foundation not only preserves his own work, but also one of the largest collections of 20th and 21st century gay art. We are proud to present a cross-section of this for the first time. (p. 91)

A self-defined purpose of the Foundation is the promotion of contemporary gay artists. Starting on page 203, we offer an insight into their diverse activities and present works by photographers, painters, illustrators and sketch artists, guests in the former home of Tom of Finland in Los Angeles as artists in residence or were supported by exhibitions and other programs.

Many artists have been inspired by Tom of Finland, such as G. B. Jones and Josh Paul Thomas (whose photograph appears on our front cover). Literary figures pay homage to the "grand master of gay art". For this volume, we asked four writers to take inspiration from one of his drawings for a short story. (p. 36)

We thank all authors and artists who have enriched this special volume of *My Gay Eye* with their text and picture contributions – and in particular the Tom of Finland Foundation, without whom this special book in this form would not have been possible.

Rinaldo Hopf & Axel Schock
Berlin, February 2018

Translation: Simon Williams

Preface • Grußwort

It was our collective destiny that Tom and I met and I became his muse, friend, partner in business, his confident, lover, pimp, and all-round protector of the realm. I have been a proud custodian of Tom's legacy for over 30 years. When Tom came to America, and started staying at 1421 Laveta Terrace, he was able to fully experience the level of success he had achieved in empowering us all with our right to be proud and free in being just who we are.
It was also his time to let go and enjoy all that California and its lifestyle offered him. It wasn't until Tom came to Los Angeles, and this house, with its environment of free expression, that he was able to live fully what he had been drawing on paper.

Welcome to this special edition of *My Gay Eye* dedicated to a wider understanding of what is the Tom of Finland Foundation, its collections, programs and over purpose for its presence in our culture– according to our motto: To educate the value of erotic art through protecting, preserving and promoting.

Durk Dehner, President & Cofounder
Tom of Finland Foundation

Es war unser gemeinsames Schicksal, dass Tom und ich uns trafen und ich seine Muse, sein Freund, Geschäftspartner, Vertrauter, Geliebter, Zuhälter und Hüter seiner Schätze wurde. Seit über 30 Jahren bin ich ein stolzer Verwalter von Toms Vermächtnis. Als Tom nach Amerika kam und in unser Haus 1421 Laveta Terrace einzog, konnte er endlich den Erfolg genießen, den er damit erreicht hatte, uns alle zu befähigen, stolz und frei und wir selbst zu sein. Es war auch der richtige Zeitpunkt, loszulassen und alles zu genießen, was Kalifornien ihm zu bieten hatte. Erst als Tom nach Los Angeles und in dieses Haus mit seinem freien Lebensstil kam, konnte er alles, was er gezeichnet hatte, auch tatsächlich leben.

Willkommen zu dieser Sonderausgabe von *Mein schwules Auge*, die ein größeres Verständnis dafür schaffen möchte, was die Tom of Finland Foundation ist, ihre Sammlung, Programme und ihre Zielsetzung – gemäß unserem Motto: den Stellenwert erotischer Kunst aufzuzeigen, indem wir sie schützen, bewahren und fördern.

Durk Dehner, Präsident und Mitbegründer
der Tom of Finland Foundation

Übersetzung: Rinaldo Hopf

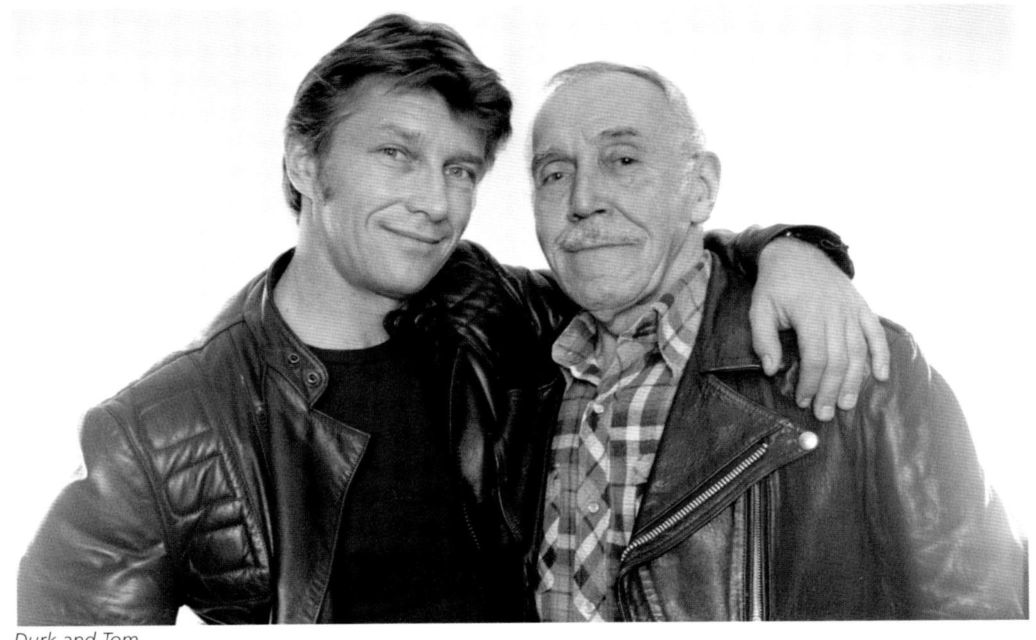

Durk and Tom

DURK DEHNER

The Perfectionist • Der Perfektionist

From Touko Laaksonen to Tom of Finland. The most important milestones in his artistic and personal development • Von Touko Laaksonen zu Tom of Finland. Die wichtigsten Stationen seiner künstlerischen und persönlichen Entwicklung

The young Finn, Touko Laaksonen, was born with a natural inclination for thriving on challenges. He was right there, ready to learn, when his parents gave him the opportunity to play the piano. His nephews recalled watching him listen to a melody on the radio and then sitting right down at the piano and playing it after only hearing it once. He liked to push himself to excel, as with his ability in drawing and painting. This nature was wide spread as he possessed the nerve to just approach men he was attracted to if he sensed they were of the same *inclination* as him. He had a leather motocross racing suit made for himself and then went to the race track and hung out with the competition motorcyclists in the inside track area, without any concerns that he didn't even *own* a motorcycle. He wanted to get up close to those guys so he determined that this was the best way to do it.

He always accepted projects offered to, or requested of him. He would do his upmost to do them at the highest level that was possible, always striving to do just a bit better each time. When he was only in his early 20s, he entered officer training for the Finnish Army. He took this opportunity in challenging himself into becoming the best he could, but he remained humble about both his merits and status. He was given charge over men for whom he did everything within his power to provide the training that would develop them into the strongest force possible to defend their homeland against the Russians. It was recounted that all of his men liked him very much, as he treated them fairly and did not put himself above them as so many other officers did. When Lieutenant Laaksonen gave the orders, his men obeyed them, for they respected and trusted him.

Den jungen Finnen Touko Laaksonen zeichnete von Kindheit an aus, dass er erst durch Herausforderungen zur vollen Entfaltung kam. So war er sofort bereit, Klavierspielen zu lernen, als seine Eltern ihm die Gelegenheit dazu gaben. Seine Neffen erinnern sich, dass er eine Melodie im Radio hörte, sich dann direkt ans Klavier setzte und sie nachspielte – obwohl er sie nur ein einziges Mal gehört hatte. Er liebte es, sich selbst zu übertreffen – das galt auch beim Zeichnen und Malen. Sein Naturell ermöglichte es ihm genauso, Männer direkt anzusprechen, zu denen er sich hingezogen fühlte und wenn er spürte, dass sie dieselbe Neigung hatten wie er. Er ließ sich einen Motocross-Leder-Rennanzug maßschneidern, ging auf die Rennstrecke und hielt sich im inneren Bereich bei den Motorradfahrern auf, ohne sich irgendwelche Gedanken darüber zu machen, dass er selbst kein Motorrad besaß. Er wollte diesen Männern nahe sein, und fand, dass das so am einfachsten ging.

Grundsätzlich nahm er alle Projekte an, die ihm angeboten oder von ihm verlangt wurden. Er gab sein Bestes, um sie so gut wie irgend möglich zu erledigen, und war immer bestrebt, jedes Mal noch ein bisschen besser zu werden. Mit Anfang zwanzig begann er eine Offiziersausbildung in der finnischen Armee. Er nutzte die Chance, so gut zu werden wie möglich, blieb dabei aber bescheiden, sowohl, was seine Verdienste als auch seinen Status betraf. Er hatte die Verantwortung für eine Gruppe von Soldaten, für die er alles in seiner Macht Stehende tat, sie so auszubilden, dass sie ihr Heimatland bestmöglich verteidigen konnten. Es wird erzählt, dass alle seine Männer ihn sehr mochten, da er sie fair behandelte und sich nicht wie viele andere Offiziere über sie stellte. Wenn Leutnant Laaksonen Befehle gab, gehorchten seine Männer, weil sie ihn respektierten und ihm vertrauten.

Tom has most likely included himself here, as the voyeur, ca. 1946 • Vermutlich porträtierte Tom sich auf diesem Bild selbst, als der Voyeur

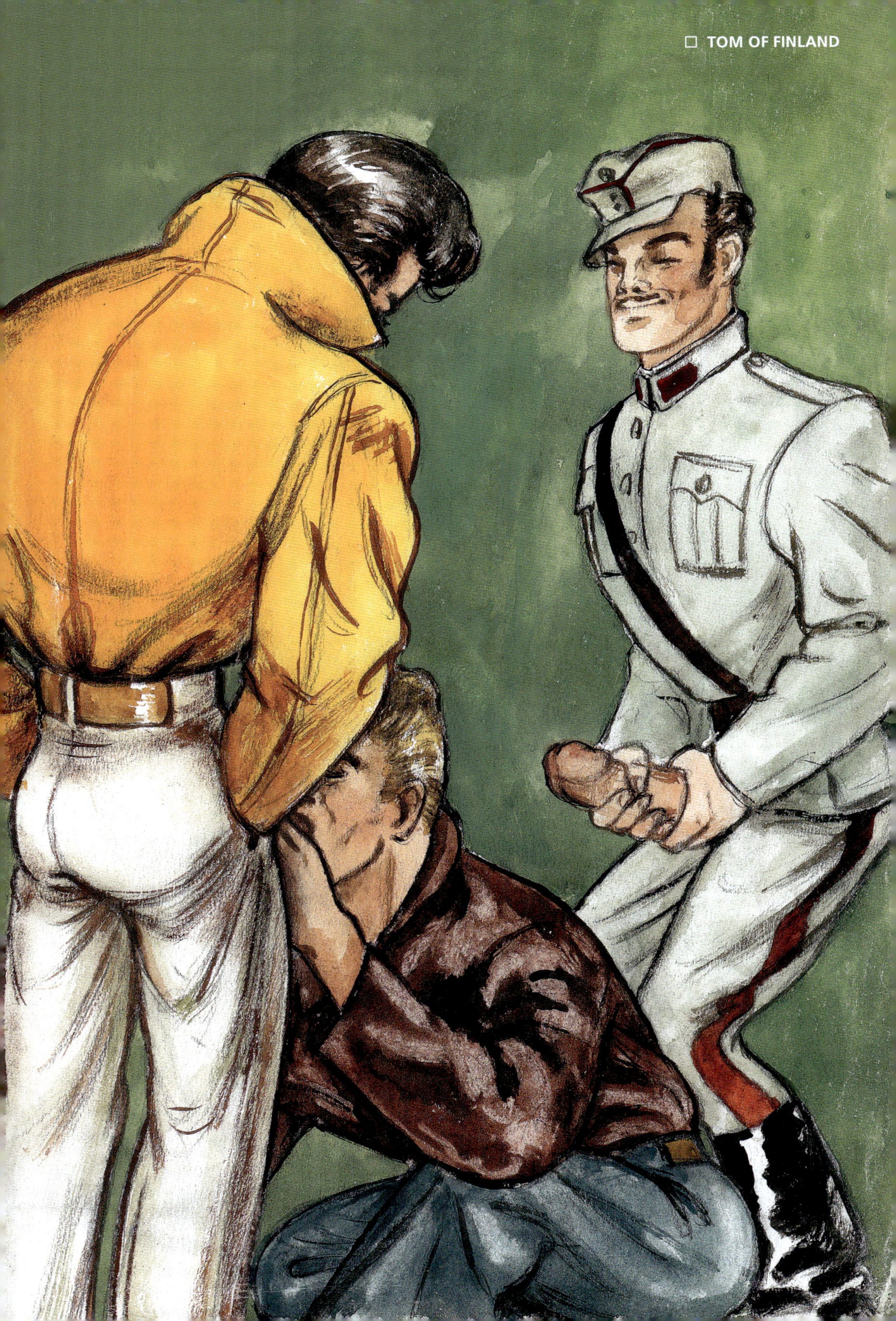
☐ TOM OF FINLAND

In life there are usually a few experiences we have that end up shaping our future and destiny. With Touko, his first infatuation was with a German officer. They met in the park cruising after dark and there was an immediate connection between them, both having a deep appreciation for boots, uniforms and the men who wore them. They had gratifying sex with each other, and lingered to have a cigarette and exchange bits of information on who they were and what they wanted in life. This went on for three nights in a row, but on the forth night the German pilot was a no show, as was the case on the fifth night. Touko then took it upon himself to go to the central office and examine the list of soldiers that had been killed or went missing in action. His

In jedem Leben gibt es in der Regel ein paar Schlüsselerlebnisse, die entscheidend unsere Zukunft und unser Schicksal prägen. Für Touko war es seine erste Liebe – zu einem deutschen Offizier. Sie trafen sich beim nächtlichen Cruisen im Park und hatten sofort eine intensive Verbindung. Beide hatten eine erotische Affinität zu Stiefeln, Uniformen und zu den Männern, die sie trugen. Sie hatten guten Sex, rauchten danach eine Zigarette und tauschten sich darüber aus, wer sie waren und was sie im Leben vorhatten. Das ging drei Nächte so, aber am vierten Abend tauchte der deutsche Pilot nicht mehr auf, und auch am fünften nicht. Touko ging daraufhin zur Zentrale und ließ sich die Liste der Soldaten zeigen, die entweder getötet oder aber verschwunden waren. Der Name seines Stuka-

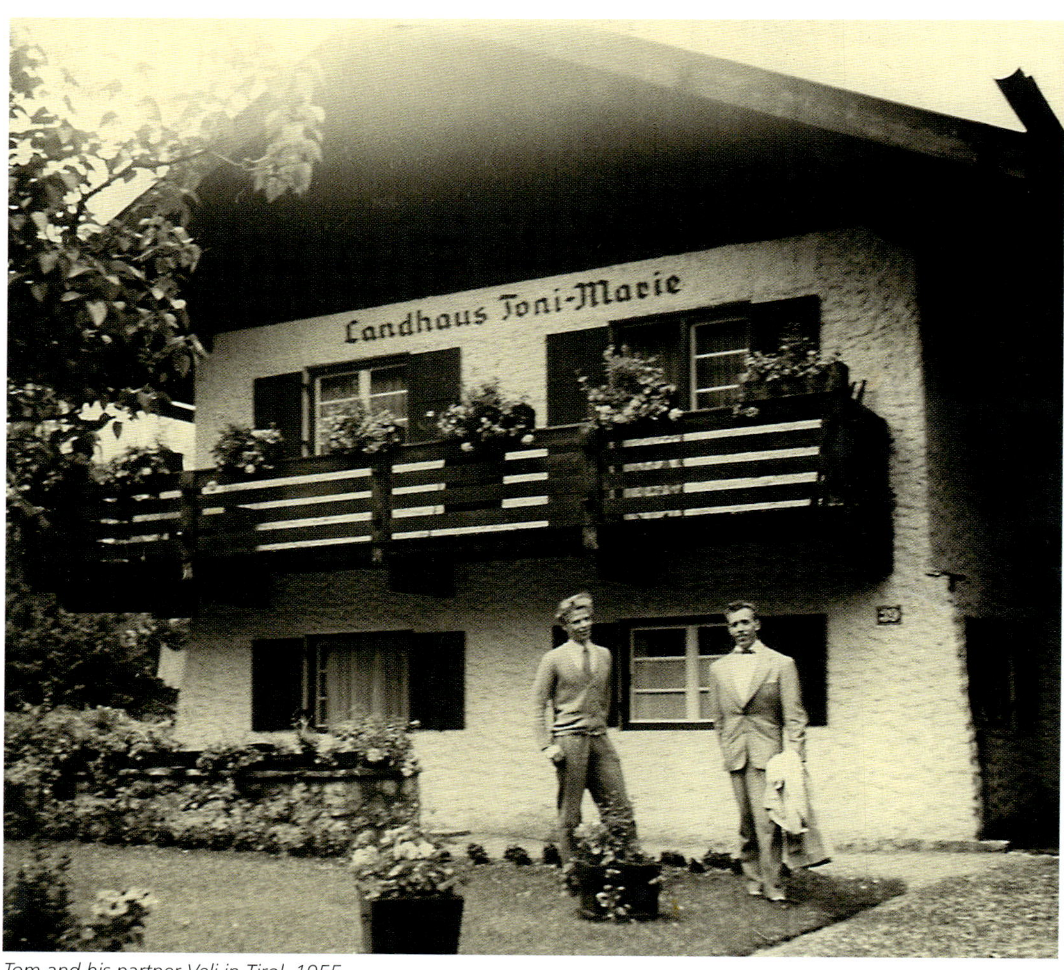

Tom and his partner Veli in Tirol, 1955

Stuka officer's name was there, apparently having been shot down over enemy territory. It was that man, in his amazing form fitting uniform, that was indelibly etched into Tom's psyche. That it was him that he was drawing over and over again. Passion, and love, have no borders.

Tom was later criticized for drawing the German uniform, as some felt it was not "politically correct" considering what they represent. Tom's response was that he was fetishizing the uniform, enjoying it sexually and that men looked so good in that uniform, he couldn't help himself. He never went along with the politics nor the horrific crimes the Nazis had committed. It seemed it did not make any difference that his first love happened to wear that uniform and it was the Germans who came to Finland's aid when they were being threatened by Russia.

Tears would well up in Tom's eyes when he would, only on very rare occasions, recount the experience with a Russian paratrooper. He spotted him coming down in the night sky. He did not know if he was one of several, or a lone scout sent ahead to determine where the Finnish soldiers were waiting within the forest. Touko, the soldier, knew he had no choice but to see if he could prevent any radio information getting back to Russian headquarters. Silence was essential. Without any further thinking, he pulled out his knife and ran up to the paratrooper just as he was landing and pushed the knife into his back all the way to the handle. He went down and Touko did not waste one minute and ran back to camp where radio messages were then sent informing of Russian scouts in the area. Early the next morning he returned to the body to ID the soldier. He took the time to process the traumatic incident, as it was the first time he had ever stabbed anyone. He turned the body over, and seeing the young man's face, he immediately started to cry and the tears turned to deep sobs. To just think that he, the one who loved and adored the male of our species beyond anything else, had actually destroyed the most beautiful man he had ever seen.

Offiziers war dabei, offenbar war er über feindlichem Territorium abgeschossen worden. Es war dieser Mann in seiner wie angegossen sitzenden Uniform, der unauslöschlich in Toms Seele eingebrannt war. Er war es, den er immer und immer wieder zeichnete. Liebe und Leidenschaft kennen keine Grenzen.

Tom wurde später dafür kritisiert, dass er deutsche Uniformen zeichnete. Einige Rezipienten befanden, diese Uniformen zu zeichnen sei nicht „politisch korrekt", wenn man bedenke, was sie repräsentieren. Toms Antwort war, dass für ihn die Uniform ein sexueller Fetisch sei und dass Männer in Uniform einfach sehr gut aussahen. Er äußerte sich nie zur Politik und zu den schrecklichen Verbrechen der Nazis. Für ihn machte es keinen Unterschied, dass seine erste Liebe zufällig diese Uniform trug. Die Deutschen waren Finnland zu Hilfe gekommen, als das Land von Russland bedroht wurde.

Tom hatte jedes Mal Tränen in den Augen, wenn er, was sehr selten vorkam, von seiner Begegnung mit einem russischen Fallschirmjäger erzählte. Er sah ihn am Nachthimmel herunterkommen. Er wusste nicht, ob er einer von mehreren war oder ein einsamer Kundschafter, der vorausgesandt worden war, um herauszufinden, wo die finnischen Soldaten im Wald warteten. Touko, der Soldat, wusste, dass er keine andere Wahl hatte, als zu verhindern, dass Funksprüche in das russische Hauptquartier gelangten. Er musste sich völlig still verhalten. Ohne zu überlegen, zückte er sein Messer, rannte zu dem Fallschirmjäger, als dieser landete, und stieß ihm das Messer bis zum Heft in den Rücken. Der Mann ging zu Boden und Touko rannte augenblicklich zurück zum Lager, wo bereits Meldungen eingegangen waren, dass russische Späher in der Gegend gesichtet worden waren. Früh am nächsten Morgen kehrte er zu dem Toten zurück, um ihn zu identifizieren. Er nahm sich Zeit, den traumatischen Zwischenfall zu verarbeiten; es war das erste Mal, dass er jemanden erstochen hatte. Er drehte den Körper auf den Rücken. Als er das Gesicht des jungen Mannes sah, brach er in Tränen aus, in heftiges Schluchzen. Unfassbar, dass er, der Männer über alles liebte und verehrte, den schönsten Mann, den er je gesehen hatte, getötet hatte!

Leaving the military after the war, the thought never left his head that he must do something good with his life, he decided he would focus on seeing if he could improve the lives of his fellow Homosexuals: To raise their self esteem and for them to have more happiness, love and beauty in their lives. Tom knew that they were a gift from Mother Nature, full, whole and complete.

In his 60s, having realized that he had actually succeeded in his ambition, he finally, verbally acknowledged that he did not sit around and think about this goal, but that it had been there deep within him from the very start. Yes, he was going to have his men happy, well adjusted, and confident of being proud of who they were by thoroughly enjoying sex with other men.

In Tom's post war era, he realized he had to improve his abilities to draw and paint to be able to communicate his messages to his brothers all over the world. At that time he was still using words within his storytelling, and of course it they were Finnish. He was going to have to get good enough that words were not necessary – it had to be communicated with the looks, the gestures, body language. He increased the hours he devoted to drawing up to six or seven. This meant he was working before heading off to his job and then after coming home before bed. He had no difficulty devoting himself to art; it was his passion.

Tom was of the attitude that if anything was worth doing, it was worth doing at the best level you could achieve. As a result, he perfected his anatomical rendering and the depiction of the look *and feel* of leather. He did *Leather Duo* in 1963, a work that is as popular today as it was when he drew it.

Tom gradually built a reference collection of over 650 pages maintained in three-ring binders. They covered every angle and position of the body, in and

Als er nach Kriegsende das Militär verließ, beschloss er, etwas Gutes aus seinem Leben zu machen und sich vor allem dafür einzusetzen, das Leben seiner homosexuellen Mitmenschen leichter zu machen. Er wollte ihr Selbstwertgefühl stärken, dass ihr Leben mit mehr Glück, Liebe und Schönheit erfüllt würde. Für Tom waren schwule Männer ein Geschenk von „Mutter Natur", und zwar uneingeschränkt.

In seinen 60ern erkannte er, dass er seine Ambitionen tatsächlich hatte verwirklichen können, nicht bloß herumgesessen und über dieses Ziel nachgedacht hatte, sondern es bereits von Anfang an tief in ihm steckte. Ja, er würde seine Männer glücklich darstellen, indem sie den Sex mit anderen Männern in vollen Zügen genossen, mit beiden Beinen im Leben stehend und zuversichtlich und stolz auf das, was sie waren.

In der Nachkriegszeit realisierte er, dass er seine zeichnerischen und malerischen Fähigkeiten verbessern musste, um seinen Brüdern auf der ganzen Welt seine Botschaft mitteilen zu können. Zu dieser Zeit verwendete er noch Text in seinen Bildgeschichten, natürlich auf Finnisch. Er wollte so gut werden, dass Worte nicht mehr nötig waren – alles musste mit Blicken, Gesten und durch Körpersprache kommuniziert werden. Seine Zeit widmete er mehr und mehr der künstlerischen Arbeit, meistens sechs bis sieben Stunden täglich. Dies bedeutete, dass er zeichnete, bevor er zu seinem Brotjob ging, und nach Feierabend wieder am Zeichentisch saß, bis es Zeit war, zu Bett zu gehen. Er hatte kein Problem damit, sich ganz auf die Kunst zu konzentrieren, sie war seine Leidenschaft.

Tom war der Ansicht, dass man alles bestmöglich tun müsse. Folglich perfektionierte er seine anatomischen Kenntnisse und auch die künstlerische Darstellung von Leder, sowohl bezogen auf die Optik wie auch auf dessen Textur. 1963 entstand *Leather Duo*, ein Werk, das heute noch genauso beliebt ist wie zur Zeit seiner Entstehung.

Tom baute über die Jahre eine Vorlagensammlung von über 650 Blättern auf, die er in Ringbüchern ablegte. Die Sammlung umfasst jede Stelle und jede Stellung des Körpers, mal mit, mal ohne Uniform, auch jede Menge Lederbiker und Gesichter. Er schnitt diese Bilder aus Bodybuilding-

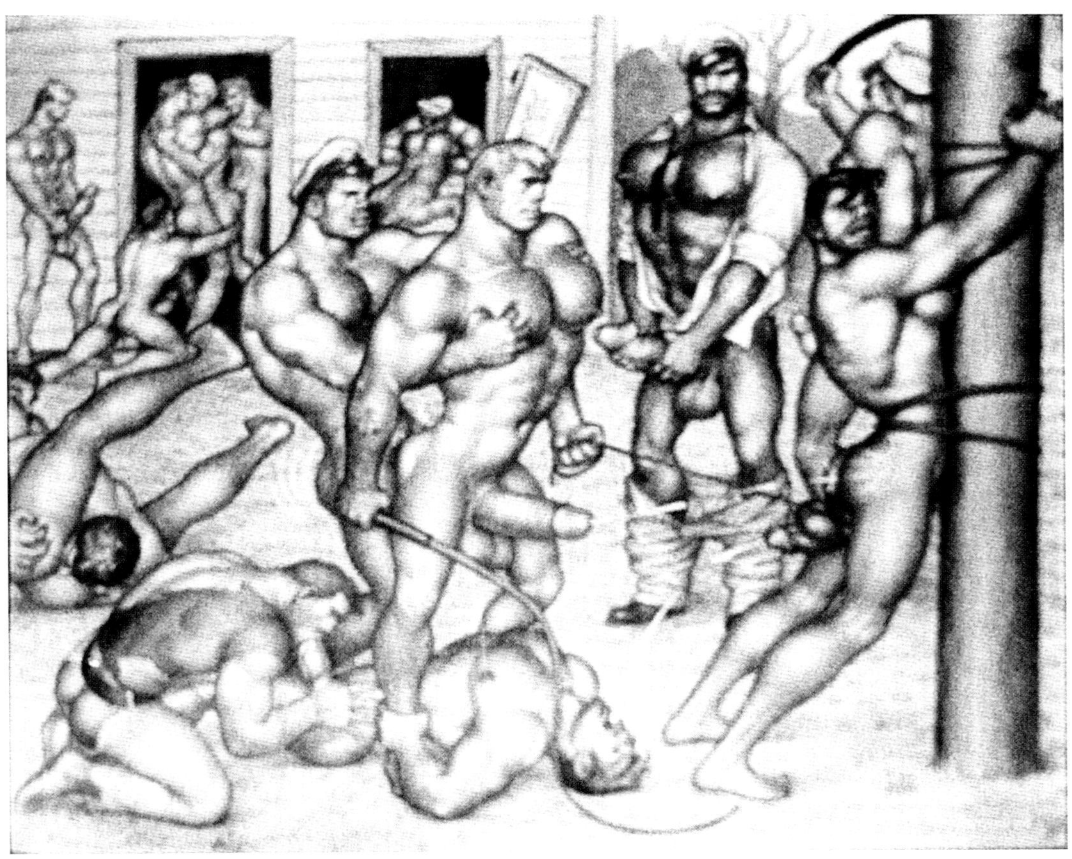

Here is an example of a drawing that Tom did not photograph well. When you compare it to works that were being done for the American market, it's revealing just how advanced Tom of Finland was in 1958.
.

Auch wenn Tom die hier abgebildete Zeichnung nicht gut abfotografiert hat, so zeigt dieses Beispiel recht gut – zumal im Vergleich zu den Arbeiten für den amerikanischen Markt – wie weit Tom of Finland seinen Stil bereits 1958 entwickelt hatte.

out of uniforms, leather bikers, faces. He gathered this resource material from male physique magazines, photo prints he received from studios and mainstream publications of the day. He soon moved into photographing his own models, developing the film and making photo prints. He would cut out all of these images and paste them artistically on sheets of paper, collage style, which he found very pleasing to his eye.

The use a camera was essential for Tom, for to mail his friends and fans examples of his drawings he had to reproduce

Magazinen aus, ließ sich Fotoabzüge von Studios schicken und durchforstete Zeitschriften aller Art. Bald fing er an, Modelle zu fotografieren, die Filme selbst zu entwickeln und Abzüge zu machen. Er schnitt die Bilder aus und ordnete sie zu Collagen, ganz so, wie es ihm am besten gefiel.

Die Arbeit mit der Kamera war für Tom sehr wichtig. Um seinen Freunden und Fans Beispiele seiner Zeichnungen schicken zu können, musste er sie reproduzieren. Er konnte sie unmöglich in den Fotoladen seines Dorfes bringen! Nein, denn seine Arbeiten hätten als Schmutzliteratur gegolten, für die Männer ins

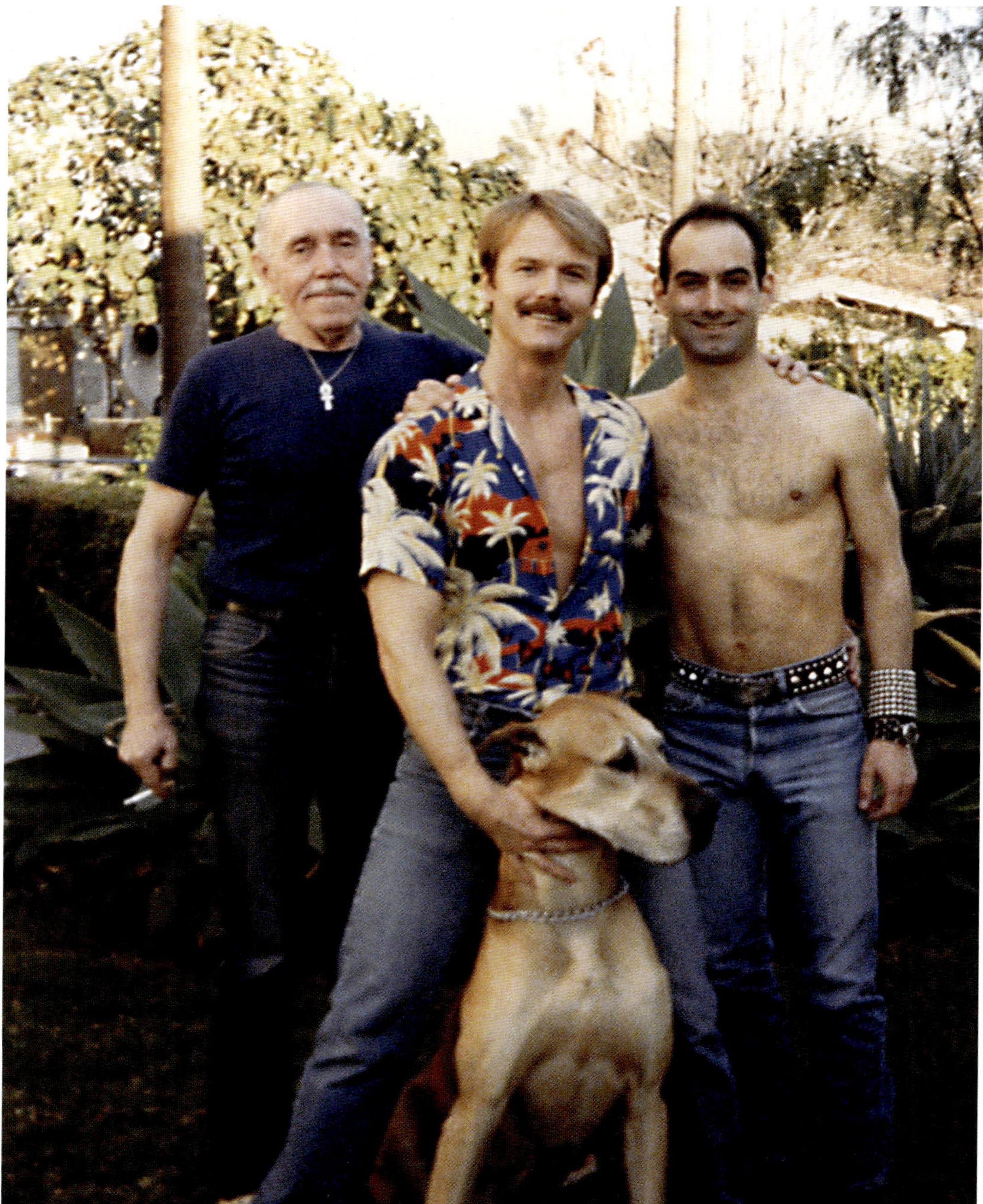

Tom, Luke, Hank and Duke, Los Angeles, ca. 1986

them. There was no possibility of taking them into the village photo shop! No, this was the smut that they put men in jail for. So, in a closet in his apartment he developed film, made prints and started a cottage mail order business. Everything

Gefängnis wanderten. Also richtete er sich in einem Abstellraum in seiner Wohnung eine Dunkelkammer ein, entwickelte die Filme, machte Abzüge und startete einen kleinen Versandhandel. Alles musste in einen Umschlag in der Größe von Luftpostumschlägen passen (ungefähr 7,5 x

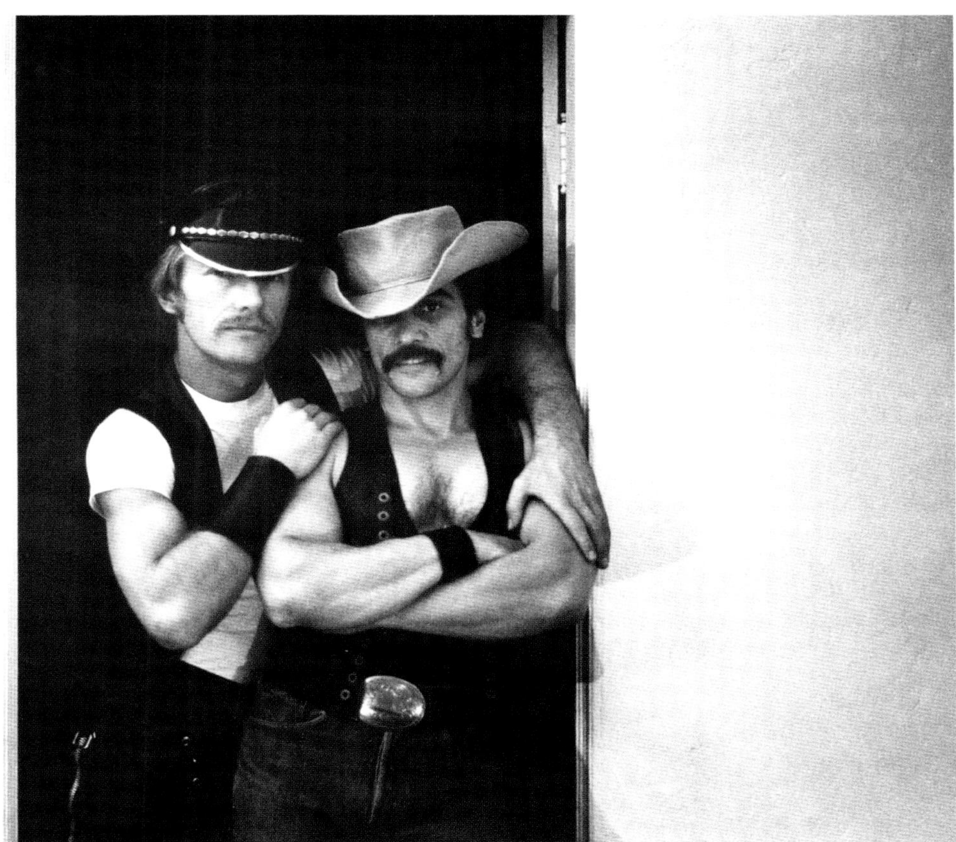

Durk and Domingo Orejudos aka Etienne, ca. 1979

had to fit inside an envelope the size of the original air mail envelops (approximately 3x5"). Anything larger would increase the chances of it being opened by postal authorities in Finland, or the receiving country, which could get his friends and fans into deep trouble. You would think that this would have made him reluctant to do this, but the drive to share his work was much stronger than the fear of him being apprehended. It was a cause, for he knew that he was right and the laws were wrong. He, and others in this business, were going to serve their fellow Homosexuals. Yes, it was a burgeoning movement: Gay liberation.

It is definitely worth noting that there were occurrences where Tom was swindled, robbed, lied to or betrayed. His first exhibition was at The Revolt Press Bookstore in Hamburg where all of his works

12,5 cm). Alles, was größer war, erhöhte die Gefahr, dass die Postbehörden in Finnland oder im Empfängerland die Sendungen öffneten, was seine Bewunderer und Fans in große Schwierigkeiten gebracht hätte. Man könnte meinen, dass ihn das alles davon abgehalten hätte, aber der Drang, seine Bilder zu verbreiten, war stärker als die Angst vor einer Festnahme. Er wusste, dass er im Recht war und die Gesetze falsch. Er und andere in diesem Gewerbe wollten für ihre Mithomosexuellen arbeiten. Dies war der Beginn der homosexuellen Befreiung.

Es muss leider erwähnt werden, dass Tom manchmal belogen, betrogen und ausgeraubt wurde. Seine allererste Ausstellung fand im Revolt Shop in Hamburg statt, wo alle seine Werke am Vorabend der Eröffnung gestohlen wurden, und zwar vom Manager. Er wurde auch von Robert Mapplethorpe betrogen, dessen Geschäftspartner (in ihrer gemeinsamen Galerie) weder den Erlös für die erfolgten Ver-

were stolen by the manager the night before the opening. He was lied to by Robert Mapplethorpe whose business partner in their gallery business withheld payment and did not return works – the entire fiasco lasted two years and Tom came away without a dozen drawings nor any compensation for them. Every time he was beaten down, he would swear to himself that that was it, he would give up. However, it would only take two to three days, and he could not keep himself away from the drawing table. It was his life's blood. He often said that when he would reach these terrible lows that this alter ego, he named Kake, would come to him and get him to lighten up , to once again get aroused over some idea or image of a man, and then he was off and drawing once again. He discovered very early that if a drawing had an arousing quality to it, and if he could keep himself in that state of mind, yes, often times with a hard on, he noticed that the finished work came out so much better than otherwise. His *stimulation* had heightened his ability to fine tune the nuisances of his works.

Tom was often labeled as a pornographer, which he did not mind at all, because he called his creations his "dirty little drawings". He respected his own work, he knew the quality, but he did not want to buy into the game of being pressured by the art world at the time. Everyone was seemingly fixated on manipulating artists. He also knew that if he could just keep his work reaching those young developing Homosexuals, then that was the purpose of his oeuvre. Of course he wanted to earn money and therefore had to go through all the abuse and disrespect that the adult publishing business put on the artists that they used in their publications. They paid them next to nothing; they hardly ever returned the original works (which were required pre computer age) to them. If they returned the artwork to the artist, it could be damaged. If it wasn't returned, it could have ended up in a garbage bin.

The process of gaining respect and honor for what he created took many years for

käufe teilte, noch ihm die nicht verkauften Werke zurückgab. Das Fiasko dauerte geschlagene zwei Jahre und Tom hatte am Schluss ein Dutzend Zeichnungen verloren und dafür keinerlei Entschädigung erhalten. Jedes Mal, wenn er übers Ohr gehauen wurde, schwor er sich, dass er jetzt aufgeben würde. Es dauerte allerdings meist nur zwei bis drei Tage, bis er wieder an den Zeichentisch zurückkehrte. Zeichnen war sein Lebenselixier. Er sagte oft, dass, wenn er völlig down war, sein Alter Ego namens Kake zu ihm kam und ihn dazu brachte, sich aufzuraffen und sich wieder einmal von einer Idee oder dem Bild eines Mannes anregen zu lassen – und schon fing er an zu zeichnen. Auch entdeckte er früh, dass er in einen sehr speziellen Geisteszustand geriet, oftmals mit einer Erektion verbunden, wenn eine Zeichnung eine besonders aufregende Qualität andeutete. Und wenn er es schaffte, in diesem Geisteszustand zu bleiben, die Zeichnung dann viel besser wurde als sonst. Diese Stimulation erhöhte seine Fähigkeit, die Nuancen der Zeichnung zu verfeinern.

Tom wurde oft als Pornograf bezeichnet, was ihn keineswegs störte, denn er bezeichnete seine Kreationen selbst als seine „schmutzigen kleinen Zeichnungen". Er hatte Respekt vor seiner eigenen Arbeit und war sich ihrer Qualität bewusst, aber er wollte sich nicht von der Kunstwelt unter Druck setzen lassen. Offenbar waren alle darauf fixiert, Künstler zu manipulieren. Er wusste, dass es der Sinn und Zweck seines Oeuvres war, junge Schwule zu erreichen und zu inspirieren. Natürlich wollte er auch Geld verdienen und musste deshalb wohl oder übel Respektlosigkeit und schlechte Behandlung von Pornoverlegern ertragen. Sie zahlten fast nichts; auch gaben sie oft Originale (die vor dem Computerzeitalter zur Reproduktion benötigt wurden) nicht zurück. Wenn Bilder zurückgegeben wurden, waren sie häufig beschädigt. Und wenn nicht, dann waren sie im Mülleimer gelandet.

Es dauerte viele Jahre, bis Tom für seine künstlerische Arbeit Respekt und Anerkennung fand. Manchmal können Künstler sich nicht selbst vermarkten und brauchen einen Helfer, wie ich es für Tom wurde. Ich konnte für ihn Forderungen stellen, die ihm nicht so leicht möglich waren. Und ich kümmerte mich bei Verträgen, um gerechten Lohn für die geleistete Arbeit, die Beachtung seines Urheberrechts und sorgte für

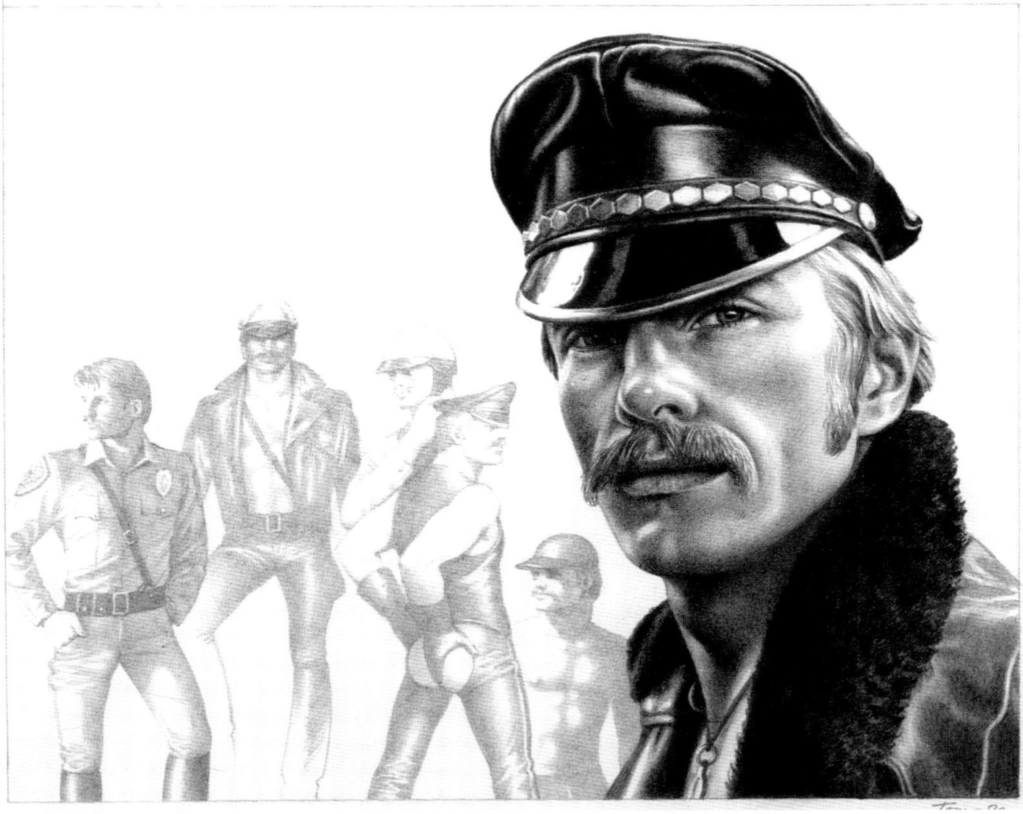

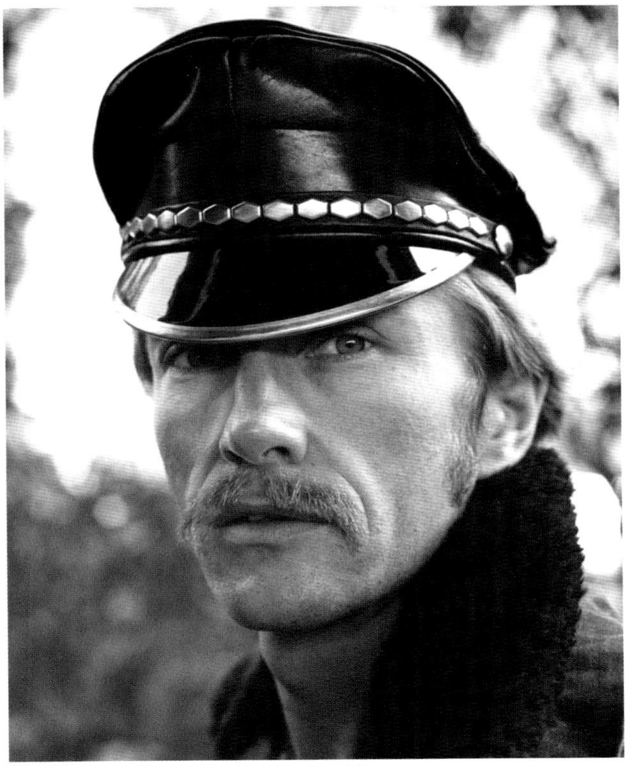

Durk Dehner, reference photo, ca. 1979

Tom. Sometimes artists are not equipped themselves and need an advocate such as I was for Tom. I was able to demand for him what he often times could not ask for himself. Contracts, fair pay for work completed, regard for his copyright, and printing at the quality that his works deserved. He often was very happy to have Leather clubs use his work without payment; it was his way of nurturing them.

In his final era of his life, the forming of Tom of Finland Company and Tom of Finland Foundation became his raison d'être. Both embodied honor and fairness for all, Tom's values. We built Tom of Finland Foundation with the principles he held. He never wanted his fellow artists to have to endure the dreadful acts of mistreatment and skullduggery that he went through. It has been his foundation's mission to educate others in preserving their legacy through documentation, record keeping, and always maintaining a high resolution catalogue. Tom's Foundation encourages self promotion, building networks and knowing artists' rights. Foremost, reinforcing pride in what artists create and that we hold them as the shaman of our tribe.

The presence of erotic art in our lives creates a sense of identity, icons to manifest oneself with. To hang these talismans on our walls projects freedom, wholeness and beauty beyond words. Erotic art exemplifies a mandala of a tolerant and accepting society.

Harvey S. Shipley Miller, trustee of The Judith Rothchild Foundation, stated in 2006 that Tom of Finland was one of the five most influential artists of the 20th century; that influence transcended into the culture and became part of it. We are part of Tom's world.

Through building a treasured relationship which crossed boundaries from professional, personal and intimate, Durk Dehner cofounded the Tom of Finland Foundation in Los Angeles with Touko Laaksonen a.k.a. Tom of Finland in 1984.

die Druckqualität, die seine Arbeit verdiente. Oft überließ er seine Zeichnungen Lederclubs auch ohne Bezahlung. Das war seine Art, sie zu unterstützen.

In seinen letzten Lebensjahren wurde die Gründung der Tom of Finland Company und der Tom of Finland Foundation zu seinem Lebensinhalt. Beide sind getragen von Toms Werten: der Fairness und Achtung anderen Künstlern gegenüber. Wir bauten die Tom of Finland Foundation mit Prinzipien auf, die ihm wichtig waren. Er wollte, dass andere die schlechte Behandlung, die er durchgemacht hatte, niemals würden ertragen müssen. Es wurde die Aufgabe seiner Stiftung, andere dahingehend zu beeinflussen, ihr Vermächtnis durch gute Dokumentation und einen Katalog mit guten Abbildungen zu bewahren. Toms Stiftung will Kollegen zur Selbstvermarktung, zum Aufbau von Netzwerken und zum Bewusstwerden ihrer Rechte als Künstler ermutigen. Besonders wichtig wurde die Stärkung des Stolzes auf die eigene künstlerische Produktion, und das Bewusstsein, dass Künstler die Schamanen unseres Stammes sind.

Die Gegenwart von erotischer Kunst in unserem Leben erzeugt ein Bewusstsein für Identität und Symbole, durch die wir uns ausdrücken können. Diese Talismane an unsere Wände zu hängen schafft ein Gefühl von Freiheit, Ganzheit und Schönheit. Erotische Kunst schafft so etwas wie ein Mandala einer toleranten Gesellschaft.

Harvey S. Shipley Miller, Stiftungstreuhänder der Judith Rothschild Foundation, erklärte 2006 Tom of Finland zu einem der fünf einflussreichsten Künstler des 20. Jahrhunderts; sein Einfluss transzendierte in die Kultur und wurde ein Teil davon. Wir sind Teil von Toms Welt.

Übersetzung: Rinaldo Hopf

Mit dem Aufbau ihrer wertvollen Beziehung, die die Grenzen von professionell, persönlich und intim überschritt, gründete Durk Dehner zusammen mit seinem langjährigen Lebensgefährten Touko Laaksonen a.k. Tom of Finland 1984 die Tom of Finland Foundation in Los Angeles.

Different Techniques
of Tom

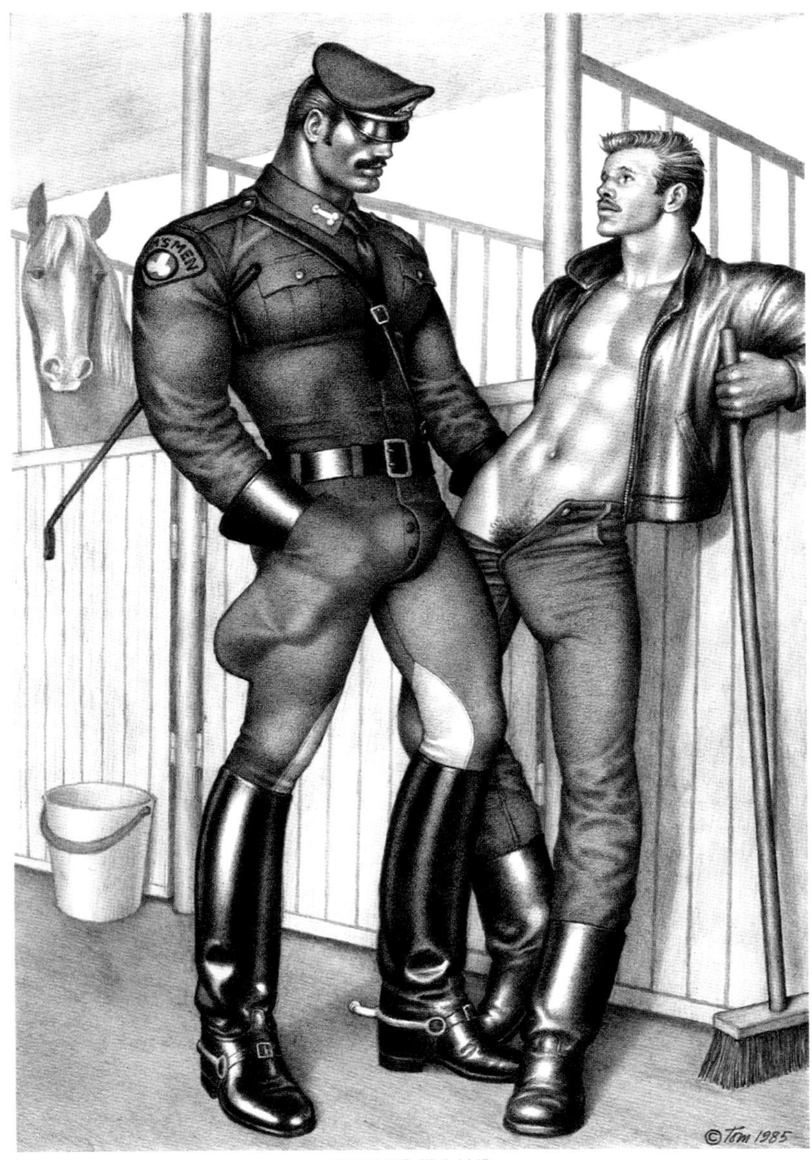

TOM OF FINLAND
Graphite • Graphit

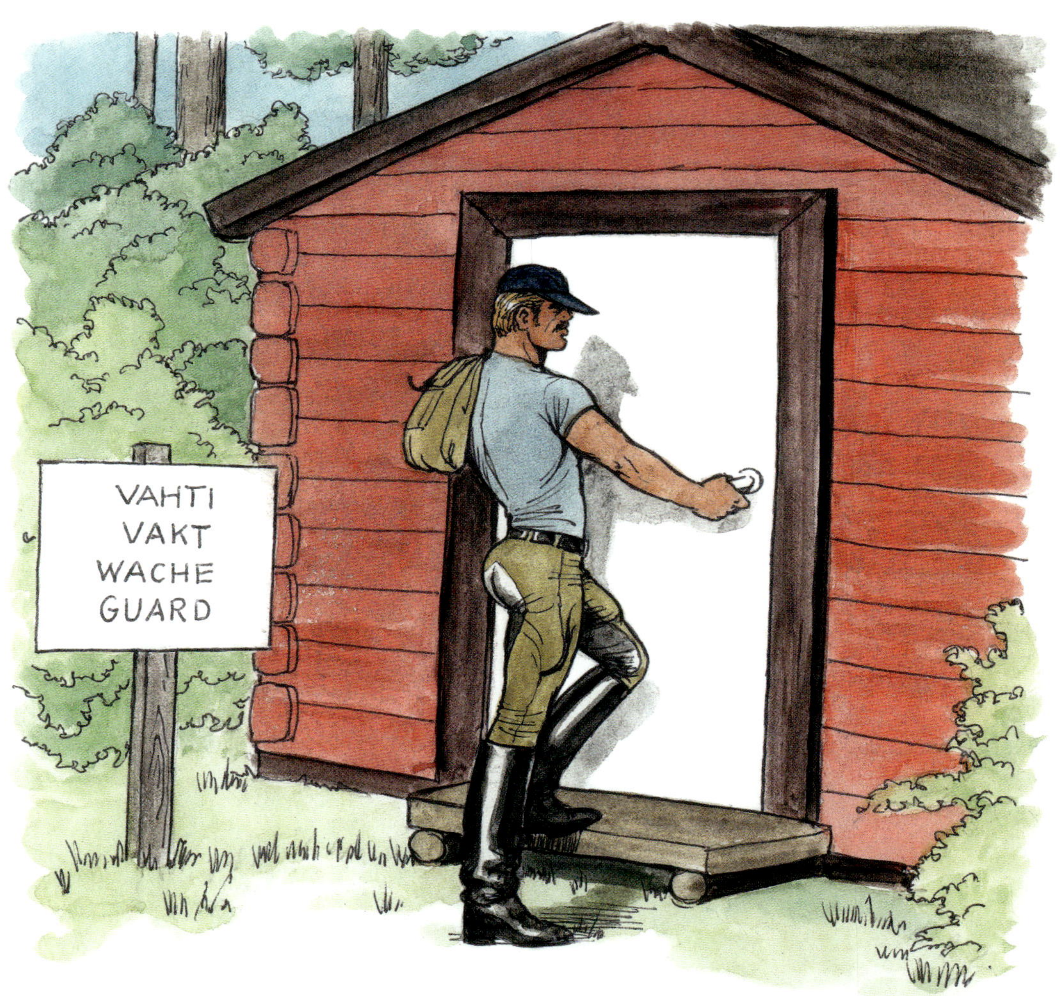

Watercolor • Aquarell

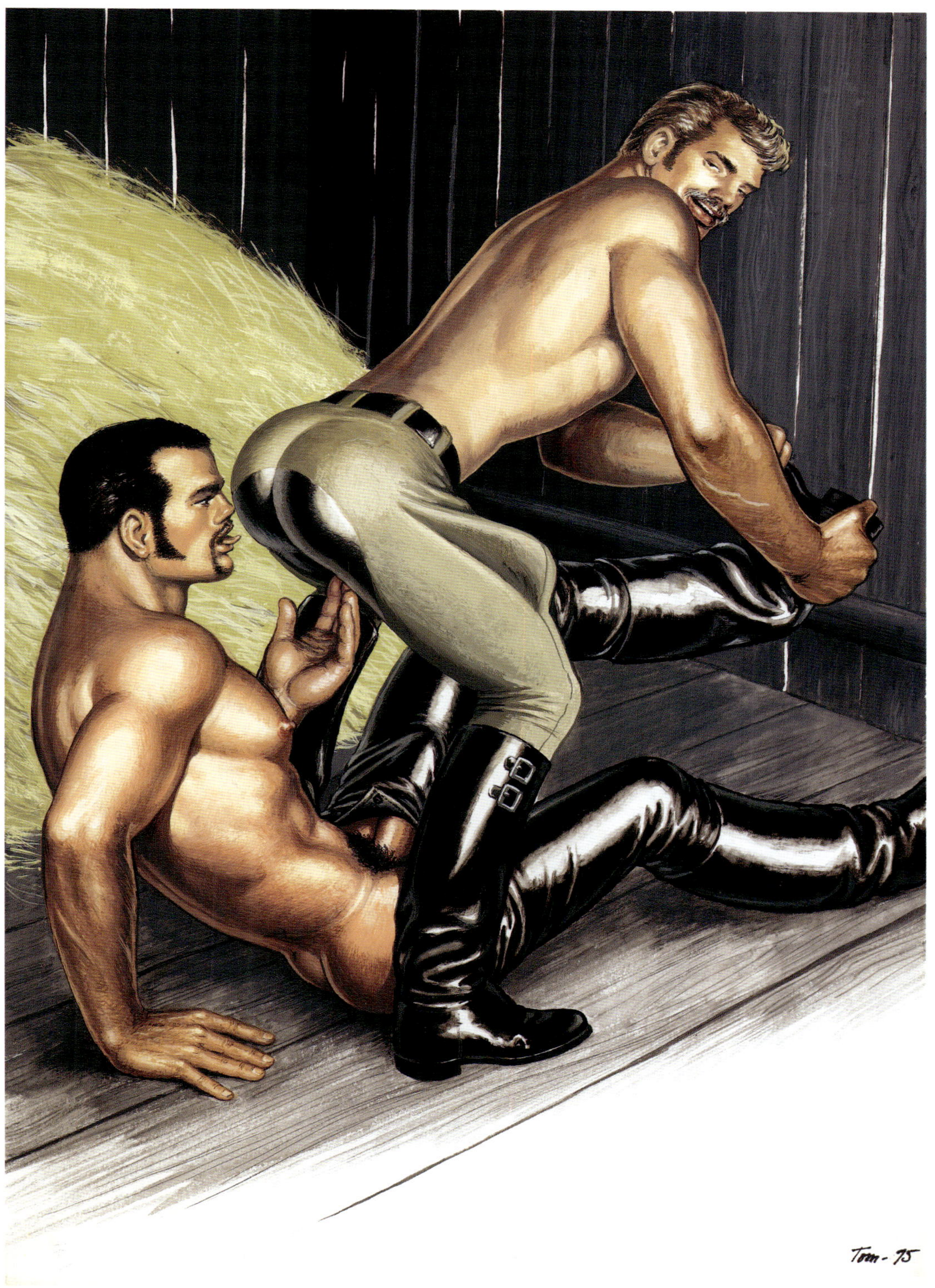

Gouache

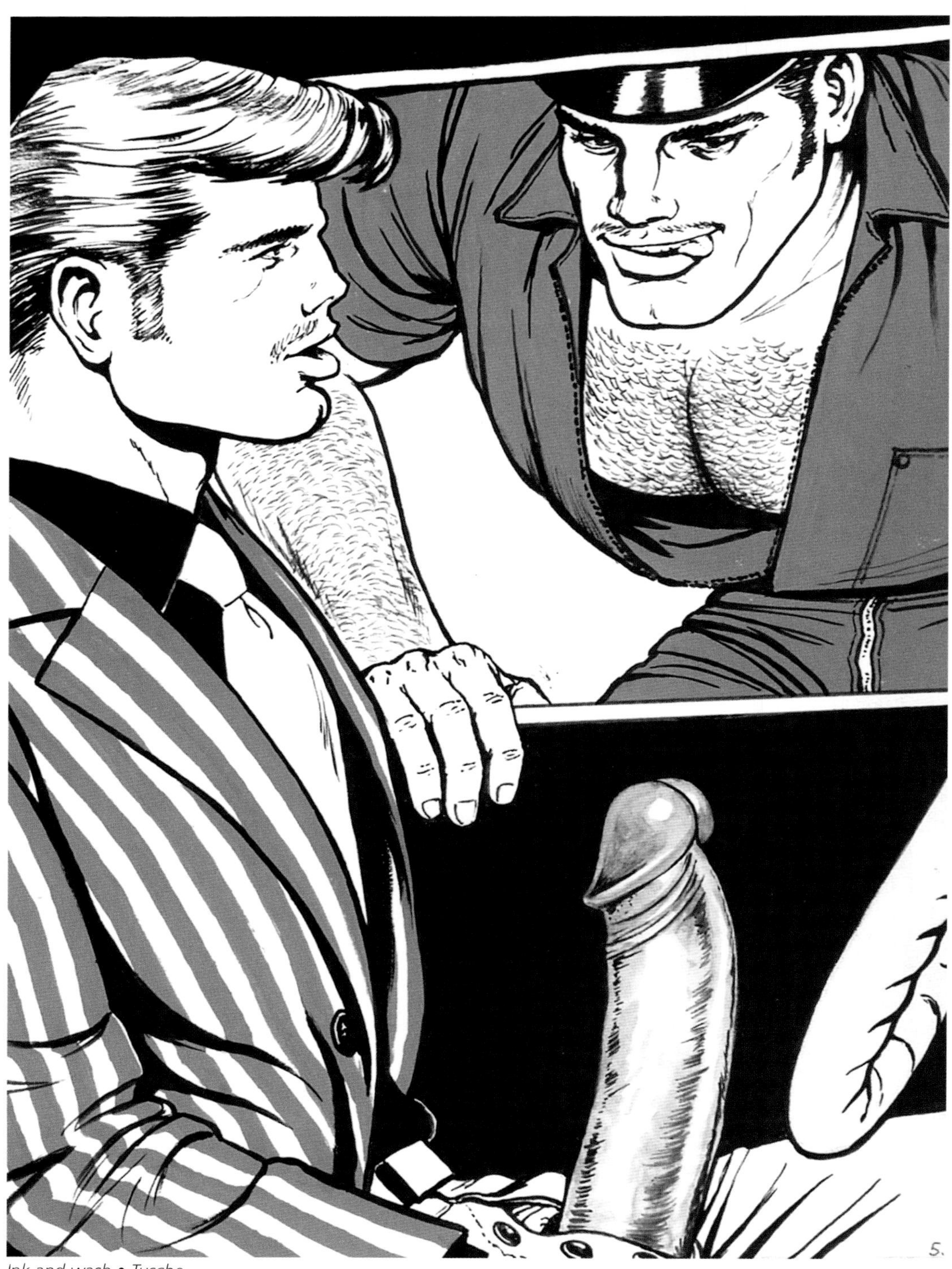

Ink and wash • Tusche

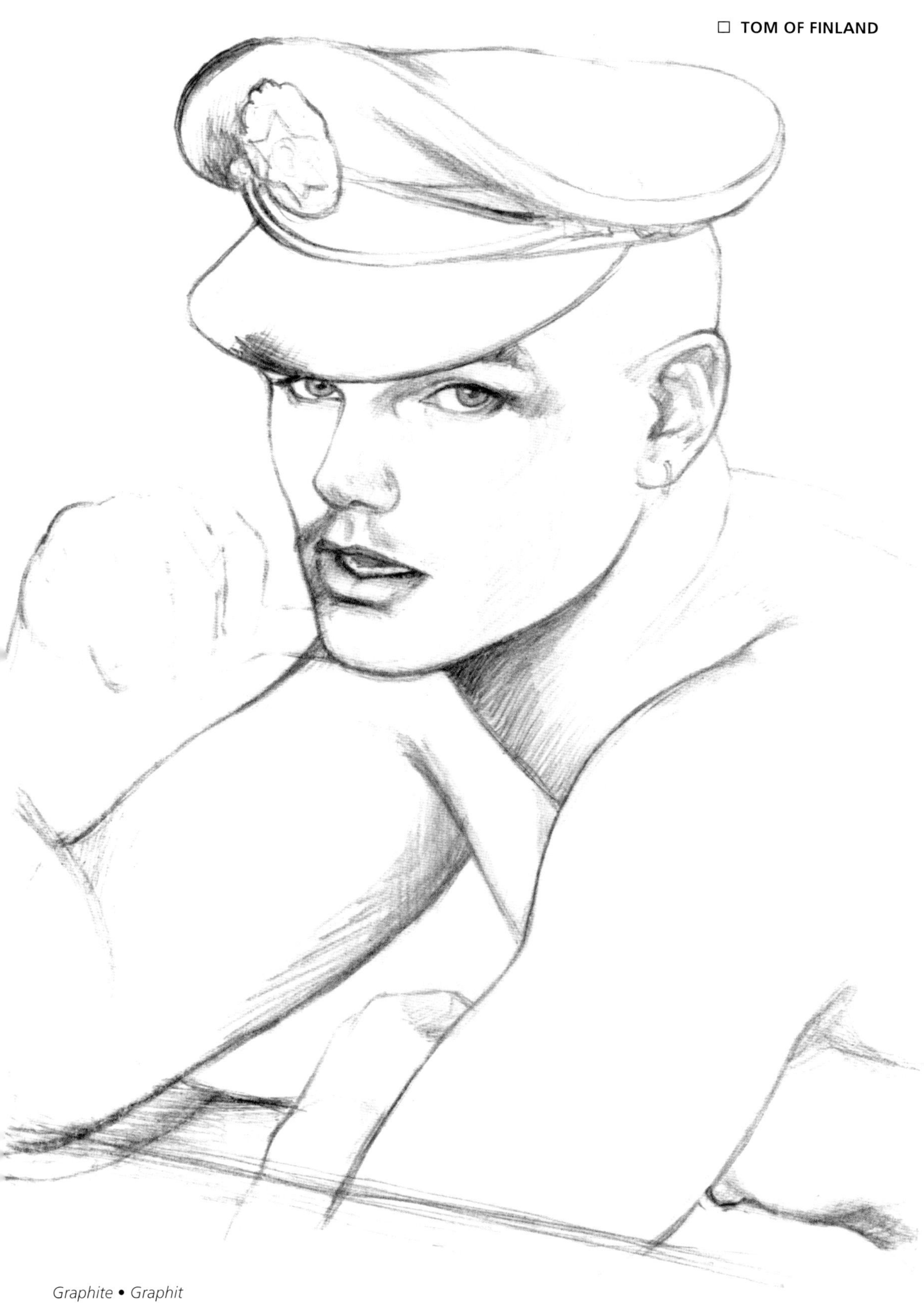

Graphite • Graphit

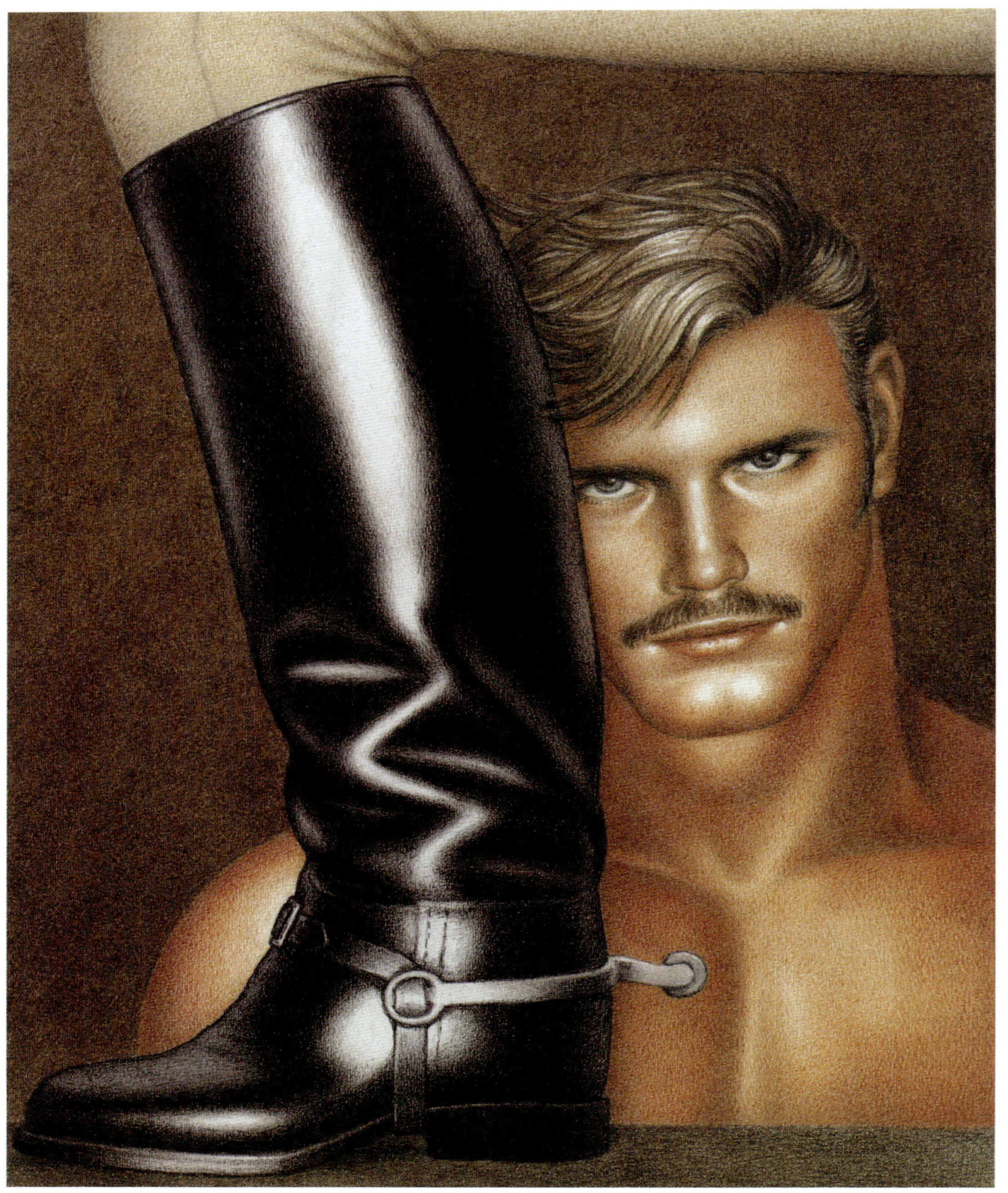

Color pencil • Farbstifte

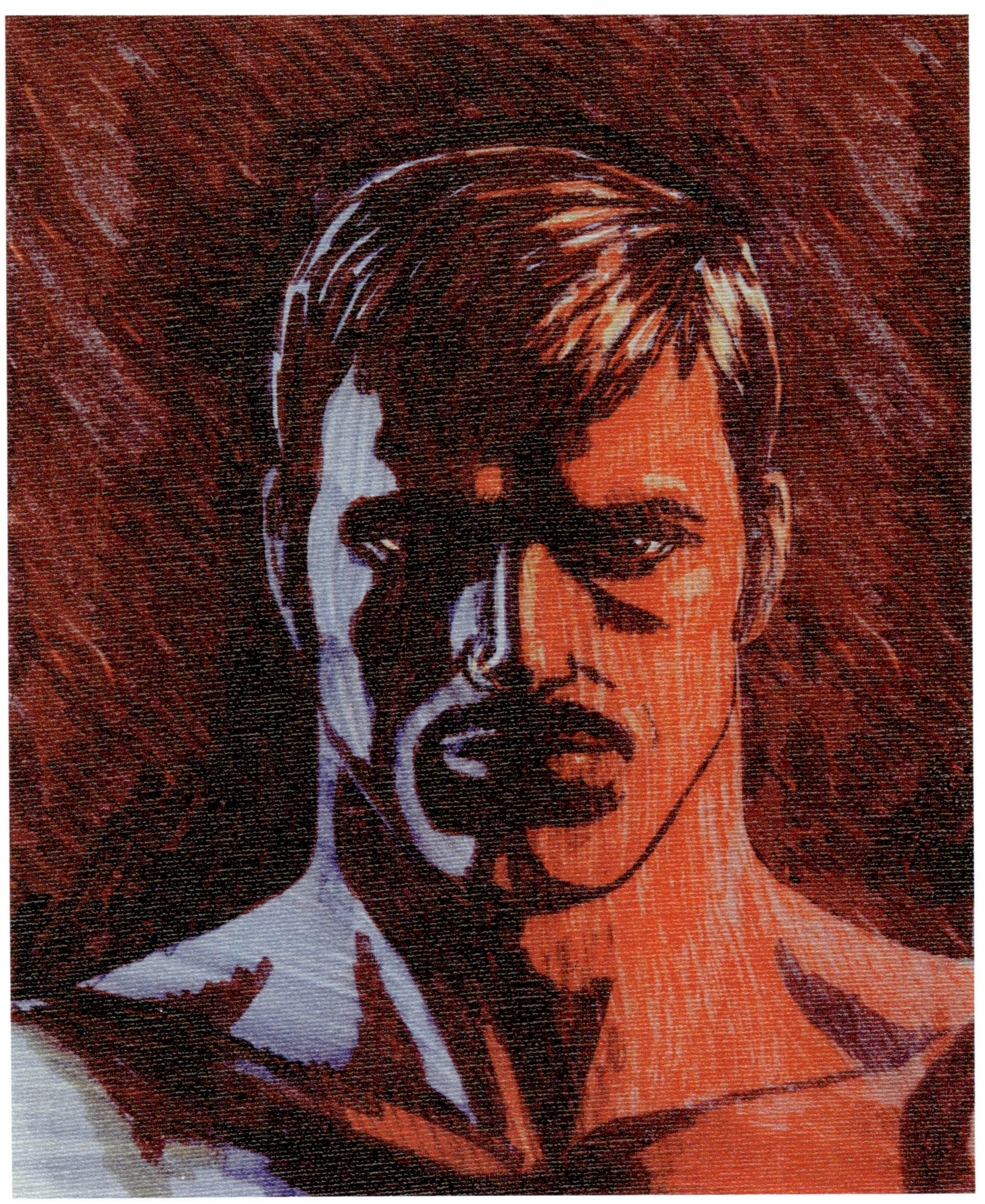

Marker pen • Marker

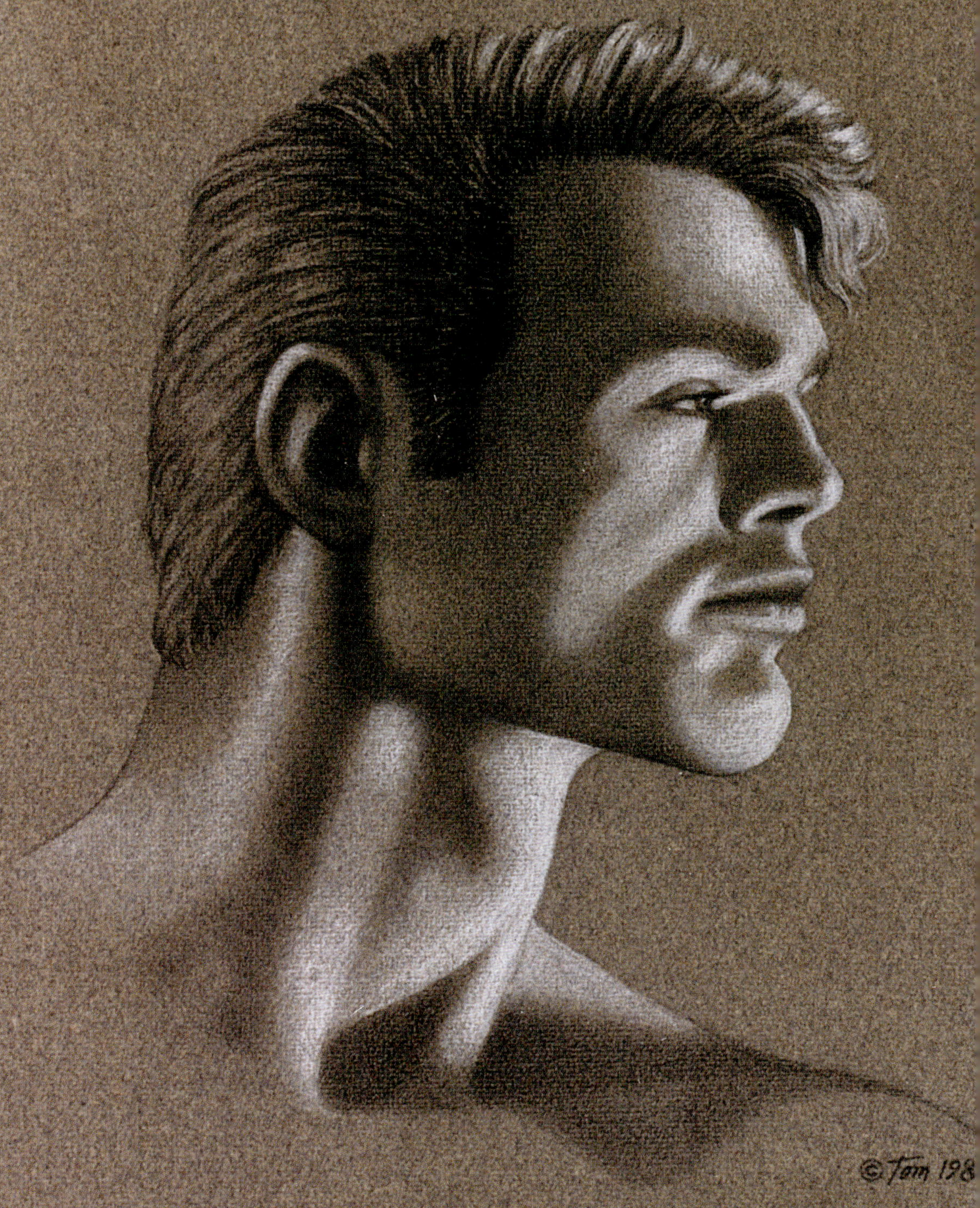

Pastel • Pastell

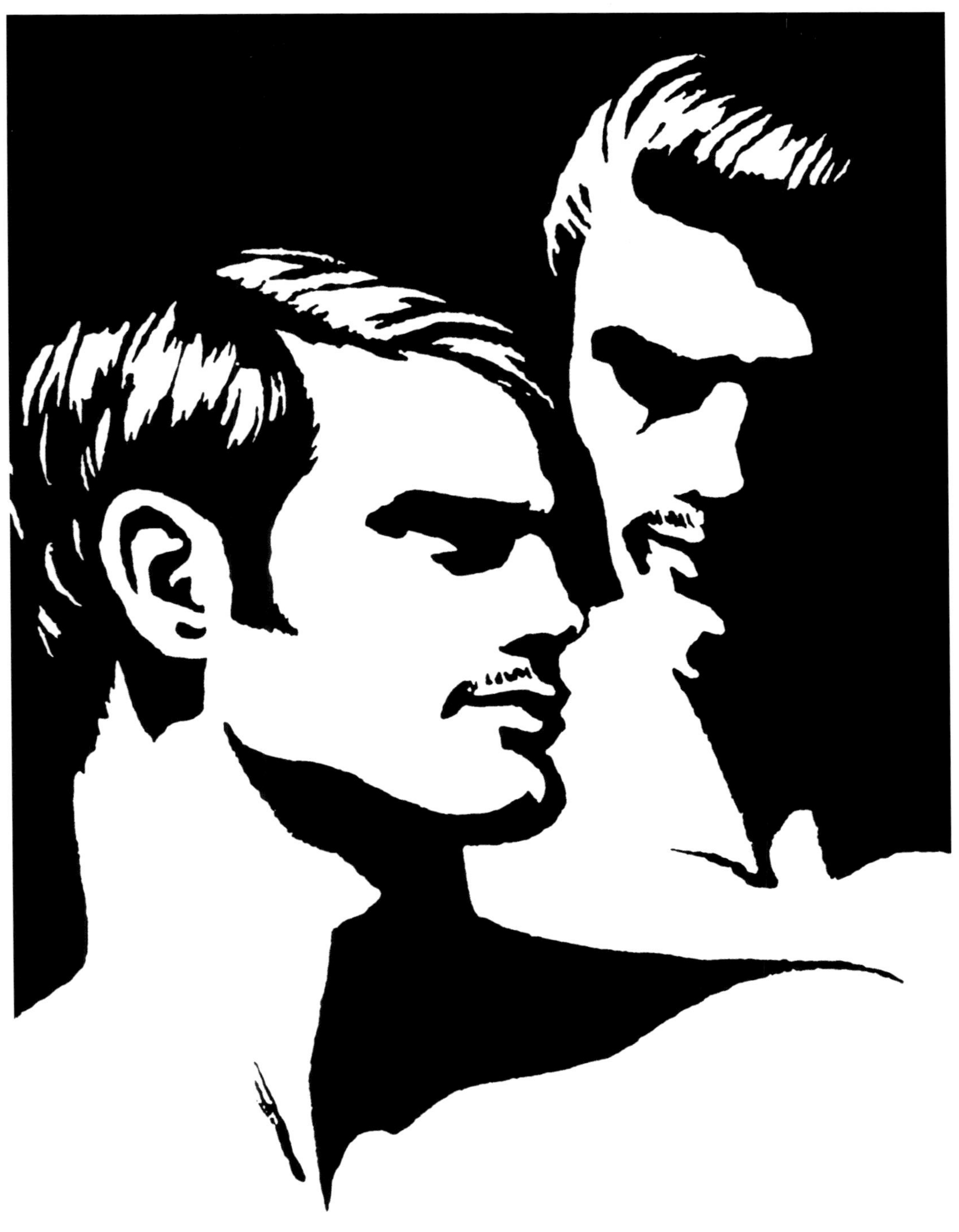

Linocut • Linolschnitt

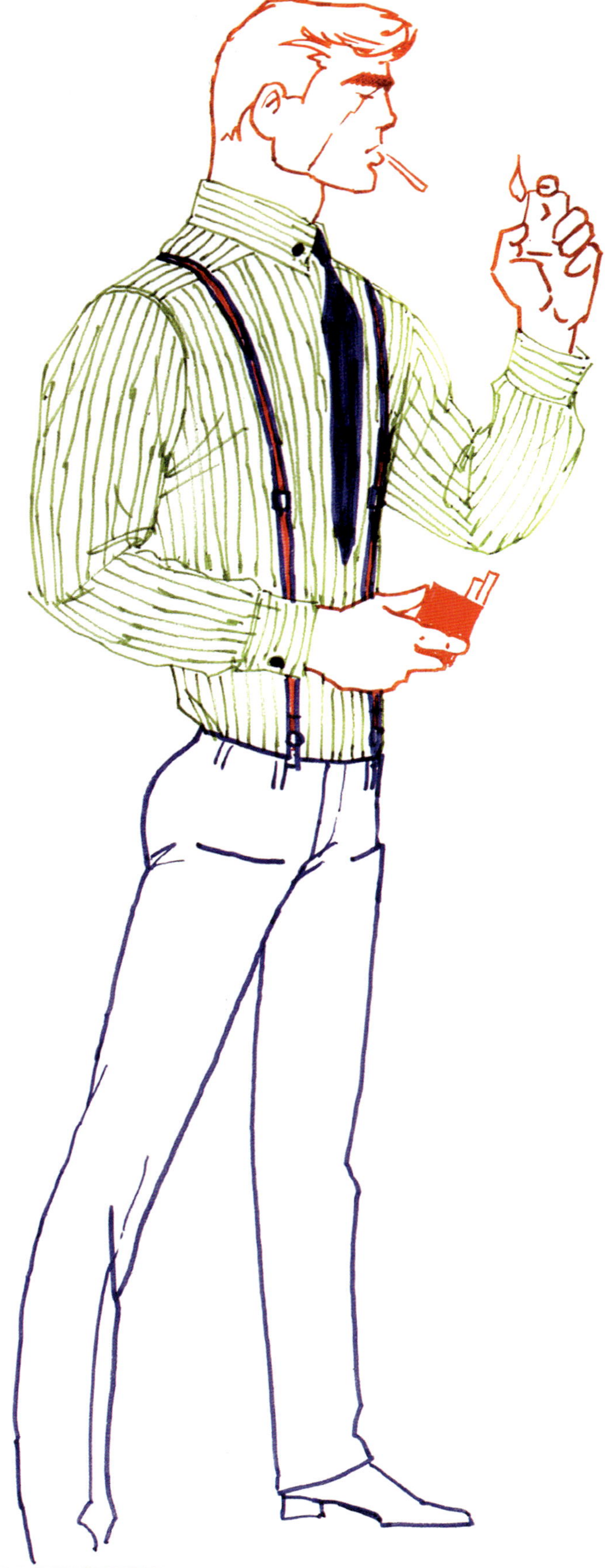

Technical pen • Rapidograph

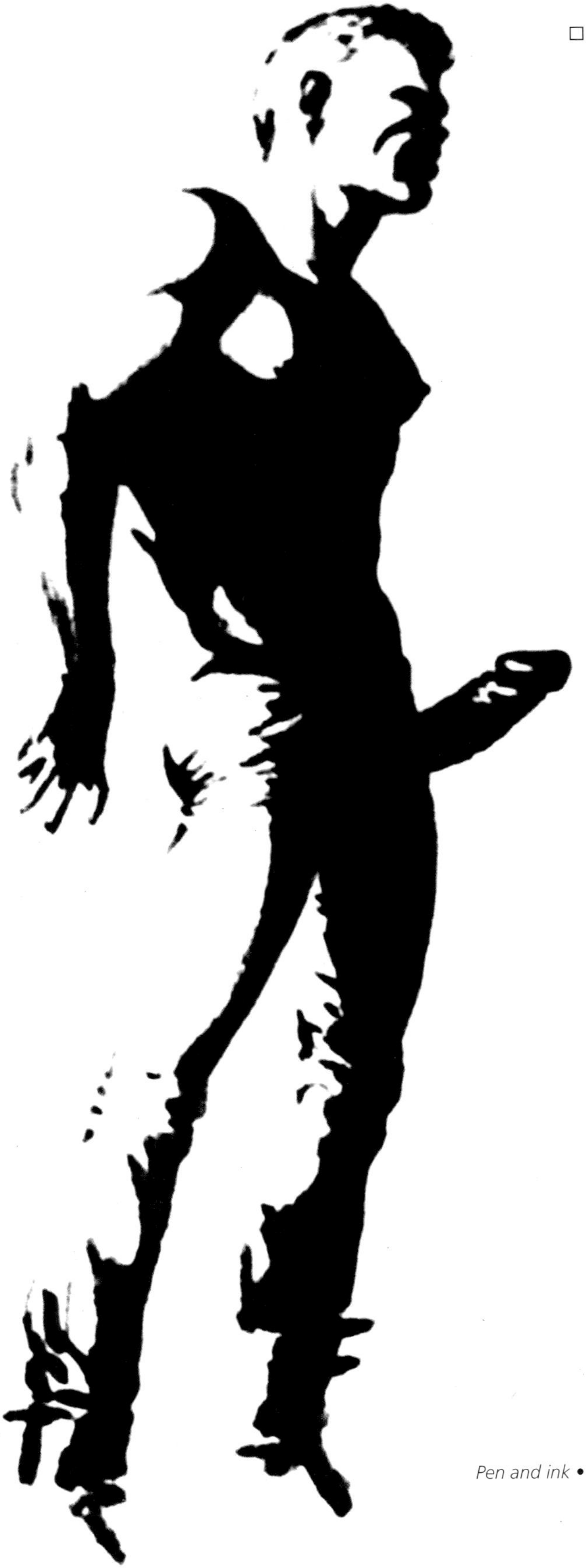

Pen and ink • Tuschezeichnung

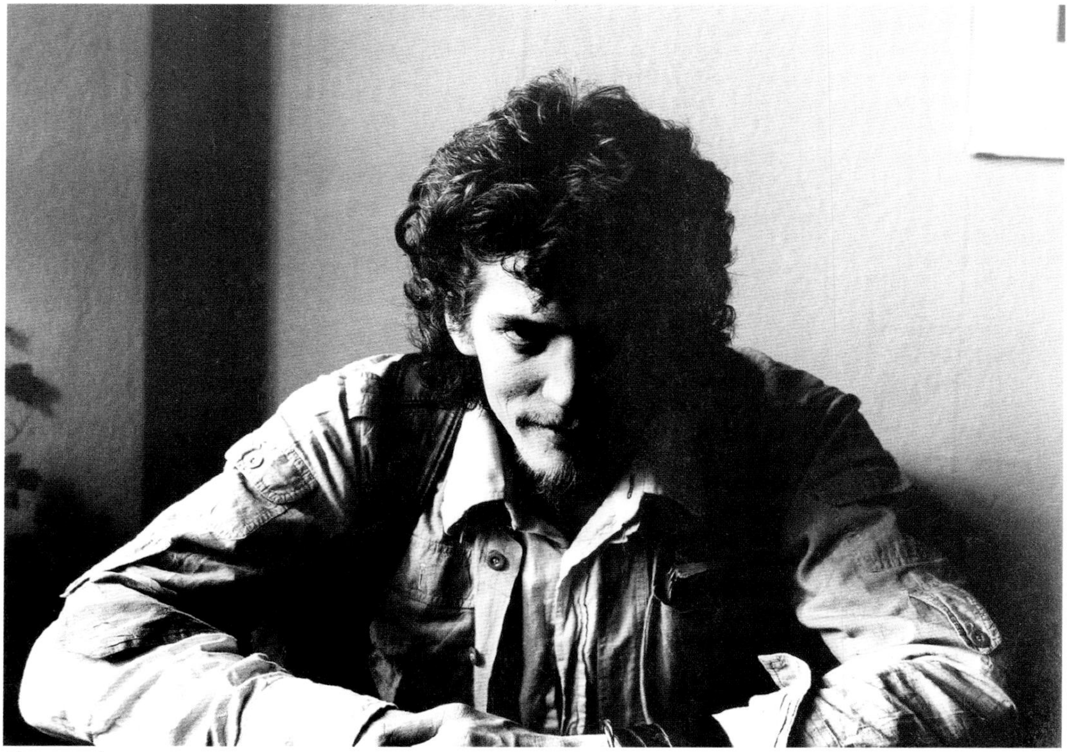

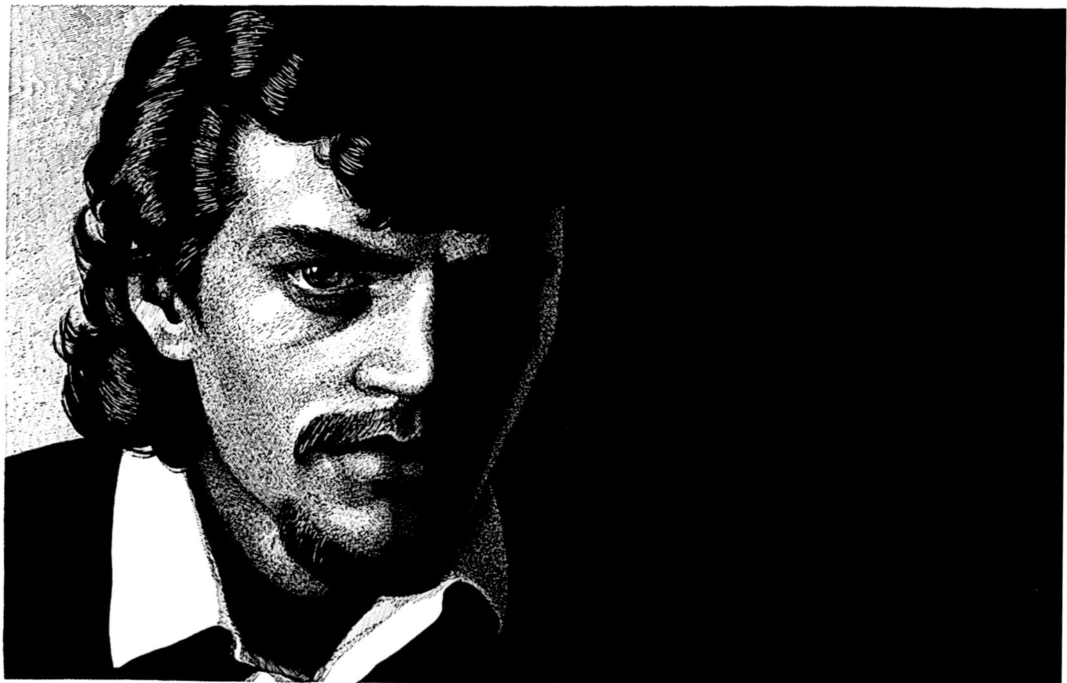

Photograph

Pen and ink • Tuschezeichnung

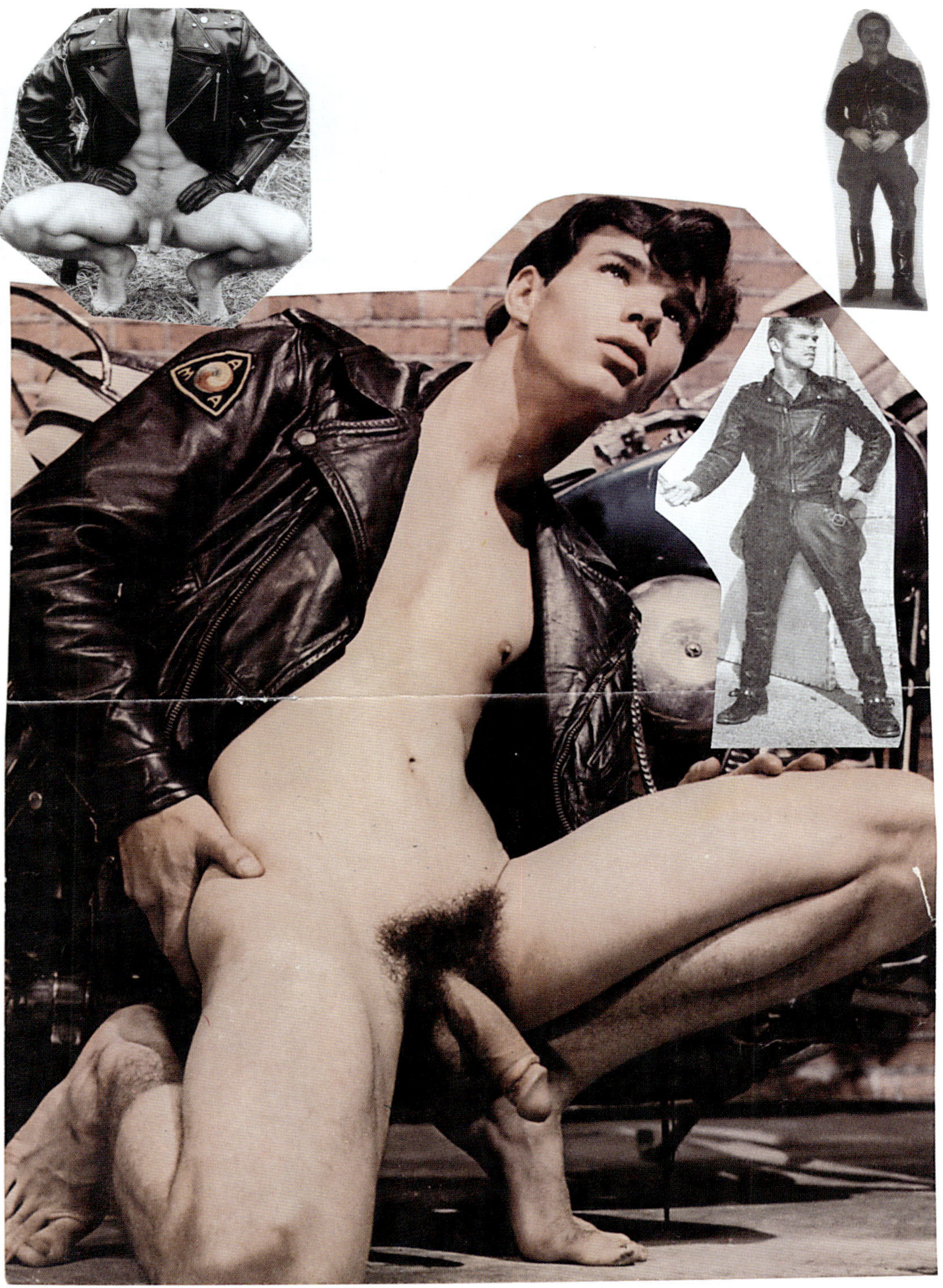

Cut and pasted paper (Reference page) • Collage (Bildvorlage)

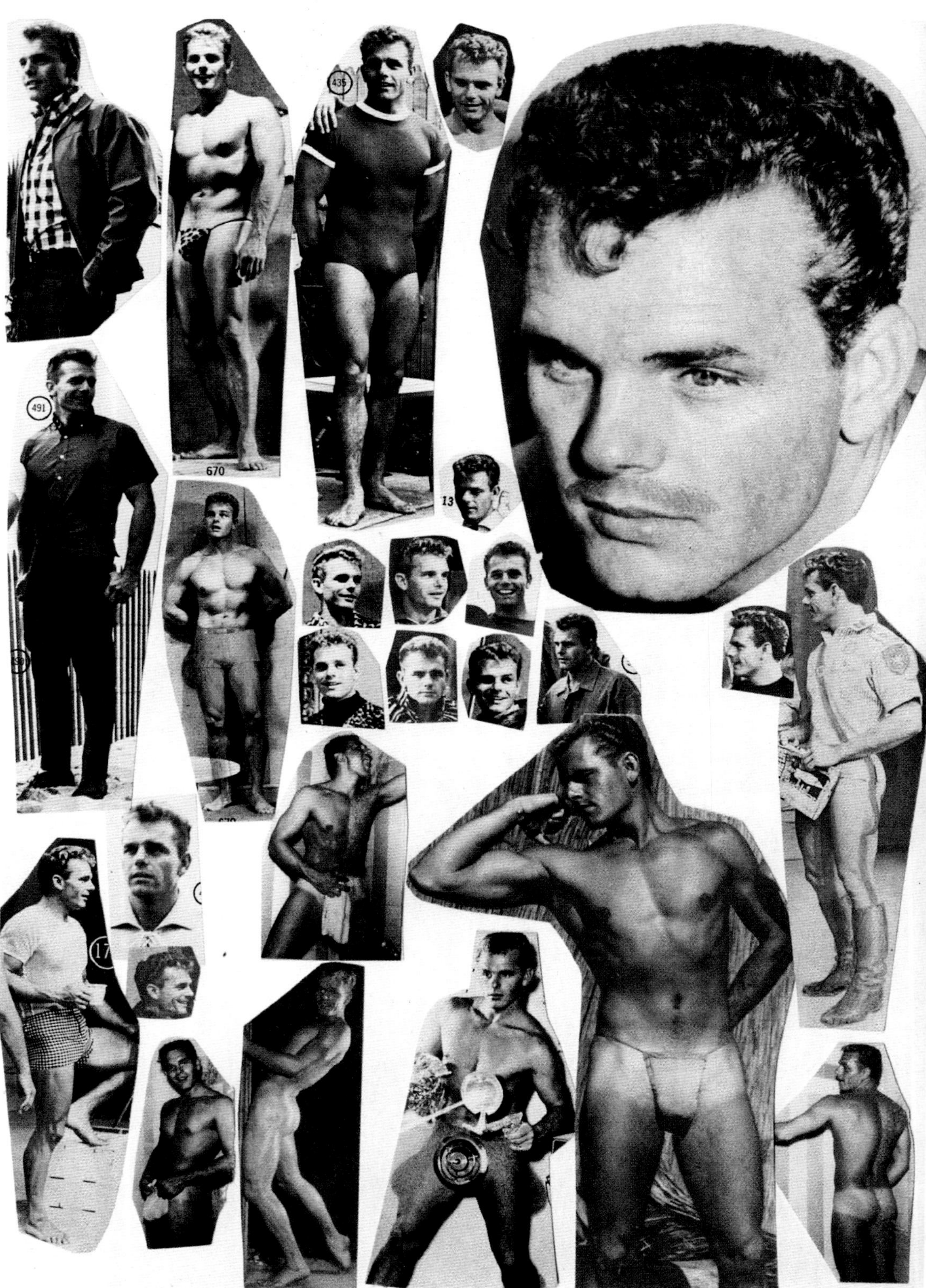

Cut and pasted paper (Reference page) • *Collage (Bildvorlage)*

Tom's Work Process

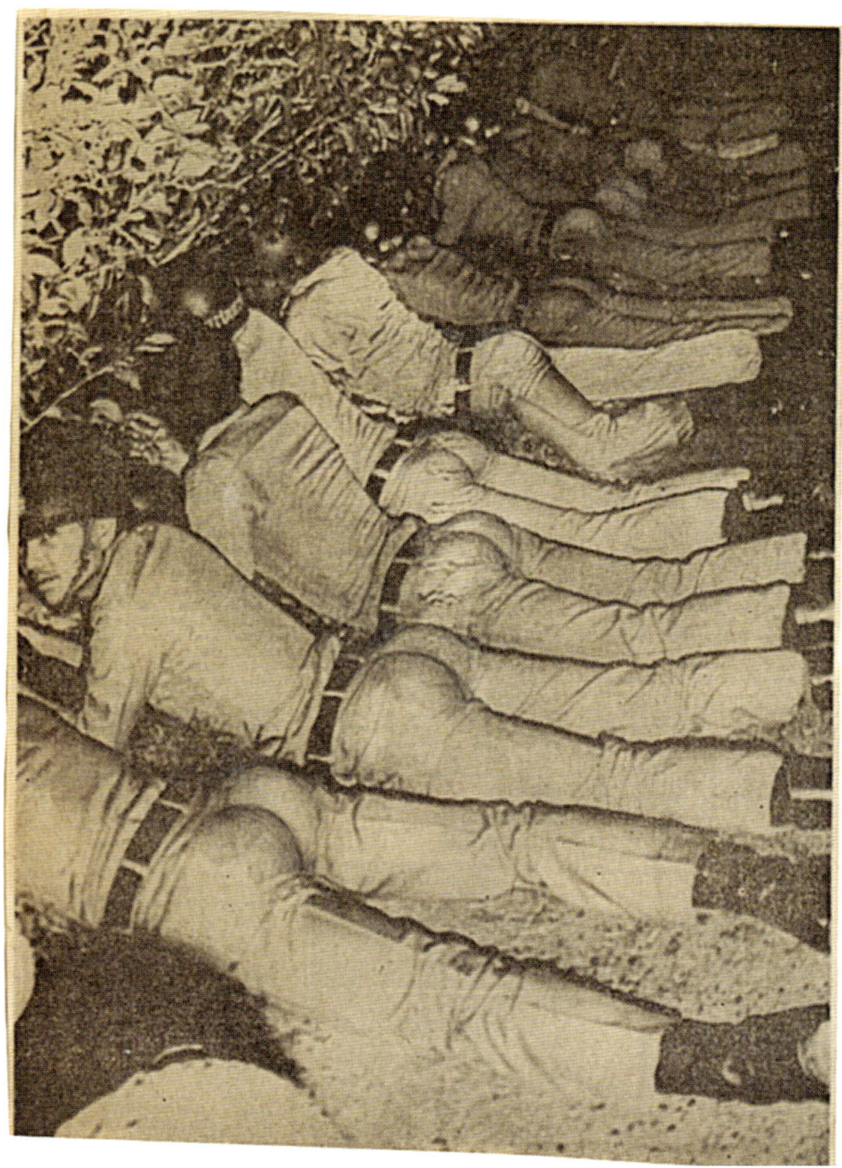

TOM OF FINLAND
Embellished newspaper • bearbeitetes Zeitungsfoto

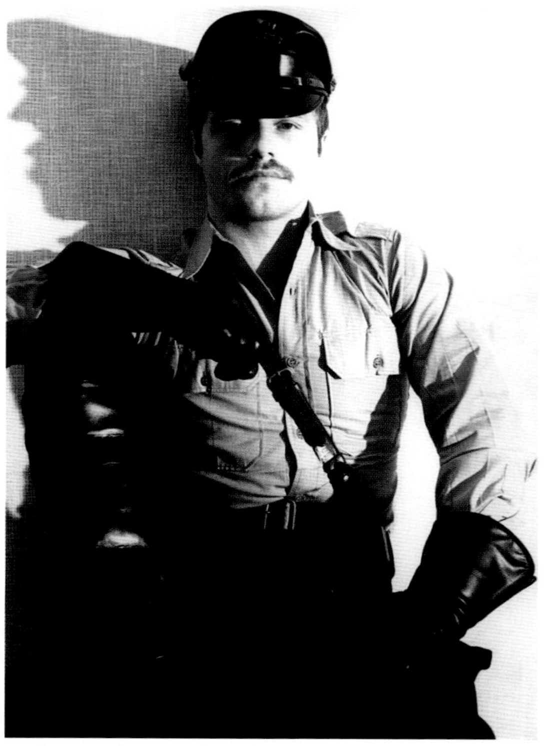

Reference photograph • Bildvorlage

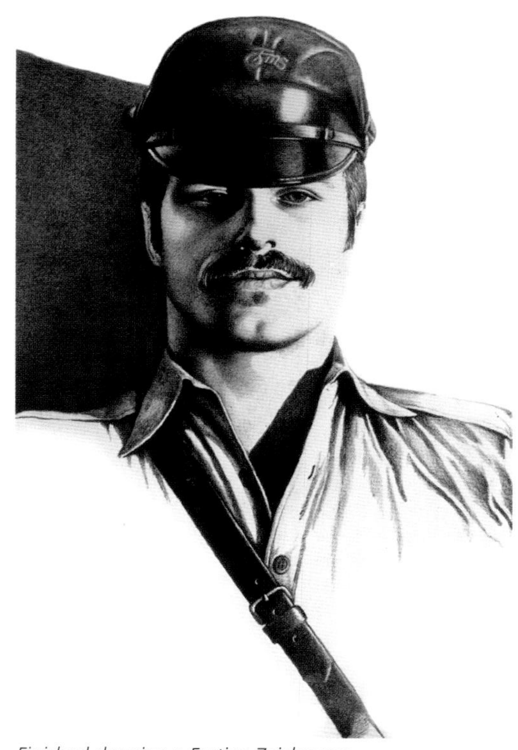

Finished drawing • Fertige Zeichnung

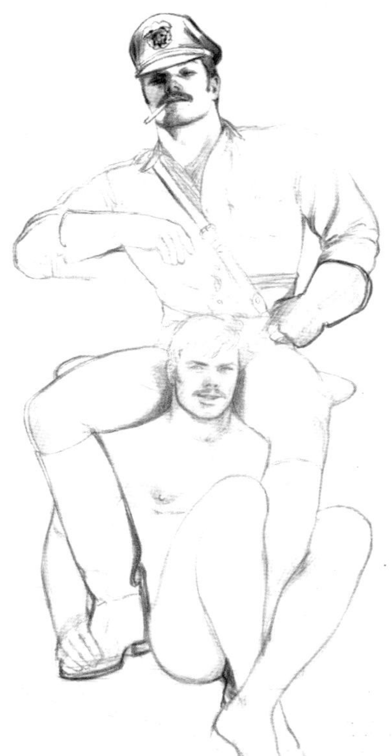

Preparatory drawing • Rohskizze

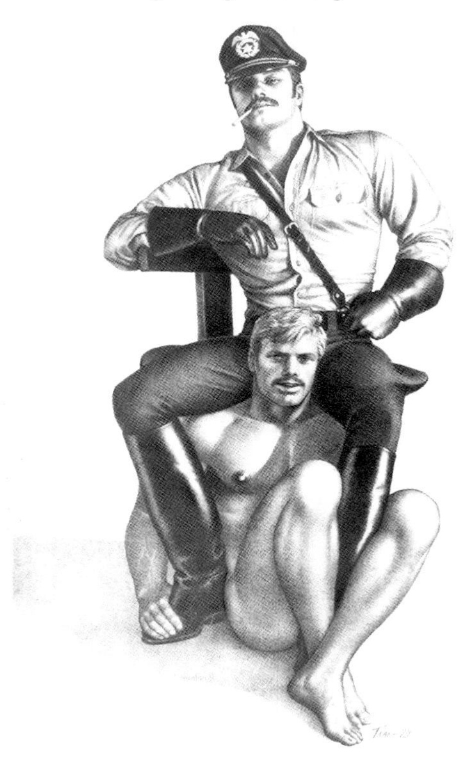

Finished drawing • Fertige Zeichnung

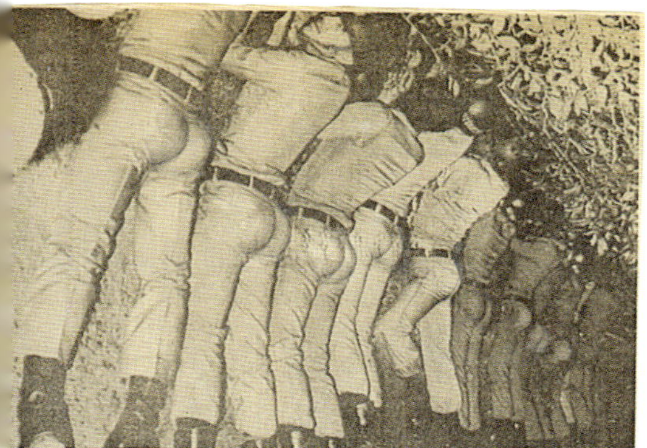

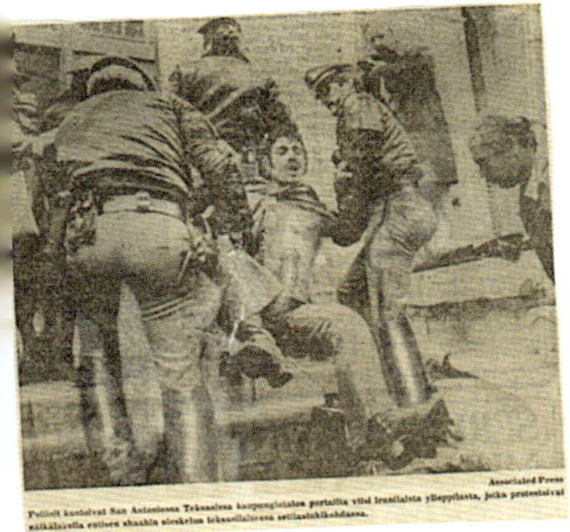

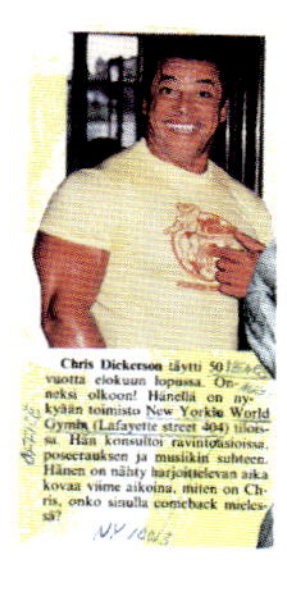

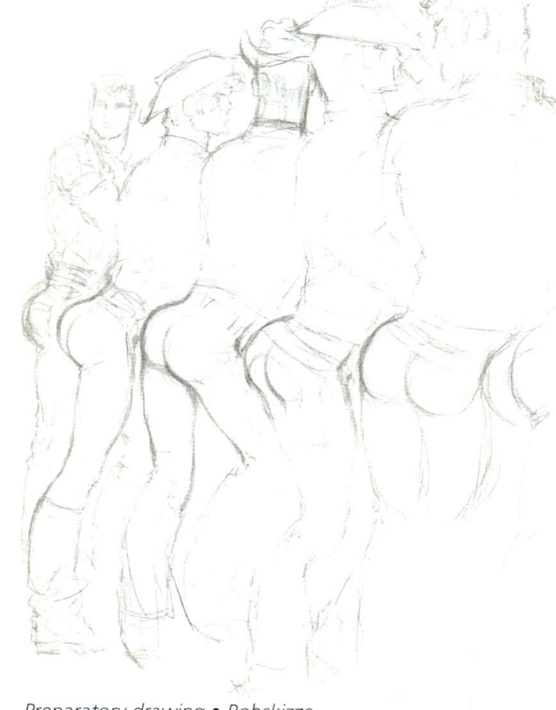

Cut and pasted paper (Reference page) • Collage (Bildvorlage)

Preparatory drawing • Rohskizze

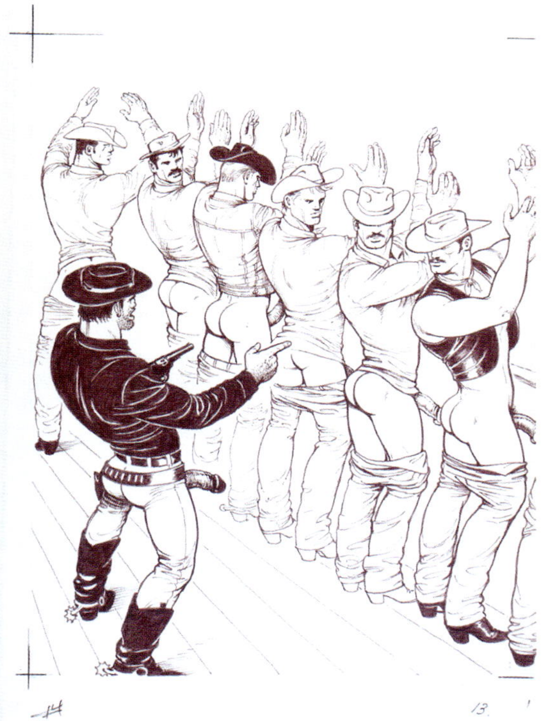

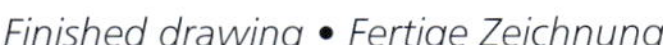

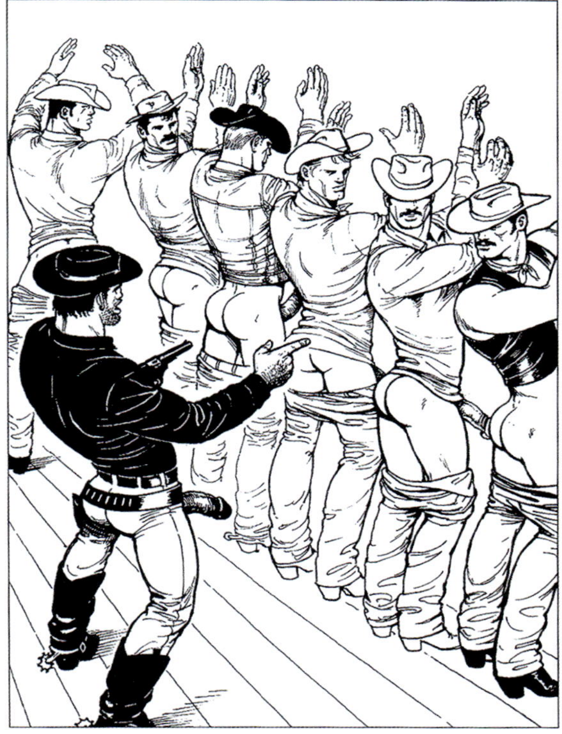

Finished drawing • Fertige Zeichnung

Published drawing • Veröffentlichte Zeichnung

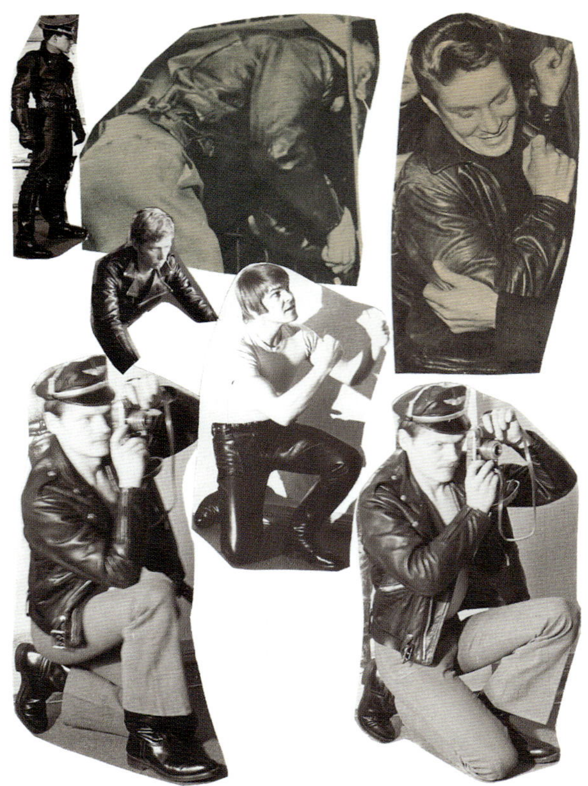

Cut and pasted paper (Reference page) • Collage (Bildvorlage)

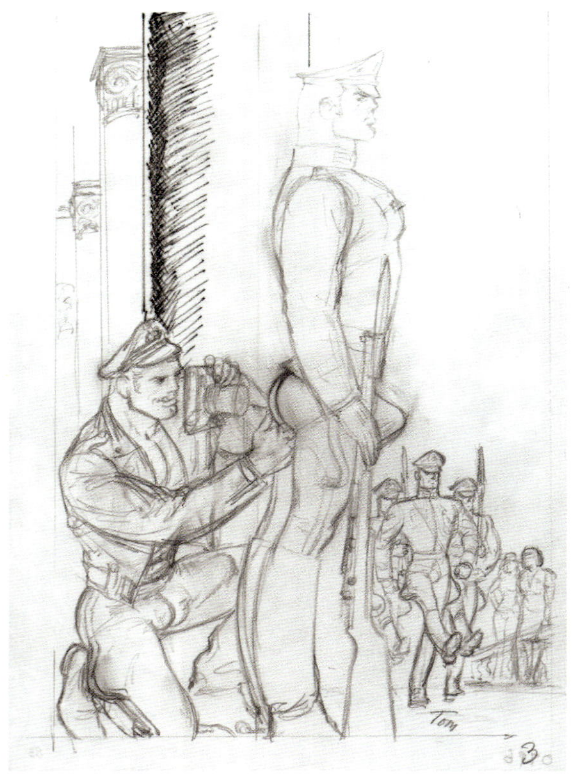

Preparatory drawing • Rohskizze

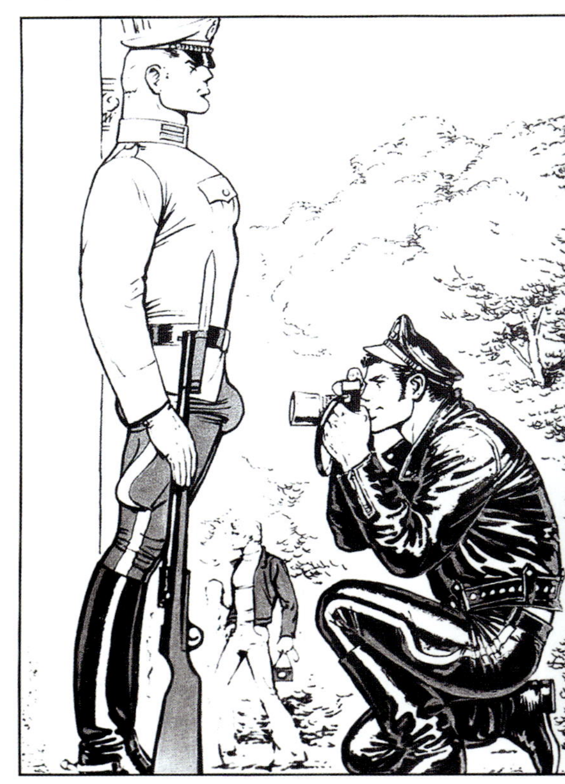

Finished drawing • Fertige Zeichnung

Hommage à Tom

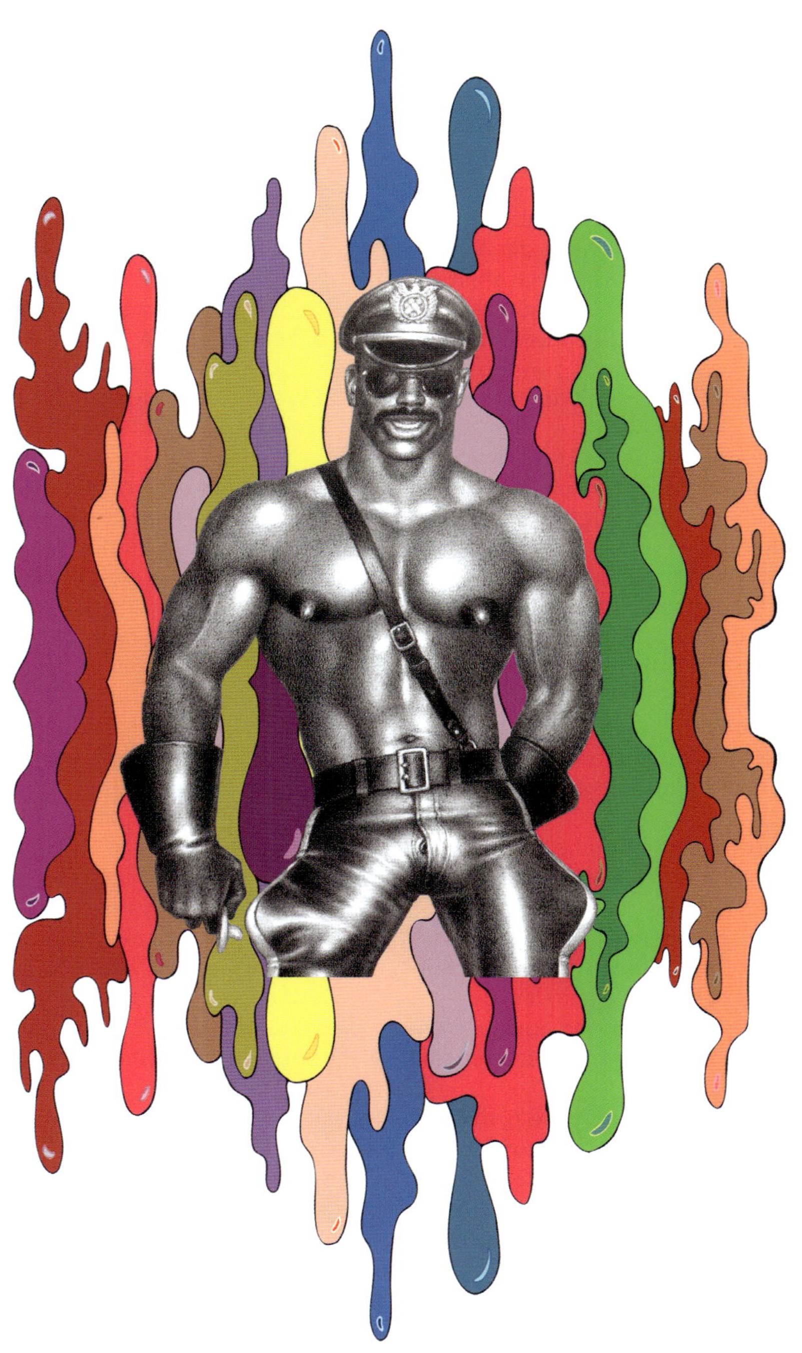

ASSUME VIVID ASTRO FOCUS

SAM BALDUCCI

... unter die Räder kommen! •
You'll end up in the gutter!

Da, wo Fred herkam – nicht weit entfernt von Frankfurt und dennoch aus einer anderen Welt –, gab es viele Dinge nicht. Man legte Wert auf adrettes Aussehen. Jugendliche wie er trugen ordentliche Hosen, gebügelte Oberhemden und wurden streng erzogen. Das Regelwerk erlaubte keine eigenmächtigen Ausbrüche, sondern man lernte für die Schule, die Ausbildung und das Leben oder half im Haushalt. Alles wie vor hundert Jahren. Er aber fühlte, wie sehr er sich von den anderen unterschied und wie es ihn fortzog. Nur nicht enden wie sie, die nichts erlebt hatten und nur ihre eigenen vier Wände kannten.

„Du wirst noch unter die Räder kommen!", keifte die Mutter und damit genau dies nicht geschehen würde, zog sein Stiefvater ihn mit schöner Regelmäßigkeit in die Scheune und dort seinen Ledergürtel aus den Schlaufen, um ihn vor dem Schlimmsten zu bewahren, machte es damit aber nur noch schlimmer.

„Sei doch vernünftig!" Die Mutter sprach mit eindringlicher Stimme und er versuchte erst gar nicht, sich an Regeln zu halten, denn es genügte, dass die anderen Jungen ihn abends aus der Wohnung lockten und es gab kein Halten mehr.

Alles, was verboten war, stachelte ihn an: ihr schamloses Reden, das heimliche Rauchen in der Scheune, das Bier. Sie waren unter sich, griffen sich beherzt gegenseitig zwischen die Beine und wälzten sich lüstern am Boden. Mit Ralf und Burkhard ging das besonders gut – zumindest so lange, bis Mädchen auftauchten, die ihre Männerrunden nachhaltig störten und alles verdarben.

Er hörte von Tunten und Schwuchteln, die Handtaschen trugen. Perverse, die auf Jungs standen und mit durchgedrückten Beinen in Stöckelschuhen! Das Wort *schwul* existierte, aber man umging es. Er zumindest konnte nicht schwul sein, weil er sich nichts weniger vorstellen konnte, als Gefallen daran zu finden, Stöckelschuhe zu tragen.

Er hatte auch kein Bedürfnis, sich zu schminken oder nach einer Frauenhandtasche Ausschau zu halten. Was er wollte, war, seinen

Not too far from Frankfurt, yet still in a whole other world – a lot of things were missing where Frank came from. You had to dress sharp. Guys like him wore ordinary pants, ironed shirts, and were raised in a strict environment. The rules were set in stone, and didn't allow for any individuality. You studied, worked, or helped around the house. Everything as it was a hundred years ago. Still, he felt very different from everyone else, and knew this difference set him apart. He didn't want to end up like the others, with no experiences outside of their own four walls.

"You'll end up in the gutter!" his mother would scream at him, as often as his stepfather would take him to the shed, removing his leather belt in the process, to keep him from going astray. In trying to save him from a bad fate, they gave him a worse one.

"Get your head on straight!" His mother would say to him, but he didn't even try. He broke the rules every chance he got, and spent more time at night with his friends than he did at home. There was no holding back.

Everything that was forbidden at home he revelled in with his friends: their vulgar way of speaking, smoking behind the school, the beer. They kept to themselves, grabbed each other between the legs and rolled around lustfully on the ground – at least until girls showed up, and their fun was ruined.

He had heard of queers and fags, who all carried purses. Perverts, who wanted to be girls instead of boys, and who wore high heels! The word *gay* existed, but you didn't say it. Fred was sure he couldn't be gay – he couldn't think of anything he would rather do less than wear high heels. He had no desire to wear make-up or prance around with a purse. What he wanted, was to watch his stepfather mow the lawn, to smell his sweat-drenched

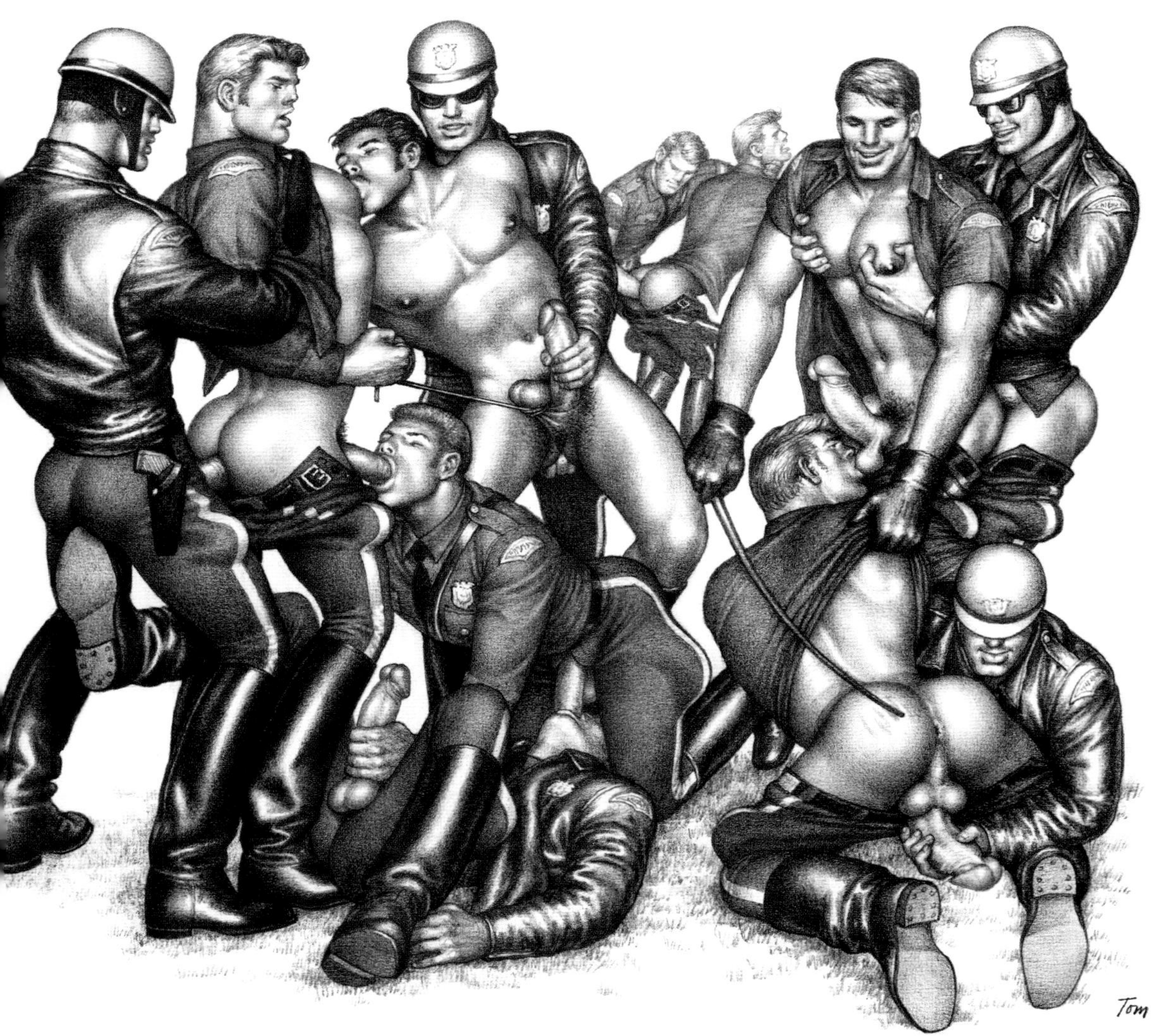

Stiefvater beim Rasenmähen zu beobachten, anschließend heimlich an dessen verschwitztem Oberhemd zu riechen und ihn beim Duschen zu beobachten. Oder seine Motorradjacke zu tragen, die im Schuppen hing, ihm aber noch viel zu groß war.

Schwule, das lernte Fred von seinen Freunden, sind Beinahefrauen und Fastmänner: Die haben nur Evolutionsreste zwischen den Beinen! Sie haben zwar Schwänze, aber sehr kleine, was an der hormonellen Unordnung liegt. Das war bedauerlich. Denn wenn Fred etwas interessierte, dann große Dinger. Richtig große! Die aber bekam er nicht wirklich zu sehen. Allenfalls ganz flüchtig, wenn sich im Stadtbad einer der Familienväter abseifte.

Mit siebzehn wurde es Zeit, in die Stadt zu ziehen.

Wie ein junger gieriger Wolf streunte er durch die Nacht, immer auf der Hut vor den Schwulen und deren Handtaschen! Manchmal aber beobachtete er Bauarbeiter oder sah Polizisten hinterher und spürte eine Sehnsucht, die er nicht einordnen konnte. Mit wachen Sinnen lauerte er, sah Männer, die bisweilen seinen Blick erwiderten, ihn aber noch verschreckten. Das Vorurteil von den weibischen Schwulen schien sich allzu oft zu bestätigen. Denn auch als er, einem starken inneren Impuls folgend, in den einzigen schwulen Buchladen geriet, hauchte ihm der Besitzer sanft entgegen. Fred wich verunsichert zurück und wollte bereits wieder gehen, als er vor einem überdimensioniert großen Buch stehen blieb: *Tom of Finland: The Art of Pleasure.* Eine unverkäufliche Sonderausgabe. So zumindest stand es auf dem Hinweisschild.

Von Tom of Finland hatte Fred noch nie etwas gehört. Als er das Buch neugierig aufschlug, konnte er es nicht glauben. Um Gottes willen! Wer kam denn auf solche Ideen? Er sah sich verlegen um. Wenn ihn jemand dabei beobachtete, dass er sich so etwas anschaute … Er schämte sich. So offensichtlich hatte ihn noch niemals eine Abbildung von Männern – richtigen Männern – in Bann gezogen.

Hier konnte er nicht länger bleiben, zumal ihm bereits die Röte ins Gesicht gekrochen war und der Buchhändler ihn beobachtete und dabei bescheuert grinste. Fred musste weg und die

shirt, to watch him while he showered. He wanted to wear his leather jacket, the one that hung in the barn, too big for Fred's smaller frame.

Gays, his friends told him, are practically women, with little, underdeveloped cocks between their legs – leftovers from a physical development void of hormones. But Fred was different. What interested him was much bigger things. Really big ones. But he never had the opportunity to see one, only once, fleetingly, in the locker room when the others were showering.

At seventeen, it was time to move to the city. Like a young, hungry wolf he dove into the night, always on the look-out for gay men with their purses. Sometimes he would watch construction workers, or would study a police officer from behind, and feel a strange longing that he didn't understand.

Often enough, the stereotype about the feminine homosexuals seemed to prove itself true. Once, on an whim, he entered a gay bookstore, and was greeted by the owner in a voice, gentler than a whisper. He turned to go, overwhelmed by insecurity, but stopped in his tracks at the sight of an overly large book: *Tom of Finland: The Art of Pleasure.* A display book, not for sale. Or at least, that's what it said on the sign.

He had never heard of a Tom of Finland before. When he opened the book, he couldn't believe his eyes. Good Lord! Who could come up with something like that? He glanced to see if anyone was around. If someone caught him looking at a book like this … he felt ashamed. Pictures of men – real men – had never cast such a strong spell over him before.

He couldn't stay any longer, especially not blushing the way he was and under the inquisitive eyes of the grinning store owner. Fred had to get away from the muscle-packed men in uniform, the cowboys and the sailors – especially from their enormous cocks!

He spent the next couple of days in the changing room of the local swimming

muskelbepackten Kerle in Uniform, die Cowboys und Seemänner wieder loswerden – und ganz besonders deren riesige Schwänze!

In den nächsten Tagen zog es ihn in die Umkleidekabinen des öffentlichen Hallenbades, die ein oder andere Klappe, immer auf der Suche nach Tom of Finland-Männern und schließlich – nur um sich zu vergewissern, dass die Sittenpolizei das Buch längst fortgeräumt hatte – schlich er wieder in den schwulen Buchladen zurück.

Der Buchhändler hatte allem Anschein nach noch einen Kollegen, der so gut aussah, dass Fred fast das Buch vergessen hätte. Der nahm aber keinerlei Notiz von ihm als neuen potenziellen Kunden, sondern packte seelenruhig eine Lieferung aus.

Mit Herzklopfen schlug Fred das Buch wahllos auf, versicherte sich, dass ihn niemand beobachtete, und sah sprachlos auf den vom Zufall gewählten Druck in der Mitte des Buches.

Tom of Finland hatte Freds geheimste Träume künstlerisch umgesetzt! Die Abbildung fesselte ihn völlig. Bewegungsunfähig und mit staubtrockenem Mund, in stiller Erwartung, seine Mutter oder der liebe Gott persönlich würden aus dem Hinterhalt auftauchen und ihn zur Rede stellen, starrte er auf das Gewimmel, das sich ihm bot, und versuchte, sich einen Überblick zu verschaffen. Vor ihm, zum Greifen nah, hatten sich hemmungslose Kerle zu einer Orgie zusammengefunden.

Dort waren sie also, die Männer, die er Nacht für Nacht suchte, aber bislang nicht gefunden hatte: große Kerle in Uniform. Halbnackte, die knieten. Polizisten mit Helmen auf den Köpfen und Pistolen an den Hüften. Dazu jede Menge enorm große, steil aufgerichtete Schwänze, die aus offenen Hosen standen und hingebungsvoll im Maul eines anderen oder – schlimmer noch – in dessen Hinterteil steckten! Derartig große Schwänze gab es nicht! Und doch: Auf diesem Druck waren sie zu sehen. Polizistenriesenschwänze!

Nie wieder würde er die Bilder loswerden können. Sie brannten sich ein. Sein Blick sprang wie ein unachtsam gezündeter Knallfrosch von einer in die andere Ecke des Drucks. Rechts unten ein blonder Typ, der mit heruntergezogenen Hosen kniete und seinen blanken, makellosen Arsch präsentierte. Die Striemen darauf stamm-

pool, and in a few gay bars, always looking for the kind of men Tom of Finland had drawn in that book. Frustrated, he ultimately slipped back into the gay bookstore, to prove to himself that the book was most definitely gone by now. The store owner seemed to have a colleague who took shifts, and who looked so good that Fred almost forgot about the book. The new guy behind the counter, however, took no notice of his potential customer, and continued to quietly unpack a delivery.

His heart beating, Fred opened the book to a random page, and, after making sure no one was watching behind him, looked breathlessly at the chosen illustration in the middle of the book.

Tom of Finland had taken Fred's most secret dreams and packed them onto the page! He was enthralled by the drawing. Unable to move, his mouth dry, and half expecting his mother or even God to appear behind him, demanding an explanation, Fred stared at the smorgasbord of men before him, and tried to take in everything with his eyes. Right in front of him, so close he could almost reach out and touch them, were men in the throes of a no-holds-barred orgy.

So that's where they had been, those men he had been searching for night after night, but had never found: massive men in uniforms. Half-naked guys on their knees. Police officers with helmets on their heads and pistols on their hips. And especially all those enormous, rock hard cocks, standing erect, jutting out of open pants and into the mouths of the others, or worse yet, in their backsides! Cocks that big couldn't exist! Yet here they were, right in front of him. Huge police cocks! He would never be able to get those images out of his head. They were permanently etched onto his brain. His gaze sprang like sparks from a wildfire from one corner of the book to the other. Bottom right, a blond, his pants pulled down and his shining, pristine ass on display. The red welts came from the man who stood above him with a knowing grin on his face and a riding crop in his

ten ganz offensichtlich von dem Kerl, der breit grinsend über ihm stand, die Gerte, die gerade niedergesaust war, in der rechten Hand. Auch seine Hose war heruntergelassen, zum Gefallen des Bullen hinter ihm, der sich bereits eingelocht hatte.

Wo gab es nur diese Stiefel? Fred musste unbedingt solche haben, beziehungsweise sie spüren. Wie der Typ ganz rechts, der damit beschäftigt war, seinen Schwanz in einem Arsch zu versenken und der die Stiefelspitze eines unter ihm liegenden Kerls aufmunternd im Schritt zu spüren bekam.

Es fiel Fred schwer, den Überblick zu behalten. Wie viele Kerle waren das? Er zählte und versuchte nicht allzu angestrengt dabei auszusehen: Elf. Nein, zwölf! Den Bullen auf der rechten Bildseite hätte er fast übersehen. Er bog jenem Typen, der die Hiebe einzustecken hatte, den steifen Schwanz nach hinten. Aus Erfahrung wusste Fred, wie geil das sein konnte. Dass es so etwas einfach in einem Buch zu sehen gab … nicht zu fassen! Wer kam nur auf solche Gedanken? Wer war derart schamlos?

Tom of Finland – diesen Namen musste er sich merken.

Freds harter Schwanz hatte sich in der Enge seiner Jeans bereits über den Bund seines Slips hochgeschoben und schmerzte, weil er gegen den Ledergürtel stieß, was Fred zusätzlich erregte. Er wollte nur noch eines: Das Seil spüren, das man dem Kerl in der Mitte des Bildes um sein Gehänge gewickelt hatte und an dem man beherzt zog. Gleichzeitig träumte er von einer streng geschlagenen Gerte und davon, wie er selbst im Schritt eines dieser Bullen kniet. Er suchte sich einen der Kerle aus, dabei sahen alle mehr oder weniger gleich aus. Alle mit Gütesiegel, Handelsklasse 1A. Keiner, der besonders intelligent wirkte. Einer mit Helm sollte es sein. Der mit Sonnenbrille! Ach was! Warum nur einer? Zwei, vielleicht drei dieser Fickmaschinen sollten es ihm gleichzeitig besorgen, ihn richtig fertigmachen! Dabei hatte er noch nie. Nicht richtig jedenfalls. Es würde wehtun. Ganz bestimmt. Er aber würde sich anstrengen und sie – so stellte er sich das vor – würden ihn zu nehmen wissen, ihn weichmachen und all seine Hemmungen mit ihren langen, harten Stößen in Luft auflösen. Danach würde Fred sich für sie, dankbar ergeben, richtig ins Zeug legen …

hand. His pants too were on the floor, to the pleasure of the cop standing behind him, and had firmly planted his manhood down, hilt deep.

Where could he find boots like that? Fred had to have them, at least he had to touch them. Like the man on the right, who was busy sinking his cock into an ass, and who blissfully felt the toe of the man's boot beneath him grinding into his crotch.

Fred couldn't keep track of them all. How many men were there? He counted, hoping his concentrating gaze didn't give him away: eleven. No, twelve! He had overlooked the cop on the right. The one busy bending the cock of his spanking victim backwards. Fred knew from experience how good that felt. That images like these were so easily on display … unbelievable! Who came up with such ideas? Who was shameless enough? Tom of Finland – he had to remember that name.

Fred's throbbing hard-on had snaked its way passed the waist of his tight jeans, pressing against his leather belt, which just added to his excitement. He wanted one thing: to feel that rope snugly around his balls like the man in the middle of the drawing, someone firmly tugging on it … At the same time he dreamt of the sound the riding crop would make and pictured himself kneeling crotch level in front of one of those cops. Which one would he pick? They all looked pretty much the same. All of them had perfect, prime-beef bodies – none seemed particularly intelligent. How about the one with the helmet? Or that one, with the sunglasses? Wait, why just one? Two, maybe three of these fuck machines should take him on at the same time, should put him through his paces! Even though it'd be his first time. Well, almost. It would hurt. Definitely. But he would try his best to please, and they, he thought, would know how to deal with him, would soften him up and slowly wear down his resistance with their long, hard thrusts. Then afterwards, Fred, blissful in his submission, would really show them what he had …

„Du wirst noch unter die Räder kommen!", hörte er die Mutter wieder, ignorierte sie aber und wollte, dass ihn endlich jemand zum Mann machte. Im Hintergrund, etwas blasser angelegt, erkannte er, was er soeben noch übersehen hatte: Ein Kerl besorgte es einem anderen mit der Faust, die er komplett in ihm versenkt hatte.

Da hatte der Künstler nun wirklich übertrieben. Eine Faust … das war nun wirklich nicht realistisch.

Gedankenverloren strich Fred mit seinen Fingerspitzen über den so schamlos entgegengereckten Arsch und wollte, dass noch ein paar Striemen hinzukamen – vielleicht auch eigene spüren. So genau konnte er das nicht sagen.

„Na, so interessiert?" Freds offensichtliche Erregung war auch dem Vertretungsbuchhändler nicht entgangen, der plötzlich hinter ihm stand und ihn fast zu Tode erschreckte. Der musste ihn schon eine ganze Weile beobachtet haben und sich seiner Sache ziemlich sicher sein, denn er schob sich näher und sein erregtes Ding ungeniert Fred in den Rücken.

„Ich werd gleich von meinem Langweiler-Chef abgelöst", sagt er mit donnernder Stimme. „Dann gehen wir zu mir nach Hause und spielen Szene für Szene nach. Was hältst du davon?"

Gar nichts! Fred hielt gar nichts davon! Diesem Typen würde er nicht gewachsen sein. Angst stieg in ihm auf. Das Atmen hatte er eingestellt und wollte nur noch schnell hier raus. Dann aber spürte Fred die große Hand auf seinem Hintern, die ihn beruhigte und ihn gleichzeitig an eine Gerte denken ließ. Er stöhnte gegen seinen Willen und ließ zu, dass man seine Hand nahm und sie nach hinten direkt zwischen die Beine des aufdringlichen Kerls führte. (Das mit dem Evolutionsrest schien nicht auf jeden Schwulen zuzutreffen). Fred wagte einen schüchternen Blick und zitterte ein wenig, was dem anderen zu gefallen schien. „Na, was ist, mein Kleiner? Bereit?"

Nein, war er nicht. Ganz sicher nicht! Er nickte, sah noch einmal auf das lustvolle Getümmel vor sich, senkte nun seinen Blick – und dann entdeckte er sie, die schwarzen Lederstiefel, die bis zu den Knien hinaufreichten.

"You'll end up in the gutter!" he heard his mother again. He ignored the voice, yearning for someone to finally make him a man. In the background, he spotted something in the drawing he had missed the first time: a guy was busy pleasuring another guy using his fist, which had completely disappeared in the guy's ass. The artist had really taken it a bit too far there. A fist … that couldn't be real. Completely in awe, Fred let the tip of his finger caress the ass so shamelessly on display and wished there were more welts to admire – maybe even wanting to feel them himself. He couldn't say exactly.

 "See something you like?" Fred's obvious arousal hadn't escaped the attention of the man behind the counter, who suddenly stood behind him scaring him half to death. He had to have been standing there watching for a long time, and must have noticed Fred's desires, seeing that his turgid manhood was firmly nudging Fred in the back. "I get off work in a few minutes," he said with a thunderous voice. "Then we can head back to my place, and act everything out, scene for scene. What do you say about that?"

Nothing! He could think of nothing to say about that! This guy was out of his league. He felt fear taking hold of him. He had almost stopped breathing and only wanted to get out of there as fast as he could. Before he could act on these thoughts, however, Fred felt a large hand on his behind, that calmed him down, and his thoughts wandered to the riding crop … He moaned against his will and let the man take his hand and place it right against his crotch. (All that talk about gay men and their underdeveloped cocks seemed not to be true after all.) Shyly, Fred looked up and trembled, which seemed to amuse the guy. "Well, what do you say? Are you ready?"

No, he wasn't ready. Definitely not! He nodded, looked one last time at the orgy on the pages of the book, and allowed his gaze to slowly sink toward the floor, until he saw them: the black leather boots on the other guy's feet, knee-high, black leather boots.

Translation: Grant Nichols and Jim Baker

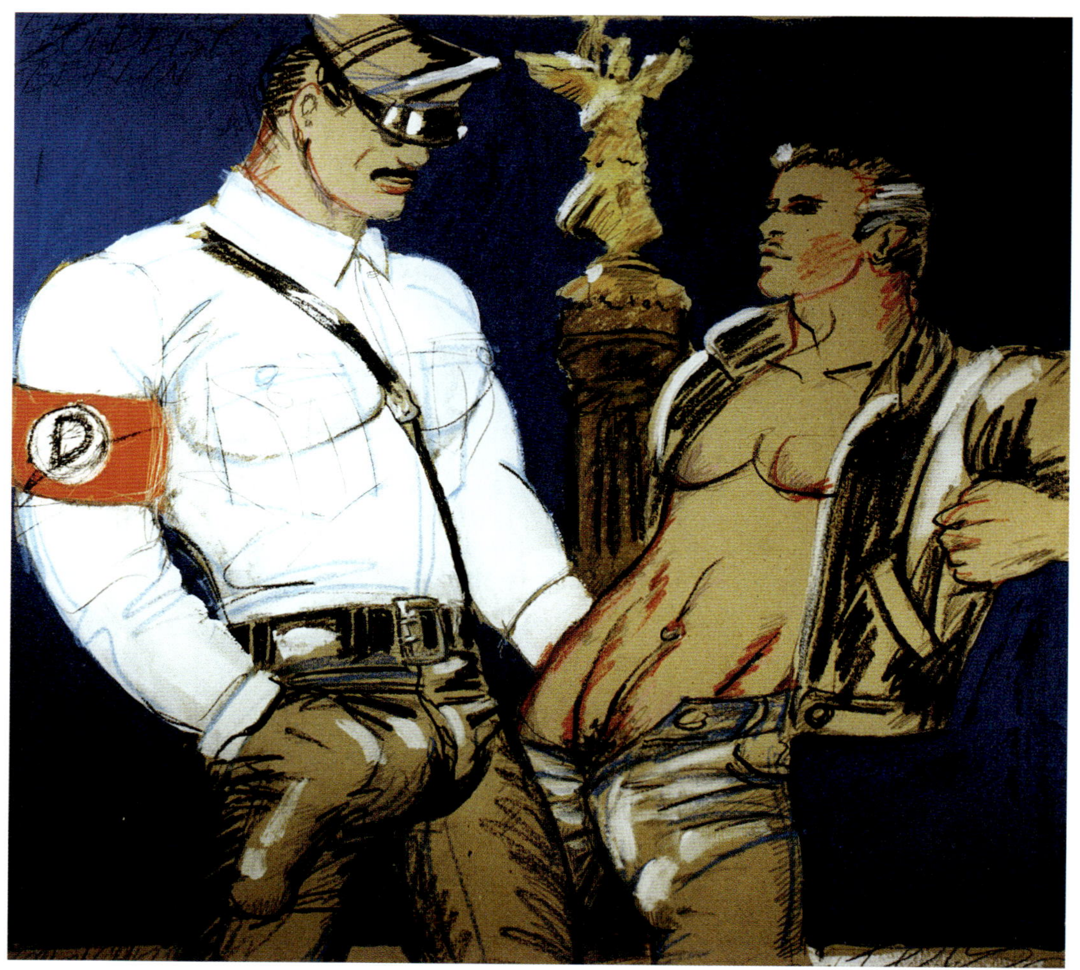

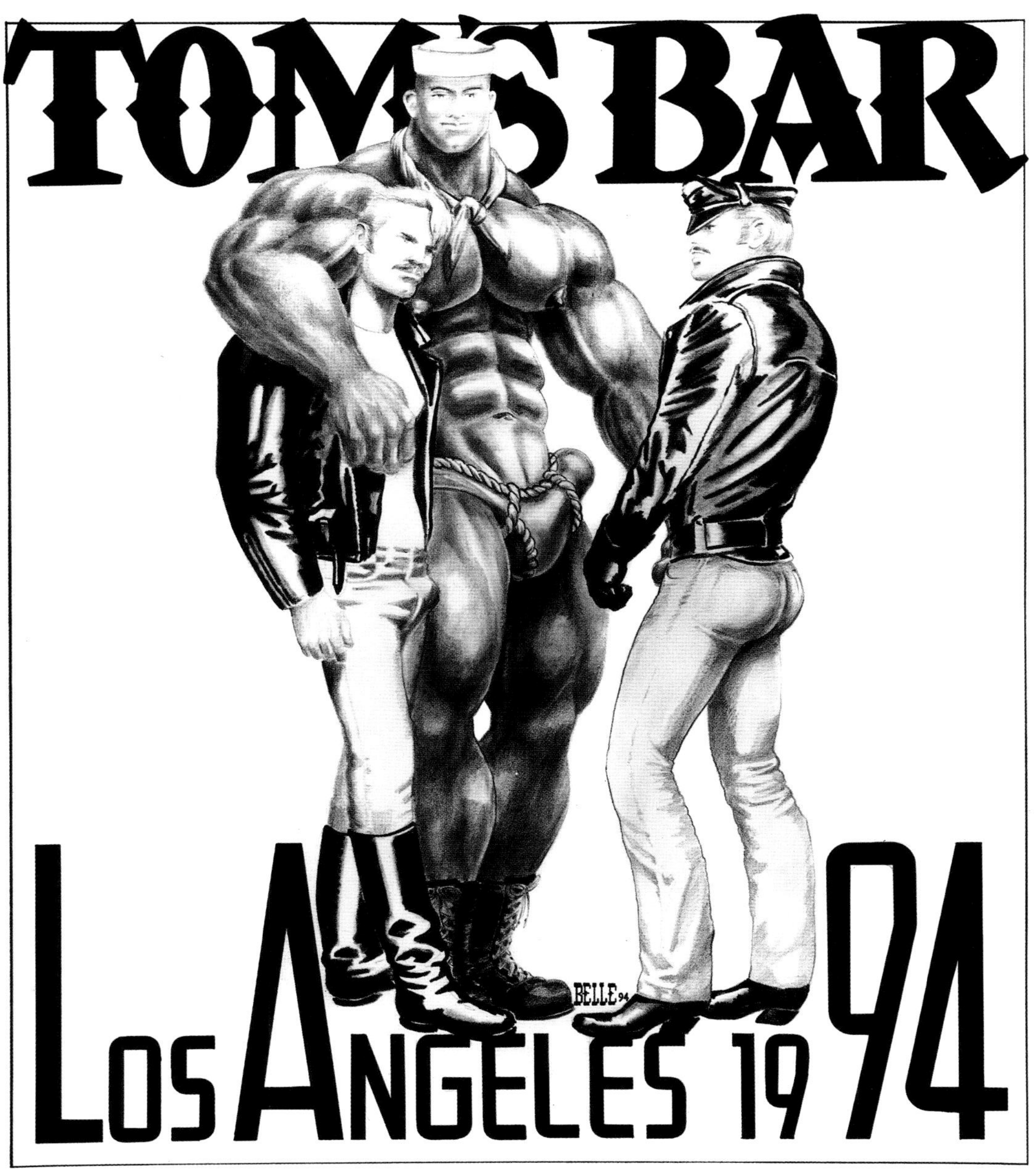
TOM'S BAR
BELLE '94
L.A. LOS ANGELES 1994

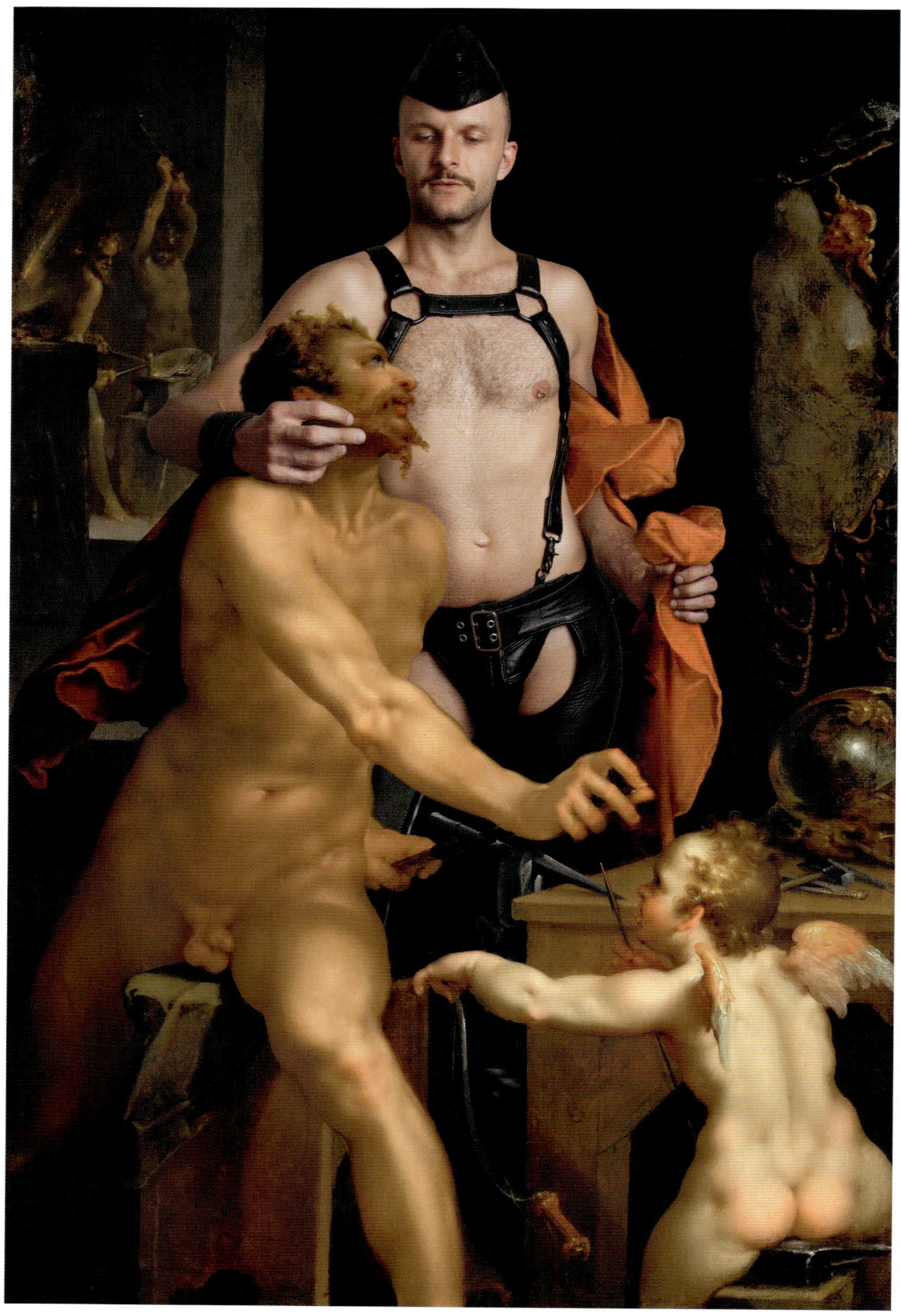

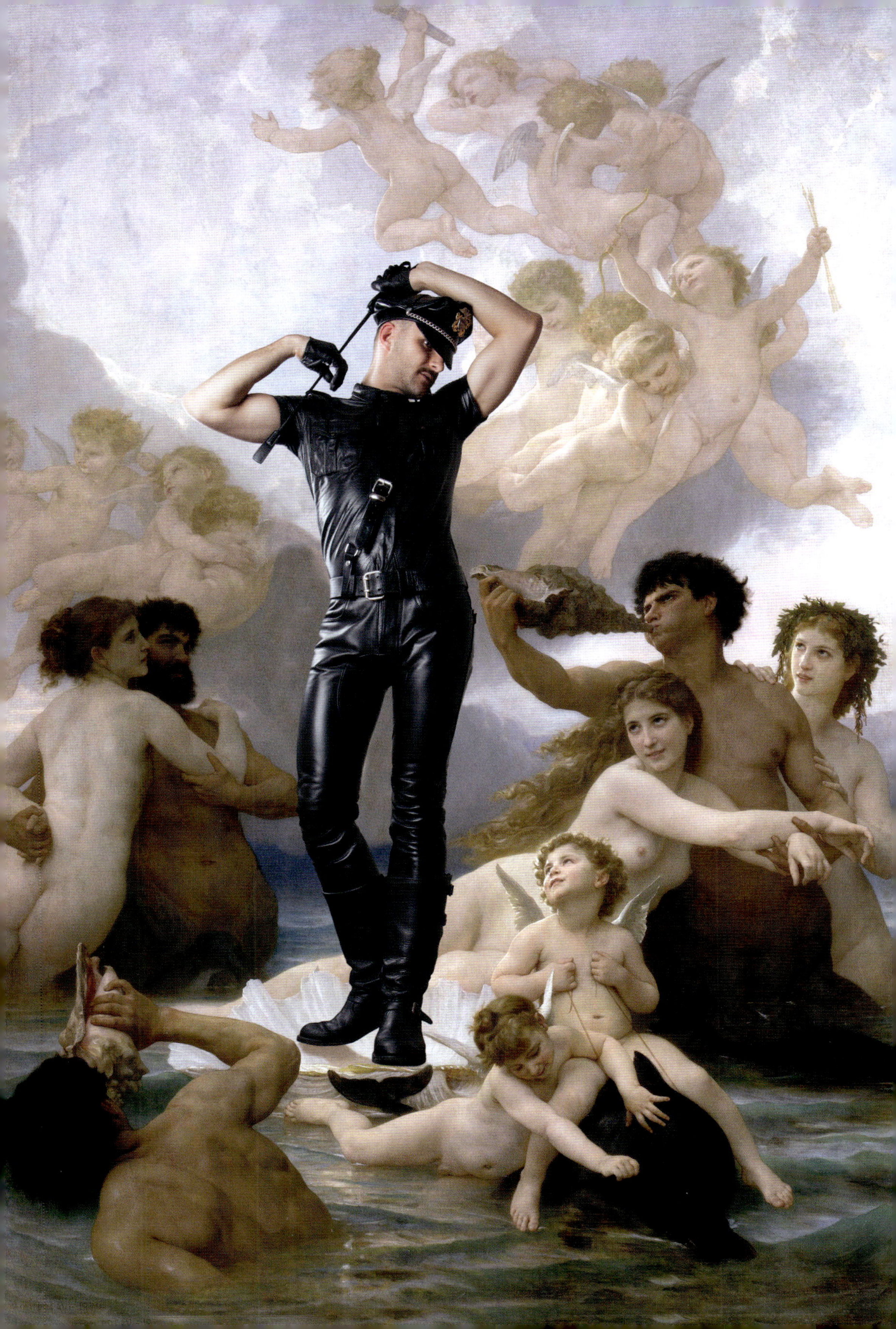

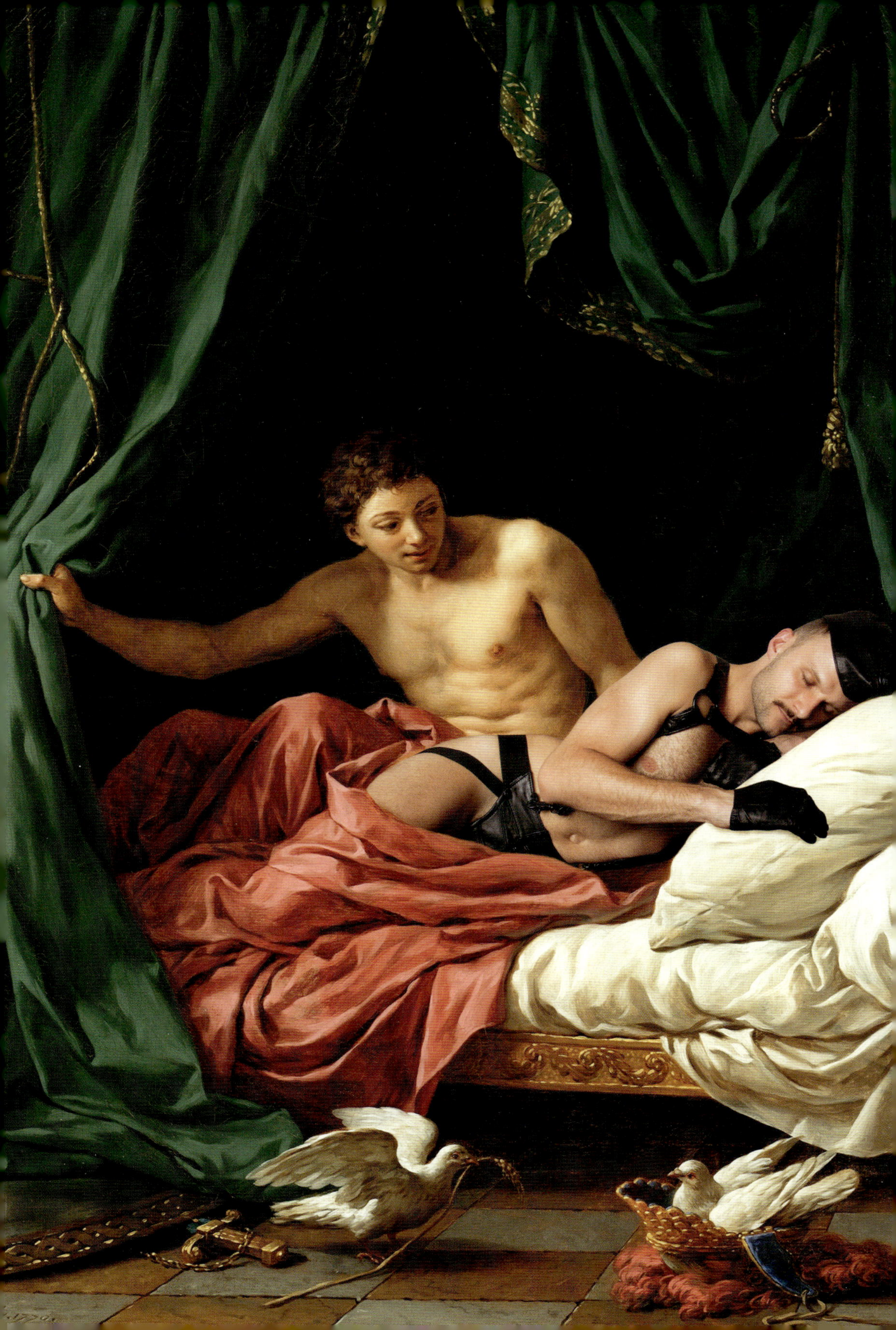

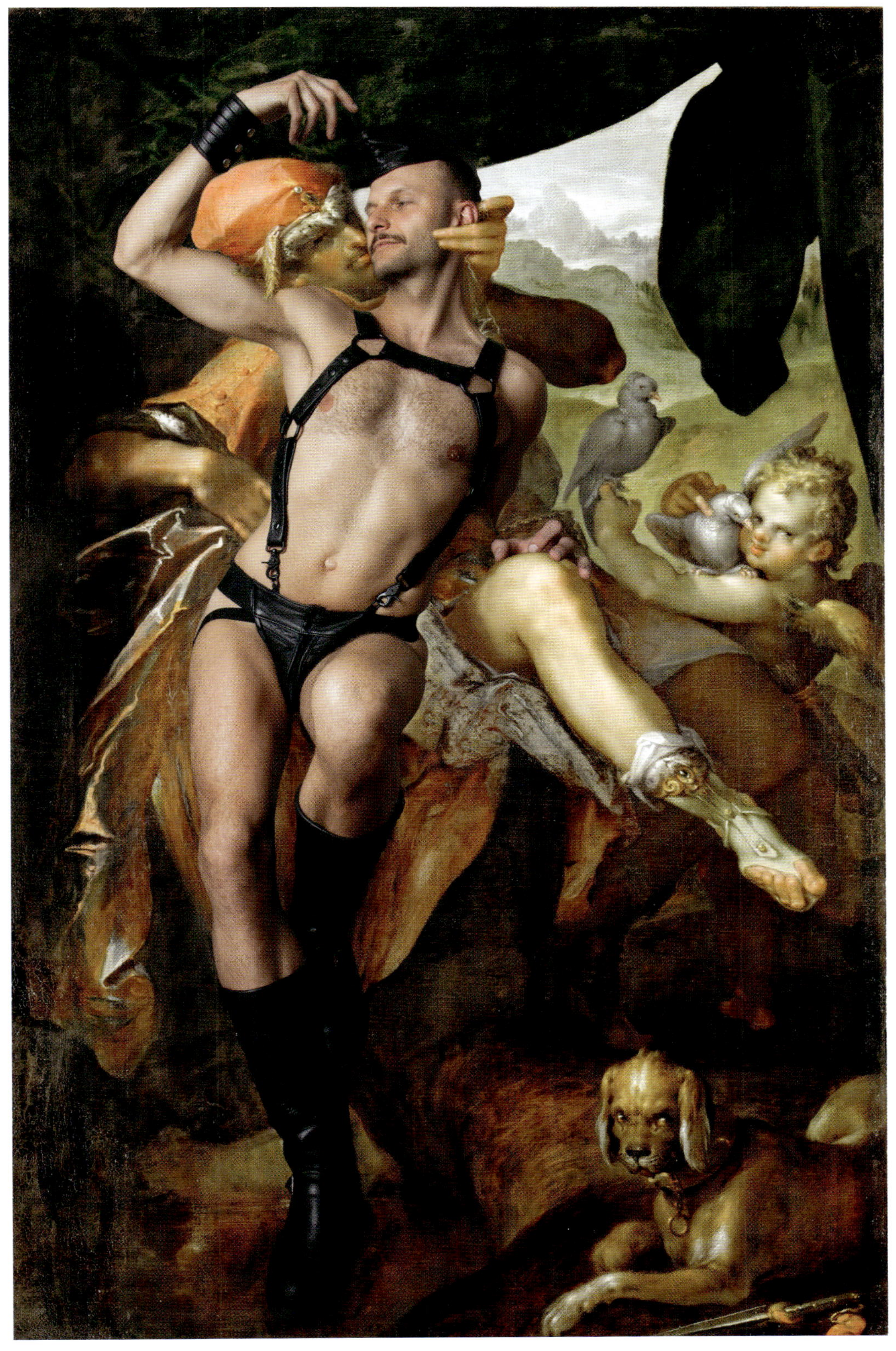

STEVEN REIGNS

The Bottom Speaks • Jetzt spricht der Bottom

My hole is an endless commodity. I give it to many, keep giving, serving, and pleasing. My hole is a secret I discovered laying on the bedroom floor of my youth, rubbed it, licked my fingers and inserted them. I loved how it made me feel as I explored beyond the hairy opening, electric with divination. I've shared the secret with thousands now, let men gaze hungrily at it puckered, pursed or budded, its pale pinkness a deceptive gate. I love when men get lost inside me. I want to consume their cocks, their loads, their body, their being. I want to consume their world in my ass, greedily engulf whatever is given. I take as much as I can, as many as I can, seeing if they can stuff me full, feed me to fulfillment. They mount me, fuck me, want me, want to own this ass as much as I want to own them. There is no limit. I am limitless, a bottomless bottom.

Their dicks or fists pound as if trying to crack me open from the inside. They want their cock to break this booty, my body, pushing and slamming hard. It's a desire they don't name, don't examine, their bodies instinctively moving to conquer and divide. They want me broken in half, as if I might reveal some essence, hoping I'll burst open like a piñata, spilling pieces of me on the floor they can put in their pocket and eat later.

They love my ass. I hear it at the gym in tight shorts, in the locker room when I'm pulling my jeans over a jockstrap. They love my ass when they're inside it; the confession comes in words and moans. But there is hate, too; in direct quantity to how much they hate themselves. The preacher, teacher, daddy beseecher telling them to turn away from instinct. They take the leftover resentment and empty it inside me. Take control, find some missing connection, fill me up with cum in search of their own fulfillment.

I can take it. This cunt is a conduit.

Mein Loch ist für alle da. Ich öffne es vielen, wieder und wieder bediene und befriedige ich sie. Mein Loch ist ein Geheimnis, das ich entdeckte, als ich in meinem Jugendzimmer auf dem Boden lag. Ich rieb es, leckte meine Finger und steckte sie mir rein. Ich fand es toll, wie es sich anfühlte, als ich es jenseits der haarigen kleinen Öffnung erforschte, ganz high von einem Gefühl der Vorahnung. Mittlerweile habe ich dieses Geheimnis mit Tausenden geteilt. Ich lasse Männer gierig zusehen, wie sich mein Loch zusammenzieht, kräuselt und aufstülpt, das blasse Rosa eine trügerische Pforte. Ich liebe es, wenn Männer sich in mir verlieren. Ich möchte ihre Schwänze, ihre Spermaladungen, ihre Körper und ihr ganzes Wesen aufsaugen. Ich möchte ihre ganze Welt in meinem Arsch aufnehmen und mir gierig alles einverleiben, was sie mir geben können. Ich nehme so viel und so viele auf, wie ich nur irgend kann. Ich bin immer darauf bedacht, dass sie mich komplett ausfüllen, mich total sättigen. Sie besteigen mich, ficken mich, wollen mich, wollen diesen Arsch genauso sehr besitzen wie ich sie besitzen will. Da gibt es keine Grenzen. Ich bin grenzenlos, ein bodenloser Bottom, ein Fass ohne Boden.

Ihr Schwänze und Fäuste stoßen zu, so als ob sie versuchten, mein Inneres aufzureißen. Sie wollen mir mit ihren Prügeln den Arsch aufreißen, meinen ganzen Körper zerteilen, sie stoßen und bolzen mit aller Kraft. Es ist ein Verlangen, das sie nicht untersuchen und benennen. Sie setzen ihre Körper instinktiv ein, um zu besiegen und aufzuteilen. Sie wollen mich entzweibrechen, als ob ich dann das Wesentliche freigeben würde; sie hoffen, dass ich aufplatze wie eine Piñata, wie ein Topf voller Süßigkeiten, sodass Teile von mir auf den Boden fallen, die sie in ihre Taschen stecken und dann später essen können.

Sie lieben meinen Arsch. Ich höre das im Fitnessstudio, wenn ich enge Shorts trage, oder im Umkleideraum, wenn ich mir die Jeans über den Jockstrap hochziehe. Sie lieben meinen Arsch, wenn sie in ihm drinstecken; ihre Bekenntnisse kommen verbal oder als Gestöhne. Aber da ist auch Hass und zwar im selben Maß, wie sie sich selbst hassen. Die Priester, Lehrer oder Väter haben ihnen eingebleut, ihren Trieben nicht

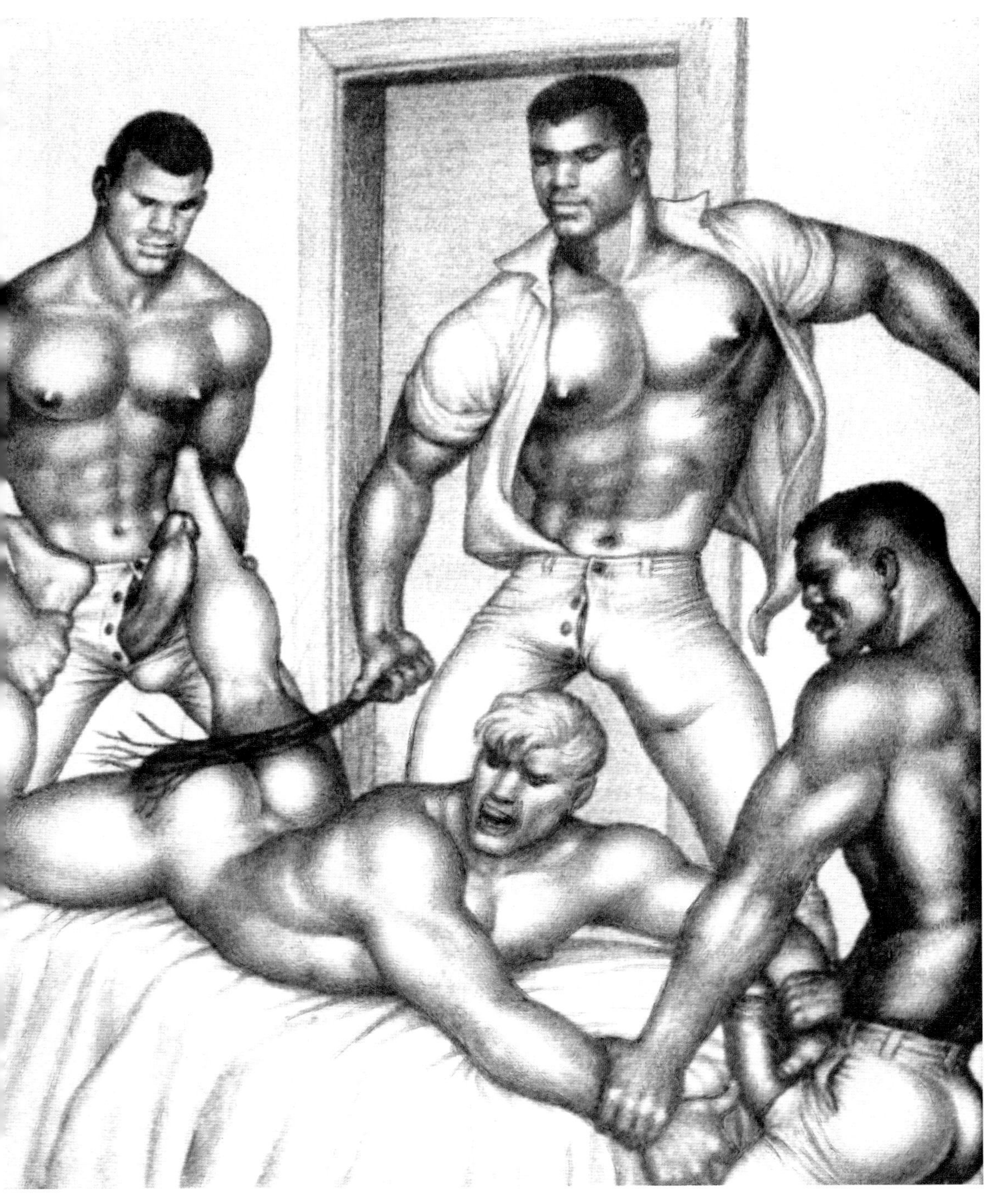

My hole has never been stolen without my wanting it stolen. There have been neither trespassers nor colonizers. I can take two at a time, the tunnel widening to a toughened lining that sponges up the cum. I'll never drown. My endless hole is inexhaustible. If it had a guestbook to sign upon entering, it would be filled with nameless cops, construction workers, cowboys, bean counters, the ugly, desperate, and dejected. Everyone is welcome here.

Here is another secret: Out of the thousands who've spent time inside me, it's never been the most attractive or the models that pleased me most. It's those who honed other skills to compensate for lesser looks and lack of muscle or their race or size. Those are the men my hole remembers most. They have channeled more power to their penises, can move and maneuver in ways those who take their bodies for granted cannot.

I'll take on groups or gangs or gargantuan cocks. Share me with friends, batter a birch on my butt, pants bulge as cocks plump inside them, yearning for the tightness I maintain. My ass can milk, stroke, delicately or in a fierce grip as if it will never let go. The men never leave the same way they entered; I take bits of them with me. I contain their multitudes deep inside. Here is the secret that remains my own; no matter how long or big their cocks, they will never arrive at their true destination. They keep pushing, higher and deeper, but my heart is the one place they will never reach. They will have to get there another way.

nachzugeben. Sie nehmen ihren aufgestauten Hass und leeren ihn in mir aus. Sie übernehmen die Kontrolle, finden eine fehlende Verbindung und füllen mich mit ihrem Sperma auf der Suche nach ihrer eigenen Erfüllung.

Ich kann das ab. Diese Fotze ist ein Kanal.

Mein Loch hat sich noch niemand genommen, ohne dass ich es nicht gewollt hätte. Es gab weder unerwünschte Eindringlinge noch Kolonisten. Ich kann zwei gleichzeitig aufnehmen, dann dehnt sich mein Arschloch zu einem strapazierfähigen Fickkanal aus, der das Sperma aufsaugt wie ein Schwamm. Ich werde niemals absaufen. Mein endloses Loch ist unerschöpflich. Wenn es ein Gästebuch hätte, in das man sich bei der Ankunft einträgt, dann wäre es gefüllt mit namenlosen Polizisten, Bauarbeitern, Cowboys, Erbsenzählern, mit Hässlichen, Verzweifelten und Entmutigten. Hier ist jeder willkommen.

Und noch ein Geheimnis: von den Tausenden, die Zeit in mir verbracht haben, waren es nie die Attraktivsten oder die Modeltypen, die mich am meisten befriedigt haben. Es waren vielmehr diejenigen, die andere Fähigkeiten verfeinert haben als Kompensation für weniger gutes Aussehen oder fehlende Muskeln, für ihre Rassenzugehörigkeit oder geringe Größe. Das sind die Männer, an die sich mein Loch am liebsten erinnert. Sie haben mehr Energie in ihre Schwänze fließen lassen und können sich auf eine Art und Weise bewegen, wie es jene Männer, die ihre Körper als Selbstverständlichkeit wahrnehmen, nicht können.

Ich stehe für ganze Gruppen, für Gangbangs und für Riesenschwänze zur Verfügung. Teile mich mit deinen Freunden, klatsche mir eine Peitsche auf den Hintern, während die Schwänze anschwellen und Hosen ausbeulen, weil sie sich nach meinem engen Loch sehnen. Mein Arschloch kann dich melken, wichsen, sanft oder so fest, als wollte es dich nie wieder loslassen. Die Männer verlassen es nie auf dieselbe Art wieder, wie sie eingedrungen sind. Ich behalte etwas von ihnen bei mir. Ich behalte ihre Masse tief in mir drin. Und hier ist mein Geheimnis: Ganz egal wie lang oder groß ihre Schwänze sind, sie werden nie bei ihrem wahren Ziel ankommen. Sie stoßen und stoßen, höher und tiefer, aber mein Herz werden sie nie erreichen. Dorthin müssen sie auf anderem Wege gelangen.

Übersetzung: Rinaldo Hopf

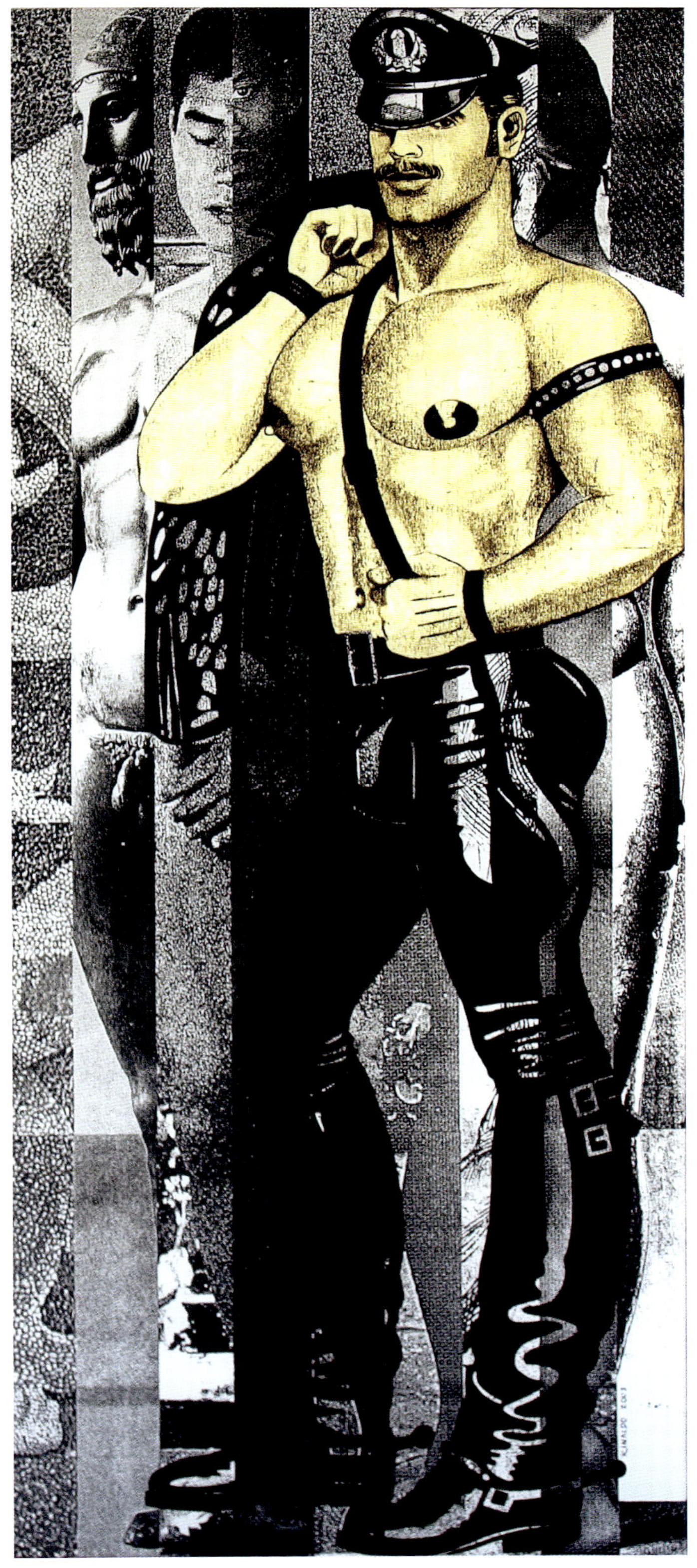

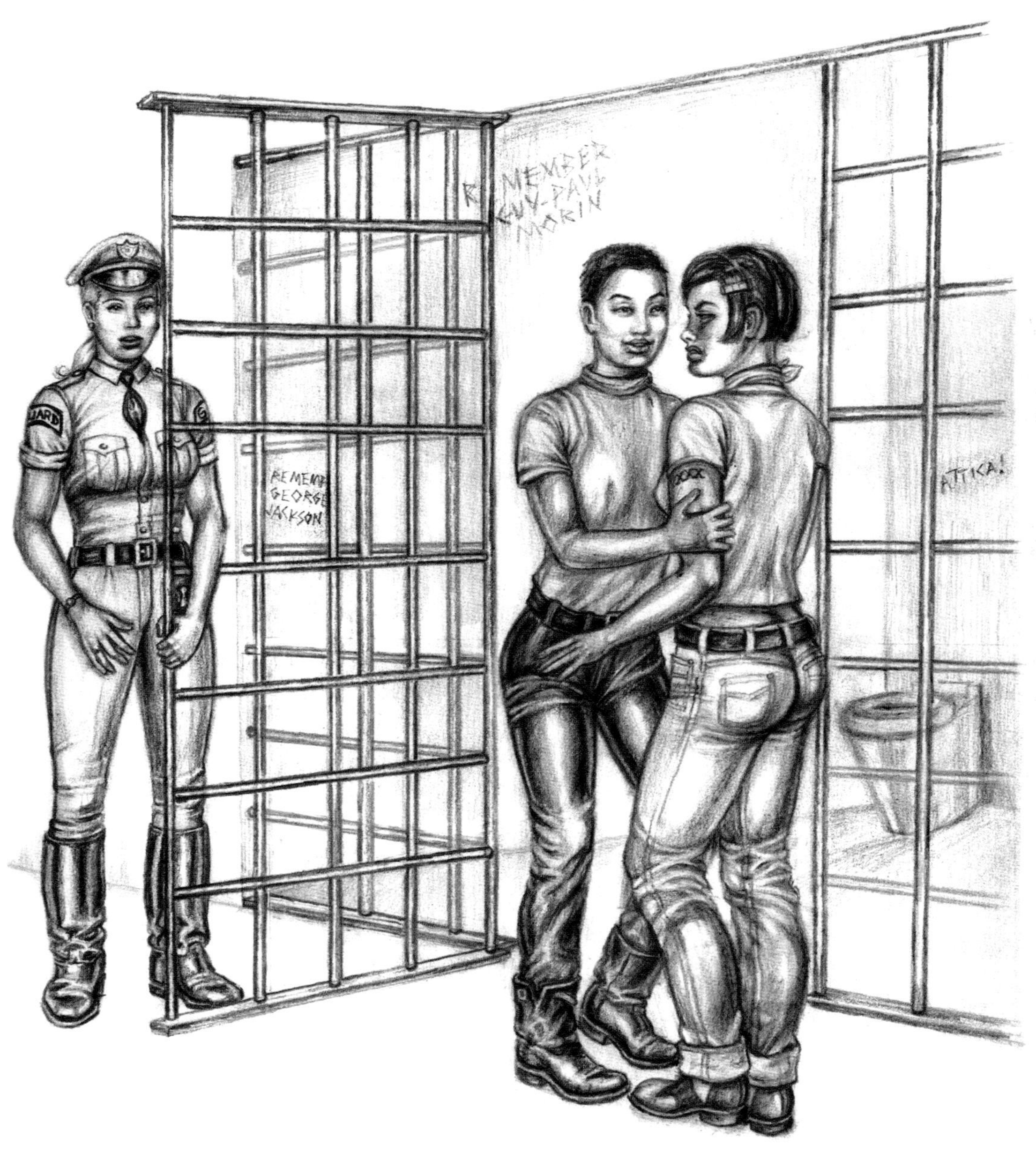
REMEMBER
GUV PAUL
MORIN
REMEMBER
GEORGE
JACKSON
GUARD
ATTICA!

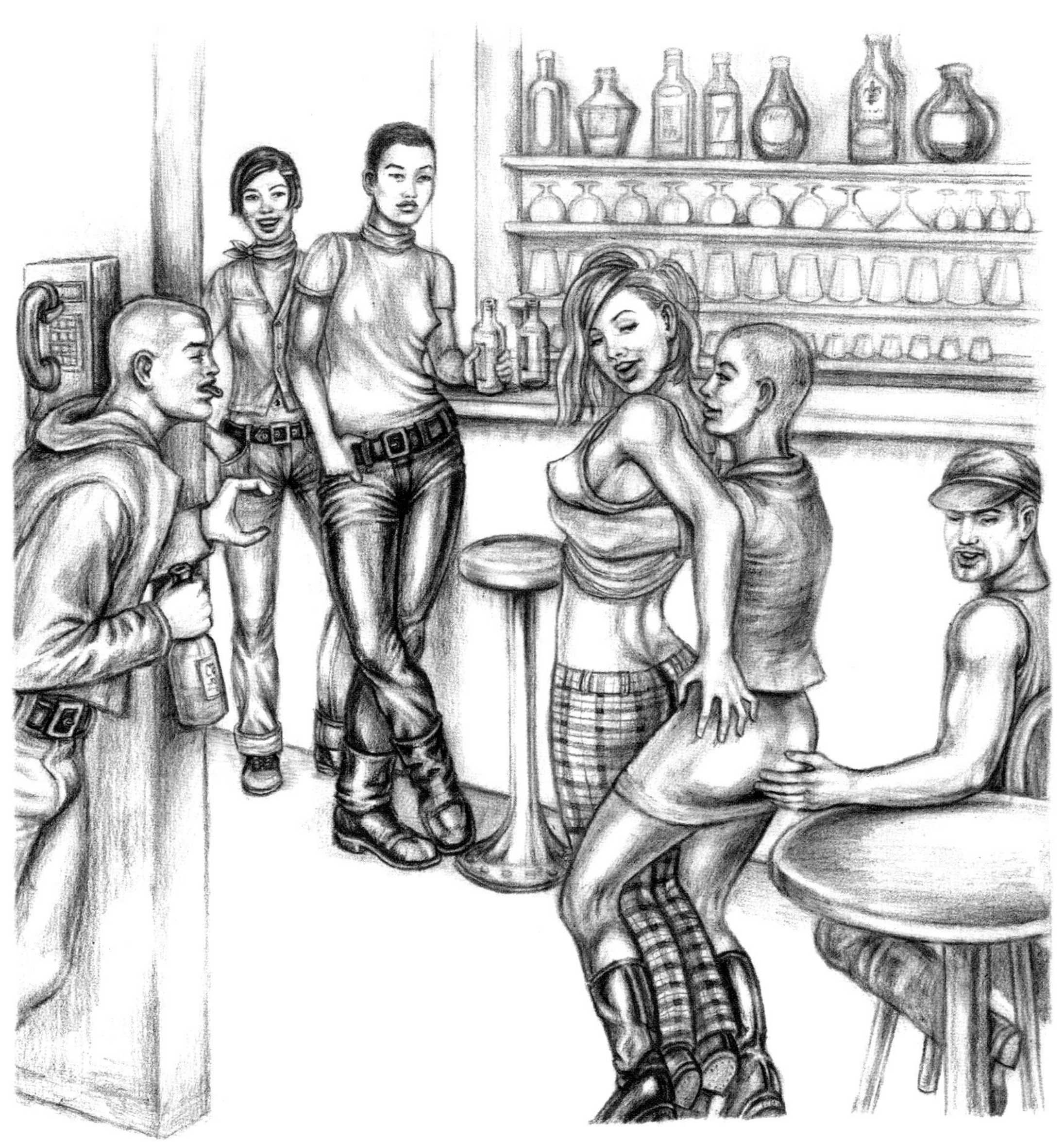

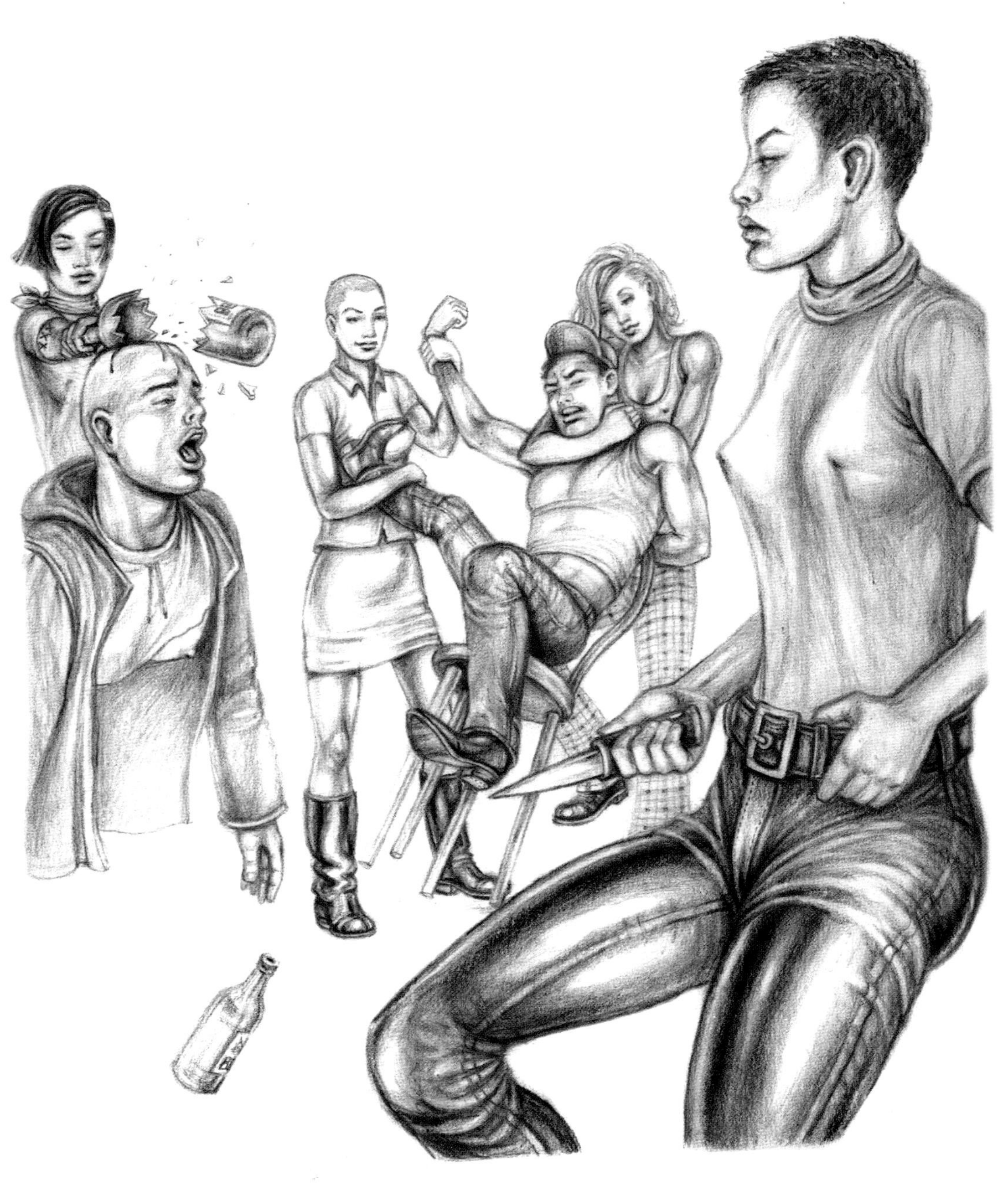

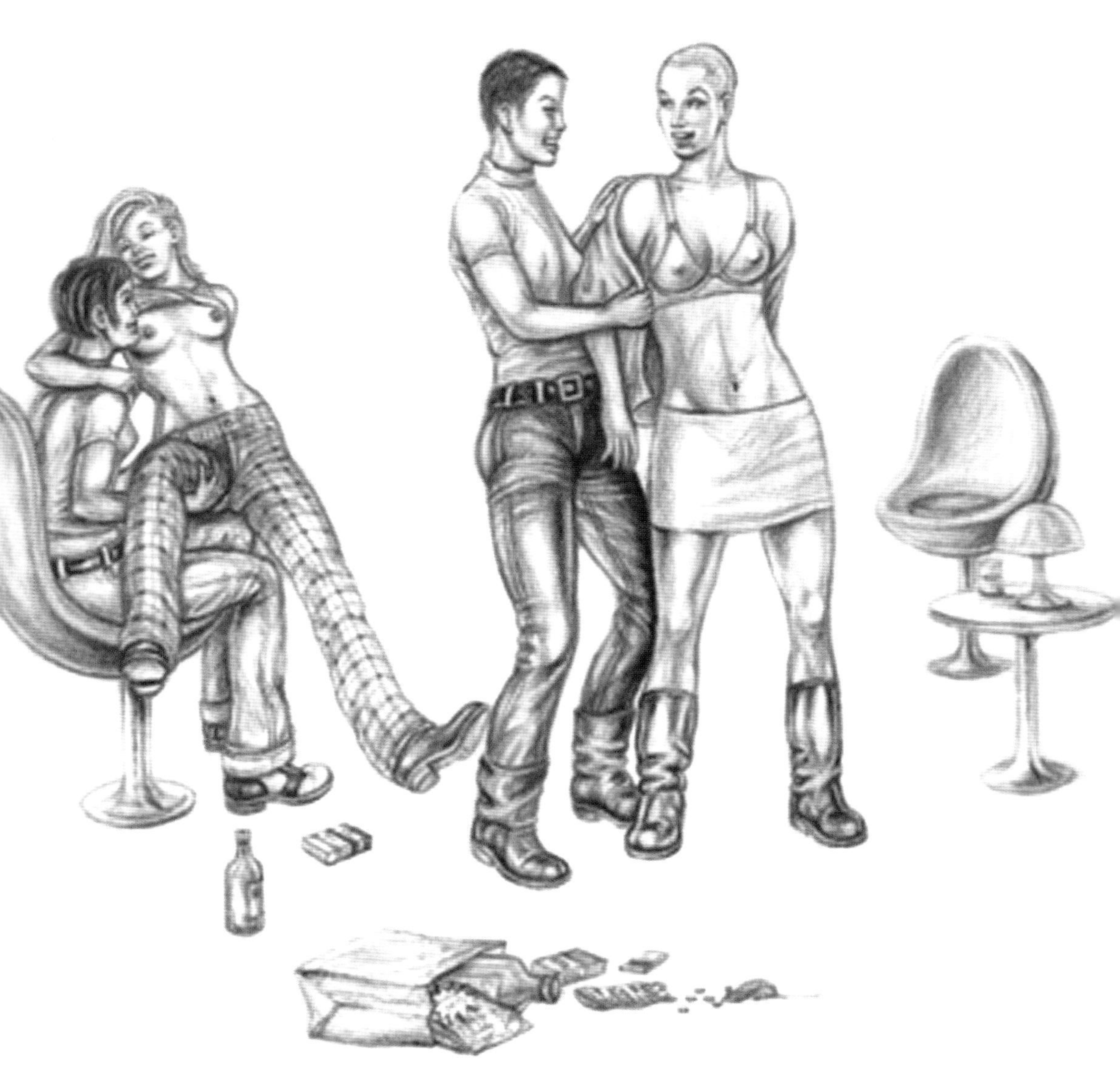

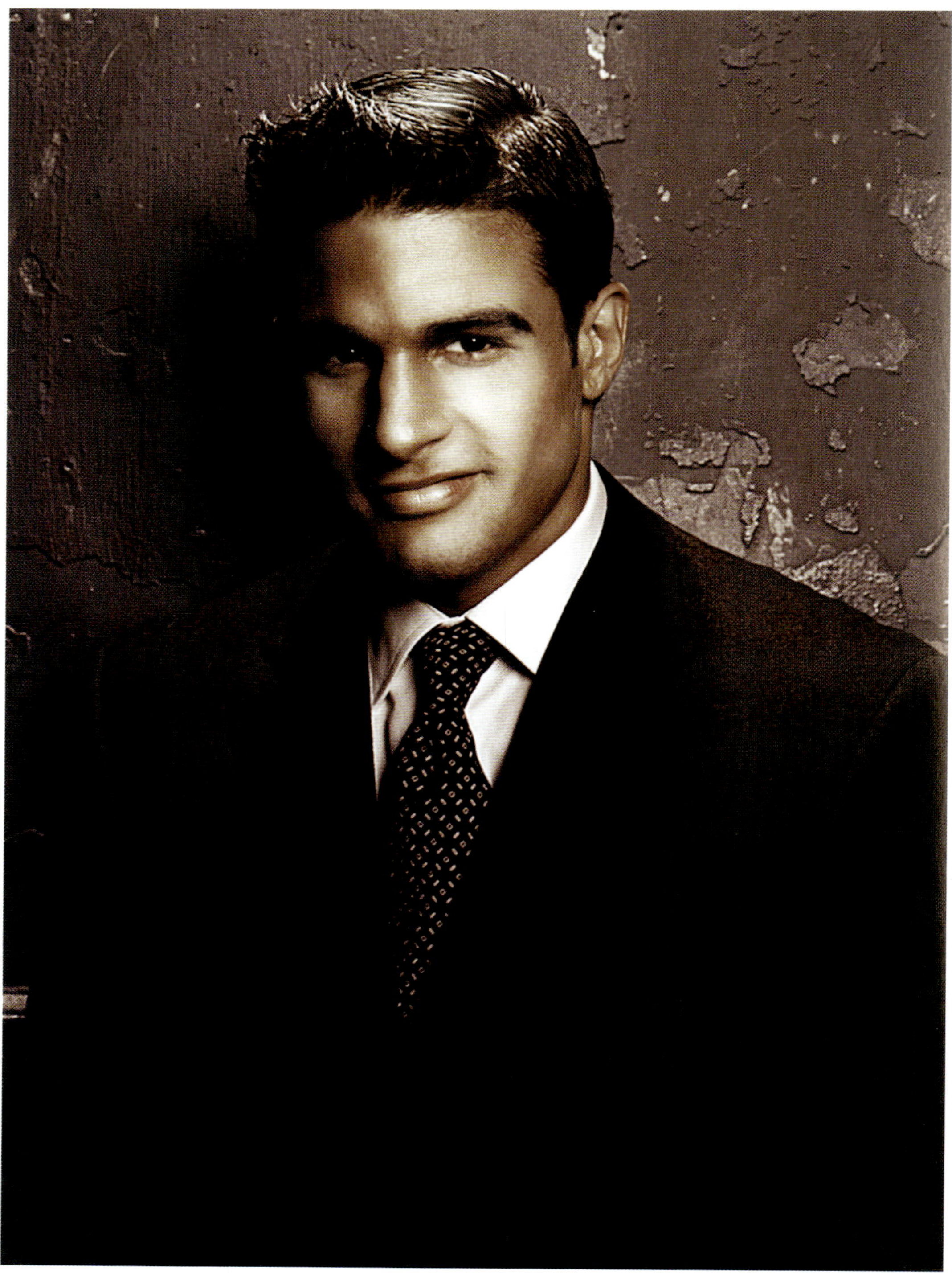

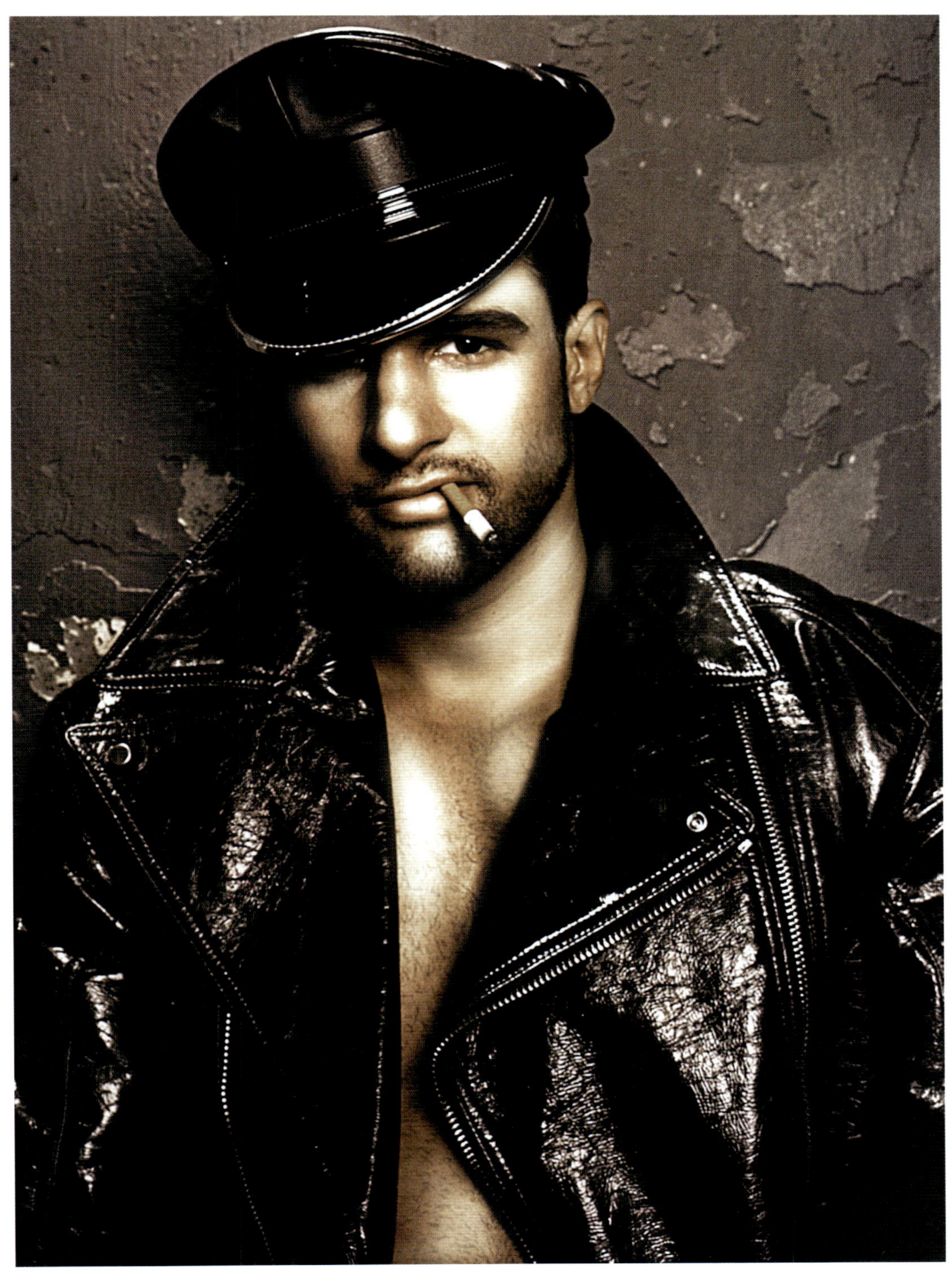

JAN GYMPEL

So ist das mit einem Heterotypen •
That's How It Goes with Straight Guys

„So, die Lampen hängen."

„Prima. Und die Wand?"

„Mach ich nachher. Jetzt hab ich erstmal Kohldampf." Er wischt sich mit dem Unterarm den Schweiß von der Stirn, nimmt einen Schluck aus der Bierflasche und schaut mich erwartungsvoll an.

„Das Fleisch braucht noch einen Moment", sage ich.

„Denn kann ich ja noch eine rauchen", erklärt er, zündet sich eine Zigarette an und kommt zu mir an den Schreibtisch. Zum Nikotingenuß auf den Balkon zu gehen, habe ich ihm gleich zu Beginn unserer Zweisamkeit untersagt: Entweder man raucht richtig oder gar nicht. Und ich will ja auch etwas davon haben. Da nörgele ich auch nicht herum, daß er sich mit der Zigarette kurz vor dem Essen die Geschmacksknospen betäubt. Ist ja seine Sache.

„Was'n das?" fragt er mit Blick auf den Bildschirm meines Computers.

„Tom of Finland. Kennst du doch."

„Welcher von den beiden?" meint er und nimmt den nächsten Zug.

„Hä?" Ich sehe ihn einen Moment lang verständnislos an. Dann sage ich: „Doofie!"

Er grinst und beugt sich hinunter zum Bildschirm, um sich die Zeichnung genauer anzuschauen. Ich konzentriere mich lieber auf seinen Geruch: nach Schweiß, Bier, Rauch … also Mann.

„Stehste darauf?" fragt er, ohne den Blick abzuwenden, etwas ungläubig.

„Och …", will ich gerade anfangen zu antworten, aber da setzt er schon ironisch nach: „Ja, ja, ich weiß, is wieder beruflich!"

„Genau!"

Dabei ist er es, der seine Augen unablässig über den Bildschirm wandern läßt und darüber sogar zu rauchen vergißt, so daß die Asche in meine Tastatur zu fallen droht.

„Sind die Typen bei dem sonst nich besser ausgestattet?" meint er.

„Na ja, es braucht ja nicht immer eine Fleischwurst zu sein."

„Da bin ich ja beruhigt", erwidert er und sieht zur Abwechslung mal wieder mich an.

"The light fixtures are up."

"Good. And the wall?"

"I'll do that later. Right now I'm starving." He wipes the sweat off his brow with his arm, takes a swig of beer, and looks at me, expectingly.

"The meat will still be a minute," I say.

"Then I have time for a cig," he responds. He lights a cigarette and walks towards the desk, towards me. I told him at the beginning of our relationship to take his nicotine addiction to the balcony – either you smoke for real or not at all. I don't nag him about how he numbs his taste buds with smoke just before the food is ready. That's his thing.

"What's that?" he asks glancing at my laptop screen.

"Tom of Finland. You know him?"

"Which of the two?" he says and takes a drag.

"Huh?" I look at him confused for a second. Then I say: "Dummy!"

He grins and bends down to the screen to see the drawings closer. I'm more concentrated on his smell: sweat, beer, smoke … man.

"And you like that?" he asks, without looking away, somewhat sceptical.

"Well …" I almost answer, before he ironically answers himself:

"Yeah, yeah, yeah, I know, it's back in style!"

"Exactly!"

But it's him who can't help but let his eyes wander across the screen, who even forgets to smoke, so long that the ash threatens to fall onto the keyboard.

"Aren't his guys normally packing more heat?" he says.

"Well, it's doesn't always have to be a sausage."

"That's a relief," he replies, and looks back to me for a change.

"Something that big is difficult to … uh … handle," I add.

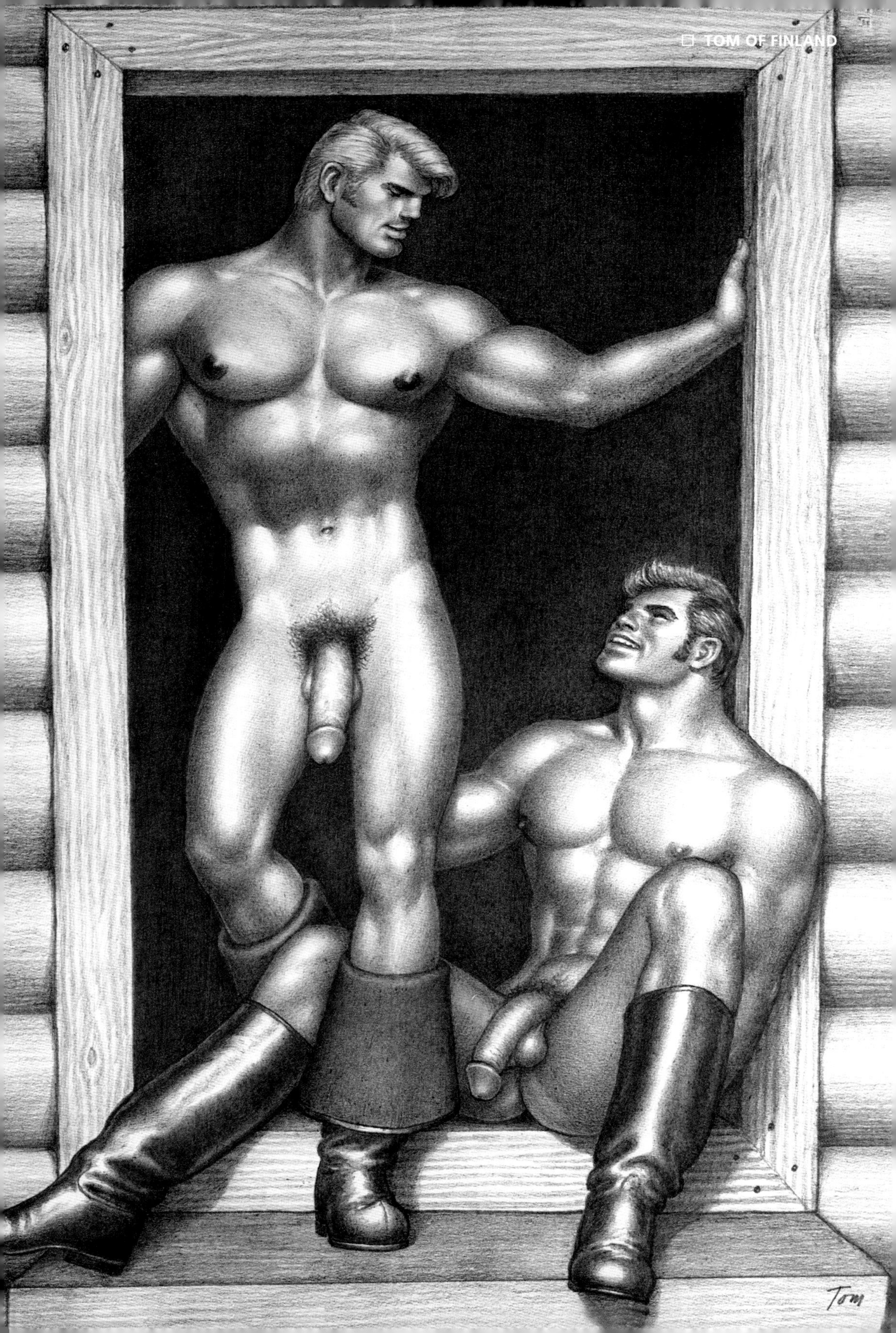

TOM OF FINLAND
Tom

„Sowas ist ja auch schwer zu … äh … handha-
ben", füge ich hinzu.
Er grinst zufrieden. „Wie is'n das eigentlich bei
Lesben?"
„Was?"
„Na, geilen die sich auch an Zeichnungen von
irgendwelchen Tittenmonstern auf, so billigen
Blondinen mit kurzen Röcken, langen Beinen,
Stöckelschuhen und Schlauchbootlippen?"
„Du meinst so Hyperfrauen? Und während die
mit ihren medizinballgroßen Brüsten, an die sie
zwei Tücher geklemmt haben, mal kurz feucht
durchwischen, kommt die Klempnerin und ver-
kündet, daß bei ihnen ein Rohr verlegt werden
muß?"
„Geht doch nicht!" konstatiert er und drückt die
Kippe aus.
„Na ja, es gibt ja Hilfsmittel …"
„Nee: Klempnerin geht nich."
Ich sehe ihn fragend an.
„Na, in schwulen Sexphantasien wimmelt's doch
auch immer von Bauarbeitern, Soldaten, Matrosen, Polizisten, Skinheads, Lkw-Fahrern, Kfz-
Mechanikern …"
„Handwerkern!"
„Ja, oder hier", er deutet mit seinem Zeigefin-
ger, der genauso rauh, schwielig und schmutzig
ist wie seine ganze Hand, auf die Zeichnung:
„Holzfäller."
„Na ja, man sieht ja nicht, daß die beiden Herrn
womöglich gerade die Hütte neu eingerichtet
und hübsch dekoriert haben. Jetzt haben sie sich
offenkundig gerade geduscht, ganzkörperrasiert
und eingeölt –"
„Und warten, daß die Cowboys vorbeikom-
men!"
„Genau. Oder die Indianer. Zum interkulturellen
Austausch."
„Aber erstens mal is das ja gar nich Ganzkörper",
fährt er unbeeindruckt fort und zeigt auf den
zentralen Bereich des stehenden Herrn. „Jetz
komm mir bloß nich damit, daß du auf einmal
darauf stehst!"
„Nein, nein", beruhige ich ihn. Ich finde ja wirklich, daß ein Mann anständig Haare haben sollte.
Auch und gerade dort. Außerdem bin ich alt
genug, um mich noch daran erinnern zu können,
als wie eigenartig bis krank es früher galt, überall
an sich herumzurasieren. Und wie aufregend es
deshalb war. Fast so aufregend wie Tätowierun-
gen, als noch nicht jeder Arsch tätowiert war. Und
wenn sich die Mode wieder ändert und es heißt:

He grins. "How does it work with Lesbians?"
"What?"
"Well, do they also stare at drawings of
some titty monsters, cheap blondes with
short skirts, long legs, high heels and thick
lips?"
"You mean like super-women? Like while
they rub their huge melon-sized breasts,
which are barely covered by a threadbare
top, then the plumber comes by and says
that pipe needs to be laid?
"No, that's not realistic!" he proclaims and
puts the cig out.
"Well, I mean there are things that help
…"
"No, plumbers never work."
I look at him questioningly.
"Well, in gay sex fantasies there are always
construction workers, soldiers, cops, skinheads, truckers, mechanics … men who
work with their hands!"
"Yeah, or here," he stabs his forefinger,
which is just as rough, callous and dirty as
the rest of his hand, at the drawing: "Lumberjacks."
"Yeah, well, what you don't see here is
that the two dudes have just reupholstered
the house and decorated it lovingly. They
apparently have just finished showering,
manscaping their bodies, and oiling up …"
"And are just waiting for the cowboys to
show up!"
"Exactly. Or the Indians. For intercultural
exchange."
"But they didn't shave everywhere," he
says unimpressed and points to the midriff
of the one guy standing. "Don't tell me
you like this stuff all of a sudden!"
"No, no," I assure him. Actually, I think
a man should have some decent body
hair. Especially down there. And I'm old
enough to remember how strange it used
to be for a guy to be completely clean-
shaven all over, and how exciting it was
for that very reason. Almost as exciting as
tattoos, before everyone and their mother had one. And when the style changes
and suddenly shaving is no longer en
vogue, then we're once again at the fore-
front of the movement.
"Secondly," he shakes me from my reverie about hairy growth in nether regions,

„Iih, rasiert! Das geht ja gar nicht!" – dann sind wir an der Spitze der Bewegung.

„Und zweitens", schreckt er mich aus den Gedanken an seinen delikaten Bewuchs, „haben die ja schon wieder ganz geschniegelte Haare. Und 'nen Fön werden se ja in der Hütte nich haben?"

„Doch. Schwule haben sowas!"

„Also, eins sag ich dir: So 'ne komische Scheitelfrisur laß ich mir –"

„Nei-hein", versuche ich ihn zu bremsen.

„Und denn tragen die ja gar keine Schnäuzer! Ich glaub, mein Hamster bohnert! Ich laß mir das blöde Ding stehen, hör mir dafür dauernd blöde Sprüche an –"

„Das sieht so männlich aus!"

„Ja, vielleicht 1980. Heute is das voll schwul. Wie wenn du in so Lederklamotten rumrennst."

„Ja", seufze ich, „die Heten haben da offenkundig im Laufe der Zeit etwas mitbekommen. War vielleicht doch nicht so gut, daß Tom of Finland so bekannt geworden ist. Und dann so viele Schwule versucht haben, sich den Masturbationsvorlagen nachzugestalten: Jetzt wirkt das, was mal als super männlich galt, super schwul."

„Pffft", schnaubt er verächtlich. „Wenn die 'n Hammer oder 'nen Akkuschrauber in die Pfoten nehmen, tun se sich doch weh."

„Das eine Mal ...", maule ich.

„Faß du mir noch mal meine Schlagbohrmaschine an, Frollein!" Mich durchfährt ein leichter Schauer bei dem kerligen Klang des Wortes „Schlagbohrmaschine". Und natürlich bei dem Gedanken daran, wie anregend er mit dem Gerät aussieht. „Das is doch alles nur Verkleidung!" ereifert er sich weiter. „Eben wie in den Pornos: Schwule wollen nich schwul sein."

Ich erinnere ihn nicht daran, wer so schwul zum Rauchen auf den Balkon gehen wollte, sondern frage: „Na, würdest du dir denn einen Porno ansehen mit Friseuren, Ballettänzern, Floristen, Flugbegleitern, Visagisten oder Buchhändlern?"

„Krankenpfleger haste vergessen."

„Genau: Nicht mal Krankenpfleger tauchen in schwulen Sexphantasien auf. Dabei gehört bei heterosexuellen Männern die Krankenschwester fest dazu."

„Sag ich doch: Und darauf rubbeln sich denn auch Lesben einen ab. Oder auf Putzfrauen, Tippsen, Friseusen."

„Friseurin! Das heißt jetzt ‚Friseurin'!"

„Aha. Und was macht jetze gerade unsere Friteurin?"

„Die brutzelt. Und wenn du nicht brav bist, gehen wir nächste Woche in das Konzert einer Diseurin."

"they all get their hair done. They definitely wouldn't have a hair dryer in their cabin in the woods would they?"

"Well, yeah. Gays have that kind of stuff!"

"Okay, well I'll tell you one thing, if you try to make me get a haircut like that I'll …"

"No no no," I try to interrupt him.

"And they don't even have mustaches! That makes me steaming mad! I let the stupid hair grow, have to constantly listen to dumb comments about it …"

"But it looks so manly!"

"Yeah, maybe in the '80s. Today it's totally gay. Like running around dressed in leather."

"Yeah," I respond, "the Straights have caught on to us over time. Maybe it wasn't so good after all that Tom of Finland got so famous. And that so many Gays tried to copy their masturbatory dream men: now everything that's super manly is super gay."

"Pfft," he snorts. "If they get a hammer or a power drill in their paws, they'll just hurt themselves."

"It was just that one time I …," I leave the sentence unfinished.

"Touch my hammer drill one more time, baby, and I swear!" A shiver courses through my body as I hear the manly sound of the words "hammer drill." And again, when I think about how arousing it is, seeing him brandish the tool. "This is all just cosplay!" he cried. "Just like in porn: Gays don't want to be gay."

I don't remind him who wanted to have an oh-so-gay smoke on the balcony, but ask: "Yeah, well, would you want to watch porn staring hairdressers, ballet dancers, florists, flight attendants, make-up artists, or book store owners?"

"You forgot nurses."

"Exactly: Not even nurses appear in gay sex fantasies. For heteros, the nurse is a staple."

"That's what I'm saying: and the Lesbians get off on that stuff too. Or on cleaning ladies, typists, stewardesses …

"Flight attendants! They're called flight attendants now!"

"Oh, brother, you all have problems!" He pulls his skin-tight shirt up, to wipe the sweat off his face. While I enjoy the sight of his abs, I ponder – if I can get him to go

„Mann, Mann, Mann, ihr habt Probleme!" Er zieht sein verwaschenes T-Shirt hoch, um sich damit den Schweiß aus dem Gesicht zu wischen. Während ich den kurzen Anblick seines Bauches genieße, überlege ich, daß ich für einen gemeinsamen Besuch bei einer Schwulenmutti oder anderen Chanteuse bestimmt auf irgend so ein schauderhaftes Rockkonzert mitgehen müßte. Wir haben uns ja auch frühzeitig auf den Kompromiß verständigt: Für jeden Action- oder gar Horrorfilm, in den ich ihn begleite, muß er – ebenso klaglos – eine romantische Komödie ertragen. Zu seinem Glück mache ich mir nichts aus dem, was heutzutage unter „Musical" verstanden wird. Allein schon das abgehackte Herumgezapple, das man jetzt für Tanz hält ... Und was Musik angeht, haben wir uns auf halber Strecke geeinigt: auf Kuschelpunk.
„Aber ich glaube nicht, daß sich Lesben an den Frauen in Heteropornos erfreuen können", versuche ich zum Thema zurückzukehren.
„Warum denn nich? Hetenfrauen sollen doch auch gerne Schwulenpornos glotzen."
„Ja, aber das ist doch etwas anderes."
„Wieso denn?"
„Na ja, das sind eben ..." Ich suche nicht nur nach Worten, sondern noch stärker nach einer politisch korrekten Erklärung. „... Lesben."
Er sieht mich an.
„Ja", fahre ich fort, dankbar, daß wir unter uns sind, „und deshalb würde ein weiblicher Tom of Finland keine solche Pin-up-Bilder zeichnen, wie sie ja sowieso schon von Männern gezeichnet worden sind. Genau!" Bei Gott, jetzt hab ich's!
„Das hat damit zu tun, daß Frauen eben eine andere Position in der Gesellschaft einnehmen. Heterosexuelle Frauen haben ja schließlich auch keine Phantasien von bis ins Absurde übersteigerten Männlichkeitsklischees gezeichnet wie Tom of Finland."
„Weiß man's?"
„Na ja, davon hätte man doch zweifellos schon einmal gehört, wenn wenigstens eine Frau so reihenweise Männer mit Fleischwurstpenissen, kleinen Kugelhintern –"
„Kleinen Köpfen." Ich grinse. „Ausladenden Oberkörpern. Ach, und übrigens", er zeigt wieder auf die Zeichnung, „bei dem Typen sind die Beine ja mal nich so dünne wie sonst bei Tom of Finland. Ich glaub, der konnte keine Beine malen."
„Glaub ich nicht", erwidere ich. „Beine haben ihn vielleicht einfach nicht besonders interessiert.

with me to see some singer, I'll definitely have to join him for some thunderously loud rock concert. We made a compromise early on: for every action film or horror flick he drags me to, he has to come along to a romantic comedy with me. He's lucky that what gets called "musicals" today is a waste of time. Not to mention the pathetic hobbling around that gets mistaken for "dancing …" And speaking of music, we met halfway: we listen to punk you can cuddle to.
"But I don't think Lesbians enjoy the women in hetero porn," I try to steer him back to the initial point.
"Well, why not? Hetero women should all watch gay porn, too."
"Yeah, but that's different."
"How so?"
"Well, yeah, I mean …" I'm not looking for a word, but for a politically correct explanation. "… Lesbians …"
He looks at me.
"Yeah," I go on, thankful, there's no one else in the room, "and that's the reason why a female version of Tom of Finland would never create these kinds of pin-ups, since they have already been created by men. Exactly!" I have it now! "That has more to do with the fact that women have a different position in society. Heterosexual women don't have the sort of overblown macho fantasies like they exist in Tom of Finland's drawings."
"How do you know that?"
"Well, you would have heard about it by now, if even one single women wanted sausages that big, little butts that tight …"
"And tiny little heads." I grin. "Boring torsos. Oh, and by the way," he points back to the laptop screen, "this guy hast not as tiny legs as some of the dudes in these drawings having little bitty legs. I don't think Tom of Finland was very good at drawing legs."
"I don't think so either," I add. "Maybe legs didn't interest him as much. Or maybe he liked the combination of huge tank-like upper bodies and slim legs. Some people like that."
He looked at me questioningly: "now don't tell me you suddenly think my thighs are too fat …"

Oder er stand auf die Kombination Riesenober-
körper – Spargelbeinchen. Manchen gefällt das."
Er blickt mich leicht pikiert an: „Also eins sag ich
dir: Jetzt komm mir bloß nich damit, daß dir meine Oberschenkel plötzlich zu dick ..."
„Bist du verrückt?" schreie ich und lange nach
seinen prachtvoll fleischigen Keulen, die deli-
kat mit blonden Härchen überzogen sind und
sich an ihrem oberen Ende aneinanderpressen.
Erfreulicherweise hat er die richtig kurzen Hosen angezogen, die ich ihm zu Weihnachten
geschenkt habe und die er sich draußen nicht
zu tragen traut. Von wegen „voll schwul", „wir
haben doch nicht mehr 1980" und „Schnäuzer
ist eh schon genug".
„Ey, nich antatschen!" ruft er, während ich über
seine kräftigen Beine streiche und versonnen
auf seine untere Körperhälfte starre. „Du hast
doch vorhin schon was gekriegt! Die nächste erst
nachher, wenn ich mit der Wand fertig bin."
„Och ..."
„Kümmre dich lieber ums Essen", fordert er,
geht einen Schritt zurück, nimmt noch einen
Schluck aus der Flasche und rülpst. „Ich muß jetz
erstmal das Bier loswerden", verkündet er dann
und stapft in Richtung Badezimmer.
„Aber nicht wieder ins Waschbecken pinkeln!",
rufe ich ihm hinterher, während ich mich auf den
Weg in die Küche mache, nicht ohne einen Blick
auf seine auch sehr erfreuliche Rückseite zu wer-
fen. „Und Händewaschen nicht vergessen!"
Ohne sich umzudrehen, erwidert er laut:
„Ho-mo!"
Ich lächle. So ist das mit einem Heterotypen.

"Are you crazy?" I cry and long for his
big fleshy tree stumps, with their delicate
blond fur. Thank goodness, he's wearing
the shorts I gave him for Christmas, the
ones he doesn't feel confidant wearing on
the street. And as far as homosexuality: "it's
not the '80s anymore; nowadays 'staches
are enough anyway."
"Hey, careful with the goods!" he pleads,
while I stroke his strong legs and gaze
lustfully at his lower body. "You already got
some earlier! You'll have to wait until I'm
finished with the wall."
"Well …"
"You figure out the food first," he de-
mands, and retreats a step, takes a swig
from the bottle, and burps. "I have to get
rid of this beer first." Then he stomps off in
the direction of the bathroom.
"Just don't piss in the sink again!" I yell,
while I make my way into the kitchen,
catching one last look at his very savory
behind. "And don't forget to wash your
hands!"
Without turning around he calls out:
"Homo!"
I laugh. That's how it goes with a straight
guy.

Translation: Grant Nichols and Jim Baker

*Cock size doesn't matter to me. I didn't start doing those gigantic cocks until
the censors let the magazines publish full frontal nudity. I had to come up with
something you couldn't get in a photograph. So those big cocks are all for the
other guys — I'm an ass man myself.*

*Die Größe eines Schwanzes ist mir nicht wirklich wichtig. Ich habe erst angefan-
gen diese Riesenschwänze zu zeichnen, als die Zensur es erlaubte, pornogra-
phische Bilder zu drucken. Da musste ich mir etwas ausdenken, was auf einem
Foto nicht möglich war. Diese Monster sind für all die anderen Kerle – ich selbst
stehe auf Ärsche!*
– Tom of Finland

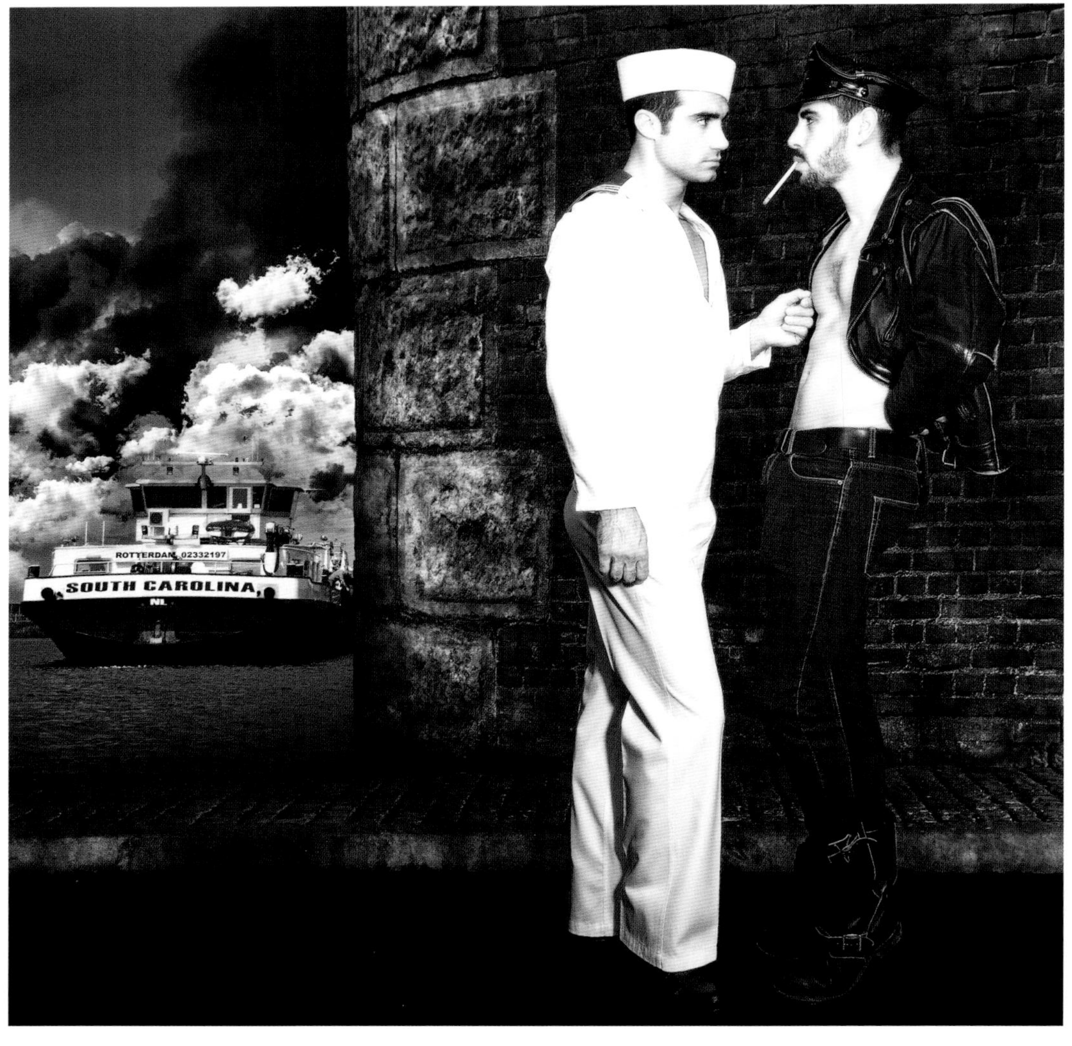
ROTTERDAM 02332197
SOUTH CAROLINA,
NL.

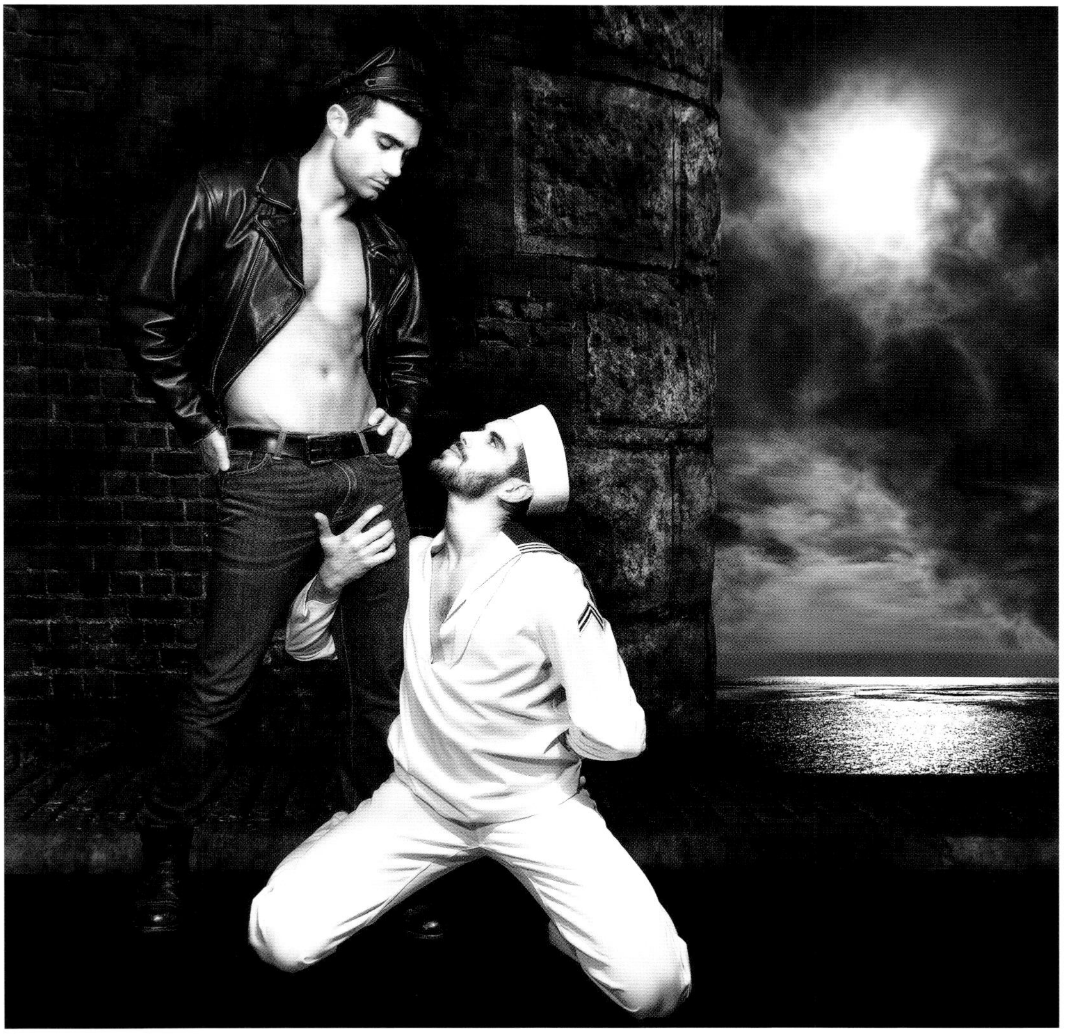

☐ ERIC LANUIT

El Cortez
HOTEL
COFFEE SHOP & BAR
FREE PARKING
GAMBL
HUSTLER
A LOTTO
OW OPEN
CE & PBR $5
GAMP
PIZZA TO $3 SLICE
LA MINE

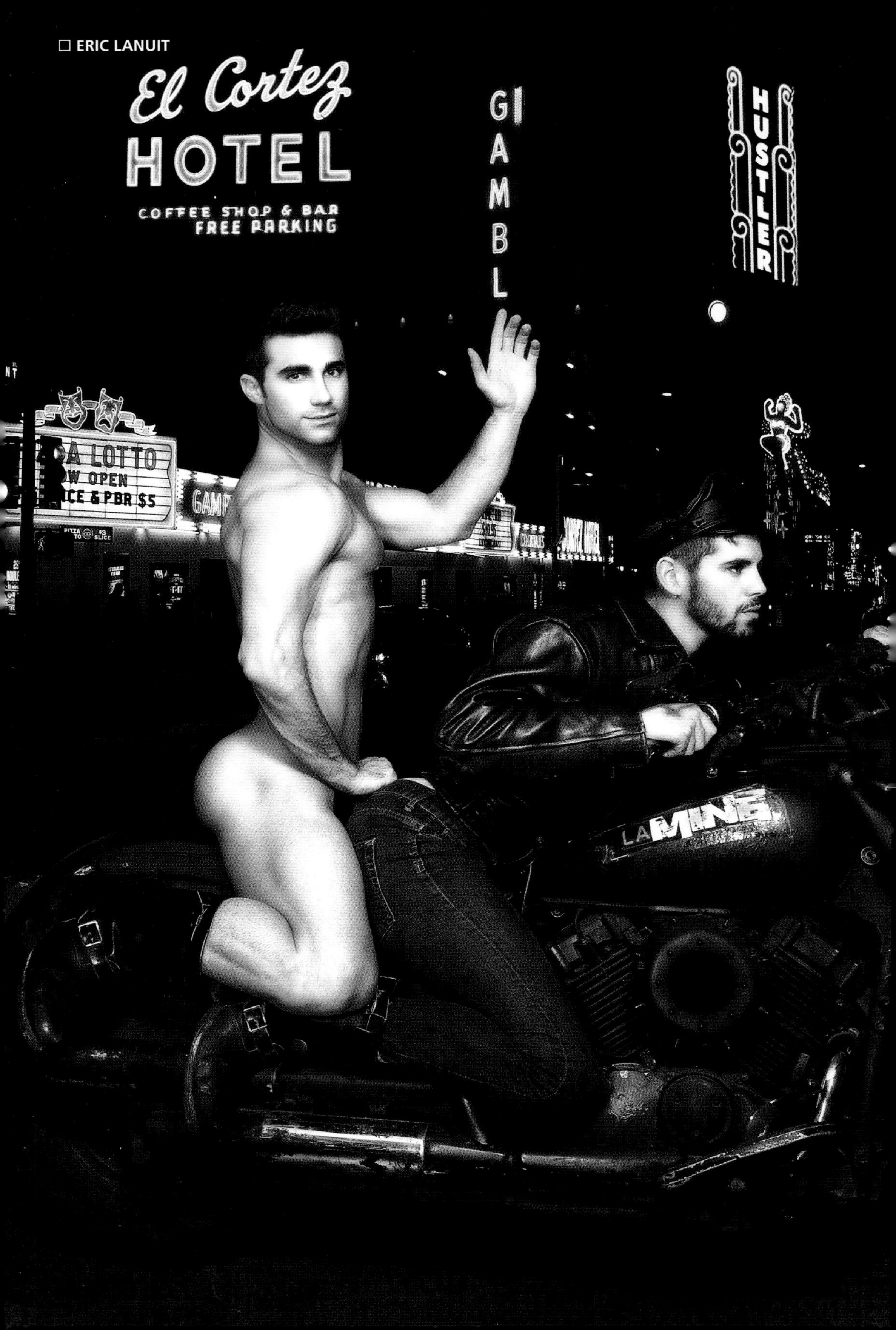

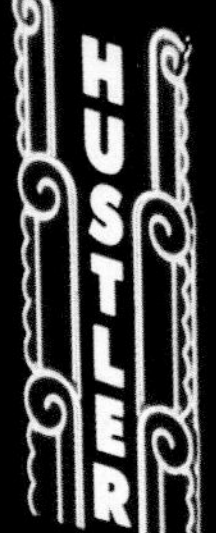

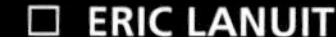

□ ERIC LANUIT

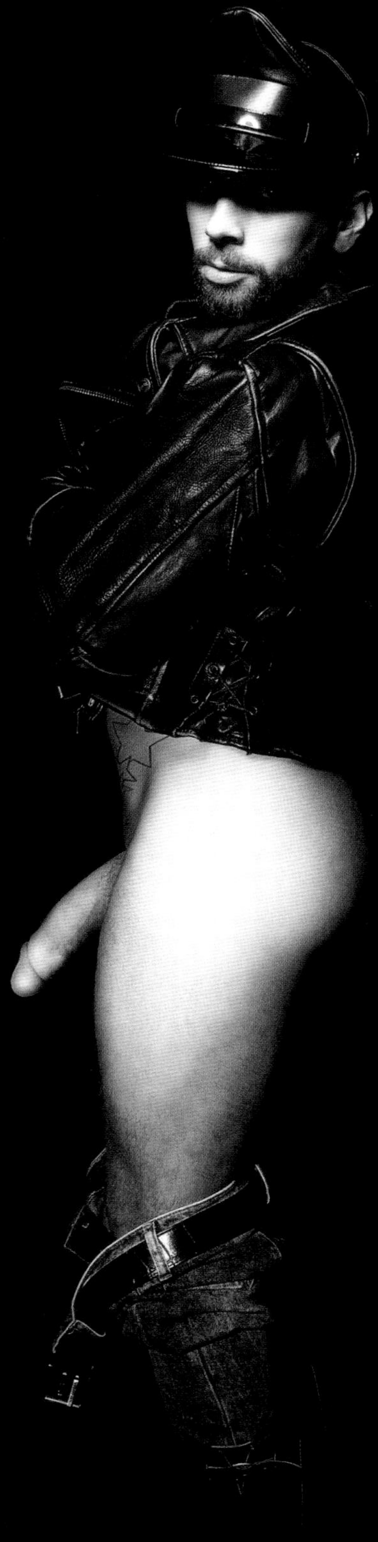

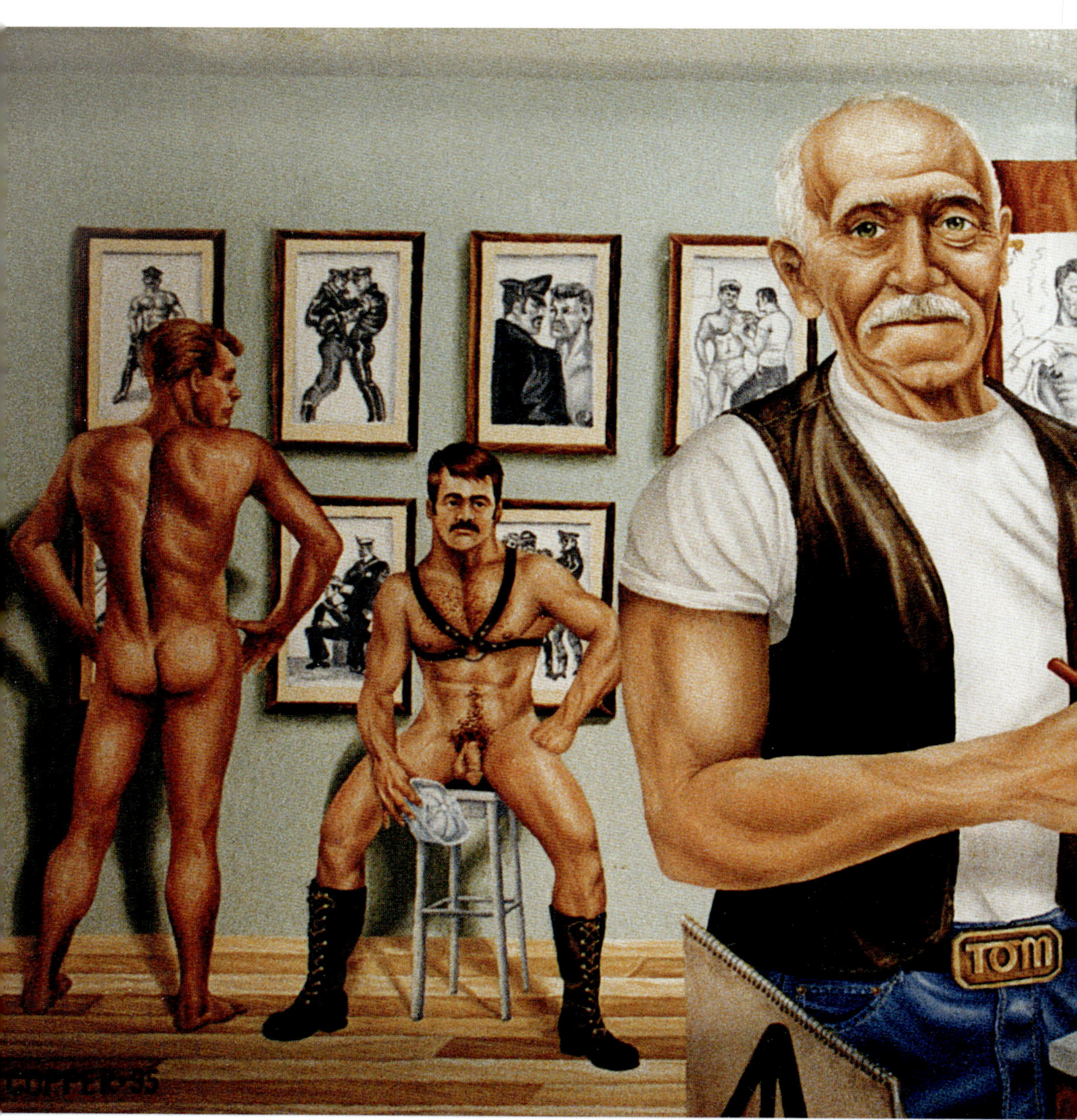

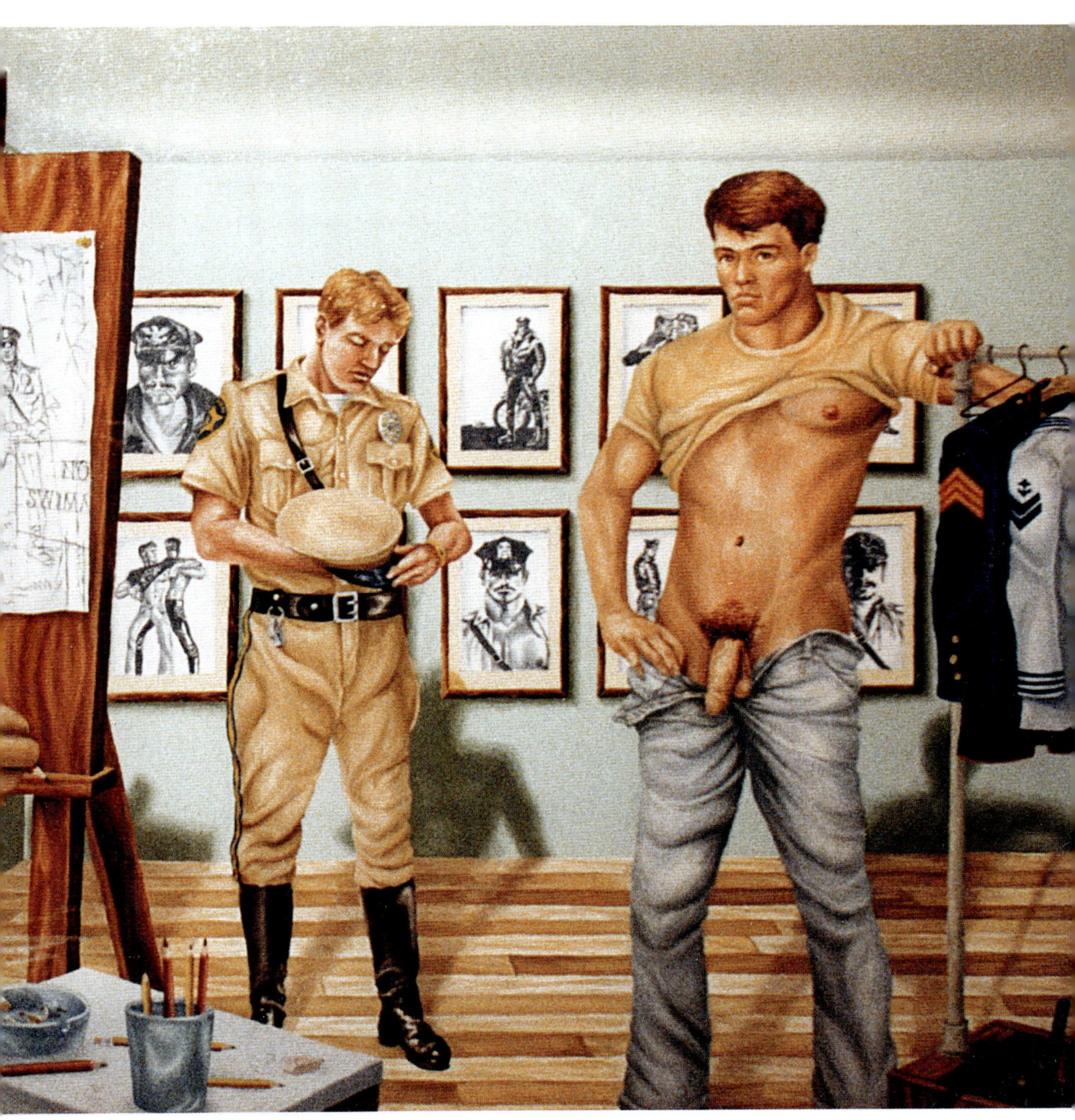

ROLF REDLIN
Schnauz • 'stache

Meine Gegenwehr erlahmt, er hat mich soweit. Markus sagt, ich sei noch jung und mein Bartwuchs nicht dicht genug. Das ist zwar nicht, was ich hören will, doch was gibt's da groß zu verlieren? Also warum die Sache nicht mal ausprobieren? Wenn sich einer in diesem Metier auskennt, dann er.

Beinahe zwei Jahre habe ich gezüchtet, doch mir will kein üppiger Hipsterbart wachsen. Er bleibt zippelig, auch wenn einzelne Haare durchaus beträchtliche Länge erreicht haben. Nun fallen sie binnen Sekunden unter flinker Schere.

„Na, das sieht doch schon ganz anders aus", sagt er.

Mein Spiegelbild erscheint mir gewöhnungsbedürftig. Allerdings, wenn ich ehrlich sein soll, hat er schon recht. „Beim Vollbart bleibt es aber! Nicht, dass ich gleich mit Schnauzbart nach Hause gehe." Ich bemühe mich, meiner Stimme einen drohenden Unterton zu geben. Unter dem Frisörumhang fühle ich mich so seltsam wehrlos.

„Keine Sorge, ich verpass' dir keinen Pornobalken!" Markus lacht und klappert mit der Schere.

Ich lache mit, wenn er auch den wunden Punkt getroffen hat. Seit Jahren beobachte ich mit Sorge und Hoffnung den Bartwuchs auf der Oberlippe. Mir scheint, er sprießt dort ganz besonders spärlich. Ganz wie ein zarter Flaum, der in die Mundwinkel hineinhängt und in dem sich höchstens die Nutella verfängt, die ich mir morgens aufs Knäckebrot schmiere.

Mehr noch als einen Hipsterbart wünschte ich mir einen Schnauzbart. Vielleicht nicht so üppig wie der aufgemalte Schnauz von Groucho Marx. Auch nicht schwungvoll gezwirbelt wie bei Wilhelm dem Zweiten. Schon gar nicht à la Salvador Dalí. Ich höre zwar für mein Leben gern die *Bohemian Rhapsody*, aber ich bin doch kein Bohémien, bitte schön. Nur ein schwuler Wirtschaftsinformatiker mit frischem Master-Abschluss. Der Bart von Freddie Mercury allerdings, der war schon ziemlich cool. Ach, was sag ich. Rattenscharf, definitiv. Breit und dunkel füllte er den Raum zwischen Nase und Oberlippe, war dabei dennoch säuberlich ge-

My resistance weakened, and he had me. Markus says that I'm still young, that my beard needs to be thicker. That's not what I want to hear, but what do I have to lose? Why not just try it once? If anyone should know, it's him.

I tended to it for two years, but still no voluptuous hipster-beard will grow for me. It remains patchy, even when individual hairs would reach the desired length. Though they fall prey within seconds to quick scissors

"Hmm, no, that looks much different," he says.

My reflection seems to take some getting used to. If I'm being honest, he's right. "The beard stays though! I won't be going home with a moustache." I try to lend my voice a threatening undertone. Still, under the barber cloth I feel so strangely defenseless.

"No worries, I won't give you a porn 'stache!" Markus laughs and clicks his scissors.

I laugh along with him, although he did hit a sore spot. For years, I have watched my hair growth on my upper lip with hope and concern. It seems to me that it grows there extra sparse. Like a soft bit of fluff, hanging onto the corners of my mouth, that can at best catch a bit of the Nutella from my breakfast.

I'd much rather have a mustache than a hipster-beard. Maybe not one as thick as Groucho Marx's. And not as waxed and spikey as the one Wilhelm the Second had. Definitely not one à la Salvadore Dalí. I'll love listening to *Bohemian Rhapsody* for the rest of my life, but I'm not Bohemian, thank you very much! Just a gay IT guy with a fresh master's degree. Freddie Mercury's mustache, now that would be cool. Ah, but what am I talking about? Uncompromisingly, definitely. His 'stache nicely filled the area between nose and upper lip, thick and dark, and was always clean, and never covered his mouth. Freddie was

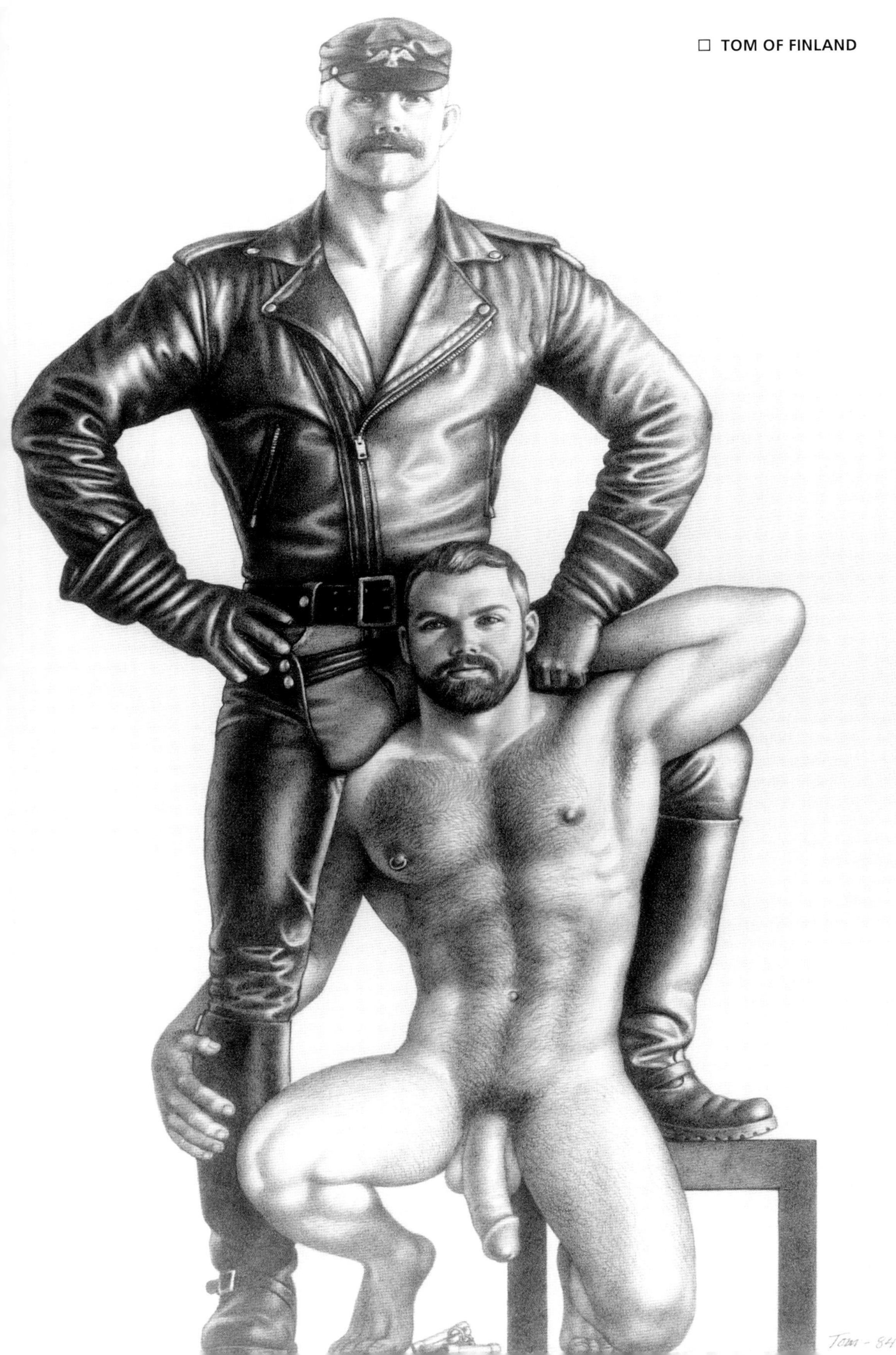
TOM OF FINLAND
Tom - 84

stutz und hing nicht in den Mund. Freddie war neunundzwanzig, als er die *Rhapsody* schrieb. Kaum älter als ich heute, der ich seinerzeit nicht einmal geboren war.

Es dauerte Jahre, bis Freddie meine Aufmerksamkeit gewann. Das gelang einem anderen Kerl viel früher. Ich weiß, es ist ein bisschen peinlich, aber schließlich hatten wir noch kein Internet. So war es beinahe unvermeidlich, dass der Marlboro-Mann aus der Zigarettenwerbung zu jenem Kerl wurde, um den sich meine jugendlich pubertierende Fantasie drehte. Männlich-markantes Gesicht und eine gestutzte blonde Schnauzbürste mit Barthaaren wie aus Draht. Was habe ich mir seinerzeit Gedanken gemacht zu der meine kleine Teenager-Welt bewegenden Frage, wie sich diese Drahtbürste wohl anfühlen mochte. Auf der Haut, hier und dort. Vor allem dort.

Als später die Fantasien meiner Pubertät nach und nach Wirklichkeit wurden, trugen die Kerle in meinem Umfeld keine Schnauzbärte mehr. Sie rasierten sich die Schädel blank und trugen dazu modische Gesichtsbehaarung, der sie den neudeutschen Namen Goatee gaben, von meiner Großmutter aber Polizisten- oder Ulbricht-Bart genannt wurde. Beides musste ich erst einmal googlen.

Heute nun sind die Ziegenbärte zur Hipsterwolle herangewuchert. Nur bei mir reicht es nicht einmal für einen Schnauz. So lebe ich allein auf der weiten Welt mit meinen Schnauzbart-Fantasien. Die lassen sich allenfalls ein klein wenig stillen, wenn sie im Fernsehen Filme mit Tom Selleck zeigen. Sämtliche Staffeln von Magnum stehen im Bücherregal gleich neben den Tom of Finland-Bänden. Im englischen Original und auf Blu-ray. Die synchronisierte Fassung gibt es nur auf DVD. Harte Zeiten für Schnäuzer-Liebhaber.

Wenn wir auch nicht diskriminiert werden, so schlägt uns doch amüsierte Ablehnung entgegen. Ich denke nur an den Begriff Pornobalken, den Markus mit gehässigem Tonfall in den Mund genommen hat. Keine Ahnung, ob er auch schwul ist, als Frisör. Ein wenig Toleranz hätte ich mir schon erhofft. Trotzdem runde ich an der Kasse auf 25 Euro auf. Er hat es verdient. Draußen schaue ich immer wieder nach meinem Spiegelbild in den Schaufenstern. Der Vollbart kommt gut so! Daheim parkt ein Lieferwagen mit Warnblinkanlage vor dem Häuserblock. Die Haustür zum Nachbarhaus steht offen. Zwei drahtige Typen tragen

29 when he wrote *Rhapsody*. Just a bit older than me, though I was born long after his day.

It took years for Freddie to finally capture my attention. For anyone else, it would have come much sooner. I know, it's a little embarrassing, but we still didn't have internet. It was almost unavoidable that the Marlboro Man from the cigarette commercials became the man of all my youthful, puberty fuelled fantasies. A manly, chiseled face and a blond, bristly mustache. The thoughts that I poured into the world-changing question of my teenager-world: how would that wire brush feel? On my skin? Here, and there? Especially there.

As my pubescent fantasies became more and more reality; the men around me stopped cultivating their mustaches. They shaved their lips bare and sported the new, more in-style facial hair: the goatee. My grandmother used to call them police beards. I had to google it. Today, there are only the unkempt woolly hipster beards around. Only thing though is I can't even grow that. So, I live alone in the world with my mustache fantasies. They certainly don't fade when I see Tom Selleck in television movies. Episodes of Magnum nestle in my bookcase next to my Tom of Finland collection. In the original English and on blu-ray. The dubbed version only exists on DVD. Hard times for 'stache lovers. If we're not being discriminated against, we're met with amused rejection. I can only think of the term "porn 'stache," which Markus used with a spiteful tone in his voice. No clue whether he's gay as well, being a hairdresser. I would have expected a bit of tolerance. I still give him his tip at the register. He earned it. Outside I look in the storefront windows at my reflection. The beard looks good! At home there's a delivery trucked parked out front, with emergency lights flashing. The neighbor's door is open. Two wiry dudes carry a sofa to the curb, blocking my way. Of course, someone is moving in; it's the beginning of the month. I watch them while fishing my

ein Sofa über den Bürgersteig und ich komme nicht an ihnen vorbei. Klar, da zieht jemand ein, es ist Monatsanfang. Ich schaue ihnen hinterher und krame meinen Haustürschlüssel aus der Jacke hervor. Im nachbarlichen Treppenhaus drängelt sich ein Kerl an den Trägern vorbei, bleibt in der offenen Tür stehen und fragt: „Ich bestell Pizza für alle. Willst du auch?"

Im Film hätte ich jetzt die Schlüssel fallen lassen. Der Typ, der mich da zur Pizza einlädt, trägt einen Schnauzbart nach meinem Geschmack. Nun ist dies kein Film und in der Realität gibt es diese Sorte Überraschung nicht. Im wahren Leben tönt die Antwort aus dem Lieferwagen in meinem Rücken. „Ich nehm' Salami mit Extra-Schinken." Und schon ist der Schnauzbartmann wieder die Treppe hinauf verschwunden.

Oben in meiner Wohnung hänge ich die Jacke auf einen Bügel und muss meine Gedanken sortieren. Verflixt, ich erinnere mich nicht mehr an sein Aussehen. Ist der Bart blond? Die Augenfarbe? Keine Ahnung. Ich glaube, er ist größer, deutlich größer als ich. Oder ist das jetzt Wunschdenken? Sein Hals erschien mir ausgesprochen kräftig. Mein Gott, er könnte ein Kraftsportler sein. Wäre ich schlagfertig gewesen, ich hätte mich mit lockerem Sprüchlein selbst eingeladen. Aber ich bin nicht schlagfertig. War ich noch nie. Allerdings könnte ich meine Hilfe beim Umzug anbieten. Am besten gehe ich sofort hinüber und …

Halt! Was bin ich für ein Idiot. Benehme mich wie eine verdammte Tusse. Ich weiß doch nicht einmal, ob er es ist, der da einzieht. Mag sein, er ist auch nur ein freundlicher Helfer. Wenn dem so ist, werde ich ihn erst recht niemals wiedersehen. Ich ziehe mir ein Bier aus dem Kühlschrank und setze mich auf einen Küchenstuhl. Ruhe bewahren! Das Bier prickelt ordentlich auf dem Gaumen. Wie so häufig steigt gleich nach dem ersten Schluck der Schaum aus der Flasche hervor. Sollte Mister Moustache tatsächlich künftig in der Nachbarschaft wohnen, so wird er mir eines Tages begegnen, unweigerlich. Vielleicht schon morgen früh beim Bäcker. Oder im Fitnessstudio um die Ecke. Wie ein Hobby-Pumper sieht er schon aus. Wer weiß, ob der auf Kardio steht. Ich stelle mir vor, wie ich ihm in der Umkleide begegne und er vor mir zu den Duschen geht. Groß und breit und mit wiegendem Django-Gang.

house keys out of my jacket. In my new neighbor's door stands a man, who asks: "I'm ordering pizza for everyone. Want some, too?"

If this were a movie, I would have dropped my keys. This guy offering me pizza is sporting exactly the kind of mustache that fits my tastes. Only this isn't a movie, and nice surprises like that don't really exist. Back in real life, I hear an answer from behind me. "I'll take salami with extra prosciutto." And just like that the mustache man has disappeared back into the stairway.

Upstairs in my apartment, I hang my jacket up and have to sort my thoughts. I already can't remember what he looked like. Was his beard blond? What color were his eyes? No clue. But I think he was taller, a lot taller than me. Or is that just wishful thinking? He seemed to have a strong neck. My God, he could be a bodybuilder. If I had been quick enough, I could have gotten myself invited in with a witty joke. But I'm not that quick. Never was. I could have offered to help him move in though. I should just go over there right now and … Wait! What kind of idiot am I? I'm acting like a damn chick. I don't even know if it's him moving in at all. Maybe he's just a friendly helper. If that's true, then I'll definitely never see him again. I grab a beer out of the fridge and sit on a kitchen chair. Keep calm! The beer tickles the roof of my mouth. Like so often, the beer is foaming out of the bottle after the first sip. If Mister Mustache really does live next door, we'll run into each other again, unavoidably. Maybe in the early morning at the bakery. Or at the gym around the corner. He looks like he enjoys pumping iron. Who knows if he also likes cardio. I imagine meeting him in the locker room, and him going into the shower before me. Tall and wide and with a Django gait.

The next day begins with stress at the office. I come home late and haven't given him another thought. I meet a friend for a work-out and we cycle together in front of a projector into the Californian

Der nächste Tag beginnt mit Stress in der Firma, ich komme erst sehr spät aus dem Büro und habe keinen Moment an ihn gedacht. Ich treffe mich mit einem Freund beim Sport und wir radeln gemeinsam vor der Monitorwand durch kalifornische Landschaften. Selbst meinem besten Kumpel verrate ich nichts von der Sichtung. Mister Schnauz gehört mir ganz allein. Beinahe drei Wochen vergehen, bis er mir wieder über den Weg läuft. Es ist dunkel und ich trage die Sporttasche lässig über die Schulter geworfen. Diese Haltung habe ich schon vor Jahren eigens vor dem Spiegel einstudiert. Er kreuzt also meinen Weg, würdigt mich keines Blicks und geht schnurstracks auf das Nachbarhaus zu. Dieses Mal kommt er mir noch kräftiger vor. Er trägt eine klassische schwarze Lederjacke, die verdammt körperbetont sitzt. Meine Güte, er sieht damit aus wie einer Zeichnung von Tom of Finland entsprungen. Ich wette, der steht auch auf Kerle. Es sei denn, er ist ein einfacher Biker in schwuler Lederjacke. Heteros sind da manchmal nicht ganz stilsicher. Ich schaue ihm hinterher, bis die Haustür ins Schloss fällt. Wenn ich nichts unternehme, wird es niemals etwas mit uns werden. Voll Sehnsucht blicke ich die Fassade hinauf. Im dritten Stockwerk rechts geht das Licht an und ich weiß plötzlich, was zu tun ist. Es sind nur ein paar Schritte bis zur Tür, ich zücke das Telefon und lichte kurzentschlossen die Klingelknöpfe ab. Eines der Namensschilder in der dritten Reihe ist nagelneu.

Oben in der Küche schaue ich mir das Foto genauer an, siegesgewiss. Ein einzelner Nachname – Behrmann. Immerhin. Adresse und Name sind schnell bei Google eingegeben. Zum Glück heißt er nicht Müller. Das erhoffte Wunder bleibt indes aus, leider. Kein Behrmann im Nachbarhaus. Ich sollte wissen, dass selbst Google nicht zaubern kann. So einfach ist es mit dem Stalking dann doch nicht. Zur Abwechslung wiederhole ich die Suche, nun aber ohne Straßenangabe und nur mit Ort. Den Suchradius erweitert, wie schlau von mir. Ganz so schlau dann doch nicht. Es gibt viele Behrmanns in der Stadt: ein Restaurant, zwei Autohäuser, mehrere Ärzte. Ein Thomas Behrmann betreibt eine Fahrschule. Gar nicht dumm. Ich mache den Führerschein und lege mir ein Motorrad zu. Vielleicht klappt es dann mit dem Nachbarn.

countryside. I don't even tell my best friend about my sighting. Mister Mustache is mine alone.

Almost three weeks roll by, until he finally crosses my path again. It's dark and I have my gym bag thrown over my shoulder. I perfected this look years ago in front of the mirror. He walks past me, doesn't even give me a second look, and makes his way directly to the neighbor's house. This time he looks even stronger. He's wearing a classic black leather jacket, incredibly form-fitting. My God, in that jacket he looks exactly like a drawing from Tom of Finland. I bet he's also into guys. Unless he's just a biker in a gay leather jacket. Heteros aren't always so style-conscious. I watch him from behind until the door clicks shut. If I don't do anything, nothing will ever happen between us. Full of desire, I gaze upwards at the front of the building. On the third floor, to the right, the light goes on and I suddenly know exactly what to do. It's just a couple of steps to the door. I grab my telephone and illuminate the buzzers. One of the names in the third row is brand-new.

Upstairs in my kitchen, I study the photo more closely. It's just a last name – Behrmann. But still. Addresses and names are easy to type into Google. Thank God he's not named Müller. The much anticipated miracle doesn't happen – there's no Behrmann next door. I should have known, not even Google can perform magic. Stalking is harder than it seems. I try to search again, only this time without the street name, just the city. The search radius is bigger, how clever of me. Maybe not so smart. There are a ton of Behrmanns in the city: one restaurant, two auto shops, a few doctors. There's a Thomas Behrmann who runs a driving school. Not so dumb. I'll get my license and buy myself a motorcycle. Maybe then it'll work with the neighbor. A dumb idea, and yet I click on the link. A do-it-yourself-website, how embarrassing is that. But there he is smiling at me, leaning on the open door of a compact car. And he's wearing the same

Eine selten dumme Idee und dennoch klicke ich auf den Eintrag. Eine Do-It-Yourself-Website, wie peinlich ist das denn. Doch dann schaut er mich lächelnd an, auf die geöffnete Tür eines Kompaktwagens gelehnt. Und er trägt dieselbe Lederjacke wie vorhin. Ich speichere das Bild, vergrößere es ein wenig und begutachte den Schnauzbart. Der Hals ist wirklich kräftig. Und wie niedlich die etwas zu kleinen Ohren abstehen. Hashtag *Husband-Material*, eindeutig. Keine Sekunde würde ich zögern, meine Arme um ihn zu schlingen. Bei der Statur gibt's feste Arschbacken inklusive. Ein Sixpack braucht er nicht, lieber ein Bäuchlein mit Haaren. Ich studiere die kleine Website, bis ich jedes Wort auswendig kenne. Natürlich bietet er auch Fahrstunden auf dem Motorrad an. Darauf genehmige ich mir einen Campari Soda.

Später, im Bett liegend, fällt mir ein, was ich mal irgendwo gelesen habe. Fahrlehrer beginnen ihre berufliche Laufbahn häufig bei der Bundeswehr. Schon erscheint mir mein Schnauzbart-Mann als Feldwebel in tarngefleckter Uniform. Wenig später werfe ich ein feuchtes Papiertaschentuch auf den Teppichboden und ziehe mir die Bettdecke über die Schultern. Mein Entschluss steht fest. Ich werde mich anmelden. Gleich morgen.

leather jacket as before. I save the picture, enlarge it a bit and admire the mustache. His neck really is strong. And how sweet his little ears stick out. Hashtag *Husband Material*, definitely. I wouldn't waste a second wrapping my arms around him. With his build, I'm sure he has a firm butt. He doesn't need a six-pack, better if he has a belly, with lots of hair. I study the little website until I know every word by heart. Of course, he also gives motorcycle lessons. I drink a Campari soda to that.

Later, as I lie in bed, I remember something I had read somewhere once. Driving instructors often begin their careers in the army. My mustache man appears before me as a foot soldier in a camouflage uniform. A bit later I throw a wet tissue on the carpet and draw the covers over my shoulders. The decision is final. I'll sign up. First thing in the morning.

Translation: Grant Nichols and Jim Baker

I almost never draw a completely naked man. He has to have at least a pair of boots or something on. To me, a fully dressed man is more erotic than a naked one. A naked man is, of course beautiful, but dress him in black leather or a uniform — ah, then he is more than beautiful, then he is sexy!

Ich habe selten ganz nackte Männer gezeichnet. Wenigstens Stiefel mussten sie noch anhaben. Für mich ist ein angezogener Mann erotischer als ein nackter. Ein nackter Mann ist natürlich schön, doch wenn du ihn in schwarzes Leder oder in eine Uniform steckst... ah... dann ist er mehr als schön, dann ist er sexy!
– Tom of Finland

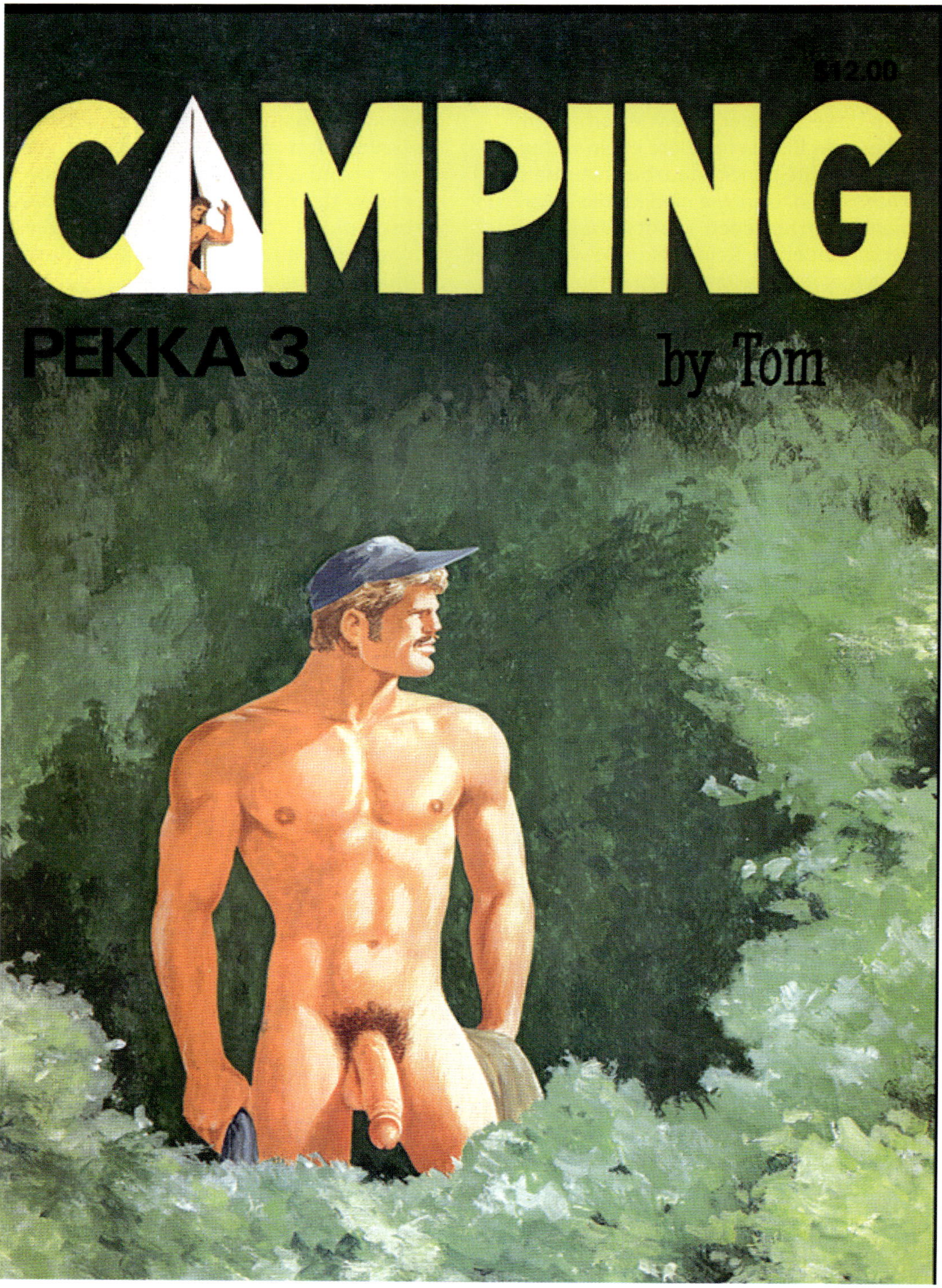

$12.00
CAMPING
PEKKA 3
by Tom

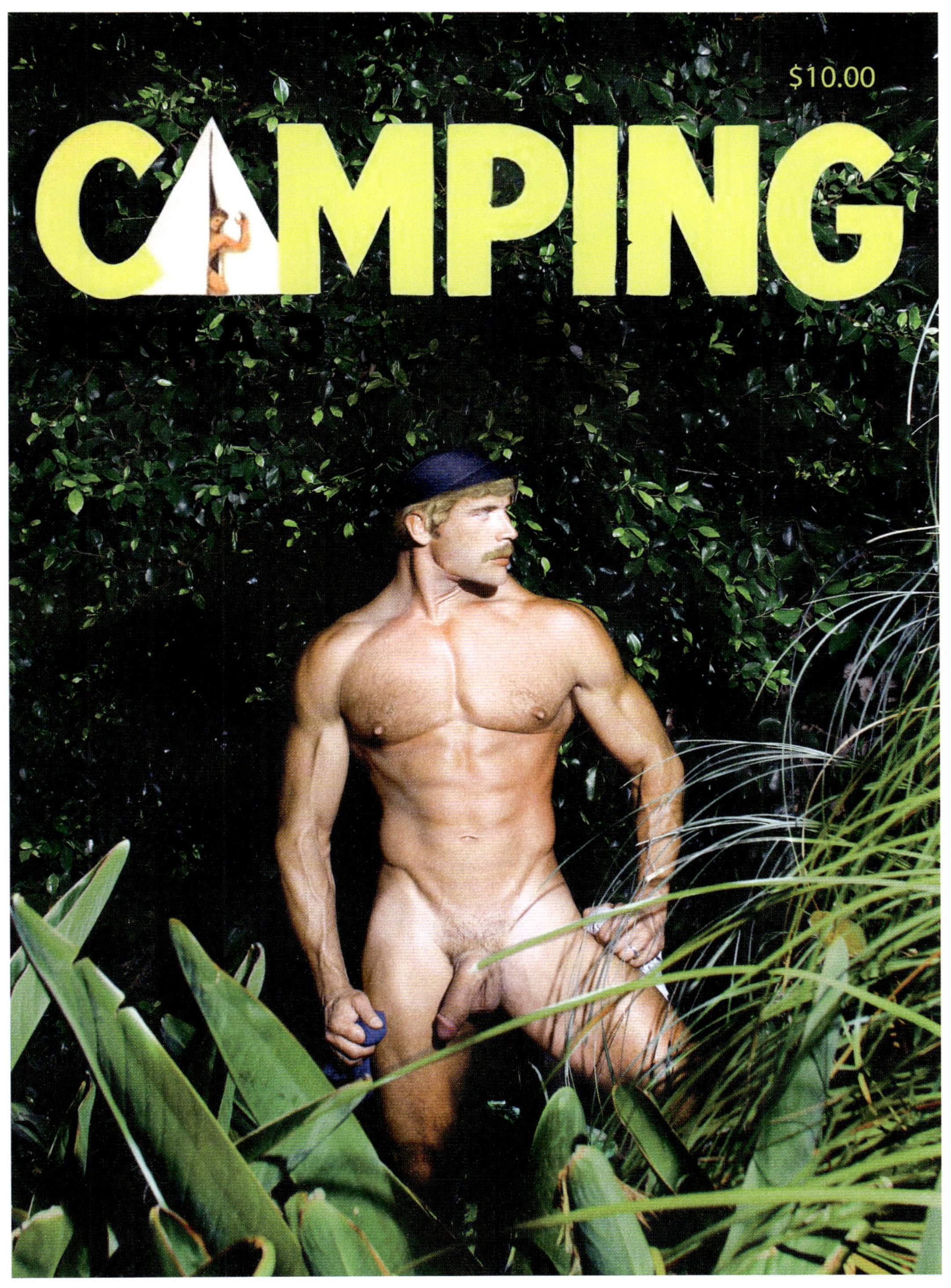
$10.00
CAMPING

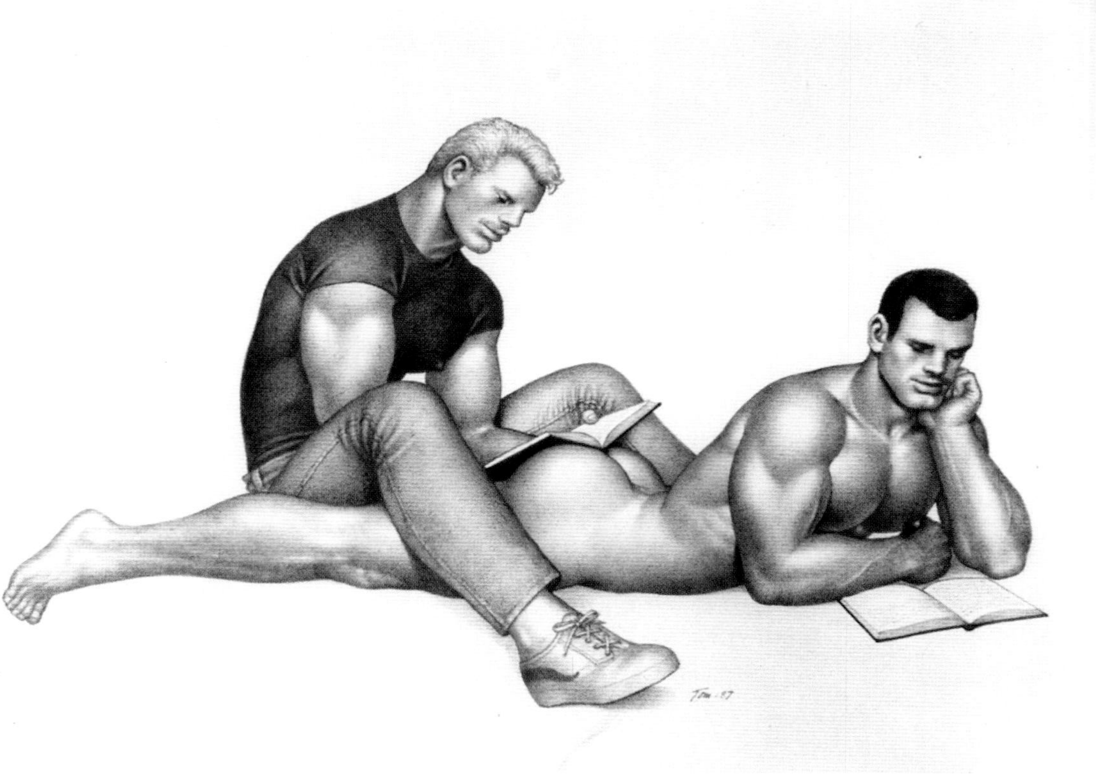

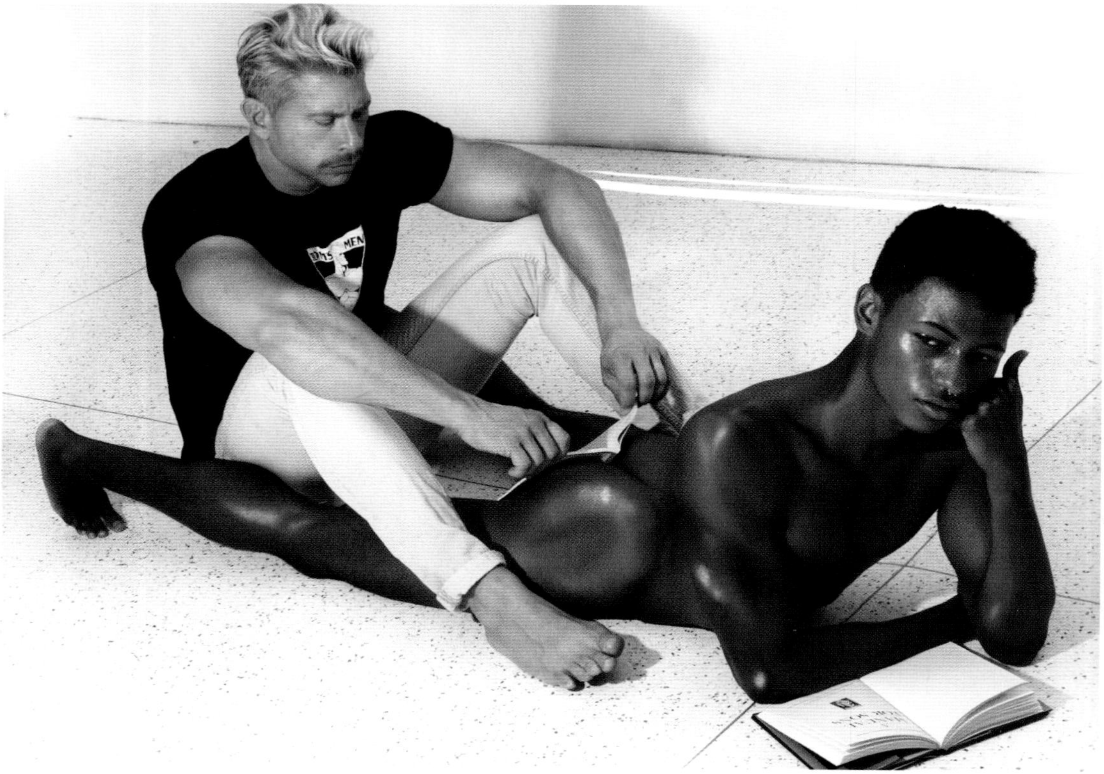

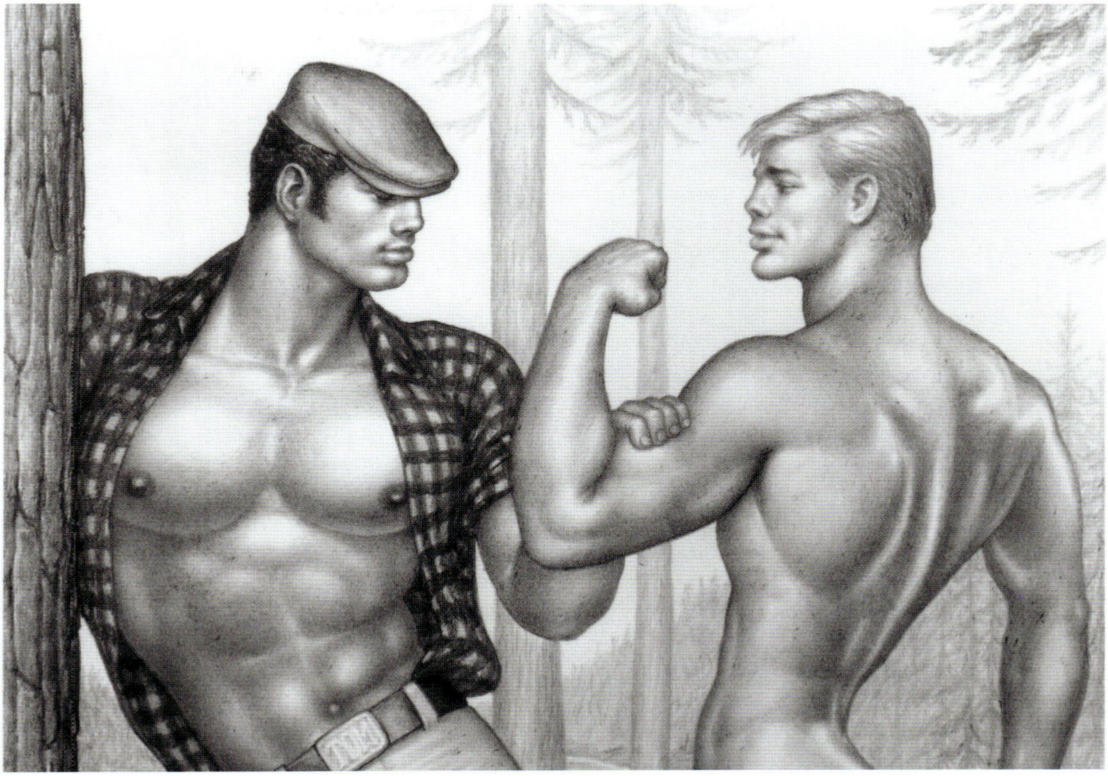

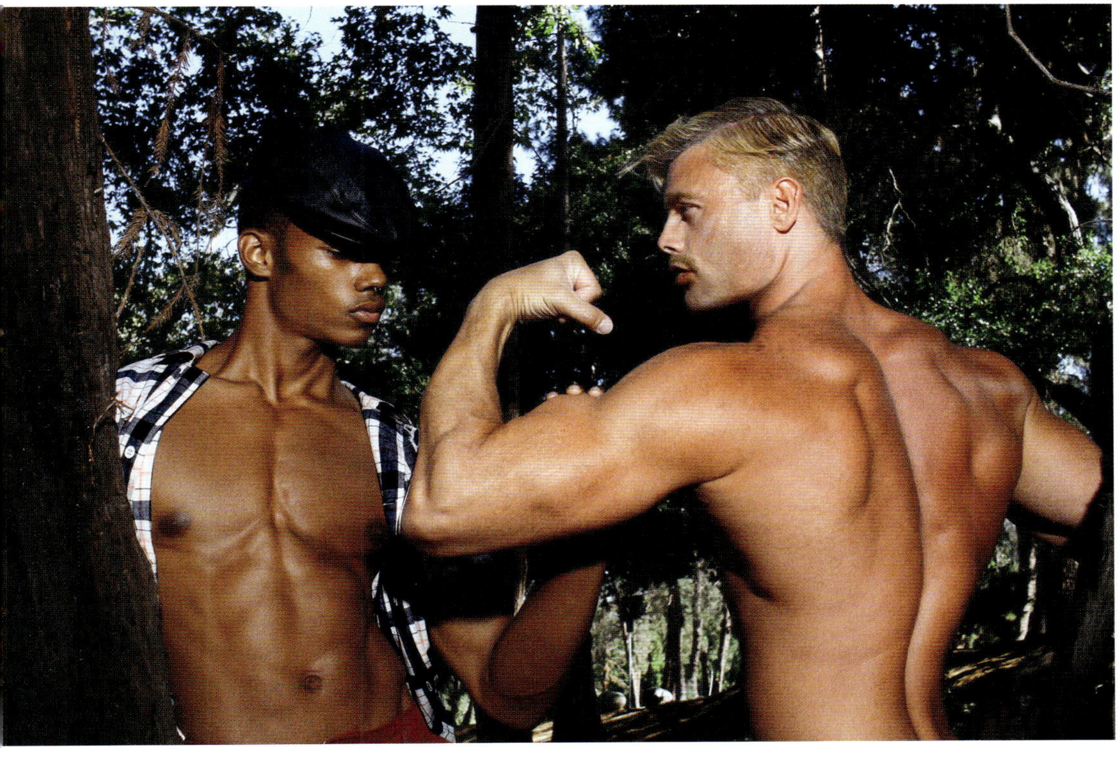

„Walt Disney mit Arschfick" • "Walt Disney with ass fucking"

Ralf König über Tom of Finland • Ralf König on Tom of Finland

Sind Tom of Finlands Zeichnungen in deinem Verständnis eigentlich Comics?
Ralf König: Jein. Tom of Finland hat Bildabfolgen gezeichnet, wenn auch nicht mit Sprechblasen und Dialog. Es sind also Comics, aber ich bin mit der Lektüre unterfordert, denn die Handlung ist ja nicht sehr kompliziert. Was mir zuerst zu ihm einfällt, ist unbedingte Lebensfreude, Lust an der Lust, ein Hohelied auf den Männerkörper, auch eine anrührende Unschuld, gepaart mit Hemmungslosigkeit. Das muss man sich heute klarmachen: Er war ein Kind seiner Zeit und Homosexualität ein Tabu. Aber er zeichnet drauflos, mit dieser unbedingten Überzeugung, dass Männer wunderschön sind und dass es an Männersex nichts, aber auch gar nichts zu schämen gibt! Er war ein großer, schamloser Zeichner schwuler Ikonen und das hatte Signalwirkung bei schwulen Männern, die meist mit Komplexen herumliefen, nicht männlich genug zu sein oder etwas Schmutziges, Unnatürliches zu tun. So erkläre ich mir auch das ständige Lächeln bei den Finland-Männern.

Wie meinst du das?
Egal, wie sie's grad treiben und was sie sich gegenseitig Monströses reinschieben, sie lächeln, als säßen sie bei Schwiegermutter auf dem Sofa und schneiden den Kuchen an. Das fand ich immer etwas ungeil an den Zeichnungen, ich lache selten beim Sex, aber ich ahne die Absicht: Selbst der derbste Fick ist fröhlich und heiter, eine vergnügliche Männersache, Genuss pur. Da ist nichts aggressiv, nichts pervers, nichts zu verstecken. Selbst wenn einer gangbangmässig rangenommen wird, sind am Ende alle happy und zufrieden. Heute gibt es ja diese Manga-Pornocomics, diese eigenartigen *Boys Love*-Büchlein für kleine Mädchen oder auch die japanischen Muskelkerle von Gengoroh Tagame, da geht es auch hart zur Sache. Aber da wird meist schmerzverzerrt das Gesicht verzogen oder gar geweint. Was am Ende vielleicht realistischer ist. Eigentlich ist es nicht der Porno, den ich mit Tom of Finland verbinde, sondern diese wunderschönen Bleistiftzeichnungen,

Are Tom of Finland's drawings comics in your understanding?
Ralf König: Yes and no. Tom of Finland drew sequences of pictures without speech bubbles and dialogue. Therefore they are comics but I'm unchallenged by reading them as the plot isn't very complicated. What comes to mind first, when I think about him, is an unconditional joy of life, a passion for passion, a song of praise of the male body, also a touching innocence paired with a lack of restraint. Today we have to remember that he was a child of his time and that homosexuality was a taboo. Nevertheless he kept drawing with an unconditional conviction that men are beautiful and that sex between men is nothing, absolutely nothing, to be ashamed of! He was a great, shameless illustrator of gay icons and this had a signal effect on gay men who often had complexes about not being manly enough or about doing something unnatural, something dirty. That's how I explain the permanent smile of the Finland men.

How do you mean that?
No matter what they are doing or what kind of monstrosity they shove into themselves, they always smile as if they were sitting on their mother in law's couch and were cutting pie. That's something I never found very arousing about these pictures. I rarely laugh during sex but I can guess the intention of it: even the roughest fuck is cheerful and fun, an man's pleasure thing, pure enjoyment. There's nothing aggressive, nothing perverse, nothing to hide. Even if a guy is taken in a gang bang manner, in the end everyone is happy and content. Today there are these manga-porncomics, these strange *Boys Love* booklets for little girls or even the Japanese beefcakes of Gengoroh Tagame, that's where things get tough. But the boys in them are mostly grimacing painfully or even cry. What might be more realistic in the end. Actually it's not porn which I link to

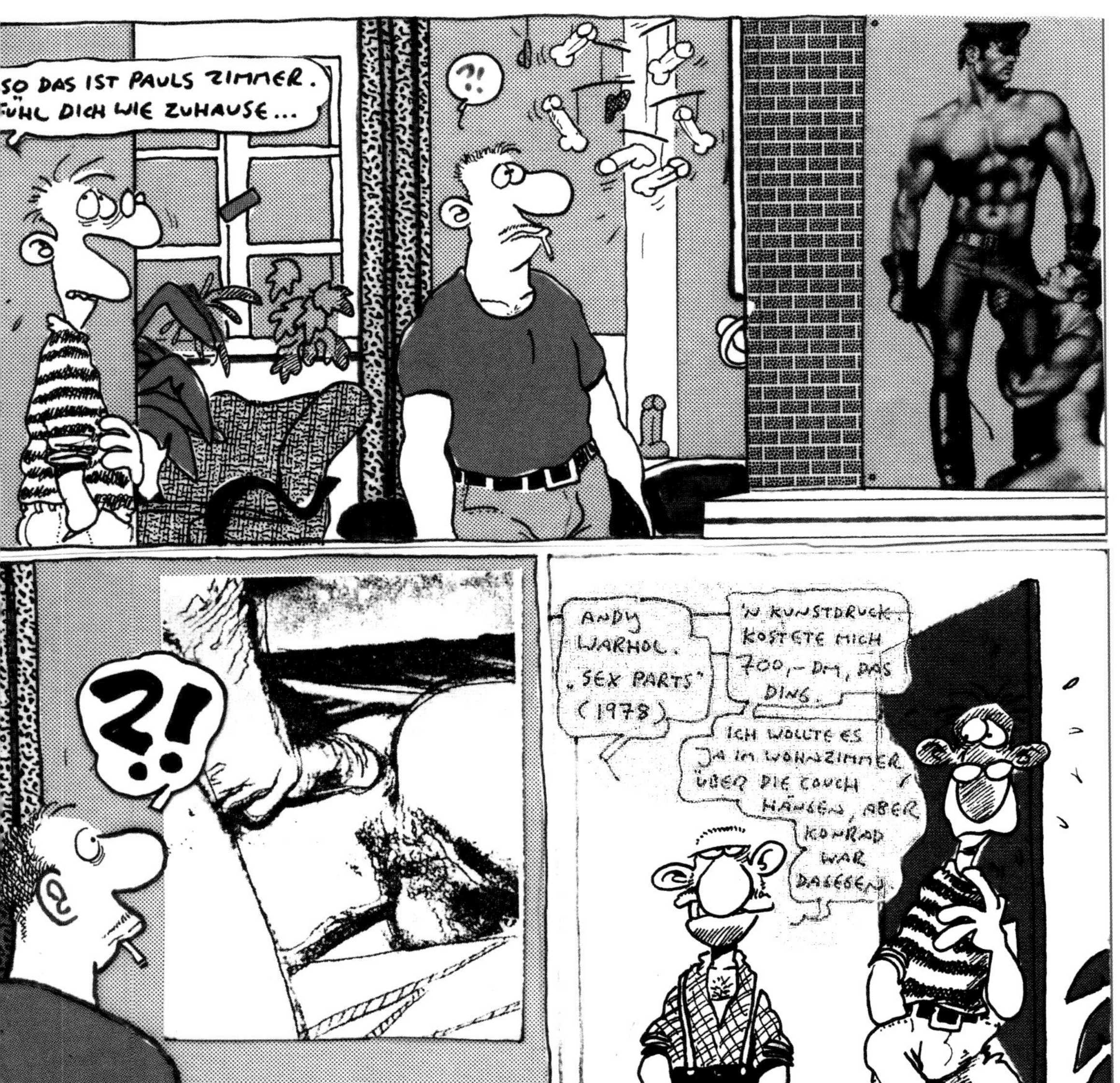

Originalseite aus einem frühen und nie veröffentlichten Konrad und Paul-Comic • Original page from an early and never published Konrad and Paul comic strip

die schimmernde Haut, das Licht, der Glanz auf dem Leder. Gleichzeitig ist es immer ein bisschen Heile Welt, immer ein bisschen märchenhaft, zu schön, um wahr zu sein. Es ist auch Kitsch, aber grandioser. Tom ist Walt Disney mit Arschfick.

Wie und wann hast du sie für dich entdeckt, und hatten sie Eindruck auf dich gemacht?
Ich kann mich nicht erinnern, wann und wo ich zum erstmal Zeichnungen von Tom of Finland sah. Ich fürchte, ich hab' schon viel früher Heftigeres gesehen, nämlich die Pornos meines Vaters im Nachtschrank. Ich kann mir aber gut vorstellen, dass es in den 50ern, 60ern für viele ungeheuerlich war, diese Zeichnungen mit den Riesenschwänzen zum ersten Mal zu sehen. Ich weiß noch, ich hatte in meiner Kindheit einen Comic aus Holland in die Finger gekriegt, eine Porno-Parodie auf Lucky Luke: „Der Mann, der schneller spritzt als sein Schatten". Sehr gekonnt gezeichnet, und Luke hatte einen Riesenschwanz und lauter Porno-Abenteuer zu bestehen, wenn auch heterosexuelle. Das hat mich mindestens genauso inspiriert wie Tom of Finland. Ich finde Lucky Luke heute noch sexy.

Wie kam's, dass du seine Zeichnungen in deinen eigenen Comics verwendet hast?
Da seine Männer quasi Heiligenbildchen waren und ich diese Überzeichnung schon damals auch etwas drüber fand, war es naheliegend, diese Perfektion ironisch hochzunehmen. Um Copyright machte ich mir Anfang der 80er überhaupt keine Gedanken, ich hatte nicht mal ansatzweise gedacht, dass ich mit meinen Comics mal erfolgreich werde. Also hab' ich in zwei, drei Geschichten zur Schere gegriffen und sozusagen als Traumprinz-Ideal diese Finland-Männer eingefügt, die dann von meinen krakeligen Knollennasen angeschmachtet wurden. Meine Nasen sind ja quasi das Gegenstück zu Finlands Männerbild. Die haben Komplexe und sind unsicher und haben ihre Probleme mit Liebeskummer, Lust und Frust. So was kommt bei Tom nicht vor. Und klar, wenn man über die Straße geht und da kommt einem so'n Typ entgegen, gutaussehend, selbstbewusst, wohlgeformt, da fiept man als gemeine Knollennase.

Tom of Finland, but these beautiful pencil drawings, the shining skin, the light, the sparkle of the leather. At the same time, it is always one bit of a perfect world, always a bit magical, too good to be true. It's kitsch, but superb kitsch. Tom is Walt Disney with ass fucking.

How and when did you discover the drawings and did they make an impression on you?
I can't remember when and where I've seen drawings by Tom of Finland for the first time. I'm afraid that I had seen rougher stuff long before, namely my dad's porn mags in his bedside cabinet. But I can imagine that for many people in the '50s and '60s it must have been outrageous to see these drawings with huge dicks for the first time. I remember that as a child I got hold of a comic from Holland, a porn parody of Lucky Luke: "The man who cums faster than his shadow." It was drawn masterfully, and Luke had a giant cock and and had to face all these porn adventures, though they were heterosexual. This fascinated me at least as much as Tom of Finland. I still find Lucky Luke sexy.

How did it happen that you used his drawings in your own comics?
Because his men were practically images of saints which I already thought to be a bit exaggerated, it wasn't hard to bust this perfection ironically. I didn't lose a thought to copyright at the beginning of the '80s, I didn't even rudimentarily think that I would be successful with my comics one day. So I grabbed my scissors together with two, three of his stories and added the Prince Charming ideal of the Finland men to my comics. They were lusted after by my scrawly bulbous noses. The noses of my characters are pretty much the opposite of Finland's image of a man. My characters have complexes and are insecure and have problems, they feel insecure and have their problems with lovesickness, lust and frustration. You can't find that in Tom's pictures. And obviously when you cross the street and such a guy is approaching you, handsome, confident, well-shaped, you whimper as a guy with a pug nose.

Sind seine Kerle heute noch zeitgemäß oder schon wieder retro-chic?
Die ganze Art zu zeichnen ist Retro, denke ich, und vielleicht ist auch diese Art Fetisch-szene ein bisschen von gestern. Klar gibt es weiterhin Ledertreffen und Military-Klamotten, aber ich habe den Eindruck, bei Tom in den 50ern war Leder wirklich noch ‚Fetisch' im eigentlichen Sinne. Heute scheint mir die Lederhose eher dem Dresscode genügen zu wollen, damit man bei der Party am Türsteher vorbeikommt.

Würde er sich freuen, dass ihm die finnische Post Sonderbriefmarken widmete, und dass unter seinem Namen Sextoys, Bettwäsche, Kaffeebohnen und Wodka verkauft werden?
Ist doch ein Triumph, aus der komplexbehafteten Schmuddelecke zur Staatsikone! Andererseits: Der Insiderkult geht natürlich ein Stück weit verloren. Ich weiß nicht. Echt, Kaffeebohnen und Wodka?

Interview: Axel Schock

Are his men still contemporary today or are they already retro-chic?
This whole kind of drawing is retro I think and maybe this kind of fetish scene is also a bit outdated. Sure, I feel the leather community is still living, there are still leather meetings and military clothing but I have the impression that for Tom in the '50s leather was still truly a fetish in its actual meaning. Today it seems like leather pants are simply meant to satisfy the dress code, to get past the bouncer.

Would Tom of Finland be happy that the Finnish Post dedicated commemorative stamps and that under his name sex toys, bedding, coffee beans and vodka be sold?
It's a triumph to make his way from the dirty corner full of complexes to being a national icon! On the other hand, the insider cult gets lost a bit. I don't know. Are there really coffee beans and vodka in his name?

Translation: Sunita Sukhana

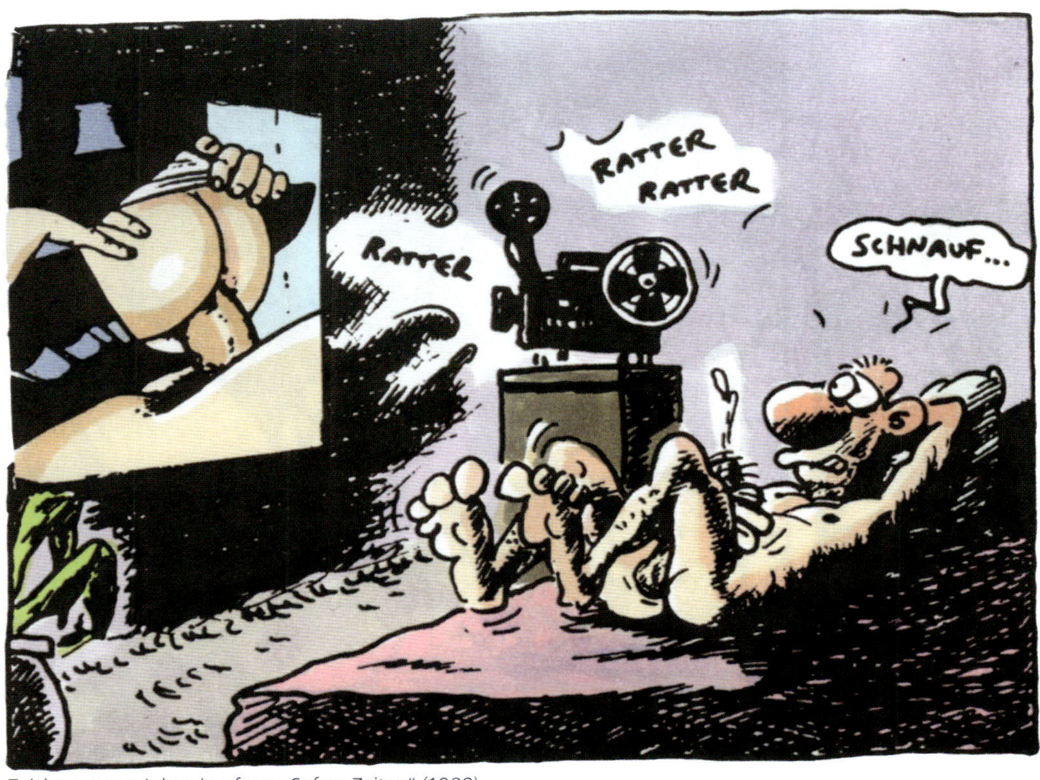

Zeichnung aus / drawing from „Safere Zeiten" (1988)

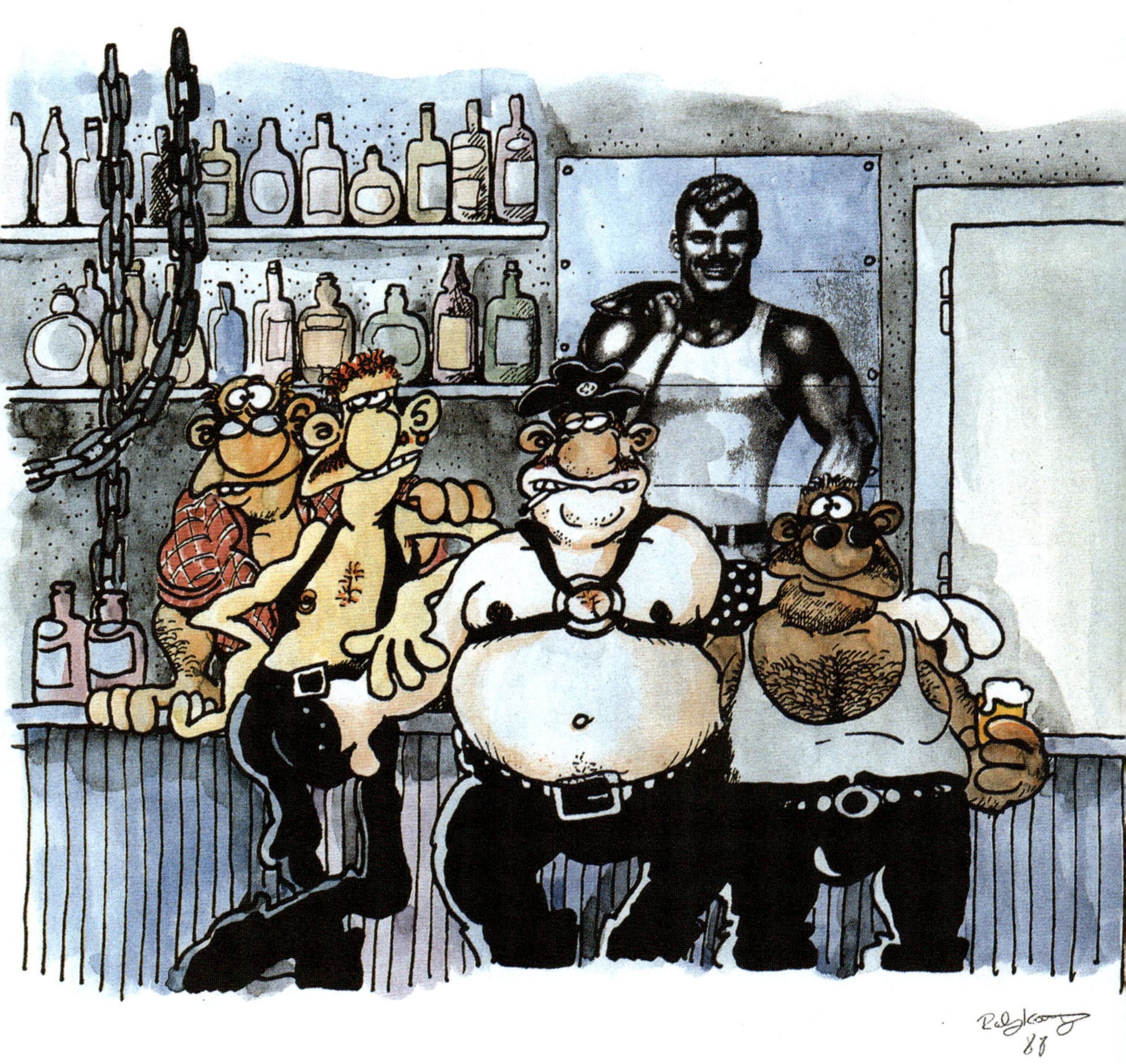

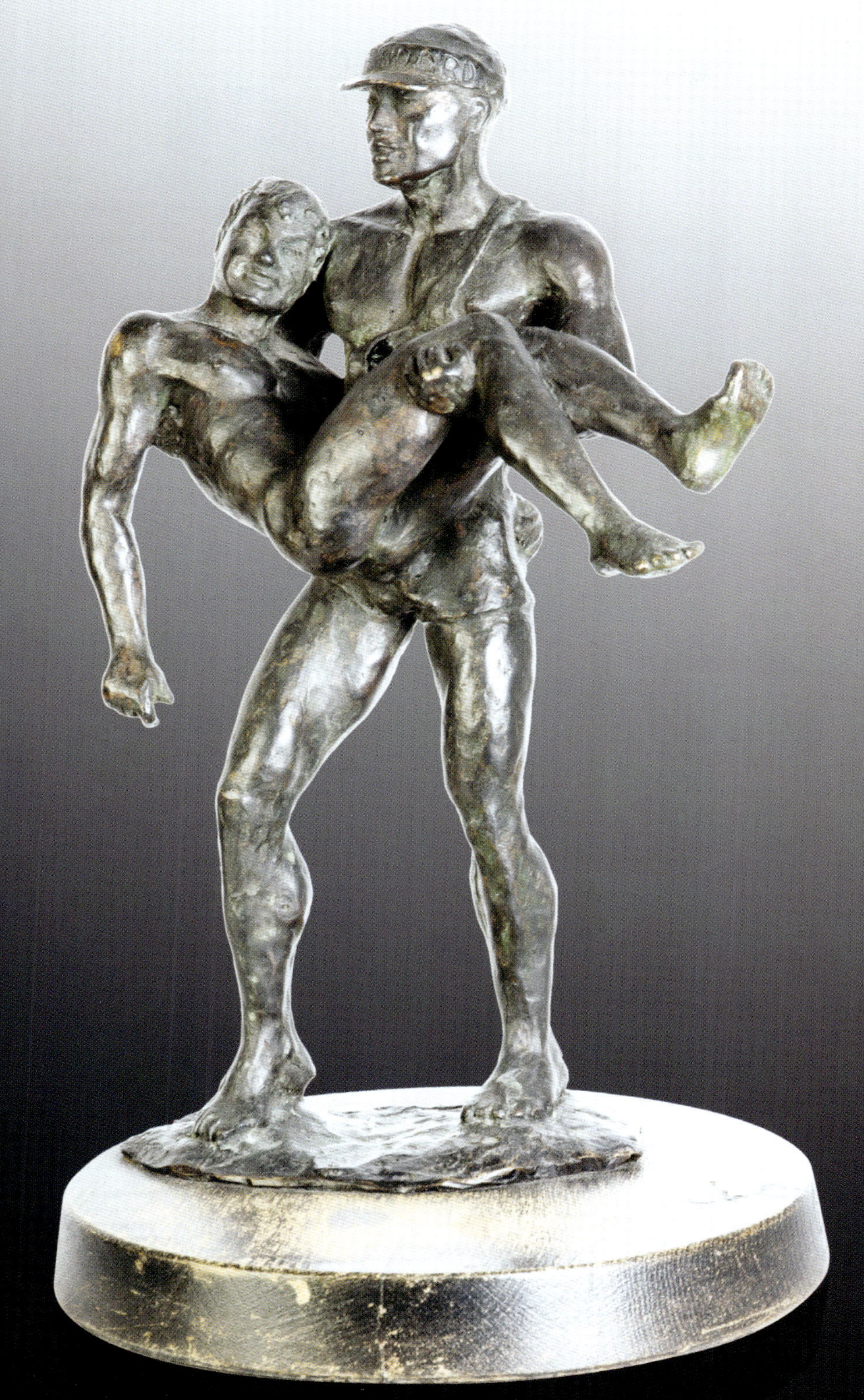

OK VAN BATENBURG

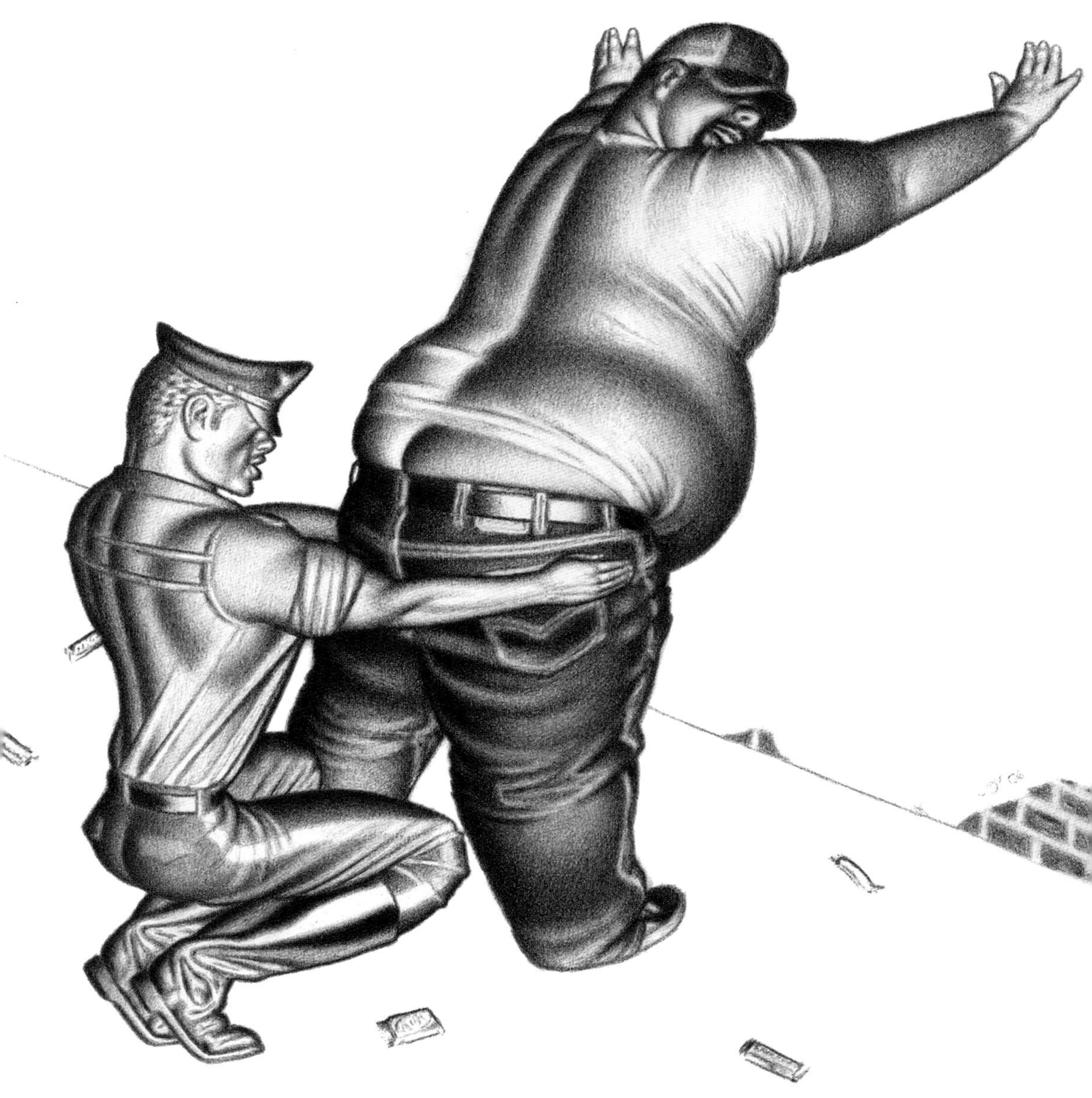

SVEN OLIVER

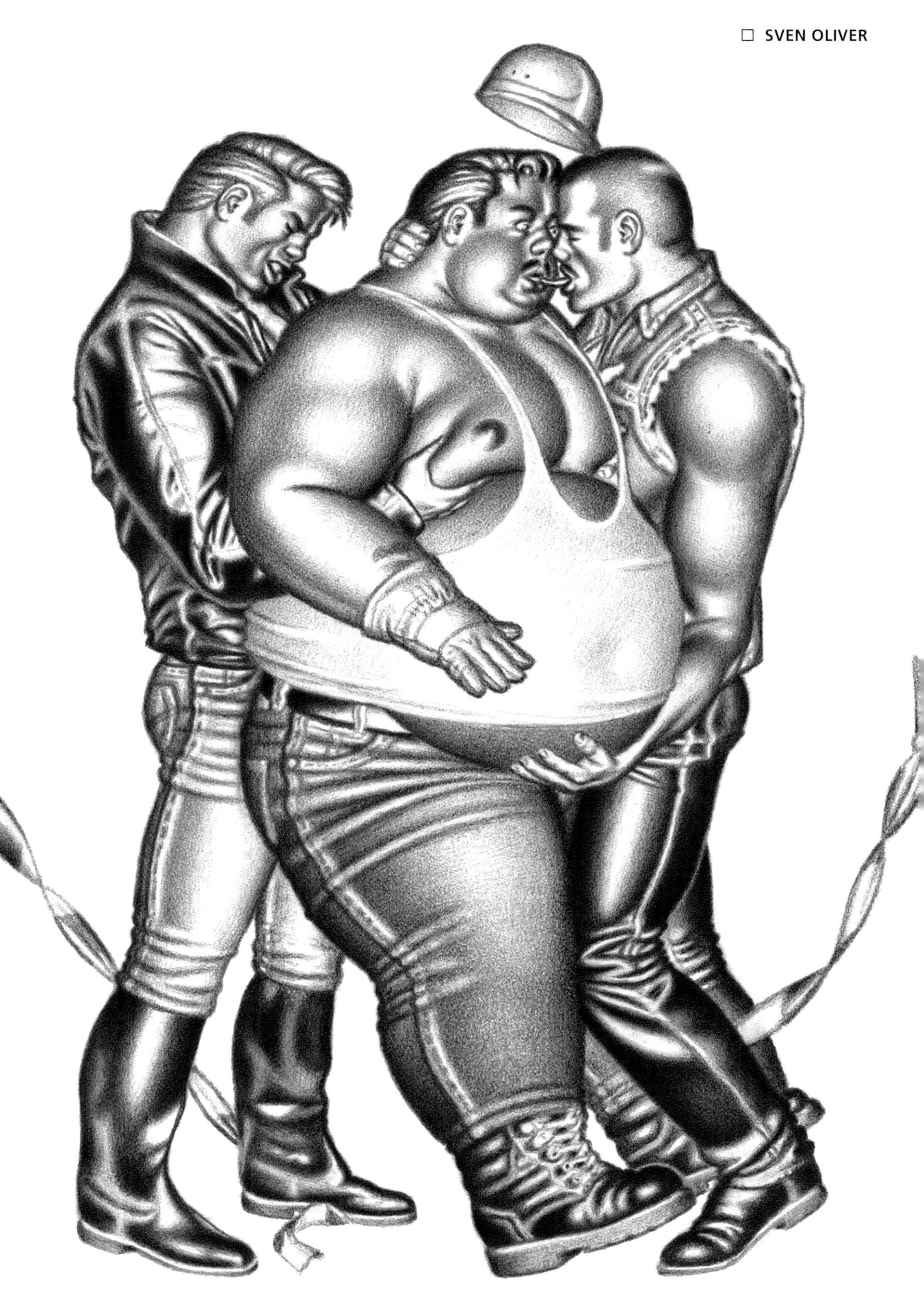

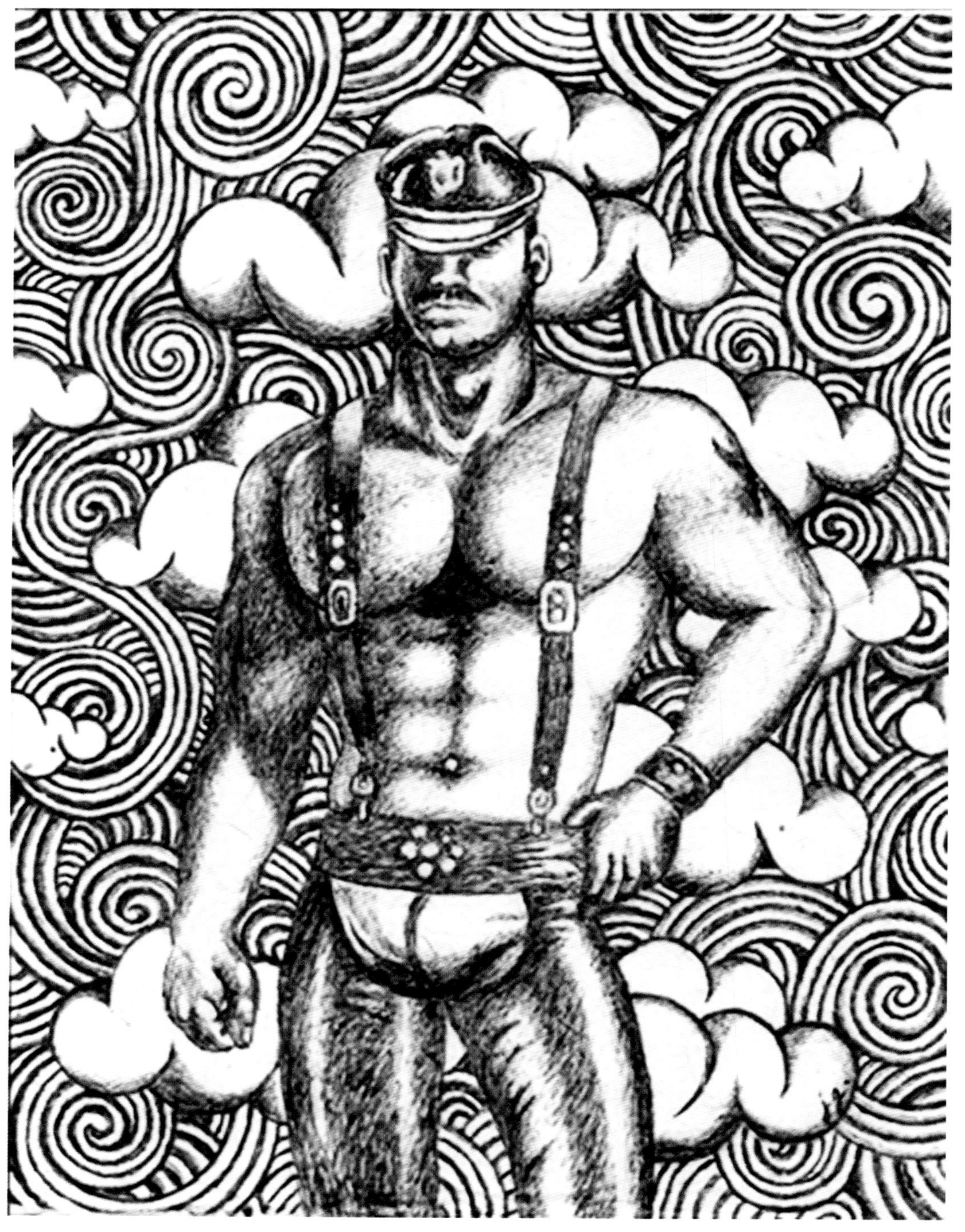

Highlights from the Collection

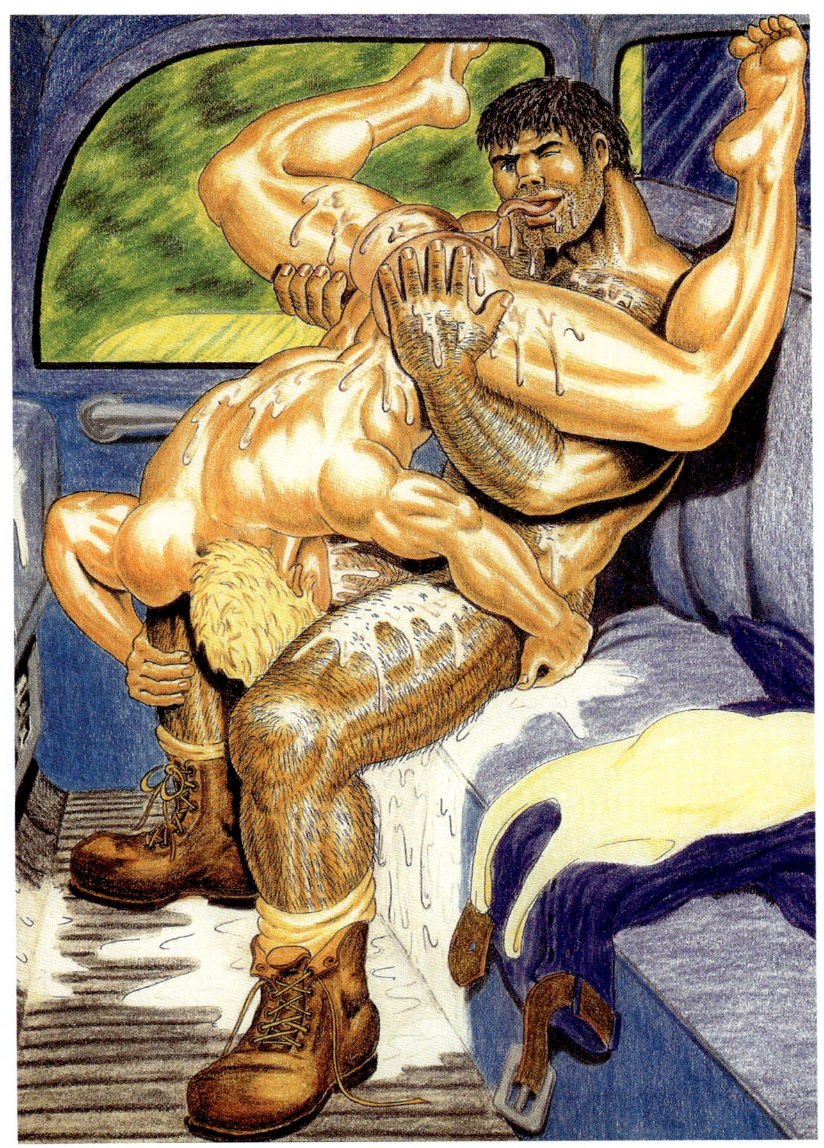

THE HUN

Life in the Largest Homoerotic Archive in the World
• Ein Leben im größten homoerotischen Archiv der Welt

Curator Marc Ransdell-Bellenger about Tom of Finland Foundation's Collecton • Kurator Marc Ransdell-Bellenger über die Kunstsammlung der Tom of Finland Foundation

I first found my way to Tom of Finland Foundation in 2009 when I attended a holiday party. I was standing on the covered front porch smoking cigars in the rain on that cold December night in the company of fellow Leathermen, many who I had previously dreamed and fantasized about. It was then I realized I was where I belonged. I had no idea at that time that it would eventually become my home and place of employment.

When I walked through the big oak door of that one hundred-year-plus Craftsman style house, as many before me and many since, I was somewhat spell bound. You could actually feel its history and the air of magic that it retained, emitting a sense of welcoming to all who passed through.

Das erste Mal kam ich 2009 zu einer Party in die Tom of Finland Foundation. Ich stand also in einer kalten Dezembernacht auf der überdachten Veranda und rauchte Zigarren in der Gesellschaft von anderen Ledermännern, von denen ich zuvor nur geträumt und phantasiert hatte. Da wurde mir klar, dass ich genau dort war, wo ich hingehörte. Damals hatte ich noch keine Ahnung, dass es irgendwann mein Zuhause und Arbeitsplatz werden sollte.

Als ich durch die große Eichentür dieses hundertjährigen Holzhauses ging, war ich verzaubert, so wie viele vor und viele nach mir. Ich konnte die Geschichte und Magie des Hauses spüren, von der alle, die hierher kommen, willkommen geheißen werden.

Ein Besuch hier kann eine transzendente Erfahrung sein; zumindest war es das für mich. Bei mei-

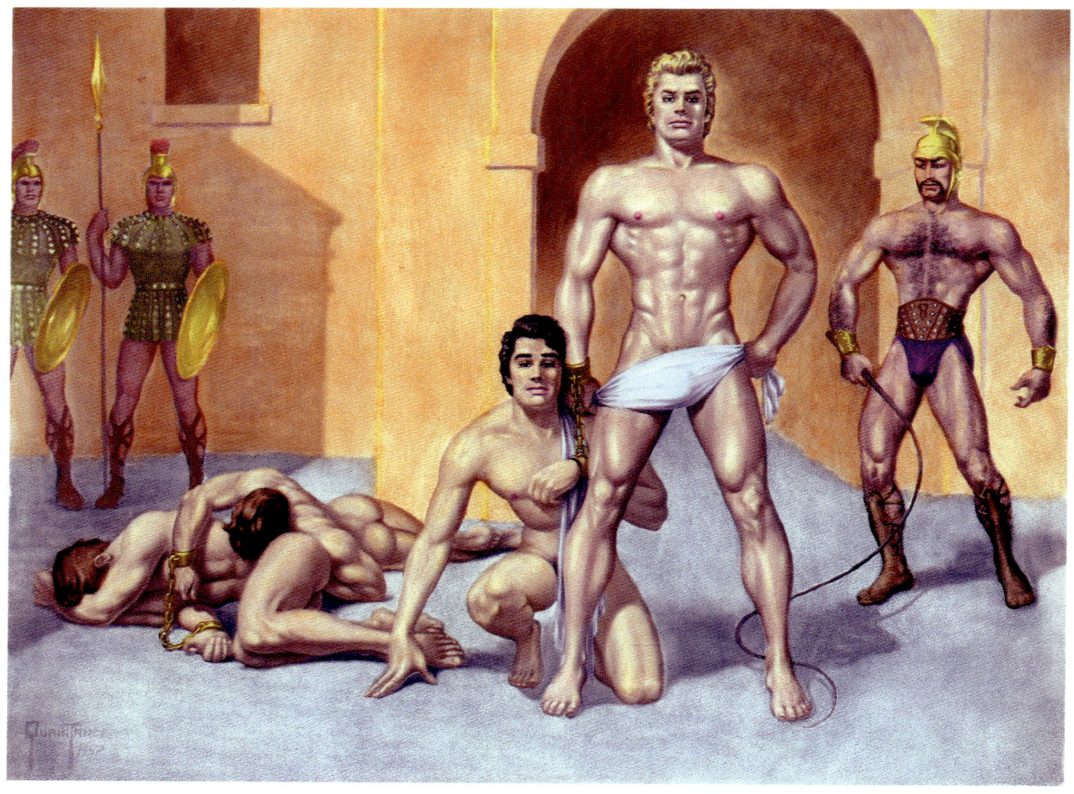

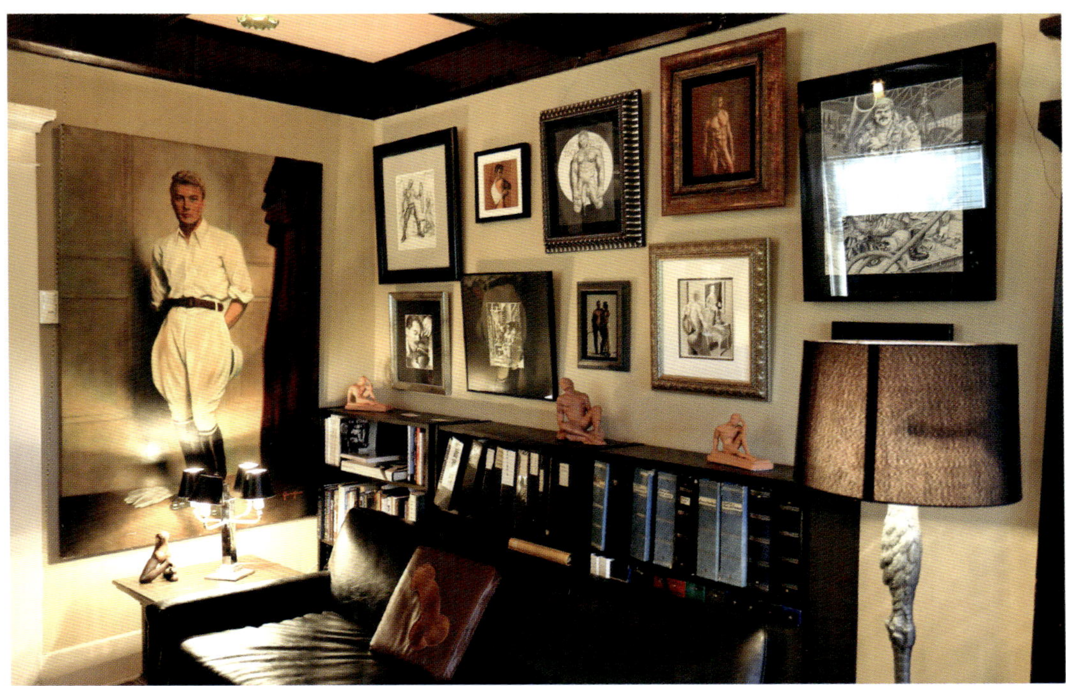

TCM House. Photo: Rinaldo Hopf

Visiting here, well it can be a transcendent experience; at least it was for me. When I arrived at the House, in many ways I was broken and drifting. The life of this home revived me. Its energy seems to grow as a result of every person that crosses over that threshold. This has in some manner been set in motion by its caretaker over these past thirty some years, Durk Dehner. Through his focus and dedication to our arts and culture the place absorbs and expresses itself in some mystical way that can only be experienced. He has given his heart and soul to TOM House and the Foundation that he and the artist Tom of Finland created together here. It is his intention to perpetuate this living, breathing, always transforming home that houses one of the largest collections of "who we are". We need only rise to the occasion and take charge of it and its future.

My life without the work of Tom would be hard to imagine. When I saw my first drawing, I knew I was not alone. There were other men out there like me and that is when I set off to find them and myself. So here I am curator at a place that fits me like a custom made pair of boots.

ner Ankunft war ich in vielerlei Hinsicht entwurzelt und gebrochen. Die Energie dieses Hauses hat mich wiederbelebt. Sie scheint mit jeder Person zu wachsen, die diese Schwelle überschreitet. Auf geheimnisvolle Weise scheint das der Hüter des Hauses, Durk Dehner, im Lauf der letzten dreißig Jahre bewirkt zu haben. Durch seine Konzentration und Hingabe an unsere homoerotische Kunst und Kultur hat dieser Ort eine mystische Ausstrahlung bekommen, die sich nur persönlich erfahren lässt. Er hat sein Herzblut für das TOM House und die Foundation gegeben, die er gemeinsam mit dem Künstler Tom of Finland hier geschaffen hat. Sein Wunsch ist, dieses lebendige, atmende, sich immer wieder verwandelnde Zuhause zu bewahren, das eine der größten Sammlungen zu unserer schwulen Identität beherbergt. Wir müssen uns nur der Aufgabe stellen und das Haus und seine Zukunft aktiv gestalten.

Mein Leben wäre ohne Toms Werk schwer vorstellbar. Als ich zum ersten Mal eine Zeichnung von Tom sah, wusste ich, dass ich nicht alleine bin. Mir wurde klar, dass es meinesgleichen gibt und ich machte mich auf, um diese Männer und auch mich selbst zu finden. Hier bin ich nun Kurator an einem Ort, der mir wie ein maßgefertigtes Paar Stiefel passt.

Interview:

The fan base of Tom of Finland is still growing, his work and life is narrated and discussed in several books and also in films. Nevertheless, the art collection of the Foundation is still quite unknown. Why is that?

This book is the first to explore the other artists in the collection. From the outside the Foundation looks like a large worldwide corporation. The reality is we have a very small sometimes paid staff (3 to 4 at any given time) and a large group of devoted fans and volunteers helping us throughout the world. Most of the time the staff is focused on just handling the day-to-day operations of keeping the organization running. I joined the Foundation about three years ago with the goal of getting the collection catalogued thus making our ability in protecting, preserving and promoting the collection and the erotic arts all the more effective. I would say that because we have been focused in more recent years on Tom's work and his legacy that the other artists' part of our collection is much less well known. The cataloguing will change that as this book will do also.

What exactly is the collection of the Tom of Finland Foundation?

Every time I walk through our storage space, it is astonishing for me to see the wide range of what we have in our care. Essentially there are two components of the collection: Tom's work and the work of other artists. The Tom collection contains his finished drawings, preparatory sketches, reference pages, ephemera, his leather outfits and his World War II uniform, several pairs of his boots, his vast collection of stamps and just about everything to do with Tom.
The other larger collection would be all of the other artists for whose work we care. Artists like Richard Hawkins. Rex, Étienne, George Quaintance and Don Bacardy. All of whom are very well known in the art world. We also have primitive works and others by naïve artists no one's ever heard of or seen before.

Interview:

Tom of Finlands Fangemeinde wächst nach wie vor, sein Werk und sein Leben werden in zahlreichen Büchern und Filmen erzählt und diskutiert. Dennoch ist die Kunstsammlung der Stiftung noch relativ unbekannt. Wie kommt das?

Dieser Band von *Mein schwules Auge* stellt als erstes auch die anderen Künstler der Sammlung vor. Von außen sieht die Stiftung wie ein großes globales Unternehmen aus. In Wirklichkeit haben wir wenige (oft unbezahlte) Mitarbeiter (es sind nie mehr als 3 bis 4 Personen) und zahlreiche hingebungsvolle Fans und Freiwillige, die uns auf der ganzen Welt helfen. Die meiste Zeit sind die Mitarbeiter darauf konzentriert, die täglichen Arbeiten zu erledigen, um das Unternehmen am Laufen zu halten. Ich bin vor etwa drei Jahren der Stiftung mit dem Ziel beigetreten, die Sammlung zu katalogisieren und so unsere Möglichkeiten zu verbessern, die Sammlung und die erotischen Künste zu schützen, zu bewahren und zu fördern. Ich würde sagen, dass der Teil unserer Sammlung, der die Werke der anderen Künstlern beinhaltet, weniger bekannt ist, weil wir uns in den letzten Jahren überwiegend auf Toms Werk konzentriert haben. Die Katalogisierung und dieses Buch werden das jetzt ändern.

Was genau ist die Sammlung der Tom of Finland Foundation?

Jedes Mal, wenn ich durch unseren Lagerraum gehe, staune ich über die große Bandbreite dessen, was wir dort alles haben. Im Wesentlichen hat die Sammlung zwei Komponenten: Toms Werke und die Werke der anderen Künstler. Die Tom-Sammlung enthält seine fertigen Zeichnungen, vorbereitende Skizzen, Nachschlagewerke, Ephemera, seine Lederoutfits und seine Uniform aus dem Zweiten Weltkrieg, dazu mehrere Paar Stiefel, eine riesige Sammlung von Briefmarken und eben alles, was mit Tom zu tun hat. Der andere und größere Teil der Sammlung enthält die Werke all unserer anderen Künstler, wie Richard Hawkins, Rex, Étienne, George Quaintance und Don Bacardy, die in der Kunstwelt bekannte Größen sind. Wir haben dort aber auch primitive Kunst und Arbeiten von naiven Künstlern, von denen noch nie jemand etwas gehört oder gesehen hat.

How did this collection get started?

The collection has its initial roots with Tom's work. The Foundation was set up to house Tom's ephemera, his correspondence, his leathers and other personal materials. Eventually other artists wanted to be a part of Tom's world and began to donate works to the Foundation. When it comes to the collections and archives, I half-jokingly refer to it as the world's largest homo-erotic archive – next to The Vatican. As the AIDS epidemic began to decimate our community, our queer histories were vanishing at an astonishing pace. At the encouragement of the Foundation, many artists and collectors made arrangements to bequest their bodies of work and collections to the Foundation upon their death. In most cases a phone call would come in, "My son just died and you have 20 minutes to come in and clear out his apartment, or everything is going to be thrown away". During that dark era, the Foundation became an emergency repository for our art, culture and history.

Wie ist diese Sammlung entstanden?

Die Sammlung hat ihre Wurzeln in Toms künstlerischer Arbeit. Die Stiftung wurde gegründet, um Toms Ephemera, seine Korrespondenz, seine Ledersachen und andere persönliche Materialien zu beherbergen. Irgendwann wollten andere Künstler zu Toms Welt dazugehören und begannen, der Stiftung einige ihrer Werke zu spenden. Wenn es um die Sammlung und das Archiv geht, spreche ich immer halb scherzhaft vom größten homoerotischen Archiv der Welt – neben dem Vatikan. Wir fingen mit dem Aufbau der Sammlung ungefähr zu der Zeit an, als die Aids-Krise begann. In der Zeit also, als unsere schwulen Geschichten in rasantem Tempo verschwanden. Mit der Unterstützung der Stiftung trafen viele Künstler und Sammler Vorkehrungen, dass ihre Werke und Kunstsammlungen nach ihrem Tod in die Stiftung übergingen. Meistens kam aber einfach nur ein Anruf: „Mein Sohn ist gerade gestorben und ihr habt 20 Minuten Zeit, seine Wohnung

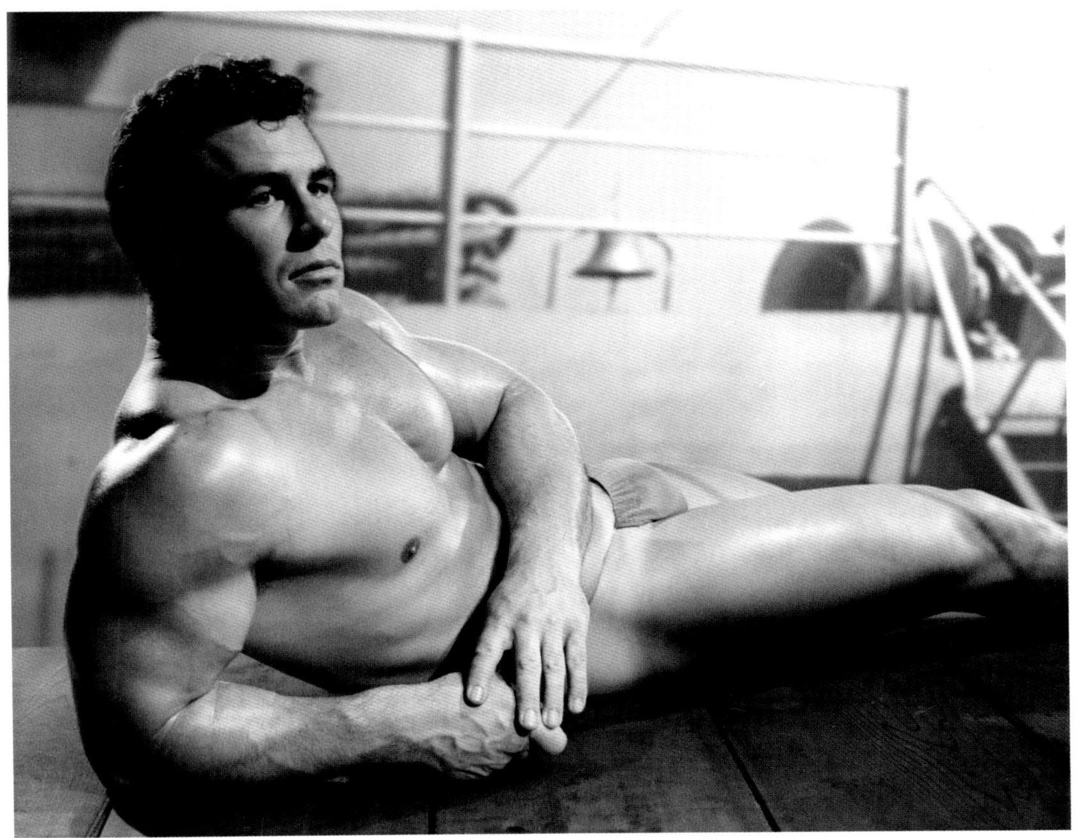

How did the Foundation obtain new art works?

The Foundation has always had the policy that we would not purchase art works for our permanent collection. We would have gone bankrupt in no time, thus we have always relied on the generosity of artists and collectors. There's one gentleman by the name of Norman Diegan who for at least the past decade has sent the Foundation one to two drawings every week just like clockwork. Rick Castro, artist and curator, unfortunately had to close his gallery Antebellum and took the opportunity to donate part of his personal collection to the Foundation. Also in recent years, we have taken in a large private collection from San Francisco as well as another from Los Angeles. Peter Fiske, a well-known member of the Leather community, and a 2017 inductee into the Leather Hall of Fame also generously donated an original Tom of Finland drawing this year.

zu räumen; sonst wird alles weggeworfen". In dieser dunklen Zeit wurde die Stiftung zu einem Notfalllager für unsere Kunst und Geschichte.

Wie hat die Stiftung neue Kunstwerke bekommen?

Die Stiftung hatte immer die Politik, keine Kunstwerke für unsere ständige Sammlung zu kaufen. Wir wären ja in kürzester Zeit pleite gewesen – deshalb haben wir immer auf die Großzügigkeit der Künstler und Sammler gebaut. Es gibt z.B. einen britischen Gentleman namens Norman Diegan, der der Stiftung seit mindestens einem Jahrzehnt jede Woche ein bis zwei Zeichnungen schickt. Der Künstler und Kurator Rick Castro musste leider seine Galerie Antebellum schließen und nahm das zum Anlass, der Stiftung einen Teil seiner persönlichen Sammlung zu spenden. In den letzten Jahren haben wir auch jeweils eine große private Sammlung aus San Francisco und aus Los Angeles bekommen. Peter Fiske, ein bekanntes Mitglied der Leder-Community, der 2017 in die Leather Hall of Fame

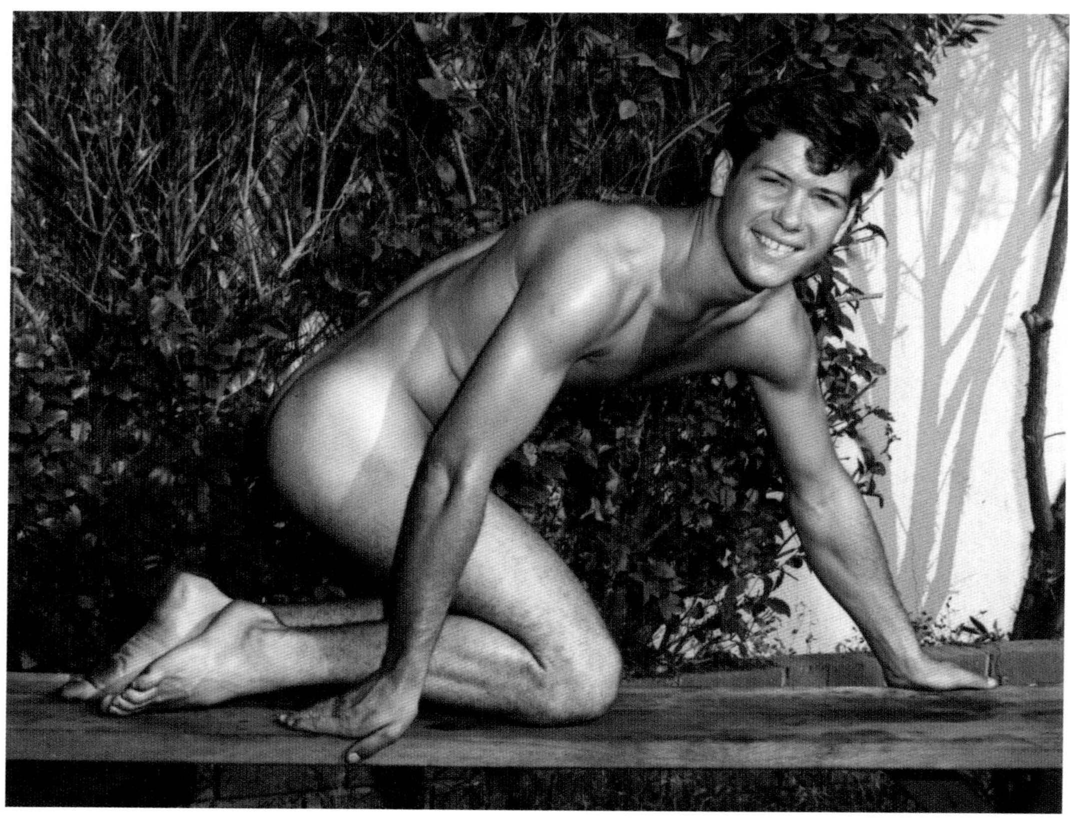

How many artists are represented in the collection?
We currently do not know exactly how many individual artists are represented in the collection. That is a task which is going to take place over the next few years. Once we have a new museum collection database software in place. I would estimate it to be in the thousands and would conservatively estimate the number of individual works of art in the collection between seven thousand to nine thousand.

What is the spectrum of the collection?
This collection encompasses every imaginable medium and material, probably even some that are unimaginable. As well as several periods in time: We have work from feudal Japan to fascist Italy to contemporary European and America. It ranges from traditional painting, drawing and sculpture to video and audio performance art pieces as well as a large collection of various media of motion pictures.

What makes the charm of the collection?
The collection encompasses the afore-mentioned Masters of the erotic arts as well as complete naïve, folk amateurs and emerging artists from our competitions. We do not discriminate: The masters hang next to the unknowns.

How are these works presented in the Foundation? Is there enough space to archive them and enough human and financial resources to preserve the works?
It is the same case for every museum from the Metropolitan to the Louvre to smaller facilities such as ourselves, there is never enough space, money or staff to do what we do and there never will be enough. The unique challenge the Foundation faces is that we are housed in a house. And not just a static museum house, but a living house where we host events and classes and lectures. We are also trying to do our laundry and go about our normal daily lives, or as normal as our lives can be in this house, add to that there are between three to seven Gay men living and fucking here at any given time.

aufgenommen wurde, spendete im selben Jahr eine eine Tom of Finland Originalzeichnung.

Wie viele Künstler sind in der Sammlung vertreten?
Wir wissen derzeit nicht genau, wie viele Künstler in der Sammlung vertreten sind. Das herauszufinden wird eine Aufgabe für die nächsten Jahre sein, sobald wir eine neue Datenbanksoftware für Museumssammlungen installiert haben. Ich würde schätzen, dass es mehrere tausend Künstler und vermutlich sieben- bis neuntausend Einzelwerke sind.

Was umfasst die Sammlung alles?
Diese Sammlung umfasst alle erdenklichen Medien und Materialien, wahrscheinlich sogar einige, die unvorstellbar sind – sowie verschiedene Epochen: Wir haben Werke aus dem kaiserlichen Japan, über das faschistische Italien bis hin zu zeitgenössischer Kunst aus Europa und den USA. Das Spektrum umfasst traditionelle Gemälde, Zeichnungen und Skulpturen, Video- und Audio-Performancekunst bis hin zu einer großen Sammlung verschiedener Filmmedien.

Was macht den Charme der Kollektion aus?
Die Sammlung umfasst alle, von den oben genannten Meistern der erotischen Kunst bis zu naiven Amateuren und den aufstrebenden Künstlern aus unseren Wettbewerben – wir machen da keine Unterschiede. Bei uns hängen die Meister neben Unbekannten.

Wie werden diese Werke in der Stiftung präsentiert? Gibt es genug Platz, um sie zu archivieren und genügend menschliche und finanzielle Ressourcen, um die Werke zu erhalten?
Für jedes Museum, vom Metropolitan Museum bis zum Louvre ebenso wie für kleinere Einrichtungen wie uns selbst gilt: Es wird nie genug Platz, Geld oder Personal geben, um das zu tun, was wir alles tun wollen.
Für unsere Stiftung besteht die besondere Herausforderung darin, dass wir in einem Wohnhaus untergebracht sind. Es handelt sich nicht um ein statisches Museum, sondern um ein lebendiges Haus, in dem wir alle Arten von Veranstaltungen haben. Wir versuchen auch, unsere Wäsche zu waschen und unseren ganz normalen Alltag zu leben – so normal wie unser

We are not the Getty, a gleaming white marble citadel on the top of a hill, with 30-foot-high walls to hang David Hockneys and Robert Motherwells.
This collection is contained in a hundred-year old – plus Craftsman style home.
It is the place, where real people live in, around and with the art of our sexual history. The artworks we put on display in our living room and dining room are the works that most people hide in their closets. It's our intention to get people to celebrate their sexuality and not be ashamed or timid about it, to bring the erotic arts out of the closets and back into the living room.
There is, to my knowledge, no other facility like TOM House on this earth, possibly the Playboy mansion in the 1970s. This house doesn't belong to those of us who live here – it belongs to our tribe. It is here so that we can continue to thrive not just merely survive. I guess that is the "charm" of the place. We're not a palace for the arts were a place for the arts.
Eventually, the collection and archive had grown to a point where the storage costs were prohibitive. In an effort to solve the problem, Durk Dehner came up with an innovative idea: An onsite climate controlled shipping container. Now, artist works from all over the world are stored in a container which itself has traveled all over the world.

Interview: Axel Schock

Leben in diesem Haus eben sein kann. Darüber hinaus leben und ficken hier zu jeder Zeit drei bis sieben schwule Männer.
Wir sind nicht das Getty-Museum, keine glänzend-weiße Marmor-Zitadelle oben auf dem Berg, mit 20 Meter hohen Wänden für Hockneys und Motherwells. Unsere Sammlung ist in einem hundert Jahre alten Holzhaus untergebracht. Es ist ein Ort, an dem echte Menschen in und mit der Kunst unserer sexuellen Geschichte leben. Die Kunstwerke, die in unserem Wohn- und Esszimmer hängen, sind die Werke, die die meisten Menschen irgendwo verstecken. Wir wollen Menschen dazu zu bringen, ihre Sexualität zu feiern, sich nicht zu schämen und die erotische Kunst in ihr Leben zu integrieren.
Soweit ich weiß gibt es auf der Welt keine andere Einrichtung wie TOM House, außer vielleicht die Playboy-Villa in den 1970ern. Dieses Haus gehört nicht uns, die wir hier leben, sondern unserem „Stamm". Es ist da, damit wir weiter gedeihen können und nicht einfach nur überleben. Ich glaube, das macht den „Charme" dieses Ortes aus. Wir sind kein Palast für die Künste, wir sind ein Ort für sie.
Die Sammlung und das Archiv sind schließlich so gewachsen, dass die Lagerungskosten kaum mehr finanzierbar wurden. Bei der Suche nach einer Lösung für dieses Problem kam Durk Dehner auf eine innovative Idee: einen Schiffscontainer mit Klimatisierung. So werden die Werke von Künstlern aus aller Welt nun in einem Container gelagert, der selbst um die ganze Welt gereist ist.

Übersetzung: Rinaldo Hopf

I know my little 'dirty drawings' are never going to hang in the main salons of the Louvre, but it would be nice if — I would like to say 'when,' but I better say 'if' — our world learns to accept all the different ways of loving. Then maybe I could have a place in one of the smaller side rooms.

Ich weiß, dass meine kleinen ‚schmutzigen Zeichnungen' nie an den Wänden eines der großen Säle des Louvre hängen werden, aber es wäre doch schön, wenn unsere Welt endlich alle unterschiedlichen Arten der Liebe anerkennen könnte. Dann könnte ich vielleicht einen Platz in einem der kleineren Nebenräume bekommen.
– Tom of Finland

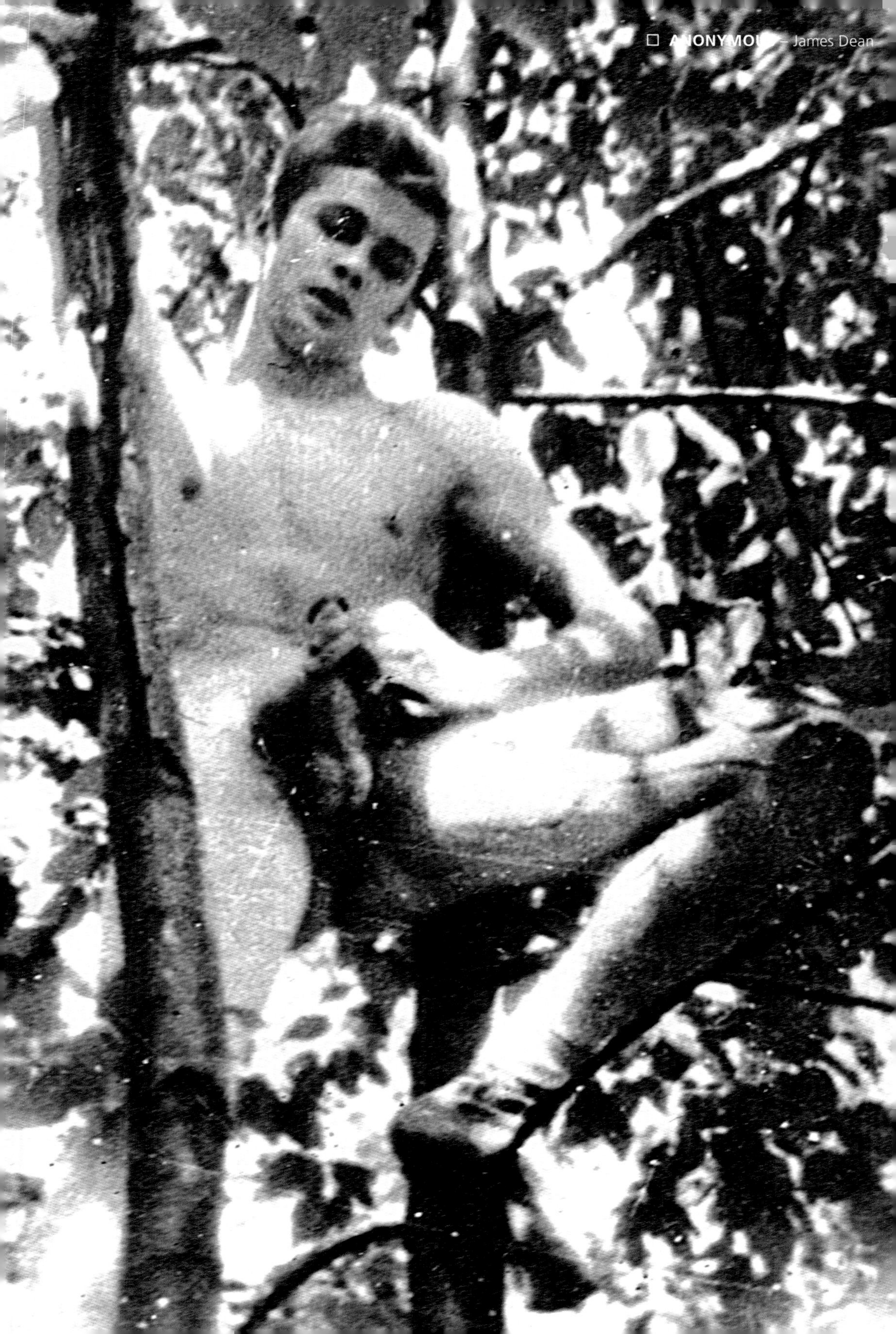
ANONYMOUS – James Dean

DURK DEHNER

Tom of Finland Foundation

Our motto: To protect, preserve and promote the erotic arts.
Unser Motto: Erotische Kunst schützen, bewahren und fördern

Tom and I started the Foundation in 1984. The first way we started to preserve was, of course, with Tom's archives. Tom was already prepared, having saved art works from crucial stages in his own development as an artist. The earliest were his childhood drawings from age eight, which have now been published.

Then there was his hand-made "war book", which documents in text and photographs, his own passage from boyhood to manhood through acquiring leadership skills as a military officer at the young age of 22. Tom's feeling was that if he and other soldiers had to wait around for actual combat with Russia, why not make the time productive? So, he established a military choir, and personally taught his men who didn't have vocal training, how to sing. A concert by the choir was even aired on national radio.

Even then, Lieutenant Laaksonen manifested what became Tom of Finland's philosophy about everything in life in which he involved himself: If you don't do something at the highest, most comprehensive level you can, what's the sense of doing it at all? Soon after the war, Tom created a series about young studs getting initiated into Gay subculture. This series gives us remarkable insights into some of the social attitudes prevalent then. For example, according to Tom, unlike today, most alpha males at the time did not seem to have concerns about getting fucked, as it appears it had no damaging impact on their positioning in the pack.

Tom held on to several thousand of his preparatory drawings, thinking they might be useful for historical purposes. Those works helped form the Foundation's permanent collection, and provided unexpected revenue sources, both for Tom while he was alive, and later for the Foundation, helping to keep our programs going and our doors open to the public.

Tom und ich haben die Stiftung 1984 gegründet. Zuallererst haben wir natürlich Toms Archiv aufgebaut, um seine Kunst zu bewahren. Tom hatte das bereits vorbereitet, indem er Werke aus entscheidenden Phasen seiner künstlerischen Entwicklung aufbewahrt hatte. Die frühesten waren seine Kinderzeichnungen aus dem achten Lebensjahr, die jetzt veröffentlicht wurden.

Dann gab es sein handgemachtes „Kriegsbuch", das mit Texten und Fotos seinen Übergang vom Jungen zum Mann dokumentiert. Im Alter von 22 Jahren hat er damals beim Militär Führungsqualitäten als Offizier entwickelt. Toms fand, dass er die Zeit produktiv nutzen könnte, solange er und die anderen Soldaten auf den eigentlichen Kampf gegen die Russen warteten. Also rief er einen Militärchor ins Leben und brachte seinen Männern, die keine Gesangsausbildung hatten, persönlich bei, wie man singt. Ein Konzert des Chores wurde sogar im finnischen Radio ausgestrahlt.

Kurz nach dem Krieg zeichnete Tom eine Serie mit jungen Kerlen, die in die schwule Subkultur eingeführt wurden. Diese Serie gibt uns einen guten Einblick in einige der damals vorherrschenden sozialen Einstellungen. Laut Tom hatten zum Beispiel die meisten Alpha-Männer damals (im Gegensatz zu heute) keine Bedenken, sich ficken zu lassen. Es scheint, als ob sich das auf ihre Stellung in der Szene nicht negativ ausgewirkt hat.

Tom bewahrte mehrere tausend seiner vorbereitenden Skizzen auf, weil er dachte, dass sie für die Zukunft nützlich sein könnten. Diese Werke bildeten später die Basis der ständigen Sammlung der Stiftung und sorgten für unerwartete Einnahmen, sowohl für Tom zu seinen Lebzeiten als auch später für die Stiftung. Sie halfen uns dabei, unsere Programme am Laufen zu halten und sicherten unsere Existenz.

Dieses Schützen und Bewahren erwies sich als eine wertvolle Lektion, die zuerst Tom und jetzt die Foundation anderen Künstlern ans Herz legt: Schaffe dein eigenes Archiv – dokumentiere zumindest deine Werke – und gehe nicht davon aus, dass irgendwelche Materialien es nicht wert

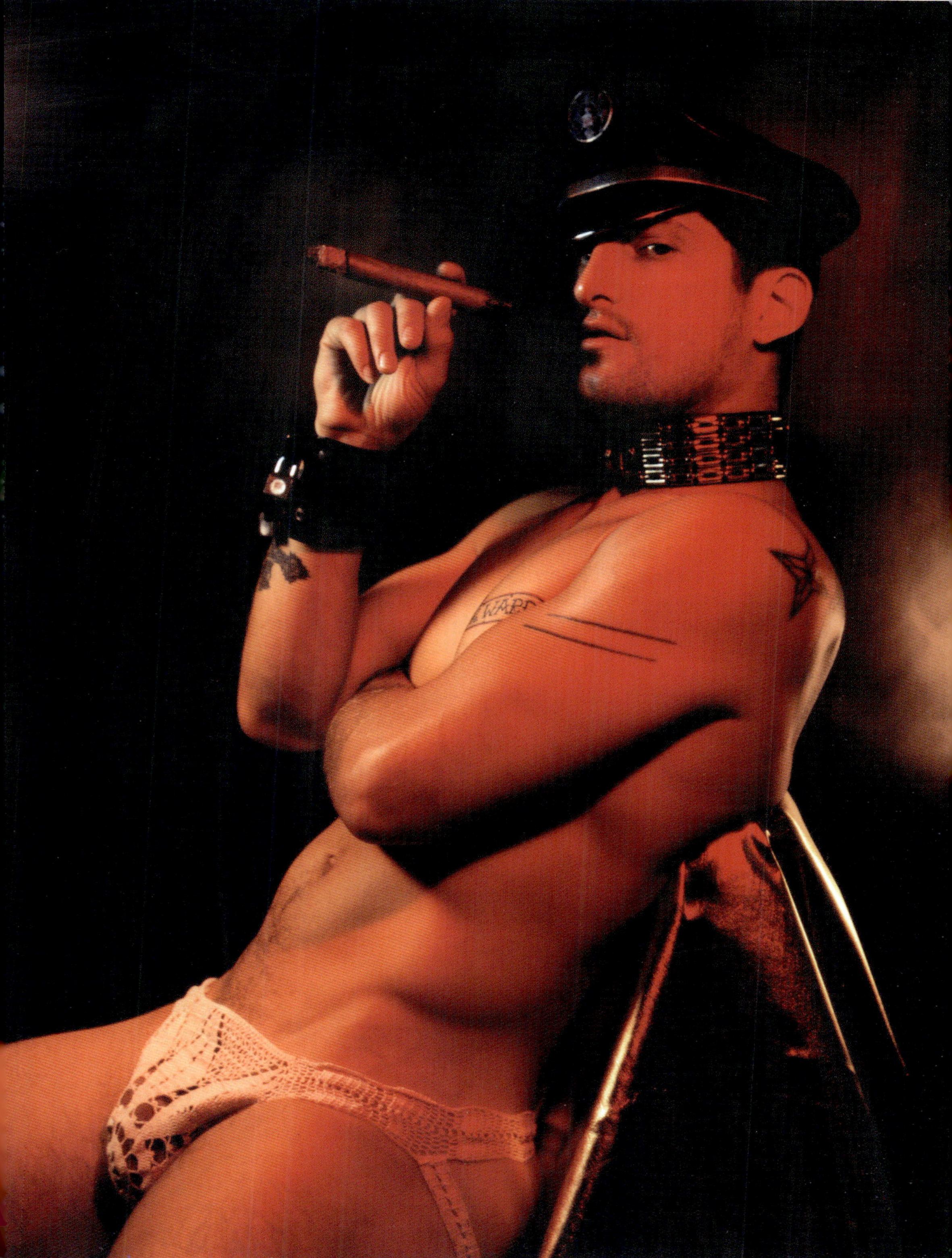

This protecting and preserving proved to be a valuable lesson, which Tom, and now the Foundation, encourages other artists to heed: Build your own archive – at least record your works – and do not assume materials are not worth keeping. Even if you don't see its value at the moment, it pays to hold on to archival objects. While Tom kept his preparatory works, he failed to safeguard his letters from fans and clients – to protect their confidentiality he disposed of their correspondence. Just think how valuable those letters would be today, as a window into Gay culture in an era of repression! While Tom's artistic work lives on, and his contributions to Gay liberation are universally recognized, his desire to protect his fellow homosexuals from possible exposure has caused us to lose potentially valuable testaments from fans of this groundbreaking artist.

Shortly after establishing his archive and starting the Foundation's permanent collection, Tom was approached by other artists, asking if they could donate one or two of their own works to the Foundation. Erotic artists were often beset by theft, denigration, and destruction of their work, and many of them saw the Foundation as their hope of being remembered.

Tom died 7th November 1991. His request was for us not to have a funeral, but rather the best Tom of Finland party ever! With that in mind, we created an event we called TOM's Bar, with the clear intention of making it as much fun for everyone as we could – and we have held the celebration every year since. The event always features sexy, fun ways for attendees to rejoice in the lifestyle Tom loved. The Best Butt Contest is one example – an always-popular excuse for some attendees to show their butts, and everyone else to admire them. Without shame, I'd have to acknowledge that there's often other hanky-panky going on as well – all in Tom's honor, of course.

But an equally important element of TOM's Bar is inviting artists to attend and showcase their works – to promote their artistry to potential collectors. This was the genesis of our Erotic Art Fairs, which have become successful events, both in Los Angeles and New

wären, aufgehoben zu werden. Selbst wenn du im Moment ihren Wert nicht erkennen kannst, lohnt es sich dennoch, Archivobjekte aufzubewahren. Während Tom aber seine Vorskizzen aufbewahrte, hat er es versäumt, seine Briefe von Fans und Kunden zu sammeln – er entsorgte ihre Korrespondenz, um ihren vertraulichen Charakter zu wahren. Man stelle sich vor, wie interessant diese Briefe heute wären, um uns Einblicke in die schwule Kultur in einer Zeit der Unterdrückung zu gewähren! Während also Toms künstlerisches Werk weiterlebt und seine Beiträge zur Homosexuellenbefreiung allgemein anerkannt sind, hat sein Wunsch, seine homosexuellen Mitmenschen vor möglicher Entlarvung zu schützen dazu geführt, dass wir möglicherweise wertvolle Zeugnisse von Fans dieses bahnbrechenden Künstlers verloren haben.

Kurz nach dem Aufbau seines Archivs und der Gründung der ständigen Sammlung der Stiftung wurde Tom von anderen Künstlern angesprochen, ob sie der Stiftung nicht ein oder zwei ihrer eigenen Werke spenden könnten. Erotische Künstler hatten oft mit Diebstahl, Verunglimpfung und Zerstörung ihrer Werke zu kämpfen und viele von ihnen sahen in der Stiftung eine Möglichkeit, als Künstler in Erinnerung zu bleiben.

Tom starb am 7. November 1991. Es war sein Wunsch, dass wir keine Trauerfeier abhalten, sondern die beste Tom of Finland Party aller Zeiten feiern! In diesem Sinne kreierten wir eine Veranstaltung, die wir TOM's Bar nannten – mit der Absicht, dass alle so viel Spaß wie möglich haben sollten – und seitdem haben wir diese Feier jedes Jahr wieder veranstaltet. Jedes Mal aufs Neue ist das für die Teilnehmer ein erregendes und unterhaltsames Event, ganz in der Art, wie Tom es liebte. Der Schönste-Hintern-Wettbewerb ist nur ein Beispiel – eine beliebte Ausrede für manchen Teilnehmer, seinen Arsch zu zeigen, und für alle anderen, ihn zu bewundern. Ohne mich zu schämen, gebe ich zu, dass es oft auch andere sexuelle Aktivitäten gibt – natürlich alles zu Toms Ehren. Ein ebenso wichtiger Teil von TOM's Bar ist es, Künstler einzuladen, ihre Werke zu präsentieren und so mit potentiellen Sammlern ins Gespräch zu kommen. Dies war die Keimzelle unserer Erotic Art Fairs, die wir sowohl in Los Angeles als auch in New York mit Erfolg veranstaltet haben. Mittlerweile haben wir mehr als 30 dieser Veranstaltungen durchgeführt, um erstens erotischen Künstlern die Möglichkeit zu geben, ihre Werke

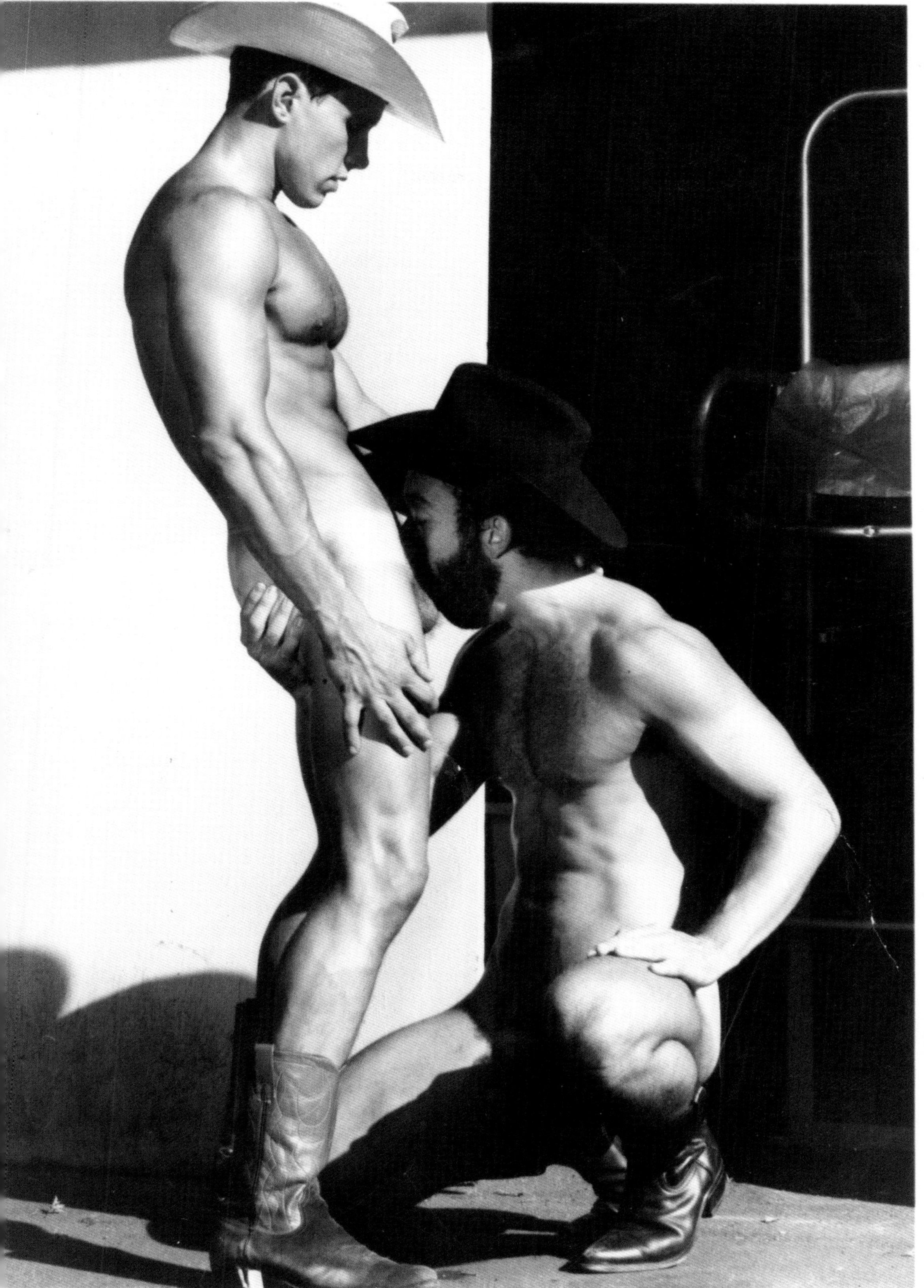

York. To date, we have produced over thirty of these events, with the triple purpose of giving erotic artists the opportunity to display and sell their work, for them to meet other artists, and to bring together the LGBTQ community to introduce them to the amazing pool of creativity which forms the world of erotic art. We emphasize the importance of displaying erotic sculptures in our homes, hanging erotic works of art on the walls, thus validating who we are and demonstrating the depth and beauty that we possess.

Once the magic between artists and potential collectors is given the space to happen, people tend to hang out and feel empowered by being in the presence of so much that speaks to them. That was the case at the first Erotic Art Fair, and is the same today. With the advent of the internet, we expanded that program and came up with galleries of art online that were available for purchase. This was fed by an ever-growing pool of artists who needed to increase their collector base, as well as collectors who wanted to sell some of the works they had. We built our website for artists, so they could benefit by directing collectors to the pages directly. Our purpose is to be useful to artists, as well as presenting to the public an opportunity to expand their appreciation of art.

Tom of Finland Foundation believes that society is a better place to live with the presence of the erotic arts, as they foster healthier and more tolerant outlooks. Tom of Finland was a rule-breaker: He did not back down and make his work less explicitly sexual. He accepted that museums might be reluctant to acquire his works because many people, including their curators, would be uncomfortable with his subject matter. He felt it was important to push limits, to make people venture outside their "safe zones", and accept work with confidence, standing behind the freedom of what art can truly express.

In the following chapter I want to pay tribute to some artists, each having a positive relationship to each other's works: REX, The Hun, Olaf, Bastille, Etienne, Domino and Jim Wigler. They created a brotherhood of belonging, where each ones' success was to be cherished, not envied.

zu zeigen und zu verkaufen, zweitens, andere Künstler zu treffen, und drittens, die LGBTQ-Community zusammenzubringen, um sie mit dem erstaunlichen Pool von Kreativität bekanntzumachen, der die Welt der erotischen Kunst bildet. Wir weisen darauf hin, wie wichtig es ist, erotische Skulpturen und andere Kunstwerke im eigenen Zuhause zu haben. Auf diese Weise können wir uns selbst bestätigen und unser Wesen und unsere Schönheit zum Ausdruck bringen.

Sobald die Möglichkeit gegeben ist, dass es zwischen den Künstlern und potentiellen Sammlern funkt, neigen die meisten dazu, sich zu entspannen und sich gestärkt zu fühlen, weil es so vieles gibt, durch das sie sich angesprochen fühlen. So war es auf der ersten Erotic Art Fair und so ist es noch heute. Mit dem Aufkommen des Internets haben wir dieses Programm erweitert und Online-Galerien entwickelt, wo man Kunst kaufen kann. Dieses Online-Portal wurde einerseits von einem ständig wachsenden Pool von Künstlern gespeist, die auf der Suche nach neuen Sammlern waren, andererseits von Sammlern, die Kunstwerke aus ihrem Besitz weiterverkaufen wollten. Wir haben unsere Website für Künstler eingerichtet, damit sie die Sammler direkt auf diese Seiten verweisen können. Wir wollen sowohl Künstler unterstützen, als auch der Öffentlichkeit die Möglichkeit bieten, ihr Kunstverständnis zu erweitern.

Die Tom of Finland Foundation ist davon überzeugt, dass erotische Kunst die Gesellschaft bereichert, da sie gesündere und tolerantere Ansichten fördert. Tom of Finland hat Regeln gebrochen: Er gab eben nicht nach und machte seine Kunst weniger explizit sexuell. Er akzeptierte, dass Museen Probleme mit seinen Werke haben könnten, weil viele Menschen, einschließlich ihrer Kuratoren, sich mit seinen Themen unwohl fühlen. Er hielt es für wichtig, Grenzen zu überschreiten und Menschen dazu zu bringen, sich außerhalb ihrer „Komfortzonen" zu bewegen, und mutige Kunst zu akzeptieren und für die Freiheit der Kunst zu kämpfen.

Im folgenden Kapitel möchte ich einige Künstler vorstellen, die jeweils das Werk der anderen schätzten: Rex, The Hun, Olaf, Bastille, Etienne, Domino und Jim Wigler. Sie schufen eine Art Bruderschaft der Zusammengehörigkeit, in der jeder sich über den Erfolg der anderen freute und ihn nicht neidete.

Übersetzung: Rinaldo Hopf

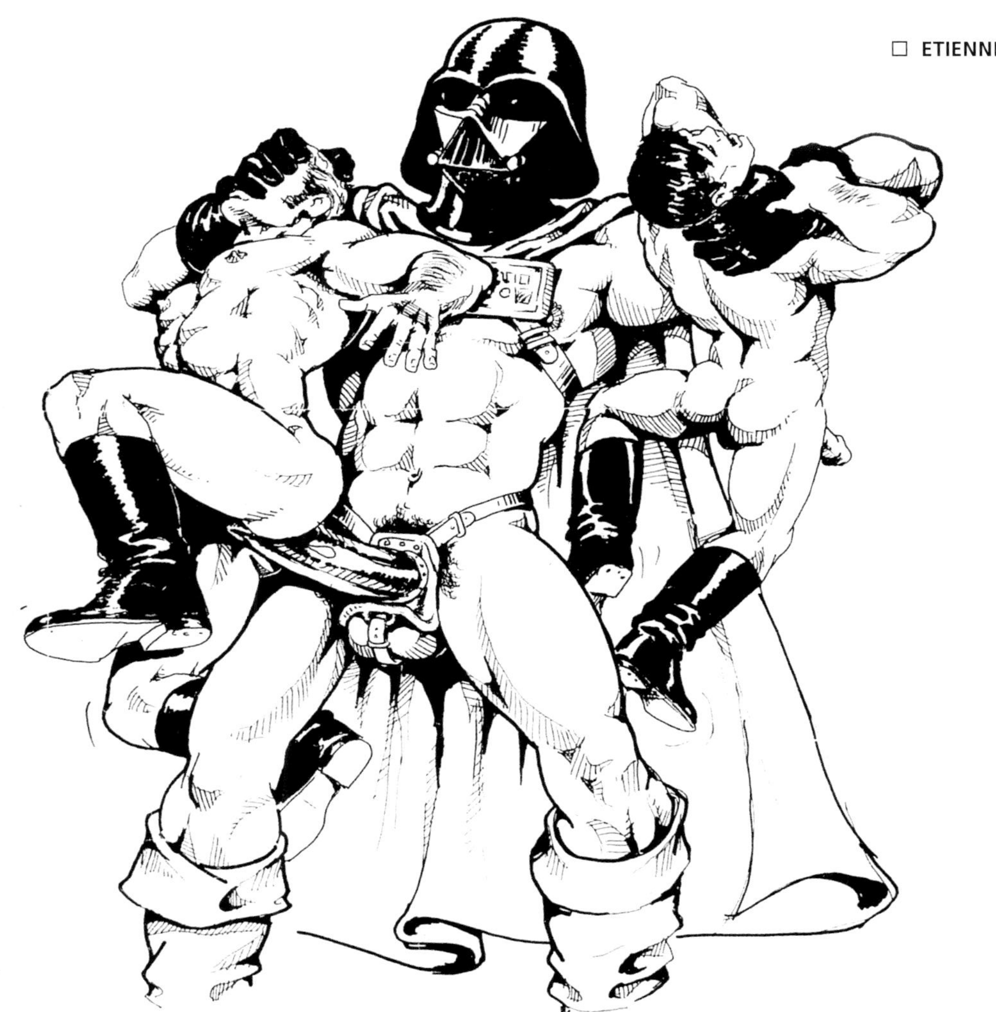

Durk, Vader and Dom

ETIENNE

Etienne and his Partner Chuck Renslow, cofounder of International Mister Leather, launched a male magazine in the '50s titled *Chris Studio*. Based out of Chicago, it naturally delved into the nightlife where the two of them opened Leather bars and discos. And not to forget: bathhouses. That is when you have a complete Homosexual diet, when all those experiences are being satisfied. This man painted a mural of me, well, let's just say it was inspired by me, and you know a model or muse's purpose is: The spark that ignites the artist's desire. I think in order for it to be really effective the artist has to fall in love with his model. Well, I won a Leather contest in NYC at the Eagle's Nest. What those men in that bar needed that night was freedom. If you've got the balls to put yourself out there, everyone is really going to be behind you, because it's infectious. And as a result, there were a lot of men that night that wanted to get behind me, so to speak.

Etienne und sein Lebenspartner Chuck Renslow, der Mitbegründer des International Mister Leather-Contest, gründeten in den 50er Jahren in Chicago das Männermagazin *Chris Studio*. Sie stürzten sich ins Nachtleben, eröffneten Lederbars und Diskotheken. Und nicht zu vergessen: Saunen. Also das komplette schwule Programm. Dieser Mann malte ein Wandbild von mir, oder besser gesagt: ein Wandbild, das von mir inspiriert wurde. Ihr kennt ja den Zweck eines Models oder einer Muse: der Funke zu sein, der das Verlangen des Künstlers entzündet. Ich denke, damit der Künstler wirklich etwas schaffen kann, muss er sich in sein Model verlieben. Nun, ich habe eine Mr. Leather-Wahl im New Yorker Eagle's Nest gewonnen. Was die Männer in dieser Bar in jener Nacht brauchten, war Freiheit. Wenn man den Mut hat, sich dort zu präsentieren, dann stehen tatsächlich alle hinter einem, das ist einfach ansteckend. Und so gab es in jener Nacht viele Männer, die im besten Sinne des Wortes hinter mir stehen wollten.

– Durk Dehner

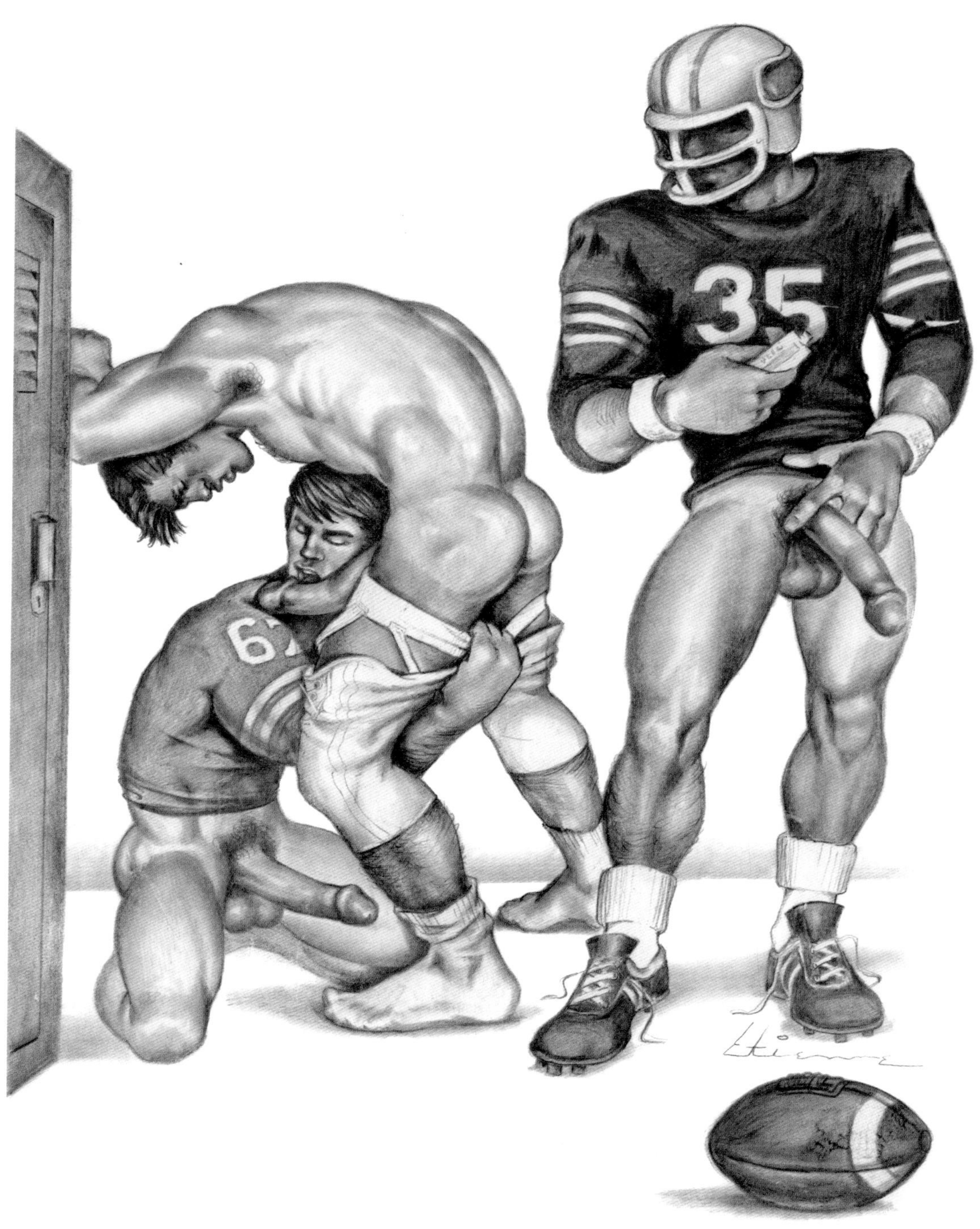

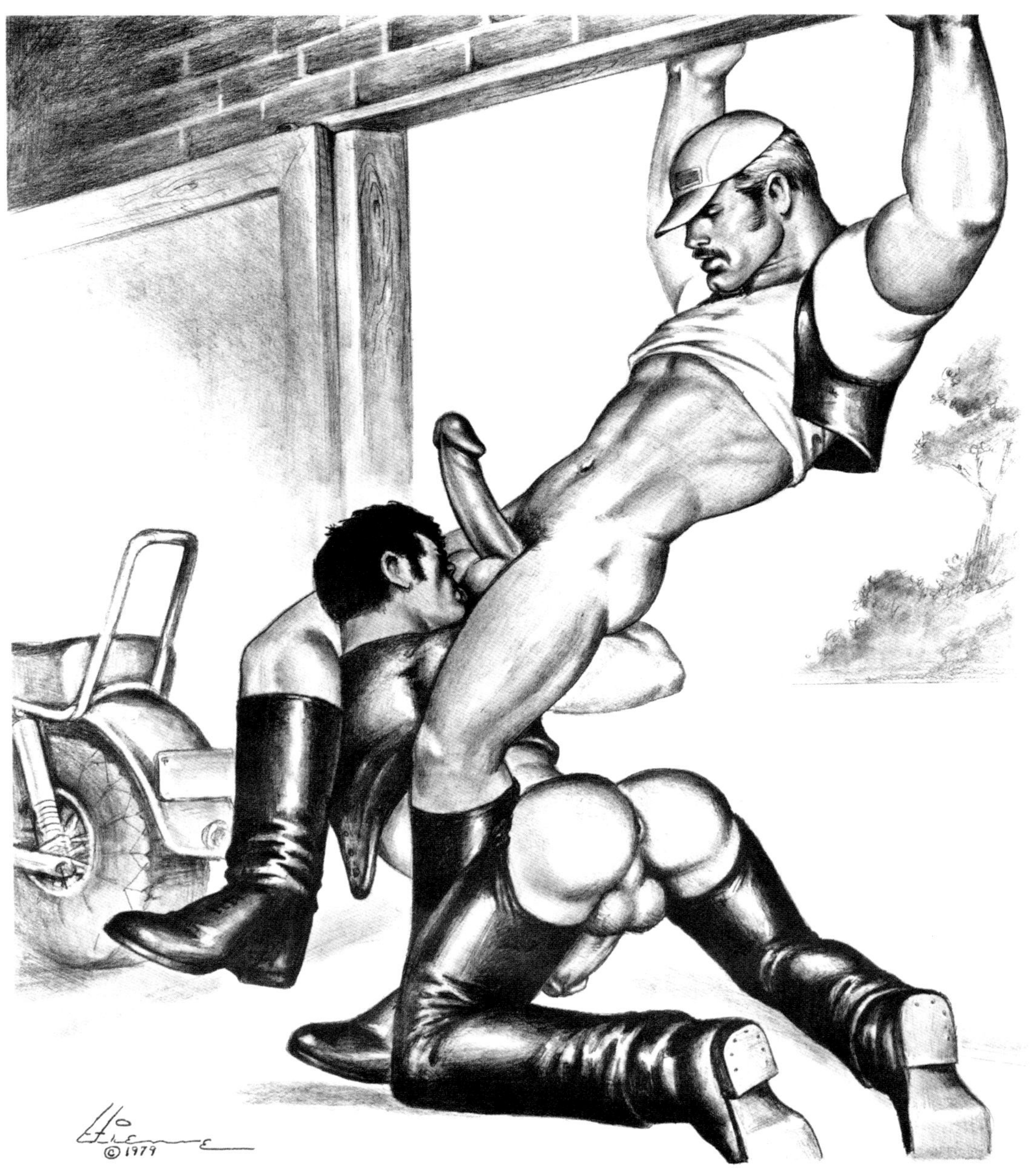

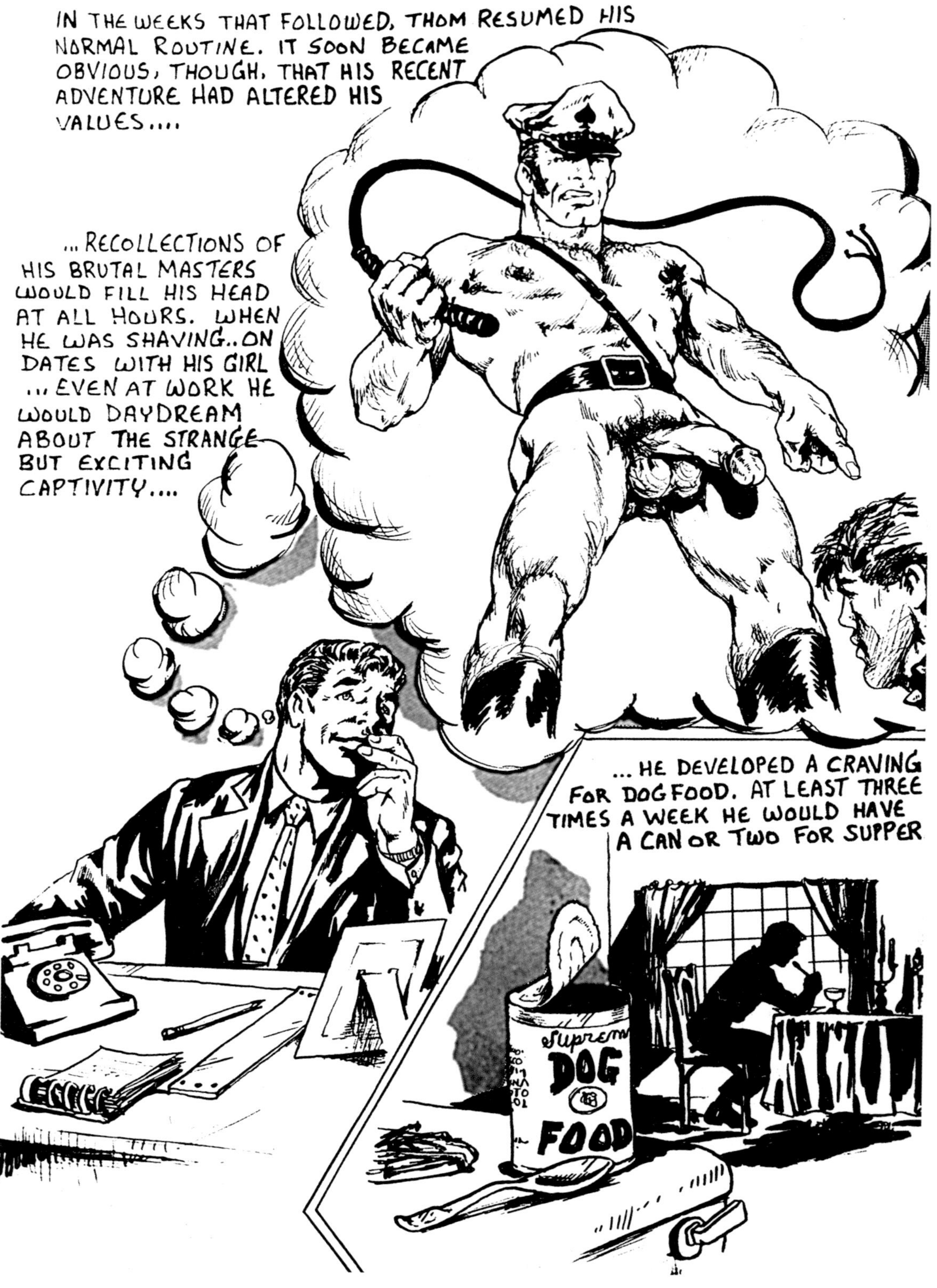
IN THE WEEKS THAT FOLLOWED, THOM RESUMED HIS NORMAL ROUTINE. IT SOON BECAME OBVIOUS, THOUGH, THAT HIS RECENT ADVENTURE HAD ALTERED HIS VALUES....
...RECOLLECTIONS OF HIS BRUTAL MASTERS WOULD FILL HIS HEAD AT ALL HOURS. WHEN HE WAS SHAVING..ON DATES WITH HIS GIRL ...EVEN AT WORK HE WOULD DAYDREAM ABOUT THE STRANGE BUT EXCITING CAPTIVITY....
...HE DEVELOPED A CRAVING FOR DOG FOOD. AT LEAST THREE TIMES A WEEK HE WOULD HAVE A CAN OR TWO FOR SUPPER
Supreme
DOG
FOOD

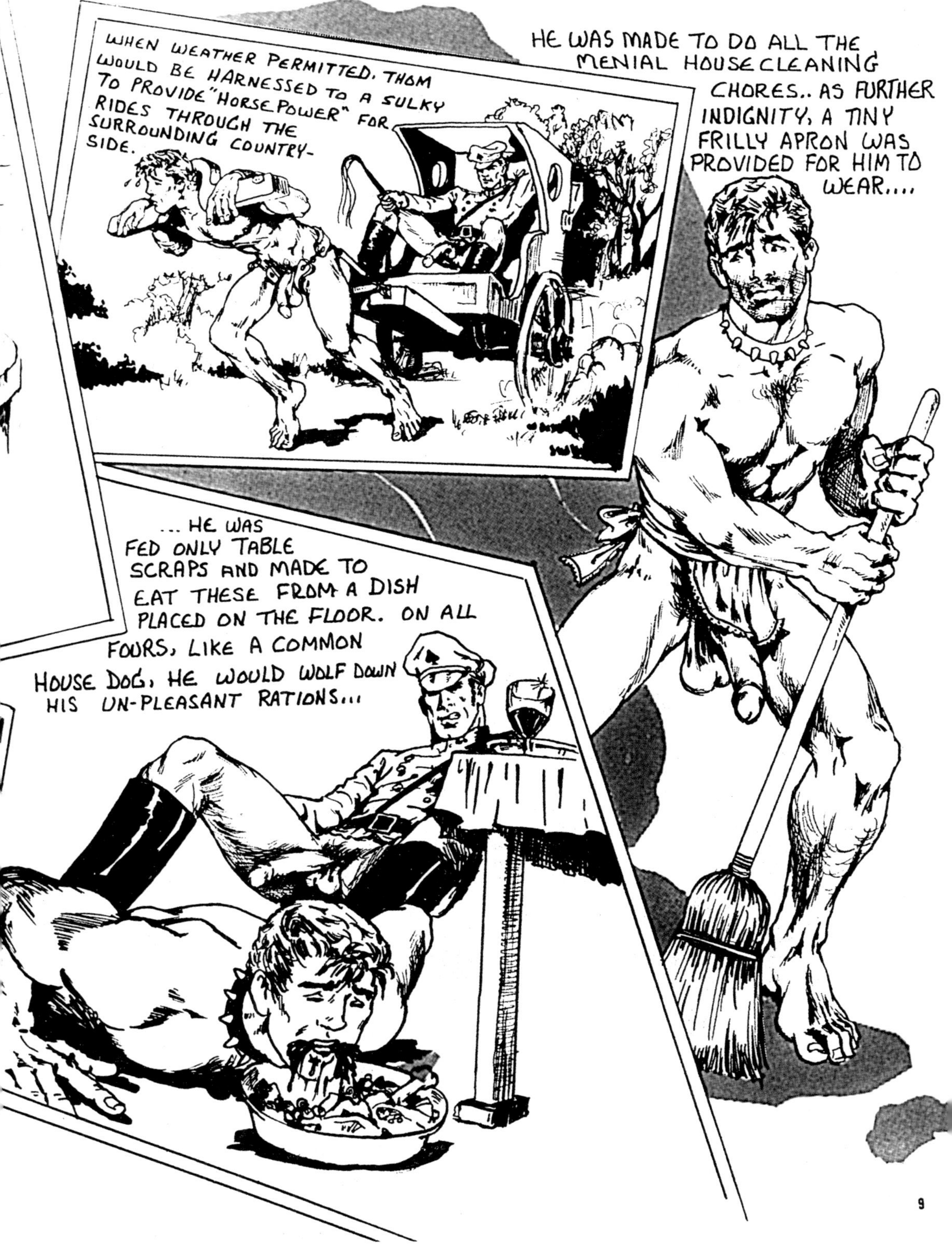
WHEN WEATHER PERMITTED, THOM WOULD BE HARNESSED TO A SULKY TO PROVIDE "HORSE POWER" FOR RIDES THROUGH THE SURROUNDING COUNTRY-SIDE.
HE WAS MADE TO DO ALL THE MENIAL HOUSECLEANING CHORES.. AS FURTHER INDIGNITY, A TINY FRILLY APRON WAS PROVIDED FOR HIM TO WEAR....
... HE WAS FED ONLY TABLE SCRAPS AND MADE TO EAT THESE FROM A DISH PLACED ON THE FLOOR. ON ALL FOURS, LIKE A COMMON HOUSE DOG, HE WOULD WOLF DOWN HIS UN-PLEASANT RATIONS...
9

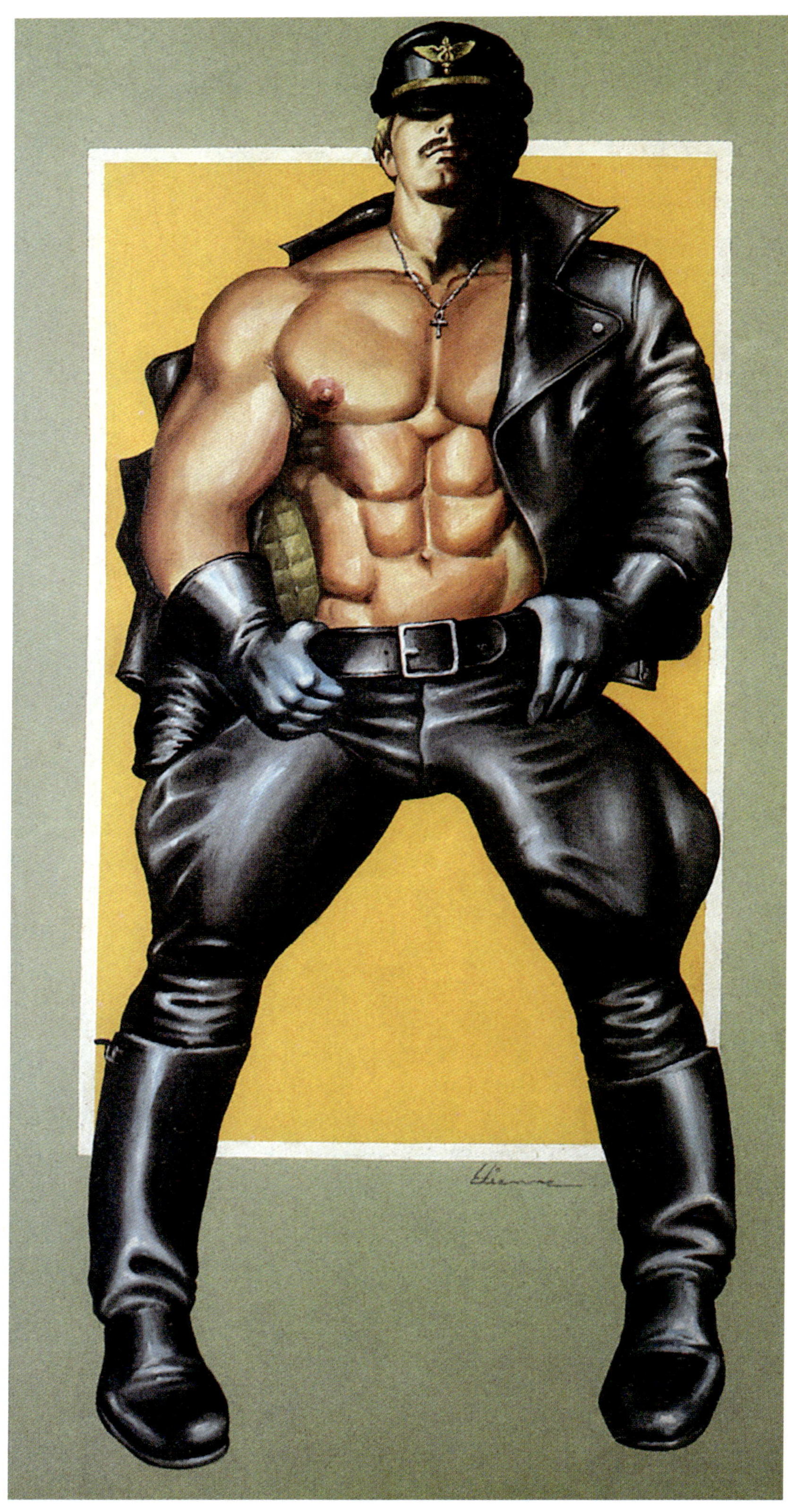

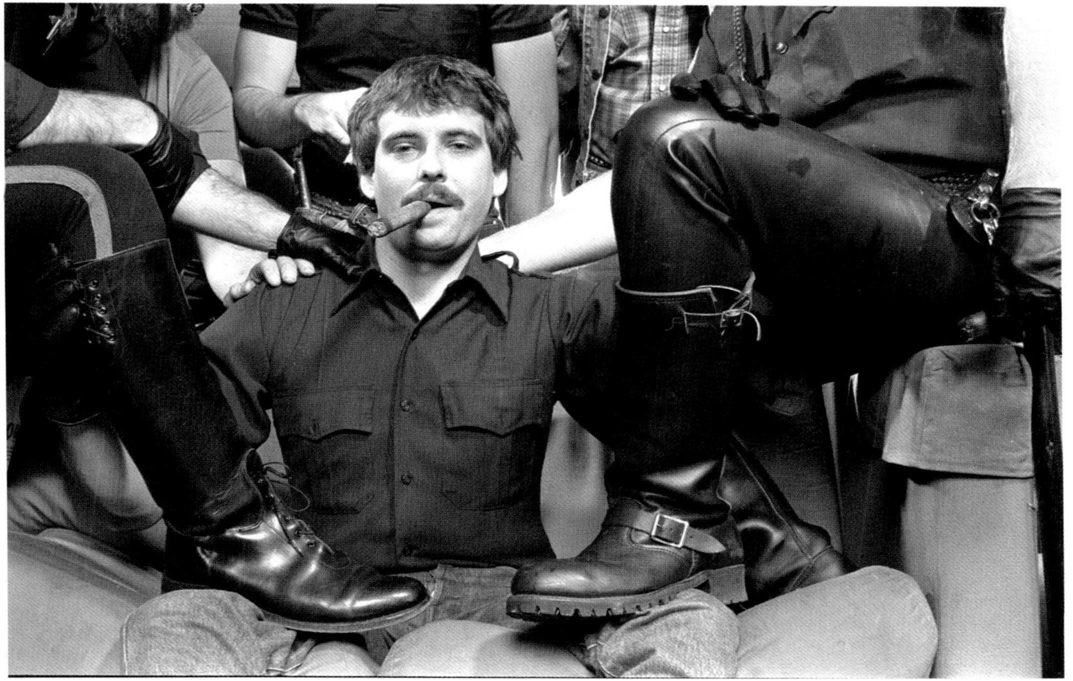

JIM WIGLER

The photographer Jim Wigler was on the streets in the '70s. He got really good in capturing the sensual, decadent, somewhat twisted mindset of the Leather and Kink world. Our unspoken mission was to be explorers; sexual rebels, who were testing the waters in S/M and bondage. We were junkies for experiencing the unknown, meeting strangers in the parks and back alleys for anonymous encounters. There were sex clubs in most neighborhoods where Gays lived or frequented.

Der Fotograf Jim Wigler war in den 70er Jahren auf der Straße unterwegs. Er war richtig gut darin, die sinnliche, dekadente, etwas verdrehte Welt der Leder- und Fetischszene einzufangen. Unsere unausgesprochene Berufung war es, Entdecker zu sein; sexuelle Rebellen, die mit S/M und Bondage experimentierten. Wir waren Junkies, auf der Suche nach dem Unbekannten, und trafen Fremde in Parks und Hinterhöfen. In den meisten Vierteln, in denen sich Schwule bewegten, gab es Sexclubs.

– Durk Dehner

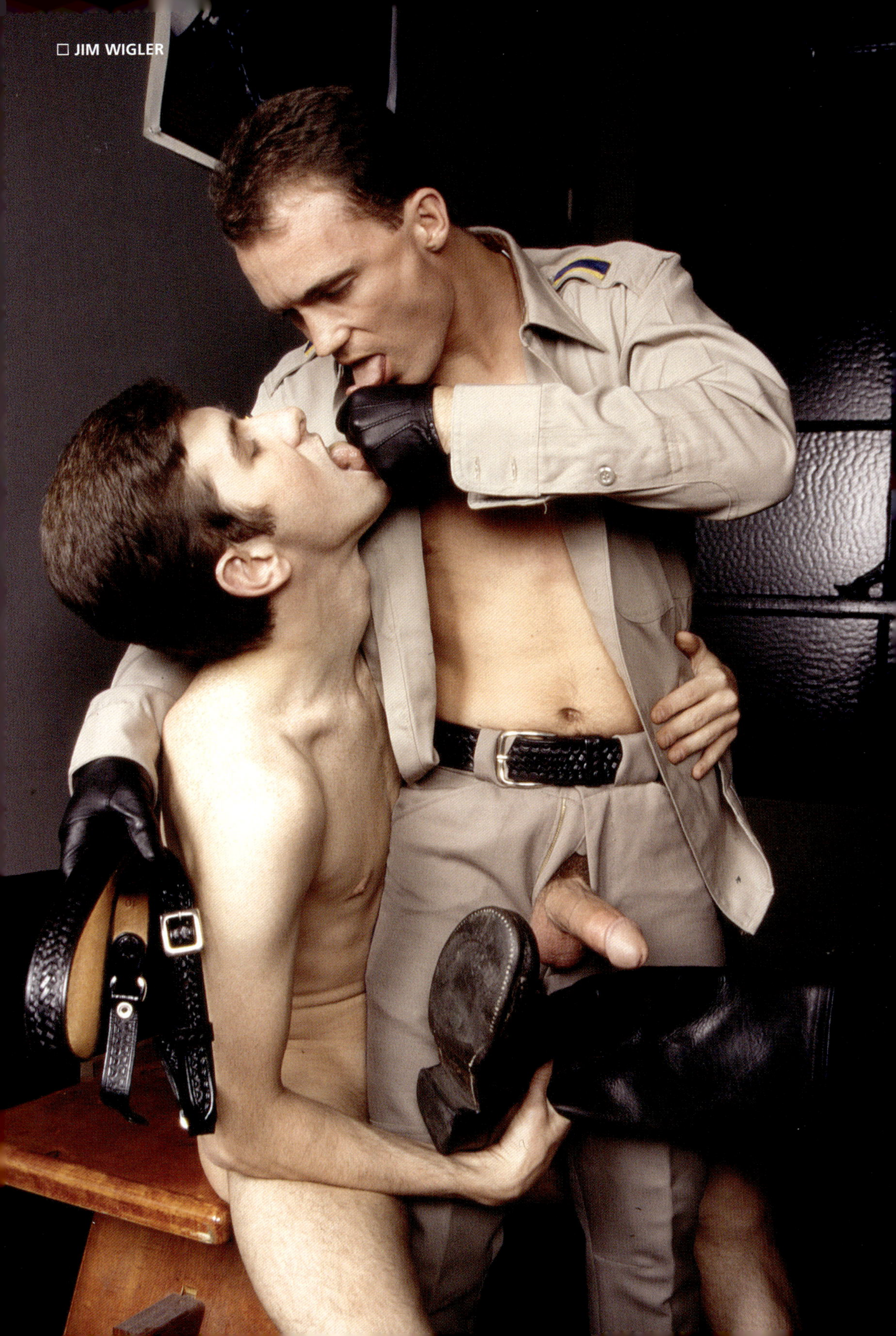
JIM WIGLER

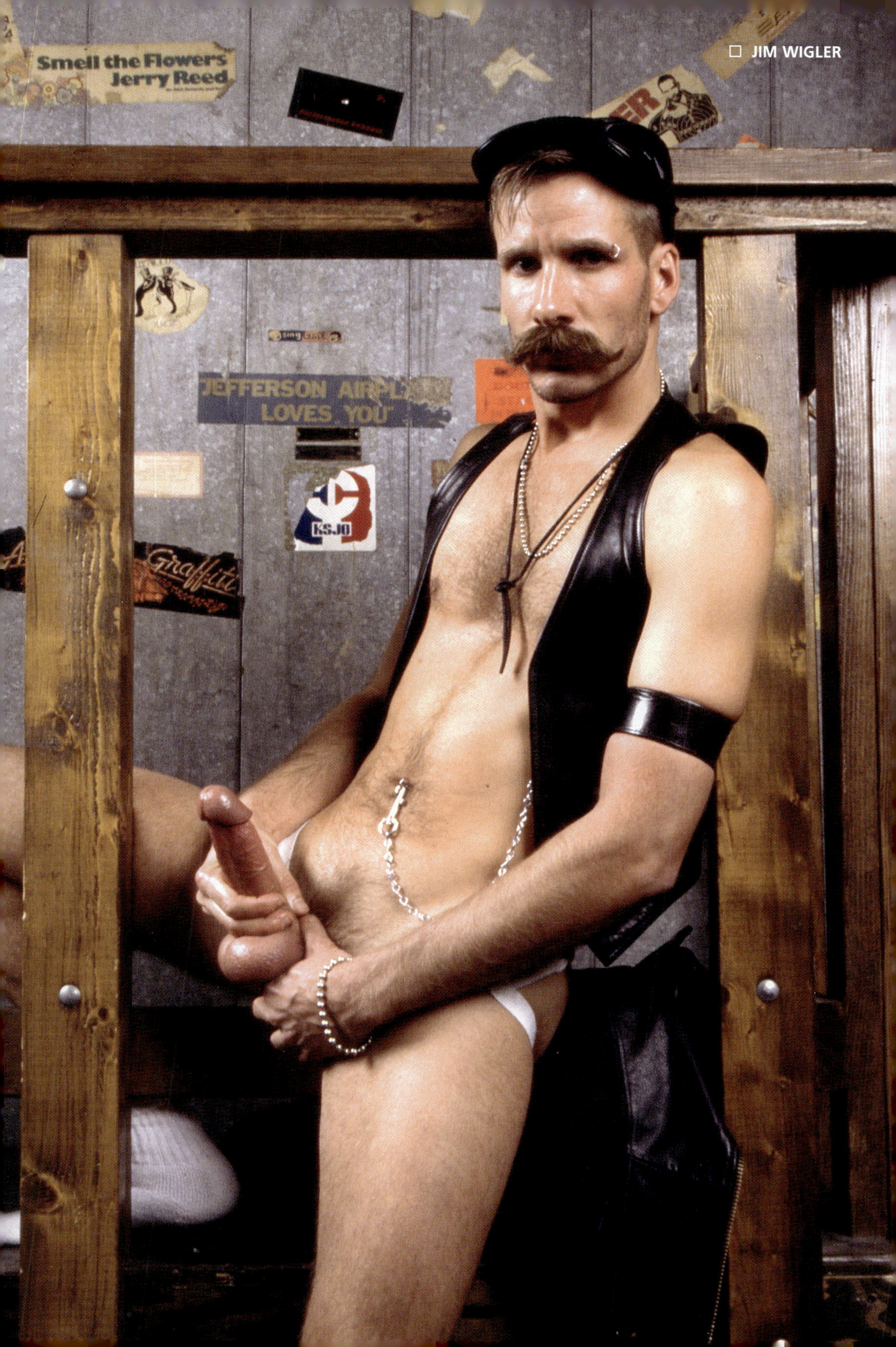

JIM WIGLER
Smell the Flowers
Jerry Reed
JEFFERSON AIRPLANE
LOVES YOU
KSJO
Graffiti

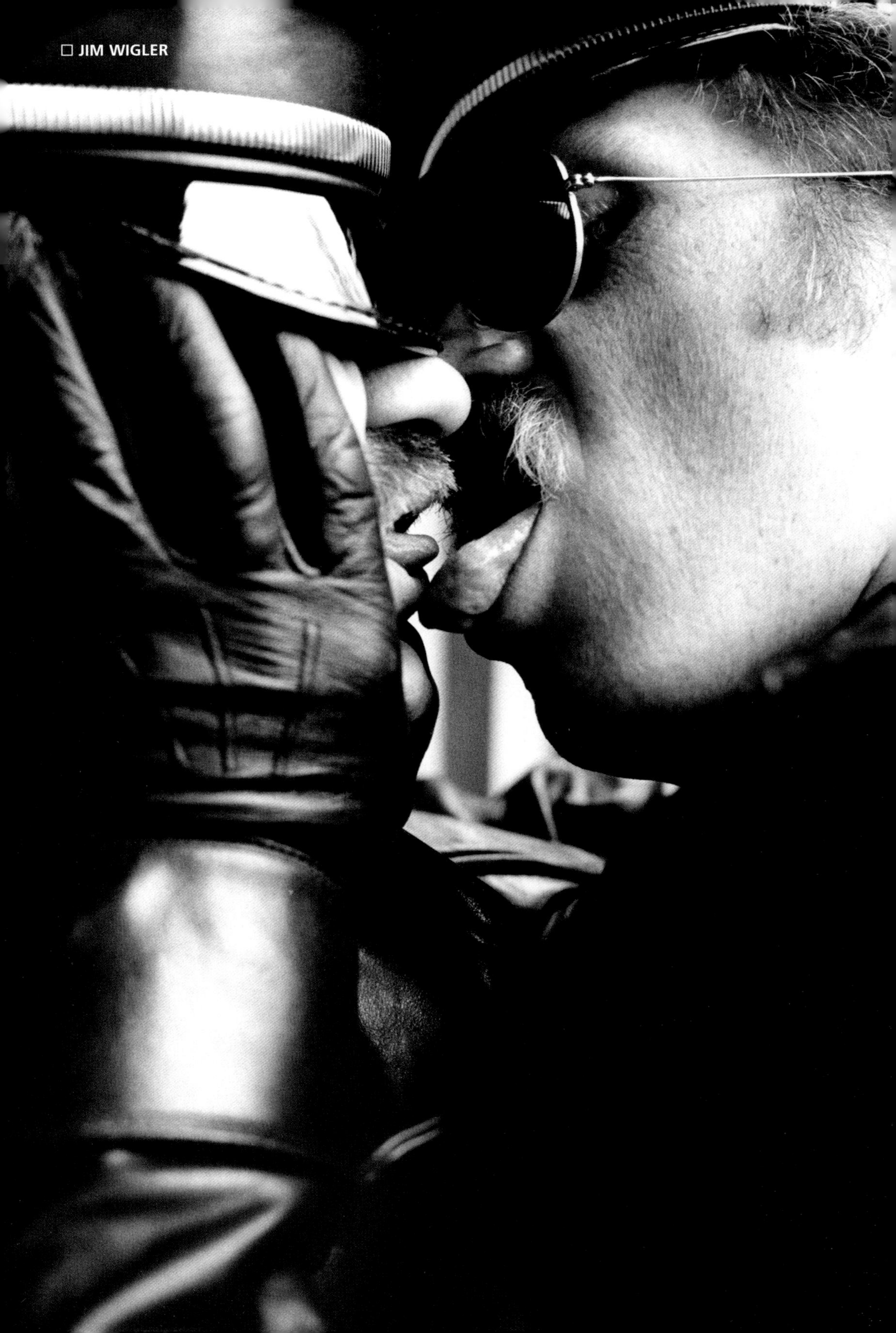

JIM WIGLER

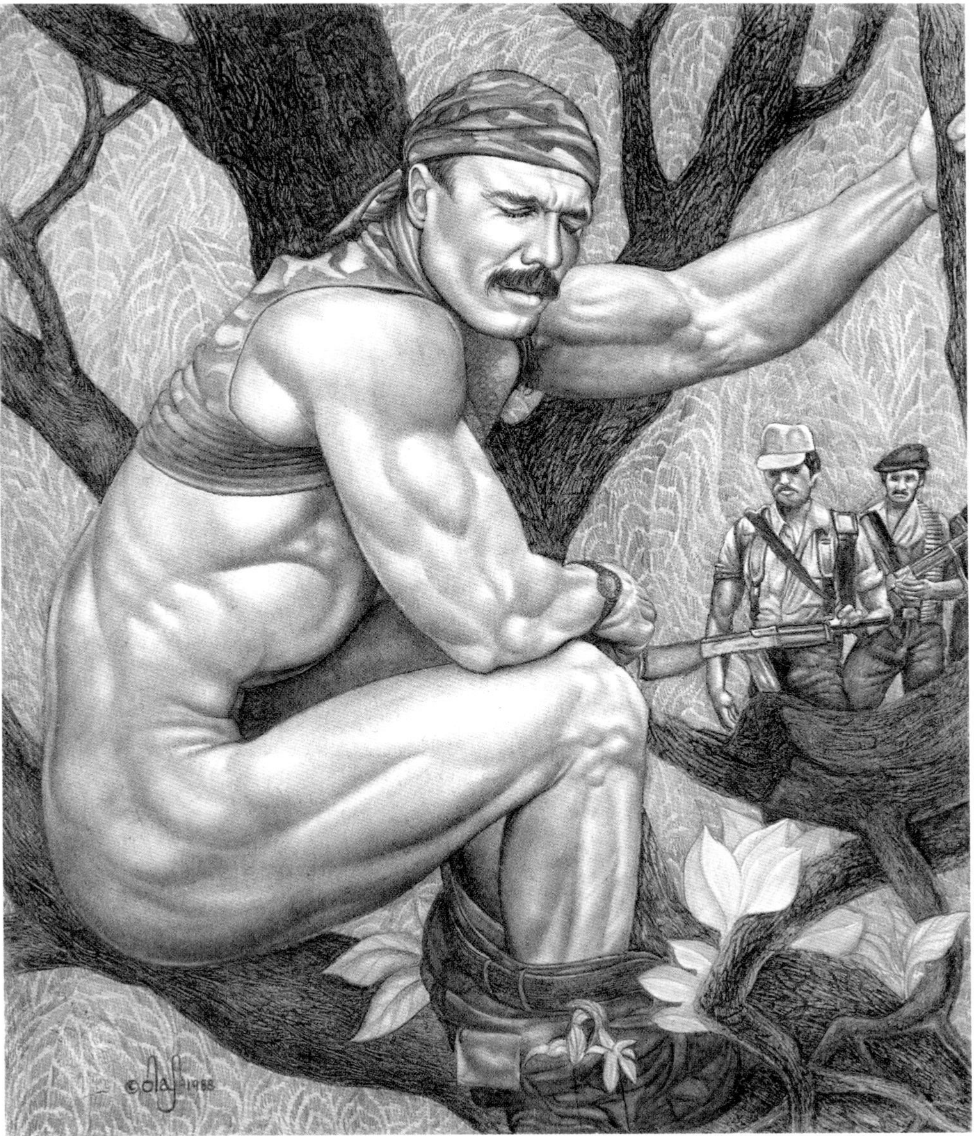

OLAF

The artist was in a sense adopted by the Tom of Finland Company in the mid '90s. He was on his way to becoming homeless, and having led a monastic life for many years, he had lost the confidence to go anywhere. So we rescued him. We got him an apartment across the street from our store in Silver Lake and everyone did their best to find buyers for his works. So he could be in a safe zone, money wise. We did it. And he lived out his life drawing, smoking and being a spiritual shaman for his community of gay men.

Der Künstler wurde Mitte der 90er Jahre von der Tom of Finland Company gewissermaßen adoptiert. Er war auf dem Weg, obdachlos zu werden. Nachdem er jahrelang ein Einsiedlerleben geführt hatte, traute er sich nicht mehr, irgendwohin zu gehen. Also haben wir ihn gerettet. Wir haben ihm eine Wohnung auf der gegenüberliegenden Straßenseite unseres Geschäfts im Stadtteil Silver Lake besorgt und jeder hat sein Bestes getan, um Käufer für seine Arbeiten zu finden und ihm so finanzielle Sicherheit zu geben. Wir haben es geschafft. Er verbrachte sein Leben damit, zu zeichnen, zu rauchen und ein spiritueller Schamane für seine schwule Gemeinschaft sein.

– Durk Dehner

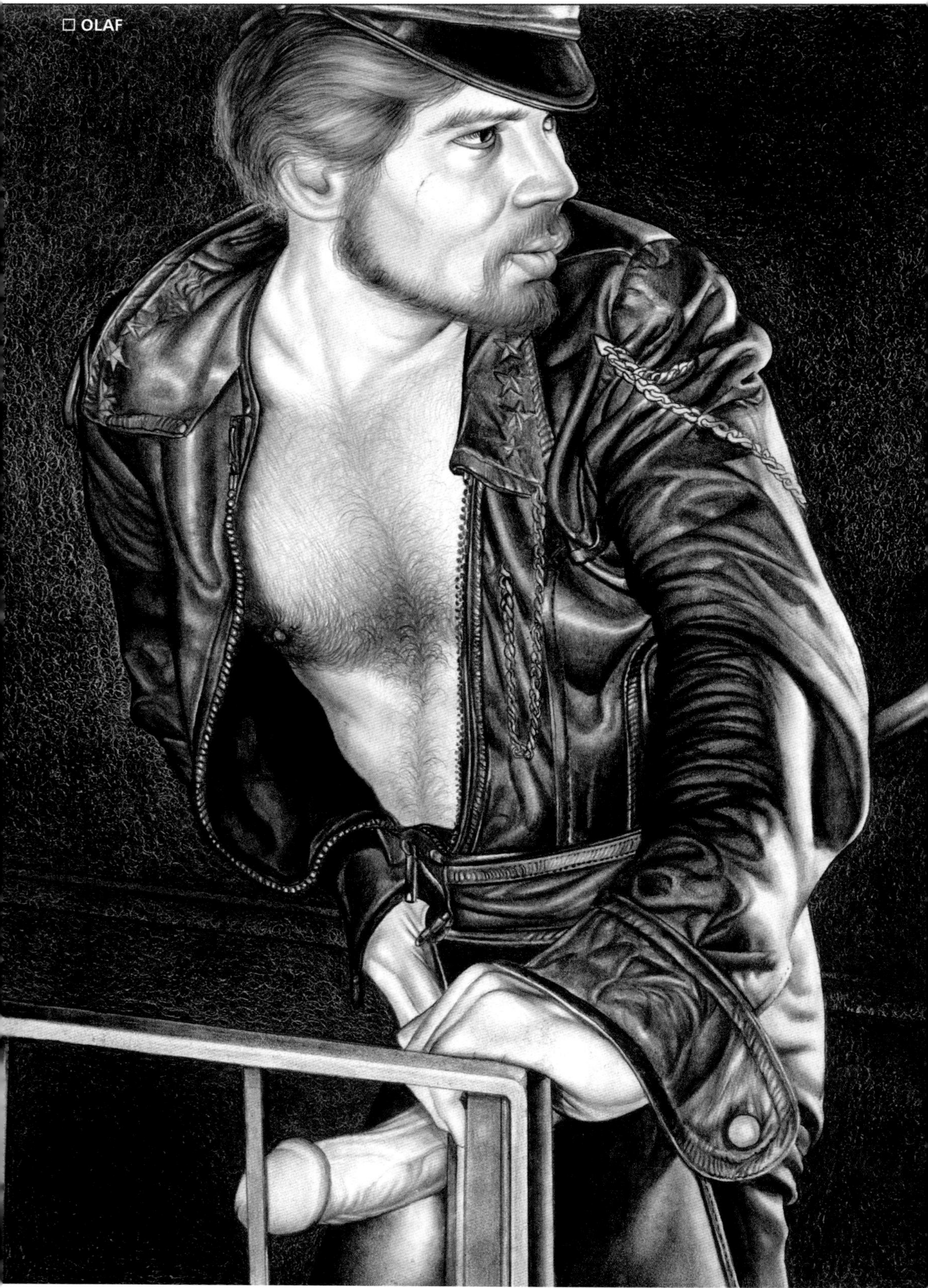

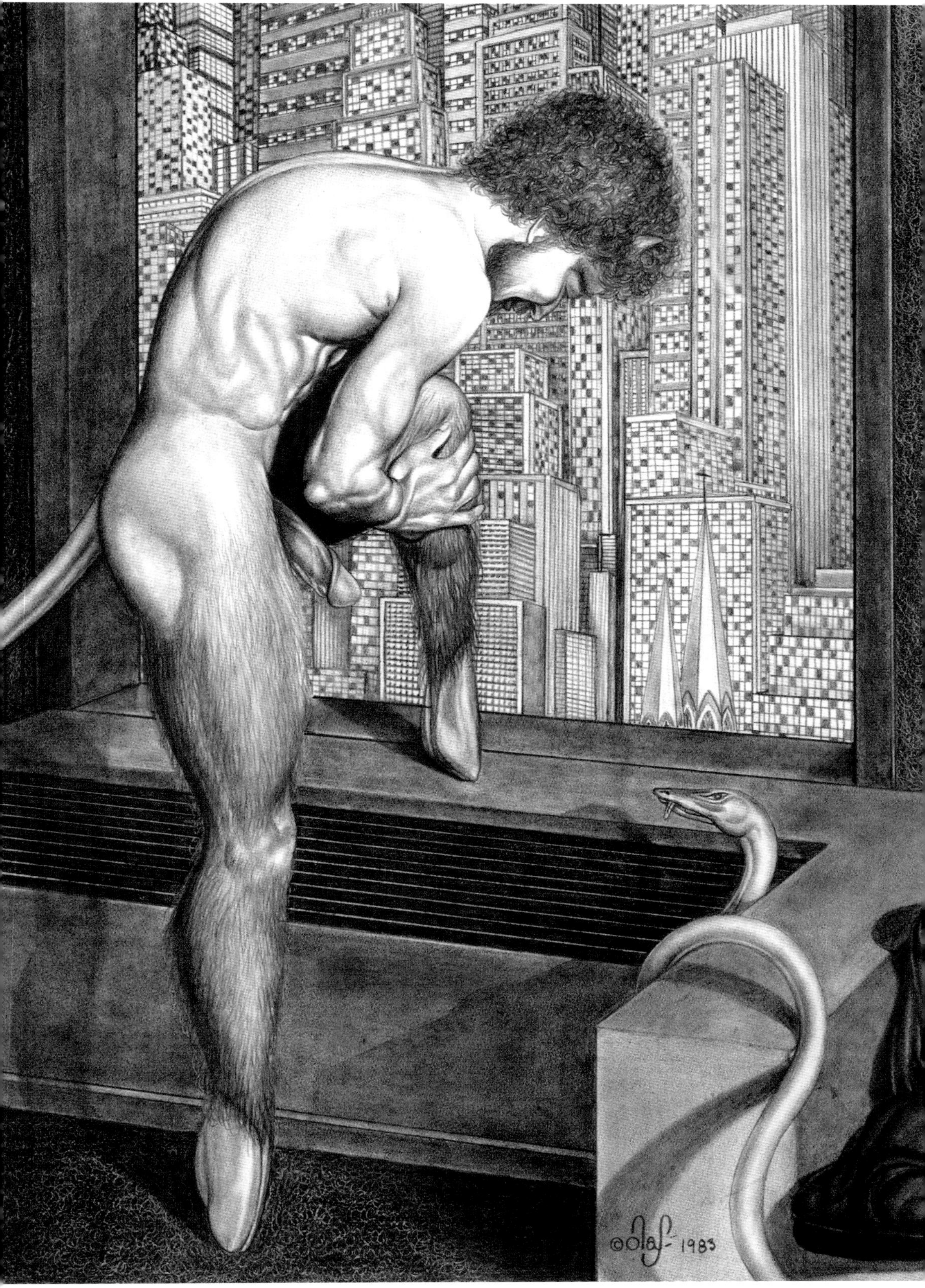

©olaf 1983

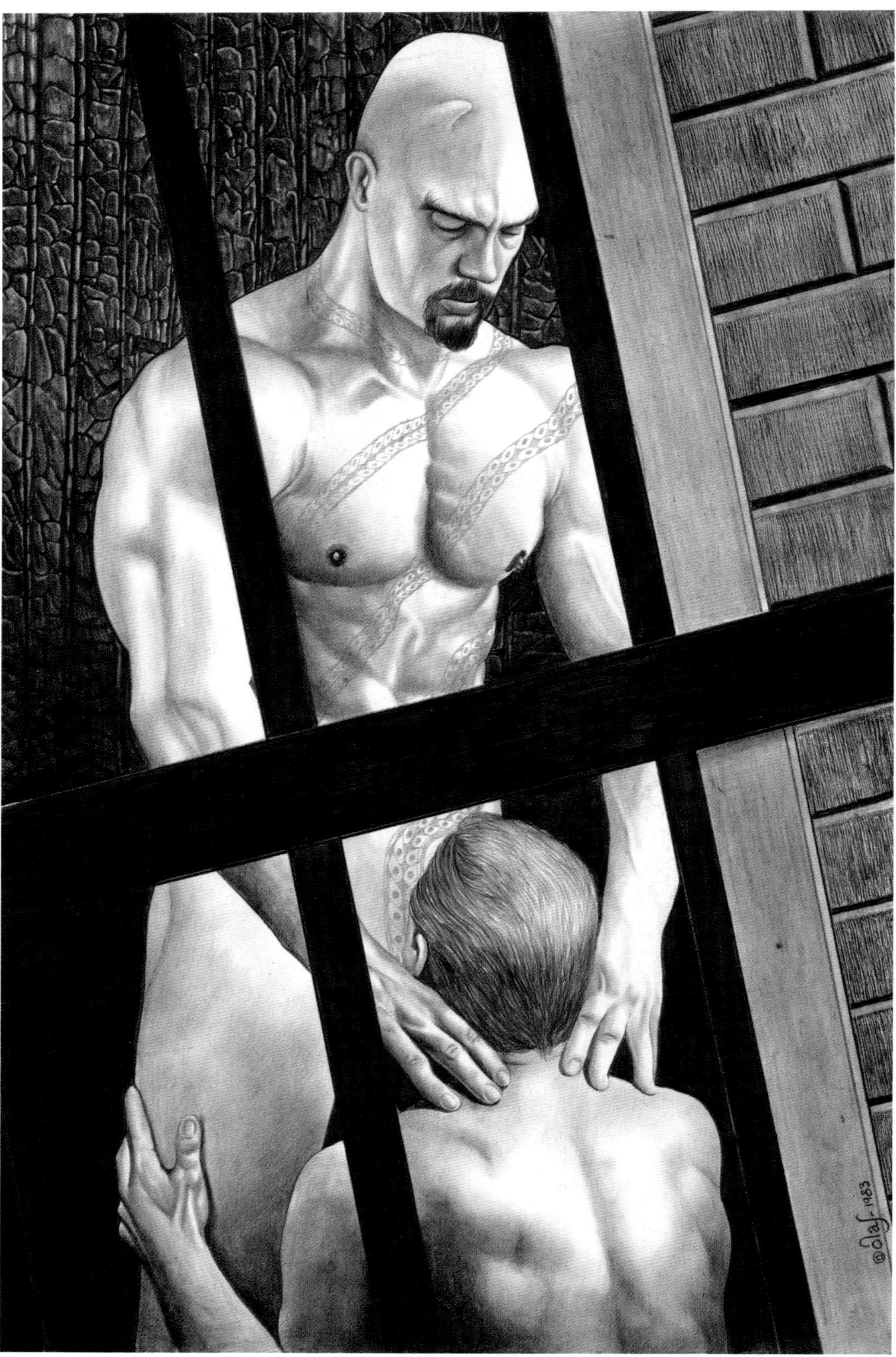

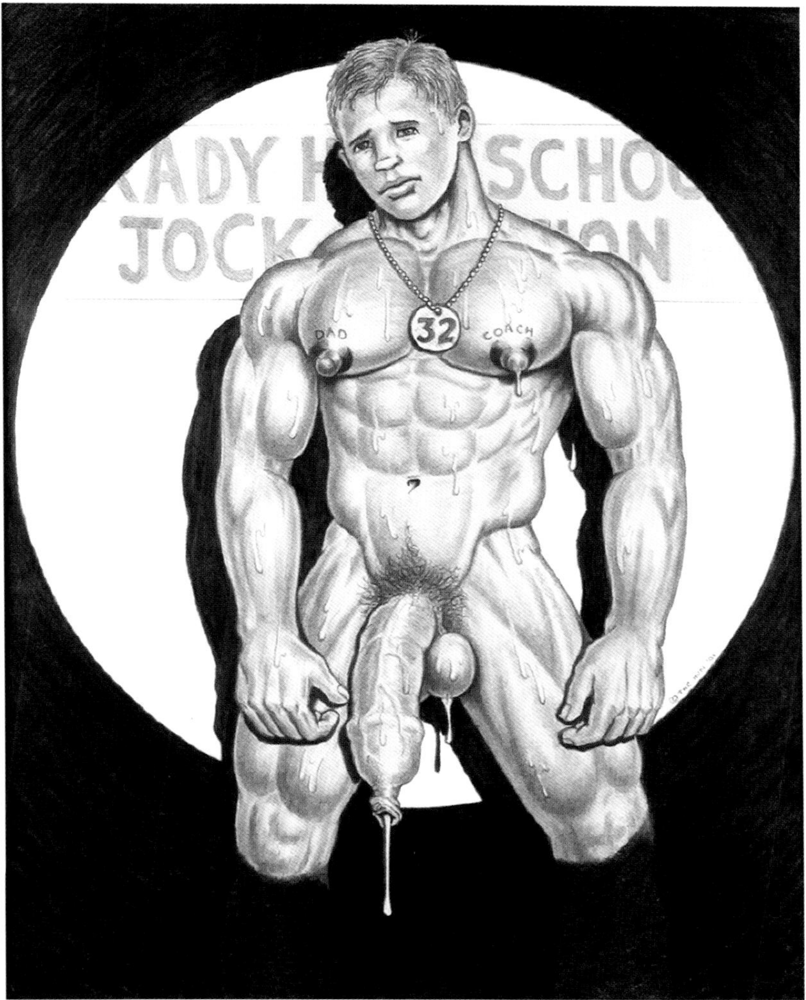

THE HUN

The Hun had a wonderfully rich relationship with Tom during the '80s, when both of them were living in Los Angeles. They set up artist salons in each of their homes and it was a wonderful coming together, full of sharing their practices and their own life experiences. During the later years after Tom had passed, Tom of Finland Company produced a book on a collection of The Hun's works. He had to be the next artist, just behind Tom, in sales for our company for maybe five or six years. His life partner is a black and it was artists like Tom, who was doing interracial works back in 1962, that forged the relationships when society was giving them the evil eye.

The Hun und Tom hatten in den 80er Jahren, als beide in Los Angeles lebten, eine wundervolle Beziehung miteiander. Beide gründeten in ihren Häusern Künstlersalons und teilten ihre Arbeitsweisen und Lebenserfahrungen bei diesen Zusammentreffen. Nach Toms Tod hat die Tom of Finland Company ein Buch mit einer Auswahl von The Huns Werken herausgebracht. Hinsichtlich der Verkäufe sollte er für unsere Firma für fünf oder sechs Jahre der zweitwichtigste Künstler nach Tom sein. Sein Lebenspartner ist schwarz, und es waren Künstler wie Tom, der schon 1962 gemischte Paare porträtierte, als die Gesellschaft diese noch mit bösen Blicken bedachte.

– Durk Dehner

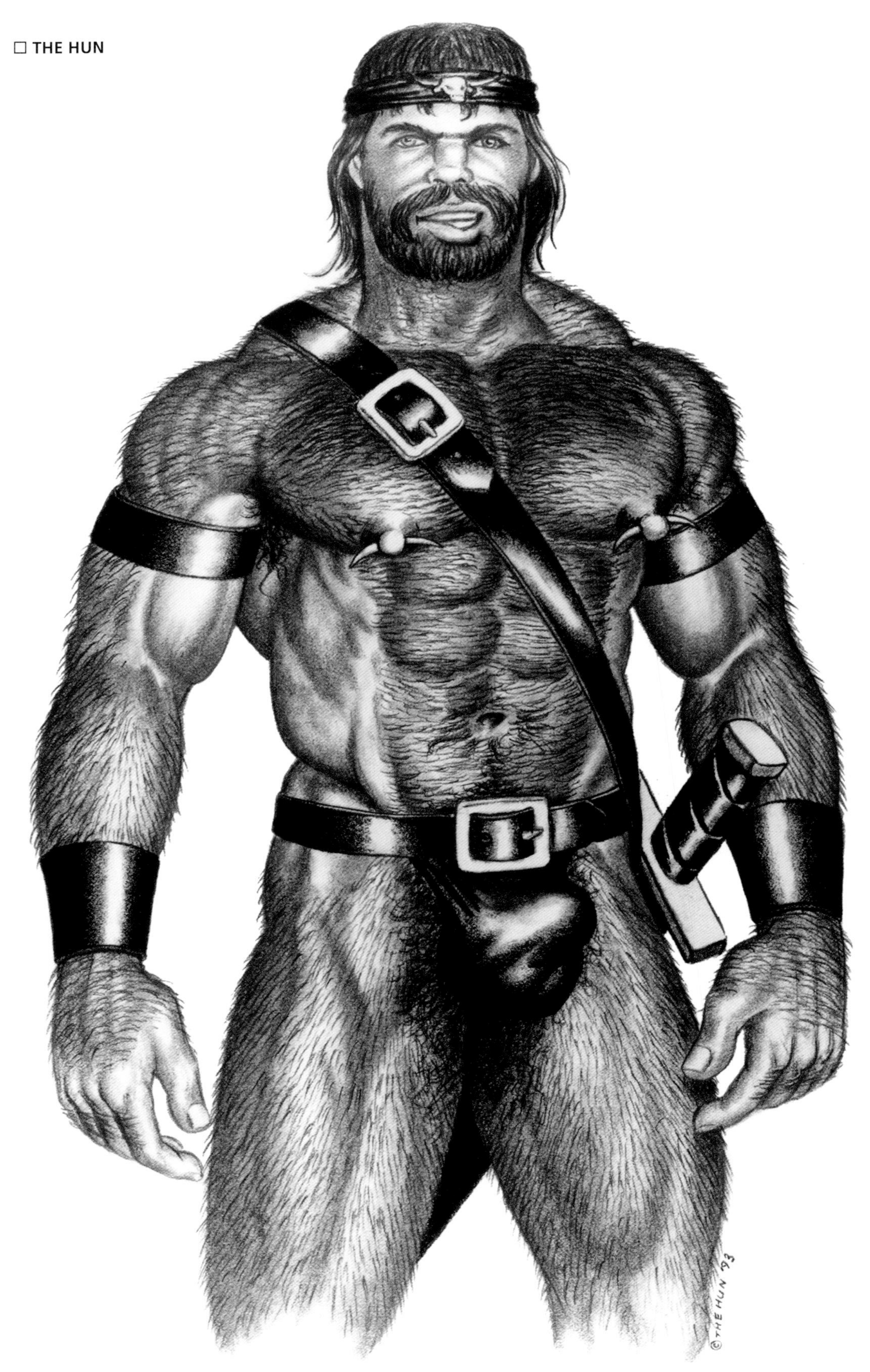

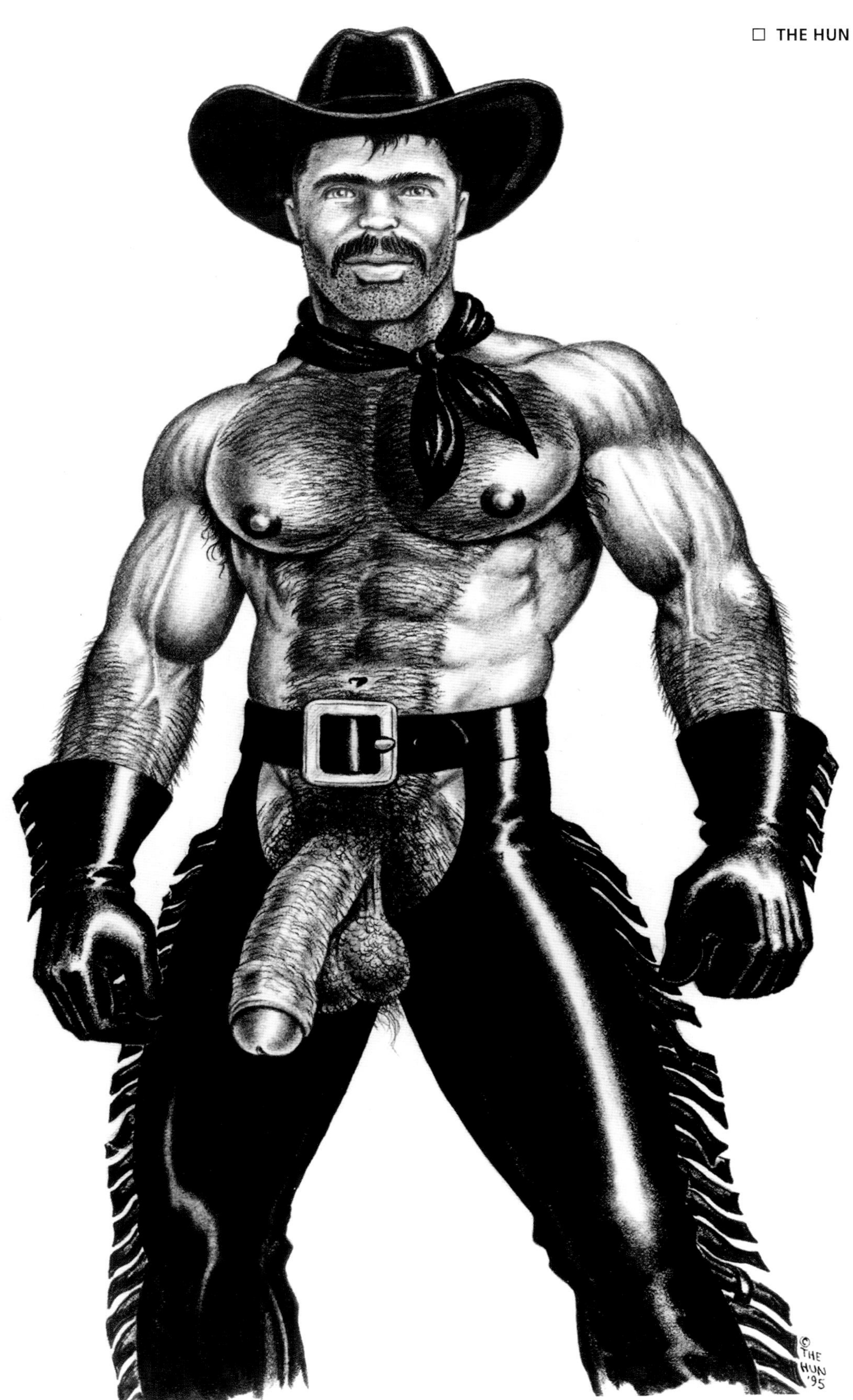

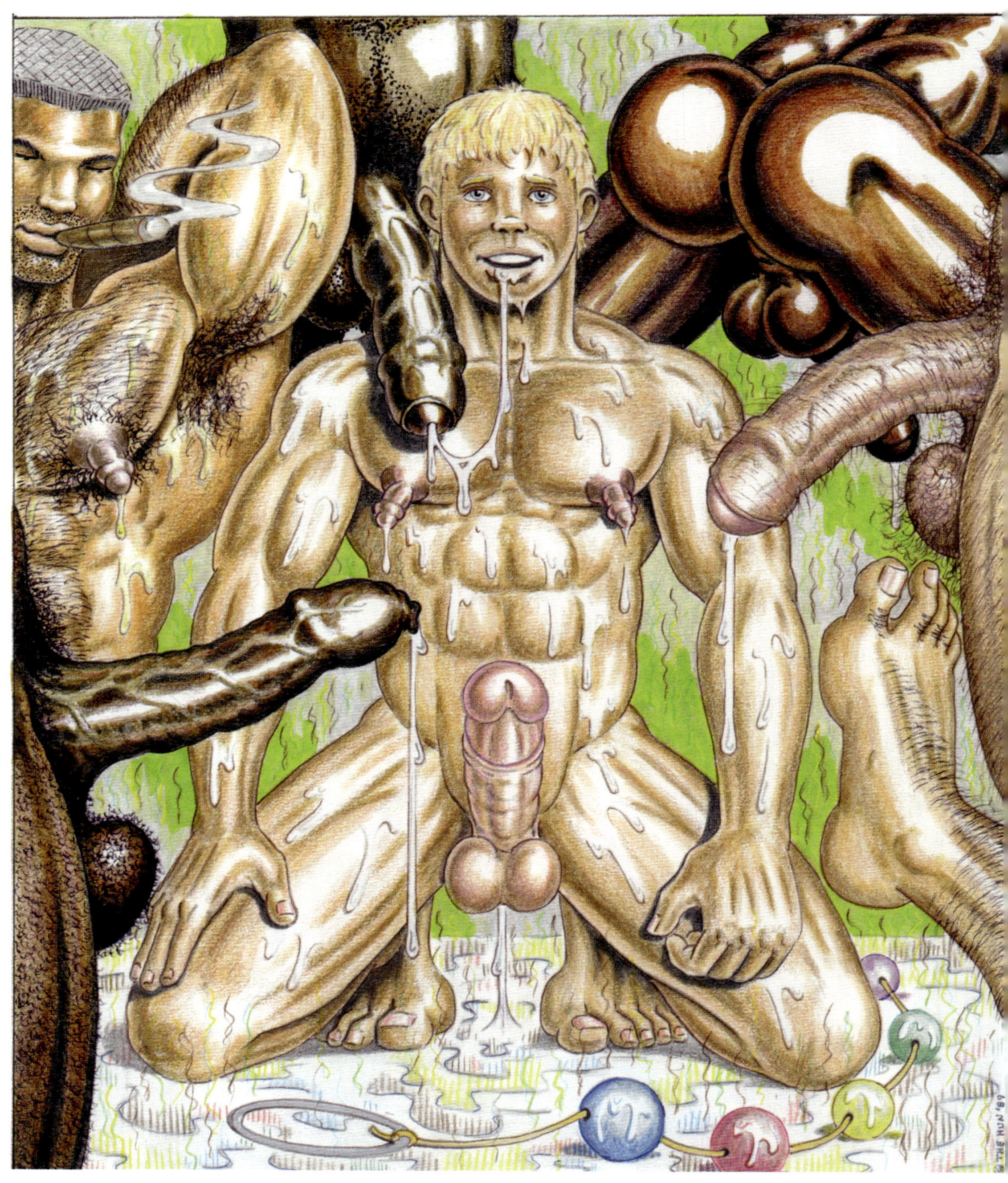

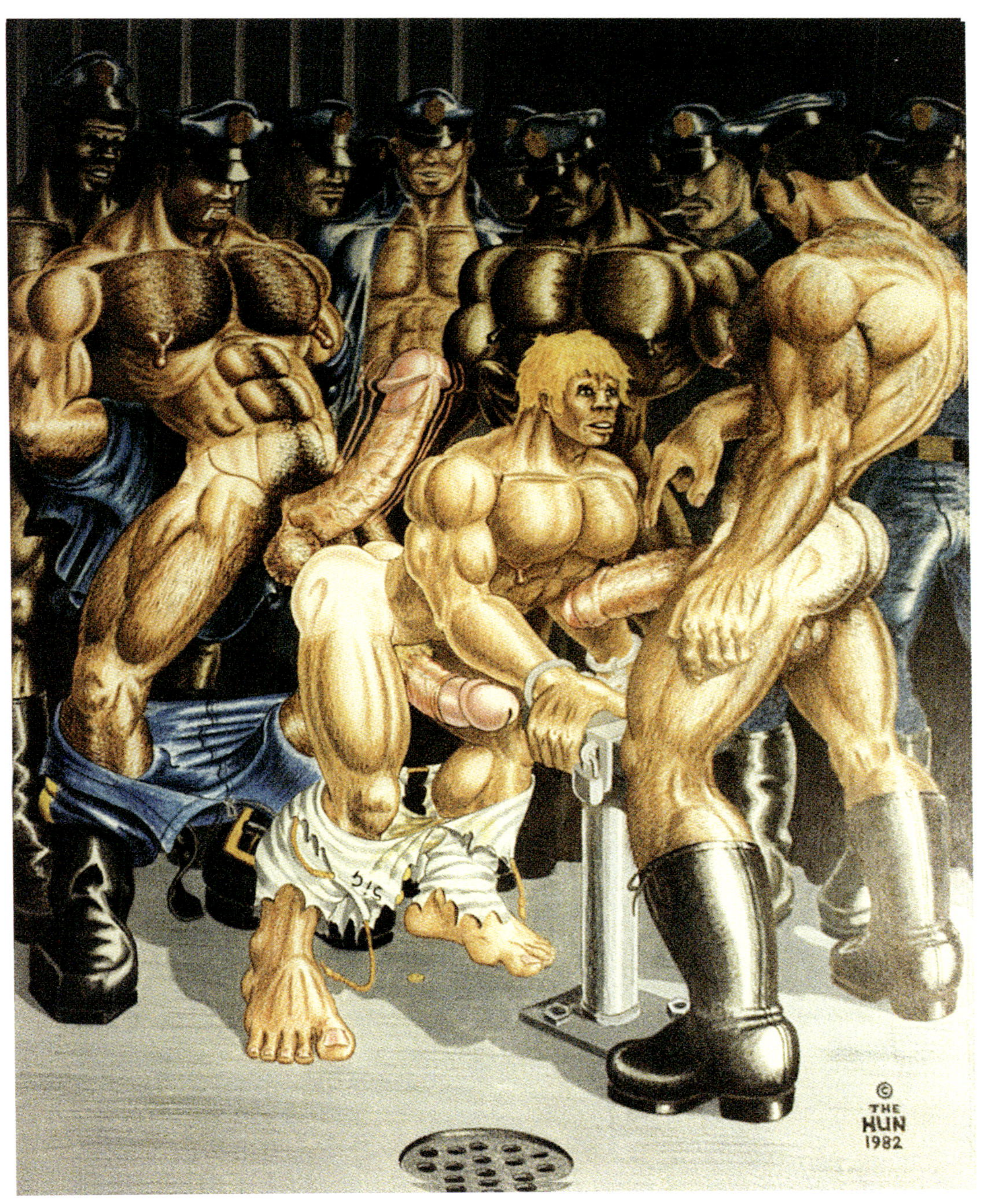

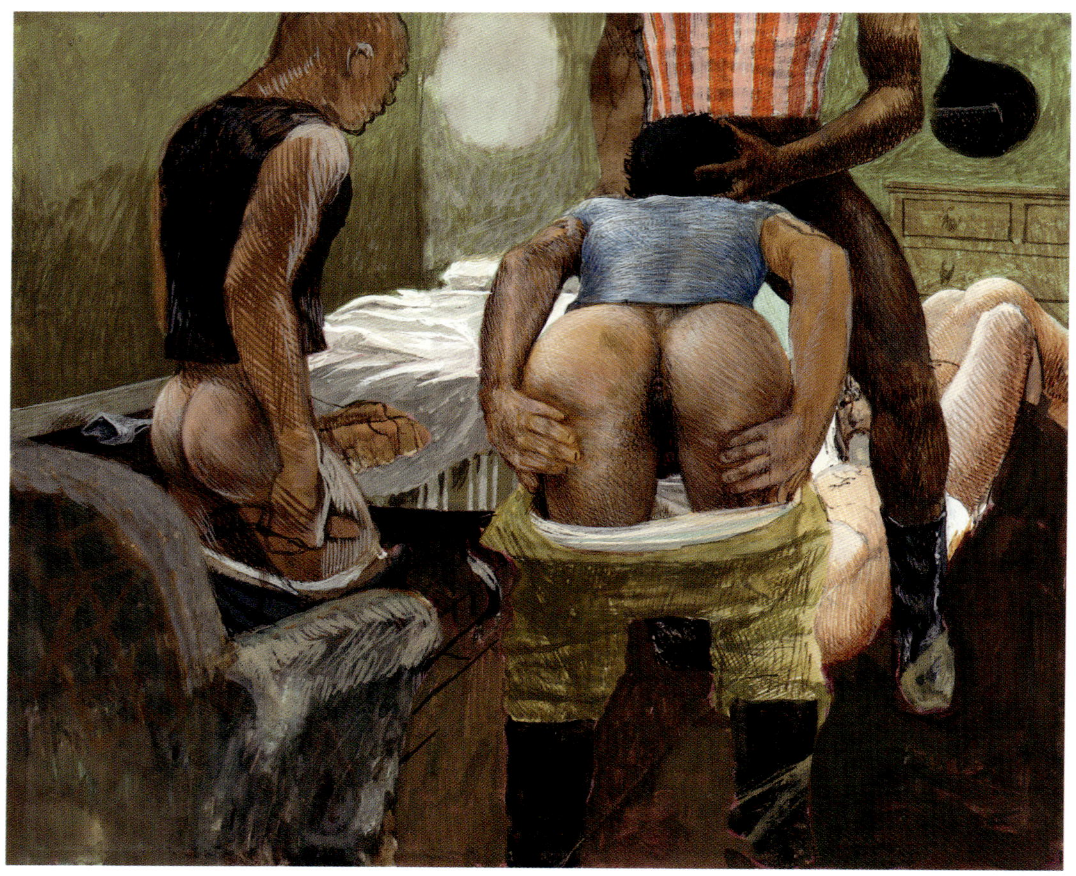

BASTILLE

The American living in Paris was working as an architectural rendering artist for large-scale building projects. His artistic works are small in size and often present dark expressions of sexuality, yet they are very spiritually based. Bastille was up for whatever he was engaging in. Tom's partner, Veli, had a brief, romantic relationship with Bastille before the artist died of AIDS-related complications.

Der in Paris lebende US-Amerikaner verdiente seinen Lebensunterhalt als technischer Zeichner bei großen Bauprojekten. Seine künstlerischen Arbeiten haben hingegen ein kleines Format und stellen oft das Dunkle der Sexualität dar, obwohl sie sehr spirituell sind. Bastille brannte förmlich für alles, was er tat. Toms Partner Veli hatte eine kurze, romantische Affäre mit Bastille, bevor der Künstler an den Folgen von Aids starb.

– Durk Dehner

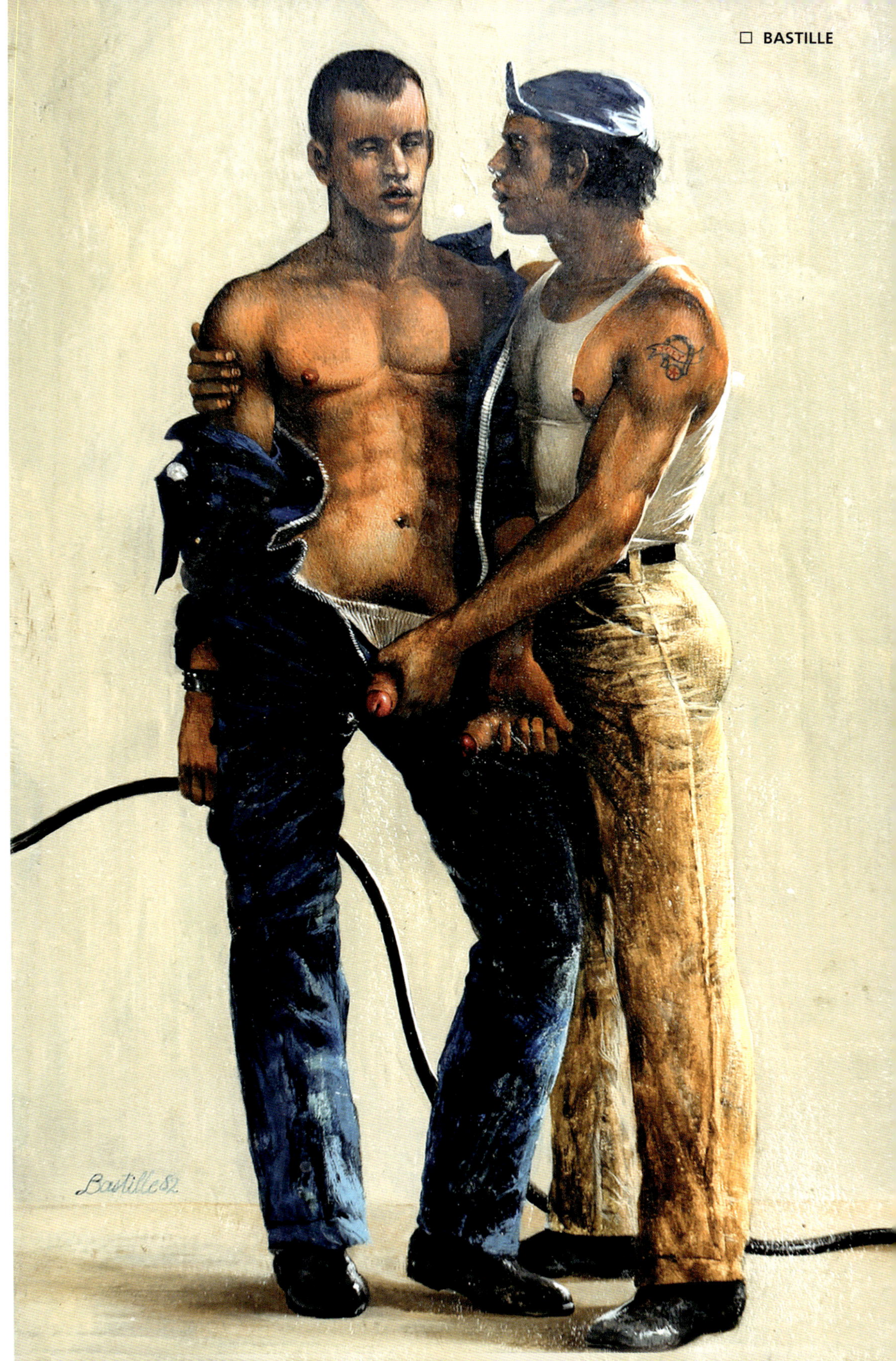
Bastille 82

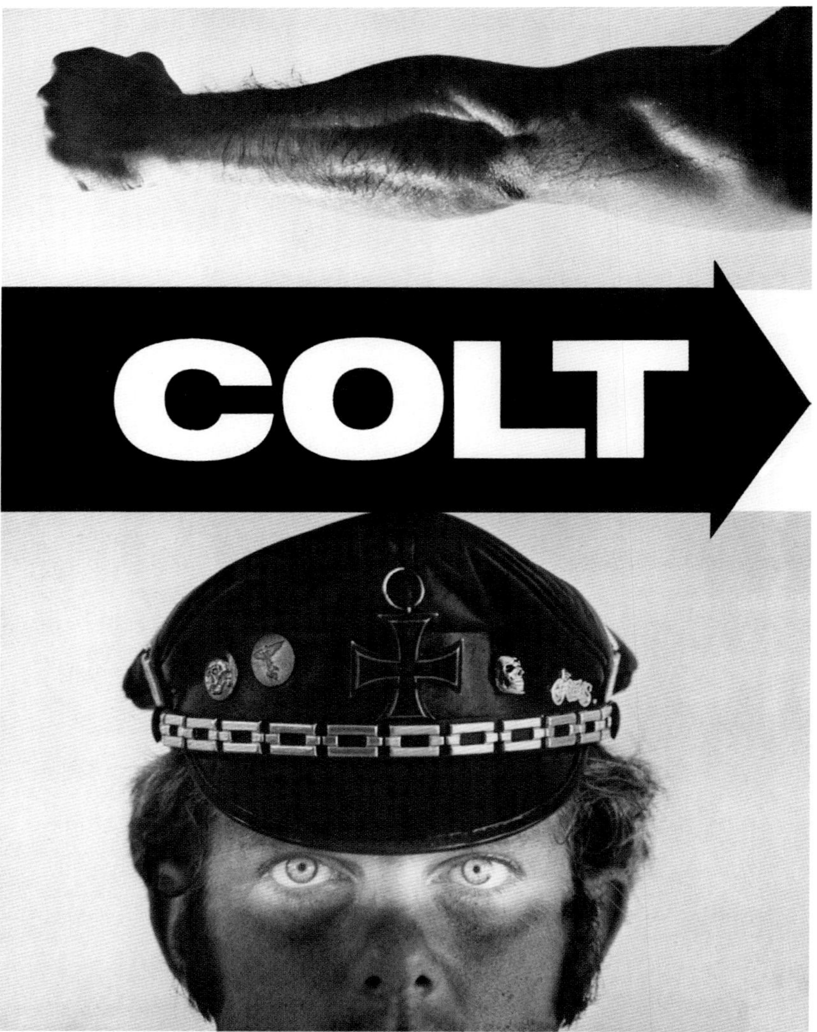

JIM FRENCH

The name "Rip Colt" is how Jim French presented his work at Colt Studio. He brought his company to the top of its league, garnering international respect. Within Gay bodybuilding circles there was no higher prestige than to be one of his subjects. Jim once invited Tom to draw several of his models and then published them in Colt's *Olympus*. Jim possessed a wide range of artistic talents, choosing to narrow his scope to photography and shooting men exclusively.

Unter dem Namen „Rip Colt" präsentierte Jim French seine Arbeit in den Colt Studios. Er hat seine Firma an die Spitze ihrer Liga geführt und iund dafür international Anerkennung bekommen. In schwulen Bodybuilding-Kreisen gab es kein höheres Prestige, als eines seiner Modelle zu sein. Jim lud Tom einmal ein, einige seiner Modelle zu zeichnen, und veröffentlichte die Zeichnungen dann in Colts Olympus. Jim besaß eine große Bandbreite künstlerischer Talente, von denen er sich jedoch zugunsten der Fotografie abwendete, um sich ausschließlich auf das Fotografieren von Männern zu konzentrieren.
– Durk Dehner

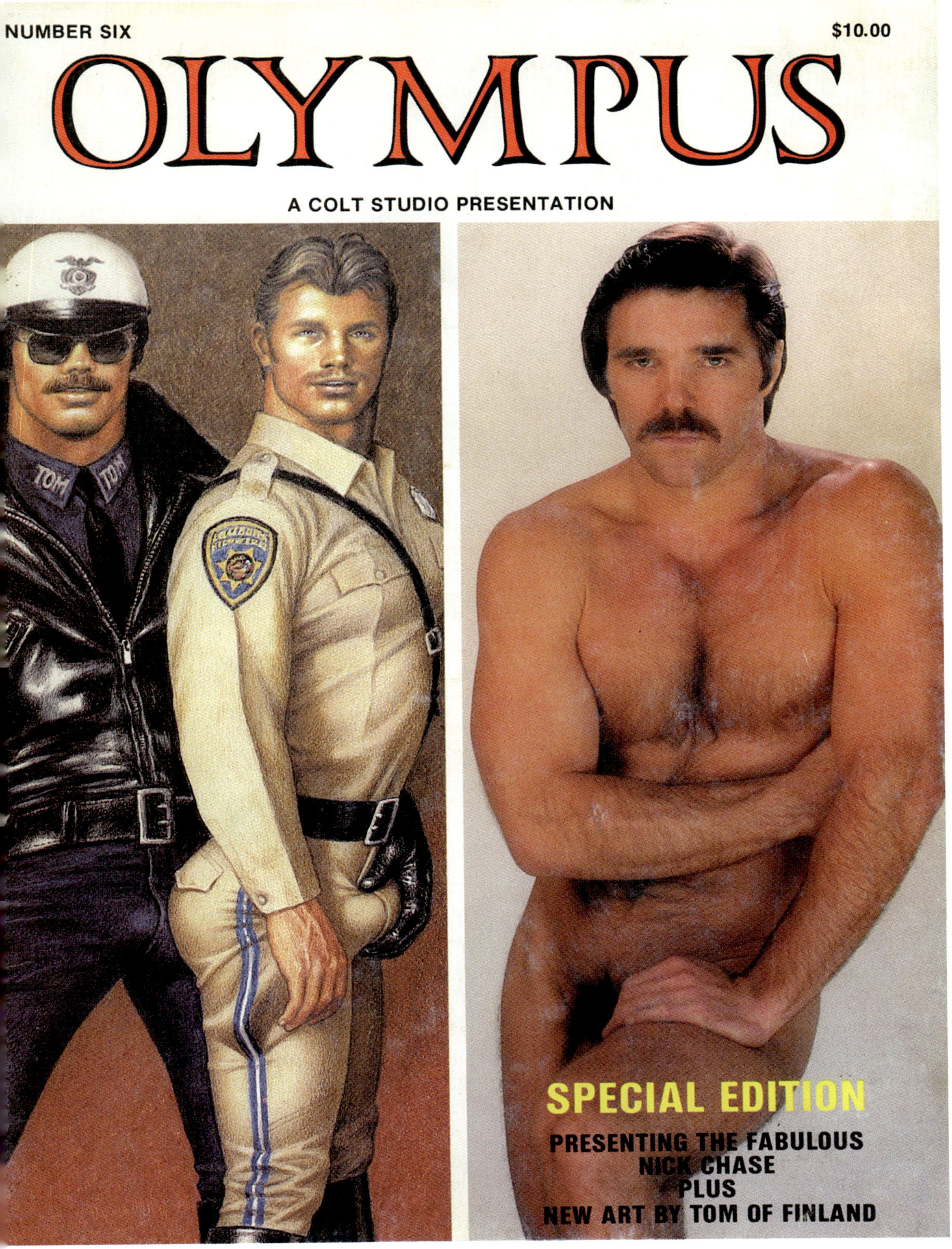

NUMBER SIX

$10.00

OLYMPUS

A COLT STUDIO PRESENTATION

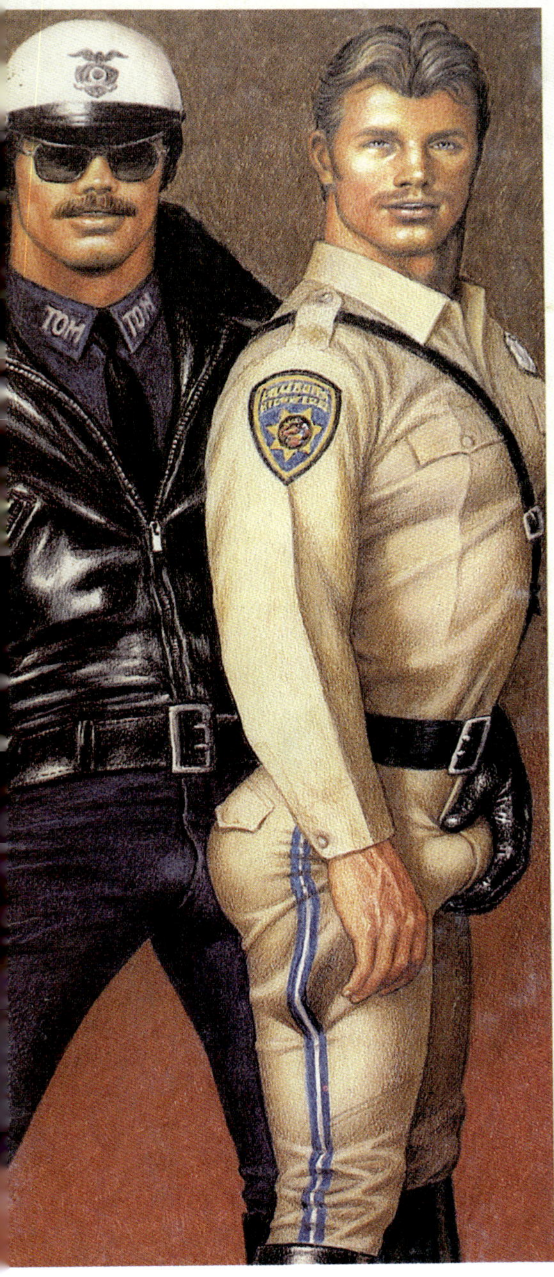

SPECIAL EDITION

**PRESENTING THE FABULOUS
NICK CHASE
PLUS
NEW ART BY TOM OF FINLAND**

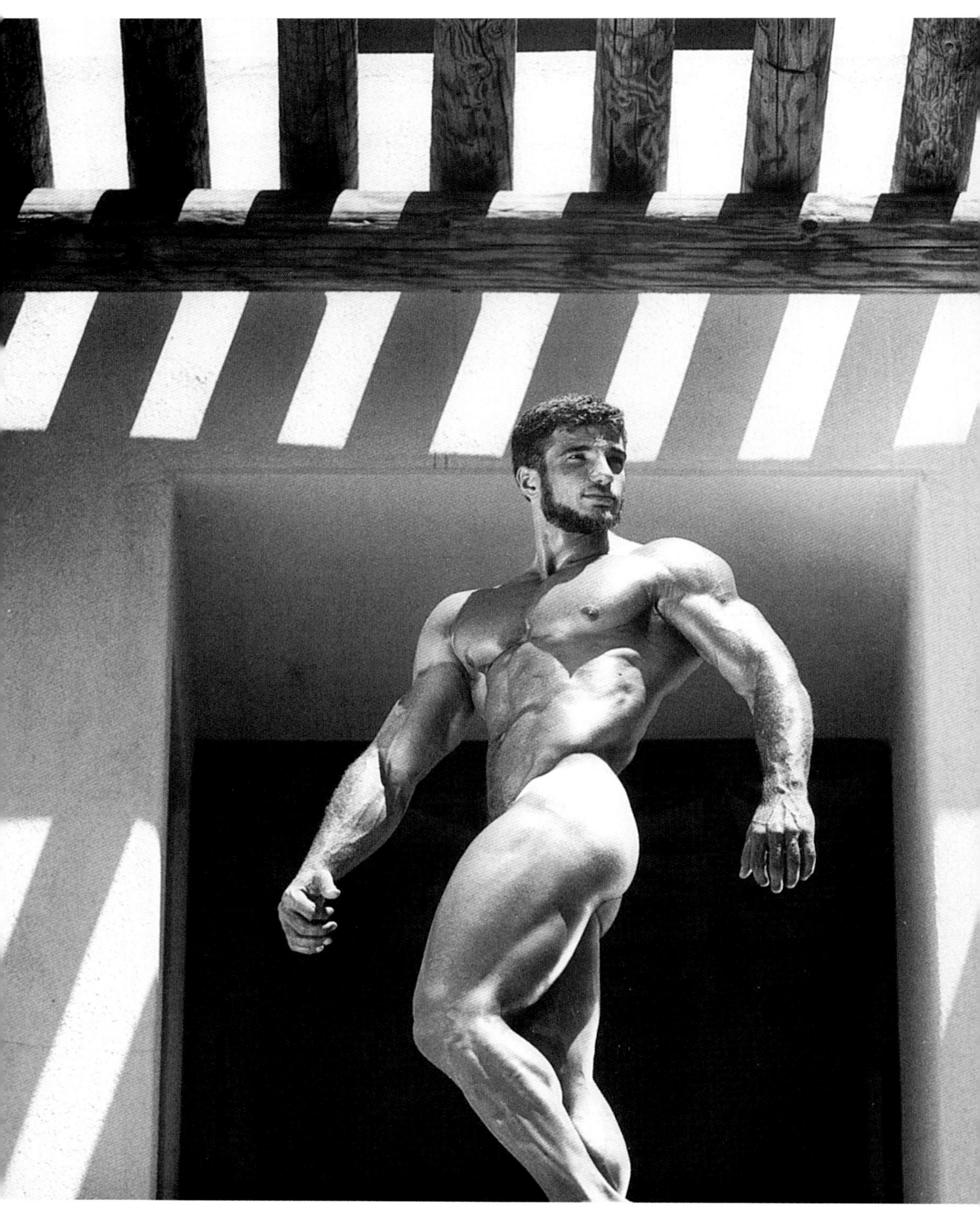

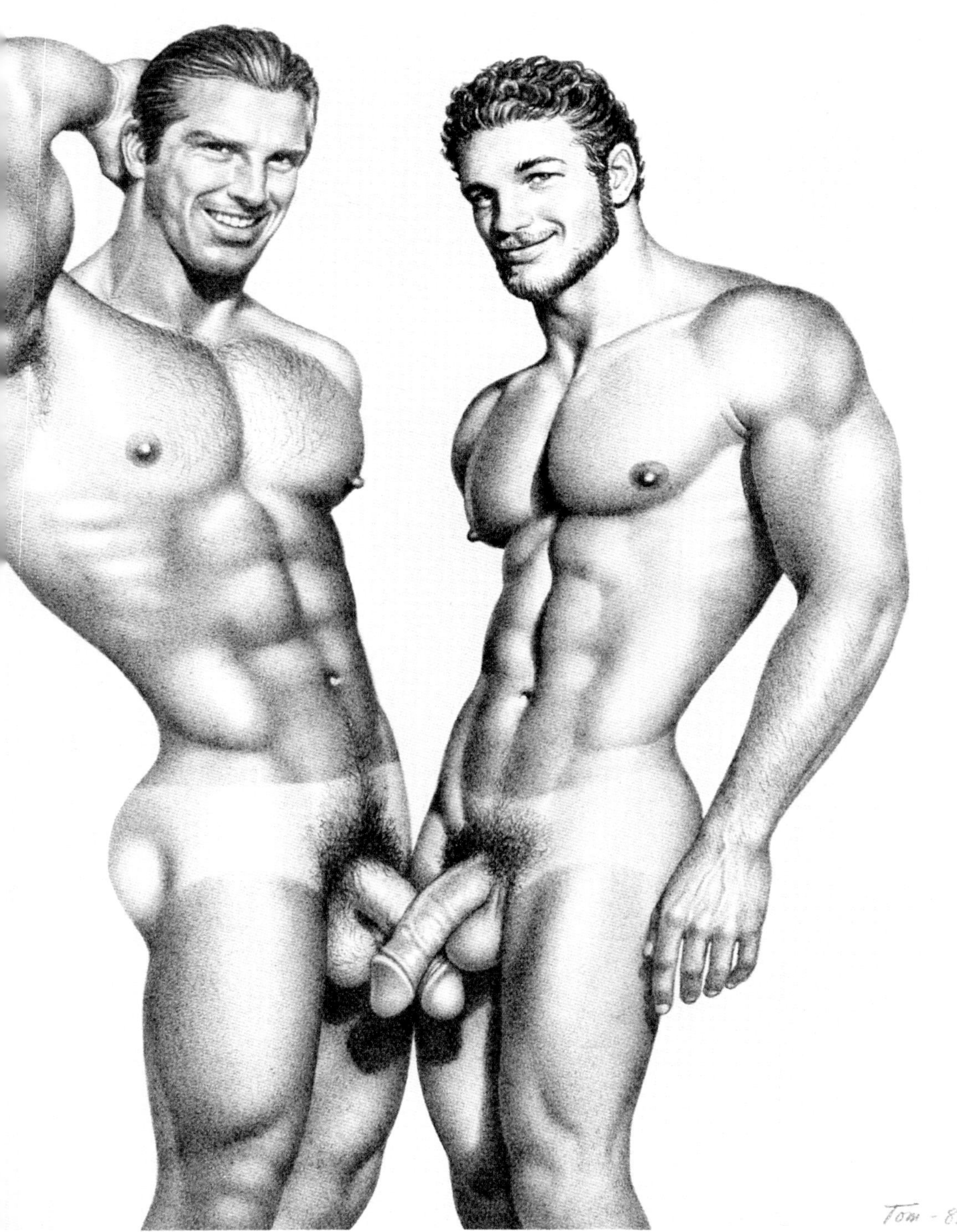

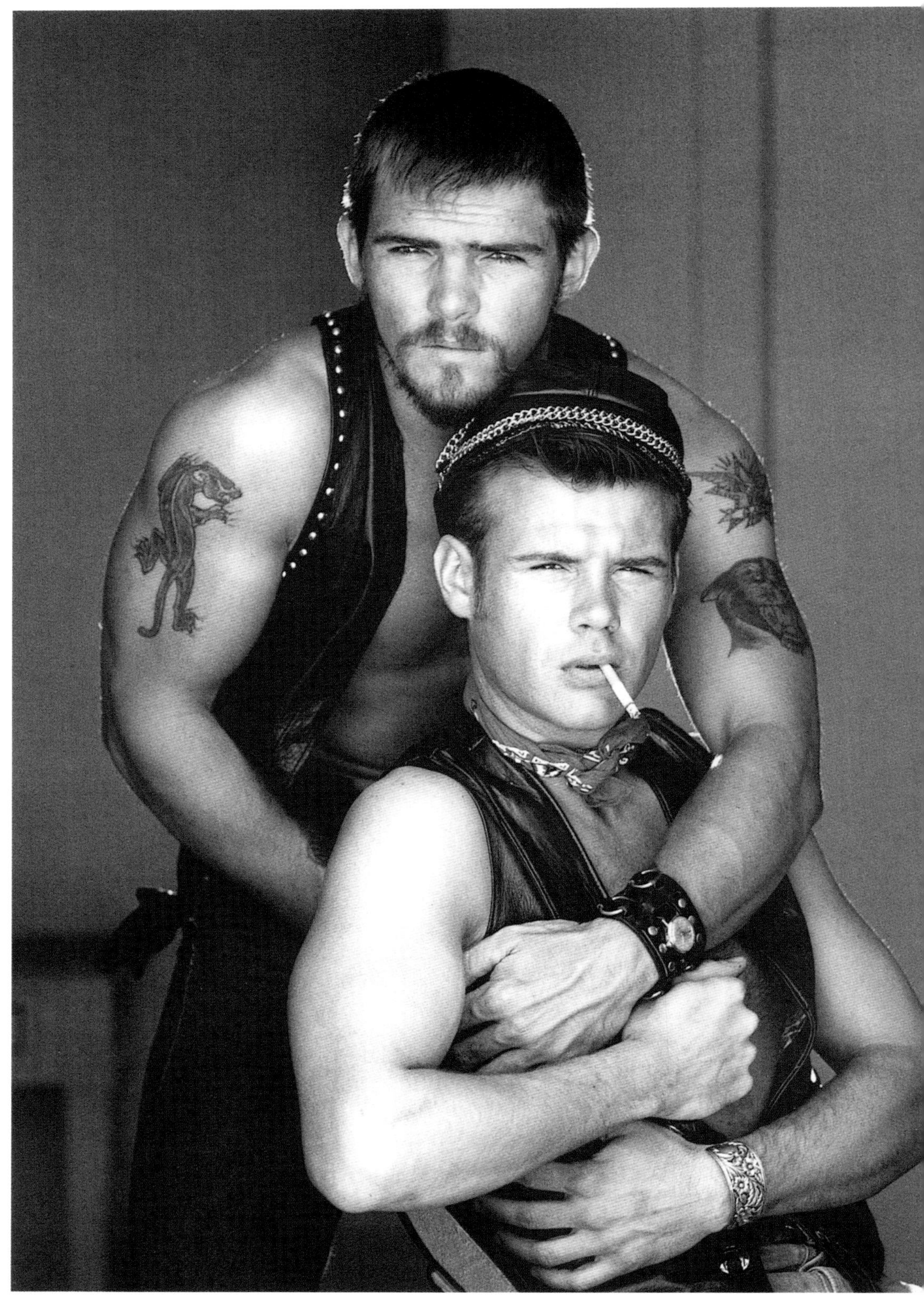

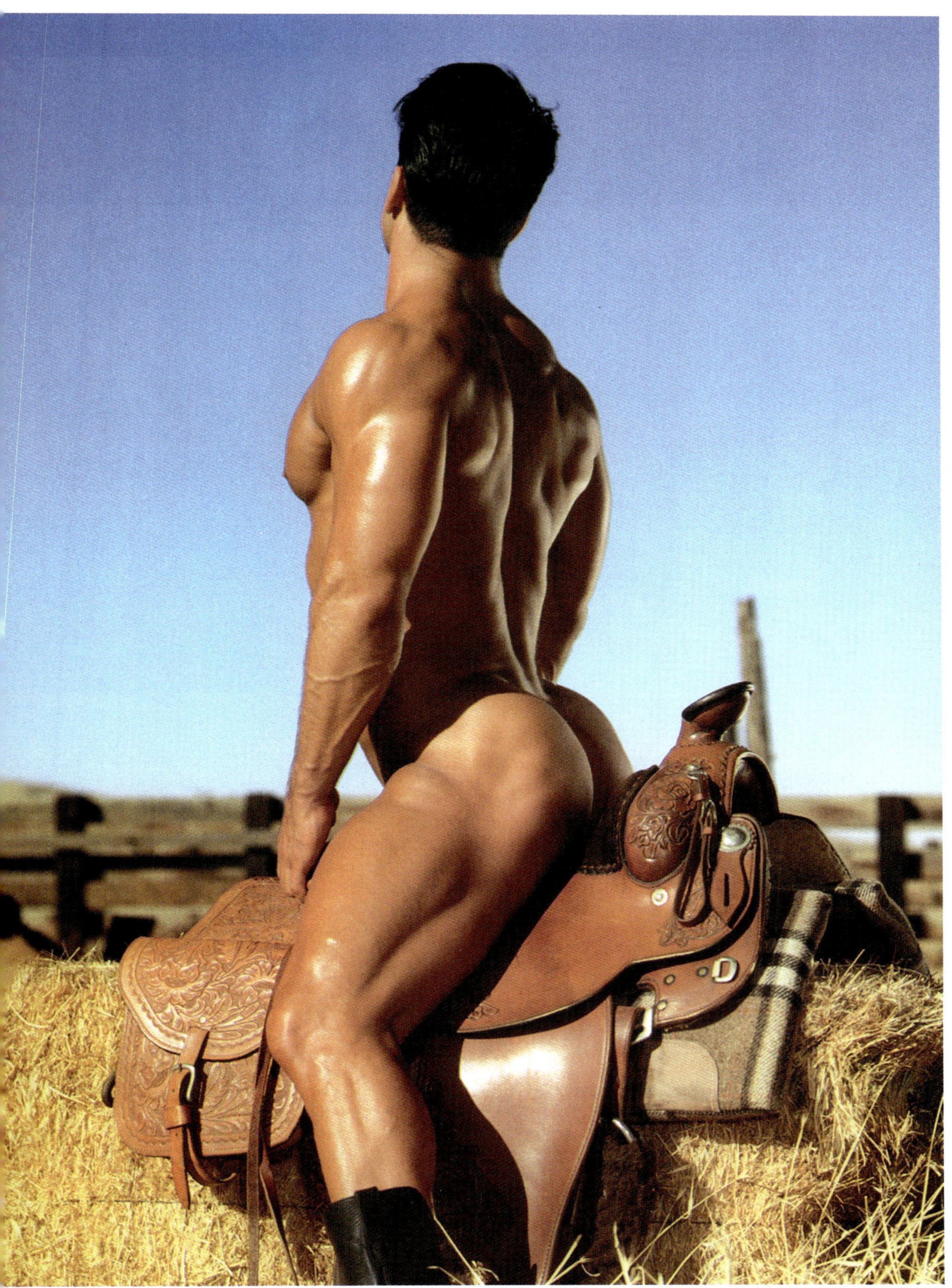

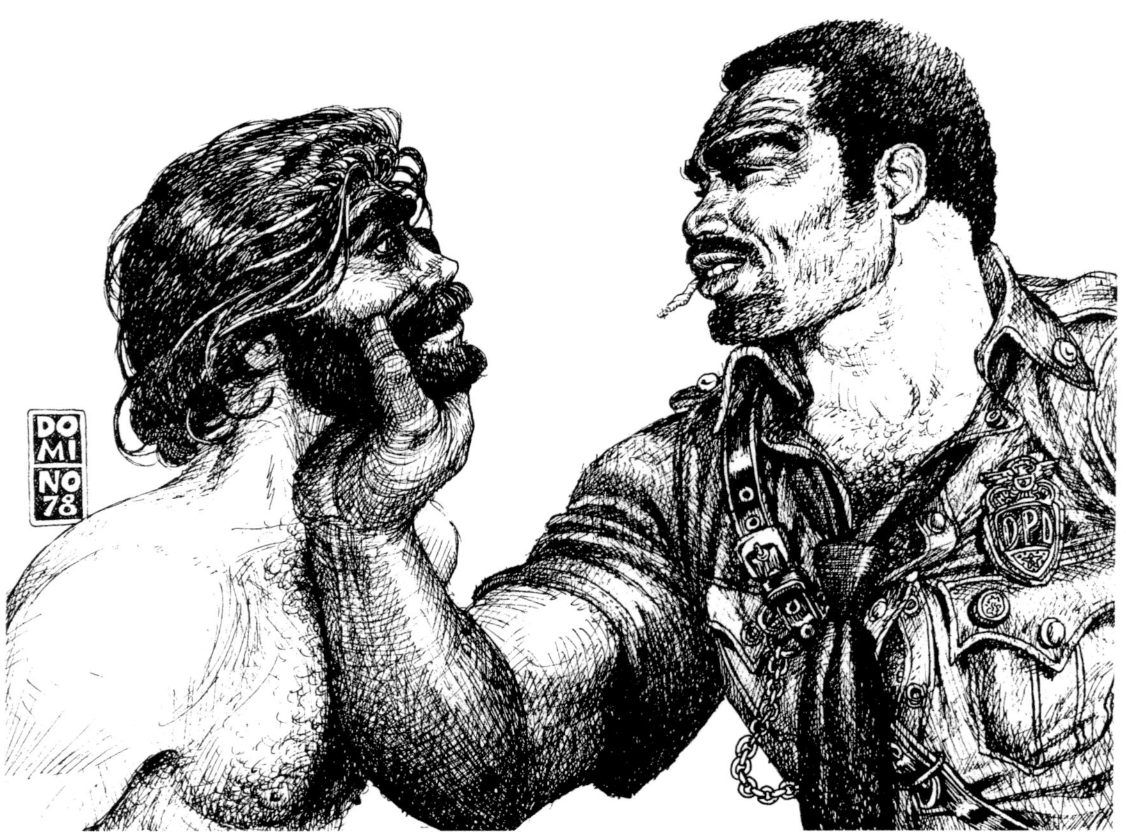

DOMINO

The man that made husky men sexy, he, and his art, basically missed the current bear era in Gay culture. He was also a master pen-and-ink artist whose work would have remained popular, if it were not for a family that was ill-advised. As a result, his work has disappeared from present day culture. So, this is a heads up: Make out your will and think twice who is going to inherit your archives or collection and where it will be most appreciated. Certainly, we encourage you to consider one of your Gay cultural establishments, and if you choose Tom of Finland Foundation, who has an international base and outreach, we would be very pleased to include you. Hopefully, by the conclusion of this book, you will have a much more defined understanding of what Tom of Finland Foundation does.

Domino ist der Mann, der stämmige Männer sexy machte. Ausgerechnet er und seine Kunst verpassten die aktuelle Ära der Bären in der schwulen Kultur. Auch er war ein Meister mit Feder und Tusche, und sicherlich wäre sein Werk noch heute bekannt – wenn da nicht seine schlecht beratene Familie gewesen wäre, die dafür gesorgt hat, dass sein Werk heute nicht mehr bekannt ist. An dieser Stelle also ein kleiner Hinweis: Macht euch beizeiten darüber Gedanken, wer einmal eure Archive und Sammlungen erben soll, und wo diese am meisten geschätzt werden. Natürlich legen wir euch nahe, hier eine schwule Einrichtung in Betracht zu ziehen – und wenn ihr euch für die Tom of Finland Foundation als international vernetzte Institution entscheidet, würden wir uns sehr freuen. Nach der Lektüre dieses Buches habt ihr hoffentlich einen guten Eindruck davon erhalten, wie die Tom of Finland Foundation funktioniert. **– Durk Dehner**

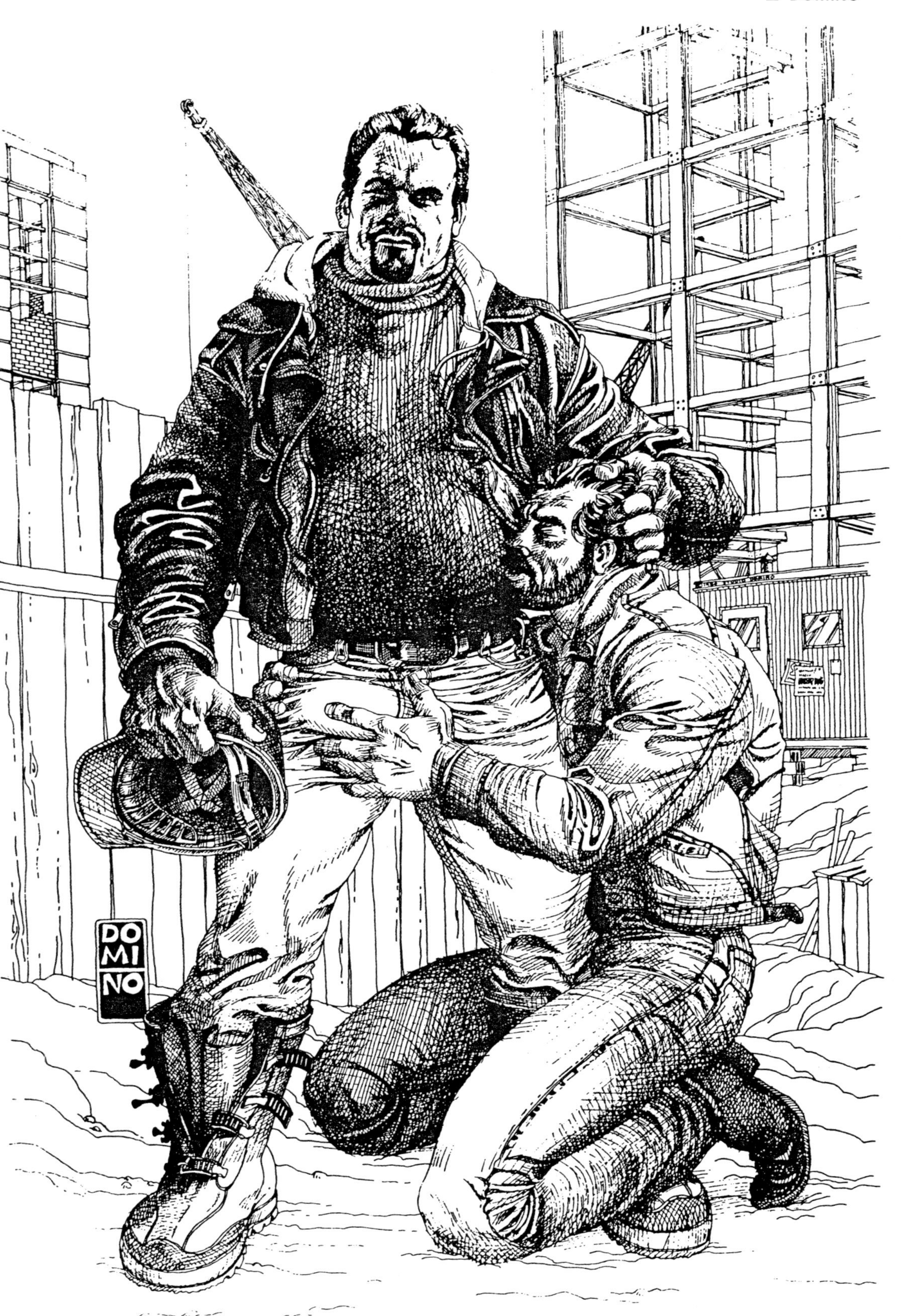

DOMINO

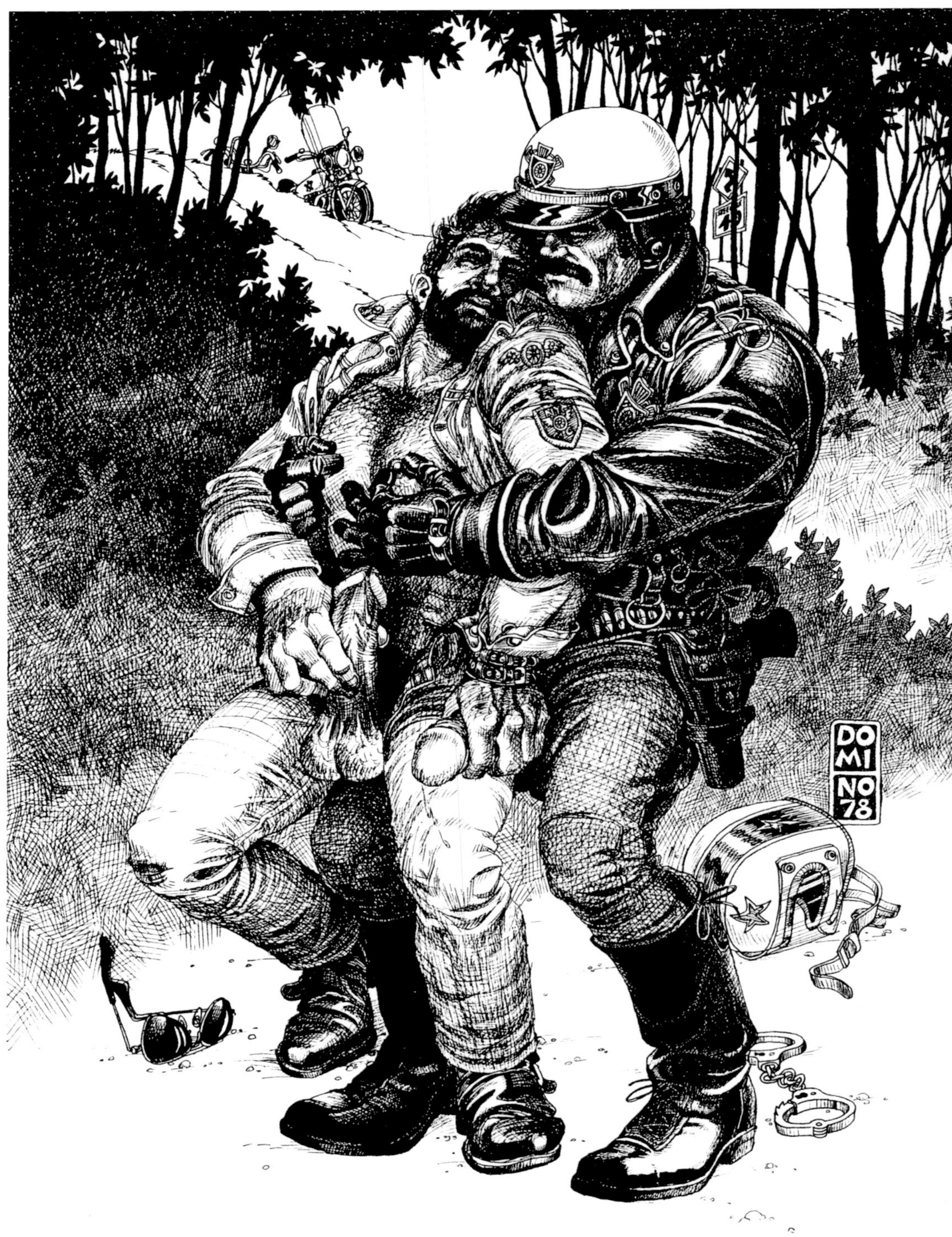

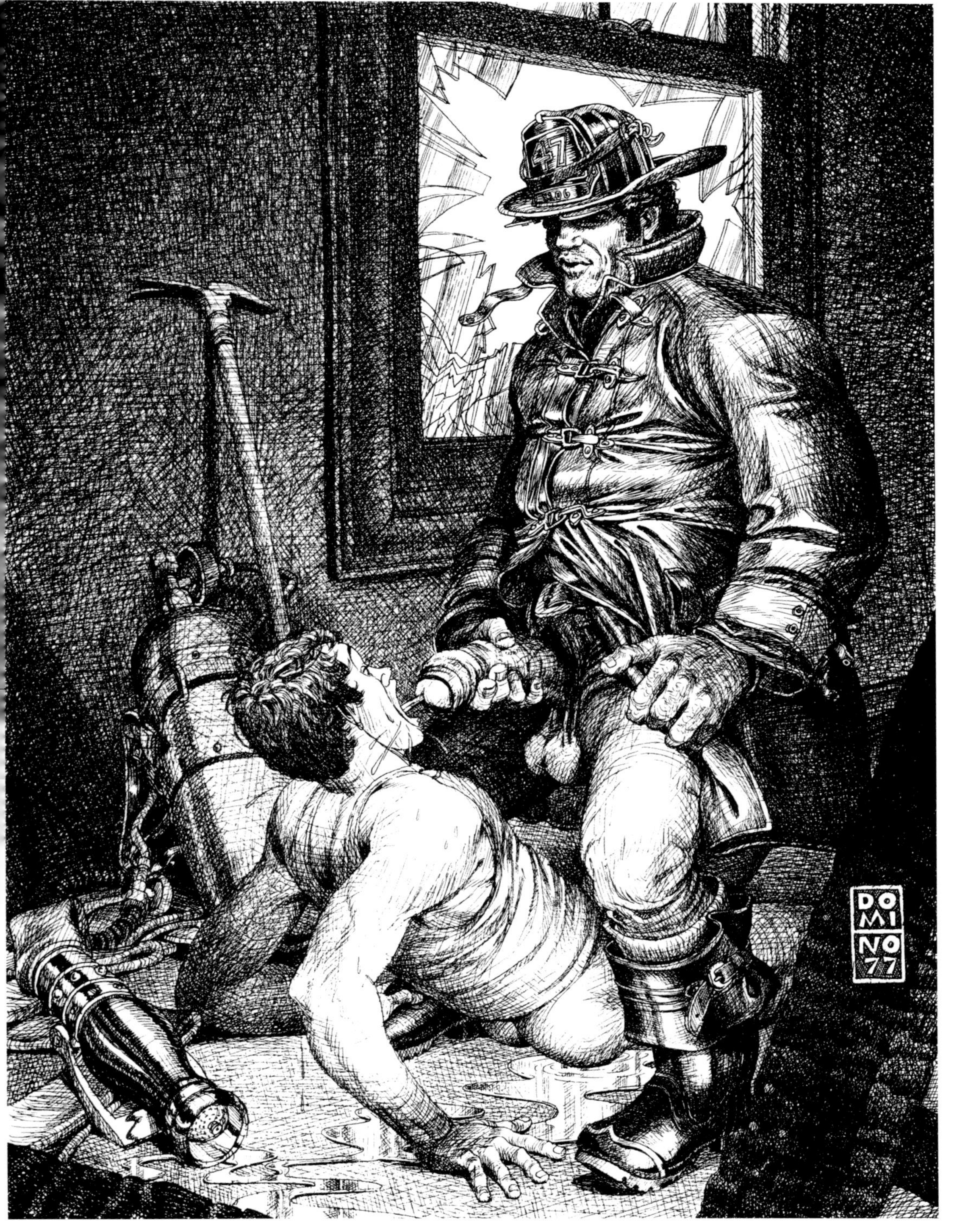

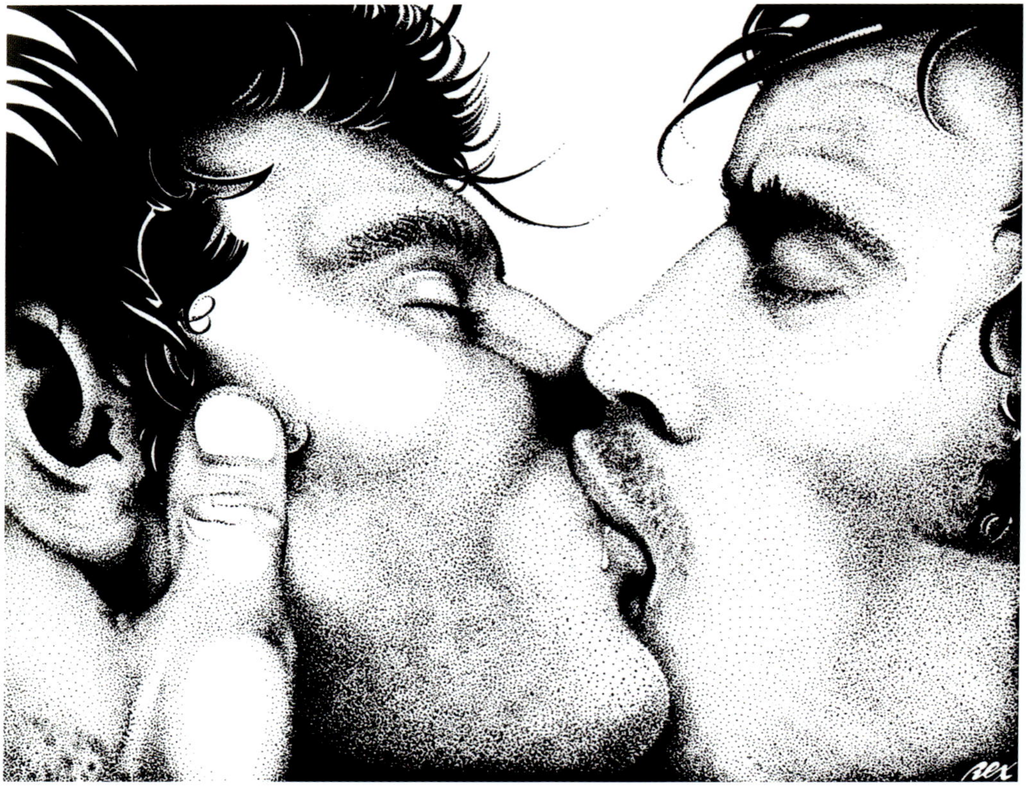

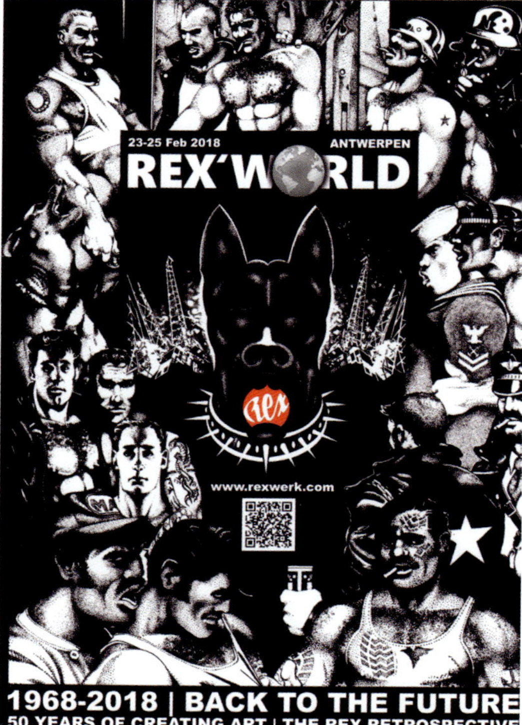

REX

Presently living and working in Amsterdam, this man is in his fifth decade as a Gay artist. He has been through many of the most formidable experiences associated with our community – including the Folsom fires which burned his apartment down with all his artwork, and the AIDS epidemic and the loss of so many friends. His work is amazing, but his technique is amazing in itself. It is one tiny dot after another. His images exude sensual feelings. REX believes that if he does not rattle someone's cage, then he has not done himself justice.

REX, der derzeit in Amsterdam lebt und arbeitet, kann bereits auf fünf Jahrzehnte als schwuler Künstler zurückblicken. Und auch auf viele prägende Erfahrungen, die mit unserer Community verbunden sind – so etwa den großen Brand im Stadtteil Folsom in San Francisco, denen auch seine Wohnung mit all seinen Kunstwerken zum Opfer fielen, sowie die Aids-Epidemie und der Verlust so vieler Freunde. Nicht nur sein Werk, auch seine Technik ist erstaunlich: Er setzt einen winzigen Punkt neben den anderen. Seine Bilder strahlen dadurch enorme Sinnlichkeit aus. REX glaubt, dass er an den Käfigen der anderen rütteln muss, um sich selbst gerecht zu werden.

– Durk Dehner

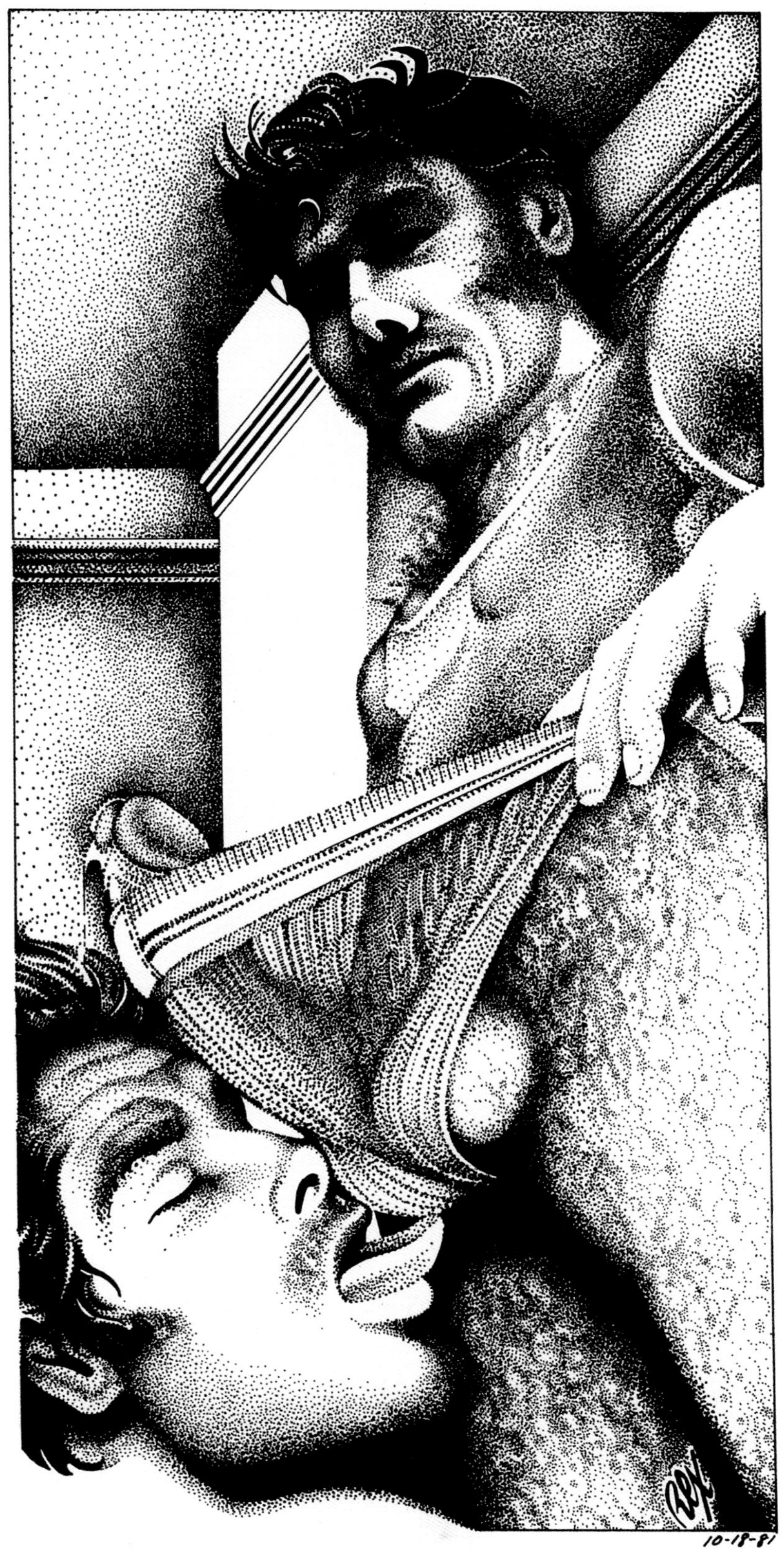

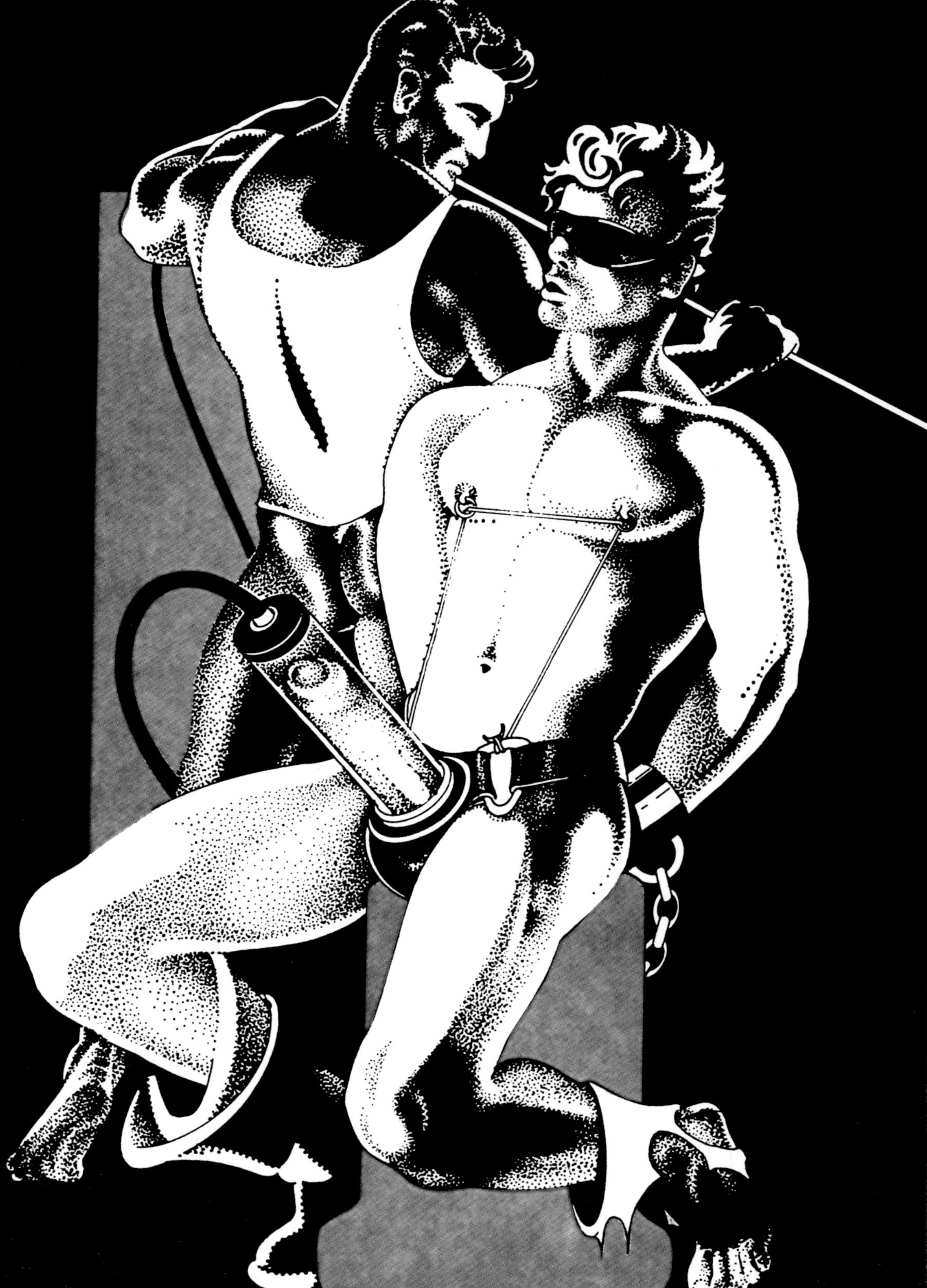
REX

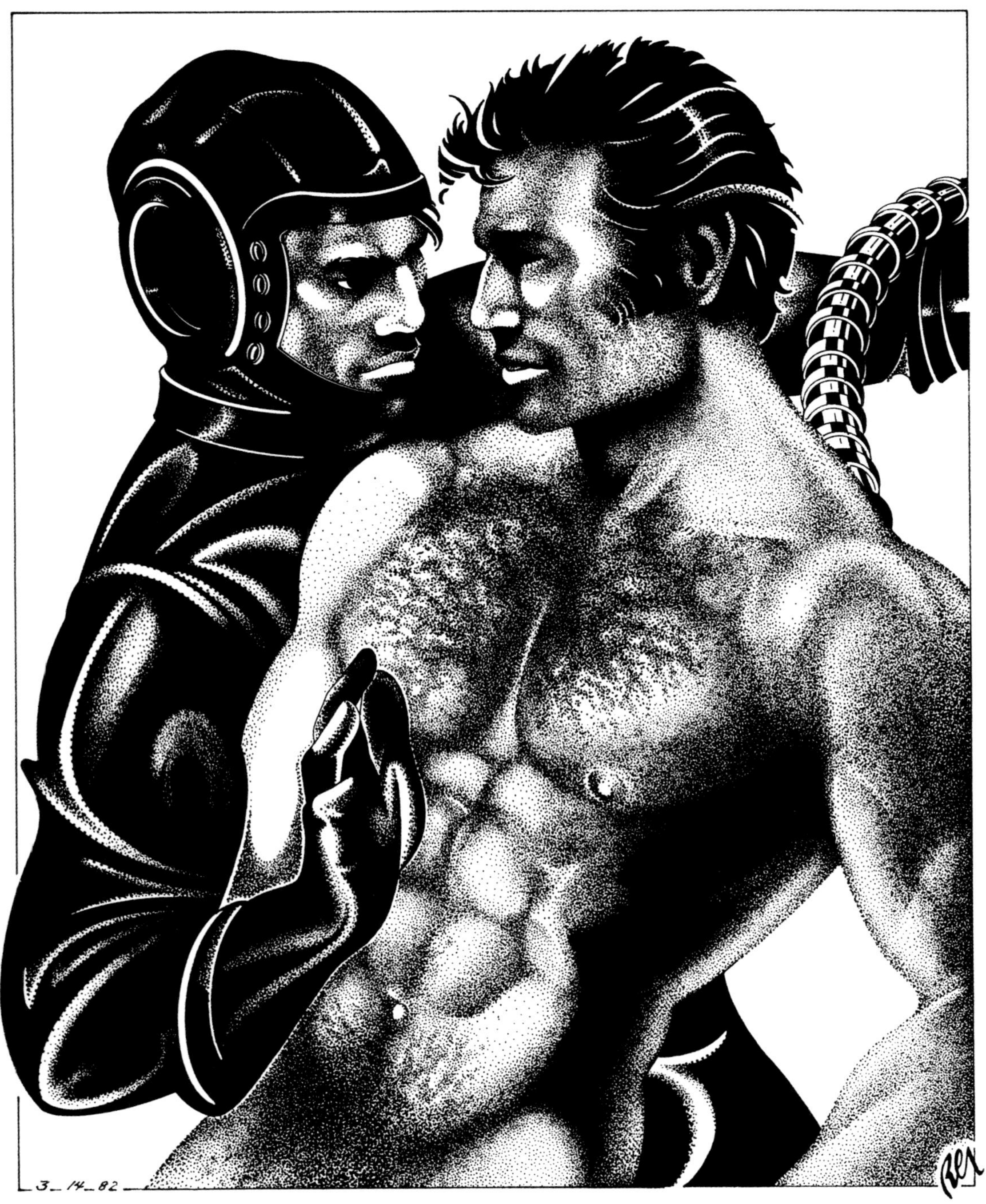

■ OLD RELIABLE
That which you are seeking . . . is also seeking you . . .

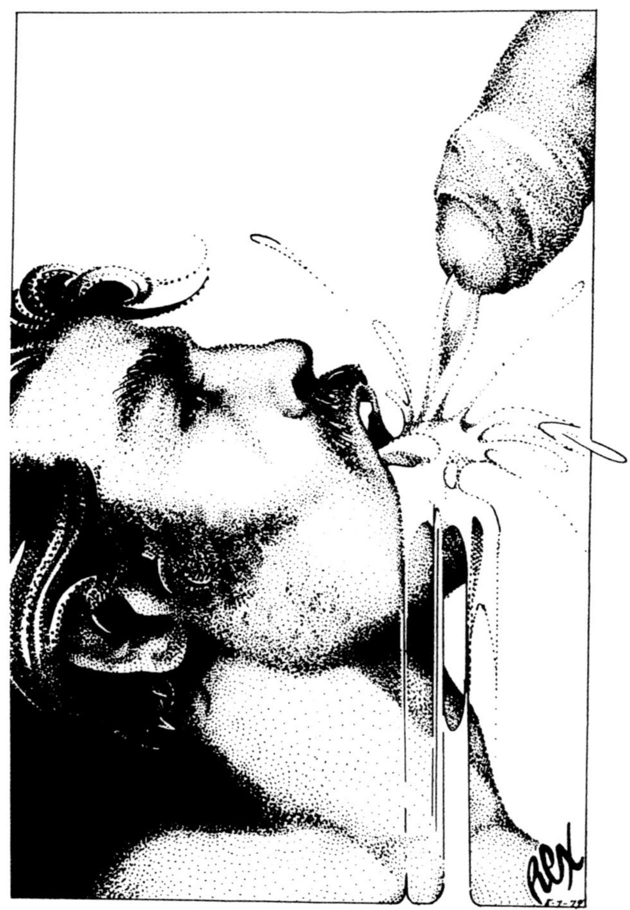

UNDER NIAGARA

What do you want most? Answers to our questionnaire said "more water sports", loud and clear. So we're going to give you a shower you won't soon forget. The title says it all. If you want to hear Dave drinking Gregg's piss, gettin' fucked and taking a piss enema, taking a whole body, face and hair shower, lappin' the suds out of the bowl, and much more, then order "Under Niagara", for a wet, wet honeymoon. **(C-10100)**

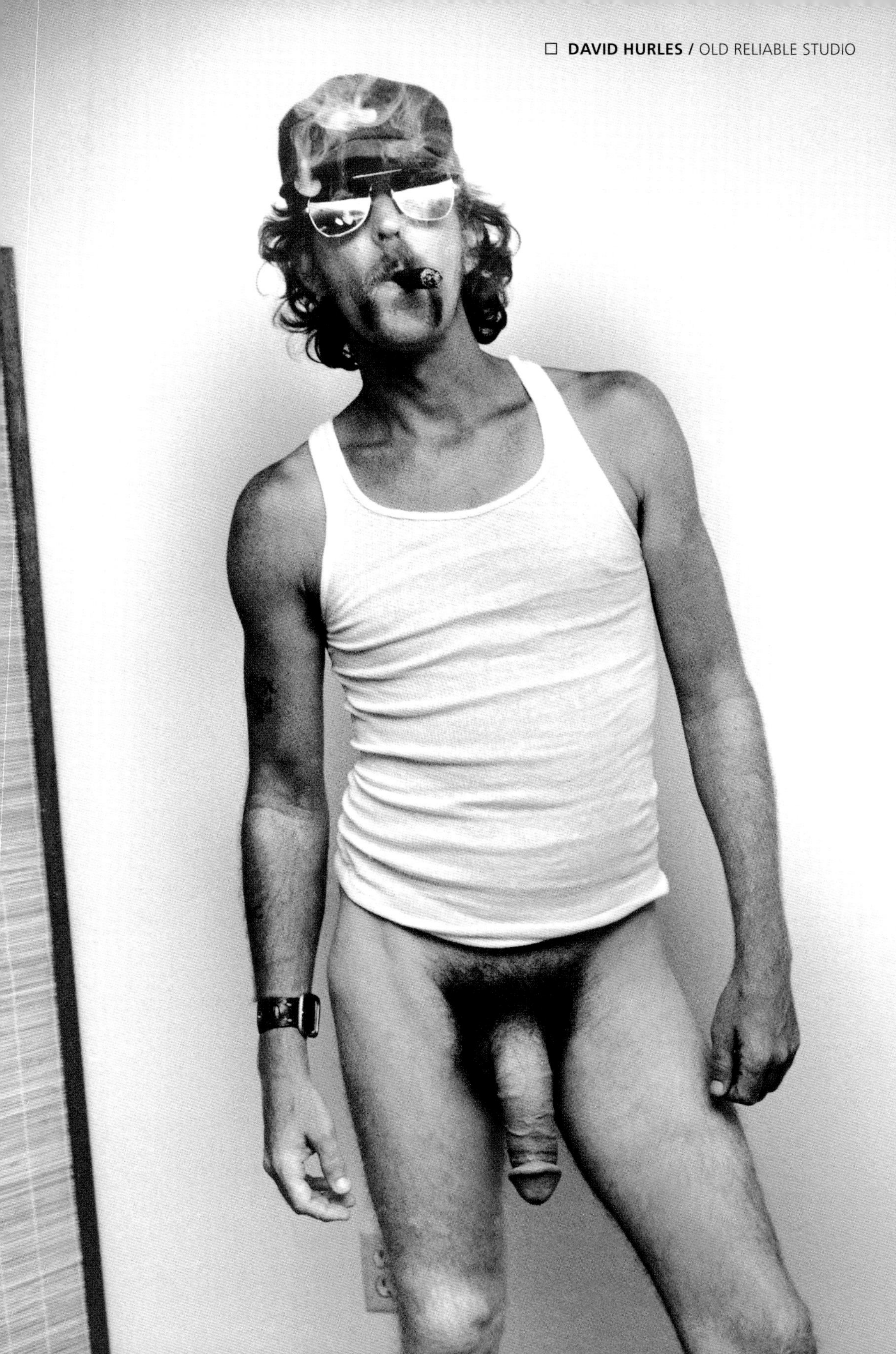

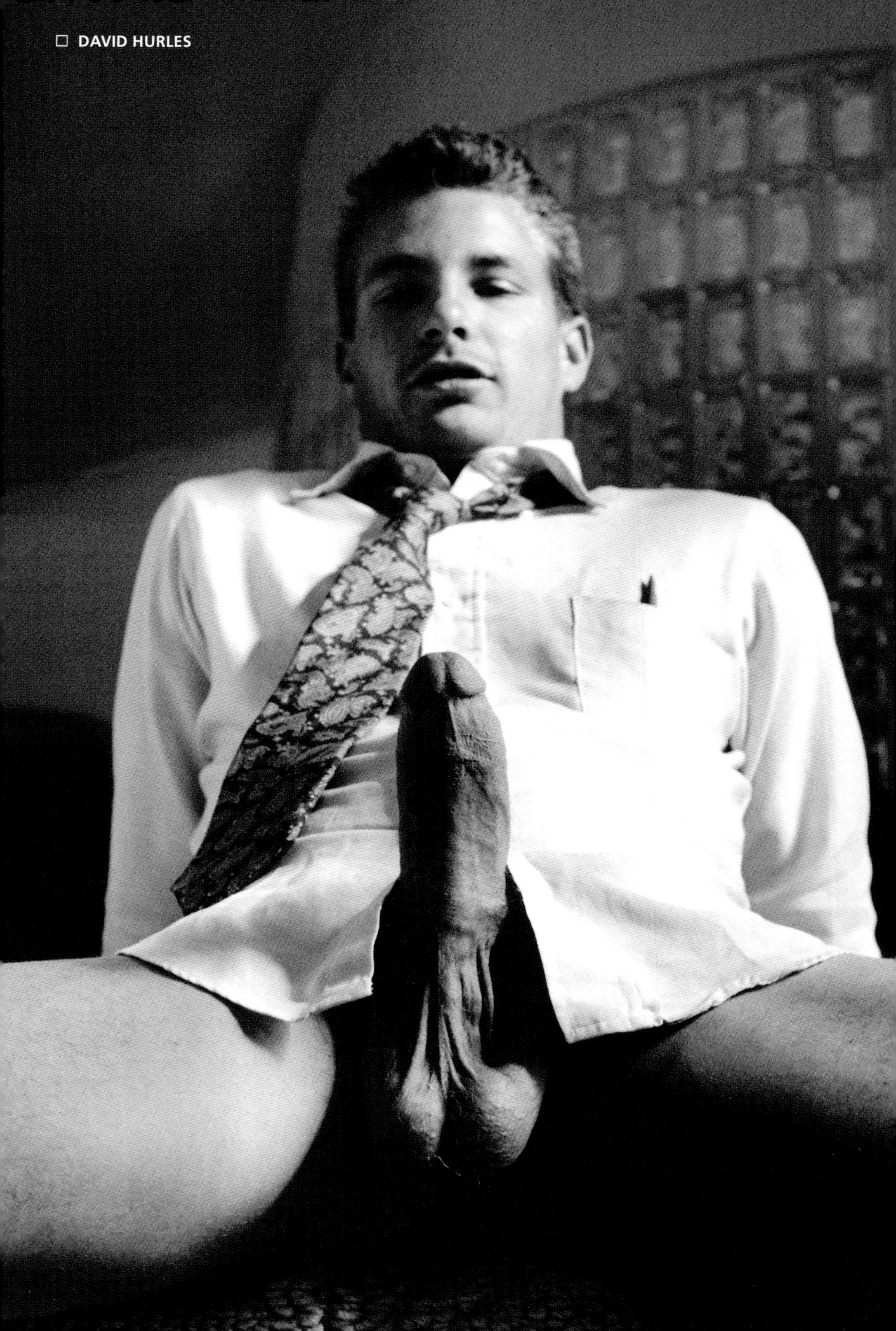

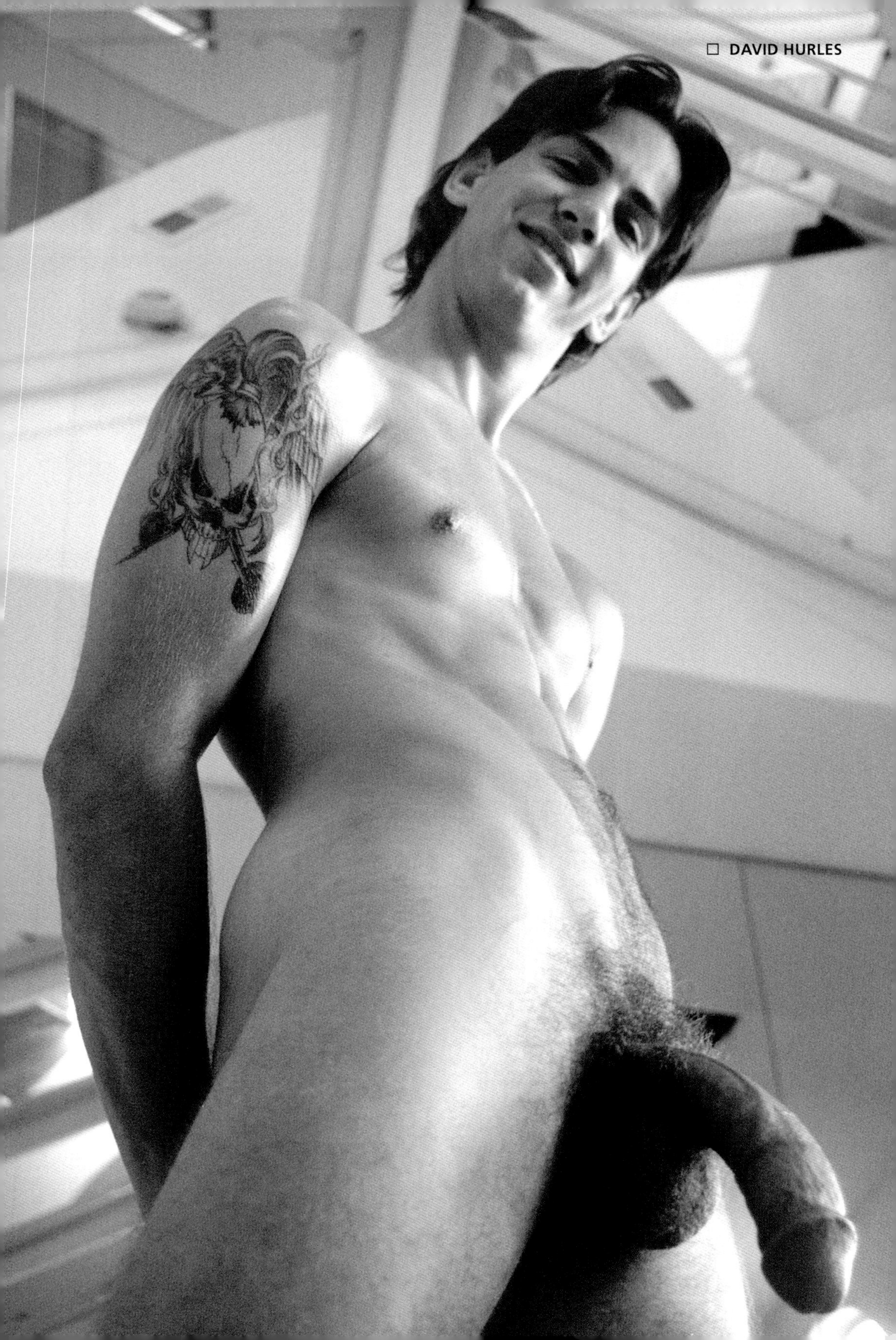
DAVID HURLES

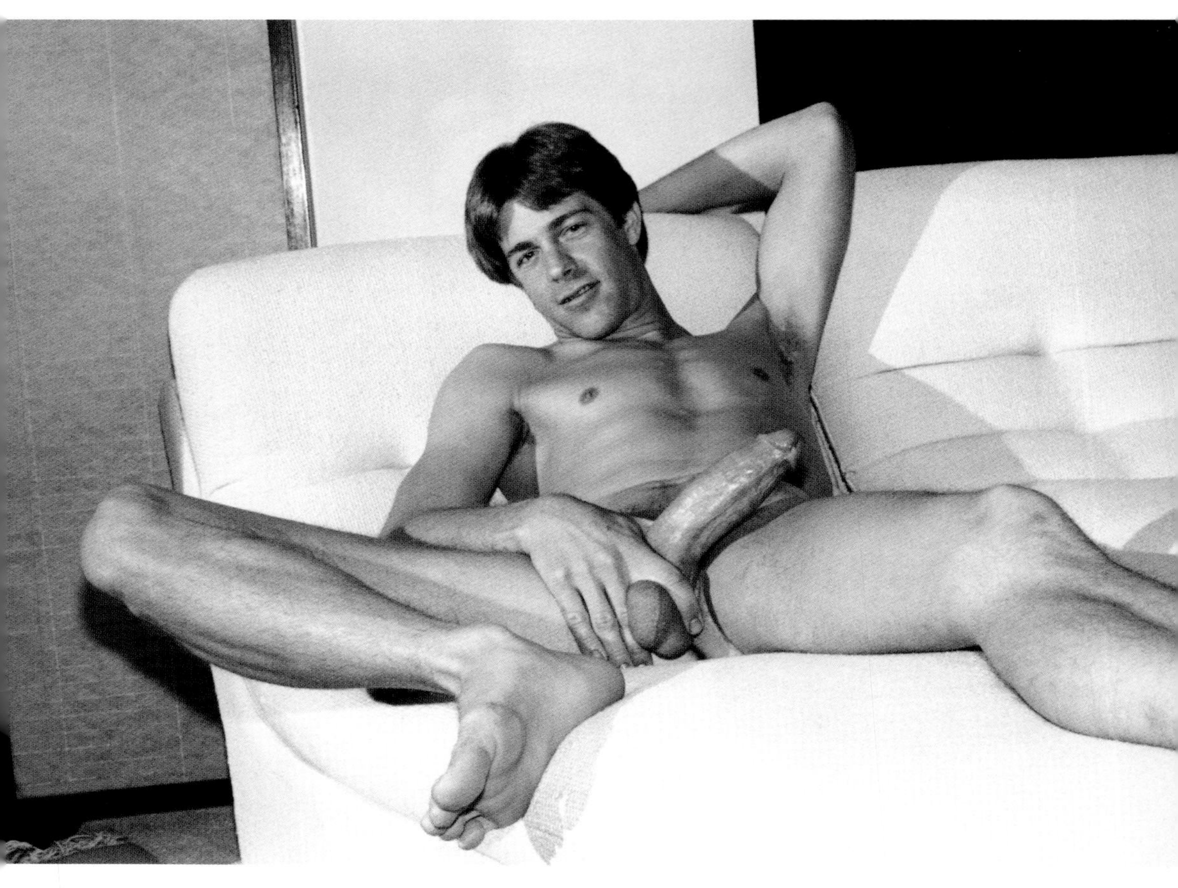

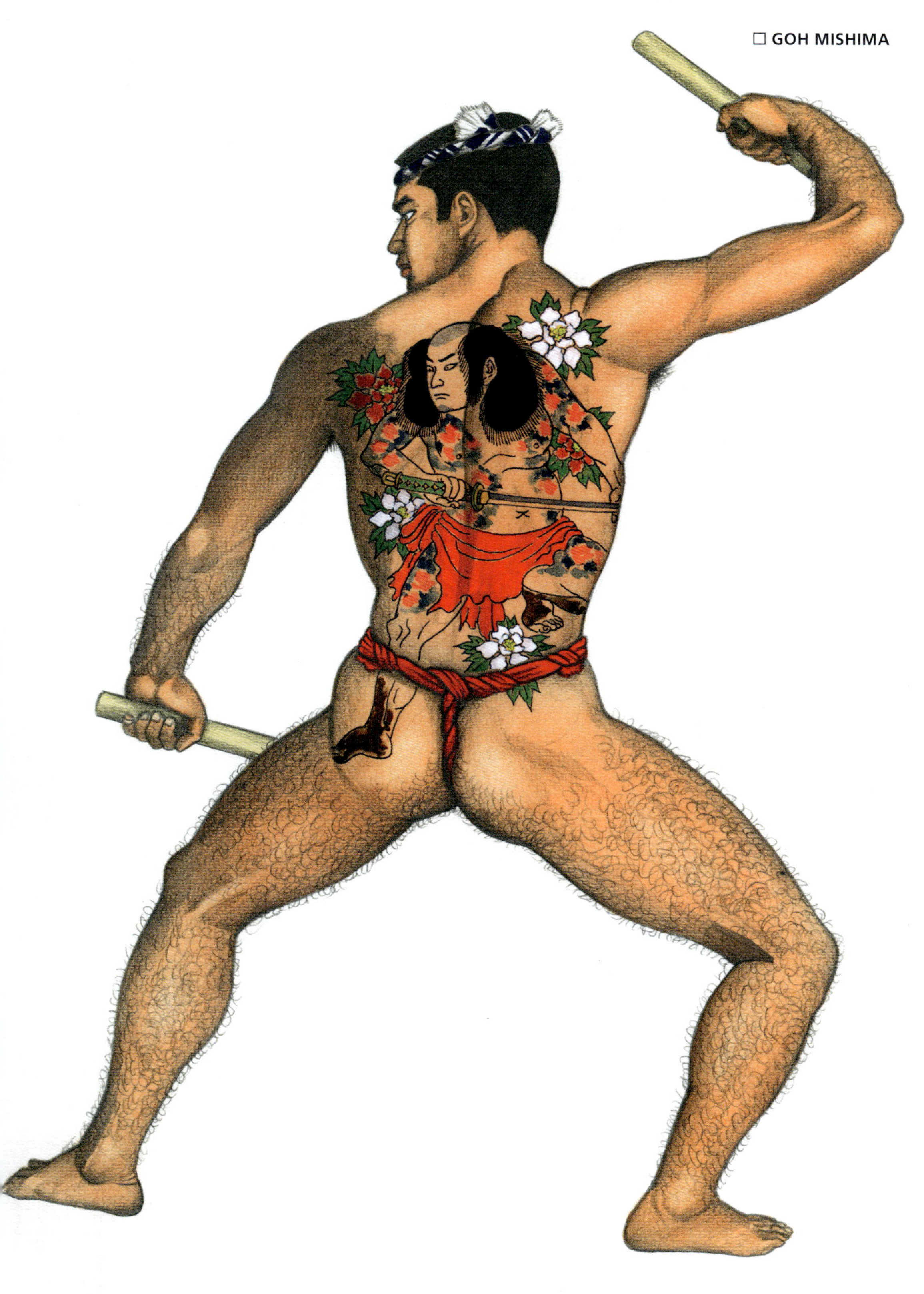

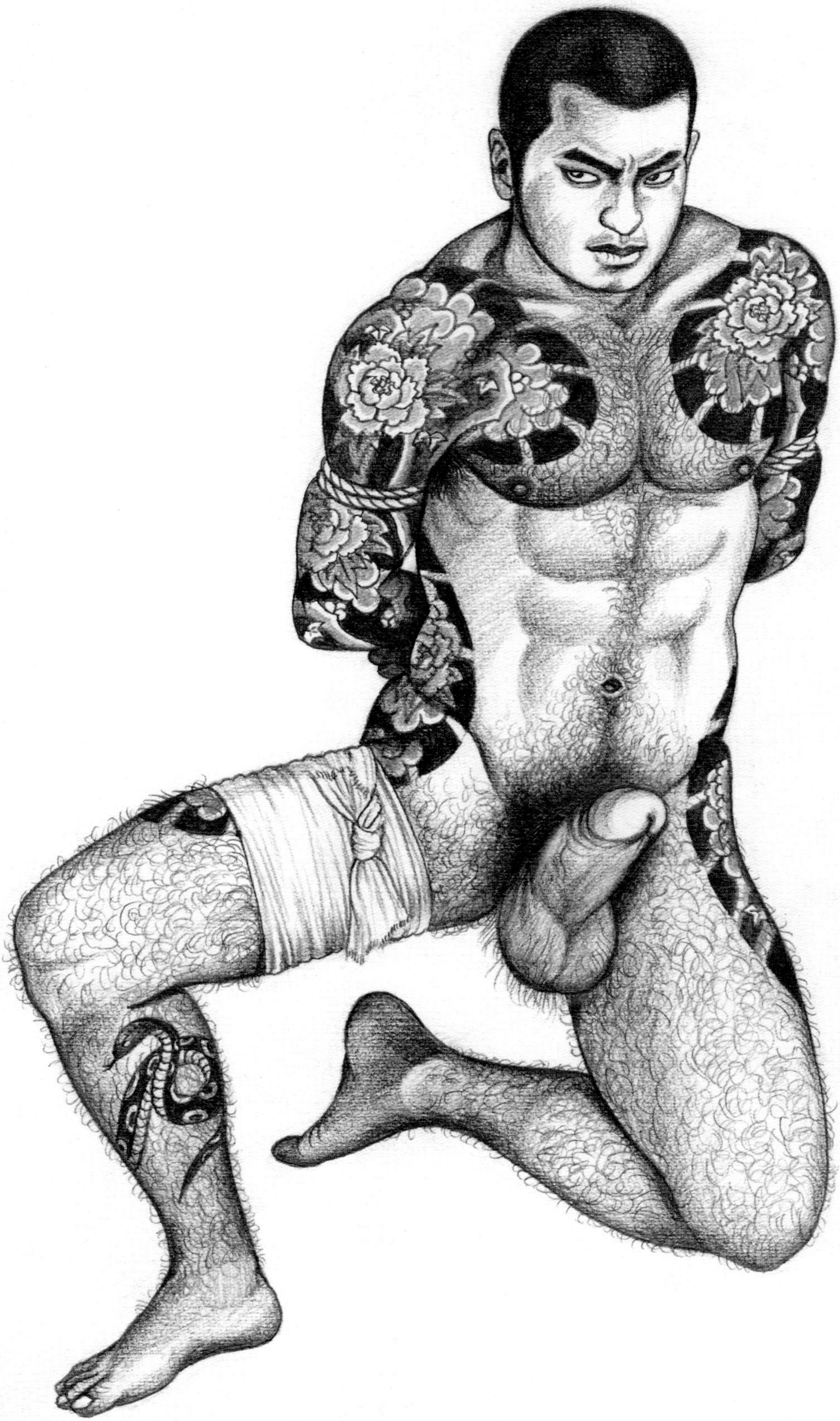

□ GOH MISHIMA

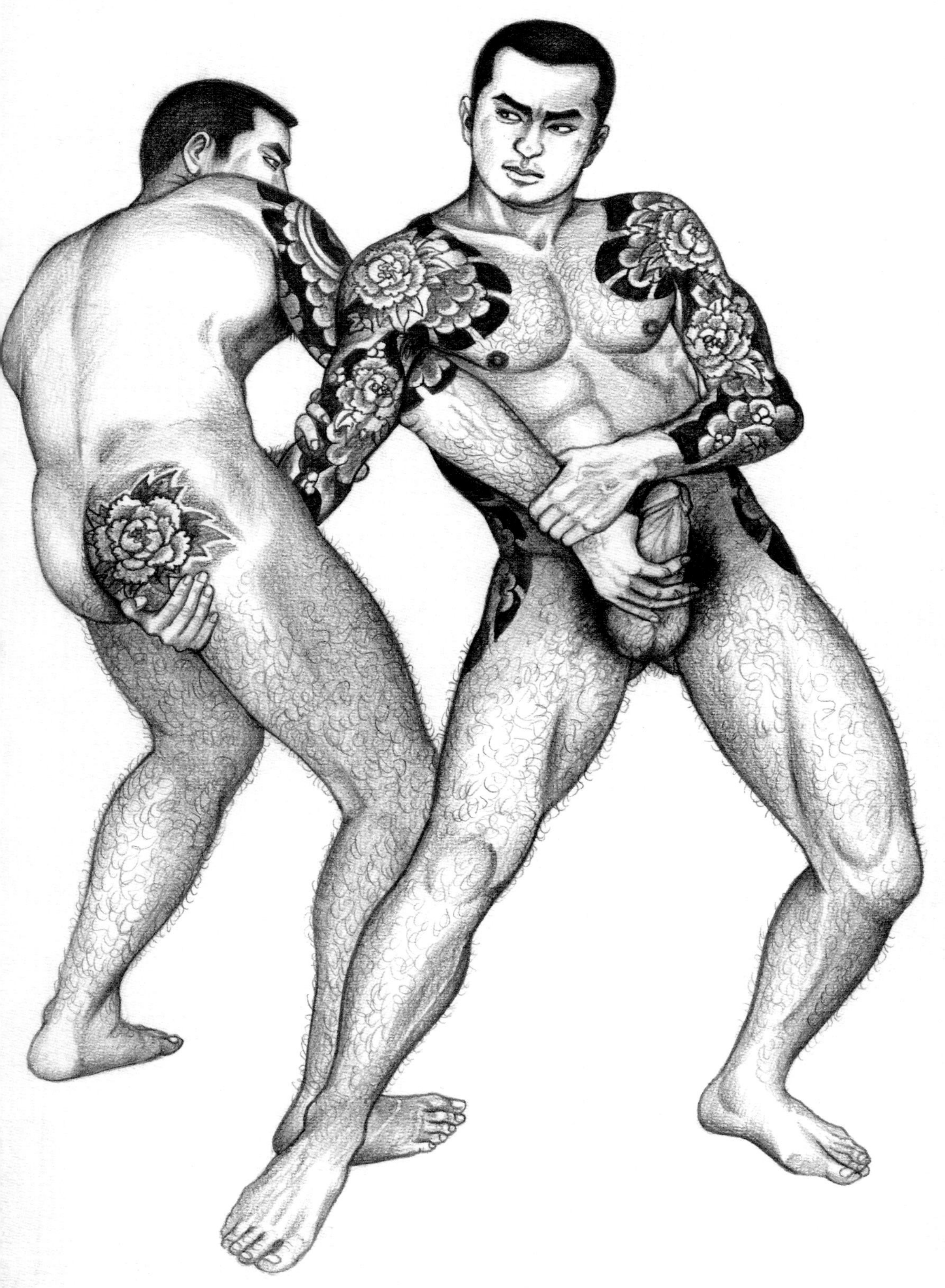
GOH MISHIMA

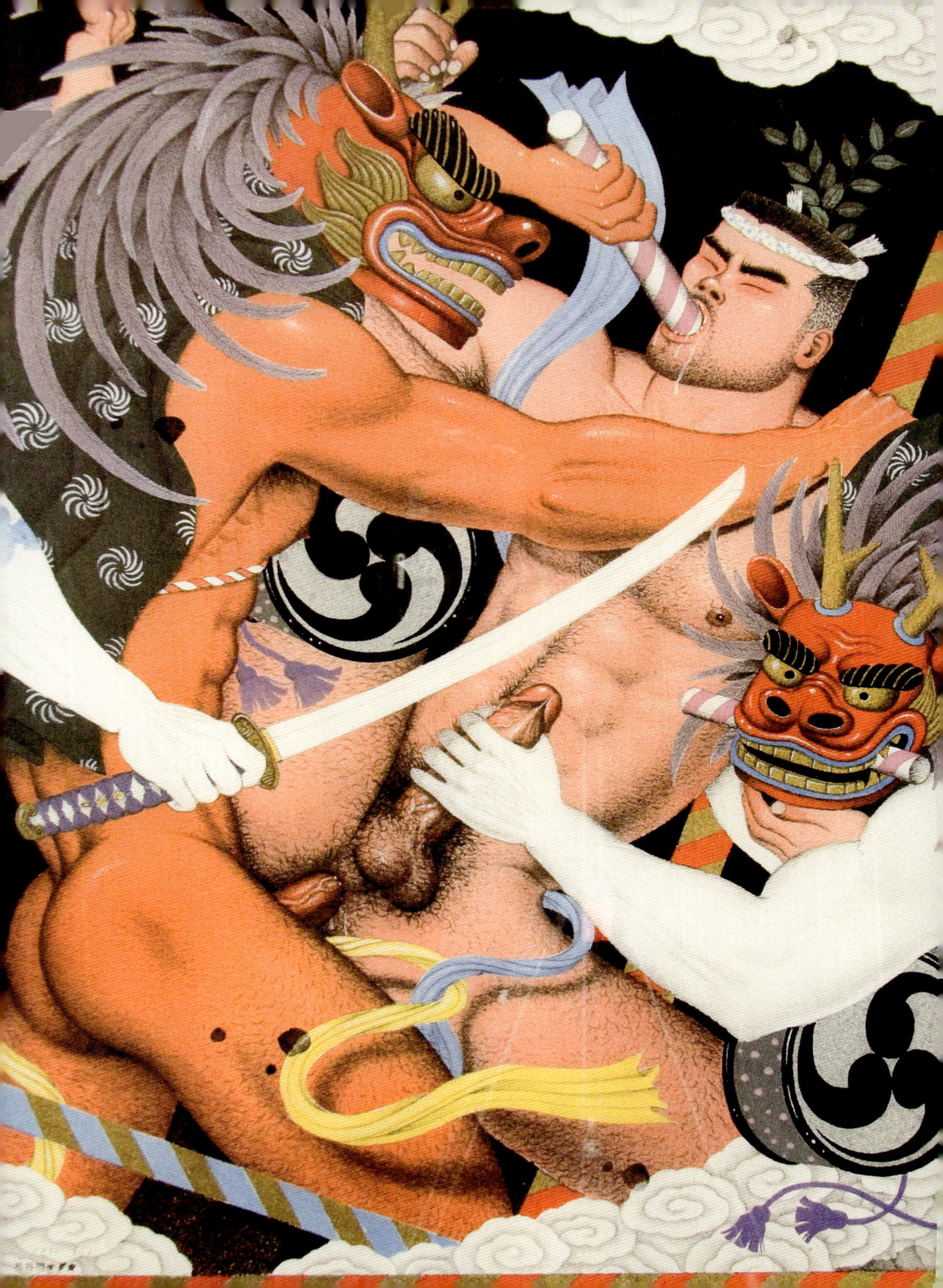

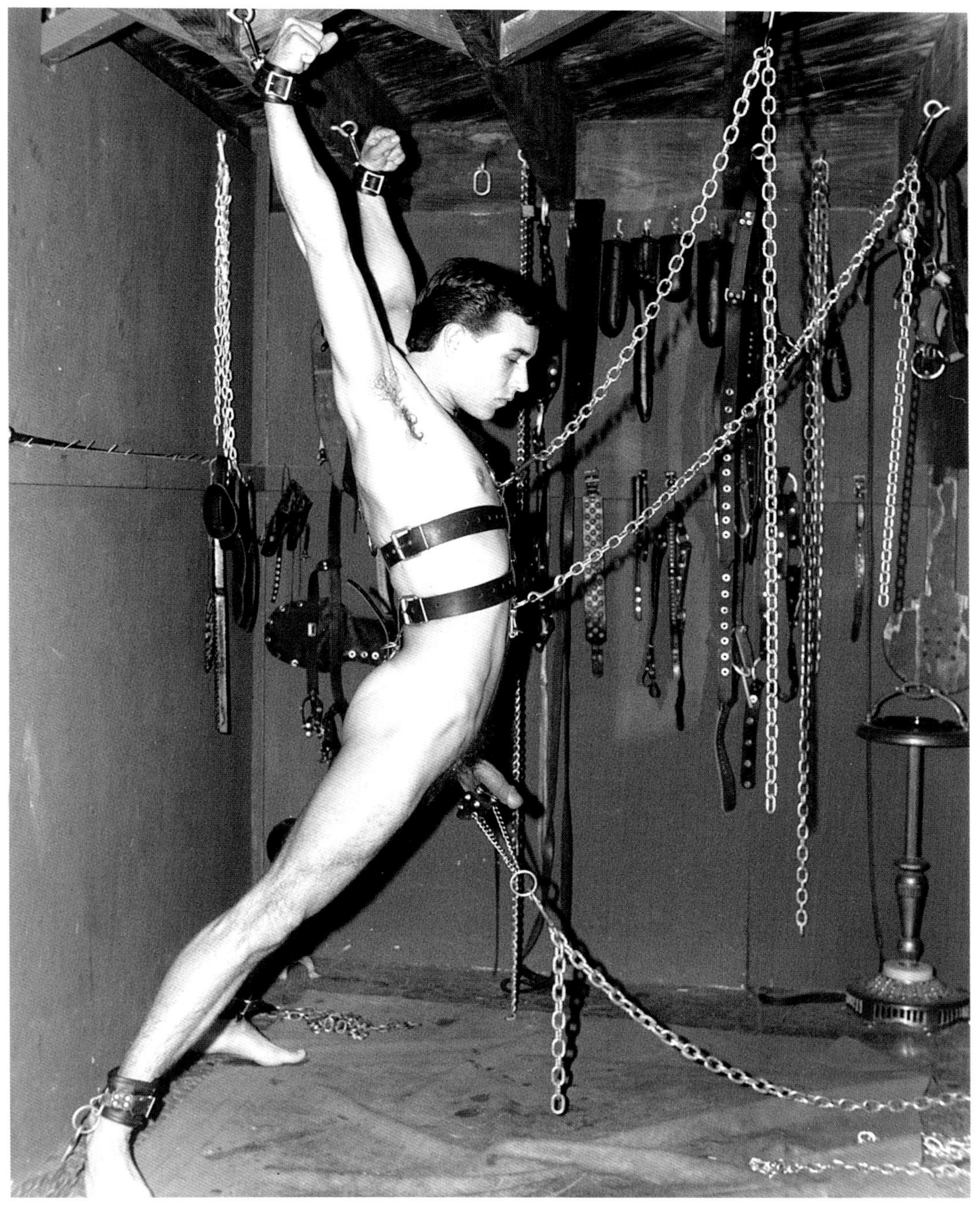

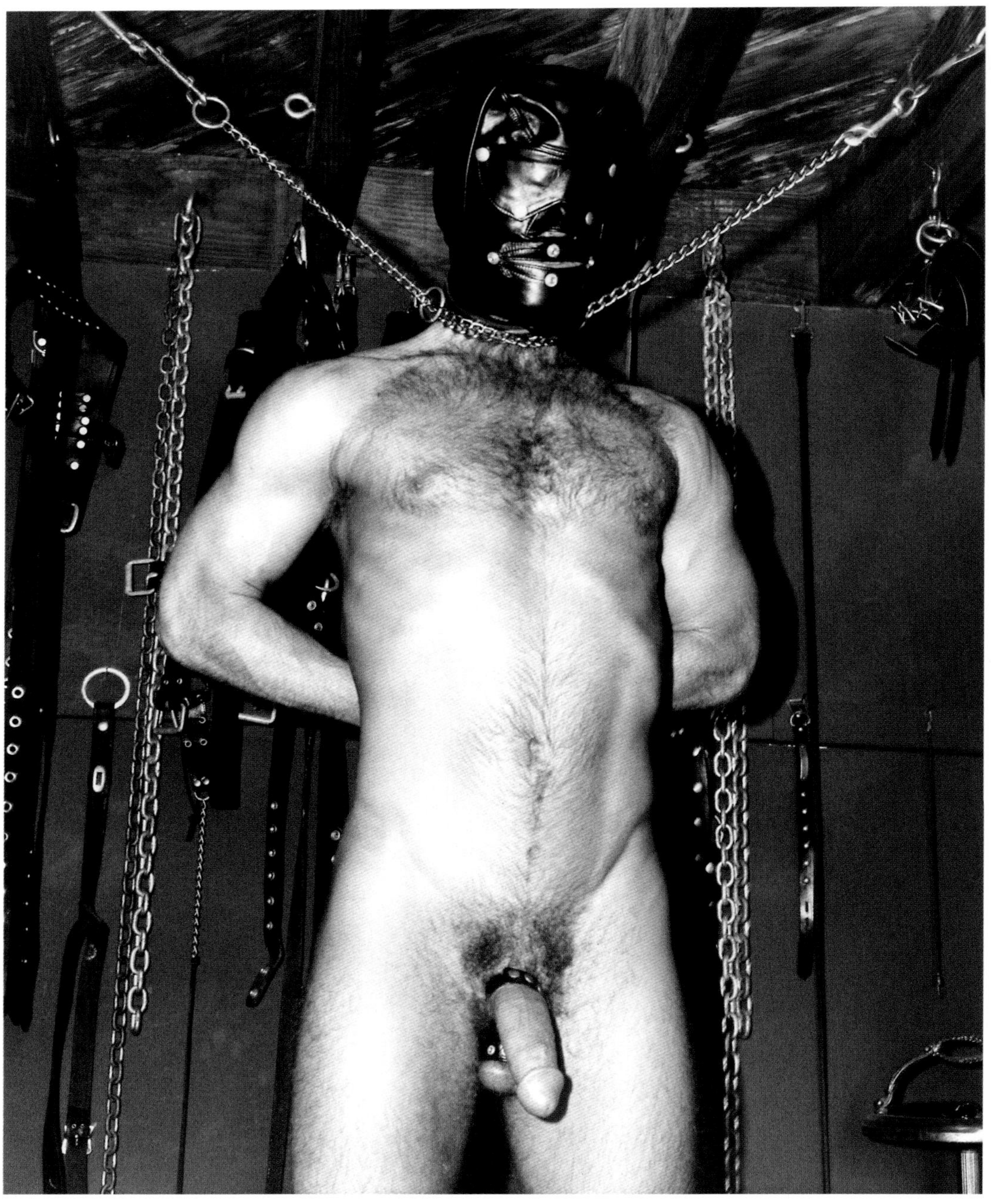

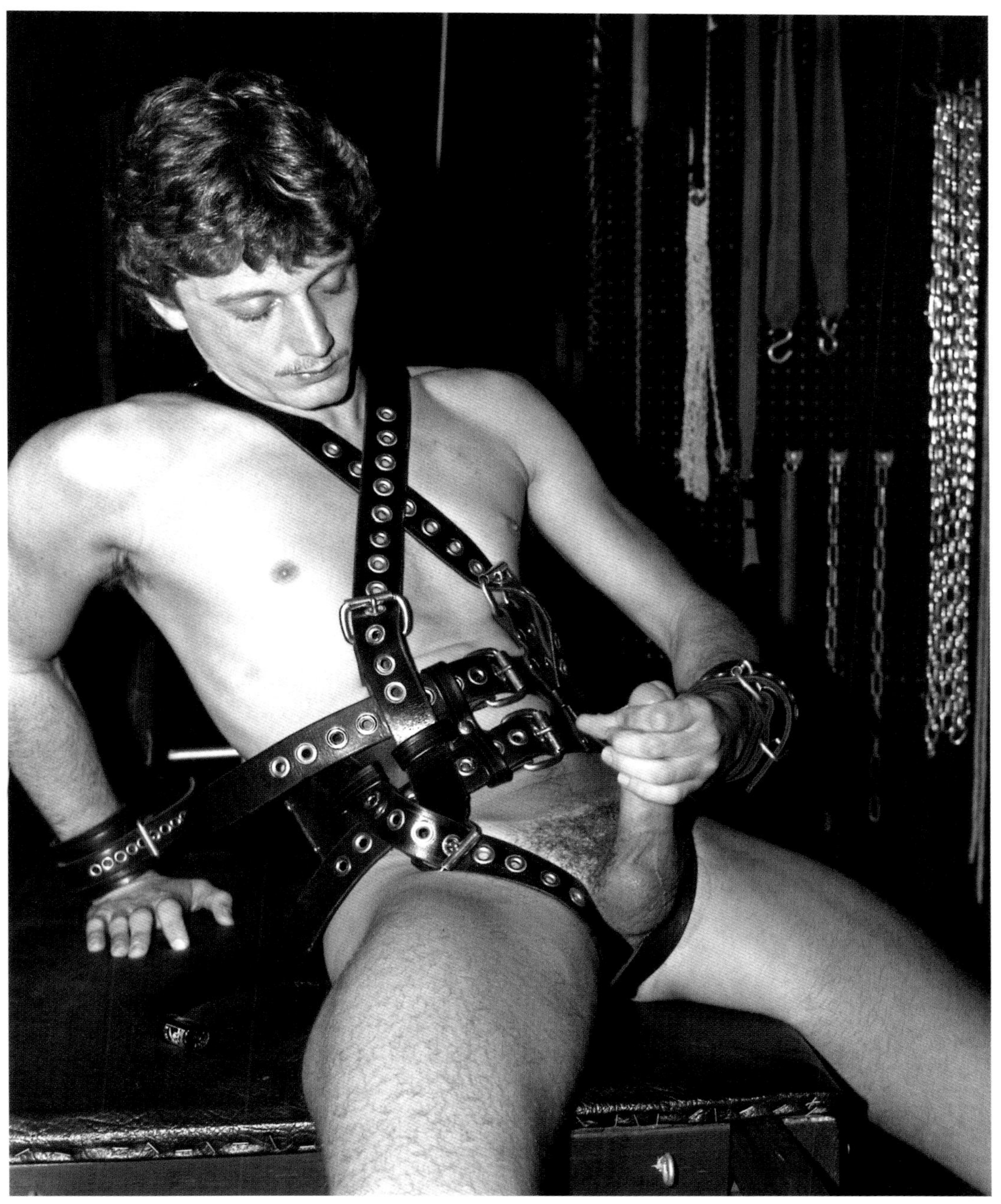

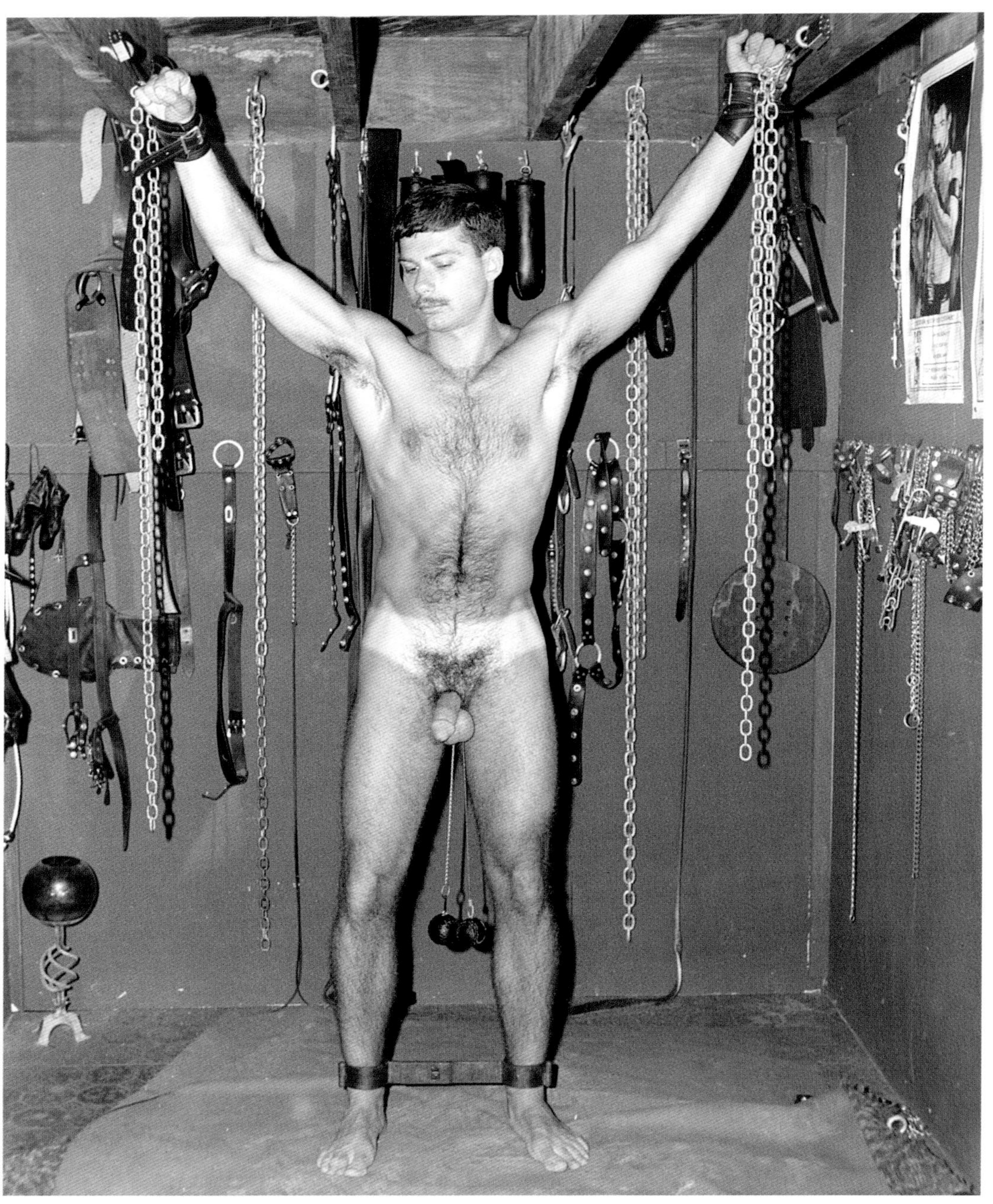

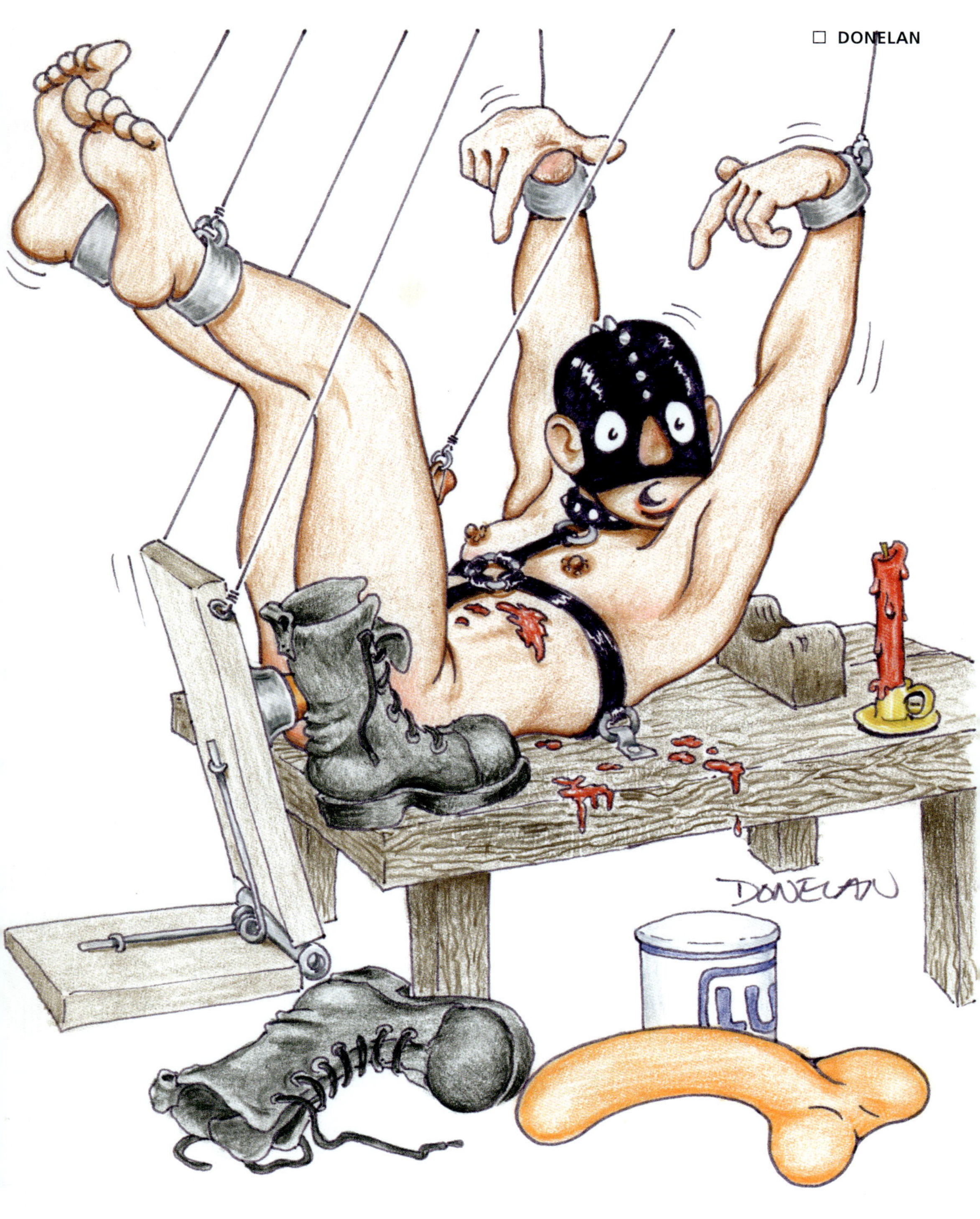

ROBERT! ROBERT! YOU CAN'T LEAVE ME LIKE THIS! ROBERT! YOU FORGOT THE TIT CLAMPS!

DAVID PARKE EPSTEIN
Beyond Narcissus on Sunset Boulevard

You & I, together hand-in-hand. We walk beyond the place where Hollywood Boulevard stops dead at the Vista movie theater. We walk down Sunset Boulevard at night. You say, "What can I get you?" I say, "Grapes." Even though all I eat is grapefruit lately. I shake inside & I worry that I've made the wrong choice. You'll be mad at me. I'll hear the knife in your voice cut another piece of me that falls to the sidewalk in front of Café Stella & I step on it. --- When did this start? When did I take you into my heart? --- We walk across Sanborn against-the-light. You say, "I'm going to Vons." I want to say, "But this isn't the best way to go." But I don't.

Instead, I walk across Sunset Boulevard to Circus of Books, where Giselle is behind the counter & I'm glad. I want to tell her about you. How I've taken you into my home & how beautiful your cock is. How I take it & how it breaks thru deep into my throat. How it slips thru a hole into my heart. How (one-at-a-time) I work three fingers up your ass, while I sing your favorite Rosemary Clooney song. --- "Come on-a my house, I'm gonna give you candy!" --- I sing Rosemary while my fingers tap out Prince & Sheena Easton lyrics on your *sugar walls.*
"Baby, cum!" I say.
"Daddy, come up here," you say.
"Whisper in my ear and use big words!"

Du & ich, zusammen Hand in Hand. Wir spazieren über den Hollywood Boulevard. Der endet am *Vista*-Kino, aber wir gehen weiter. Nachts schlendern wir den Sunset Boulevard hinab. „Was willst du?", sagst du. „Weintrauben", sage ich. Obwohl ich in letzter Zeit nur Grapefruit esse. Mir wird schwindelig und ich mache mir Sorgen, dass ich die falsche Wahl getroffen habe. Du wirst sauer auf mich sein. Ich höre das Messer in deiner Stimme ein weiteres Stück von mir abschneiden, es fällt auf den Bürgersteig vor dem Café Stella; ich trete darauf. – Wann hat das angefangen? Wann habe ich dich in mein Herz gelassen? – Wir gehen bei Rot über die Sanborn Avenue. Du sagst: „Ich gehe zu Vons." Ich will sagen: „Aber das ist ein Umweg." Doch ich tue es nicht.

Stattdessen laufe ich über den Sunset Boulevard zum Circus of Books, wo Giselle hinter dem Tresen steht. Ich bin froh. Ich möchte ihr von dir erzählen. Wie ich dich mit zu mir nach Hause genommen habe und wie schön dein Schwanz ist. Wie ich ihn verschlinge und wie tief er in meine Kehle stößt. Wie er durch ein Loch in mein Herz rutscht. Wie ich nacheinander drei Finger in deinen Arsch stecke und dabei deinen Lieblingssong von Rosemary Clooney singe. – „Come on-a my house, I'm gonna give you candy!" – Ich singe Rosemary, während meine Finger Prince- & Sheena Easton-Texte auf deine *sugar walls* klopfen.
„Komm, Baby!", sage ich.
„Komm hoch, Daddy", sagst du. „Flüster mir große Worte ins Ohr!"

Übersetzung: Florian Rogge

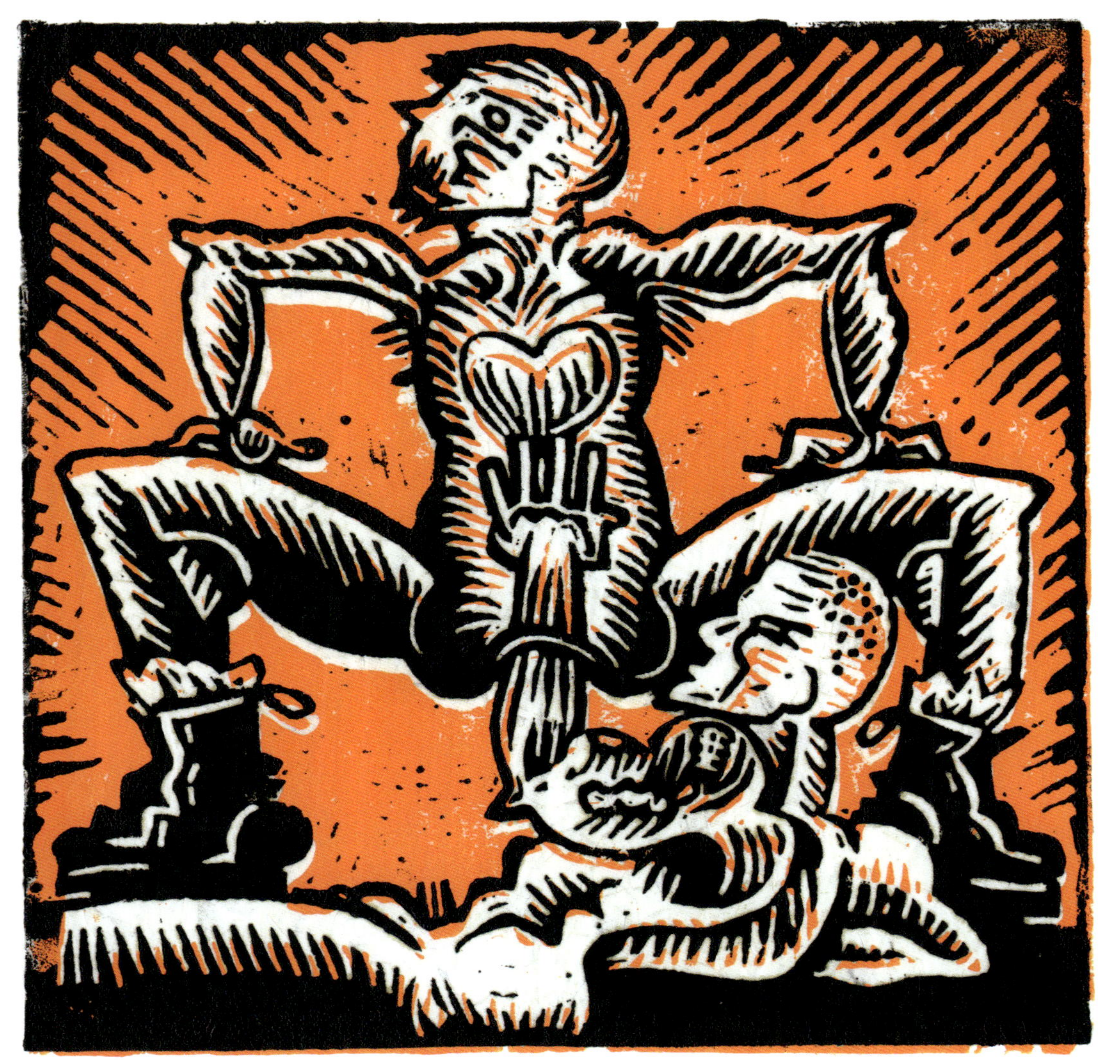

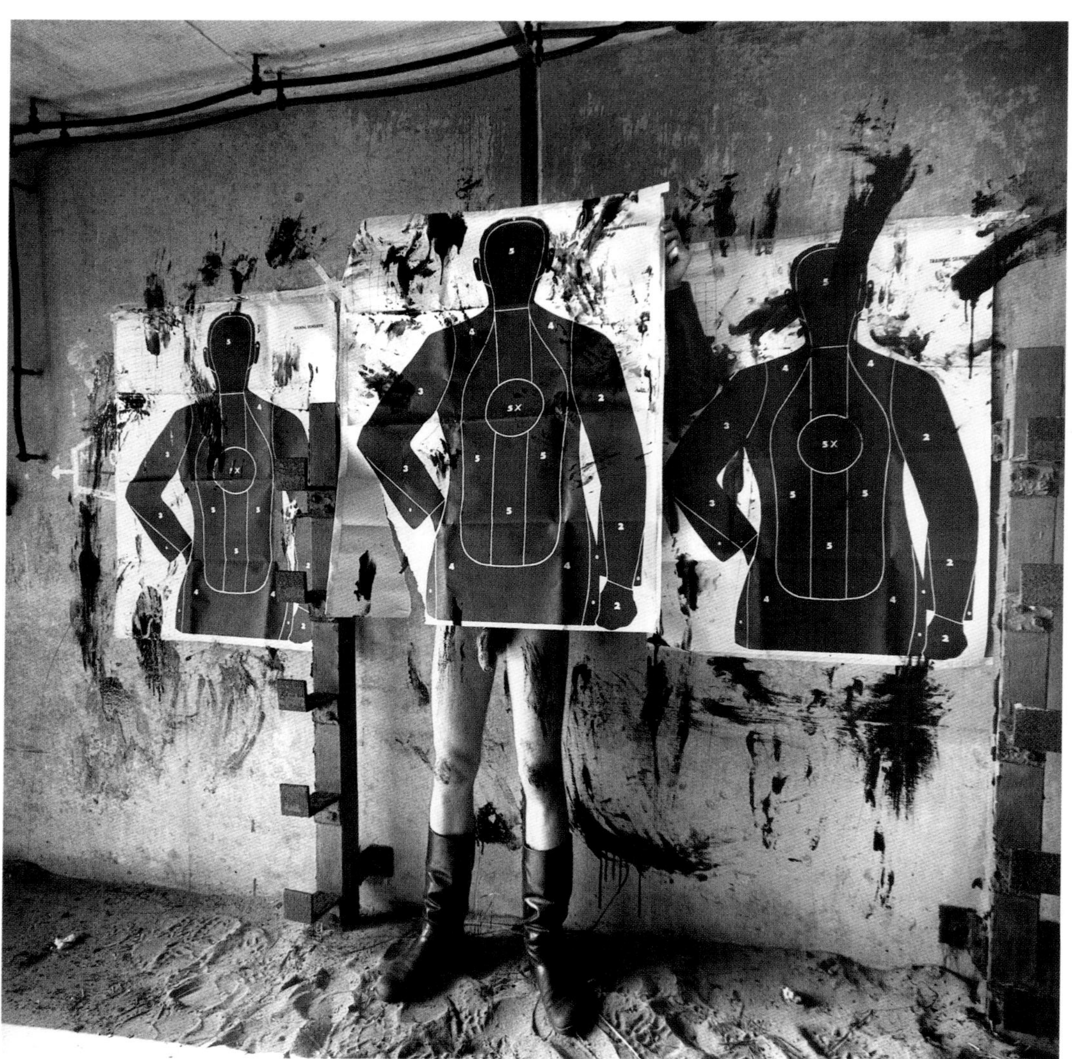

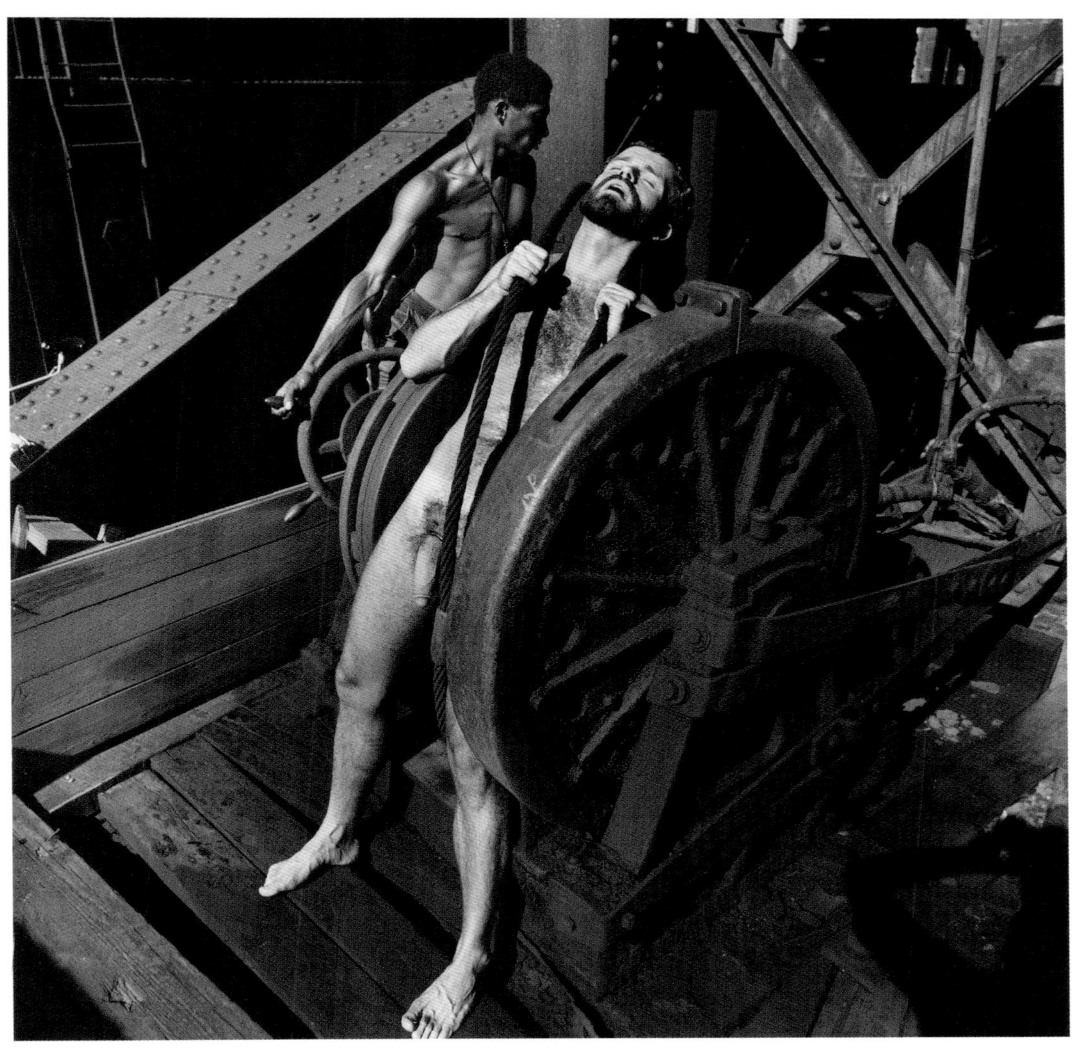

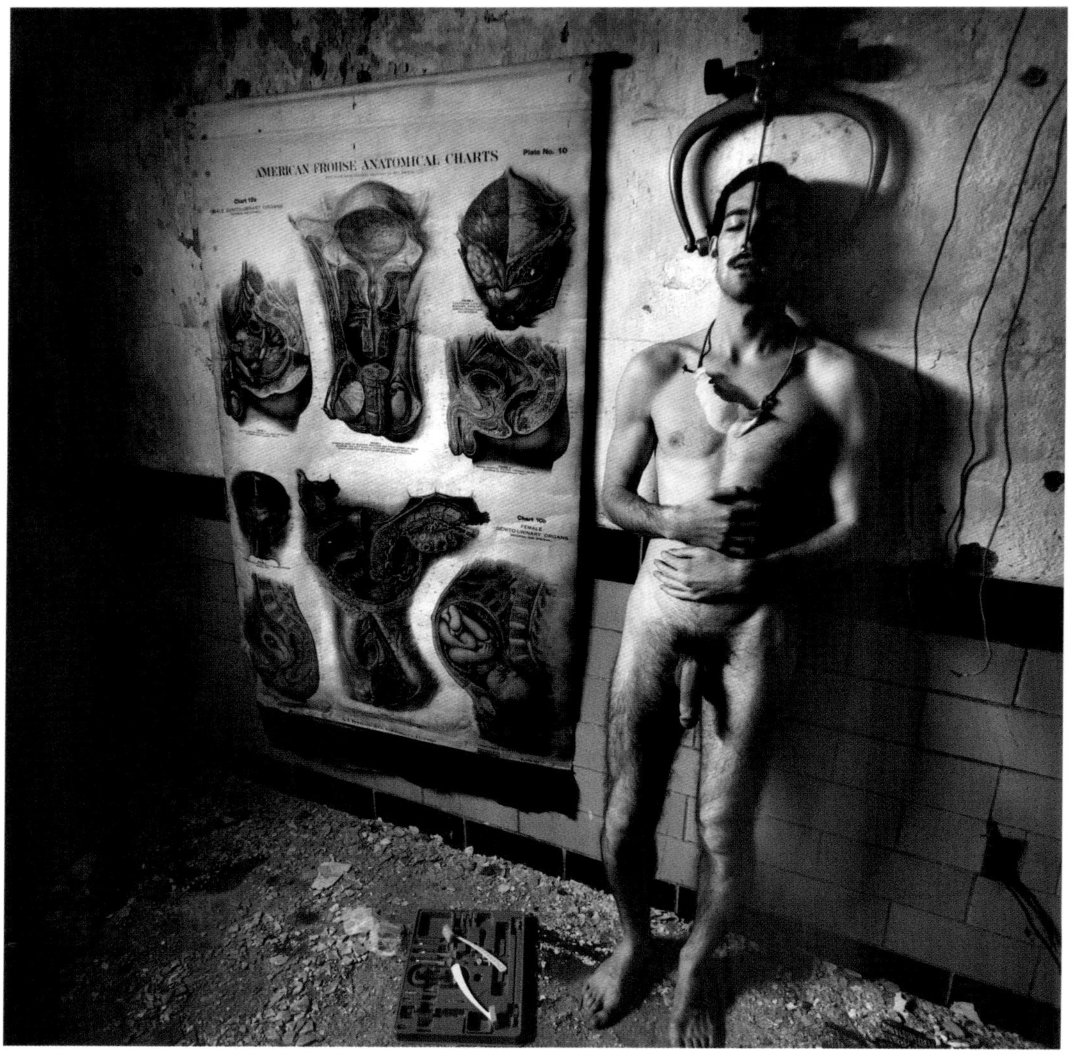

AMERICAN FROHSE ANATOMICAL CHARTS Plate No. 10

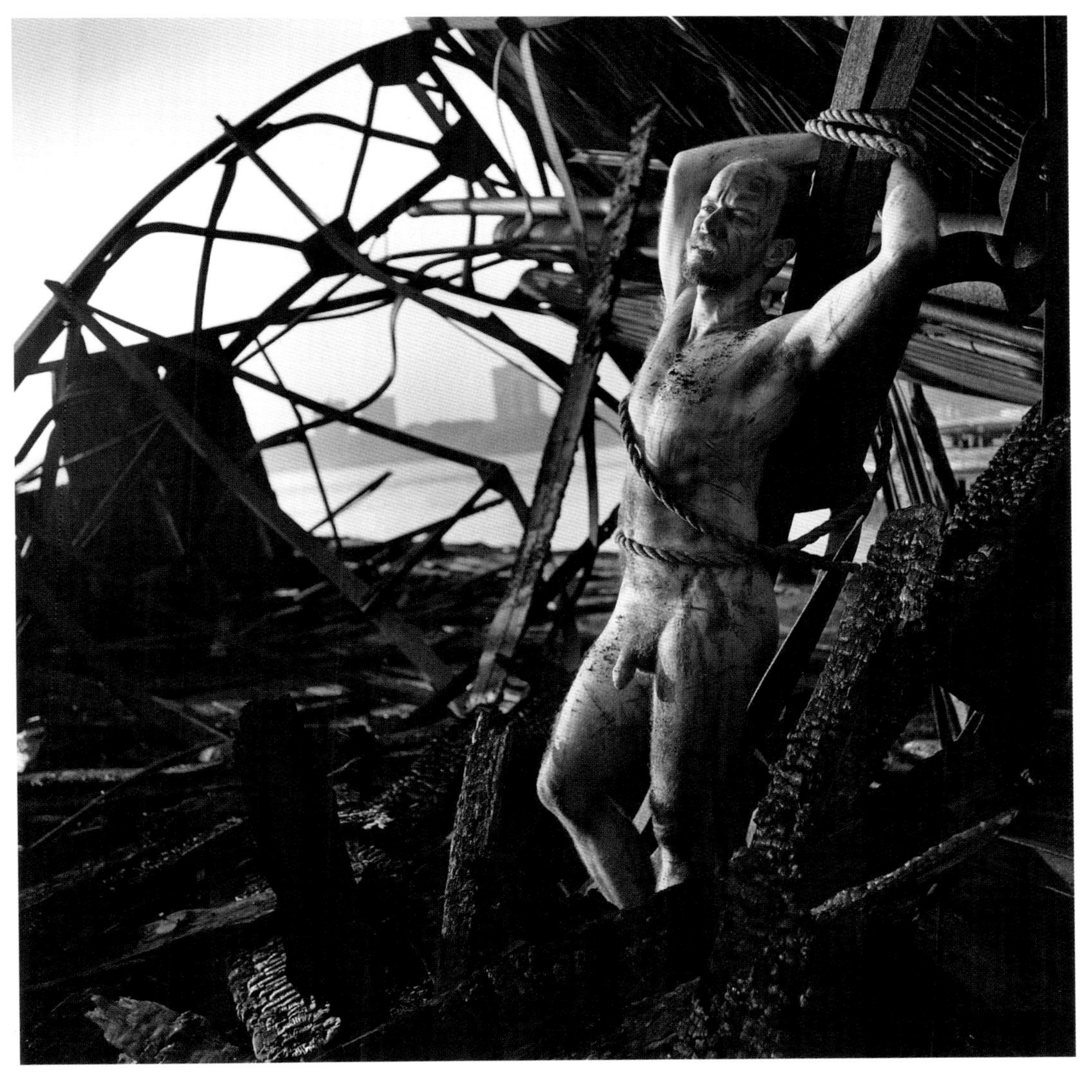

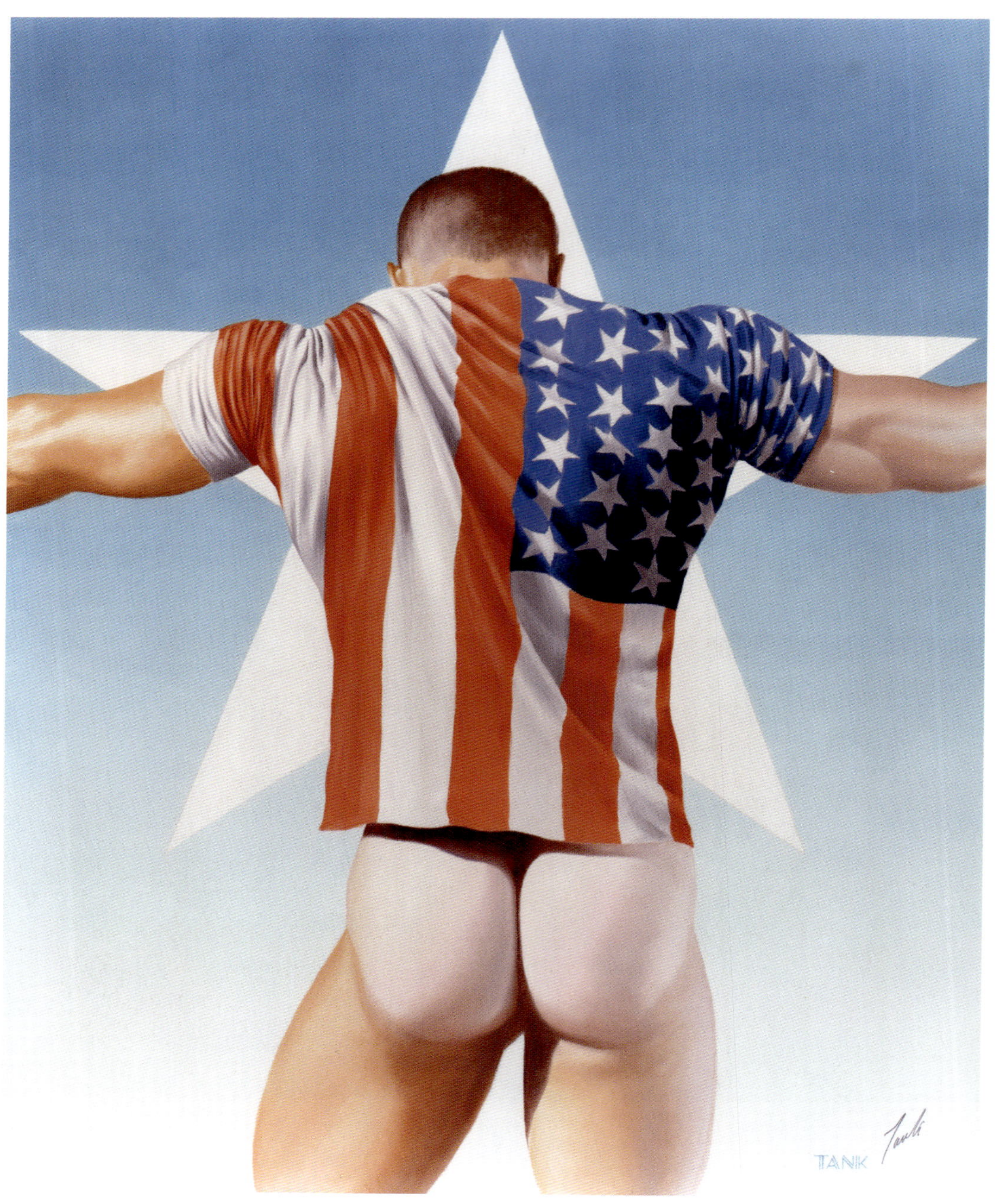
TANK

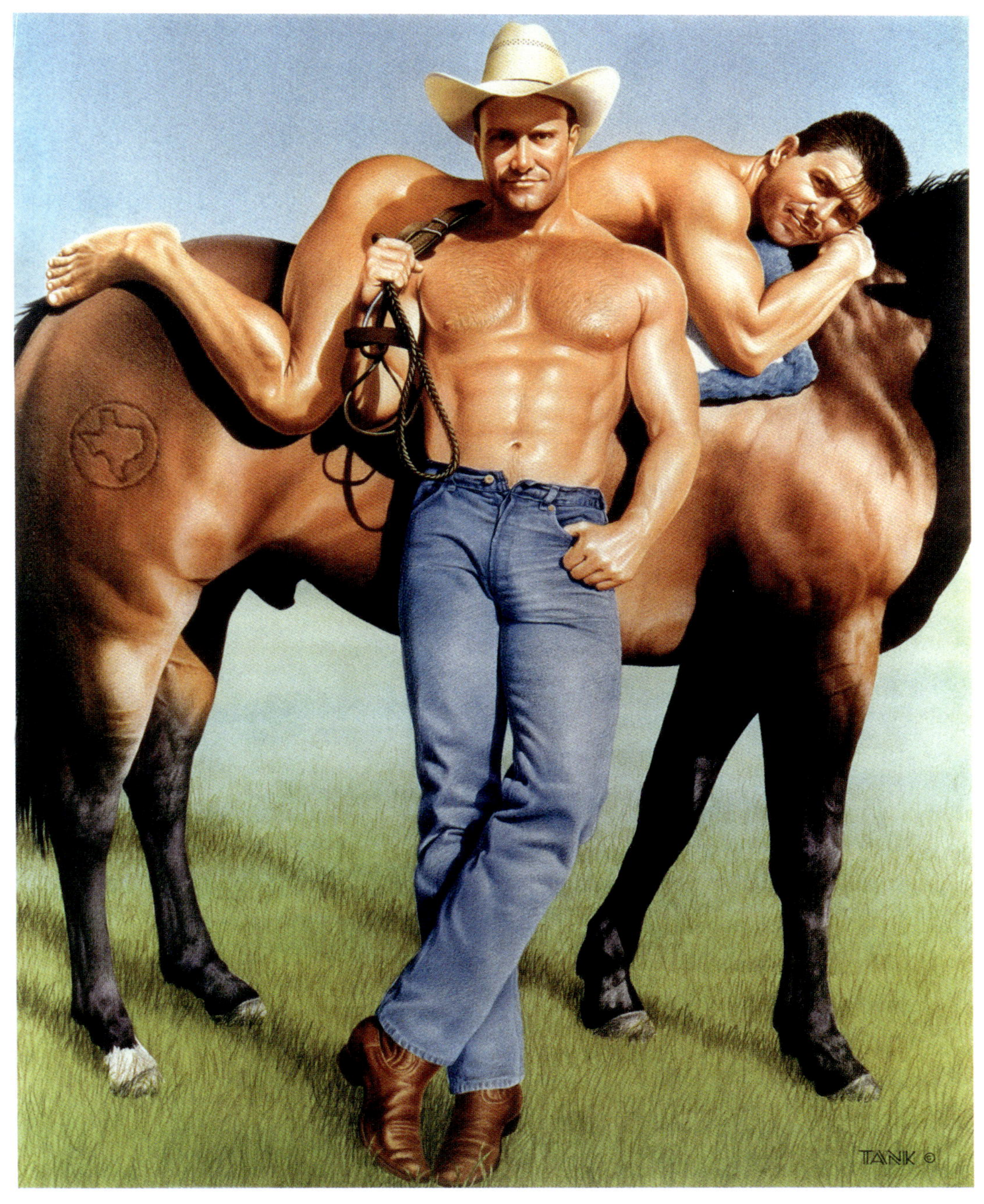
TANK ®

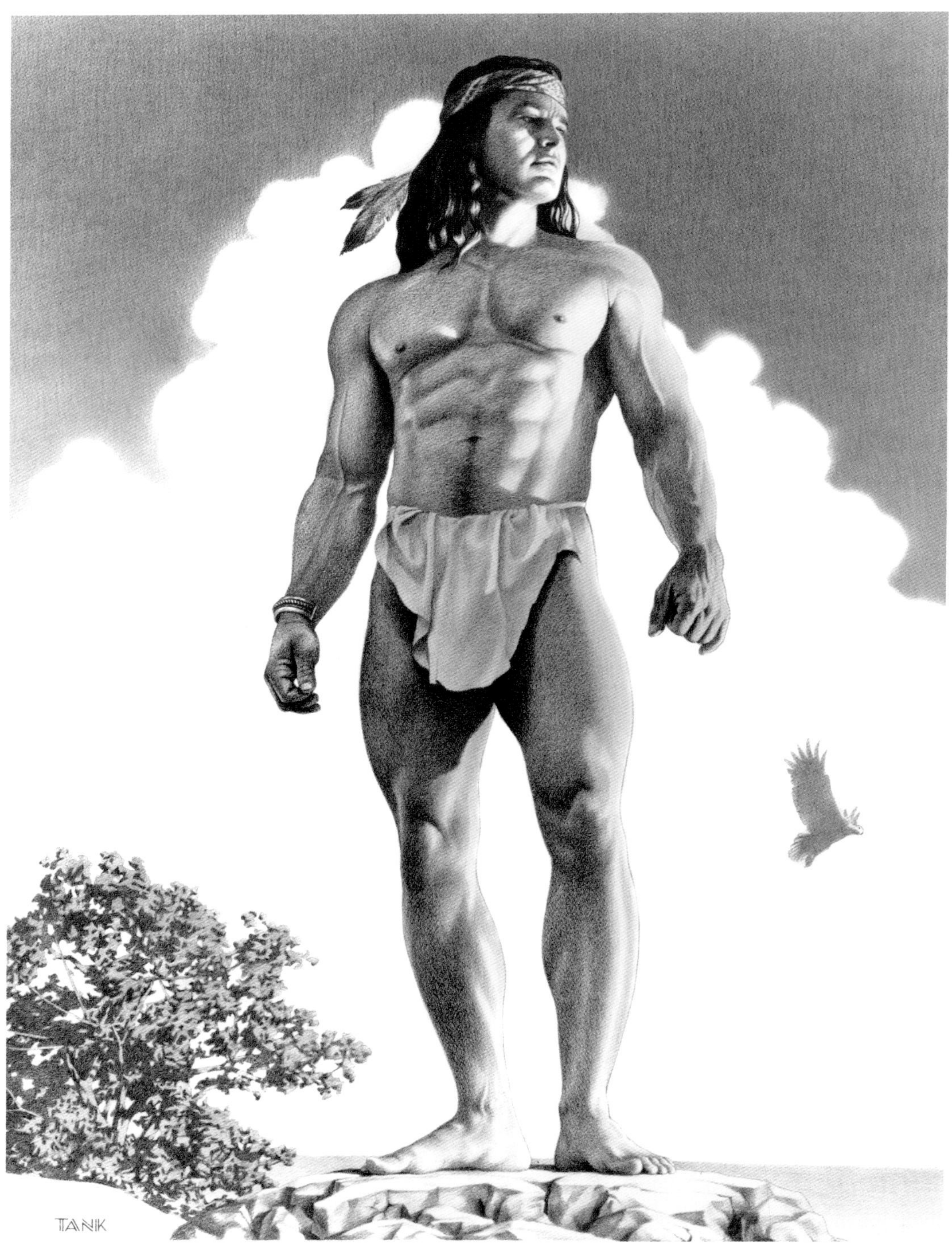

TANK

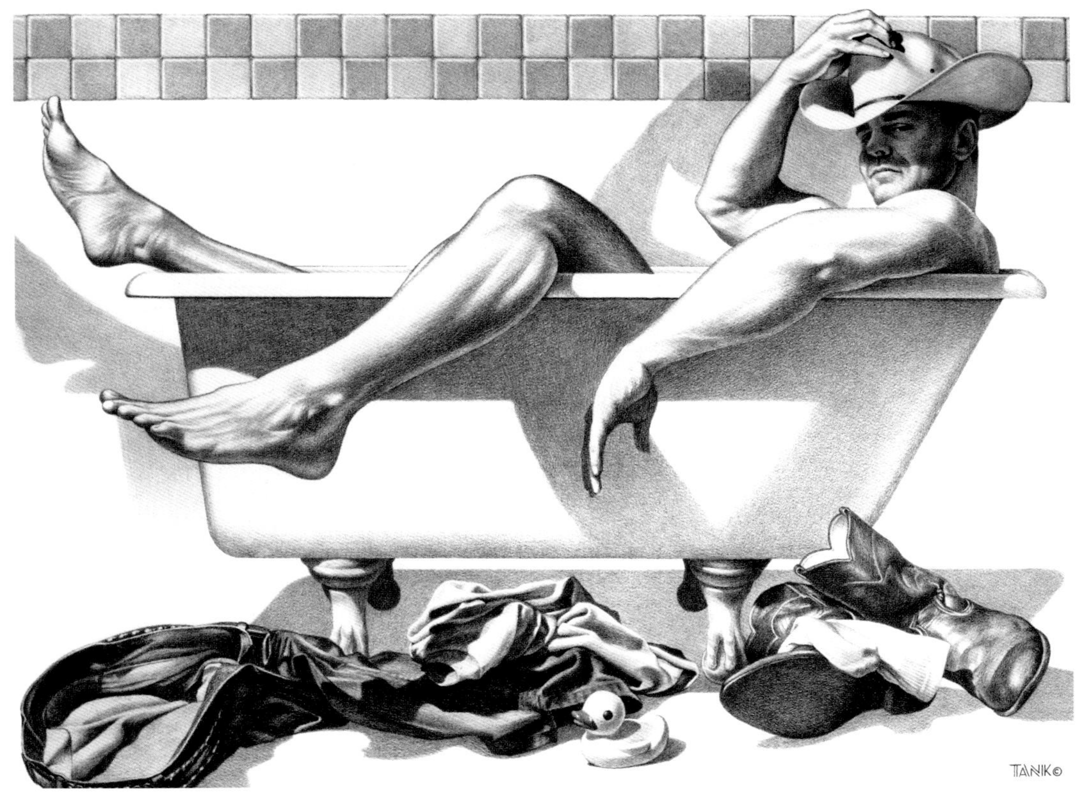

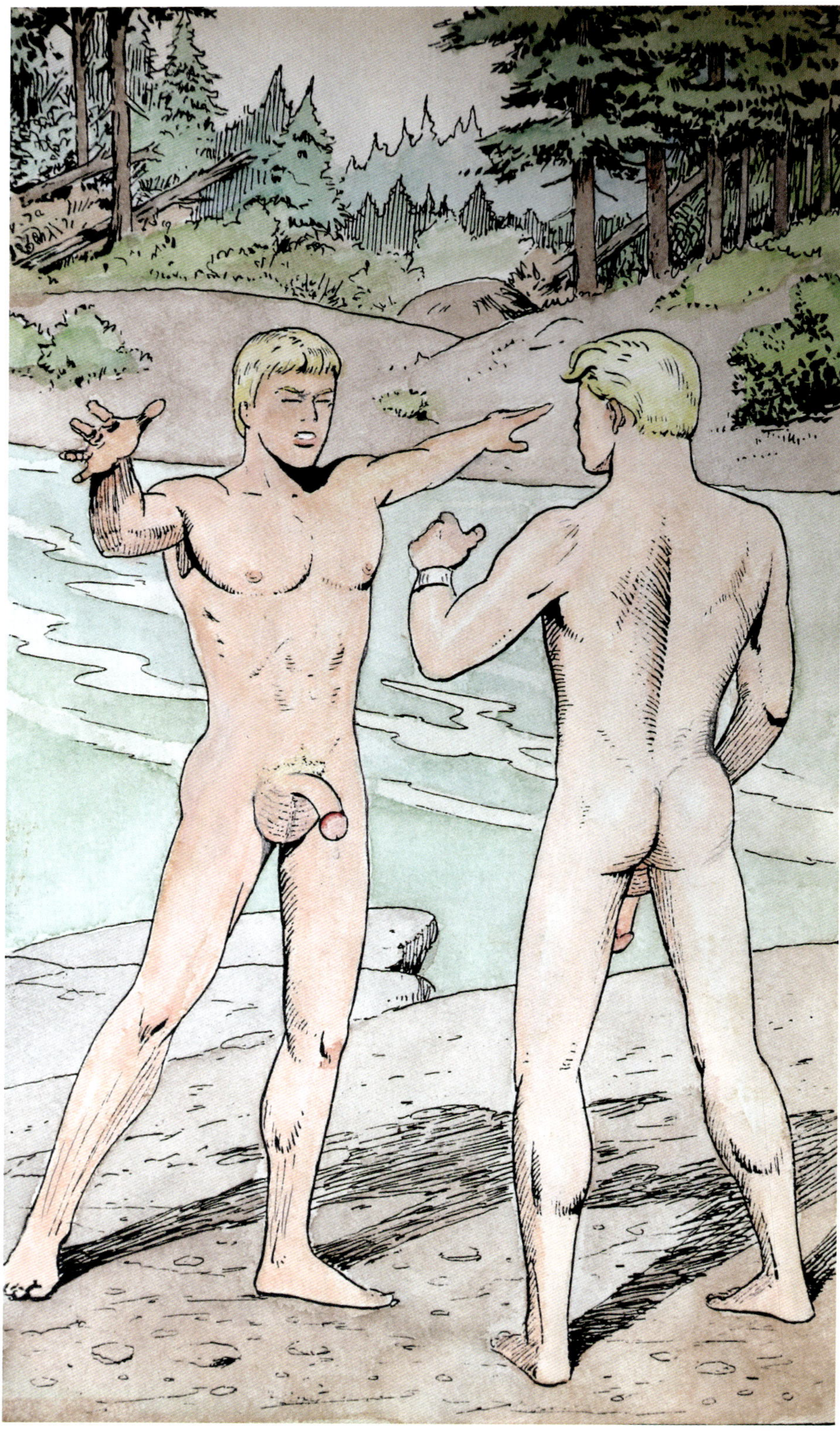

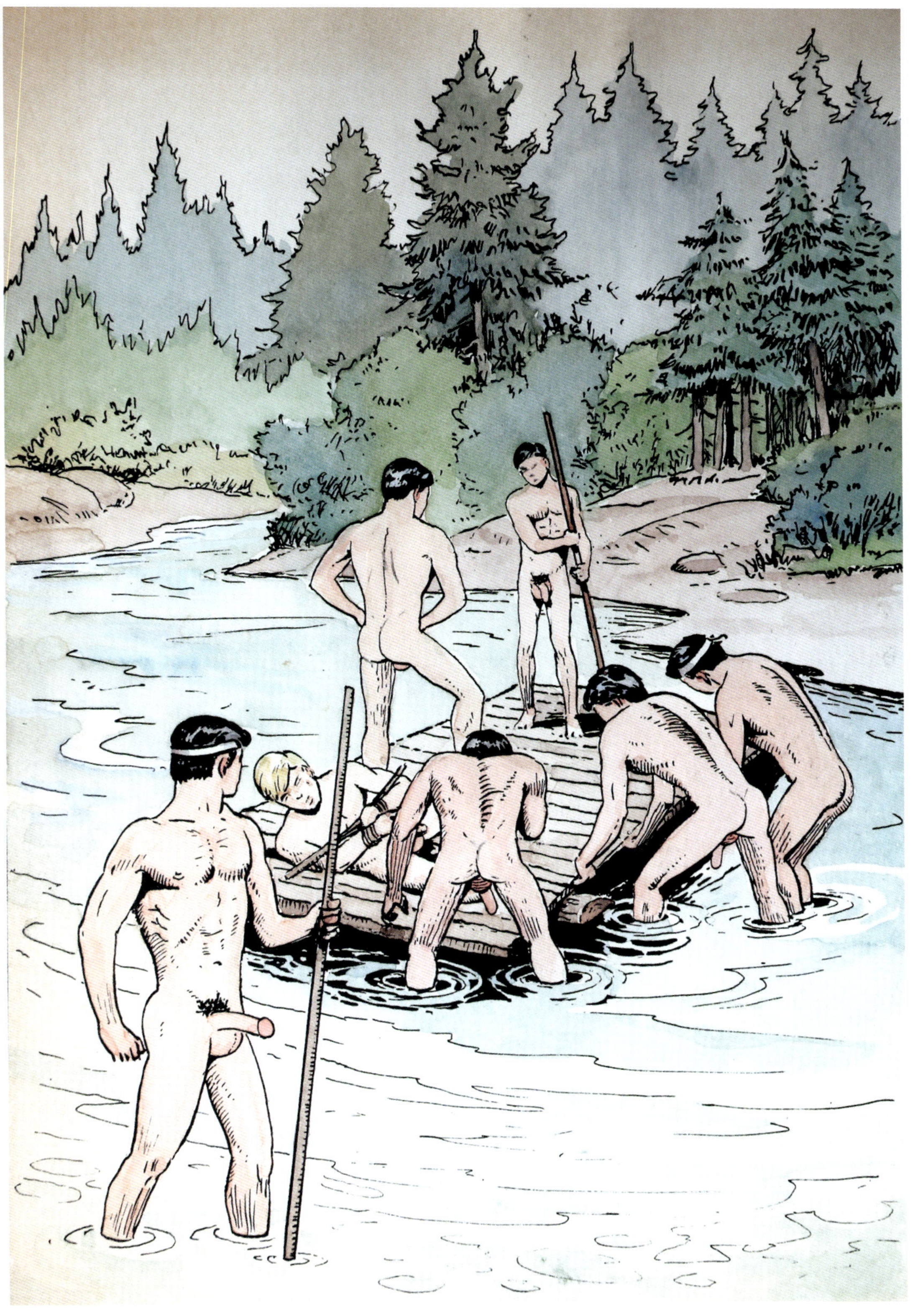

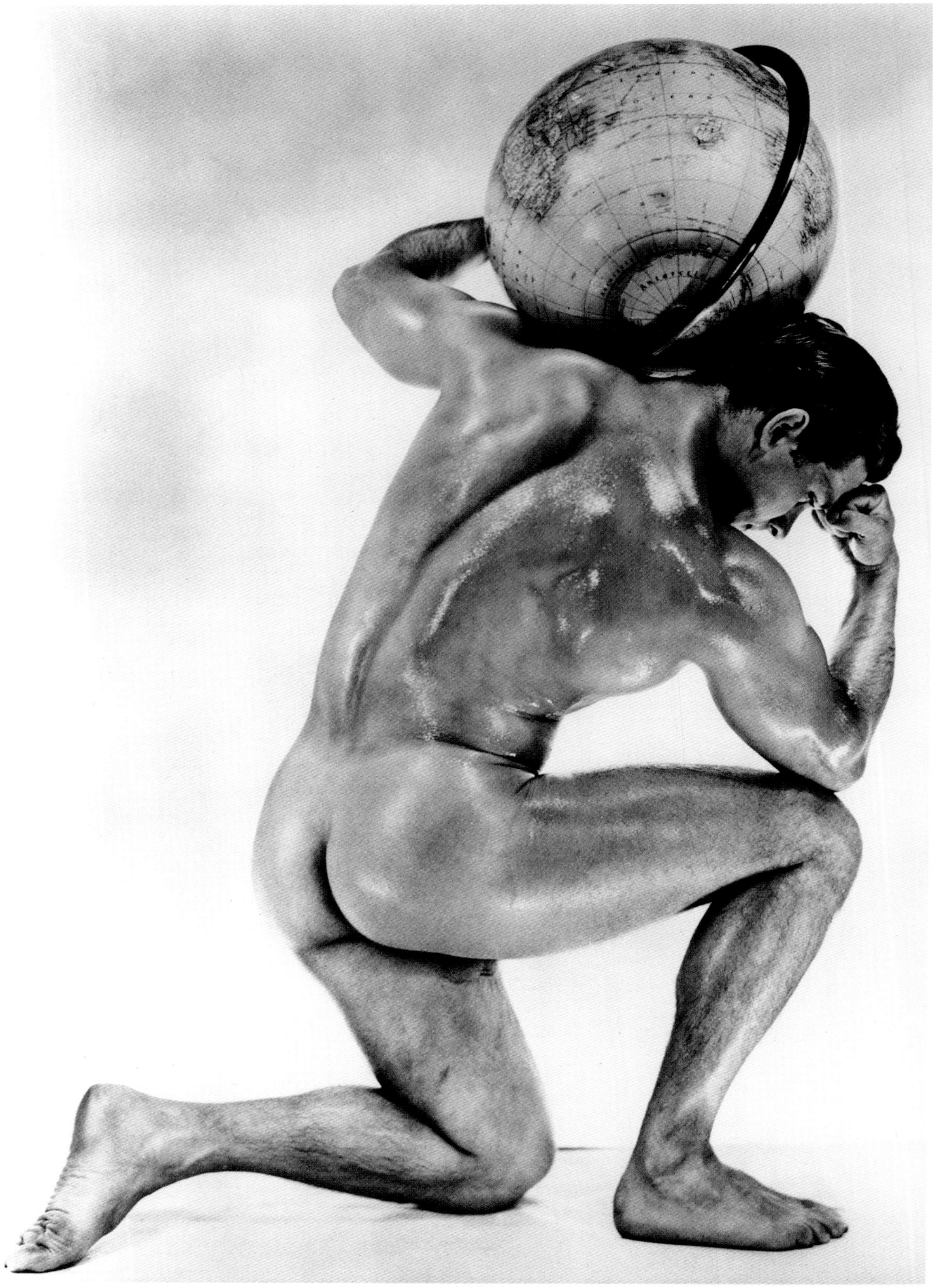

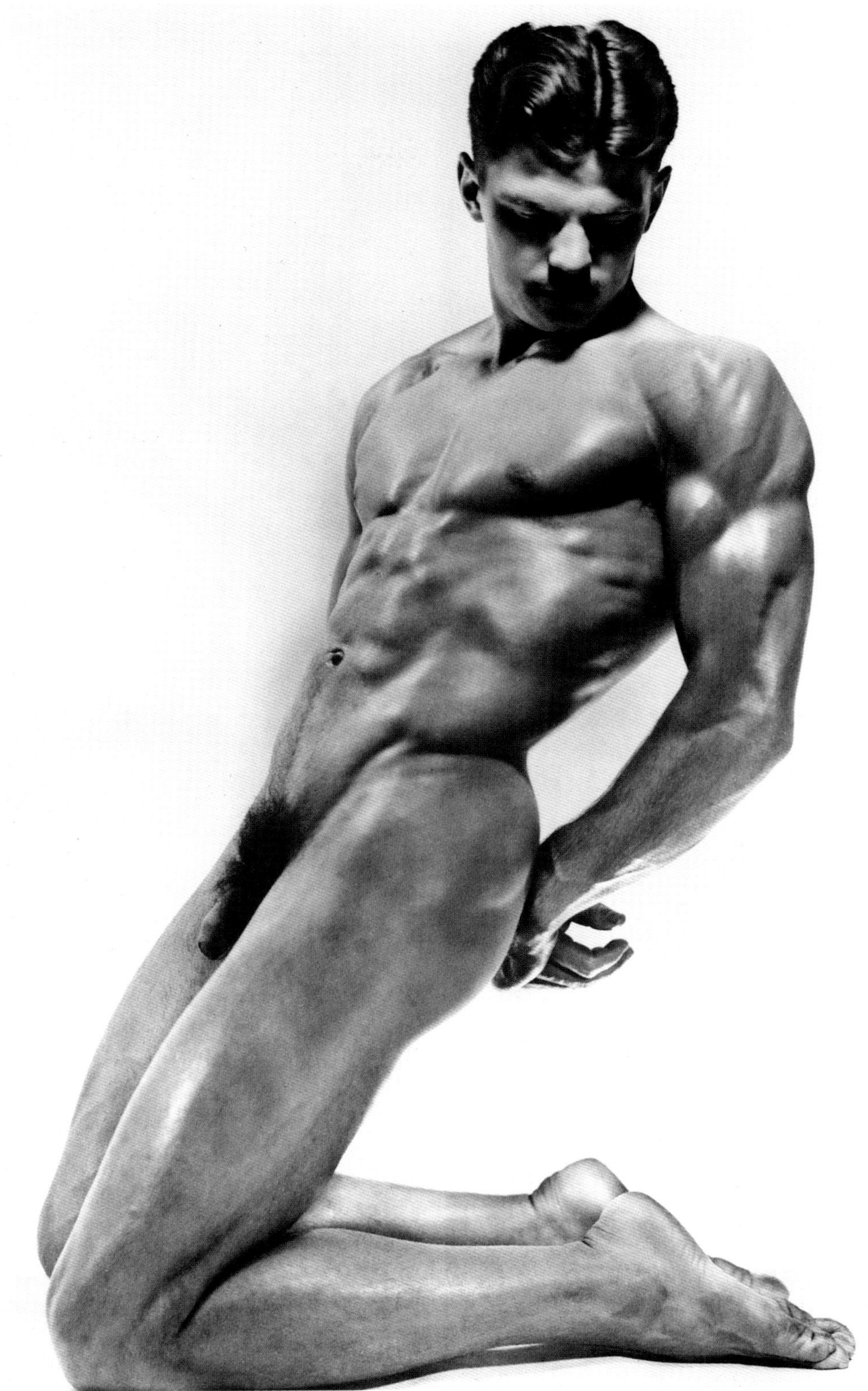

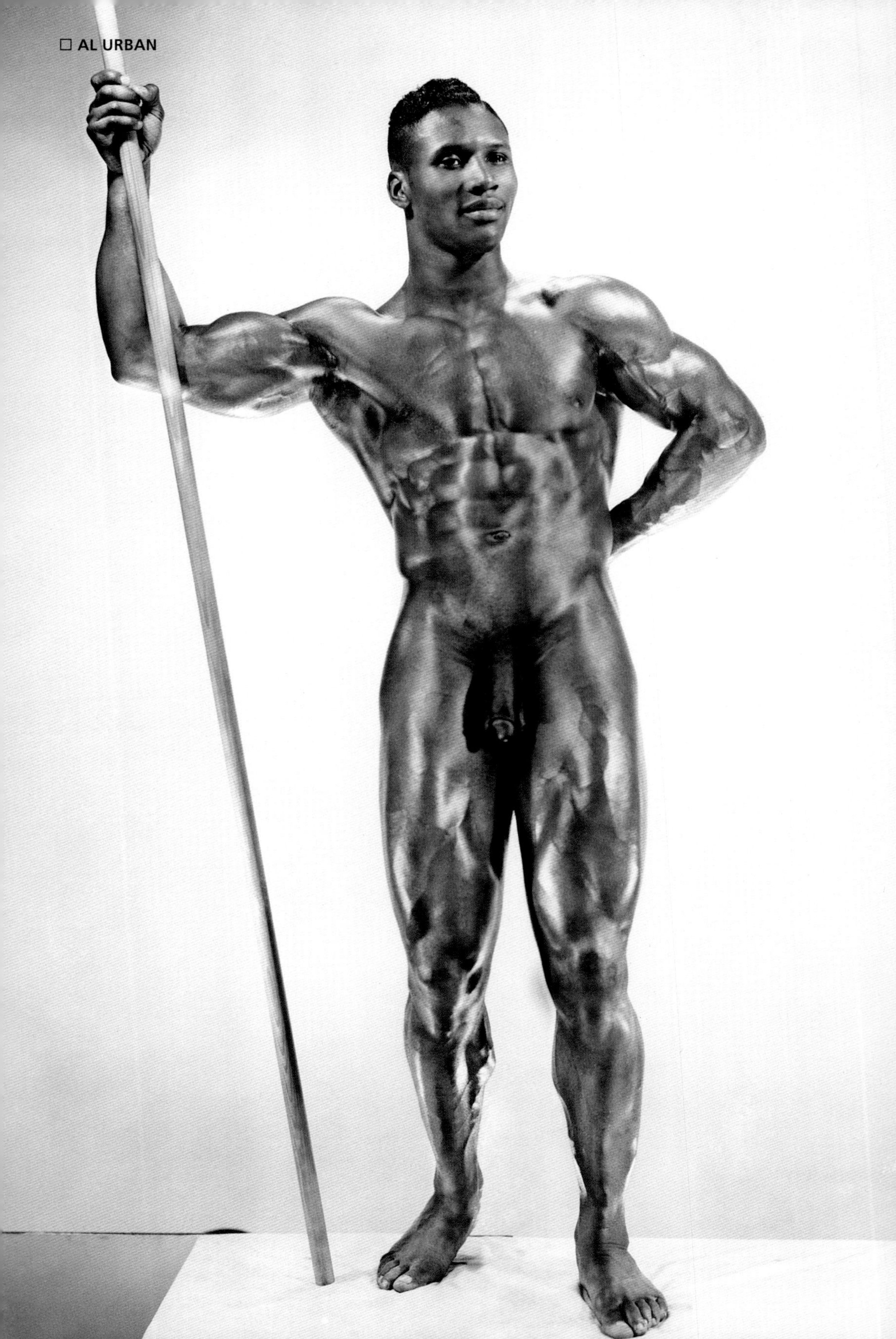

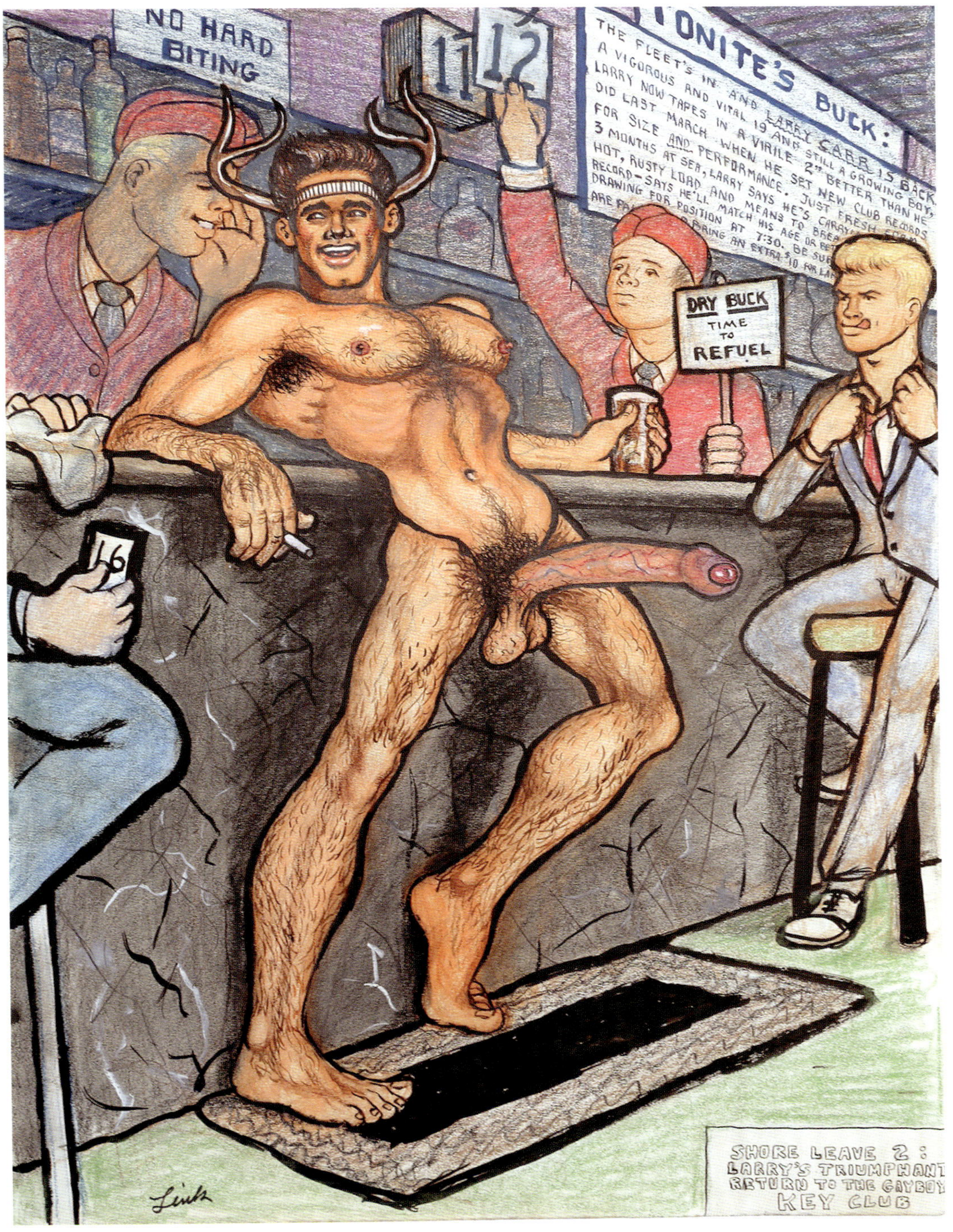
NO HARD BITING
11 12
ONITE'S BUCK:
THE FLEET'S IN AND LARRY CARR IS BACK.
A VIGOROUS AND VITAL 19 AND STILL A GROWING BOY,
LARRY NOW TAPES IN A VIRILE 2" BETTER THAN HE
DID LAST MARCH WHEN HE SET NEW CLUB RECORDS
FOR SIZE AND PERFORMANCE. JUST FRESH FROM
3 MONTHS AT SEA, LARRY SAYS HE'S CARRYING A
HOT, RUSTY LOAD, AND MEANS TO BREAK HIS OWN
RECORD—SAYS HE'LL MATCH HIS AGE OR RETIRE.
DRAWING FOR POSITION AT 7:30. BE SURE TO
BRING AN EXTRA $10 FOR LAST
ARE FA
DRY BUCK
TIME
TO
REFUEL
16
Link
SHORE LEAVE 2:
LARRY'S TRIUMPHANT
RETURN TO THE GAYBOY
KEY CLUB

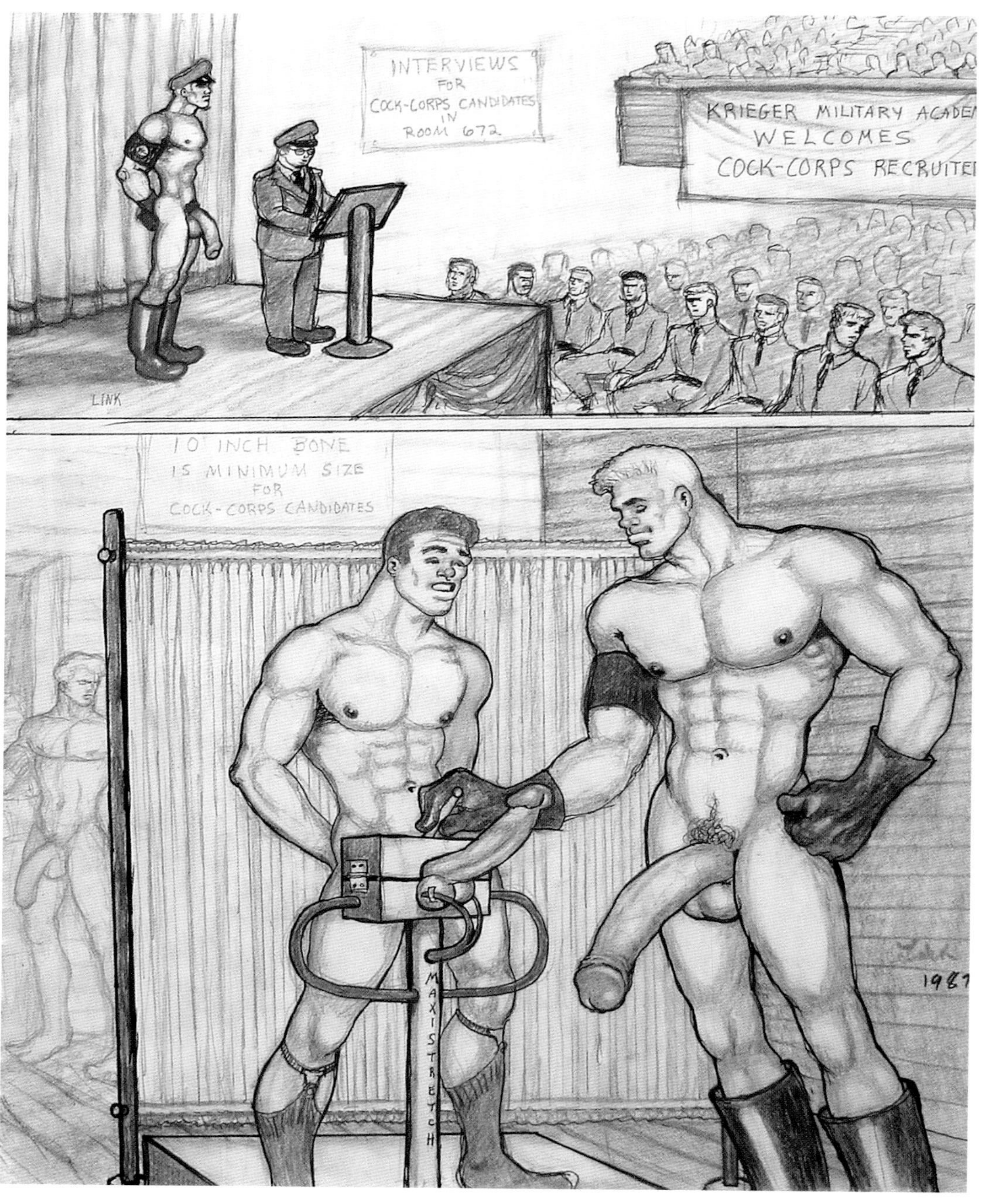
INTERVIEWS
FOR
COCK-CORPS CANDIDATES
IN
ROOM 672
KRIEGER MILITARY ACADEM
WELCOMES
COCK-CORPS RECRUITE
LINK
10 INCH BONE
IS MINIMUM SIZE
FOR
COCK-CORPS CANDIDATES
MAXI STRETCH
1987

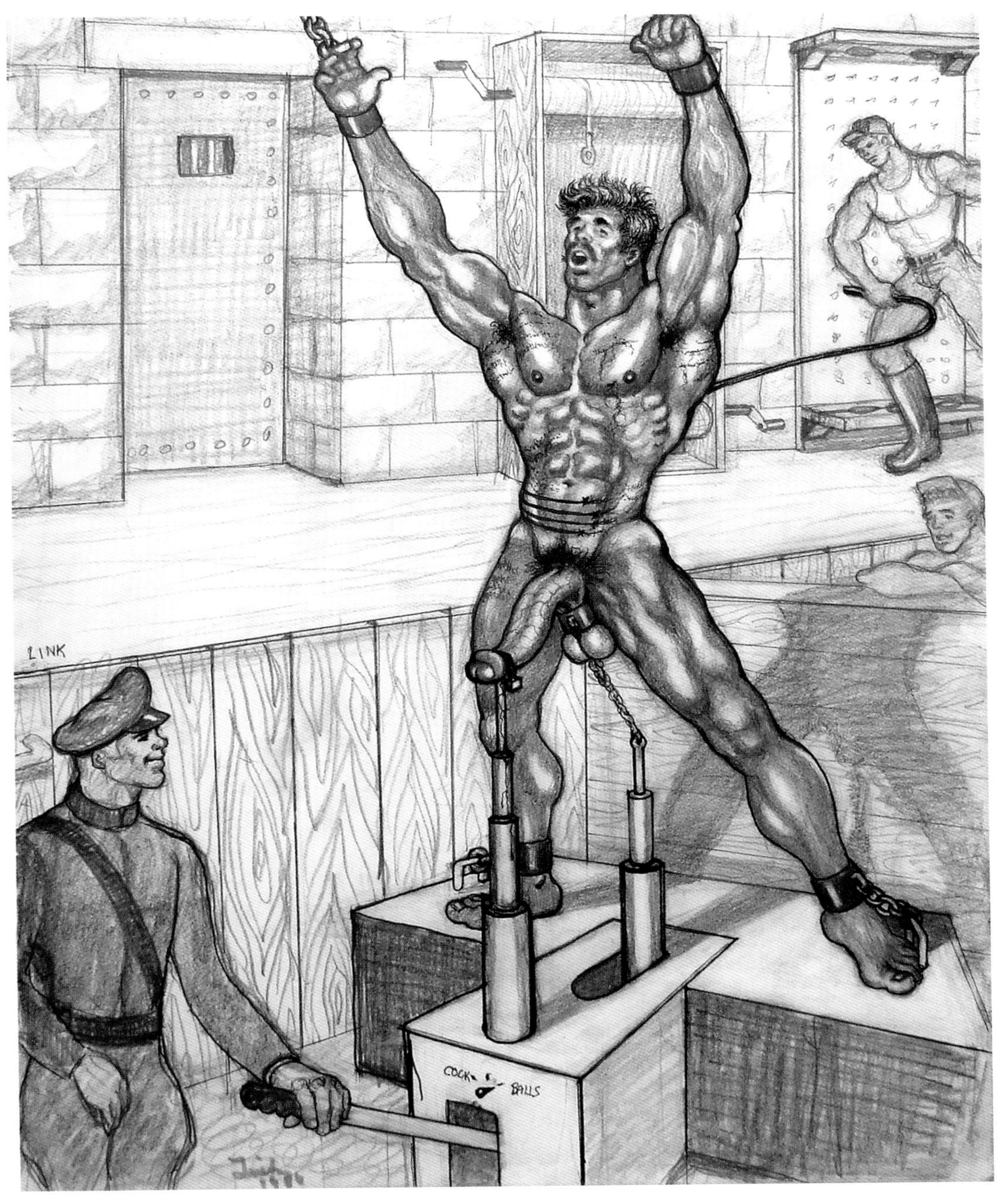
LINK
COCK- BALLS

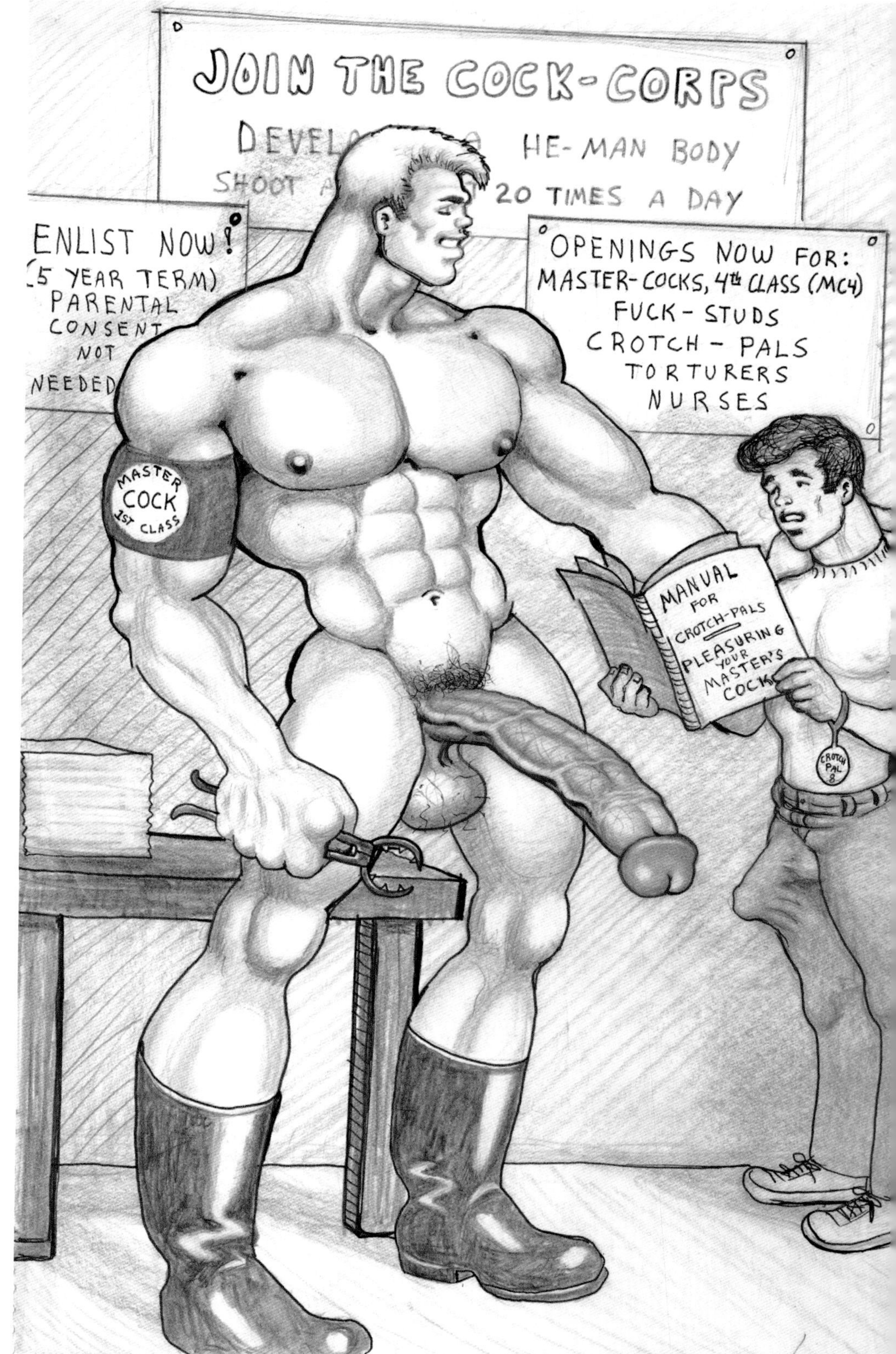
JOIN THE COCK-CORPS
DEVELOP A HE-MAN BODY
SHOOT A LOAD 20 TIMES A DAY
ENLIST NOW!
(5 YEAR TERM)
PARENTAL CONSENT NOT NEEDED
OPENINGS NOW FOR:
MASTER-COCKS, 4TH CLASS (MC4)
FUCK-STUDS
CROTCH-PALS
TORTURERS
NURSES
MASTER COCK 1ST CLASS
MANUAL FOR CROTCH-PALS PLEASURING YOUR MASTER'S COCK
CROTCH PAL 8

STRIP AND RAISE A BONE
COCK-RATINGS:
MC4 - 8" Soft
11 INCHES Hard
FUCK-STUDS:
9" HARD
These are minimum
KOCKLICK MILITARY ACADEMY
MC4
ORGASM COUNT
SPERM RATING
15
16
SUPER-COCK & FUCK-STUD PHYSICALS -
ENTER ON UPPER LEVEL OF GYM
APPRENTICE TORTURERS
REPOPT TO BOILER ROOM
Link - 1986

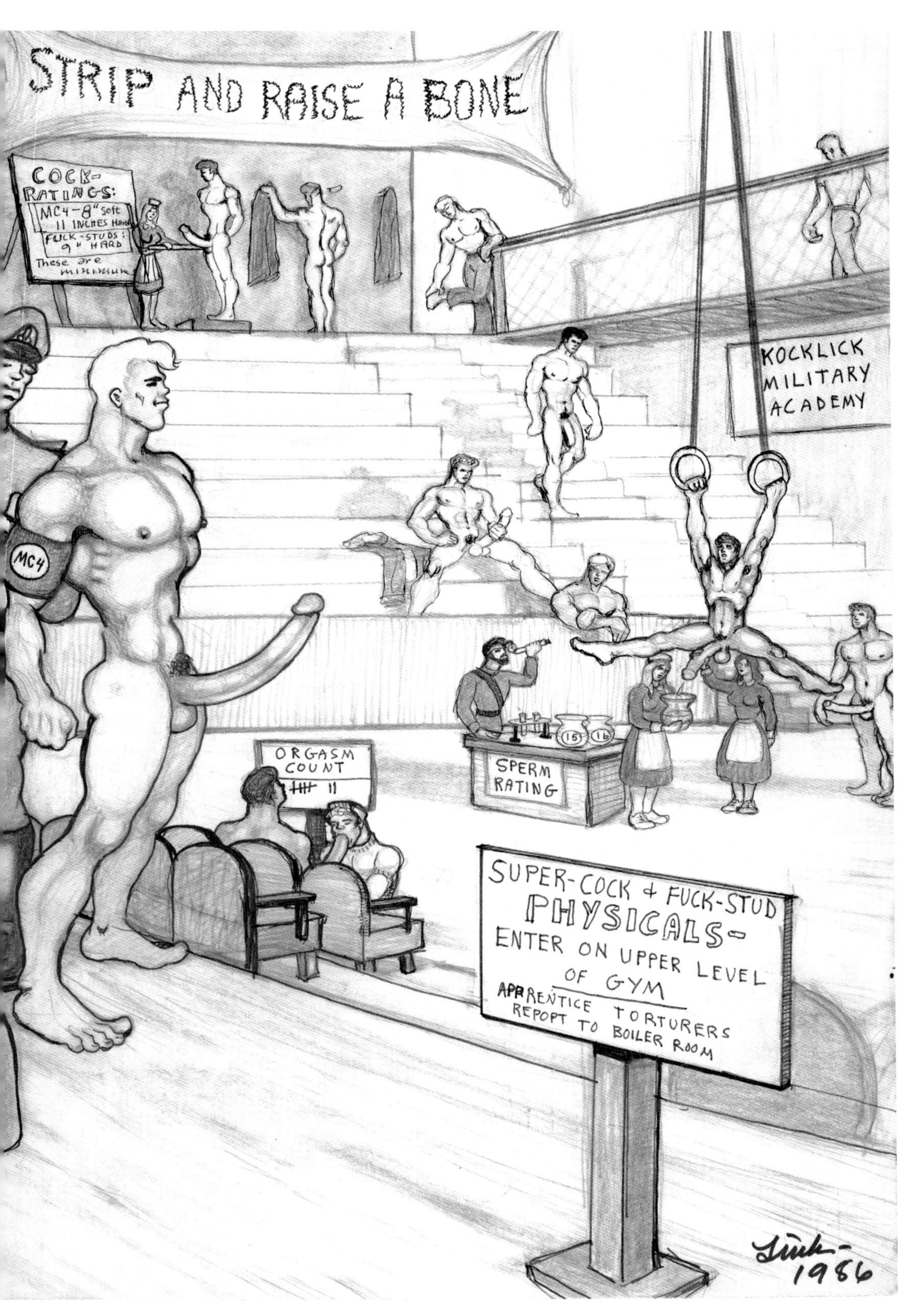

173

JIM BAKER

Tom of Finland – Defying the Laws of Physics •
Die Kunst, den Gesetzen der Physik zu widersprechen

I always had a somewhat inexplicable interest in physics. During my emotionally turbulent High School years, there was just something immensely reassuring about the cut-and-dry laws, steadfast theorems, and unyielding rules governing the world of physics that captured my attention and fascinated my young mind.

To equate the art of Tom of Finland with the laws of physics is to many surely a stretch of the imagination. But still, the straining muscles, the bulging biceps, the taut material covering the massive thighs of the men who inhabit the visual world of Tom of Finland exerted an almost surreal attraction to my inquisitive scientific mind. I would gaze at the black-and-white drawings and marvel at the perfect arcs, the tight contours of muscle, the unrelenting lines of black ink, demarking where his world started and my world ended.

I could spend hours tracing the frame of a square jawline, the rigid clefts, the mountainous plateaus of mass, conscious of the impossibility of such beings, and yet in awe of their creation, defying as they did the very laws of the physical world. As if Newton's apple had fallen not profanely to the ground but rather had been entrapped beneath the leather-encased loins of Tom's many men.

Ah, the gravity they exerted, those images. Drawing, pulling, enticing all objects around them closer and closer, until the inevitable collision occurred. It comes as no surprise that the inertia of the initial years following my coming out was irrevocably disturbed by this unknown force.

Es mag seltsam klingen, aber Physik hat mich immer schon fasziniert. Während des Chaos meiner Adoleszenz übten die trockenen Gesetze, die klaren Regeln und die festen Lehrsätze, die die Welt der Physik beherrschen, eine erstaunlich beruhigende Wirkung auf mich aus. Es war vielleicht nur die Neugierde eines „Jugend forscht"-Möchtegernwissenschaftlers, der Ordnung in seiner sonst so aufgewühlten Gefühlswelt herzustellen suchte.

Es mag manchen verwundern, wenn die Gesetze der Physik mit der Kunst von Tom of Finland verglichen werden, doch es waren diese vor Spannung strotzenden Muskelstränge, die sich wölbenden Bizepse, der enge zum Bersten angespannte Stoff um die prallen Oberschenkel der Männer in Toms Welt, die in meinem Entdeckergeist eine beinahe surreale Anziehungskraft auf mich entwickelten. Ich konnte schier endlos lange dasitzen, die Schwarz-Weiß-Zeichnungen betrachten und die perfekten Bögen bewundern, die kräftigen Konturen der skizzierten Muskeln und die Unnachgiebigkeit der schwarzen Linienzeichnung, die eine Grenze deutlich markierte, wo seine Welt anfing und meine aufhörte.

Stundenlang konnte ich die markanten Kieferpartien mit dem Finger liebevoll nachzeichnen, über die prallen Beulen, die Berge einladenden Männerfleisches streichen, dabei im vollen Bewusstsein, dass solche Wesen in der realen Welt gar nicht existieren dürften, und doch in respektvoller Ehrfurcht vor deren Schöpfer, der mit seinem Schaffenswillen die Gesetze der Physik scheinbar aufhob. Als ob Newtons berühmter Apfel nicht profan zu Boden gefallen wäre, sondern vielmehr wie durch Geisterhand unter dem prallen Ledergemächt von Toms Kerlen bloß gefangen gehalten würde.

Ach, diese Anziehungskraft, die seine gezeichneten Himmelskörper auf mich ausübten! Ihre Sogwirkung, die mich immer enger in ihre Umlaufbahn zu ziehen drohte, bis der unvermeidliche Aufprall erfolgte. Es überrascht daher nicht, dass meine Trägheit, die vor allem in der Zeit nach

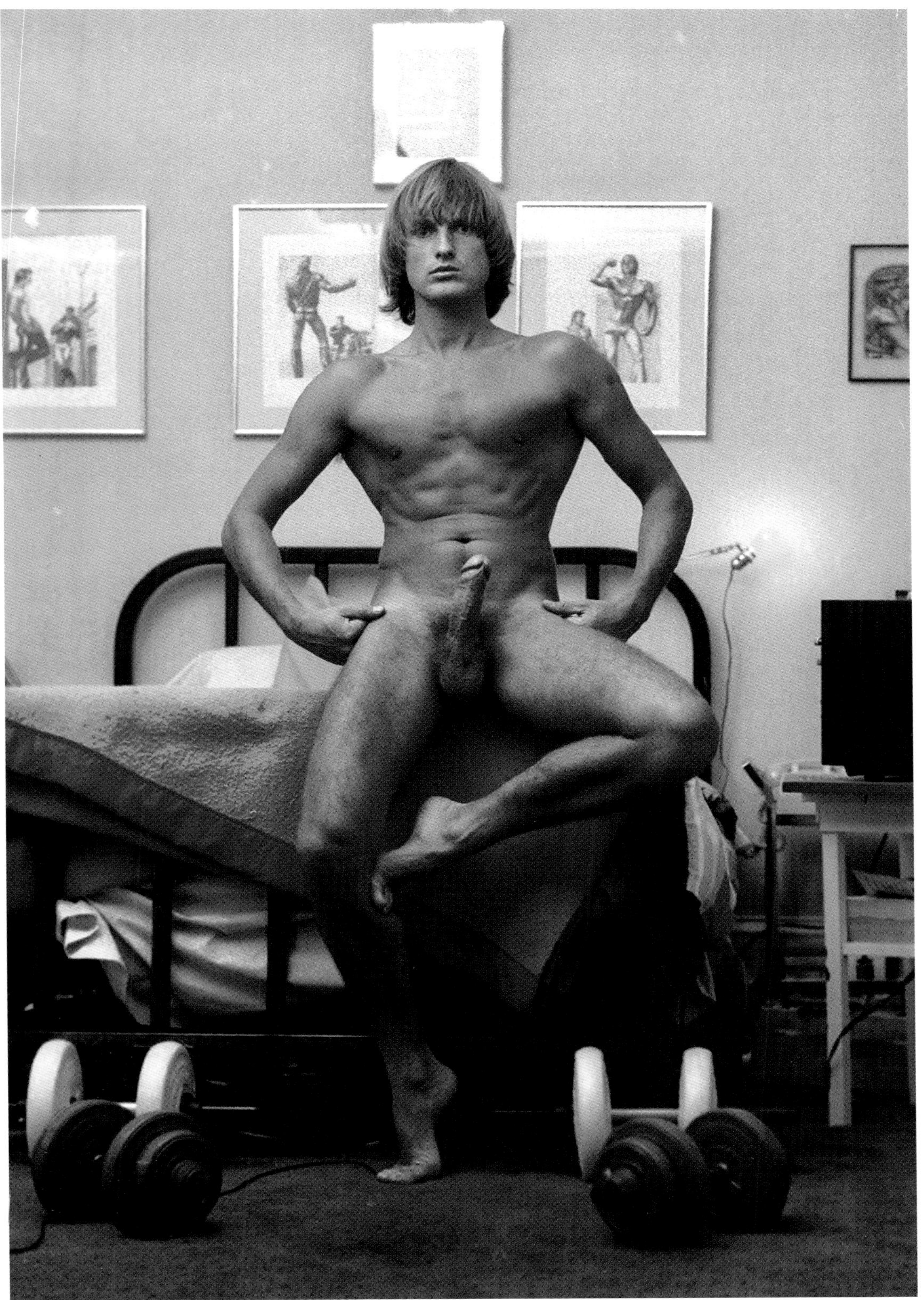

If Newton's Third Law is correct and for every action, there is an equal and opposite reaction, then the laws of Tom's fictitious realm caused a multitude of actions as well as reactions in my life – many of which govern my motions to this very day.

meinem Coming-out eintrat, durch Toms Männer gewaltig aufgewirbelt wurde, ausgelöst durch eine mir bis dahin unbekannte physische Kraft.

Wenn es stimmt, was uns das dritte Newton'sche Gesetz lehrt, „actio gleich reactio", dann besitzt die Wechselwirkung zwischen Tom of Finland und meinem schwulen Selbstbewusstsein durchaus eine Gültigkeit – damals wie heute.

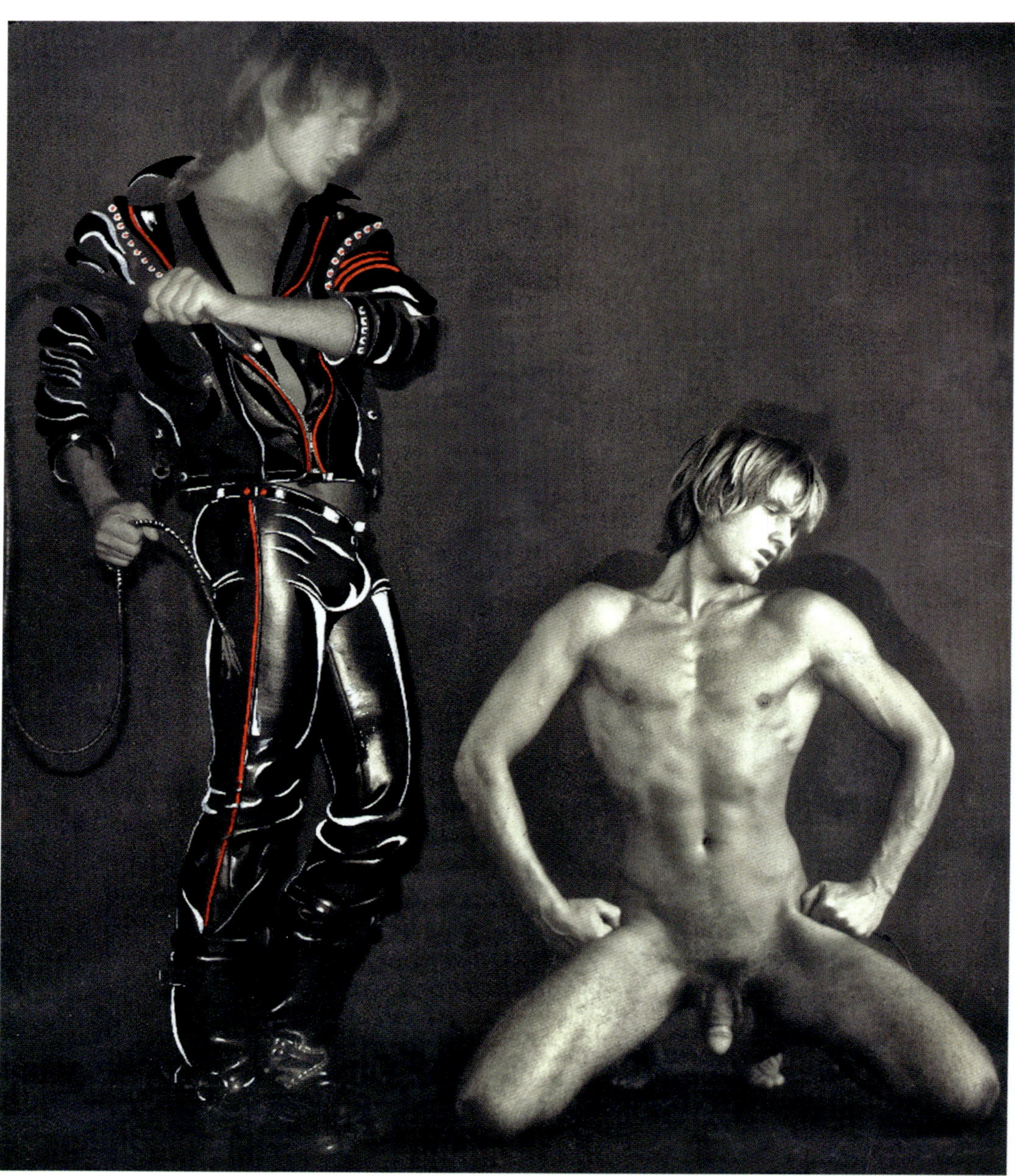

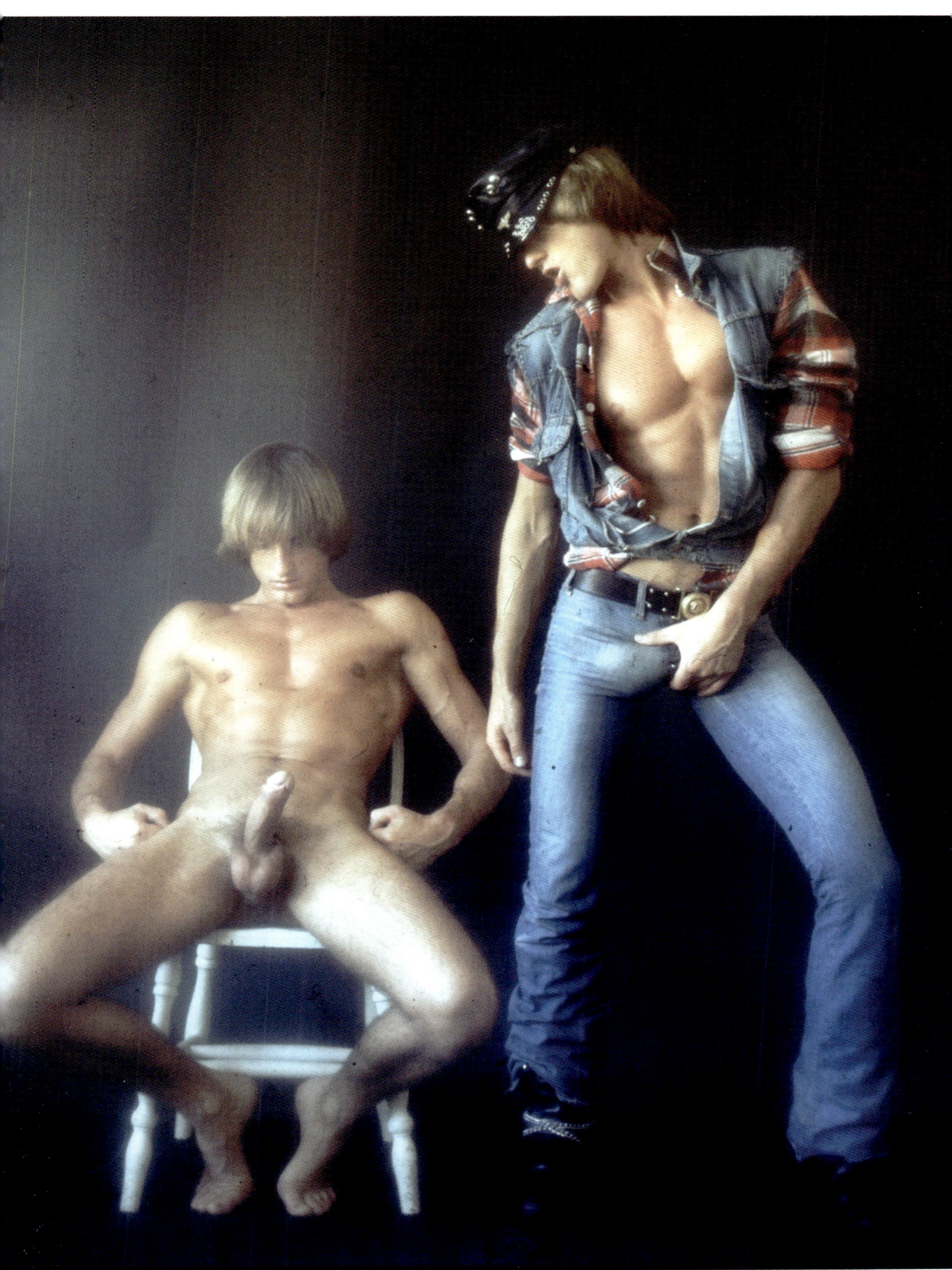

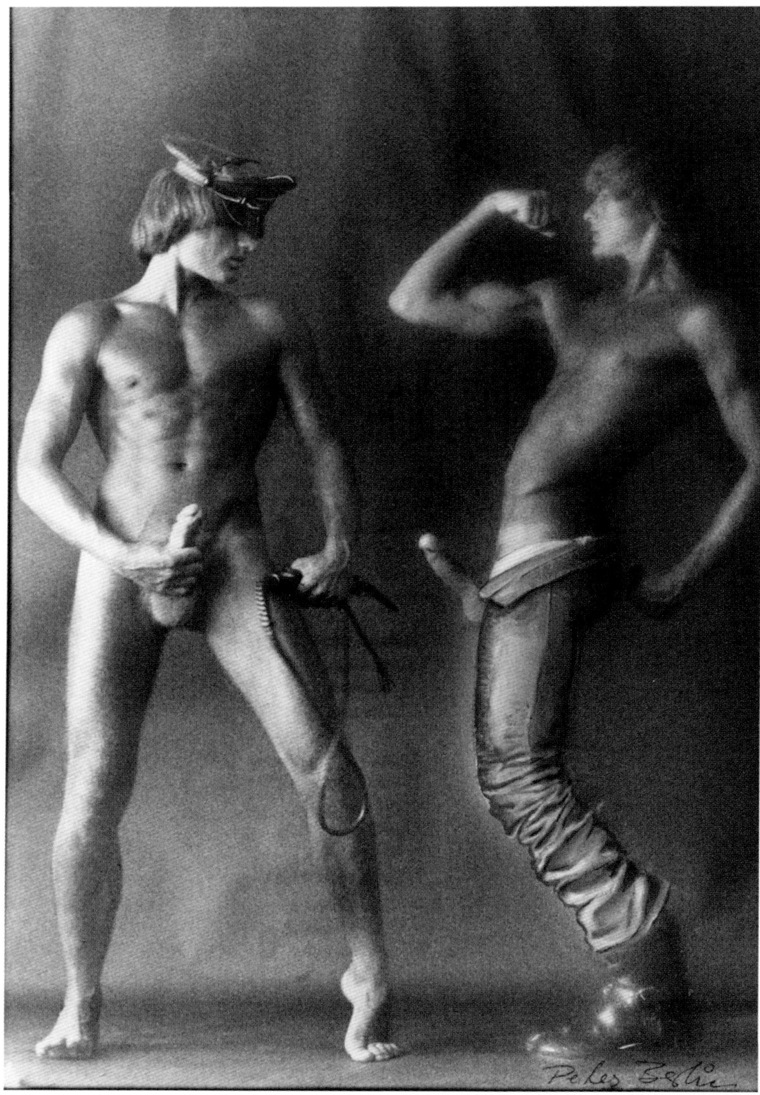

PETER BERLIN

Known as a narcissist, he truly is the definition of an artist. He has created his name, his image, his persona. He fashions his own clothes. He photographs himself, develops the film, and makes his own prints. He is director and star of his own films. An original originator, he is always taking full control of the final work.

Er ist Narzisst und verkörpert den wahrhaften Künstlertypus. Er hat seinen Namen selbst gewählt und eine Kunstfigur kreiert. Er schneidert nicht nur seine Kleidung selbst, er fotografiert sich selbst, entwickelt seine Filme und macht die Abzüge. Er ist Regisseur und Star seiner eigenen Filme. Als alleiniger Urheber hat er immer die volle Kontrolle über sein Werk.

– Durk Dehner

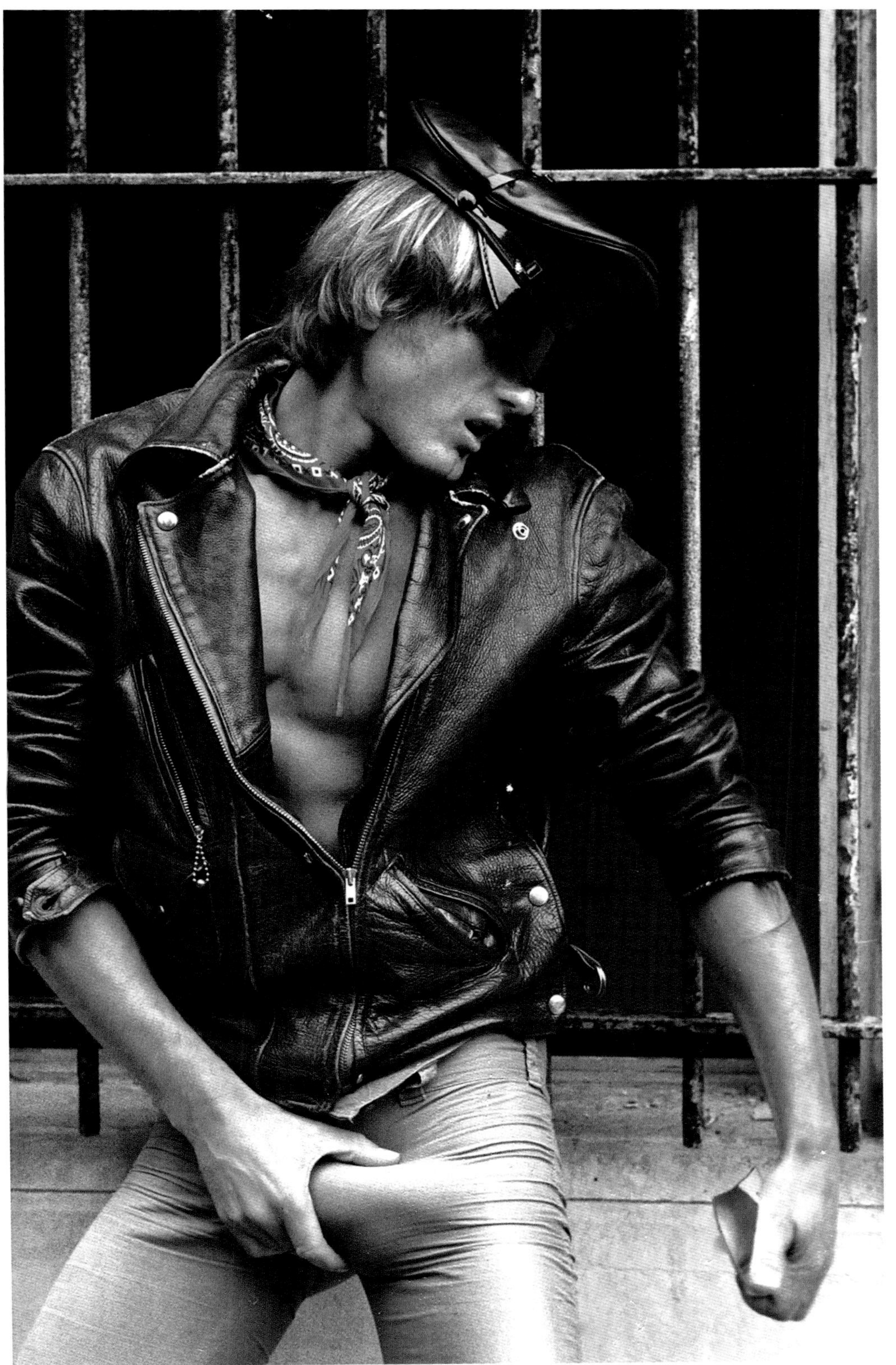

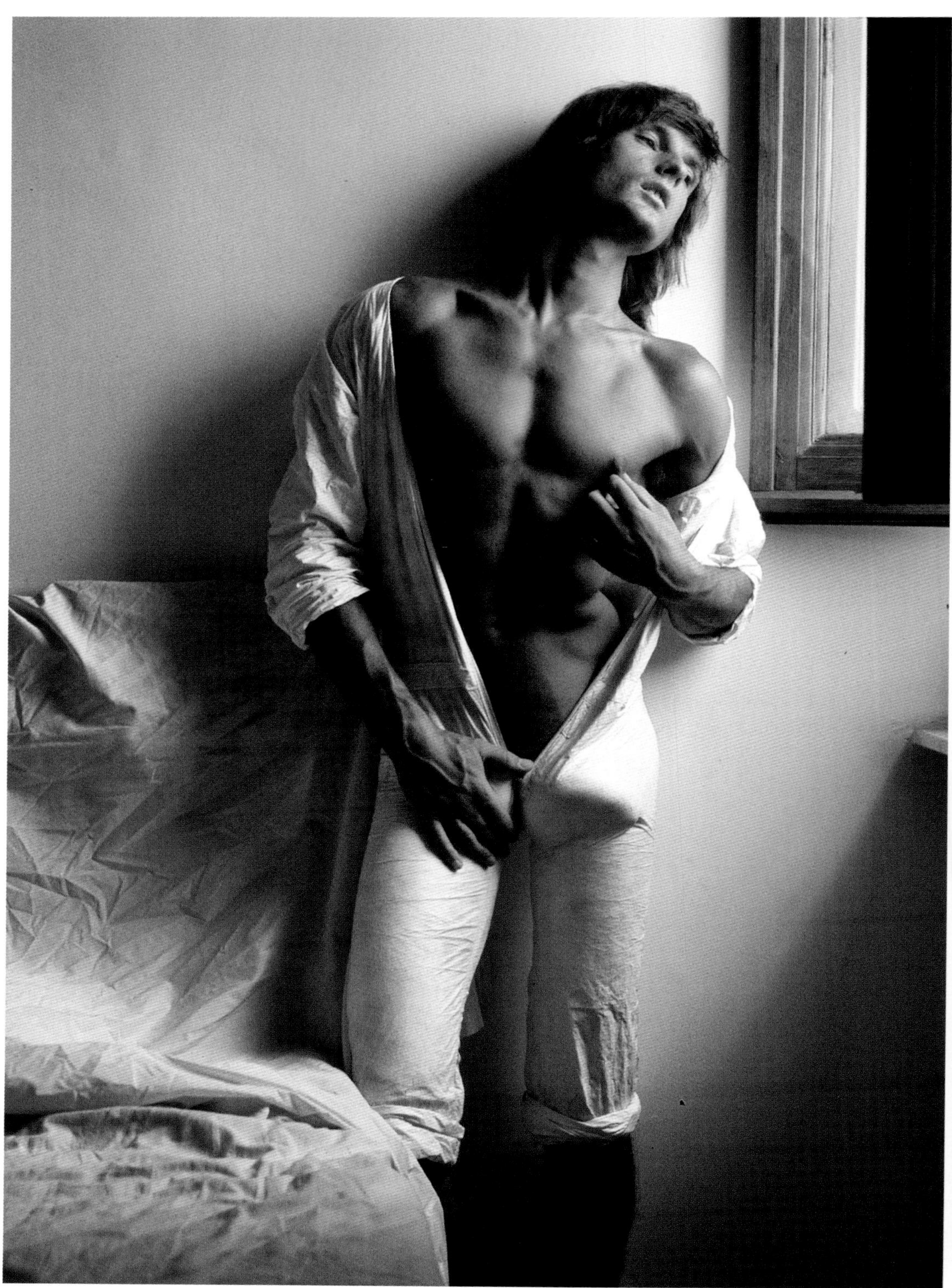

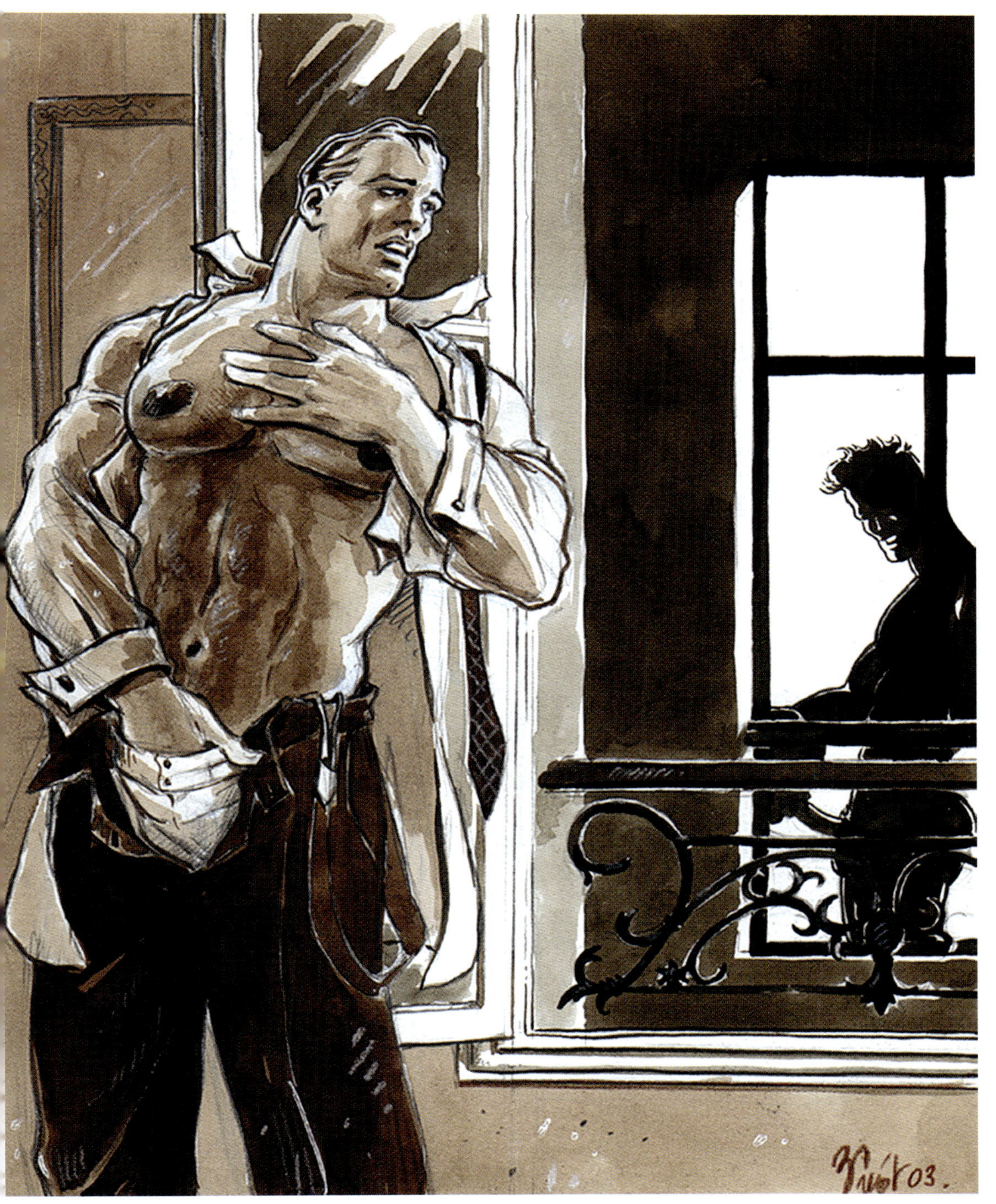

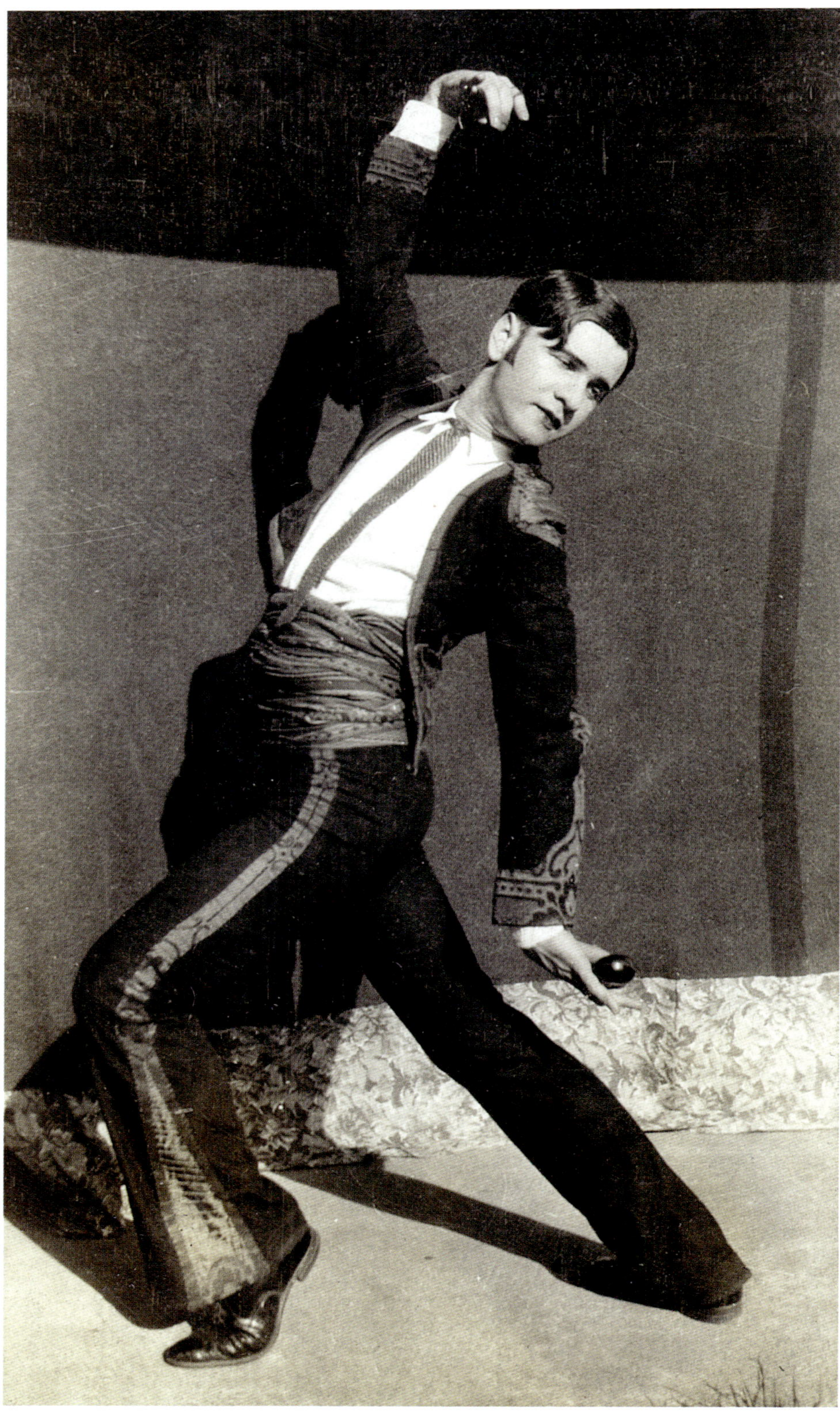

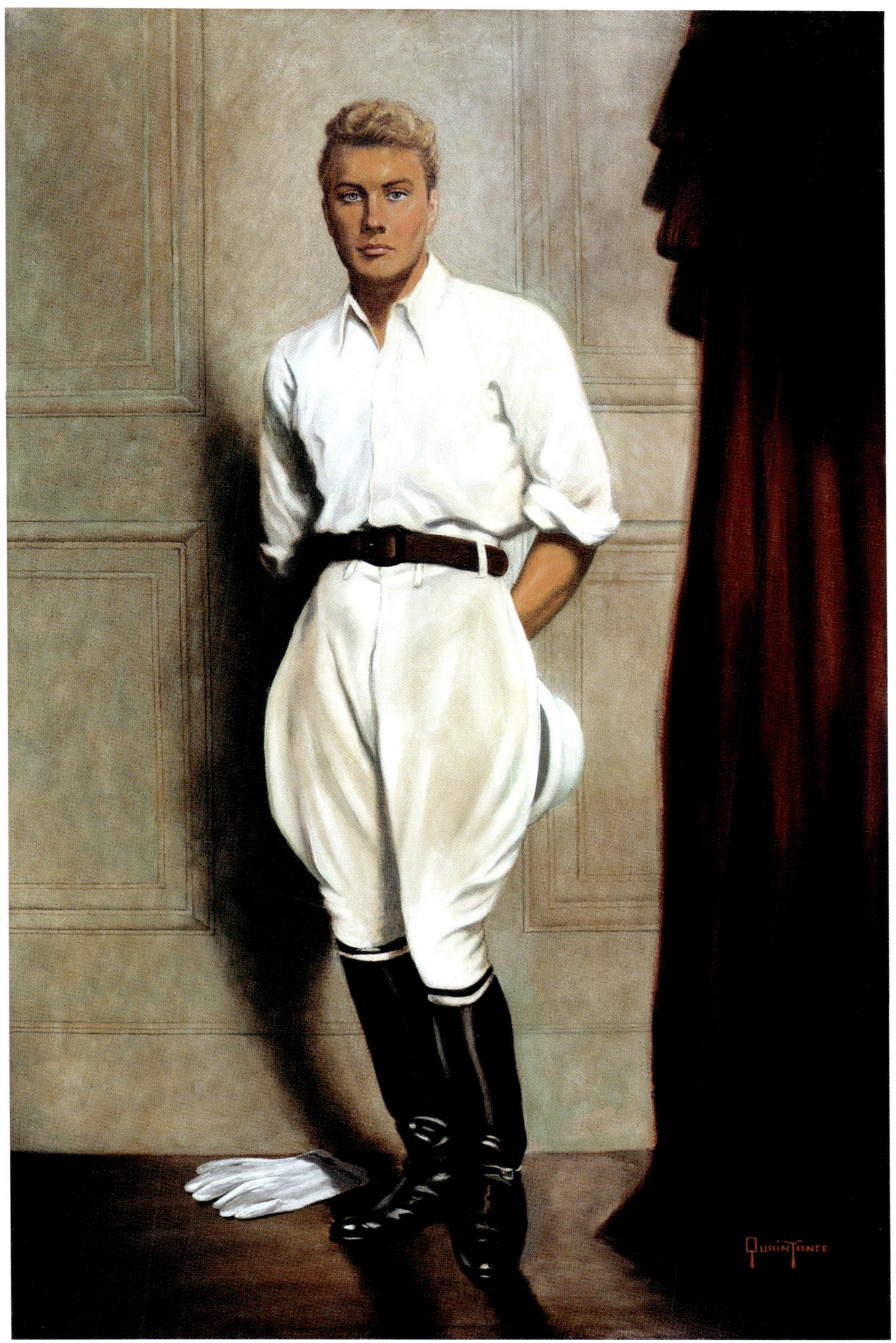

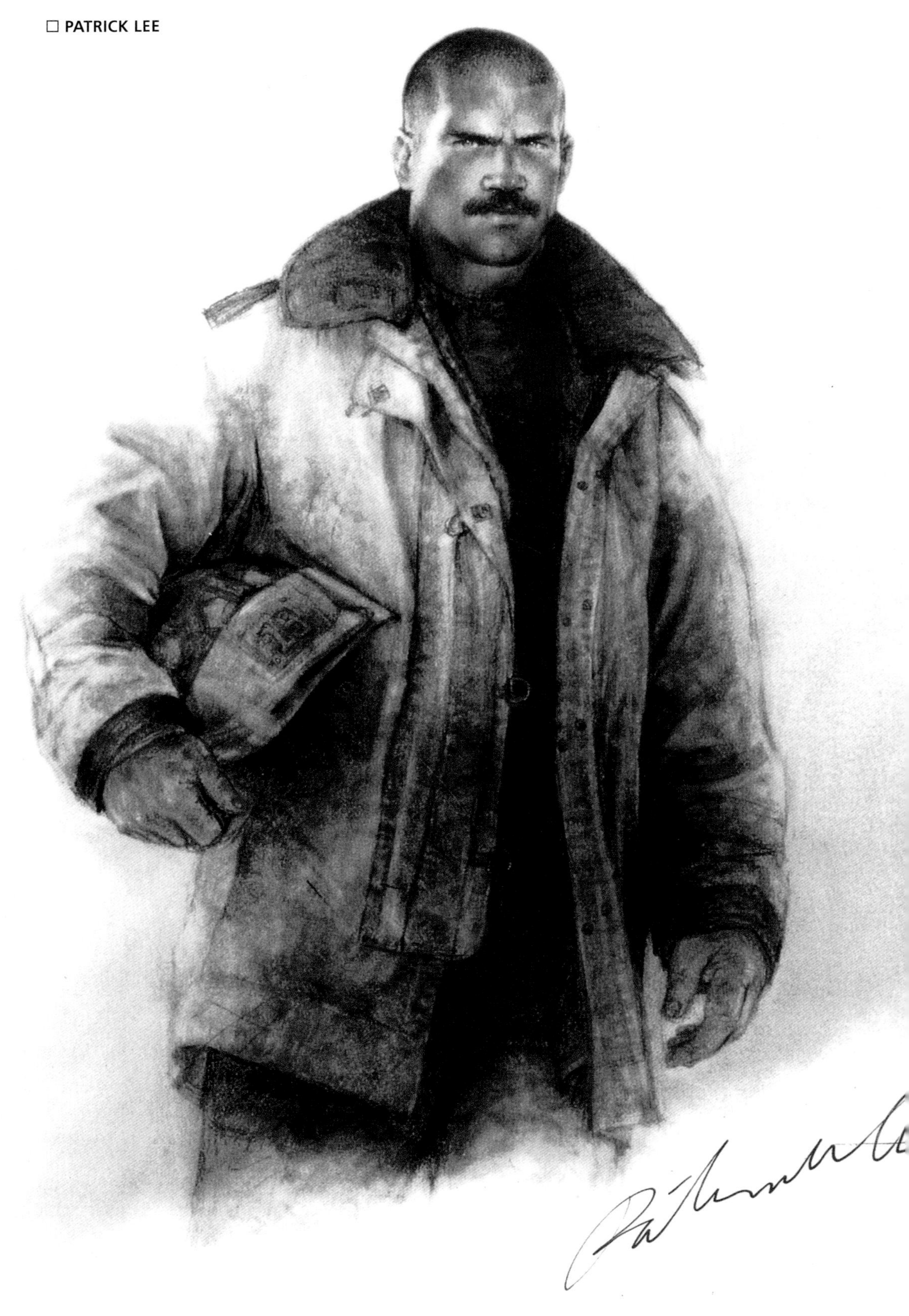

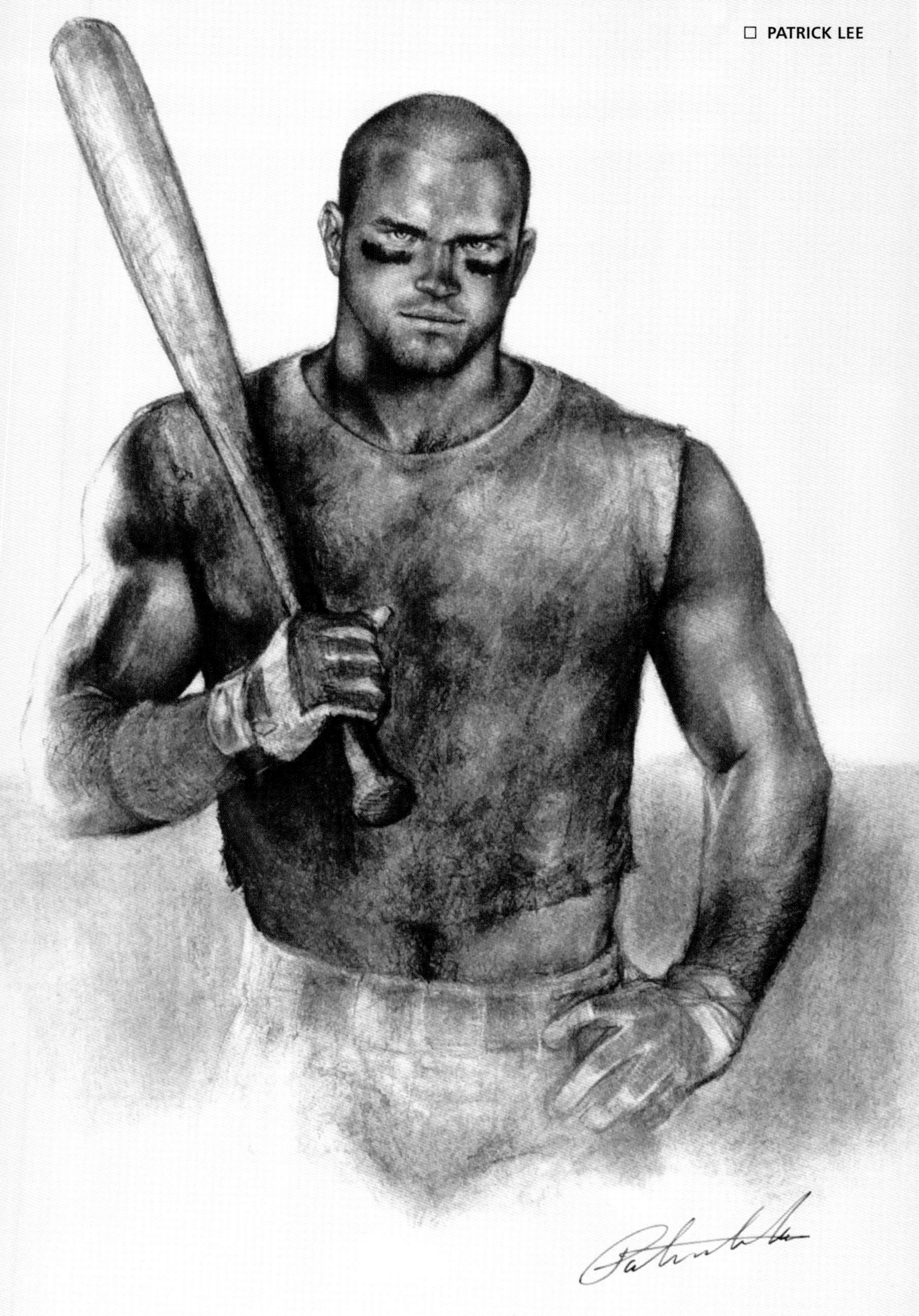
PATRICK LEE

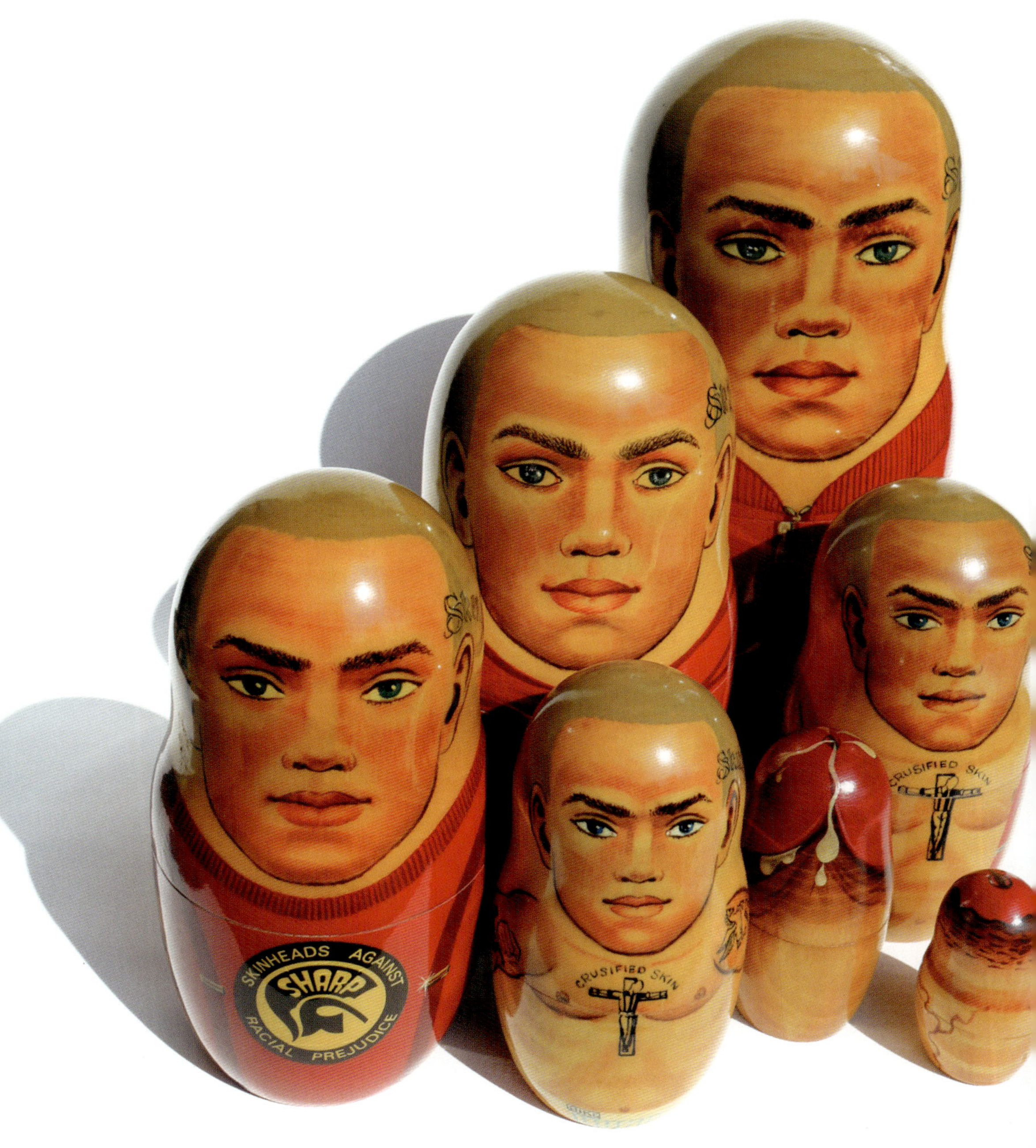

SKINHEADS AGAINST
SHARP
RACIAL PREJUDICE
CRUSIFIED SKIN
CRUSIFIED SKIN

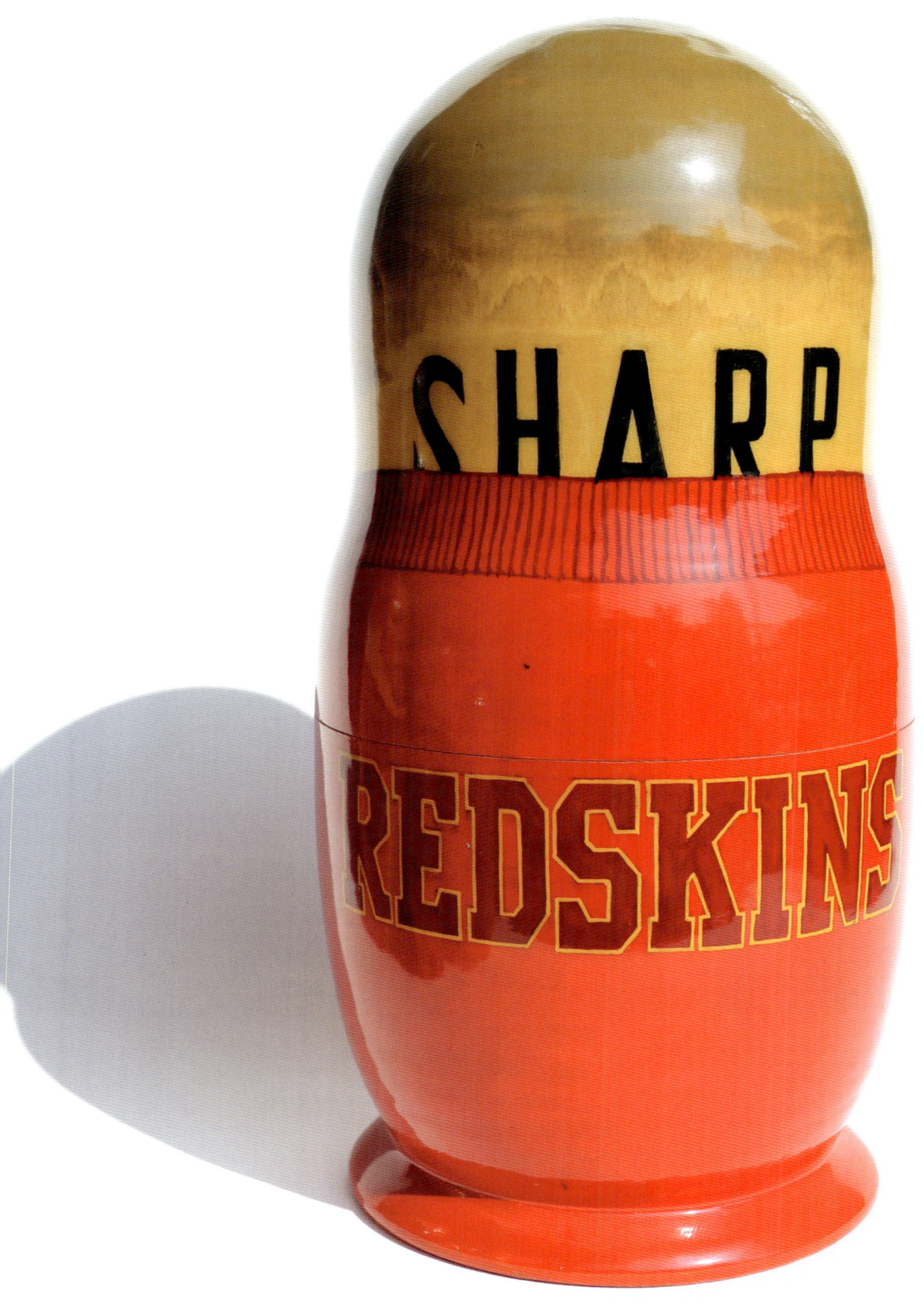
SHARP
REDSKINS

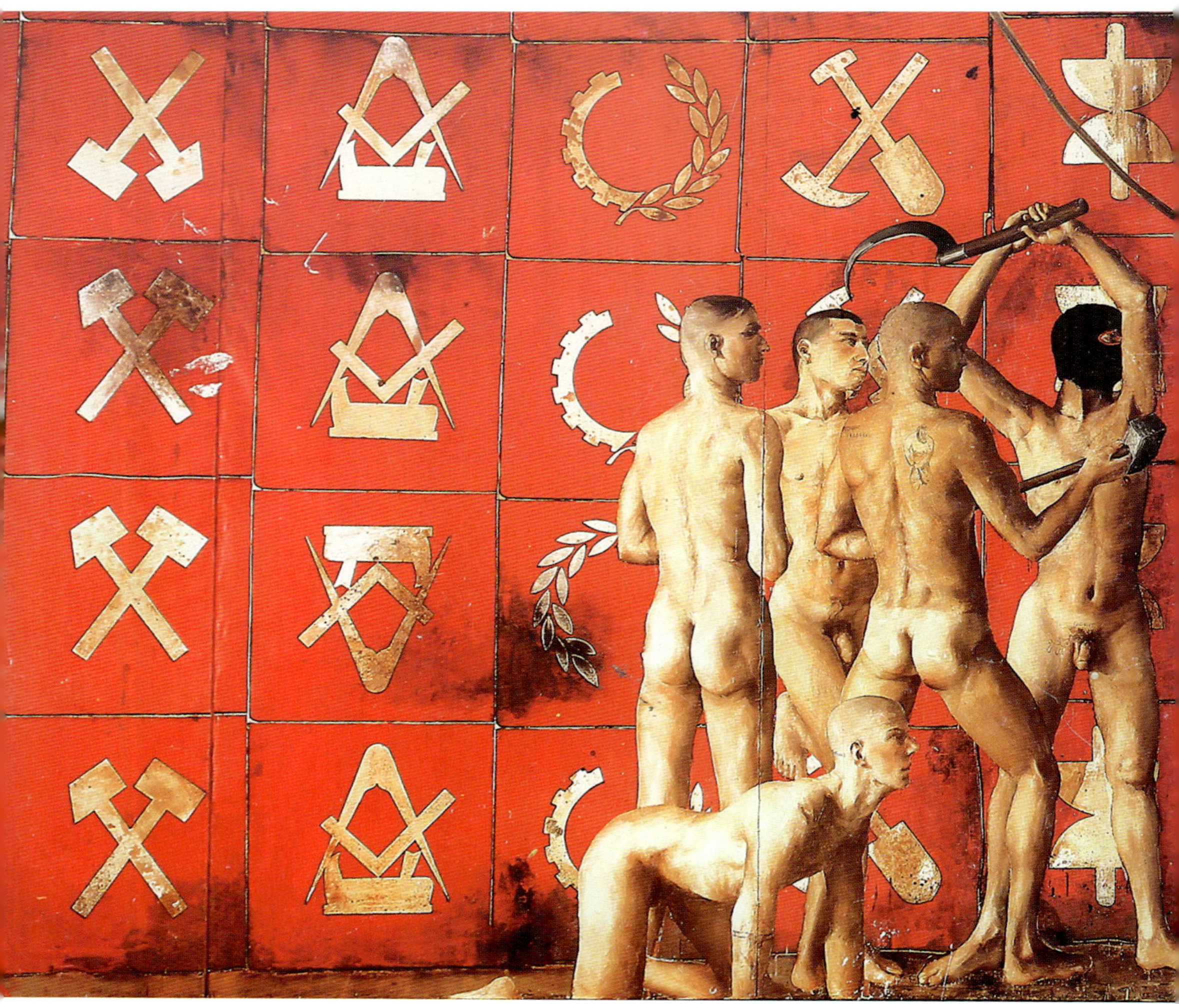

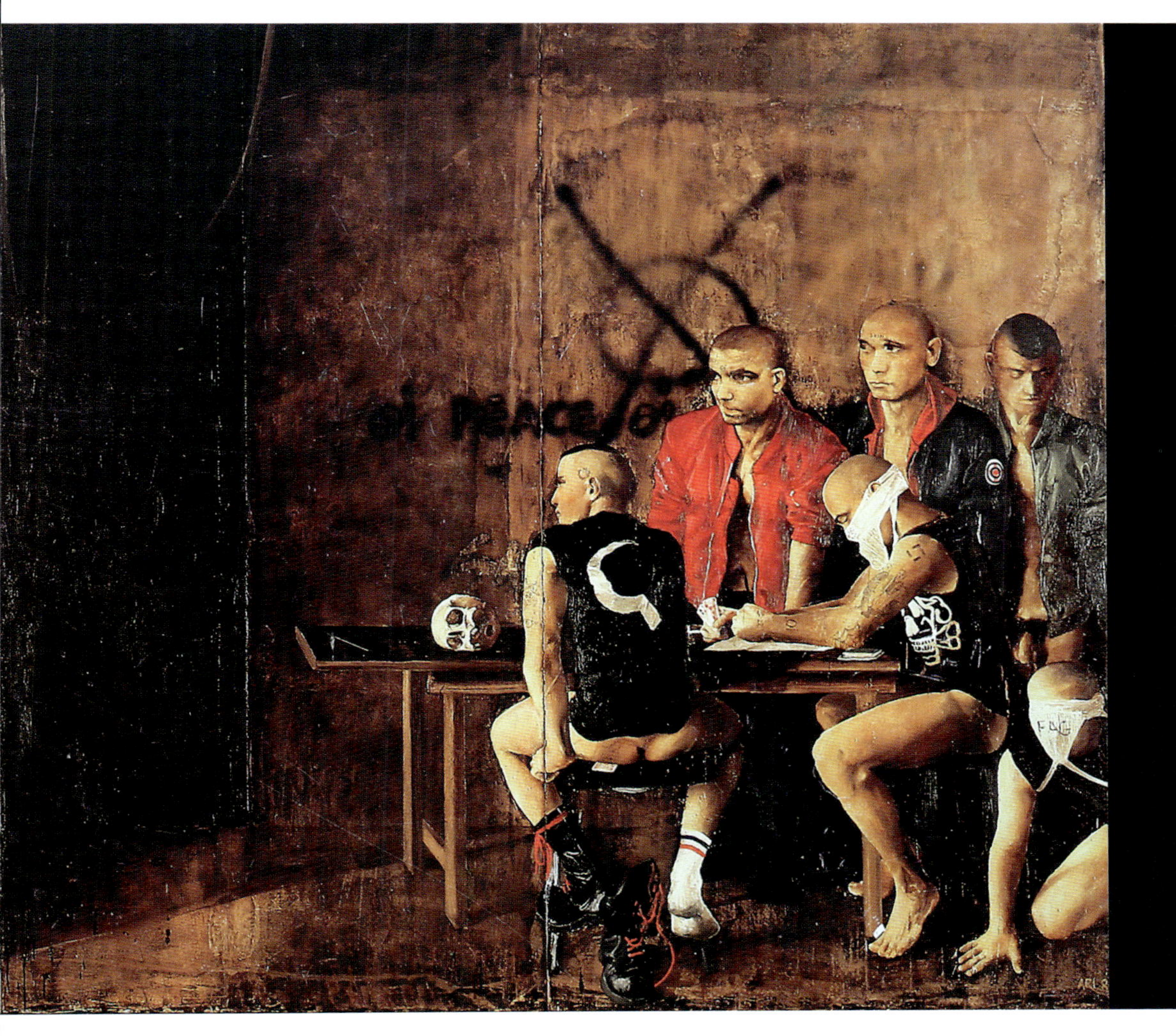

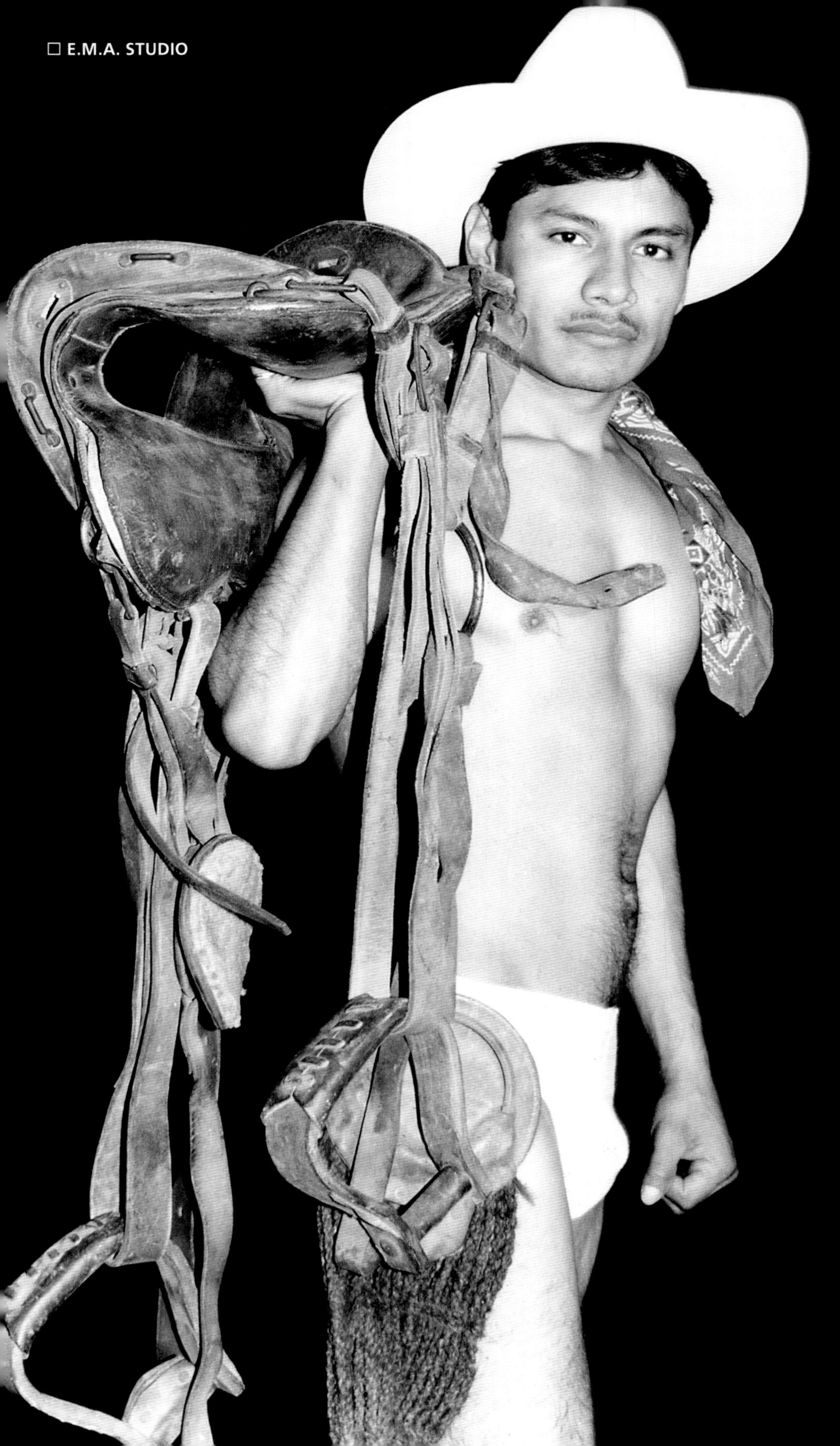
E.M.A. STUDIO

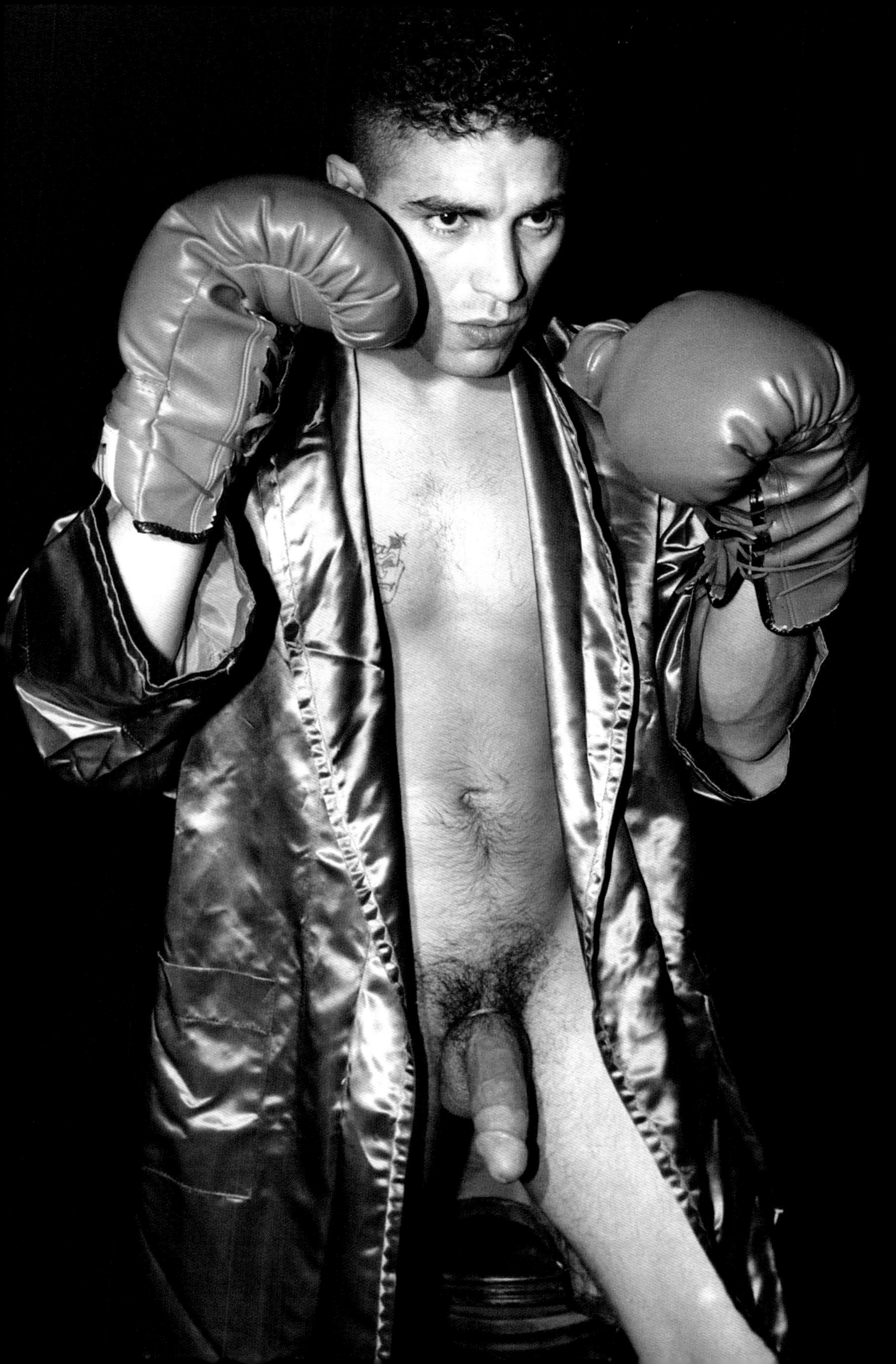

□ E.M.A. STUDIO

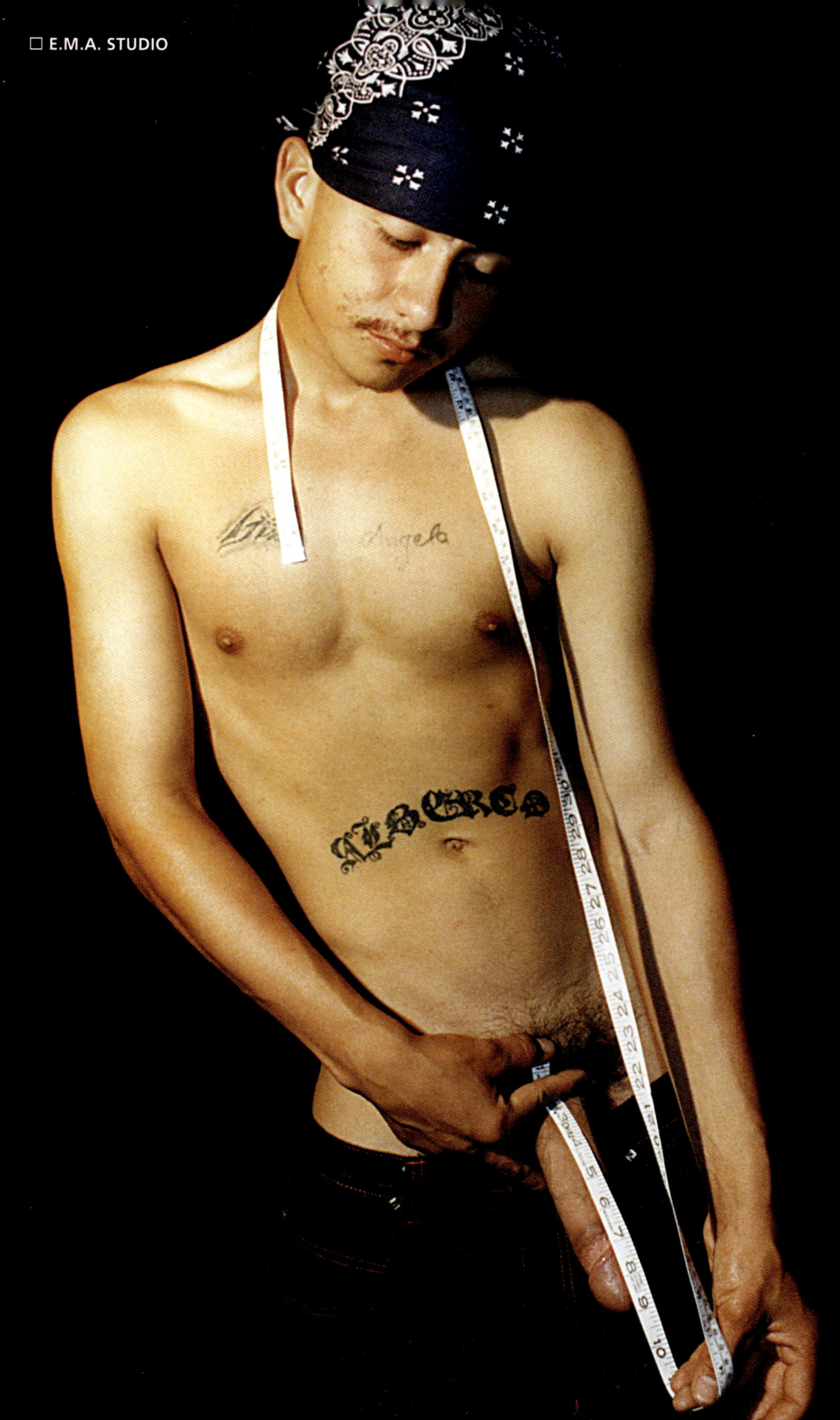

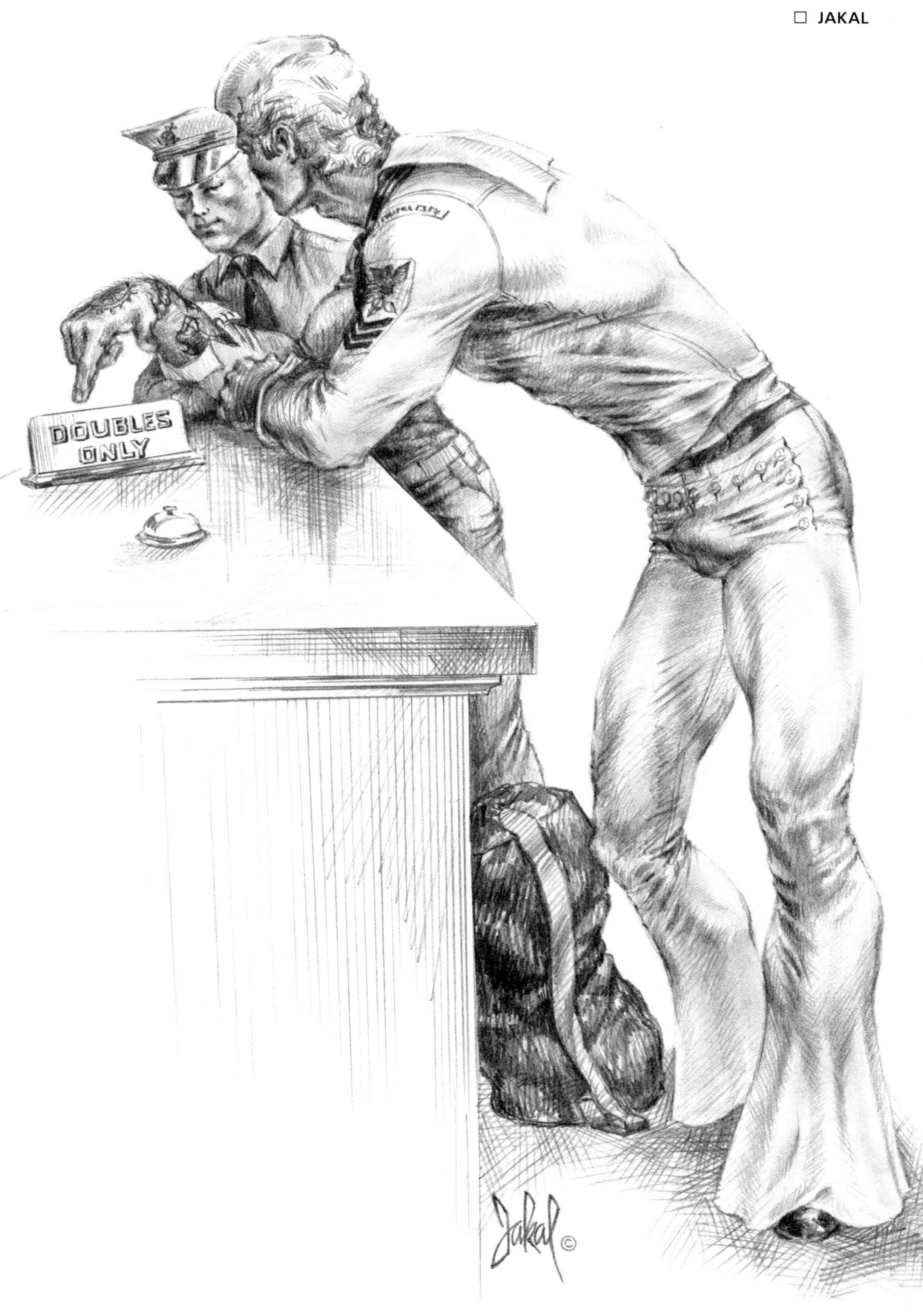
DOUBLES ONLY

☐ JAKAL

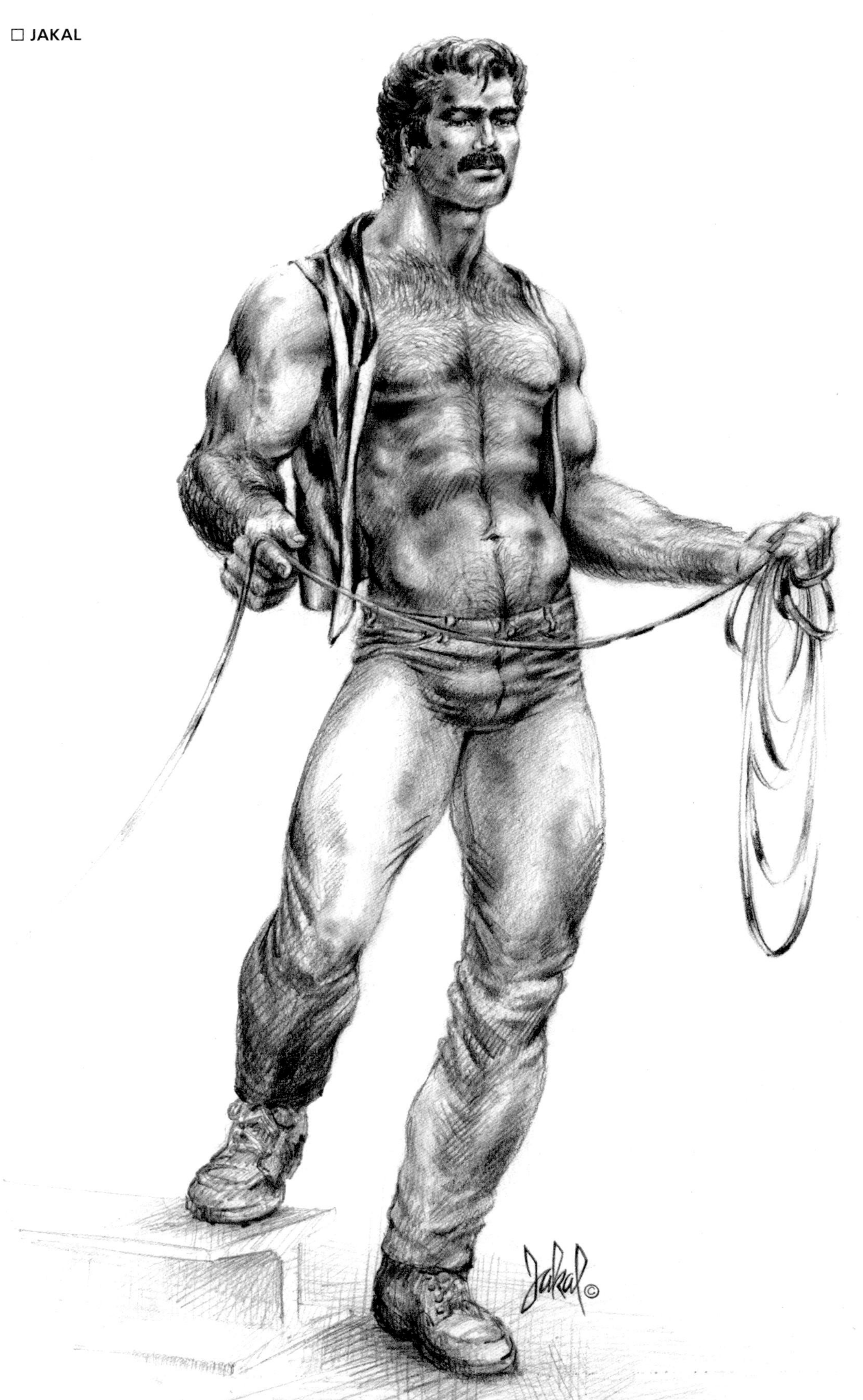

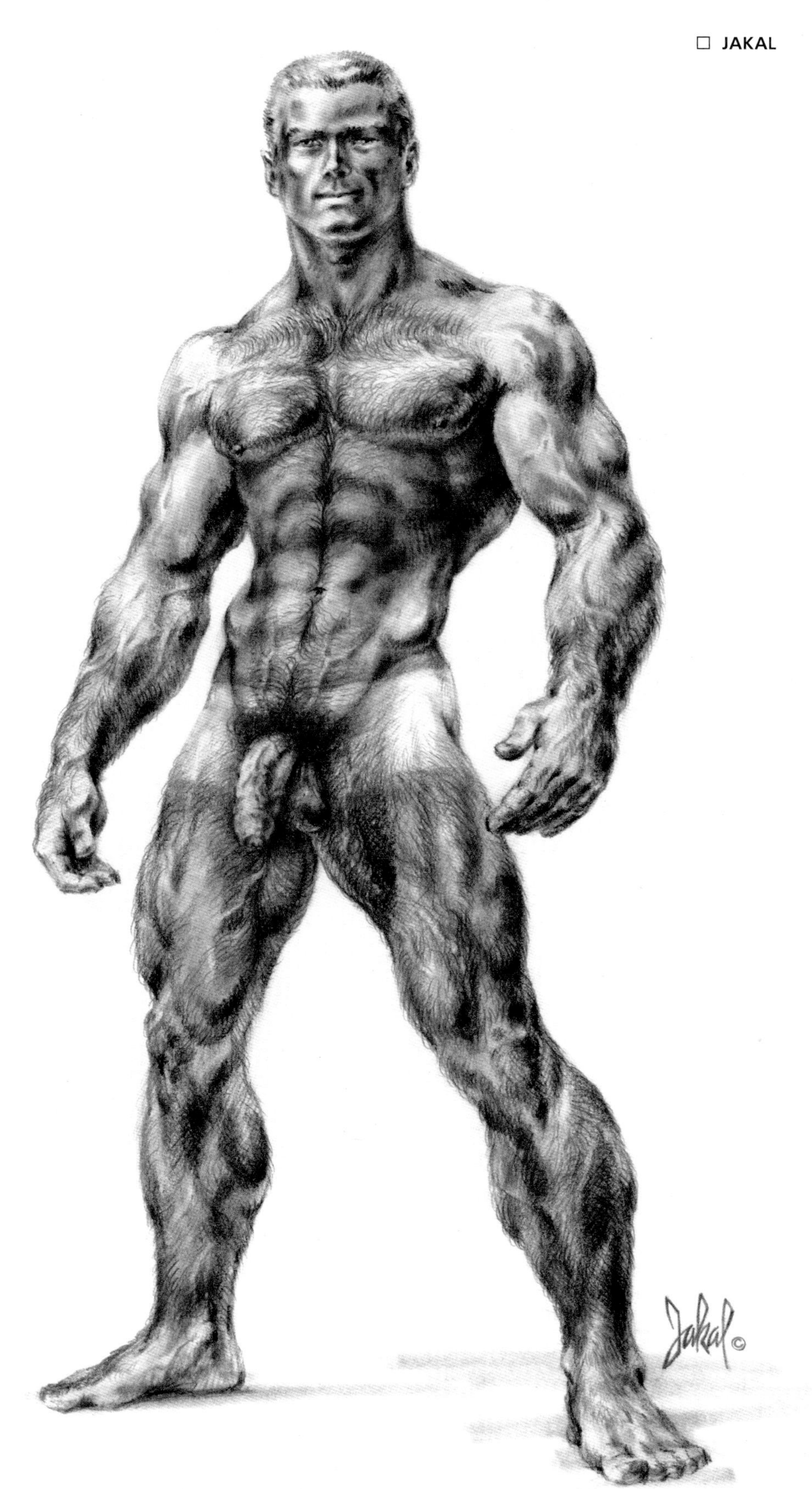

JAKAL

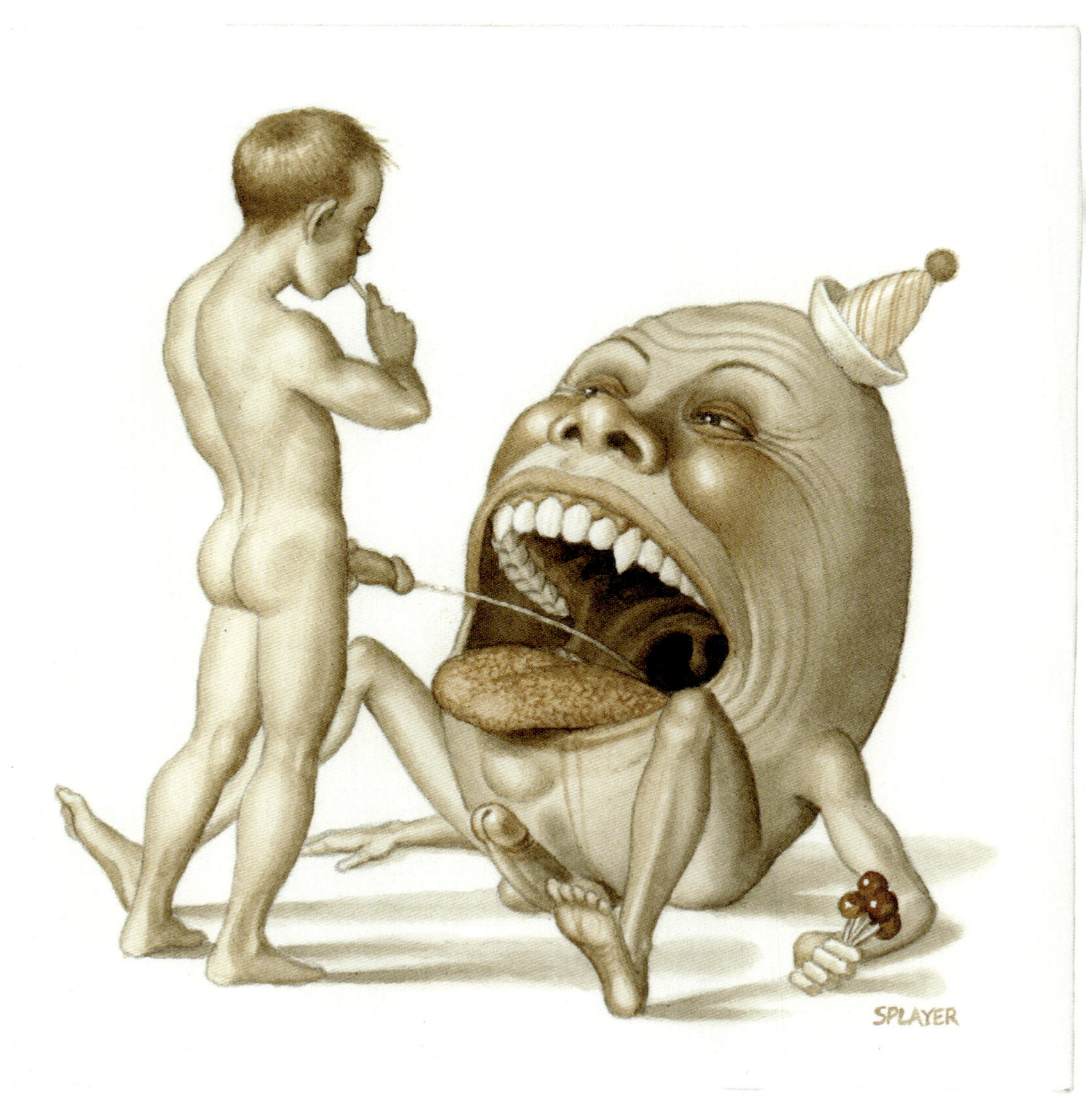
SPLAYER

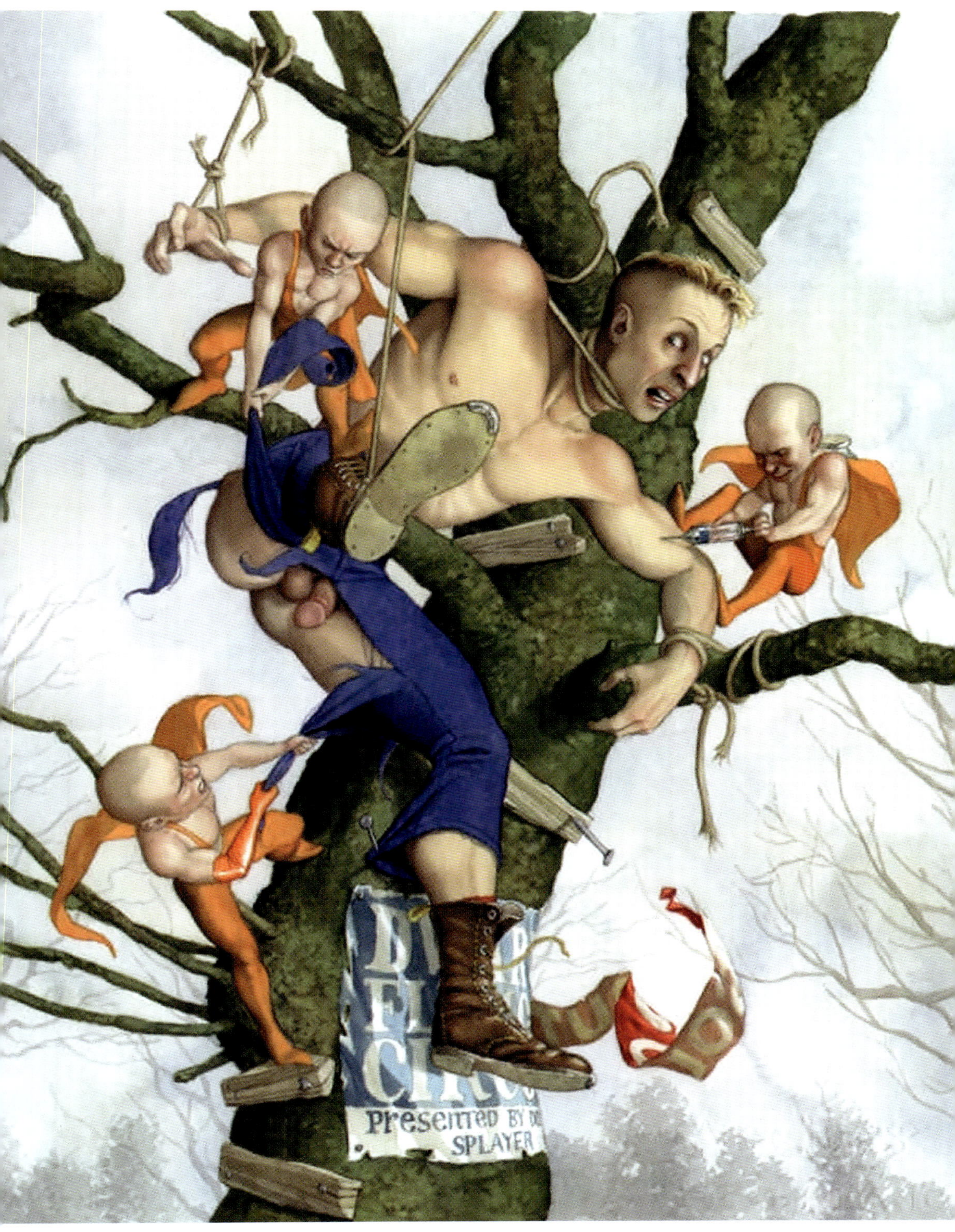

PRESENTED BY D...
SPLAYER

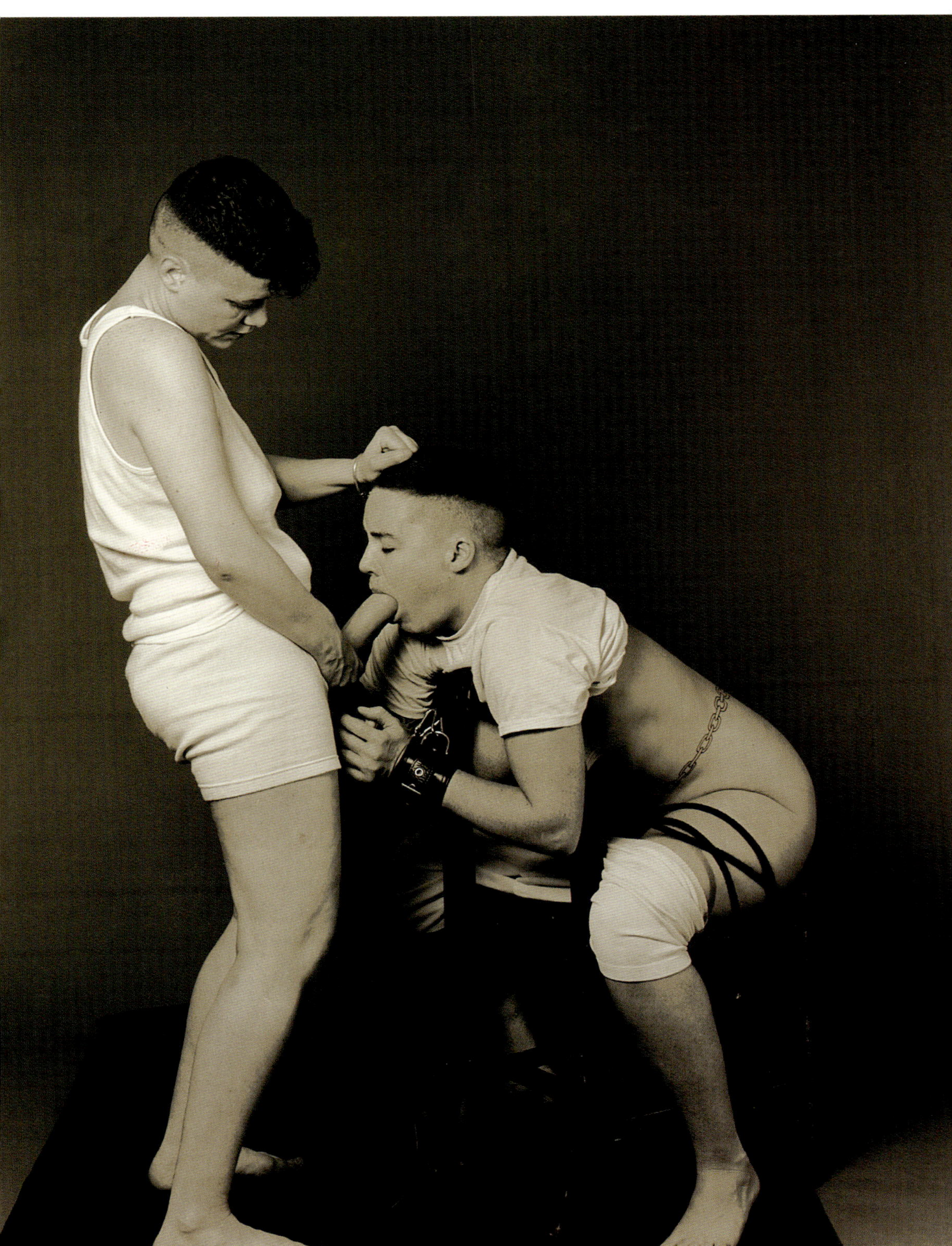

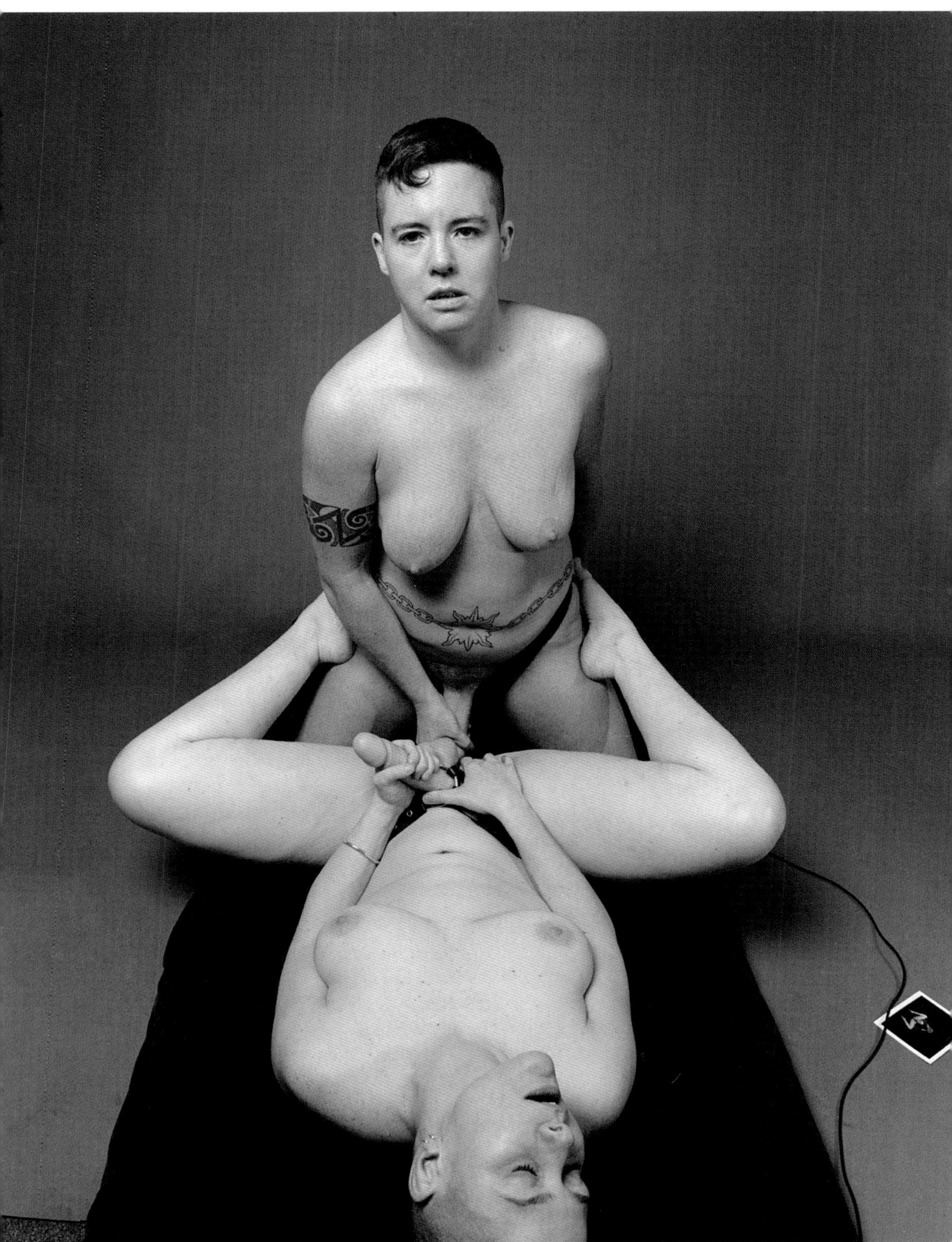

KEVIN CLARKE

Wer hat Angst vorm Riesenschwanz? •
Who's Afraid of the Big Bad Dick?

Tom of Finland in der internationalen Museums- und Kunstszene. Oder: Die neue Macht
der Heterofrauen vs. Diskussionen in der LGBTQQIAAP* Community •
Tom of Finland's position in the international museum and art world, or: The new power
of straight women buying gay erotica vs. discussions within the LGBTQQIAAP* community

Es lässt sich schwer leugnen, dass die Sache mit der Darstellung von Sex in öffentlichen Räumen schwierig ist. Wenn es um Homosexualität geht, wird's noch schwieriger. Zur Erinnerung: Ein Bild wie Gustave Courbets *L'origine du monde (Der Ursprung der Welt)*, 1866 für den türkisch-ägyptischen Diplomaten Khalil Bey entstanden und von diesem in seine berüchtigte Erotiksammlung aufgenommen, wurde von einem grünen Vorhang vor den Augen der Welt verborgen. Nur ausgewählte Gäste durften das Gemälde sehen. Weil aber so gut wie jeder davon gehört hatte, war es das berühmteste ungesehene Kunstwerk des 19. Jahrhunderts, ein „chef d'oeuvre inconnu". Dass es 1995 ins Museum d'Orsay in Paris kam und heute prominent platziert dort hängt, empfinden viele nach wie vor als Provokation. Auch die kalifornische Firma Facebook.

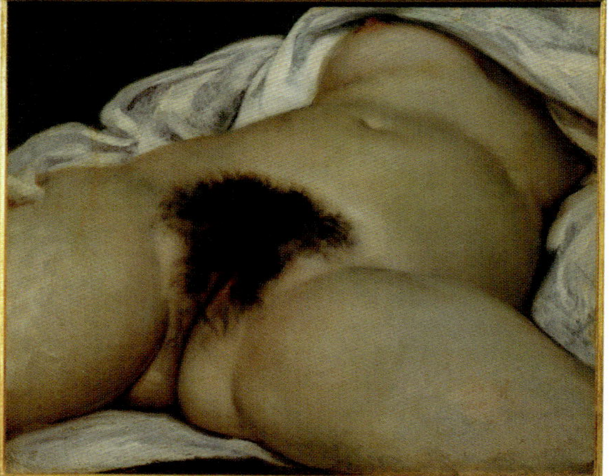

GUSTAVE COURBET *L'Origine du monde*

Sie klassifizierte Courbet-Posts 2011 als Verstoß gegen die Standards ihrer Gemeinschaft. Daraufhin kam es zu einem Gerichtsverfahren in Frankreich wegen Einschränkung der Kunstfreiheit. 2016 wurde die US-Firma verurteilt, Posts des Bildes von Usern in Frankreich zuzulassen. Für die restliche Welt gilt weiterhin: fotorealistisch gemalte weibliche Schamlippen und -haare bleiben im neo-prüden Internetzeitalter unerwünscht.

Dabei handelt es sich beim *Ursprung der Welt* um ein eindeutig heterosexuell konnotiertes Gemälde und um weibliche Nacktheit. Dafür

There's no denying that it's difficult to show portrayals of sex in public spaces. A little reminder is a picture by Gustave Courbet, *L'origine du monde (The Origin of the World)*. It was created in 1866 for the Turkish-Egyptian diplomat Khalil Bey, and as part of his notorious erotica collection, was covered by a green curtain and hidden from the world's gaze. Only special guests were allowed to see the painting, and only after dinner. But because almost everyone had heard about it, it became the most famous unseen piece of art of the 19th century, a *chef d'oeuvre inconnu*. In 1995 it was acquired by the Musée d'Orsay in Paris and it is now prominently displayed at that museum. Many apparently-till consider this a provocation, among them, the California company Facebook. In 2011 they classified a social media post showing Courbet's picture a "violation of community standards." This action prompted a lawsuit in France, claiming that Facebook was limiting the freedom of the arts. In 2016 the US-firm was ordered to allow posts of the painting – but only by users in France. For the rest of the world, a realistic painting of a labia with pubic hair was still a "violation." Welcome to the neo-prude internet age!

When it comes to homosexuality, matters get even worse. At least *The Origin of the World* is clearly a heterosexually oriented painting, showing female nudity for the pleasure of straight men. And a heterosexual French school teacher was willing to go to court

war ein französischer Lehrer bereit, kämpfend vor Gericht zu ziehen. 2012 zeigte dagegen das Museum Leopold in Wien die Schau *Nackte Männer. Von 1800 bis heute* und wählte als Poster das Bild *Vive la France* vom schwulen Künstlerduo Pierre et Gilles aus. Es zeigt drei Fußballer unterschiedlicher Hautfarbe – bekleidet nur vom Knie abwärts. Ein Murren über die drei „Nackerten" im Wiener Stadtbild ließ nicht lange auf sich warten. Die Proteste führten dazu, dass die „Wiener Würstchen" publicityträchtig überklebt werden mussten, zur Vermeidung öffentlichen Ärgernisses. Und Facebook zensierte das Motiv ebenfalls; es wurde nur im Genitalbereich verpixelt zugelassen für Posts rund um die Ausstellung in einem staatlichen Museum. Diesmal klagte niemand. Weil das Bild homoerotisch ist? Weil männliche Nacktheit anders behandelt wird als weibliche? Weil die Gemeinschaftsstandards von Privatfirmen wie Facebook, Apple, Amazon oder Google inzwischen hart erfochtene gesetzliche Grundlagen in Bezug auf die Darstellung von Nacktheit aushebeln? Gefechte, die besonders die Pioniere schwuler Pornografie in den USA einst ausgefochten hatten und damit eine Befreiung für *alle* Menschen durchsetzen konnten.

Es mag zwar stimmen, dass die Kunst der letzten 100 Jahre den „classical drag" abgeschüttelt hat – also die Notwendigkeit, queere Sexualität_en in antike Kontexte zu verpacken, wie Alex Pilcher in *A Queer Little History of Art* 2017 behauptet.[1] Aber sobald entsprechende Darstellungen das Label „Porno" angeheftet bekommen, ist es mit der Toleranz der Hüter öffentlicher Moral, Museen und Steuergelder vorbei. Schließlich müssen Minderjährige geschützt werden, heißt es. Selbst bahnbrechende Ausstellungen wie *Queer British Art 1861-1967* in der Tate Britain oder *La mirada del otro. Escenarios para la diferencia* im Prado-Museum, beide 2017, vermieden homoerotische Sexdarstellungen, die nicht eindeutig als „Kunst" klassifiziert werden können.

Umso erstaunlicher ist es, dass ausgerechnet das Oeuvre Tom of Finlands solche Sichtbarkeit

for his right to enjoy this painting and share his enjoyment with others on social media. In 2012, however, the Leopold Museum in Vienna presented the exhibition *Nackte Männer. Von 1800 bis heute (Nude Men. From 1800 Till Today)* and chose the picture *Vive la France* by gay artist duo Pierre et Gilles for their poster. It showed three soccer players of different skin colors, only dressed from the knees downward. It didn't take long for protests about the three "Nackerten" (nudes) polluting downtown Vienna to emerge. The protests got so fierce that eventually the advertising company pasted over the "Wiener Würstchen" (Vienna sausages) to avoid public outrage. Of course, Facebook also censored the picture; it was only allowed to be posted with the genital area pixelated. Even the state funded museum itself, when advertising the exhibition on their own social media platforms, had to use the pixilated image. No one sued this time. Was this because the picture was homoerotic? Because male nudity is treated in a different manner from female nudity? Because the community standards of private companies such as Facebook, Apple, Amazon and Google now restrict rigorously fought for rights regarding public nudity; rights that were once fought for by the pioneers of gay pornography in the US and which lead to liberation of *all* people?

It might be true, as Alex Pilcher states in *A Queer Little History of Art* 2017[1], that homoerotic art has finally cast off the necessity for "classical drag," i.e. the need to wrap queer sexualities into contexts of Greek or Roman antiquity to be presentable. But as soon as such homoerotic portrayals get labeled as "porn," the tax money for museums, the guardians of public morality, comes to an immediate stop. Even groundbreaking exhibitions like *Queer British Art 1861-1967* at the Tate Britain or *La mirada del otro. Escenarios para la diferencia* at the Prado Museum in Madrid, both 2017, avoided explicit homoerotic pictures which couldn't be clearly identified as "art." There was no "sex" anywhere in sight there, no erections, no penetrations and of course there was no sperm spurting about.

---

[1] Alex Pilcher, *A Queer Little History of Art*, London: Tate Publishing 2017, S. 9.

[1] Alex Pilcher, A Queer Little History of Art, London: Tate Publishing 2017, p. 9

im internationalen Museumsbetrieb erlangen konnte, und dass seine übersteigerten Darstellungen von Männern, Männersex und Maskulinität eine derart singuläre Stellung in der westlichen Popkultur eingenommen haben. Das reicht von T-Shirts über Bettwäsche, Kaffeeverpackungen, Kalendern, Spielfilmen bis zu Ausstellungen im Los Angeles Country Museum of Art, Museum of Modern Art (MoMA) oder der Biennale in Venedig. Wie passt das zusammen?

Als sich Touko Laaksonen 1957 mit dem Cover und Einzelseiten in *Physique Pictorial* der Öffentlichkeit erstmals als „Tom of Finland" vorstellte, tat er dies mit heroisch überhöhten Männerdarstellungen: Holzfäller aus der Serie *Men in the Forrest*. Sie stellen oberflächlich betrachtet den gesunden *All American Guy* dar, wie er kraftstrotzend die Welt in Besitz nimmt. Entsprechend konnten diese Beefcake-Bilder in jedem US-Supermarkt der 1950er Jahre verkauft werden. Als Vorbild für die Nachkriegsjugend im Kalten Krieg. Eingeweihte ‚warme' Leser, die wussten, dass es mehr zu sehen gab, mussten entsprechende Bilder bei Herausgeber Bob Mizer bestellen, unter der Hand. Die postalisch verschickten Arbeiten kursierten nicht öffentlich. Weswegen Tom of Finland-Sexbilder nur einem überschaubaren Zirkel von Fans bekannt waren.

Das änderte sich drastisch, als Ende der 1960er Jahre schwule Pornografie in den USA nach mehreren Gerichtsurteilen allgemein sichtbar werden konnte und schwule Pornozeitschriften an Kiosken auslagen – vielfach mit Illustrationen von Tom of Finland. Damit wurden dessen Bilder mit einem Schlag einem Massenpublikum zugänglich, zusammen mit Arbeiten anderer Erotikillustratoren. Robert W. Richards und Hunter O'Hanian kuratierten 2014 im Leslie + Lohman Museum for Gay and Lesbian Art die Ausstellung *Stroke: From Under the Mattress to Out in the Open* über diese pornografischen Zeichnungen. Im Ausstellungskatalog schreiben sie: „By the late 1960s, with the impact of the 'sexual revolution,' the rise of feminism, and the Stonewall Inn riot, the demand for [sex] magazines mushroomed. [T]itles included *Blueboy, Torso, Honcho, Mandate*, and *InTouch*. Each issue typi-

This makes it all the more astonishing that the oeuvre of Tom of Finland (ToF) has reached such prominence in the international museum world. His portrayals of monstrously endowed men having exaggerated sex have become a regular feature within Western pop culture. There are T-shirts with ToF images, bed clothes, coffee packages, calendars, movies about his life, as well as, exhibitions in the Los Angeles County Museum of Art, Museum of Modern Art (MoMA) and Biennale in Venice. How does this fit with the attitudes just described?

In 1957, when artist Touko Laaksonen was introduced on the cover and in the pages of *Physique Pictorial* as "Tom of Finland," it was with heroic portrayals of men: the lumberjacks from the series *Men in the Forest*. On the surface, they showed healthy all-American guys powerfully conquering the world. And, so, these beefcake pictures could be sold at grocery stores of the 1950s in the USA; they represented the prototype of postwar ideals during the Cold War years. Well-informed gay readers knew there was more to these images, because they knew you could order additional sets from editor Bob Mizer. These additional art works were far more explicit because they were sent privately by mail and never circulated publically. That's why Tom of Finland's men-having-sex pictures were only known by a small circle of dilettanti.

This changed dramatically in the late 1960s. Gay pornography became more visible after several legal battles were won in the United States. These allowed pornographic magazines to be sold at newsstands. Many of these had illustrations by Tom of Finland. Thus his pictures, together with works by other erotic illustrators, suddenly became accessible to a mass audience. In 2014 Robert W. Richards and Hunter O'Hanian curated an exhibition about pornographic drawings: *Stroke: From Under the Mattress to Out in the Open* at the Leslie + Lohman Museum for Gay and Lesbian Art. "By the late 1960s, with the impact of the 'sexual revolution,' the rise of feminism, and the Stonewall Inn riot, the demand for [sex] magazines mushroomed. [T]itles included *Blueboy, Torso,Honcho, Mandate*, and *InTouch*. Each issue typically featured masterful illustrations

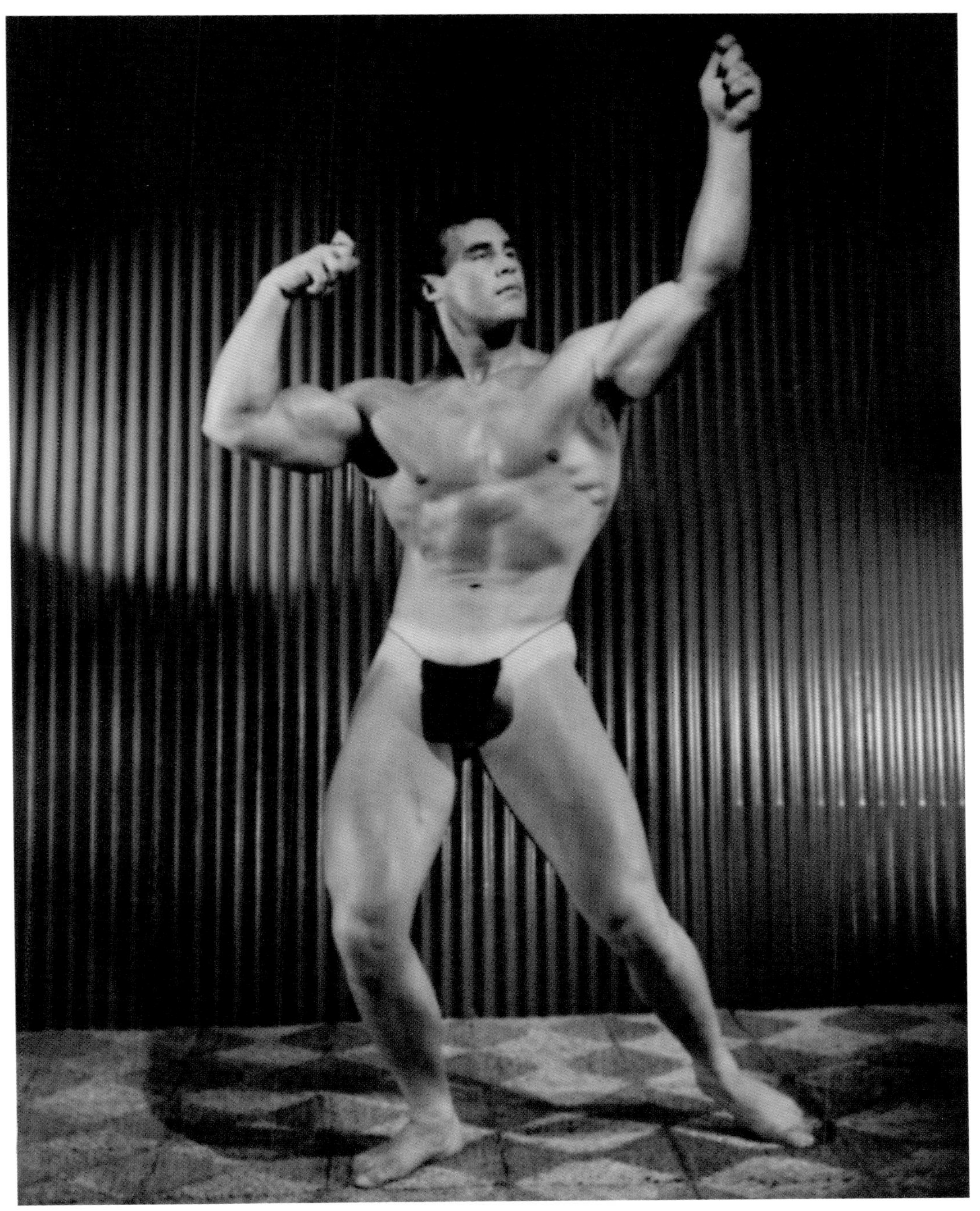

cally featured masterful illustrations by major artists."[2] Allerdings zirkulierten die Sexbilder von **Blade, Etienne, The Hun und anderen** aus dem *Stroke*-Universum primär in der schwulen Community, nicht in Museen oder renommierten Galerien. Auch nicht in Kunstbänden, die in regulären Kunstbuchhandlungen standen. Das schaffte einzig Tom of Finland.

Ein zentraler Unterschied ist, dass Tom zusammen mit Durk Dehner 1979 anfing, seine Arbeiten über die Tom of Finland Company zu vermarkten. Im Gegensatz zu anderen Erotikkünstlern ohne Agent professionalisierte Durk den Umgang mit Tom of Finland, kreierte ein Markenbewusstsein. Und er entriss die *dirty drawings* der Zirkulation in Hinterzimmern von Sexshops. 1989 wurde erstmals ein Tom of Finland-Werk beim Auktionshaus Christie's versteigert. 1991 hingen Tom of Finland-Werke in der Whitney Biennale zusammen mit Arbeiten von Jasper Johns, Roy Lichtenstein, Robert Rauschenberg und Frank Stella. Damit beschritt das Tom of Finland-Werk einen Weg, den bis dahin niemand sonst aus dem pornografischen Untergrund eingeschlagen hatte, mit Ausnahme von Fred Halsted, dessen experimentelle „Gay Phantasies" *L.A. Plays Itself* und *Sex Garage* (beide 1972) vom MoMA für die eigene Sammlung angekauft wurden, als bislang einzige dort vertretene Titel des Genres. Tom of Finland folgte erst 2006: in die Judith Rothschild Foundation Contemporary Drawings Collection des MoMA.

Bemerkenswerterweise handelt es sich bei vielen dieser Tom of Finland-Arbeiten nicht um schwanz- und penetrationslose Werke. Ganz im Gegenteil. Durk schaffte es mit seinem ständig wiederholten Mantra, die Bilder zeigten Homosexualität ohne jegliches Schuldgefühl (*„Tom went about creating the archetype of masculine homosexuals who participate freely together in sex – a decree from Nature herself"*)[3], Kuratoren zu überzeugen, dass es sich bei Tom of Finland um eine „Bastion der Freiheit" handle, wie die Fotografin Rachel Laurent es formuliert: *„[These] are the works of a man that didn't cower or inhibit himself*

by major artists."[2] However, explicit pictures by other artists circulated in gay subculture such as Blade, Etienne and The Hun, were not in museums or prestigious galleries. Nor were they included in art books displayed in regular bookstores. Only Tom of Finland succeeded in crossing that line.

One major reason was Tom, together with Durk Dehner, started to market his works through the Tom of Finland Company in 1979. In contrast to other erotic artists without agents, Dehner professionalized the handling of Tom of Finland and created brand awareness. He took the "dirty little drawings" out of the backrooms of sex shops. In 1989, a Tom of Finland drawing was sold at the auction house Christie's for the first time. In 1991 Tom of Finland pictures were shown at the Whitney Biennale together with works of Jasper Johns, Roy Lichtenstein, Robert Rauschenberg and Frank Stella. In this way, Tom of Finland took a path few from the pornographic underground had ever walked, with the possible exception of Fred Halsted's experimental "gay phantasies," *L.A. Plays Itself* and *Sex Garage* (both 1972), which were acquired by MoMA as sole representatives of the genre. In 2006, Tom of Finland followed when his works were incorporated into the Judith Rothschild Foundation Contemporary Drawings Collection at MoMA.

Remarkably, many of these works show erect dicks and penetration. Durk repeated over and over again, that these ToF pictures depicted homosexuality without any shame, *"Tom went about creating the archetype of masculine homosexuals who participate freely together in sex – a decree from Nature herself,"*[3] convincing curators that ToF was a, "bastion of freedom." As photographer Rachel Laurent expressed it: *"[These] are the works of a man that didn't cower or inhibit himself in his expression of what was in his heart. He represents freedom for us all."*[4] Additional help in this crusade to conquer mainstream institutions was won through the monographs of publisher Benedikt Taschen. These started with *Tom of Finland* in 1995

[2] Robert W. Richards und Hunter O'Hanian, *Stroke: From Under the Mattress to Out in the Open,* Berlin: Bruno Gmünder Verlag 2015, S. 7
[3] F. Valentine Hooven III, Durk Dehner, S. R. Sharp, *Tom of Finland. Life and Work of a Gay Hero,* Berlin: Bruno Gmünder Verlag 2012, S. 13.

[2] Robert W. Richards and Hunter O'Hanian, Stroke: From Under the Mattress to Out in the Open, Berlin: Bruno Gmünder Verlag 2015, p. 7
[3] F. Valentine Hooven III, Durk Dehner, S. R. Sharp, Tom of Finland. Life and Work of a Gay Hero, Berlin: Bruno Gmünder Verlag 2012, p. 13

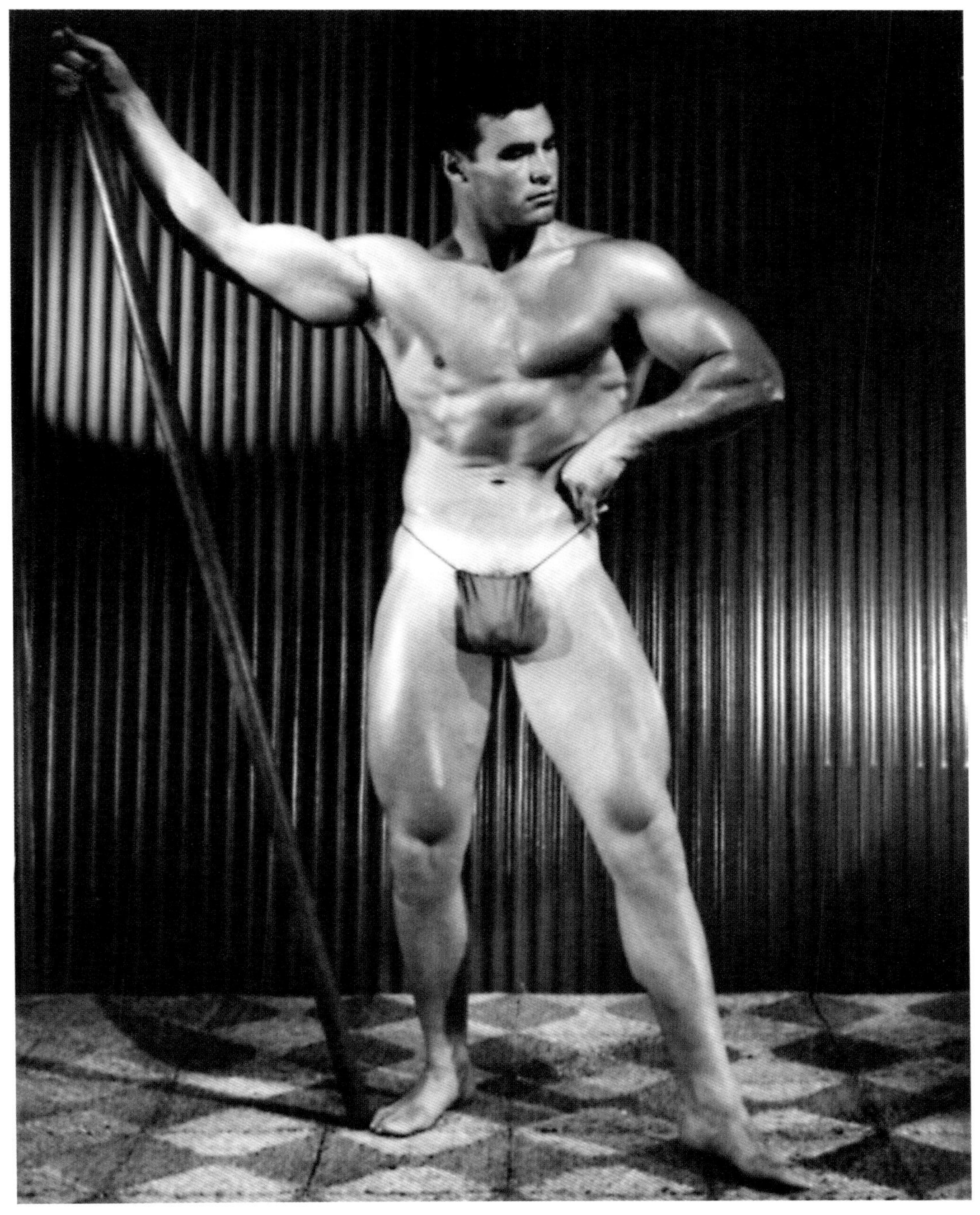

in his expression of what was in his heart. He represents freedom for us all."[4] Sehr hilfreich bei diesem Kreuzzug in die Institutionen und den Mainstream waren die Monografien des Kunstverlags Benedikt Taschen, die 1995 mit *Tom of Finland* begannen und sich bis in die Gegenwart fortsetzen: u. a. *Art of Pleasure* (2002), *Tom of Finland: The Comic Collection* (2005), *Tom of Finland XXL* (2009).

Im Zuge der Professionalisierung des Umgangs mit Tom of Finland-Erotikkunst und mit Blick auf den Nachruhm gründete Durk 1984 zusammen mit Tom die Tom of Finland Foundation (ToFF) in Los Angeles. Eine Non-Profit-Organisation, deren zentrale Ziele lauten: Bewahren, Dokumentieren, Restaurieren, Ausstellen. Die Notwendigkeit zum Bewahren wurde besonders in den Jahren der Aids-Krise deutlich, als viele Familien die angeblichen ‚Schmuddelwerke' im Nachlass von Verstorbenen entsorgten. Im Zuge der Neupositionierung von Tom of Finland initiierte Durk eine erste Biografie. Sie erschien 1991 auf Finnisch. Durch die Veröffentlichung des Buchs in seiner Heimat durchbrach Tom die lange Geheimhaltung seines Doppellebens. Es war ein für die Epoche bemerkenswertes Coming-out, das durch die Diagnose einer Lungenerkrankung 1988 befördert wurde und durch Toms Wissen um seinen baldigen Tod. Parallel zur Biografie überredete Durk die Finnish Film Foundation, die Doku *Daddy and the Muscle Academy* von Ilppo Pohjola zu fördern und den Film im finnischen Fernsehen auszustrahlen, bevor er weltweit in den Kinos anlief. Ein für die frühen 1990er Jahre singulärer Akt staatlicher Unterstützung für Homothematiken auf dem Höhepunkt des Aids-Sterbens. Die Finnen kürten Tom of Finland über Nacht zu ihrem „number one son". Tom erlebte das noch, bevor er Ende 1991 starb. Mehrere finnische Museen kauften Tom of Finland-Werke, zum Beispiel das Kiasma, Helsinkis Museum für Zeitgenössische Kunst, aber auch die Stadt Kaarina, wo Tom 1920 geboren worden war. Sie wurden im dortigen Rathaus ausgestellt.

Aber der eigentliche Siegeszug stand noch bevor. Durk als Sachverwalter und Erbe gelang es mit konstant weitergeführter Lobbyarbeit, dass Tom of Finland-Bilder in weitere Museums-

and continue right up to the present: *Art of Pleasure* (2002), *Tom of Finland: The Comic Collection* (2005), *Tom of Finland XXL* (2009).

While the two men were professionalizing the handling of ToF erotic art with an eye on Tom's posthumous reputation, Durk and Tom founded the Tom of Finland Foundation in Los Angeles in 1984. It is a non-profit organization with the following goals: preserve, document, restore and exhibit. The necessity to preserve became especially clear during the years of the AIDS crisis when many families disposed of the "dirty works" they found in the apartments of their dead relatives. In his quest to position Tom of Finland in the market, Durk initiated the first biography published in 1991 in Finnish. With this publication Tom overcame the secrecy of the double life he had been leading for decades in his home country. It was a remarkable coming-out, coinciding with his diagnosis of a fatal lung disease in 1988 and Tom's knowledge of his imminent death. Parallel to the biography, Durk supported the Finnish Film Foundations backing of the documentary *Daddy and the Muscle Academy* by Ilppo Pohjola. The film was broadcast on Finnish TV before being shown in movie theaters worldwide. This was a singular act of official state support of queer topics at the peak of the AIDS crisis in the 90s. The Finns, it seemed, elevated Tom of Finland to the status of their "number one son." Tom was able to witness all of this before he died at the end of 1991. Several Finnish institutions bought Tom of Finland works: the Kiasma and Helsinki's Museum for Contemporary Art. The town, Kaarina, where Laaksonen was born in 1920, purchased and exhibited the works publicly in the city hall.

Durk, as agent and champion, succeeded in having Tom of Finland pictures included in additional museum collections, but the main triumph was yet to come. In 1994, Schwules Museum in Berlin had their first solo ToF exhibition, which was a pioneering act. In 2006 the Helsinki City Museum presented the next big solo exhibition: *Ennennäkemätöntä – Unforeseen.* Between those two shows there were several group exhibitions. The inclusion

---

[4] Zit. ebd., S. 13.

[4] quote ib., p. 13

kollektionen aufgenommen wurden. 1994 gab es eine erste museale Soloausstellung im Schwulen Museum Berlin. Eine Pioniertat. Es dauerte dann bis 2006, bis das Helsinki Stadtmuseum die nächste große Soloausstellung *Ennennäkemätöntä – Unforeseen* präsentierte. Dazwischen liegen zahllose Gruppenausstellungen, in denen Tom of Finland-Arbeiten gezeigt wurden. Die Inklusion bei der Biennale in Venedig 2009 stellt einen Höhepunkt dar: Tom of Finland war vertreten im Nordischen Pavillon, kuratiert vom schwulen Künstlerduo Elmgreen & Dragset. Neben Penetrationen, frei schwingenden Erektionen und Fetischuniformen war auch Tom of Finlands *David* nach Michelangelo zu sehen, der 1981 als Auftragsarbeit für den italienischen Film- und Opernregisseur Franco Zeffirelli entstanden war.

Mit der finnischen Regierung hat Durk nach wie vor einen unschlagbar ‚respektablen' Partner an seiner Seite, der seinerseits davon profitiert, dass der Tom of Finland-Ruhm Menschen für Finnland begeistert, die sonst nicht mal von der besten Touristikabteilung erreicht werden könnten. Dass ein Land so wenig Berührungsängste mit Riesenerektionen und Fetischsex hat – diese sogar als Marketingtool für den Fremdenverkehr nutzt – ist erstaunlich. Dass die finnische Post auch den Streit mit Nachbarländern nicht scheute und 2014 eine Tom of Finland-Briefmarkenserie herausbrachte (auf Anregung der Tom of Finland Foundation) ist nicht minder erstaunlich.

Ob die Tom of Finland-Kanonisierung irgendwann auch zu einer Wiederentdeckung seiner einstigen Illustratorenkollegen aus der Erotikwelt führen wird? Ob der liberale Umgang mit Tom of Finland-Sexfantasien in Post- und Kunstwelt irgendwann dazu führen wird, dass auch die Internetgiganten von Silicon Valley ihre Standards lockern und einen befreiteren Umgang mit Nacktheit zulassen werden? Darauf wird man vermutlich warten müssen, vielleicht lange. Aber es ist gut zu wissen, dass Tom of Finland eine zentrale Rolle spielt im Kampf um die Akzeptanz schwuler Pornografie – und dass dieses neuerdings auch Nichtschwule interessiert. Indiz dafür ist der Anstieg von Heterofrauen als Konsumentinnen und neuerdings sogar die Gründung schwuler Pornostudios durch Heterofrauen wie Nica Noelle. Für viele dieser Frauen ist es eine Befreiung zu bestimmen, was

of ToF at the Biennale in Venice in 2009 was a highlight. Tom of Finland was represented in the Nordic Pavilion. Curated by gay artist duo Elmgreen & Dragset the show featured penetrations, freely swinging erections and fetish scenes, next to Tom of Finland's *David* (after Michelangelo). It had been commissioned for Italian film and opera director Franco Zeffirelli in 1981.

In the Finnish government, Durk has found an unimpeachably "respectable" partner standing by his side. And this partner profits, in turn, from Tom of Finland's fame and enhancement of the "cool" image of the country. As a result, Finland has no reservations in featuring huge erections, uniforms and fetish sex, using them as a brilliant marketing tool for tourism. Even the Finish postal service created a Tom of Finland stamps series (Tom of Finland Foundation made the application) in 2014 and didn't shun a conflict with neighboring countries such as Russia. On the contrary, the conflict put the Finns into the headlines, worldwide, as an open and ultra-cool place. And people apparently flock to the county in search of "real" ToF men which they expect to be running around, like Hobbits in New Zealand, in the wild.

Will Tom's "canonization" someday lead to a rediscovery of his former colleagues from the erotic world, as represented in the *Stroke* exhibition and catalog? Will the liberal handling of ToF sex fantasies by Finnish postal services and the international art world one day make internet giants of Silicon Valley loosen their "standards" and allow a freer depiction of nudity? We'll probably have to wait a bit for this to happen, possible a very long time. But it's good to know that Tom of Finland plays a key role in the fight for acceptance of gay pornographic imagery – and that, lately, even non-Gays are showing a growing interest in this. Evidence of this is the increasing popularity of gay pornography by straight women and the founding of gay porn studios by a straight woman such as Nica Noelle. For many of these women it's liberating to dictate what they want to see men do in front of a camera, instead of the other way round.

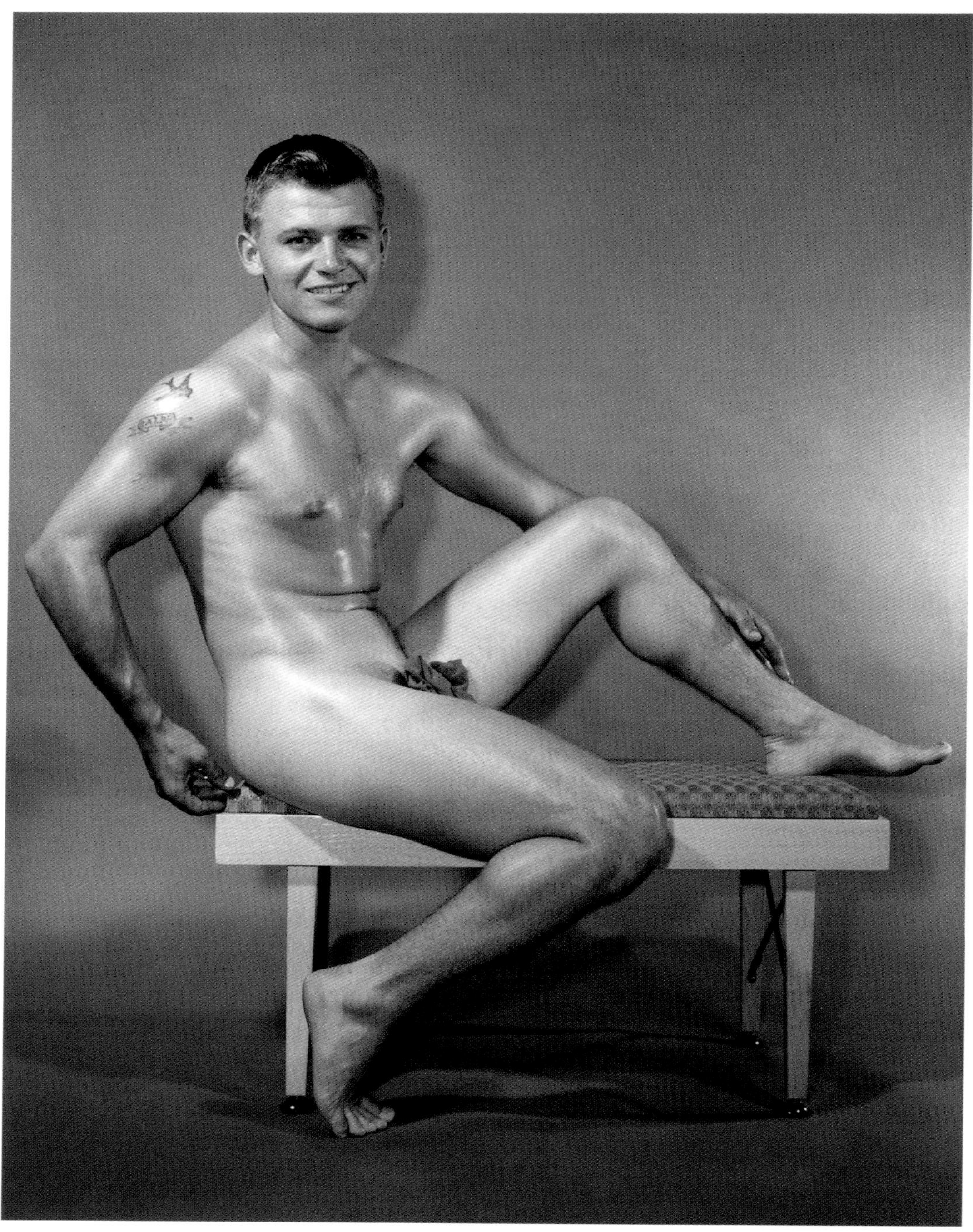

sie sehen wollen von Männern, die nunmehr ihren Wünschen als Sexarbeiter vor der Kamera zu folgen haben, statt umgekehrt.

Noch 2009 hatte Elke Krystufek im Kunstforum International der Biennale von Venedig behaupten können, dass der Männerakt „eine gesellschaftliche Unmöglichkeit" sei, „weil er scheinbar keinem weiblichen Begehren" entspreche „und daher in Nischen verdrängt" sei.[5] Das hat sich geändert. „Wer Geld hat, bestimmt, worauf er Lust hat zu schauen", sagte Krystufek.[6] Und es scheint, als habe eine nachgerückte Generation von Frauen Geld und Lust, auf nackte Männer zu schauen. „More and more women are joining the field, women who are CEOs with enough money to invest in art", sagt Kurator und Kunstberater Thomas Knapp 2016. „Such women buy art for themselves, and what they chose is different."[7] Claus Matthes vom Pornfilmfestival Berlin ergänzt: „Grundsätzlich ist es ja so, dass heterosexuelle Frauen, ebenso wie Schwule, von Männerkörpern sexuell erregt werden. Das ist im Hetero-Mainstream-Porno ein Grund gewesen, warum Frauen keinen Spaß an diesen Streifen hatten, weil die Männer in diesen Filmen in der Regel kaum zu sehen sind. Und schwule Pornos zeigen nun mal Männerkörper im Überfluss, dazu in der Regel recht ansehnliche."[8] Nicht zufällig ist die Herausgeberin des letzten XXL-Bands *Tom of Finland* im Taschen Verlag: Dian Hanson.

Liegt die Rettung der schwulen Erotikwelt also in den Händen von Powerfrauen, die ihr Geld und ihren Einfluss spürbar machen? An Frauen, die anders als Heteromänner keine Angst vorm „körperlichen Vergleich mit anderen Männern" haben und diesen „abwehren", wie Sabine Fellner 2012 bemerkte, dabei ein Buch von Beate Hofstadler und Birgit Buchinger von 2001 zitierend?[9] Fellner ist eine der drei Kurator*innen* der Linzer Ausstellung *Der nackte Mann* im LENTOS Museum, die anschließend ans Ludwig

In 2009, Elke Krystufek could still say in *Art Forum International* of the Biennale of Venice that nude portraits of men are a "social impossibility," "because it apparently doesn't match any female desire." According the Krystufek male nudity was still "suppressed into niches".[5] This has changed. "Whoever has the money decides what he wants to see," Krystufek said.[6] And it seems that a new generation of women has money and wishes to see naked men. "More and more women are joining the field, women who are CEOs with enough money to invest in art," art consultant Thomas Knapp said in 2016. "Such women buy art for themselves, and what they choose is different."[7] Claus Matthes from the Pornfilm Festival in Berlin adds: "Basically, straight women as well as gay men are sexually aroused by male bodies. That was a reason why women didn't enjoy mainstream straight porn, because the men in these movies were barely shown. And gay porn presents male bodies in abundance, usually pretty handsome ones too."[8] It's no accident that the editor of the latest XXL-book *Tom of Finland* from Taschen is Dian Hanson.

So does the re-evaluation of gay erotica and Tom's introduction into mainstream society lie in the hands of powerful women using their money and newfound influence? Women who, in contrast to straight men, aren't afraid of a "body comparison with other men" and who don't "fight it off", as Sabine Fellner noted in 2012, citing a book by Beate Hofstadler and Birgit Buchinger from 2001?[9] Fellner is one of the three curators of the exhibition *Der nackte Mann* (The Nude Man) at the LENTOS Museum in Linz which was later also shown at the Ludwig Museum of Contemporary Art in Budapest. Included in the exhibition was Tom of Finland's 1979 drawing of a monumentally-endowed white police man in uniform who fucks a white man in the ass in a park, while another white man watches from behind a bush. In the

---

[5] Elke Krystufek, „Die weitergeschriebene Identität: Ein Gespräch von Heinz-Norbert Jocks", in: Kunstforum International, Biennale von Venedig 2009. Zit. n. Sabine Fellner, „Der nackte Mann – ein Tabu", in: *Der nackte Mann. Texte* [Katalog LENTOS Kunstmuseum Linz / Ludwig Museum – Museum of Contemporary Art, Budapest, Bd. 1], Nürnberg: Verlag für moderne Kunst 2012, S. 11.

[6] Ebd., S. 12.

[7] Thomas Knapp, Interview mit dem Autor zu Charles-James-Erotikzeichnungen, New York, September 2016.

[8] Claus Matthes, Email an den Autor, 22. März 2017.

[9] Fellner zitiert *KörperNormen, KörperFormen. Männer über Körper, Geschlecht und Sexualität*, hrsg. Vom Bundesministerium für Bildung, Wissenschaft und Kultur, Wien 2001, in: Sabine Fellner, a.a.O., S. 13.

[5] Elke Krystufek, „Die weitergeschriebene Identität: Ein Gespräch von Heinz-Norbert Jocks", in: Art Forum International, Biennale of Venice 2009, Sabine Fellner, „Der nackte Mann – ein Tabu", in: *Der nackte Mann. Texte* [catalouge LENTOS art museum Linz / Ludwig Museum – Museum of Contemporary Art, Budapest, Issue 1], Nürnberg: Verlag für moderne Kunst 2012, p. 11

[6] ib. p. 12

[7] Thomas Knapp, interview with the author about the Charles James erotic drawings, New York, September 2016

[8] Claus Matthes, email to the author, 03-22-2017

[9] Fellner cites KörperNormen, KörperFormen. Männer über Körper, Geschlecht und Sexualität, edited by Bundesministerium für Bildung, Wissenschaft und Kultur, Vienna 2001, in: Sabine Fellner, a.a.O., p. 13

Museum für Zeitgenössische Kunst in Budapest ging. In der Ausstellung kam auch Tom of Finland vor, mit einem Bild von 1979, auf dem ein überdimensional bestückter weißer Polizist in Uniform einen nackten weißen Mann im Park in den Arsch fickt, während ein anderer weißer Mann im Gebüsch zuschaut. Das Bild ist im Katalog direkt neben Andy Warhols *Two male models* (1986) positioniert, gefolgt von Wilhelm von Gloeden und Guglielmo Plüschow. Zufällig ist es genau diese aquarellierte Zeichnung, die im Dezember 2016 vom Amsterdamer Auktionshaus Arts & Antiques Group für 12.500 Euro versteigert wurde. Der bislang höchste Preis, der je für ein Tom of Finland-Blatt bei einer Auktion erzielt wurde.

Inzwischen ist es aber auch so, dass Queerfeministinnen wie die lesbischen Kurator_innen von *Homosexualität_en* im Deutschen Historischen Museum sich 2015 bewusst entschieden, Tom of Finland aus ihrer Ausstellung herauszuhalten. Denn: Es sollte deutlicher die Rolle von Frauen/Lesben im Befreiungskampf betont werden und es sollten die traditionellen „schwulen" und „weißen" Narrative überwunden werden. Ein Schlachtruf der beiden (weißen) Kuratorinnen Brigit Bosold und Dorothee Brill lautete: „Kein Tom of Finland mehr!" Während lange Jahre der Kampf der Homosexuellen gegen die übermächtige heterosexuelle Mehrheitsgesellschaft verlief, hat er sich verlagert. Heute kämpfen die einzelnen Gruppen der LGBTQQIAAP* Community (Lesbian, Gay, Bisexual, Transgendered, Queer, Questioning, Intersex, Asexual, Allies and Pansexual) gegeneinander. Wobei sich speziell Frauen – insbesondere Lesben, die über mangelnde Sichtbarkeit in der Gay Community klagen – von weißen schwulen Cis-Männern dominiert und unterdrückt fühlen. Was zur Folge hat, dass sie diese ihrerseits mit Intersektionalitätsdebatten versuchen an den Rand zu drängen. Tom of Finland als Ikone genau dieser weißen schwulen Cis-Community taugt dabei als perfektes Exempel.

Zweifellos ist die Diskussion um Tom of Finland, sein Werk und dessen Bedeutung in eine neue Runde getreten. Es wird spannend sein zu beobachten, wie sie sich weiterentwickeln wird. Angesichts des ideologischen Streits um „Critical Whiteness" hatte Dehner schon 2012

catalog the image is placed right next to Andy Warhol's *Two Male Models* (1986), followed by Wilhelm von Gloeden and Guglielmo Plüschow. Incidentally, it's precisely this water colored drawing which was auctioned off for 12,500€ at the Amsterdam Auction House Arts & Antiques Group in 2016. It was the highest price ever achieved for a Tom of Finland art work at an auction.

Meanwhile, radical queer feminists like the lesbian curators of *Homosexualität_en* (Homosexualit_ies) at the National History Museum in Berlin decided in 2015 to exclude Tom of Finland from their exhibition. Their reason: the role of women/lesbians in the struggle for liberation should be emphasized and traditional "gay" and "white" narratives should be overcome. The battle cry of the two (white) curators, Birgit Bosold and Dorothee Brill was, "No more Tom of Finland!" For many years the battle was fought between homosexuals and the heterosexual majority, it has now shifted. Today the sub-groups of the LGBTQQIAAP* community (Lesbian, Gay, Bisexual, Transgendered, Queer, Questioning, Intersex, Asexual, Allies and Pansexual) seem to be fighting against each other. Especially women – particularly Lesbians who complain about an insufficient visibility within the gay community – feel suppressed and dominated by white gay Cis-men. As a consequence, they try to push them to the margins with intersectionality debates. Tom of Finland, as an icon of exactly this white gay Cis-Community is seen, by them, as a perfect example of everything that needs to be overcome.

Without doubt the discussion about Tom of Finland, his work and its meaning has entered a new phase. It will be interesting to see how it will develop. Because of the ideological fight about "Critical Whiteness," Durk included a new chapter titled "Black Magic" in the 2012 edition of the Tom of Finland biography.10Tom incorporated interracial couplings in the early '60s, when it was both progressive and taboo. The champions of racial debate will have a lot to discuss, including trying to evaluate the images in that Black Magic chapter. Similarly, Queer Nations has ac-

in die Neuausgabe der Tom of Finland-Biografie[10] ein Kapitel mit der Überschrift „Black Magic" eingefügt. An den entsprechenden Darstellungen werden sich Vorkämpfer_innen der aktuellen Rassismusdebatten abarbeiten können (bedenkend, dass Tom of Finland bereits in den frühen 60ern gemischte Paare gezeichnet hat, was damals zugleich progressiv und tabu war). Genau wie Queer Nations Tom of Finland seit Jahren vorwirft, er sei ein „Sell Out", weil er nur „Straights" gezeichnet habe, statt eines breit(er)en Spektrums „queerer" Menschen, die nicht alle „super-masculine" sind.[11]

Der Ausschluss von Tom of Finland aus *Homosexualität_en* bzw. die Kritik von Queer Nations muss nicht schlecht sein. Schließlich geht es nicht darum, wer recht hat, sondern darum, mitzudiskutieren in einer sich stetig wandelnden Gesellschaft, auch einer queeren Gesellschaft. Solche Diskussionen halten Kunst lebendig. Das gilt für Courbets *L'origine du monde* genauso wie für Tom of Finland. Angesichts der momentanen „Beißreflexe" [12] innerhalb der zersplitterten Community wird allerdings die Darstellung von Sexualität und Homosexualität in öffentlichen Räumen neuerlich schwierig. Weil inzwischen debattiert wird, was eigentlich „Homosexualität" sei. Heute könnte man in Courbets Weltenursprung genauso gut einen schwulen Trans*-Mann erblicken wie in Tom of Finland-Figuren butche Trans*Lesben mit Schwänzen. Die Frage lautet dann: Wer darf solche Sexualität_en darstellen ohne sich dem Vorwurf von Aneignung oder Ausbeutung auszusetzen, wo dürfen solche Sexualität_en gezeigt werden, ohne gleich Trigger-Warnungen für Menschen auszugeben, die sich von Schamlippen oder Riesenschwänzen „verletzt" fühlen könnten? So kollidieren plötzlich Neo-Prüderie mit Genderkrieger_innen und ein konservatives gesellschaftspolitisches Roll-back mit einer radikalen „queeren" Neuinterpretation der Welt. Kurz: Es wird spannend, innerhalb und außerhalb der Museumswelt, auch für Tom of Finland!

cused Tom of Finland for years of being a "sell out" because he only drew "straight acting men" instead of a broader range of "queer" people who aren't all "super-masculine."[11]

The exclusion of Tom of Finland from *Homosexualität_en* and the criticism by Queer Nations are not necessarily bad. After all, it's not about who is right, but about participating in the broad discussions of a continuously changing society, as well as, our evolving queer society. These discussions keep art alive. This is true for Courbet's *L'origine du monde* and for Tom of Finland. The current "snapping reflexes"[12] between divisions within the queer community make the portrayal of sexuality and homosexuality in public spaces difficult once again, but for different reasons. Now the debate questions what homosexuality is fundamentally. Today, one could see a gay trans* man in Courbet's "The Origin of the World," or Butch Trans* Lesbians with dicks in Tom of Finland characters. The question is: who is "allowed" to depict such sexualities without accusations of exploitation; where can such sexualities be shown without issuing trigger warnings for people who feel "offended" and "injured" by a labia or huge dick? Suddenly internet neo-prudery clashes with radical gender fighters, and a conservative sociopolitical roll-back collides with a fundamental queer reinterpretation of the world. In short: It will stay interesting for Tom of Finland within and outside of the museum world.

Translation: Sunita Sukhana,
Mark Timothy Hayward

---

[10] F. Valentine Hooven III, Durk Dehner, S. R. Sharp, a.a.O., S. 229
[11] Vgl. ebd., S. 235.
[12] Patsy L'Amour LaLove, Beißreflexe – Kritik an queerem Aktivismus, autoritären Sehnsüchten, Sprechverboten, Berlin: Querverlag 2017

[10] F. Valentine Hooven III, Durk Dehner, S. R. Sharp, a.a.O., p. 229
[11] see ib. p. 235
[12] see Patsy L'Amour LaLove, Beißreflexe – Kritik an queerem Aktivismus, autoritären Sehnsüchten, Sprechverboten, Berlin: Querverlag 2017

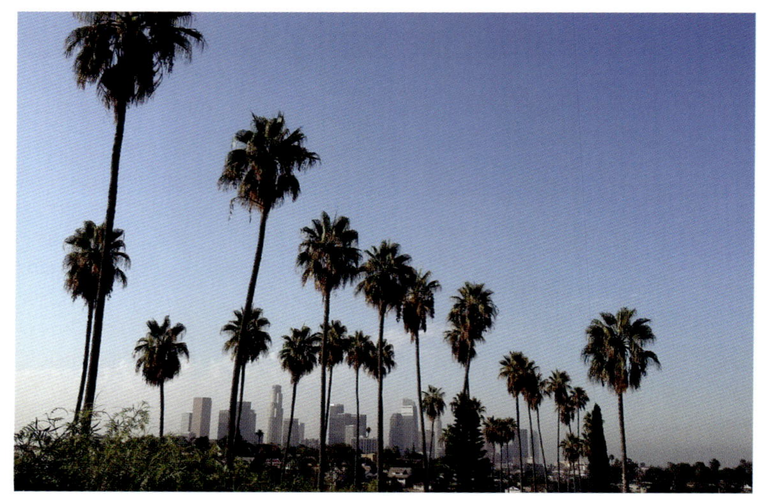

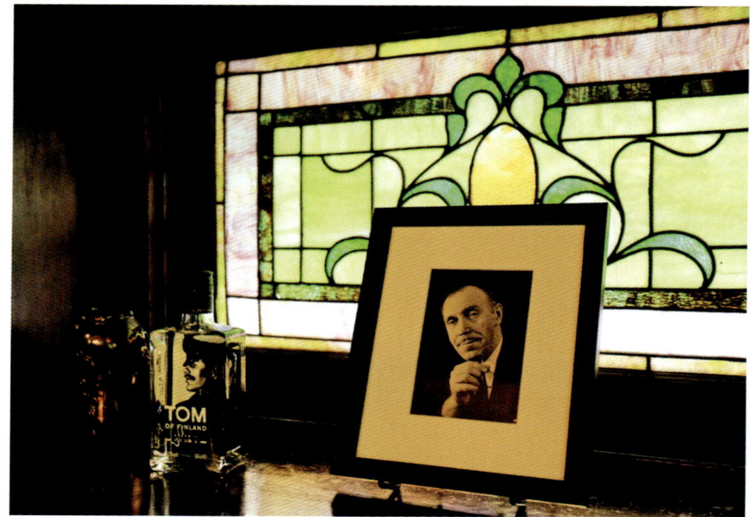
TOM
OF FINLAND

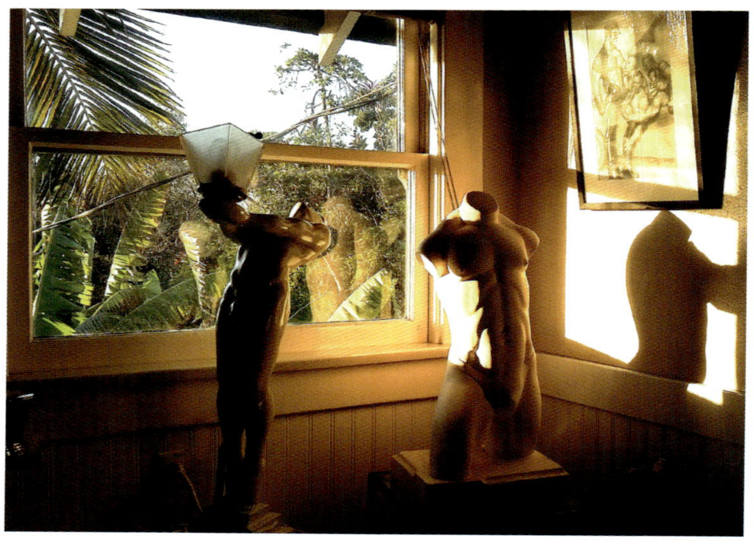

TOM House

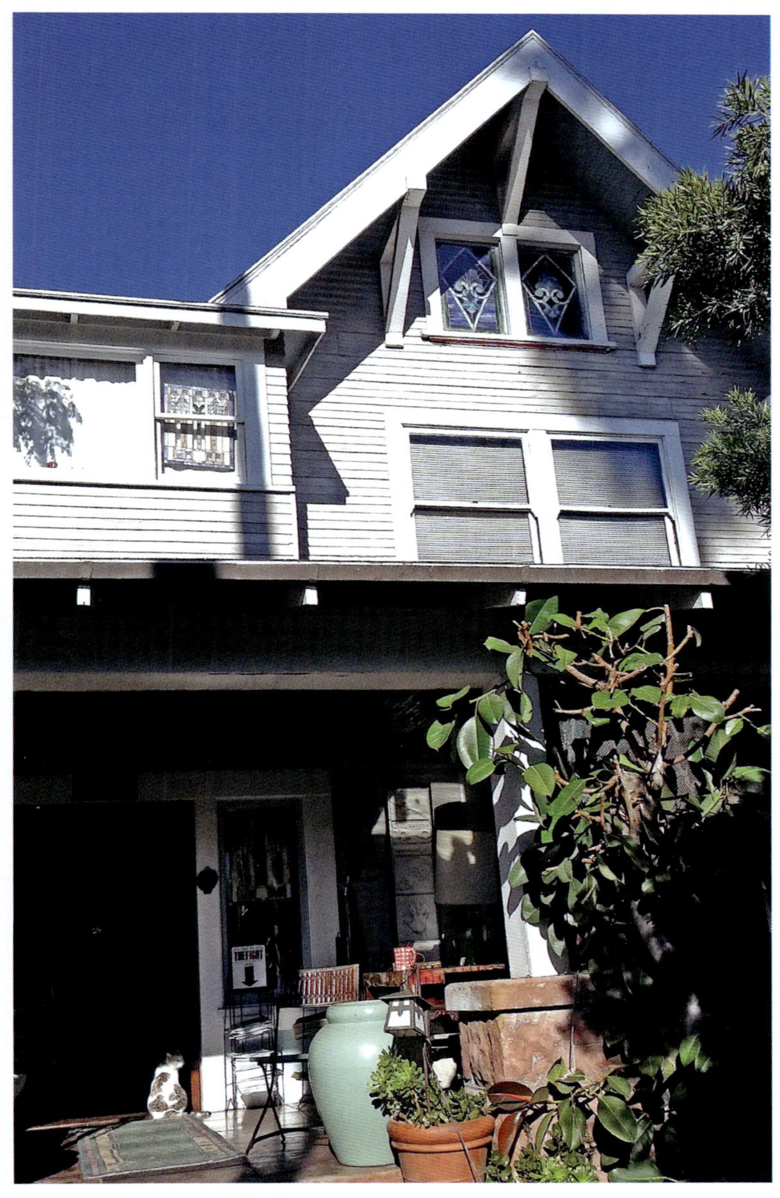

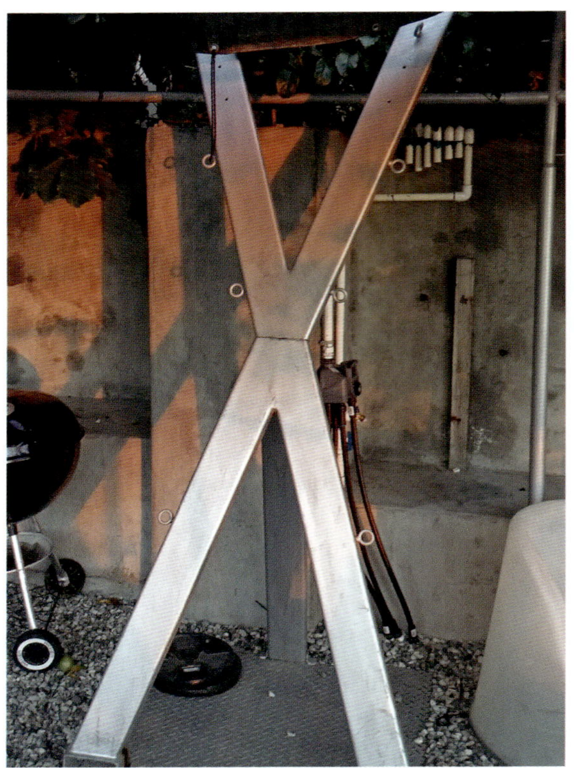

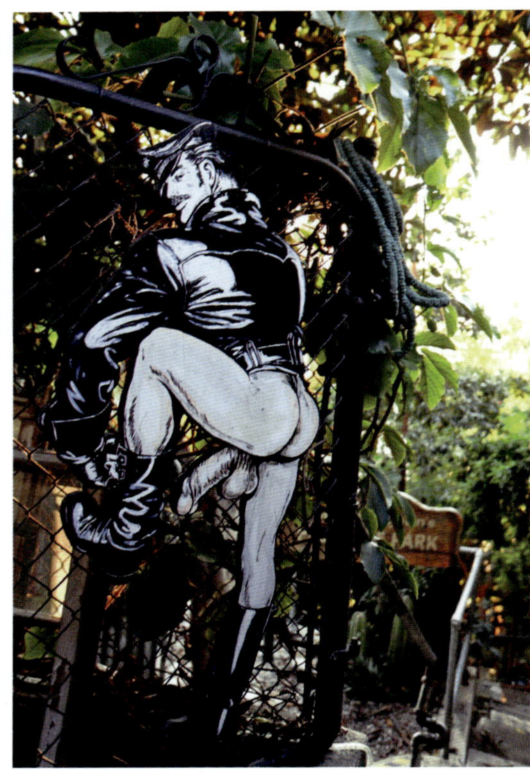

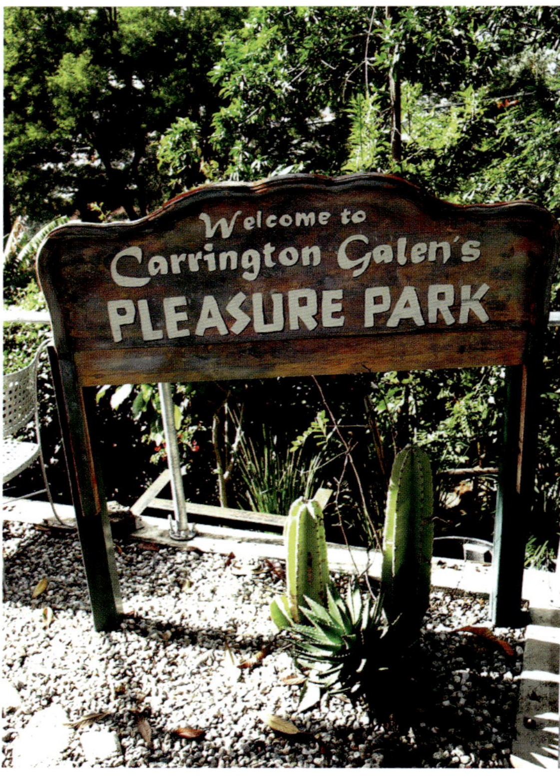
Welcome to
Carrington Galen's
PLEASURE PARK

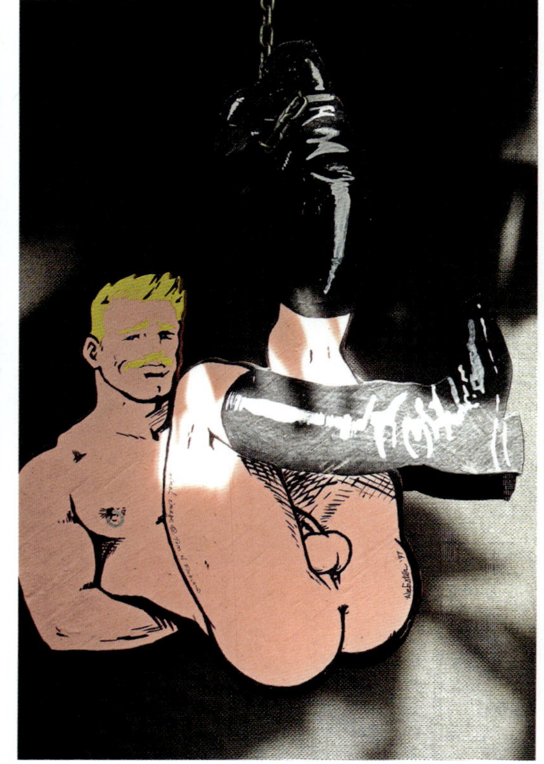

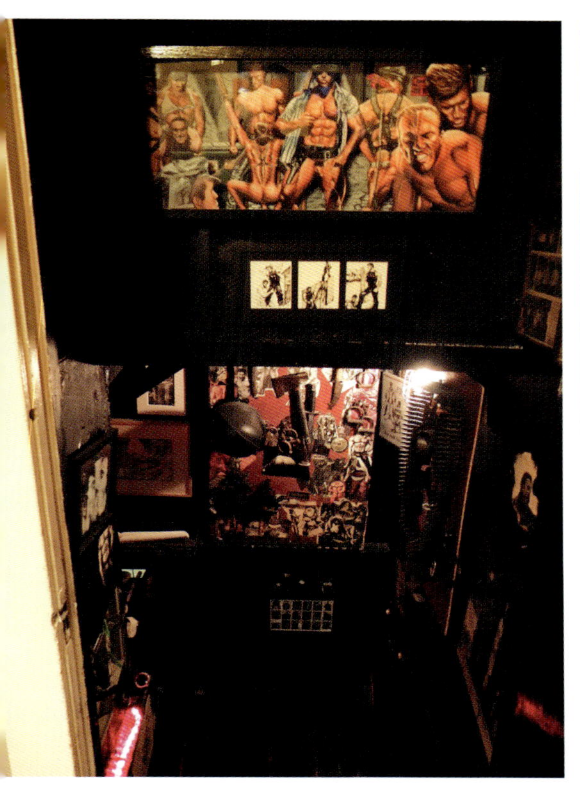

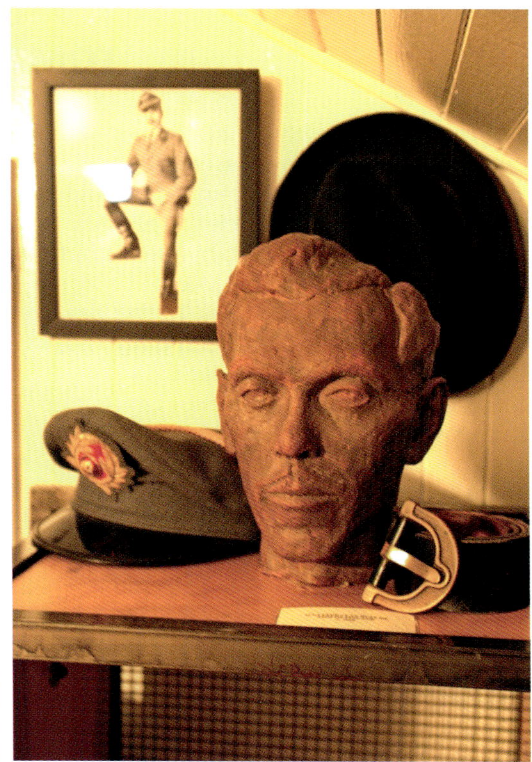

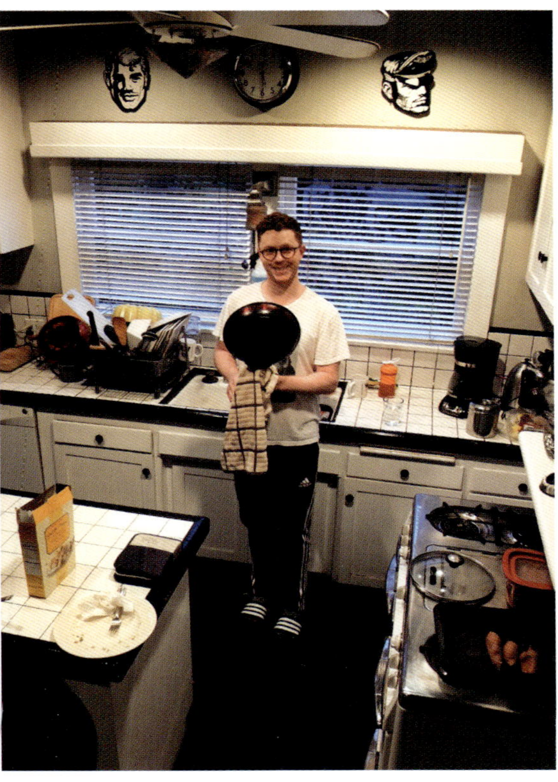

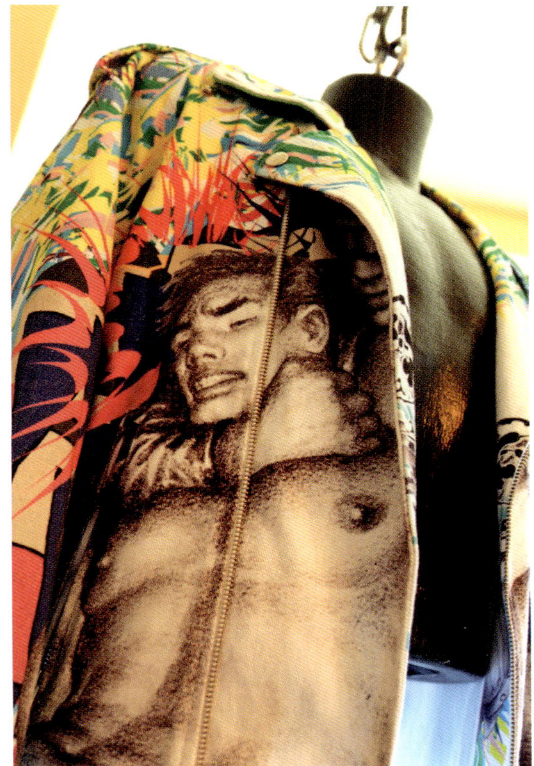

DURK DEHNER

TOM House

It started in 1979 with my ex-partner and his partner, along with my present-at-the-time partner. We collectively bought this house as a family. It was the Dehner family and Tom had his room reserved by me so that he settled into the garret that was both his studio and his sleeping quarters. To this day, we have kept it with only his belongings, books and catalog binders in the room.

When I miss him, and I still do, I can just go up to his room and lie down and have a sleep. I wake up renewed and ready to make things happen in the world.

TOM House, Tom of Finland House, was given special status in November of last year when the City of Los Angeles voted to make the residence an Historic-Cultural Monument because of the personage who lived here and after whom the property is now named. The years of significance were the 1980s when Tom called sunny California his second home.

TOM House is always evolving, always authentic in how it expresses itself to visitors through our artists in residence and programming associated with the culture of the community.

Es begann im Jahr 1979 mit meinem Ex-partner sowie seinem und meinem damaligen Partner. Wir haben dieses Haus alle zusammen als Familie gekauft. Wir waren die Dehner-Familie, und für Tom hatte ich das Mansardenzimmer reserviert, das er sowohl als Atelier als auch als Schlafquartier nutzte. Noch heute befinden sich in diesem Zimmer allein seine Habseligkeiten, seine Bücher und Sammelmappen. Wenn ich ihn vermisse, was ich immer noch tue, kann ich einfach in sein Zimmer gehen, mich hinlegen und einschlafen. Wenn ich dann aufwache, fühle ich mich erneuert, gestärkt und bin bereit, etwas zu bewegen.

Das TOM House, das Tom of Finland House, erhielt im November 2017 einen besonderen Status. Die Stadt Los Angeles erklärte die Residenz, in Würdigung des Künstlers, der hier lebte und nach dem das Anwesen benannt ist, zu einem historisch-kulturellen Denkmal. Die ausschlaggebende Zeit waren die 1980er Jahre, als Tom das sonnige Kalifornien als sein zweites Zuhause bezeichnete.

Das TOM House entwickelt sich immer weiter und bleibt sich dabei treu, durch unsere Artists in Residence und unser Veranstaltungsprogramm sind wir fest mit der Kultur der Community verbunden.

Übersetzung: Florian Rogge

t

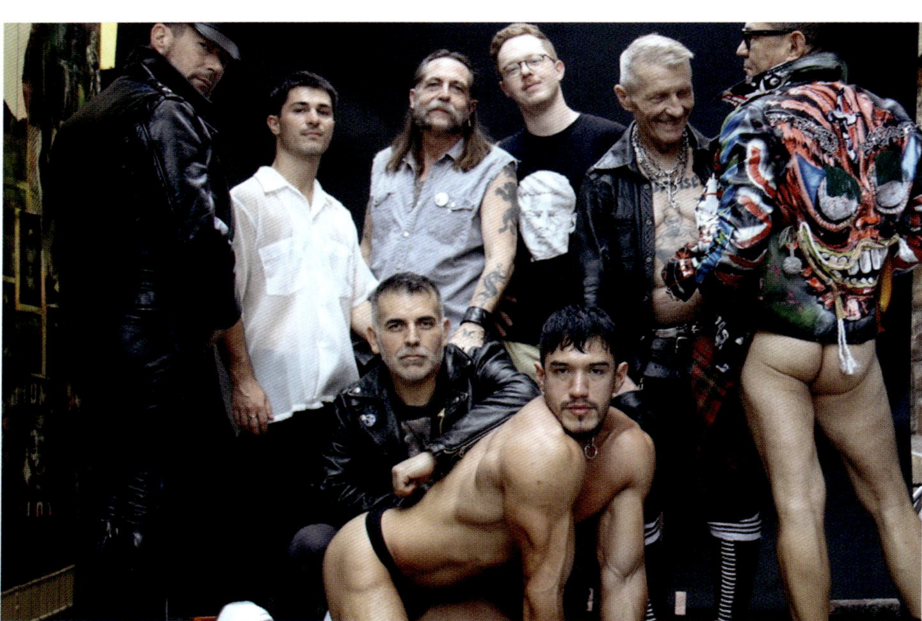

Marc Ransdall-Bellenger, Jamison Karon, Sharp, Stuart Sandford, Durk Dehner, Rubén Esparza, Miguel Angel Reyes, Jon Vaz Gar

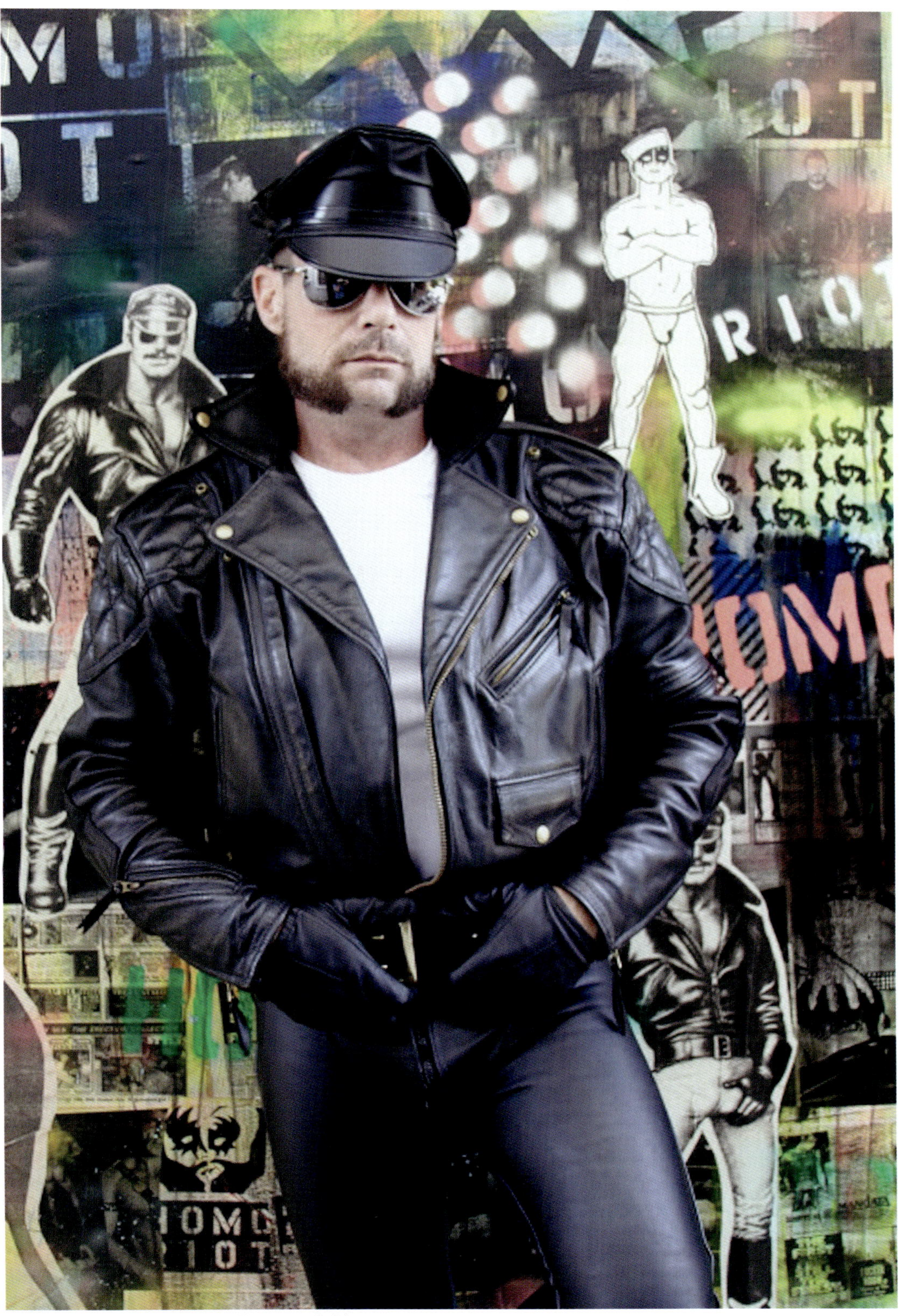

Marc Ransdall-Bellenger, mural by / Wandbild von HOMO RIOT

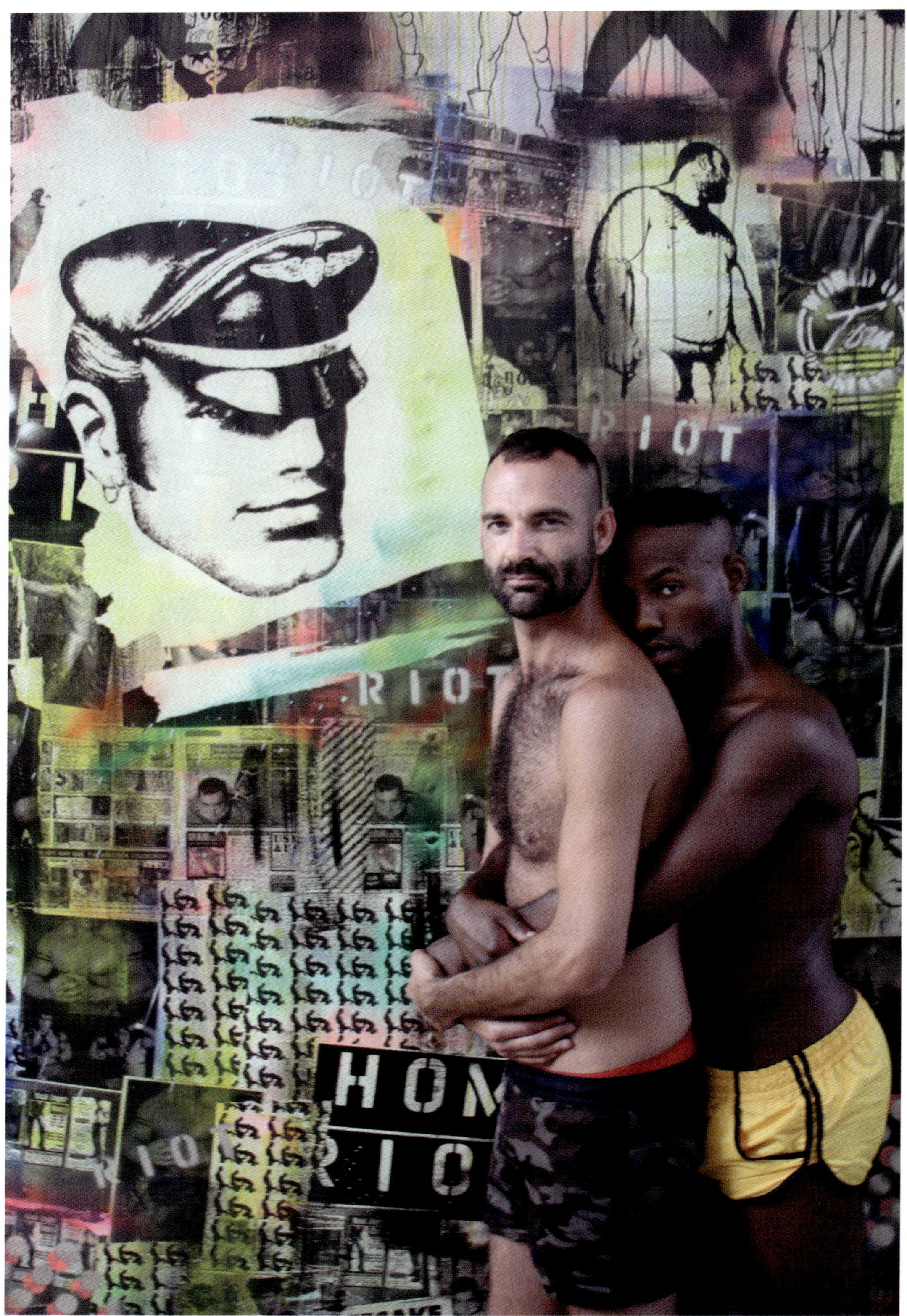

Joshua and Jordan Green, mural by / Wandbild von HOMO RIOT

Hello, TOM House

In the street of a changing Los Angeles neighborhood I stripped off my button down and rifled through the trunk of my car for a dirty sheer black t-shirt I knew was somewhere in hiding. Upon finding the crumpled shred of fabric, I impulsively brought it to my nose. The shirt was rancid with body odor. I slipped it on. At the chic neighborhood gallery full of eccentric leathered patrons I was totally overdressed and this weathered cotton shirt made me feel a little less alien.

At the gallery, the most remarkable crowd congregated: leather daddies and biker babes and gorgeous costumed men acting as pedestrian as any Sunday School boy in Ralph Lauren. On the stark white walls a few original sketches by Tom of Finland hung in stoic reverie. At the time, though I knew—perhaps instinctively—that Tom's work was prolific, I was unaware of the impact the work would have on me. That was before I saw the house.

The gallery event was a release party for a book Rizzoli published called *TOM House*, a collection of photos and words documenting the LA home Tom of Finland inhabited for the last decade of his life. The book, and subsequently the release party, brought with it the leather fetish and glorified homoeroticism of what I thought was a bygone era. The creators of the book were sat at a counter signing copies. The most alluring character being Tom of Finland's partner and Muse, Durk Dehner—a windswept, magnetic man completely clad in polished black leather and heavy silver. Terrified, but also desperate to be noticed by this rare creature I passed him my book for an autograph. This is all really cool, I mustered more boyish than I meant. He grumbled at me, asked for my name, and then scribbled eloquently with a flourish: *Jamison is a good beginning. January starts the year out right.* I had just moved to Los Angeles, I took his words as a premonition.

Auf der Straße eines wohlhabenden Viertels von Los Angeles zog ich mir das Oxford-Hemd aus und wühlte im Kofferraum nach einem schmutzigen schwarzen T-Shirt, das sich ganz unten befand. Spontan brachte ich den hauchdünnen Fetzen Stoff an meine Nase, sog den heftigen Geruch ein und streifte es mir flink über. In dieser schicken Kiezgalerie voller exzentrischer Ledermänner wäre ich in einem Oxford-Hemd viel zu overdressed. Dieses abgewetzte Stück Baumwolle ließ mich seltsamerweise weniger wie ein Außerirdischer wirken.

In der Galerie hatte sich eine bemerkenswerte Gruppe versammelt: Lederdaddys und Motorradjungs, umwerfend schöne Männer in Verkleidung, die harmloser wirkten als jeder Kirchenjunge in einer Ralph-Lauren-Werbung. An den kargen, weißen Wänden hingen einige Originalskizzen Tom of Finlands in stoischer Ehrerbietung. An diesem Abend, auch wenn ich durchaus – womöglich instinktiv – wusste, wie produktiv sein Schaffen war, ahnte ich noch nicht, welchen Einfluss sein Werk auf mich ausüben würde. Das war, bevor ich das Haus überhaupt erblickt hatte.

Die Vernissage war eine Buchpremiere für *TOM House*, einen Bildband, den der Verlag Rizzoli herausgebracht hatte. Das Buch enthielt eine Auswahl an Fotos und Texten, die das Haus in Los Angeles dokumentierten, in dem Tom of Finland die letzten zehn Jahre seines Lebens verbracht hatte. In meinen Augen hafteten dem Buch – und daher auch der Release-Party – der Fetisch Leder sowie die huldvolle Homoerotik einer längst vergangenen Ära an. Die Herausgeber des Bandes saßen hinter einem Tresen und signierten Bücher; der charismatischste von allen war dabei Toms Ex-Freund und Muse Durk Dehner: ein verwegener Mann mit einer unglaublichen Ausstrahlung, ganz in glänzendes Leder und schweres Silber gekleidet. Obwohl er mich einschüchterte, spürte ich gleichzeitig den Drang, seine Aufmerksamkeit auf mich zu lenken, also ging ich zu ihm hin, das soeben erworbene Buch in der Hand. „Das ist ja hier alles total cool", brachte ich etwas knabenhafter hervor als beabsichtigt. Er grummelte etwas, verlangte nach meinem Namen, dann schrieb er schwungvoll: *Jamison ist ein guter Anfang. Mit Januar fängt das Jahr auch gut an.* Da ich erst vor kurzem nach Los Angeles gezogen war, nahm ich seine Worte als Omen.

David Crotty, a well-connected photographer friend had invited me to the event, which was to be followed by a different gallery opening and dinner. I tottered back to him, my inscribed book dangling from sweating palms. He was chatting with the editor of *TOM House*, Michael Reynolds, a handsome salt and pepper Jew from New York, with whom I was immediately smitten. David made the introductions like any proper socialite would and the Michael invited me to the after party, commenting casually on my looks. Turning bright red I declined, as David and I had conflicting plans that evening. Go to the party, David said. We'll catch up later. He winked.
I felt something unfolding inside of me that both frightened and electrified me. On the way to TOM House I made an impromptu pit-stop at a girlfriend's, demanding she lend me a leather jacket and boots. Already drunk with anticipation, I convinced her to drop me off down the hill from the private Echo Park residence; I was euphoric at the prospect of knowing any of "TOM's Men" on a personal level. At a retro Dodger's themed bar I pounded two dirty martinis and twirled alone on the empty dance floor before spilling back onto Sunset Boulevard with newfound courage. Downtown LA glistened like a mirage behind me as I climbed a crumbling set of steps toward the palm tree lined Laveta Terrace.
Down this mystical street, I walked slow. Ahead of me, I could spot a small crowd funneling into a wooden gate. As I approached I noticed that an impenetrable two-story hedge encased this gate and the house it protected. From behind the lush Californian wall came the echoes of a lavish party. A warm glow oozed from the glowing gate and little puzzle piece orifices of that looming hedge.
I slipped into the anterior courtyard, nodding at the valet as if we were somehow acquainted. My eyes beheld the sprawling house for the first time. With every light bulb blazing, the sinister relic was smoldering in that crisp Angelino night.

David Crotty, ein gut vernetzter befreundeter Fotograf, hatte mich zur Party eingeladen, die nahtlos in eine andere Vernissage überging und mit einem Dinner endete. Ich ging ganz benommen zu ihm zurück, das frisch signierte Exemplar in meinen verschwitzten Händen. David unterhielt sich gerade mit Michael Reynolds, dem Lektor von *TOM House*, einem gutaussehenden, graumelierten Juden aus New York, von dem ich sofort hin und weg war. Ganz der Mann aus gutem Hause stellte David mich gleich vor, woraufhin Michael mich zur Afterparty einlud, nicht ohne beiläufig zu bemerken, wie gut ich denn aussehe. Ich lief rot an, lehnte aber ab, da ich an dem Abend bereits verplant war. „Geh doch mit", sagte David zu mir, „ich komme auch später nach." Dann zwinkerte er mir zu.
Ich spürte, wie sich tief in mir etwas regte, das mich verängstigte und zugleich elektrifizierte. Auf dem Weg zurück zum TOM House legte ich aber erst einmal einen unangemeldeten Zwischenstopp bei einer Freundin ein, von der ich die sofortige Aushändigung ihrer Lederjacke und Stiefel als Leihgabe verlangte. Trunken vor Erwartung überredete ich sie sogar, mich hinzufahren, und ich stieg nicht weit von der Privatadresse im Echo Park am Ende der Straße aus. Da mich die Vorstellung, ich würde bald einige von „Tom's Men" persönlich kennenlernen, euphorisierte, kippte ich in einer Baseball-Kneipe im Retro-Look gleich zwei Dirty Martinis hinunter, drehte mich eine Weile selbstvergessen auf der leeren Tanzfläche, bevor ich mich endlich auf den Weg machte und beflügelt vom neuentdeckten Mut den Sunset Boulevard entlanglief. Hinter mir glitzerte die Innenstadt von L.A. wie eine Fata Morgana, als ich eine baufällige Treppe hinaufstieg in Richtung der von Palmen gesäumten Laveta Terrace.
Gemächlich lief ich diese sagenumwobene Straße entlang. Direkt vor mir entdeckte ich eine Menschentraube, die sich langsam durch das hölzerne Eingangstor hindurchzwängte. Als ich mich ihr näherte, fiel mir die gewaltige Hecke auf, fast zwei Stockwerke hoch, die das Tor umsäumte und die Residenz dahinter schützte. Hinter dieser üppigen kalifornischen Mauer drangen die Geräusche einer fulminanten Party zu mir hindurch. Ein warmer Schein sickerte durch das Tor aus Licht und malte durch die Öffnungen im mächtigen Laub der Hecke kleine Puzzlestücke auf dem Boden.
Ich schlich in den Vorgarten und grüßte den Türsteher mit einem Kopfnicken, als ob wir alte Freunde wären. Meine Augen blieben auf einem

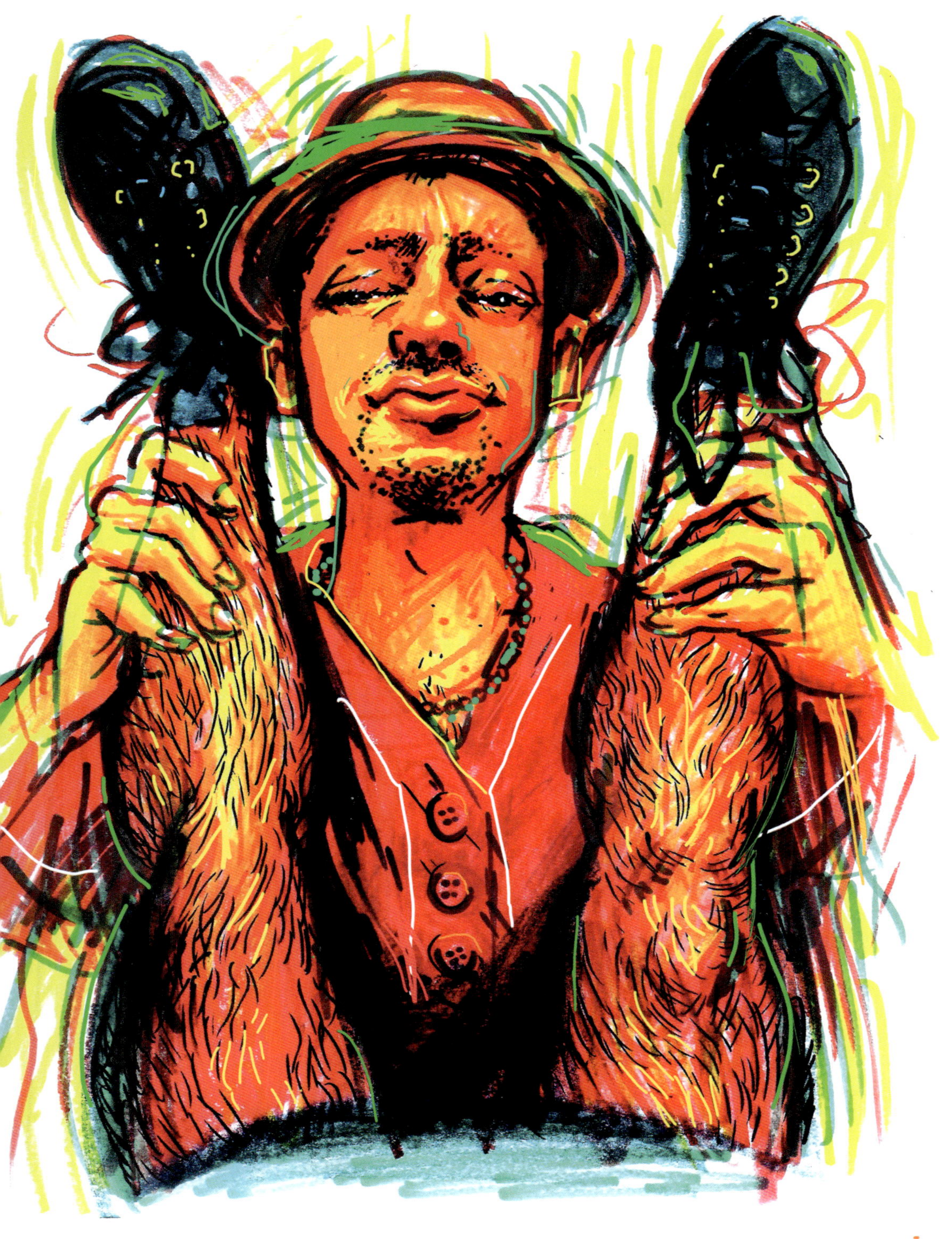

The beast was in full heat as party guests spilled in and out of its mouth; from inside came a steady moaning sound. A man in leather was sat on the front porch managing the guest list, and as I mumbled my name to him (I was not on any list), some stranger from within pulled me inside, cooing, he's with me. I smiled wearily at my lustful savior, worried of what favor he might expect from me, but as soon as I breached the sentry I found myself alone in the stomach of that house.

Laden with an incredibly fetching crowd, I pressed into what appeared to be a sex-crazed cock worshiping carnival. The walls were heavy with phallic imagery, paintings, and photographs; every surface was adorned with erect figurines and what appeared to be usable dildos of alarming magnitude. Seemingly private fantasies spilled from the very bowels of the craftsman home—on the walls and ceilings illustrations of sodomy in every manifestation were scrawled and collaged. Pigskin cloaked men passed out coquettish hors d'oeuvres, glasses of champagne, and aperitifs which spilled merrily from flamboyant jeweled hands. The handsome crowd meandered from room to room in a steady sensual flow. I found myself at an outdoor bar "The Cock Pit" plastered with Tom of Finland imagery: a police officer penetrating a prisoner with his billy club, a hundred sailors thick cocks bursting from within their trousers, every archetype of the brawny masculine male: big dicked, tight assed and dripping with cum. The bartender passed me a mixed drink just before I was swept to the edge of the patio by a new wave of people. Below me terraced garden dissolved into the hillside, glittering effervescently with miscellaneous light installations: a cock shaped lamp, Christmas strands, and rogue bulbs strung up in the greenery. A man coaxed me down the steps for a tour of "Pleasure Park," a series of fuck corners and hiding holes each more dank than the next. Though the park was relatively quiet at this time, the opportunity

weitverzweigten Gebäude ruhen. Im gleißenden Schein unzähliger Lampen leuchtete dieses Relikt in der kühlen kalifornischen Nacht. Das läufige Biest von einem Gebäude spie einen Menschenstrom hervor, während von innen ein stetiges Stöhnen zu vernehmen war. Ein Mann ganz in Leder saß vor dem Haus und kontrollierte die Gästeliste und ich murmelte meinen Namen (ich stand ja auf keiner Liste). Plötzlich zogen mich fremde Hände hinein, und eine Männerstimme gurrte: „Er gehört zu mir." Ich lächelte meinen lüsternen Retter vorsichtig an, besorgt, welche Gegenleistung er von mir wohl erwartete. Doch sobald ich die Wache hinter mir gelassen hatte, befand ich mich tief im Eingeweide des Hauses. Getragen von einer Unzahl attraktiver Männer ließ ich mich durch einen scheinbar schwanzfixierten, sexbesessenen Karneval der Lüste treiben. An den Wänden hingen zahlreiche phallische Symbole, Gemälde und Fotografien: jede Fläche wurde geschmückt von einer schier beängstigenden Anzahl erigierter Nippes-Figuren und scheinbar tatsächlich einsatzbereiter Dildos. Die intimsten Fantasien schienen aus allen Ecken dieses alten Holzhauses förmlich auf mich einzustürzen – an den Wänden und Decken wurde Sodomie in jeder denkbaren Erscheinungsform in Skizzen und Collagen illustriert. Männer, ganz in Leder gehüllt, verteilten dabei kokett Häppchen, Sekt und Aperitifs, die lustig über schwer beringte Hände schwappten. Die Massen wanderten von einem Zimmer ins nächste, einem stetigen sinnlichen Fluss gleich.

Ich landete draußen vor „The Cock Pit", einer mit Tom-of-Finland-Bildern beklebten Bar: ein Polizist, der mit seinem Knüppel in einen Gefangenen eindringt; Hunderte von Matrosen, deren steife Schwänze den Stoff ihrer Hosenlatze zum Platzen zu bringen drohen; jeder erdenkliche Archetyp des virilen maskulinen Mannes: mit gigantischem Schwanz, prallem Arsch, spermatriefend. Der Barkeeper hatte gerade noch Zeit, mir einen Cocktail in die Hand zu drücken, bevor ich von der nächsten Welle hereinströmender Männer an den Rand der Terrasse gespült wurde. Unter mir sah ich, wie sich der terrassierte Garten sanft an den Hügel schmiegte und mit seinen unterschiedlichen Lichtinstallationen magisch glitzerte: eine Lampe in Schwanzform, Weihnachtslichterketten, zufällig platzierte Leuchten im Grün der Sträucher. Ein Mann drängte mich, mit ihm die Stufen in den „Pleasure Park" hinabzusteigen, eine Ansammlung mehrerer

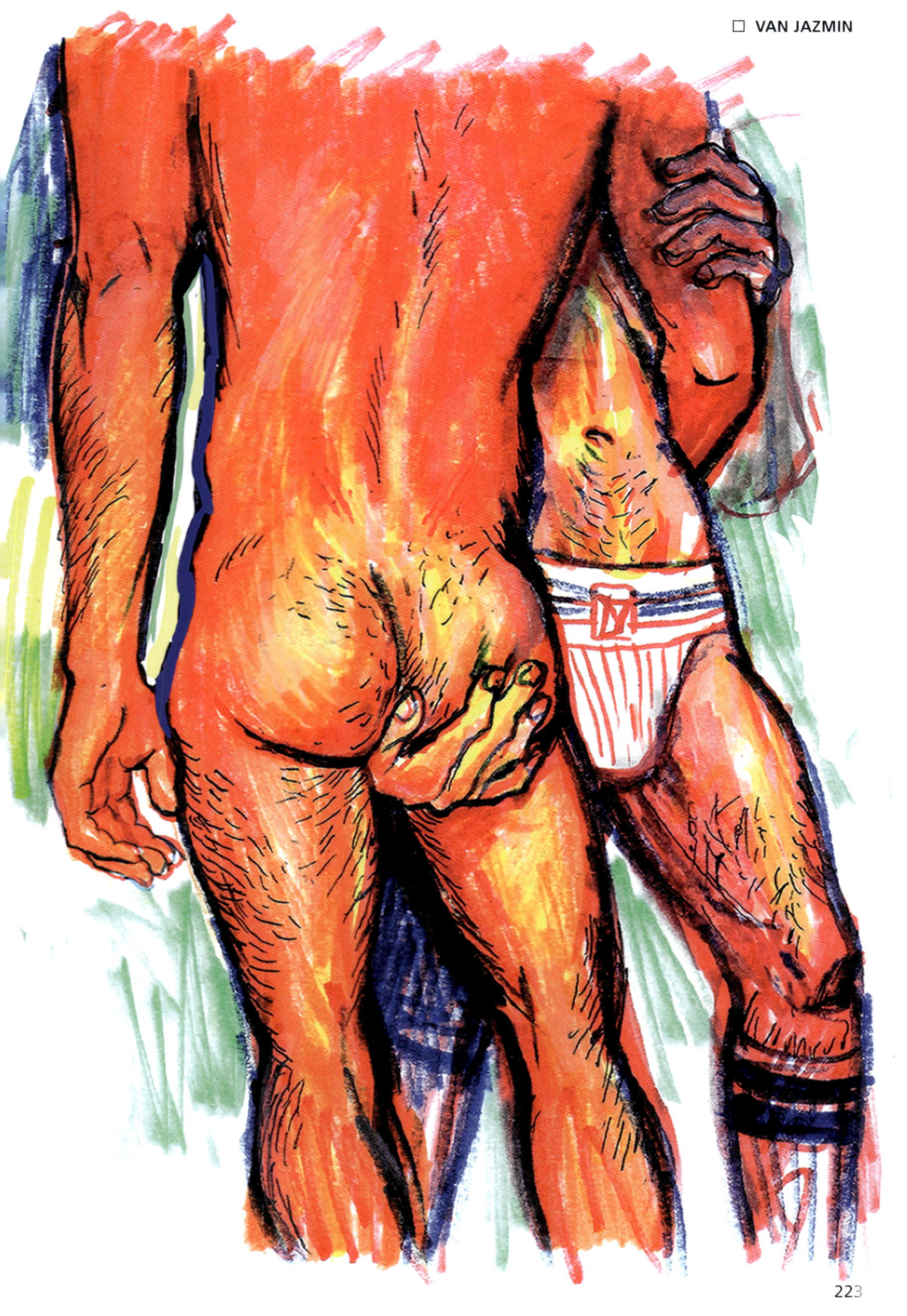

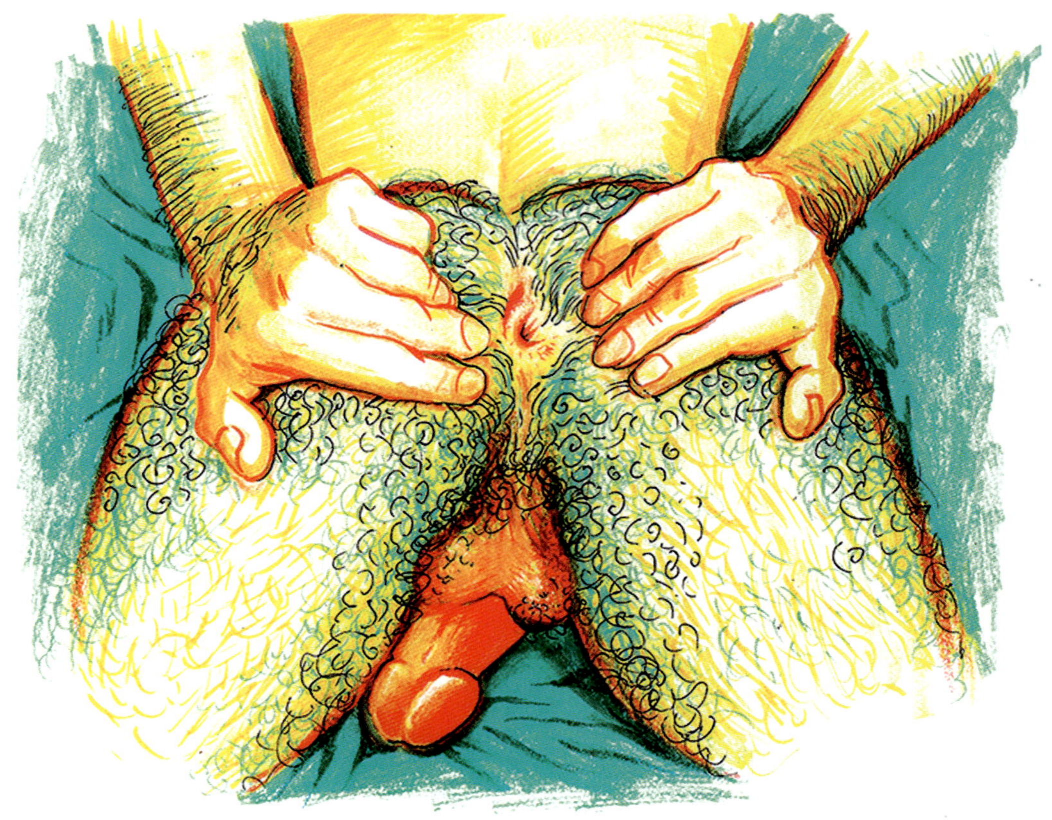

to feel the night breeze inside of me was palpable.
As I walked back up the steps, out of the gardens and toward the house, I felt the tour guide's meaty hands pressing into my backside—I retreated into the crowd. In the gift shop (the house serves as an artist foundation by day) a small group had taken pause beside an inconspicuous door. The door groaned open and a staircase descending into dim red light was revealed. I followed the group into "The Pit", a sweating hole of leather straps and penetrating props and hostile statues, among them an erotic German bust. I did not ask questions with my mouth, but I inhaled the sticky air and drank in the cages and ropes and masks with my eyes, and in some way I understood.
I was late for dinner already as I hopped into the Uber, which deposited me at a

Ficknischen und -verstecke, ein jedes feucht vor Verlangen. Obwohl um diese Zeit der Garten noch ruhig dalag, war ich dankbar für die Gelegenheit, die Abendbrise auf meiner Haut zu spüren.
Als ich die Treppe hochstieg und den Garten in Richtung Haus verließ, spürte ich die fleischigen Hände meines Begleiters auf meinem Hintern; schnell ließ ich mich von der Menge verschlucken. Im Verkaufsladen (das Haus dient ja tagsüber als Künstlerstiftung) hatte sich eine kleine Männerrunde vor einer unscheinbaren Tür versammelt, die mit einem Knarzen aufging und eine Treppe freigab, die in schummriges, rotes Licht hinabführte. Ich lief der Gruppe nach, in den „Pit" hinunter, ein schweißtreibendes Loch voller Lederriemen, erigierter Requisiten und bedrohlicher Statuen, unten denen ich sogar eine erotische deutsche Büste entdeckte. Mein Mund formte zwar keine Fragen, doch ich atmete die stickige Luft gierig ein und ließ meine Augen auf Käfigen, Seilen und Masken verweilen. Instinktiv verstand ich alles sofort.

nearby dining establishment in Silver Lake—an old industry settlement where Hollywood stars used to dine. There I gushed to David about my new sanctuary, eager to get through dinner so that I might return to TOM House. Dinner was languorous and never ending and by the time we finished it was very late and I was very drunk, but I was dropped off at TOM House anyway.

Though the party guests were gone, the energy lingered and I found myself sitting on the porch with the residents—people actually live in this house—as they chain-smoked cigarettes and talked about things I no longer remember. There was a redheaded boy there who sat next to me, but almost on top of me, and we fingered at each other through our clothes and exchanged numbers and kissed on the mouth. He walked me out and said I was lovely—he's British—and I didn't hear from him, but I kept running into him at queer events and eventually he invited me back to the House.

Mit dem Dinner war ich spät dran, also schnappte ich mir ein „Uber", der mich kurz darauf in Silver Lake direkt vor dem Restaurant ablieferte, einem alten Industriegebäude, in dem vor Urzeiten Hollywoodgrößen dinierten. Kaum angekommen, schwärmte ich David von meinem soeben entdeckten Refugium vor und fieberte bereits dem Ende der Mahlzeit entgegen, damit ich zurück zum TOM House gehen konnte. Das gemütliche Abendessen zog sich ewig hin, und als ich endlich aufbrach, hatte ich bereits reichlich viel Alkohol intus, doch man brachte mich trotzdem zurück zum TOM House. Obwohl die Partygäste inzwischen alle weg waren, lag die Energie noch in der Luft und ich setzte mich zu den Mitbewohnern auf die Veranda – das Haus wird tatsächlich bewohnt –, während sie Kette rauchten und sich über Dinge unterhielten, an die ich mich nicht mehr erinnere. Ein Rothaariger saß neben mir, quasi auf mir drauf, und wir befummelten uns gegenseitig durch den Stoff unserer Kleidung, tauschten Nummern aus und küssten uns. Er begleitete mich zur Straße und sagte, ich sei „entzückend" – er war ja Brite. Doch er meldete sich danach nicht bei mir, obwohl ich ihm bei queeren Veranstaltungen ständig über den Weg lief, bis er mich dann doch wieder ins Haus einlud.

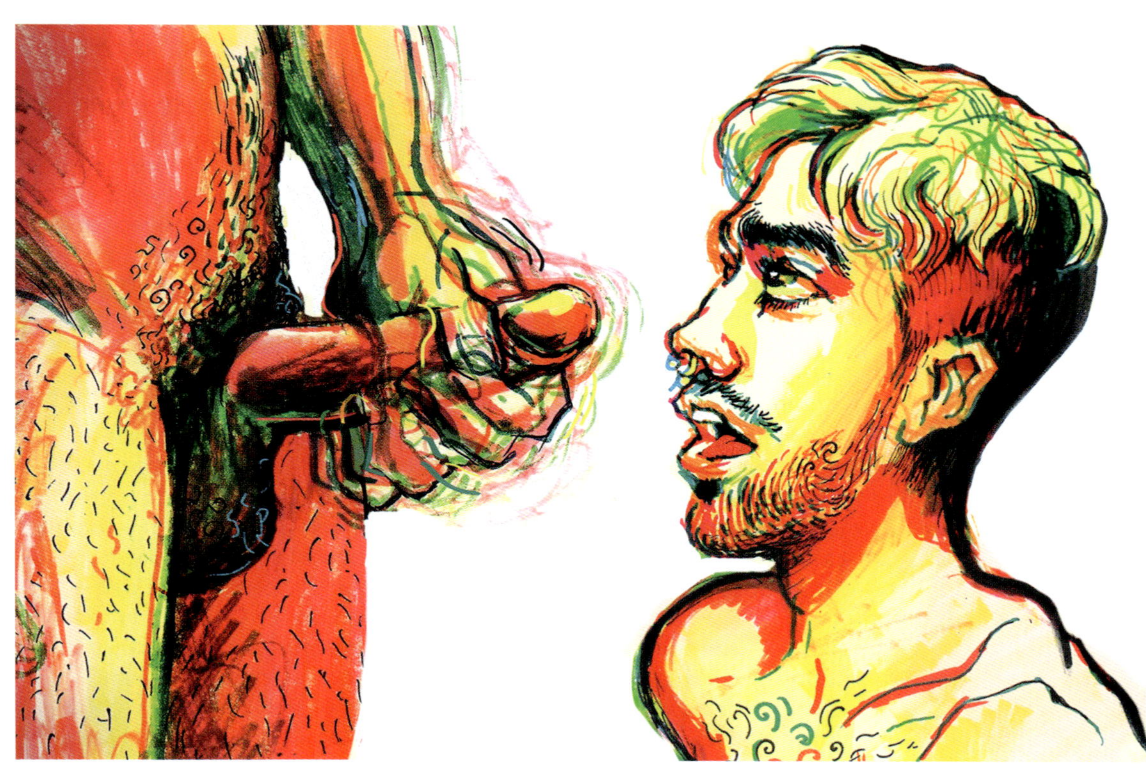

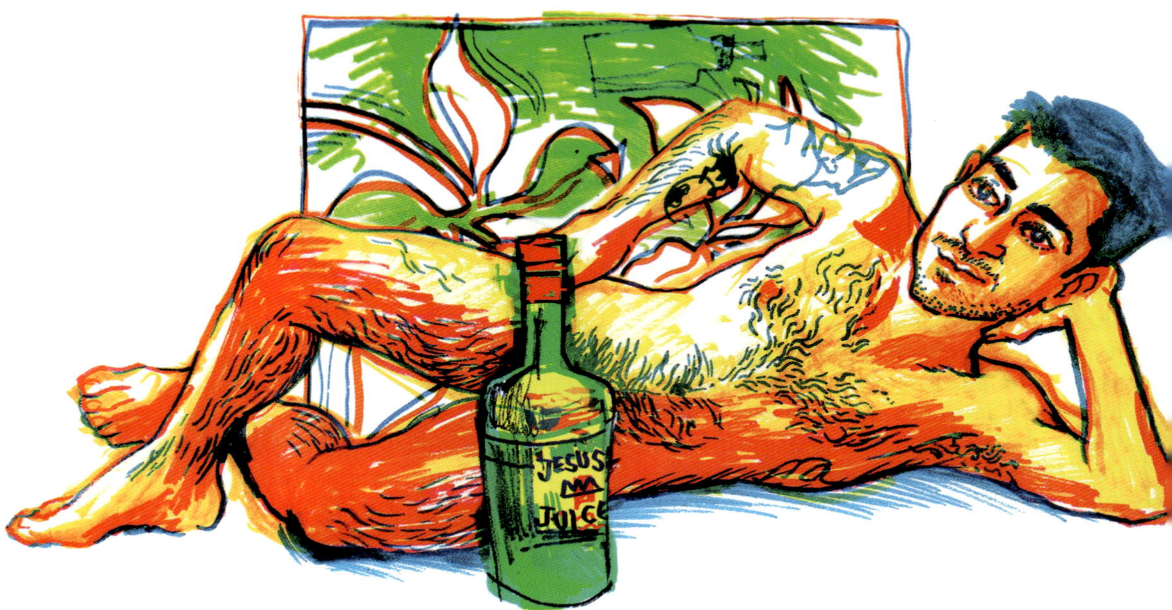

That was nearly a year ago. Since then, the redheaded boy Stuart has become one of my best friends and housemates, along with Durk, Sharp, Marc, and the slew of other transient creatives that wander in and out of this holy place. Currently, I am the artist in residence and resident sweetheart of TOM House. I have become well acquainted with the space, exploring it, filming it, sharing meals, conversation, and my body in it, and creating this collection of erotic non-fiction. The more time I spend here, the more enamored I become. This has little to do with the overwhelming amount of dick displayed in and around the house, and more to do with the significance of queer sanctuary. The necessity of such a space is immeasurable. For a people who have been banned from their churches and fired from their jobs, who have been kicked, killed, name-called, and criticized, a space to fuck freely is as close to God as any of us get.

Tom embodied in his work a free spirited gay man, glorified in body and sexually liberated. He took society's sadistic view of the faggot and empowered it, cel-

Das war vor einem Jahr. Inzwischen ist Stuart, der Rothaarige, zu einem meiner besten Freunde geworden und wir wohnen sogar in einer WG, zusammen mit Durk, Sharp und Mark sowie einer Menge anderer Kreativer auf der Durchreise, die diese heilige Stätte zeitweise bevölkern. Zurzeit bin ich sowohl der „Artist in Residence", als auch der gute Geist im TOM House. Mit dem Ort kenne ich mich inzwischen gut aus, habe alles gründlich ausgekundschaftet und alles auf Video festgehalten, habe Mahlzeiten, Gespräche sowie meinen Körper mit den anderen geteilt und schuf eine Sammlung erotischer Sachtexte. Je länger ich mich hier aufhalte, desto mehr fesselt mich dieser Ort. Das liegt weniger an den allgegenwärtigen Schwänzen, die ausgestellt werden, viel eher ist es die Bedeutung dieses queeren Refugiums. Die Notwendigkeit eines solchen Ortes lässt sich kaum in Worte fassen. Für diejenigen, die von Gotteshäusern verbannt wurden und Arbeitsstellen verloren haben, die getreten, ermordet, beleidigt und kritisiert wurden, kommt ein solcher Ort ungehemmten Fickens einer Gottesnähe gleich. Viel näher an Gott werden wir vermutlich nie kommen. In seinem Werk verkörpert Tom einen unkonventionellen schwulen Mann, befreit in seiner

ebrating the male form with a religious oeuvre.
TOM House has immortalized this work, and thus its power, creating a rare space where gay men get to be exactly who they want to be, to love who they want to love. A space where no fantasy is without merit. There is solidarity in that, and it is cleansing. In the time that I have lived in this iconic home, I have witnessed many men enter the wooden gates in search of healing. I have watched them find it.
A year ago, I stumbled into this vortex, a stroke of serendipity I am still grappling to understand. Before TOM House, I was unaware of the libertine spirit I suppressed inside of me. As an out and proud millennial gay with an affinity for queer literature and progressive attitudes, I didn't think I had more growing to do in my queerness. My time here has humbled that self-righteousness. These grounds and the men who inhabit them have birthed a revolution in me, which has largely inspired this body of work.

Sexualität, seinen Körper zelebrierend. Tom nahm den sadistischen Blick auf die Schwuchtel und verlieh ihm eine Kraft, feierte den männlichen Körper mit einem religiösen Oeuvre.
Das TOM House hat sein Schaffen verewigt und dadurch auch dessen Macht. Dadurch entstand ein seltener Raum, in dem Schwule die Freiheit haben, diejenigen zu sein, die sie sein wollen und diejenigen zu lieben, die sie lieben wollen. Ein Raum, in dem keine Fantasie ohne Wert ist. Und darin liegt eine reinigende Solidarität. Während meiner Zeit in diesem sagenumwobenen Haus durfte ich zusehen, wie zahlreiche Männer das Eingangstor passierten, auf der Suche nach Heilung. Zusehen durfte ich auch, wie sie sie fanden.
Vor einem Jahr stolperte ich selbst in diesen Strudel, ein Glücksfall, mit dem ich mich noch heute auseinandersetze. Vor meiner Zeit im TOM House hatte ich den lange unterdrückten Freigeist in mir nicht wahrgenommen. Als ein stolzer schwuler Mann der nuller Jahre mit Hang zu queerer Literatur und fortschrittlichen Gedanken bildete ich mir ein, in meinem Queersein längst erwachsen zu sein. Meine Zeit hier hat meine Überheblichkeit Lügen gestraft und mich Demut gelehrt. Dieser Ort sowie seine Bewohner haben in mir eine Revolution entfacht, die maßgeblich zur Gestaltung meiner Werke beigetragen hat.

Übersetzung: Jim Baker

My drawings are primarily meant for guys who may have experienced misunderstanding and oppression and feel that they have somehow failed in their lives. I want to encourage them. I want to encourage this minority group, to tell them not to give up, to think positively about their act and whole being.

Meine Zeichnungen sind besonders für diejenigen bestimmt, die Unverständnis und Unterdrückung erleiden mussten und die das Gefühl haben, im Leben irgendwie versagt zu haben. Ich will ihnen Mut machen. Ich will diese Minderheit ermutigen, nicht aufzugeben und positiv über ihr Dasein sowie ihr Handeln zu denken.
– Tom of Finland

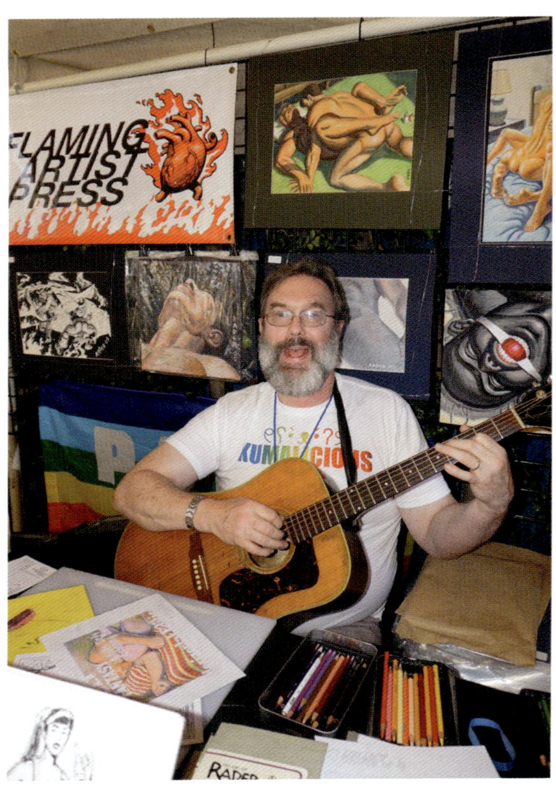

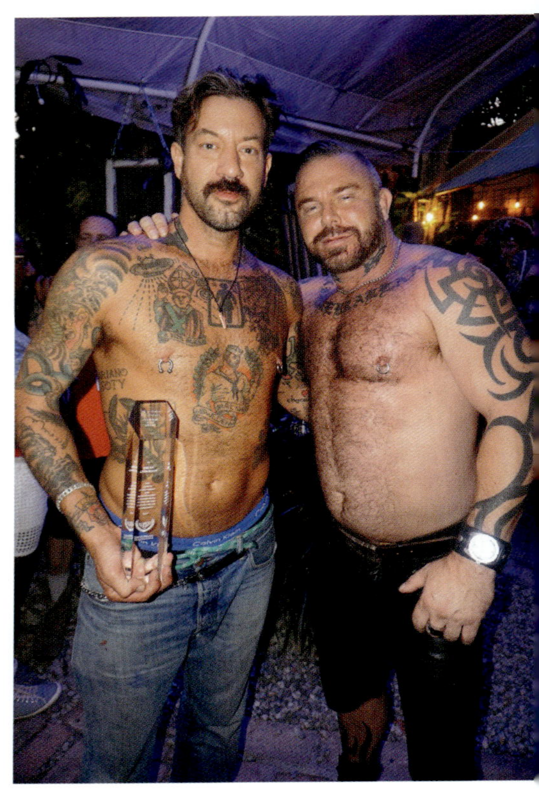

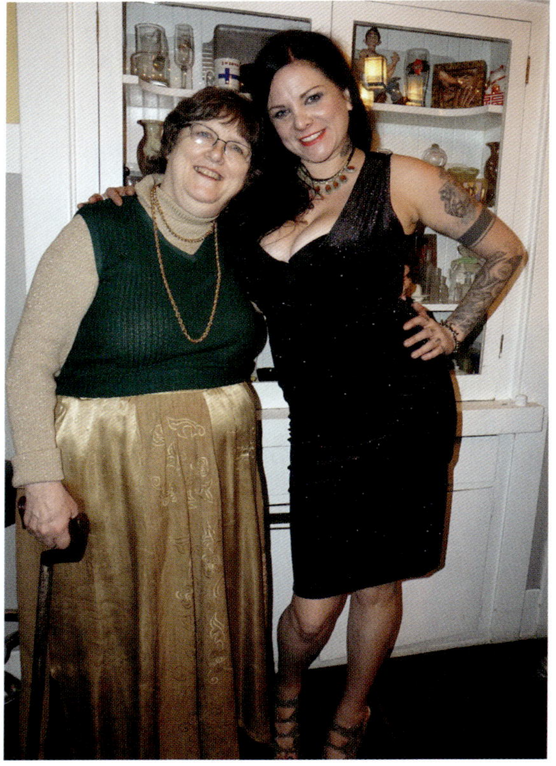

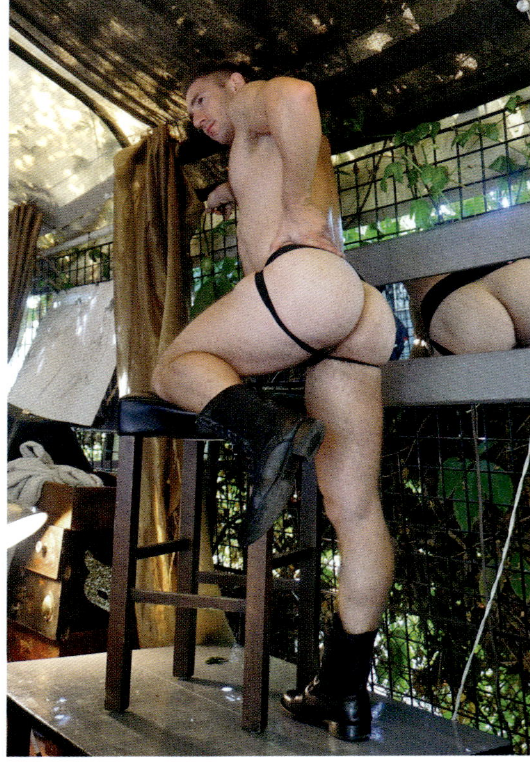

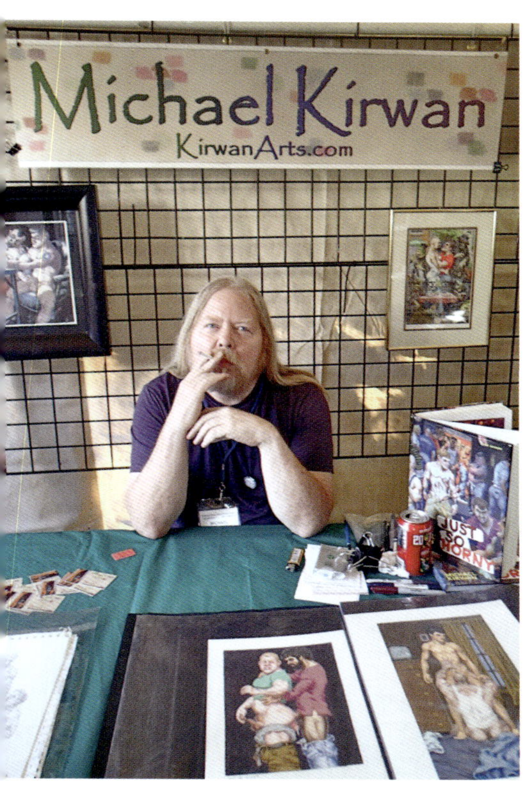
Michael Kirwan
KirwanArts.com

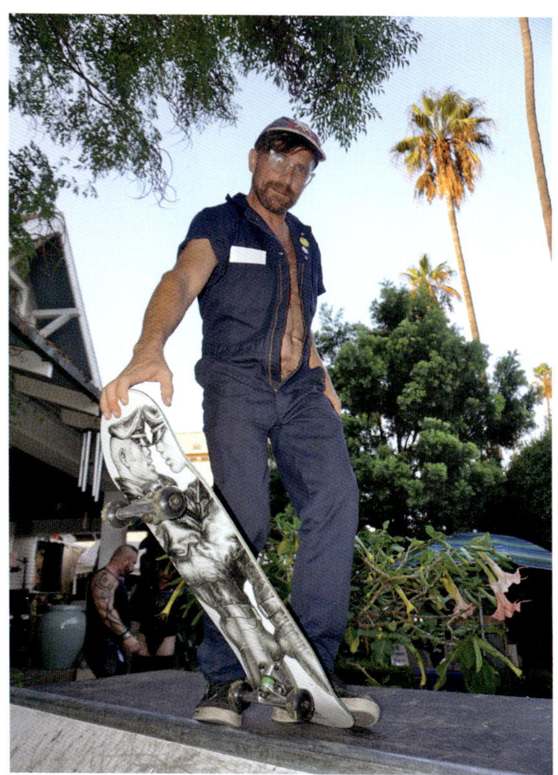

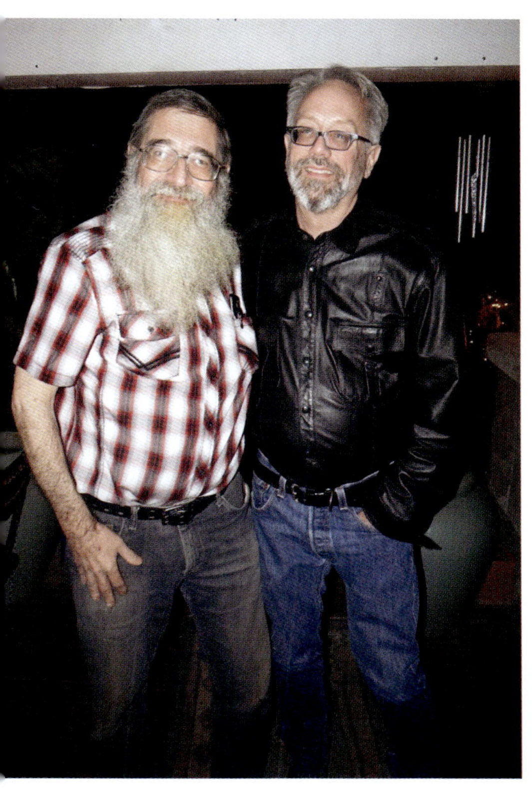

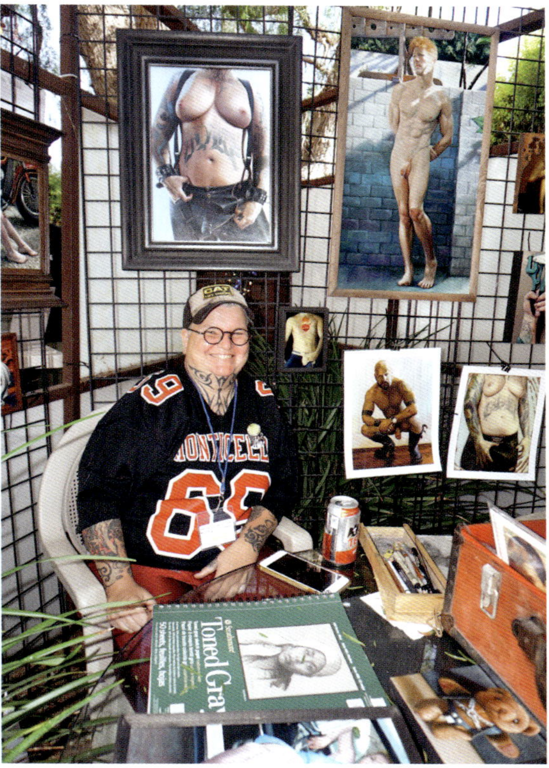

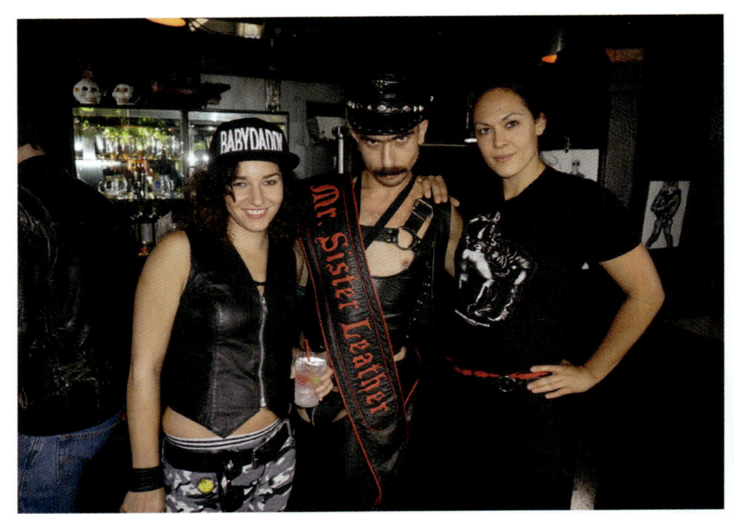
BABYDADDY
Mr. Sister Leather

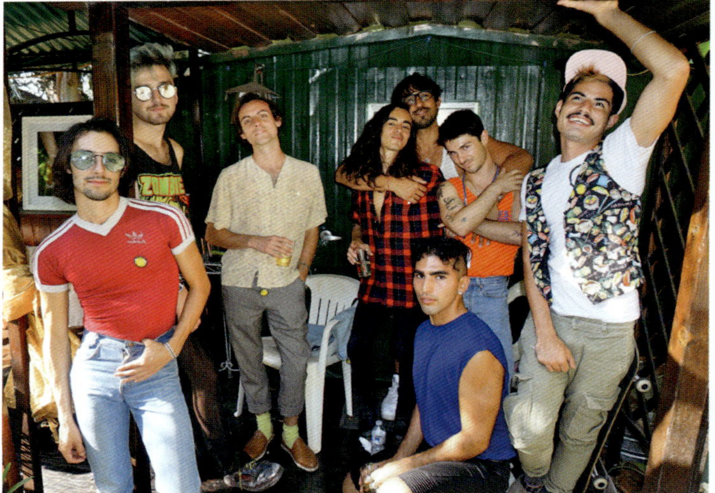

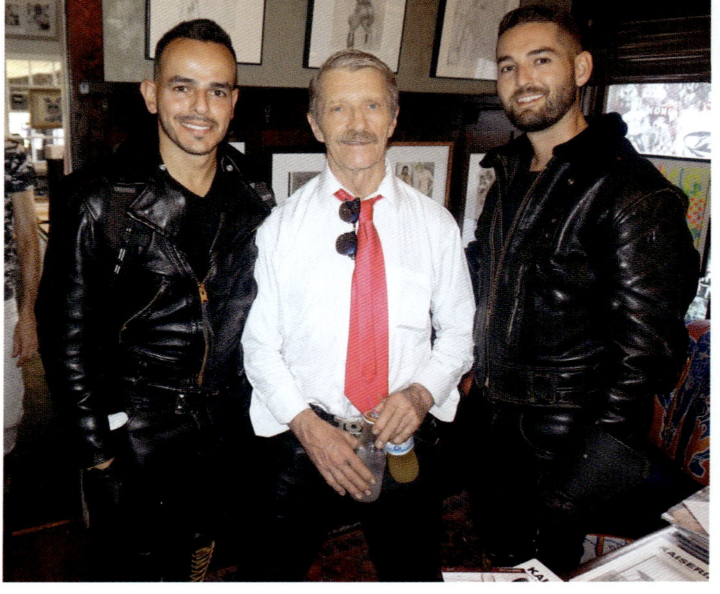

Art and Culture Festivals

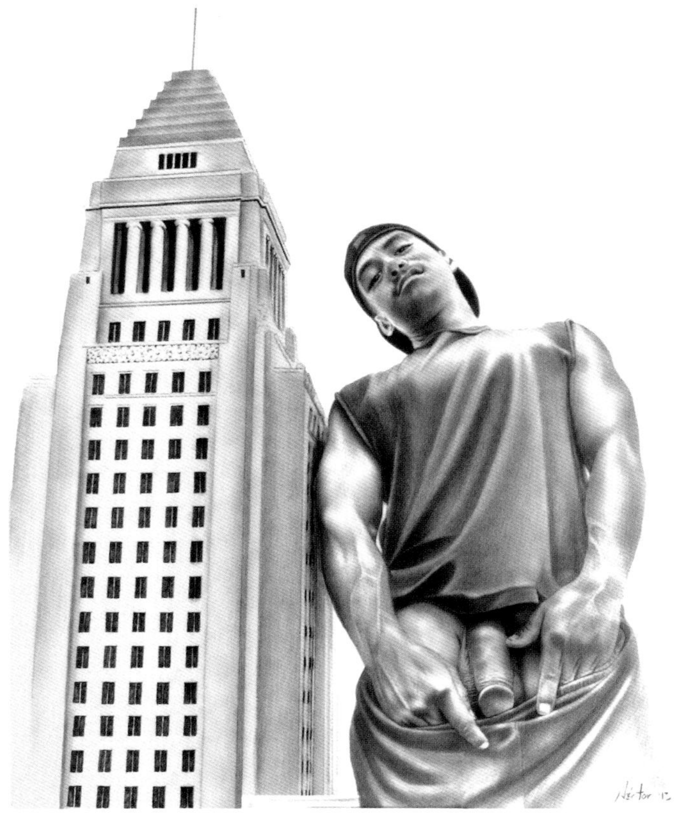

HECTOR SILVA

Tom of Finland Foundation hosts social events throughout the year to provide a sense of community for supporters of erotic art. An example is the annual TOM's Bar which promotes and exhibits erotic art in a very popular party setting and raises funds to support the Foundation's activities at the same time. The rapidly growing Tom of Finland Art and Culture Festival brings together artists and patrons from many parts of the globe. It provides them with a social environment in which to network, opportunities to explore the archives and most importantly, the opportunity to buy and sell works over the two-day weekend event.

In der Tom of Finland Foundation finden das ganze Jahr über Veranstaltungen statt, die dazu beitragen sollen, ein Gemeinschaftsgefühl unter den Förderern erotischer Kunst zu erzeugen. Ein Beispiel ist die einmal jährlich stattfindende TOMS Bar, wo Kunst in einem sehr beliebten Party-Setting ausgestellt und beworben wird. Zugleich werden Mittel gesammelt, um die Aktivitäten der Foundation zu unterstützen. Das schnell wachsende Tom of Finland Art and Culture Festival bringt Künstler und Mäzene aus aller Welt zusammen. Es bietet ihnen die Möglichkeit, sich zu vernetzen und das Archiv zu erkunden, aber vor allem auch das ganze Wochenende lang Kunst zu kaufen und zu verkaufen.

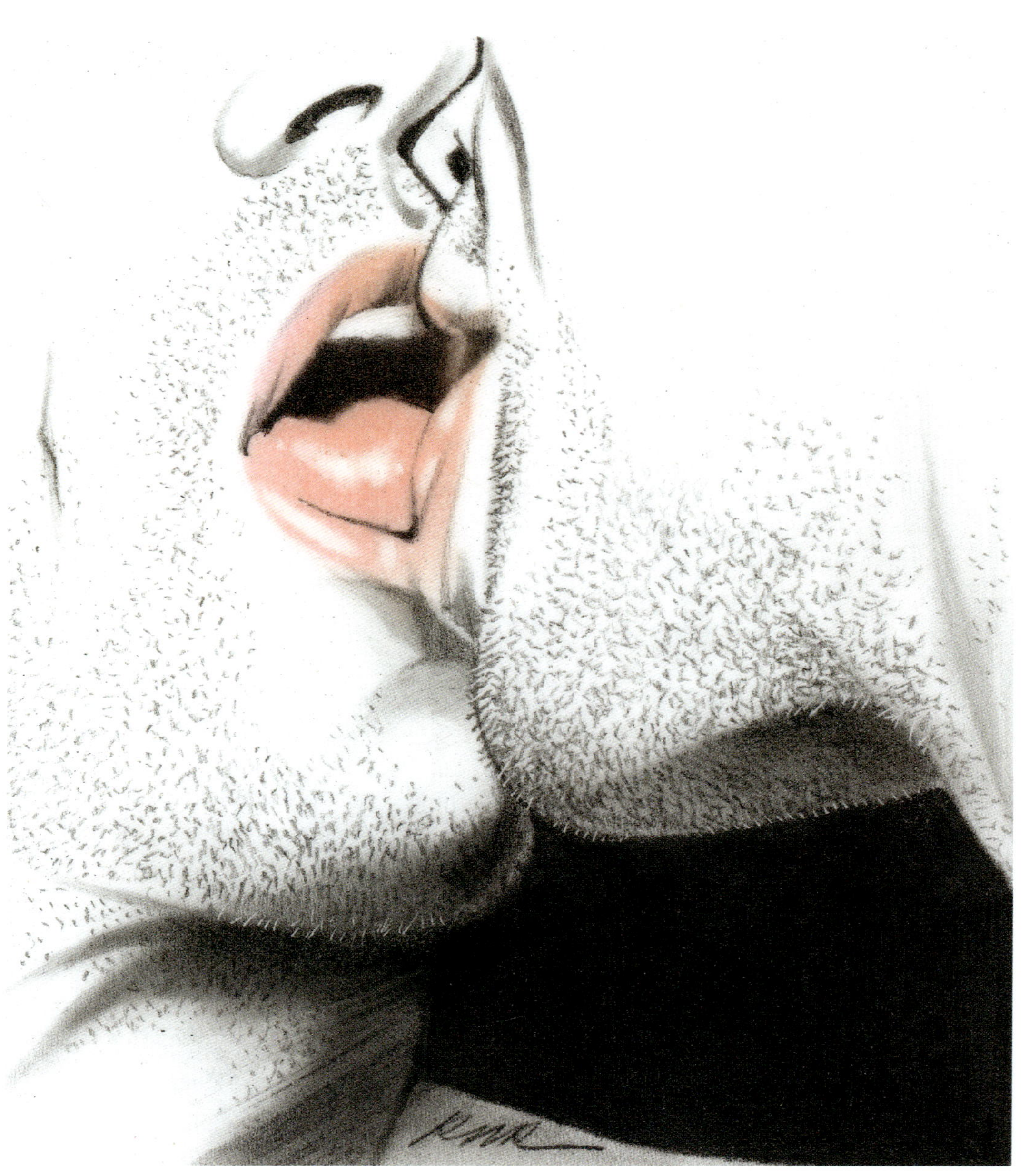

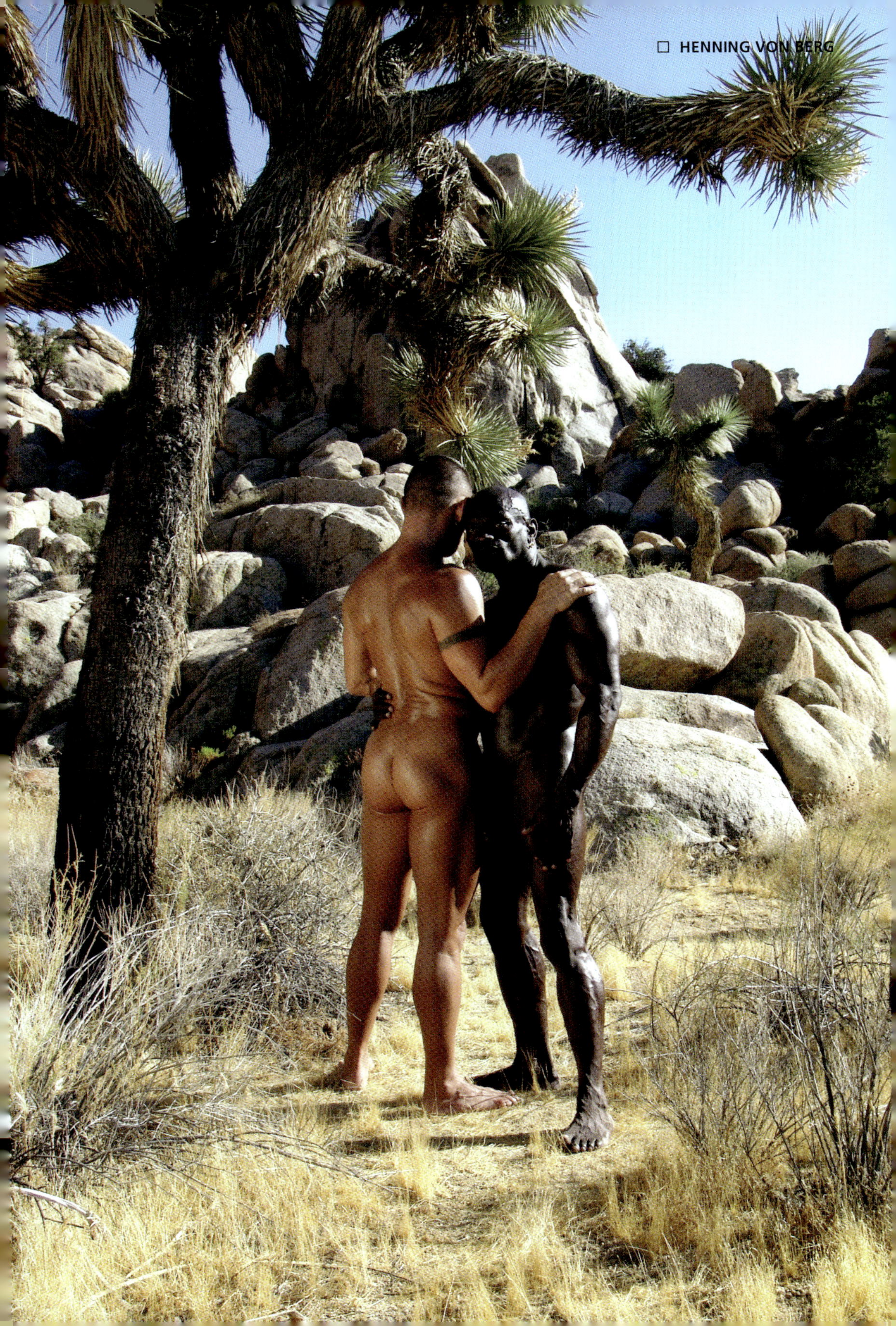

HENNING VON BERG

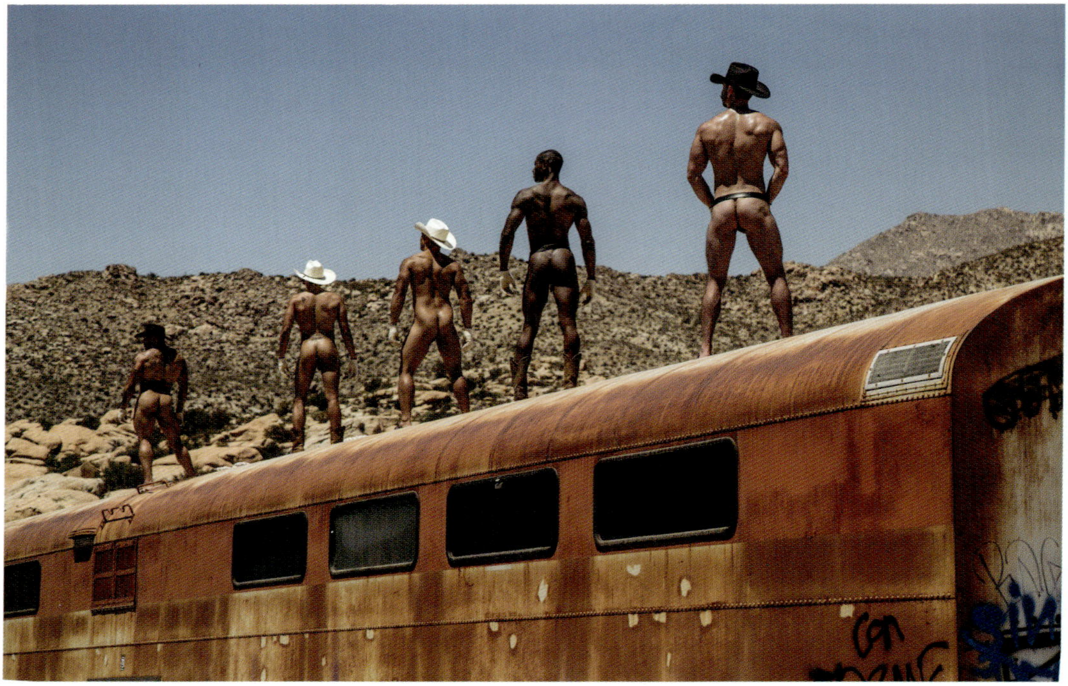

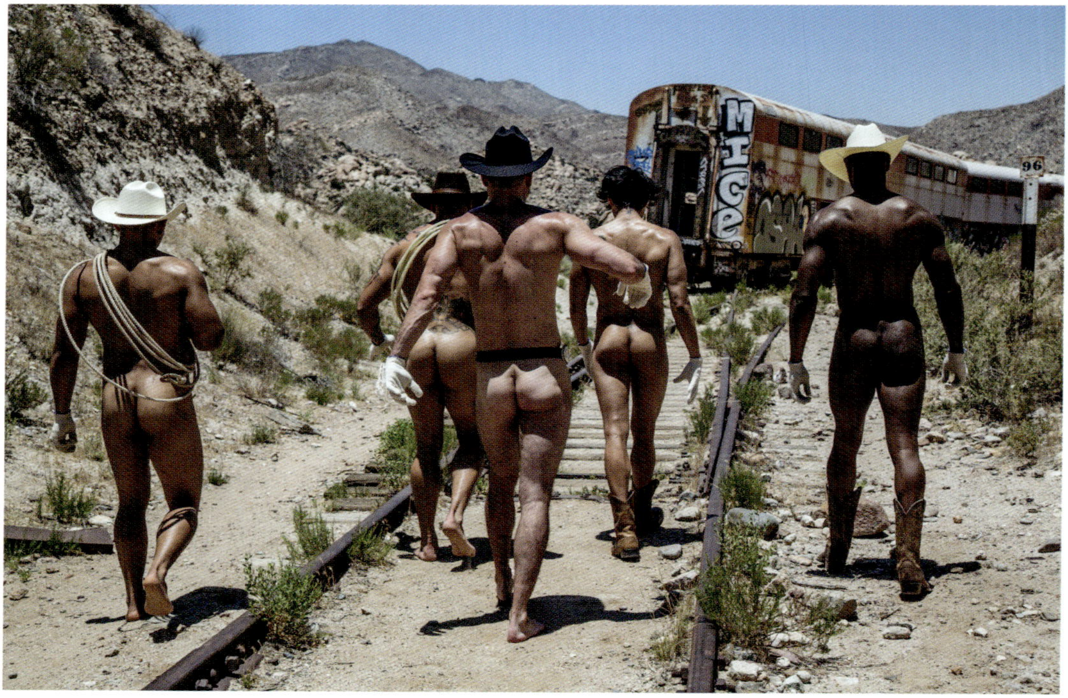

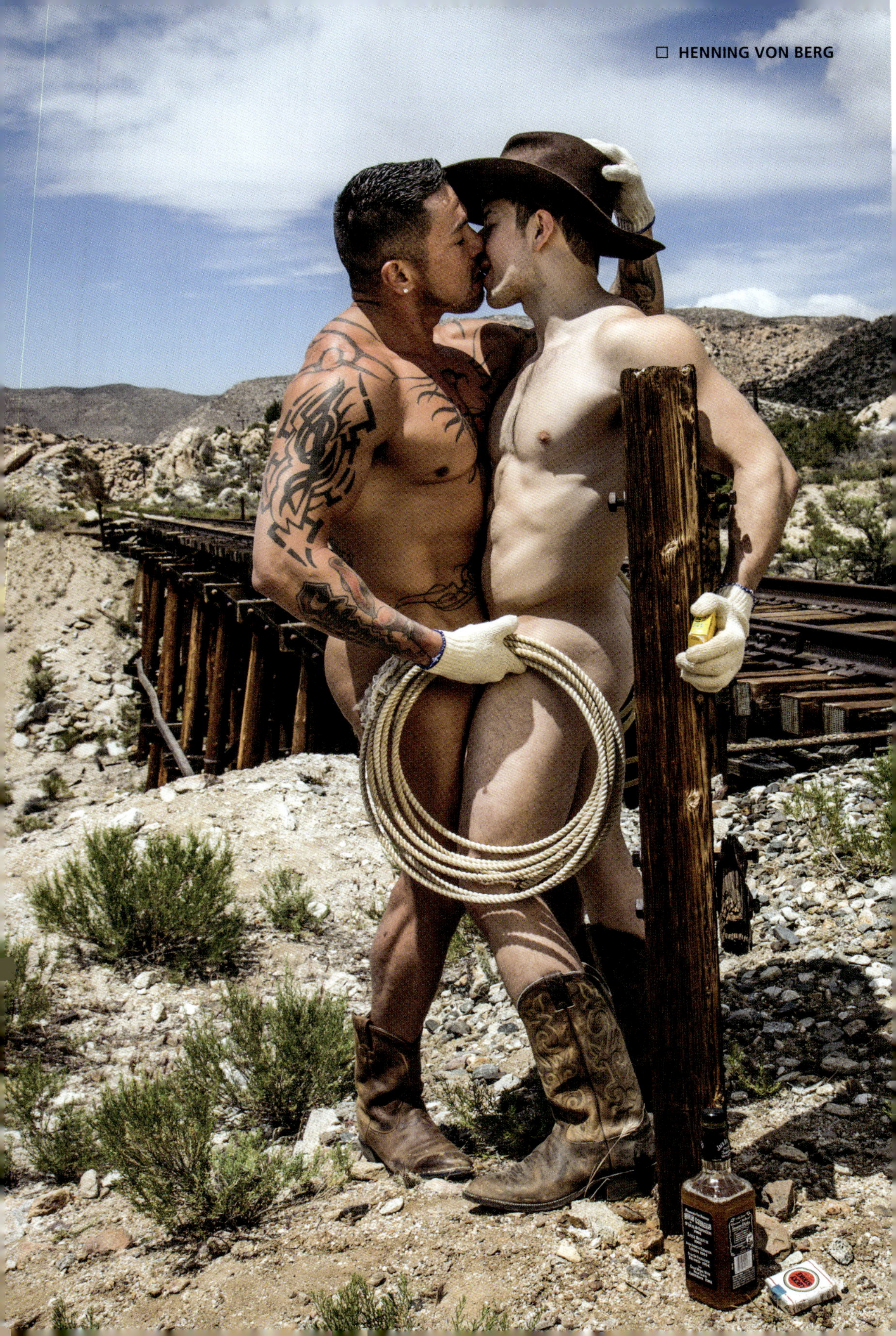

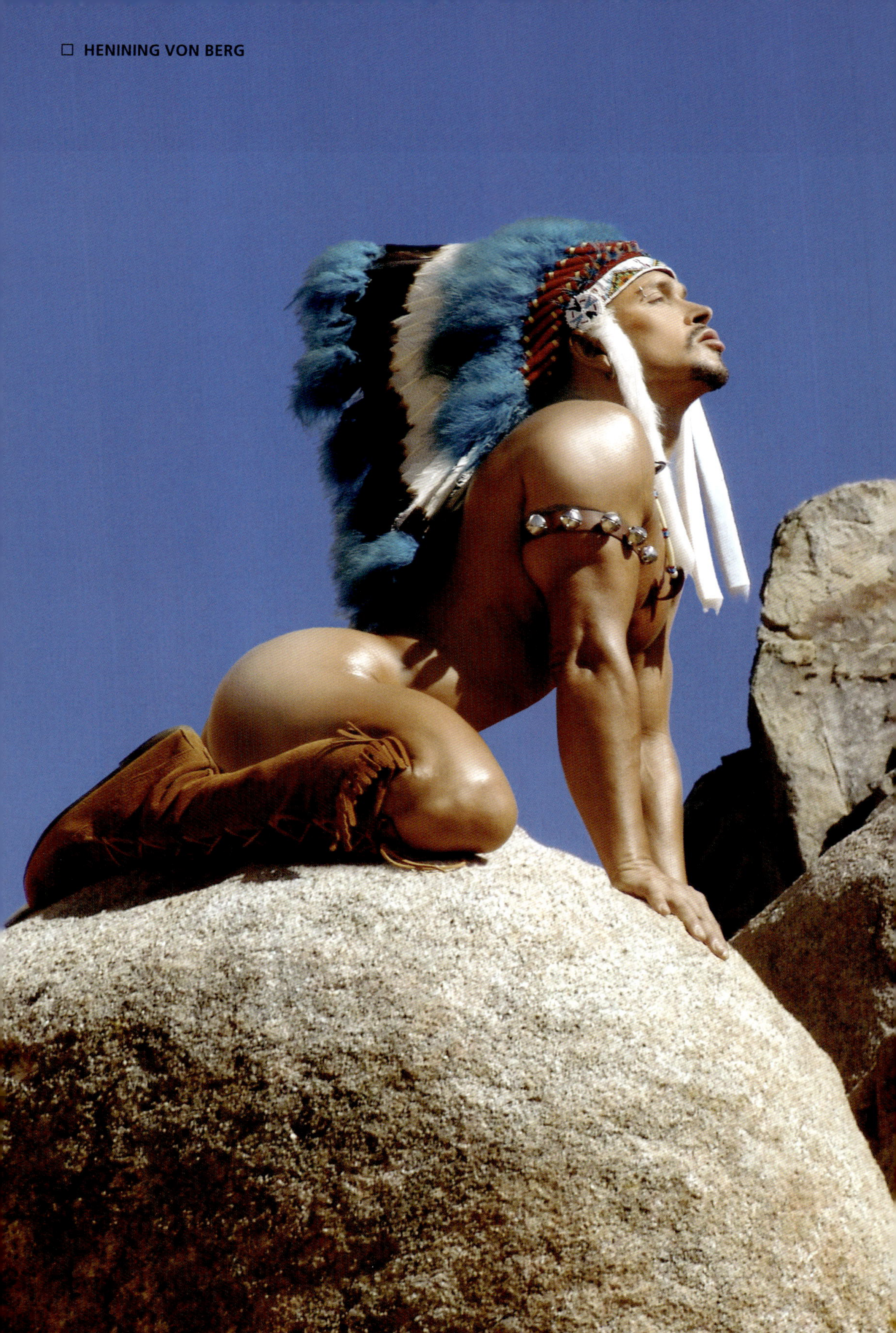

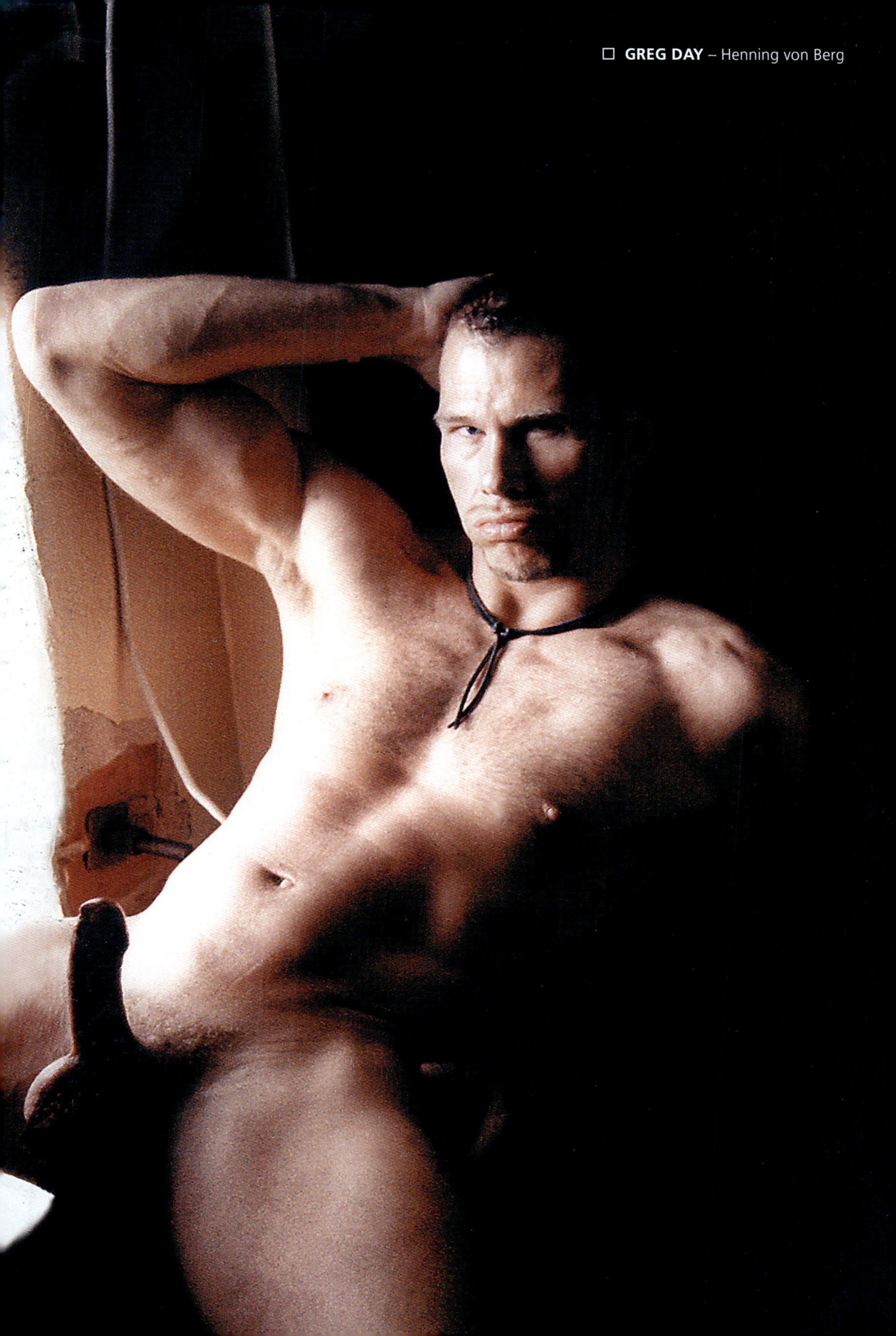

GREG DAY – Henning von Berg

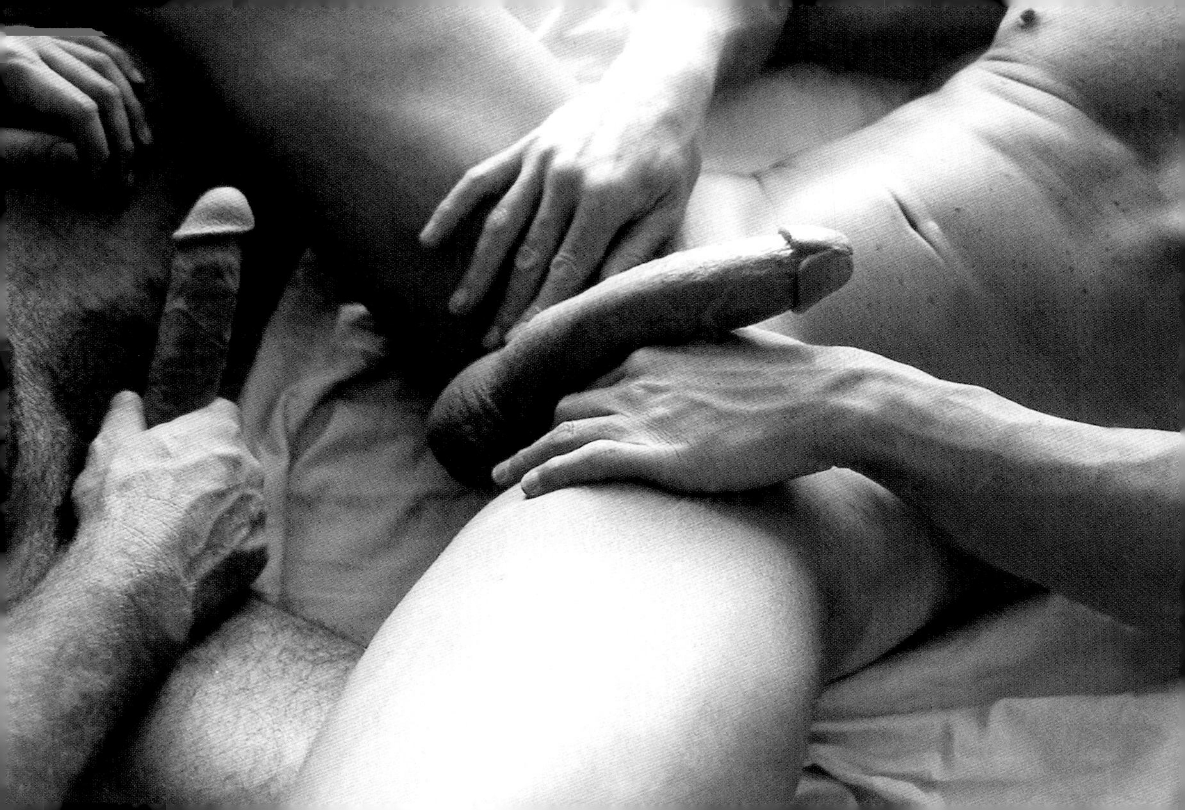

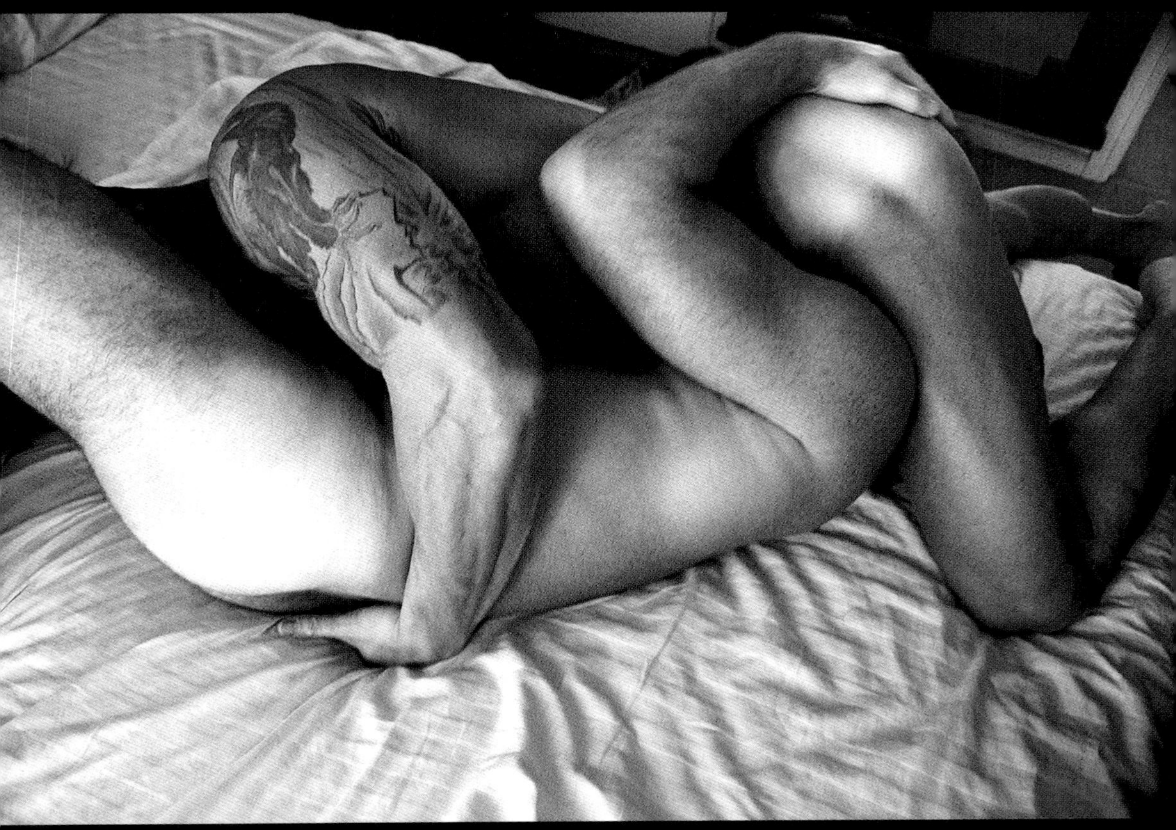

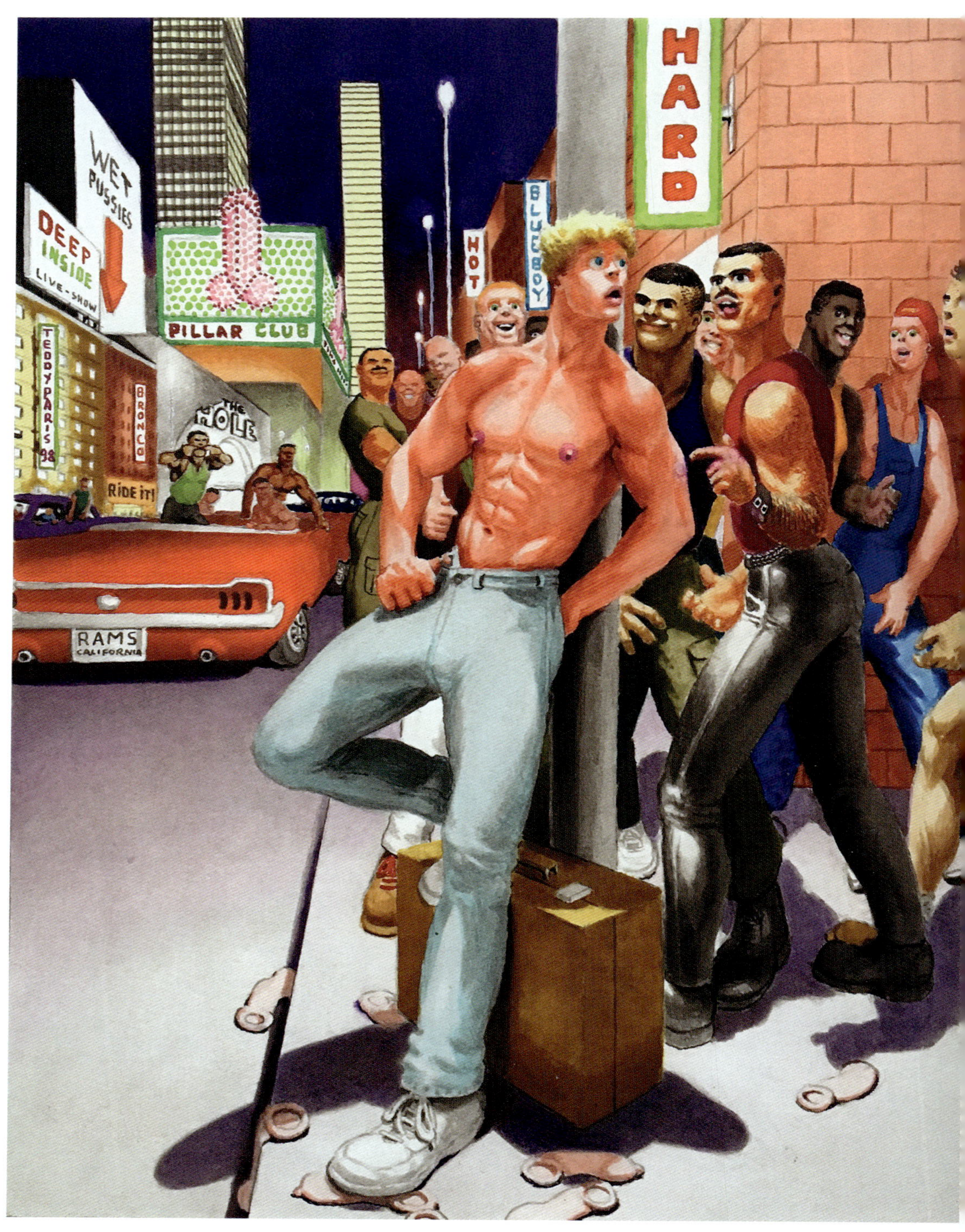
WET
PUSSIES
DEEP
INSIDE
LIVE-SHOW
PILLAR CLUB
TEDDY PARIS 98
BRONCO
THE HOLE
RIDE it!
RAMS
CALIFORNIA
HARD
HOT
BLUEBOY

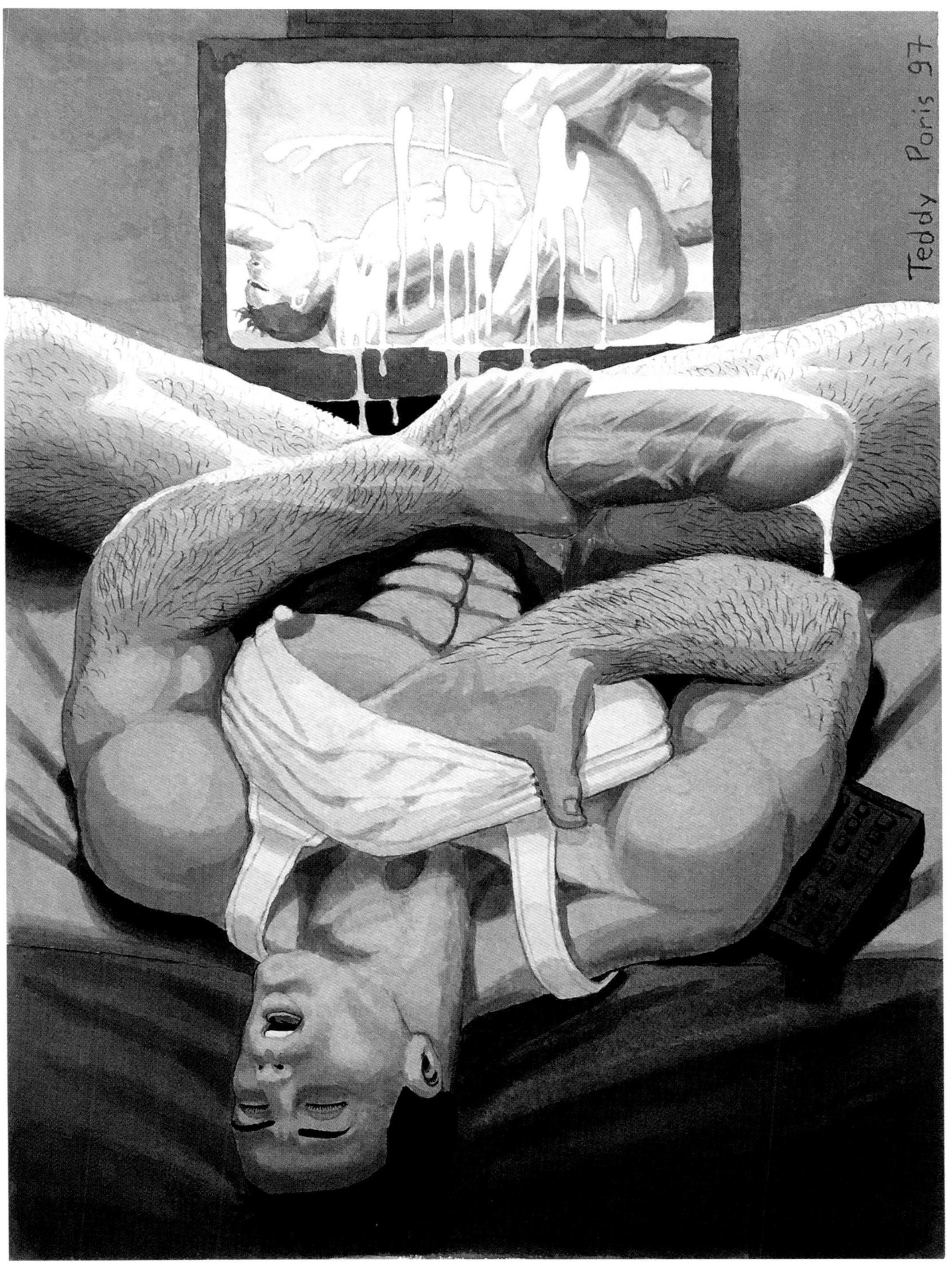
Teddy Paris 97

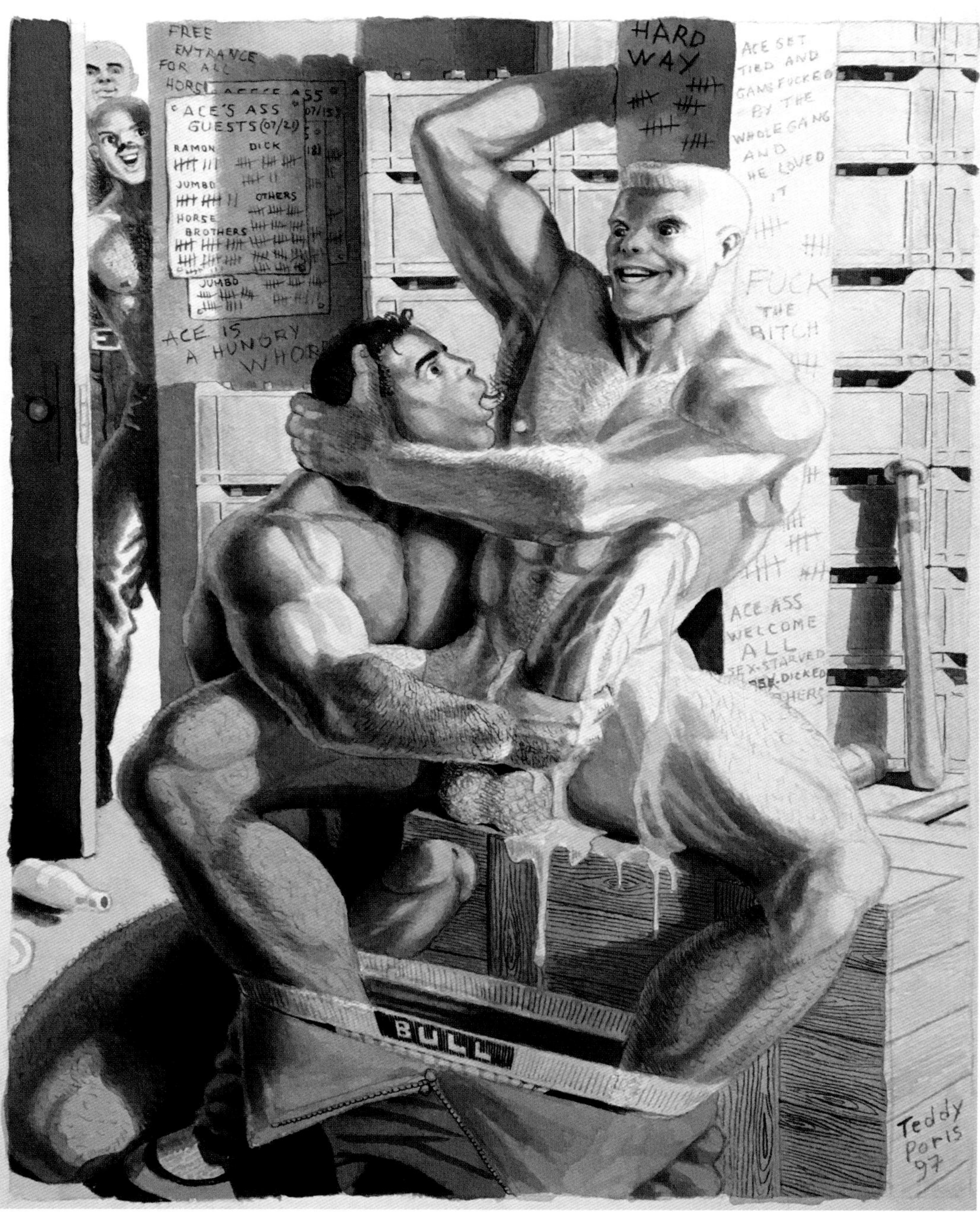
FREE ENTRANCE FOR ALL HORSE
HARD WAY
ACE'S ASS GUESTS (07/21)
RAMON
JUMBO
HORSE BROTHERS
DICK
OTHERS
JUMBO
ACE IS A HUNGRY WHORE
ACE SET TIED AND GANGFUCKED BY THE WHOLE GANG AND HE LOVED IT
FUCK THE BITCH
ACE ASS WELCOME ALL SEX-STARVED
BULL
Teddy Paris 97

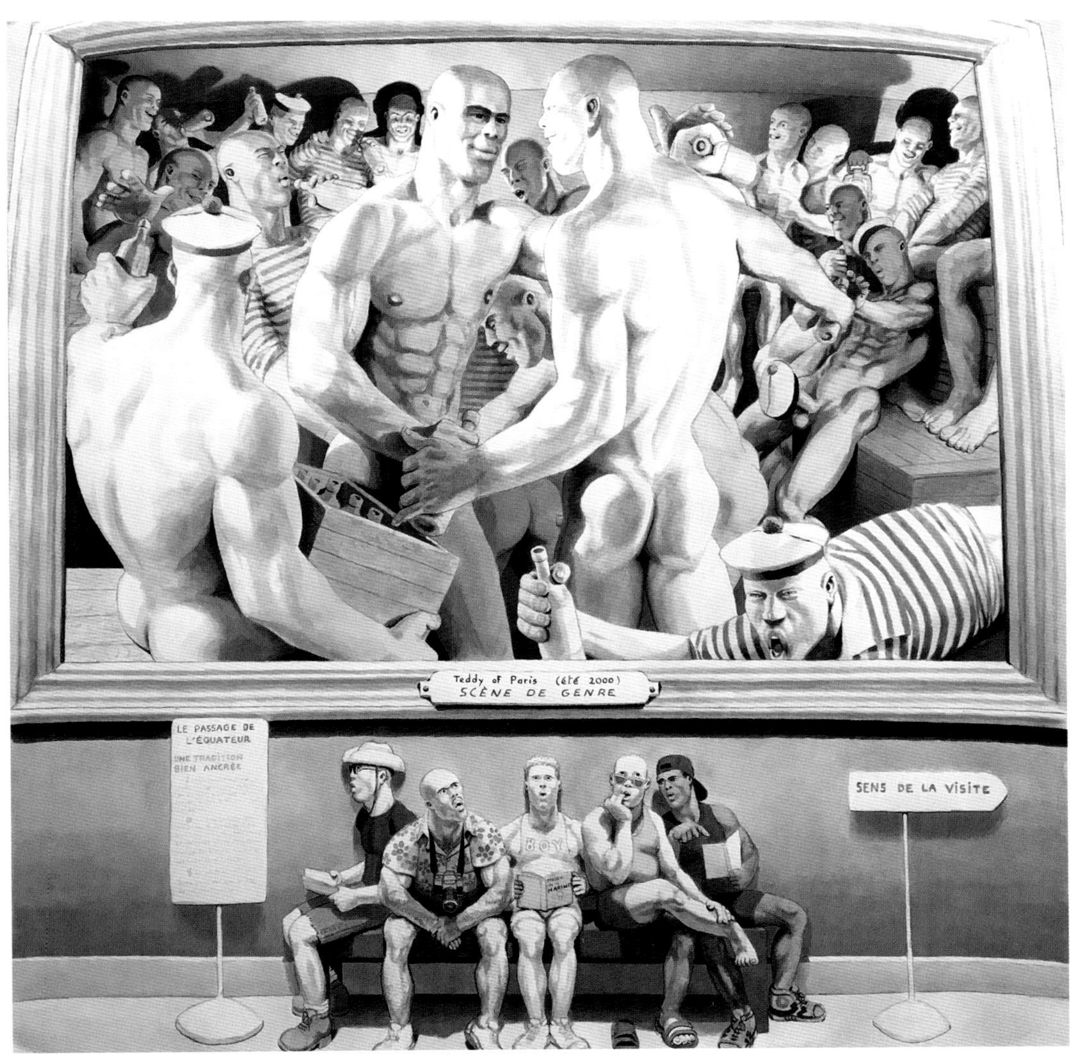
Teddy of Paris (été 2000)
SCÈNE DE GENRE
LE PASSAGE DE L'ÉQUATEUR
UNE TRADITION BIEN ANCRÉE
SENS DE LA VISITE

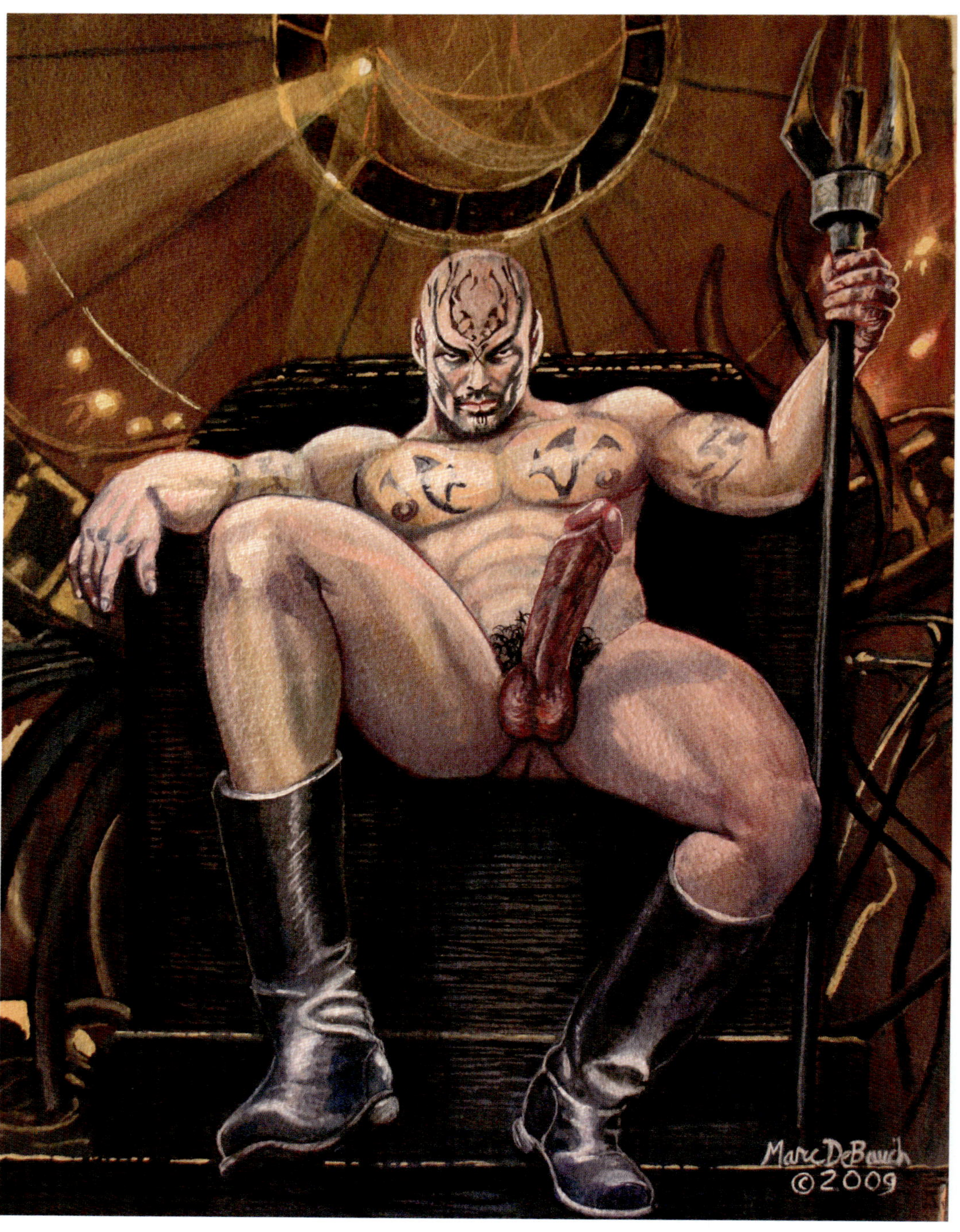

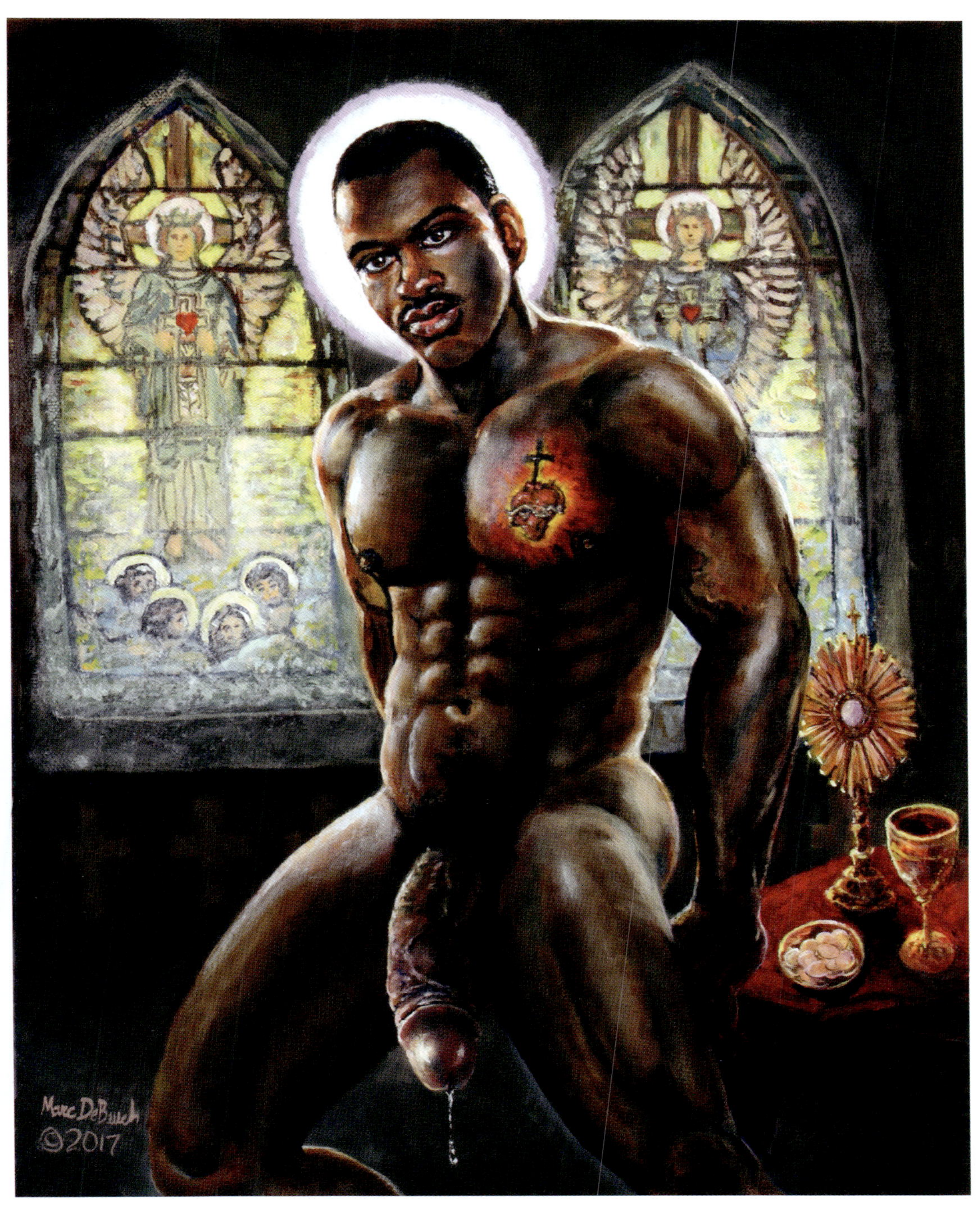

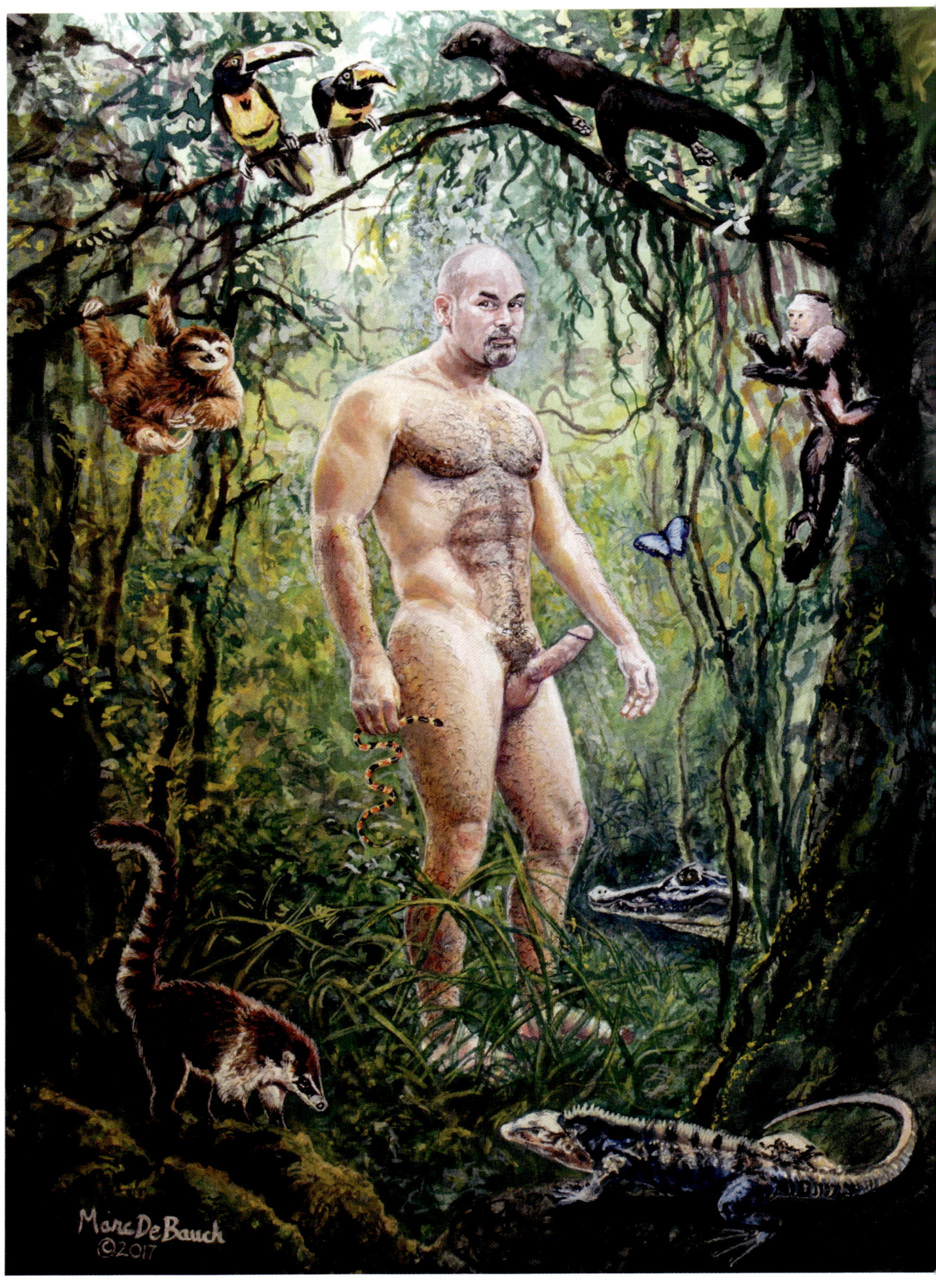
Marc De Bauch
©2017

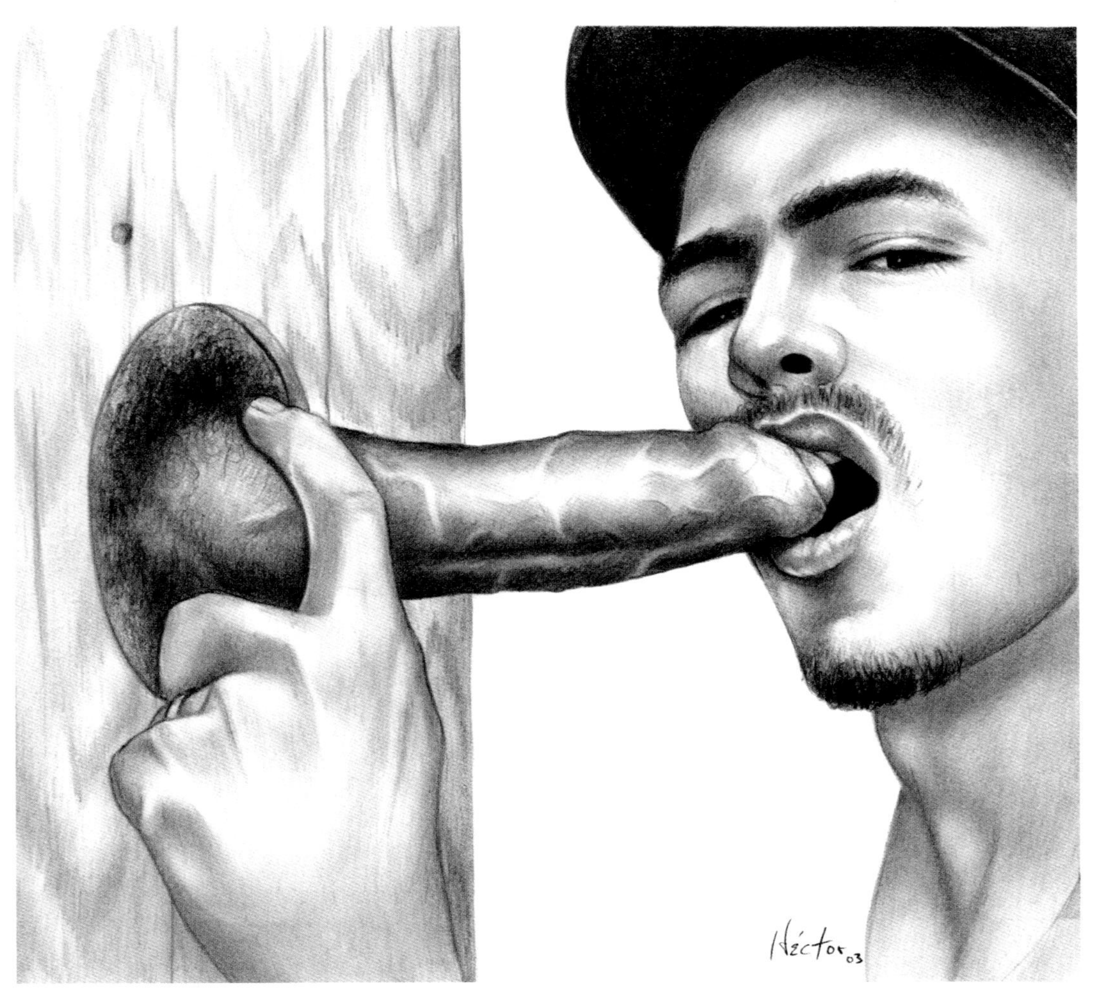

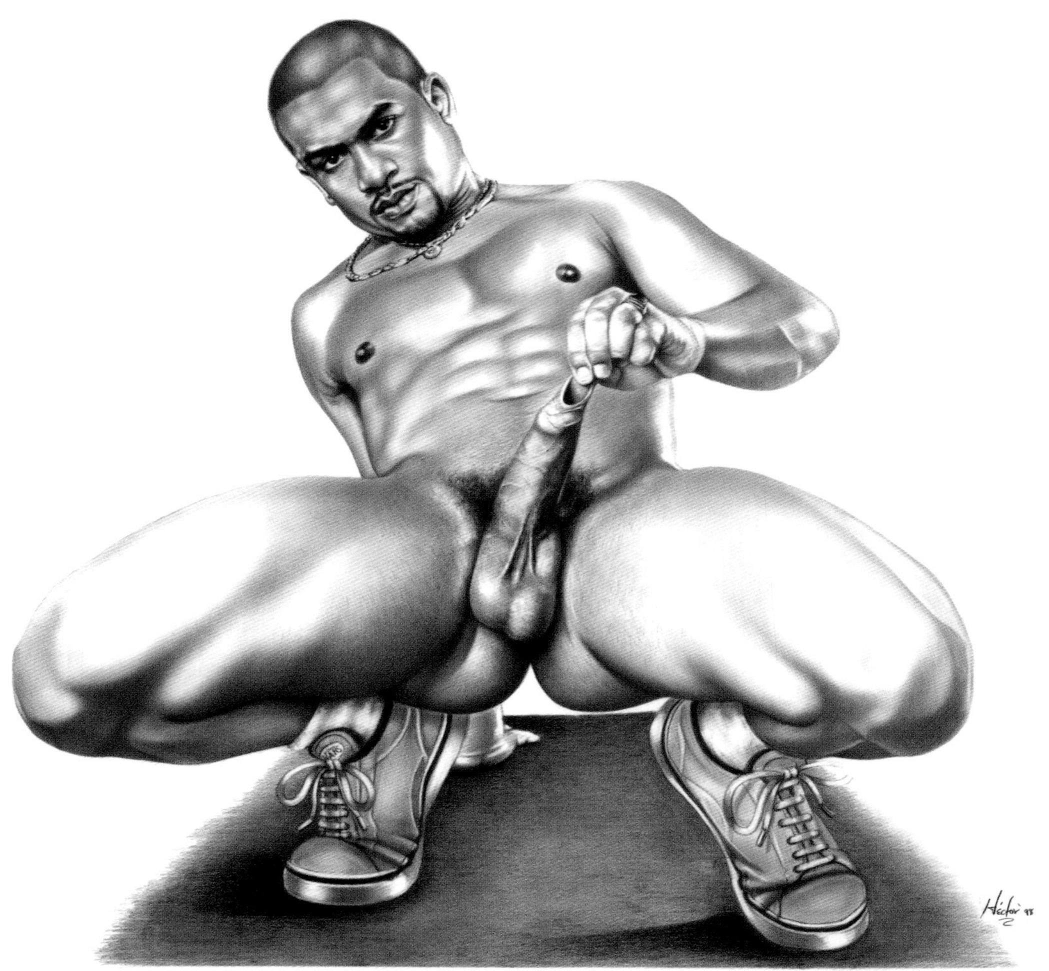

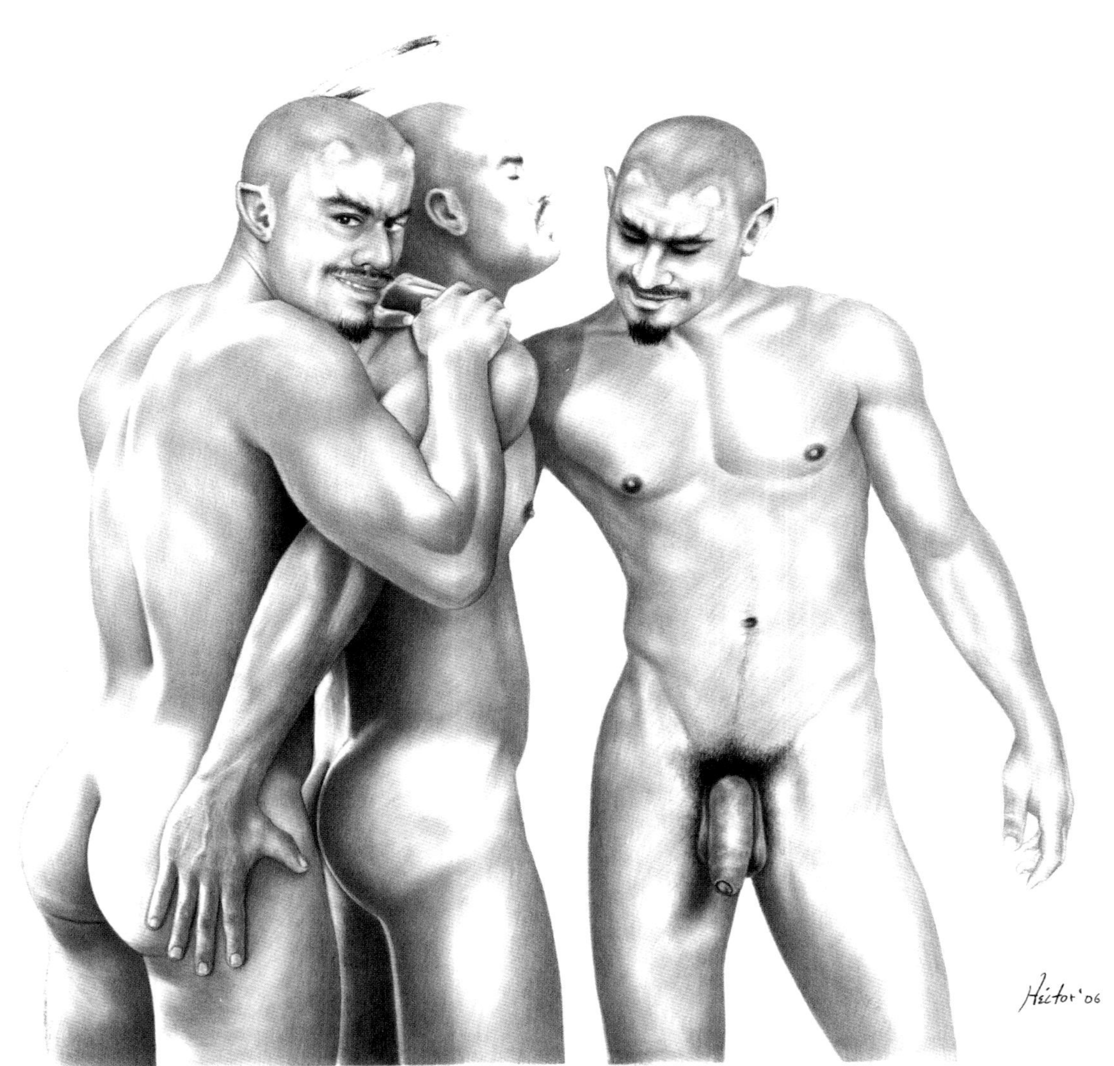

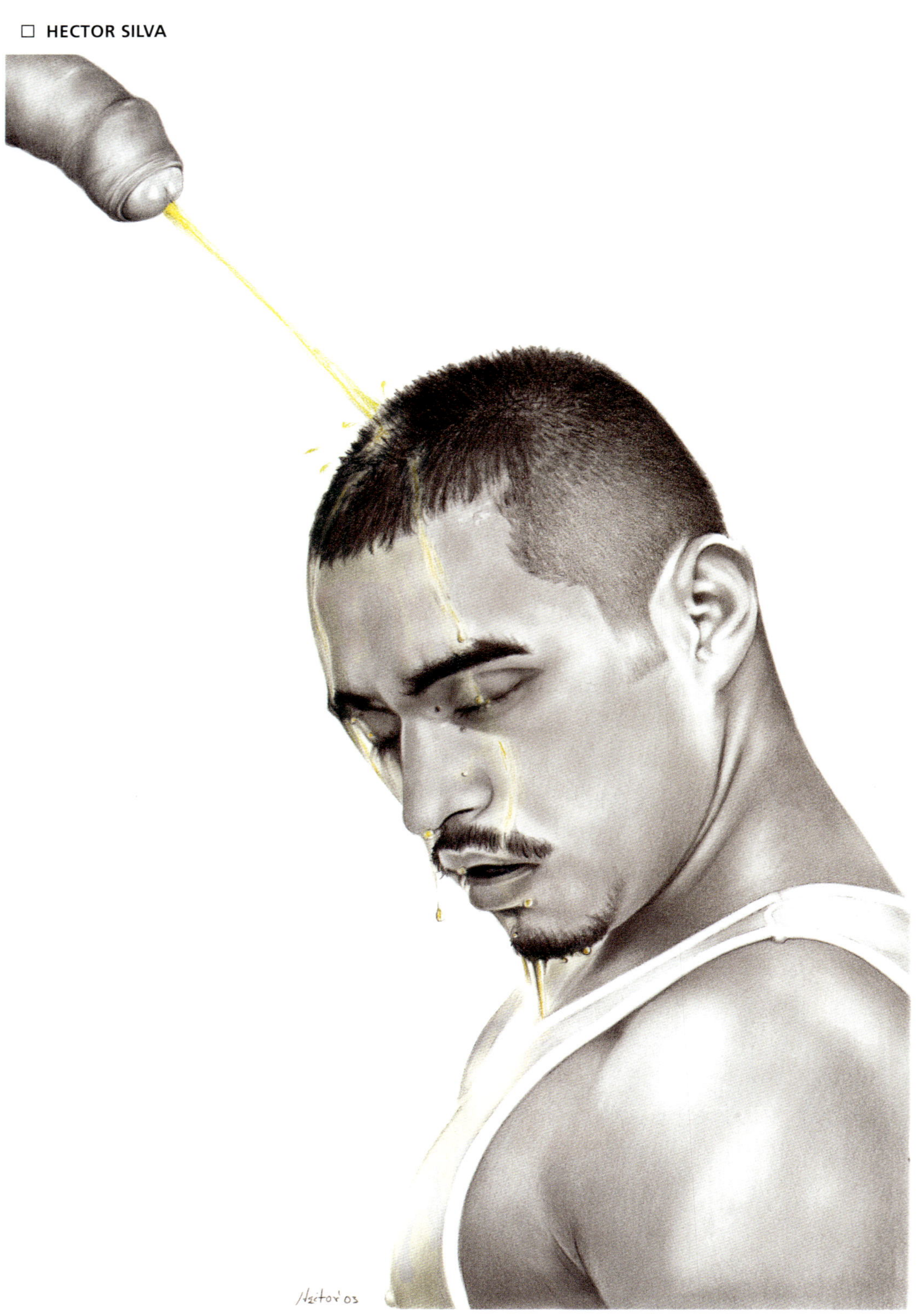

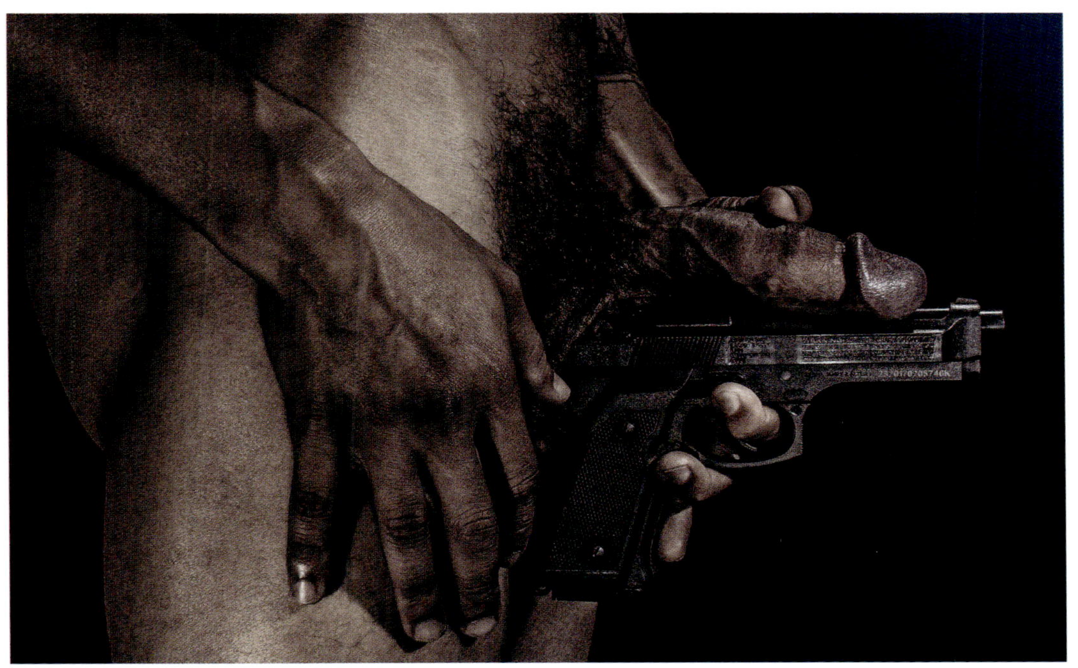

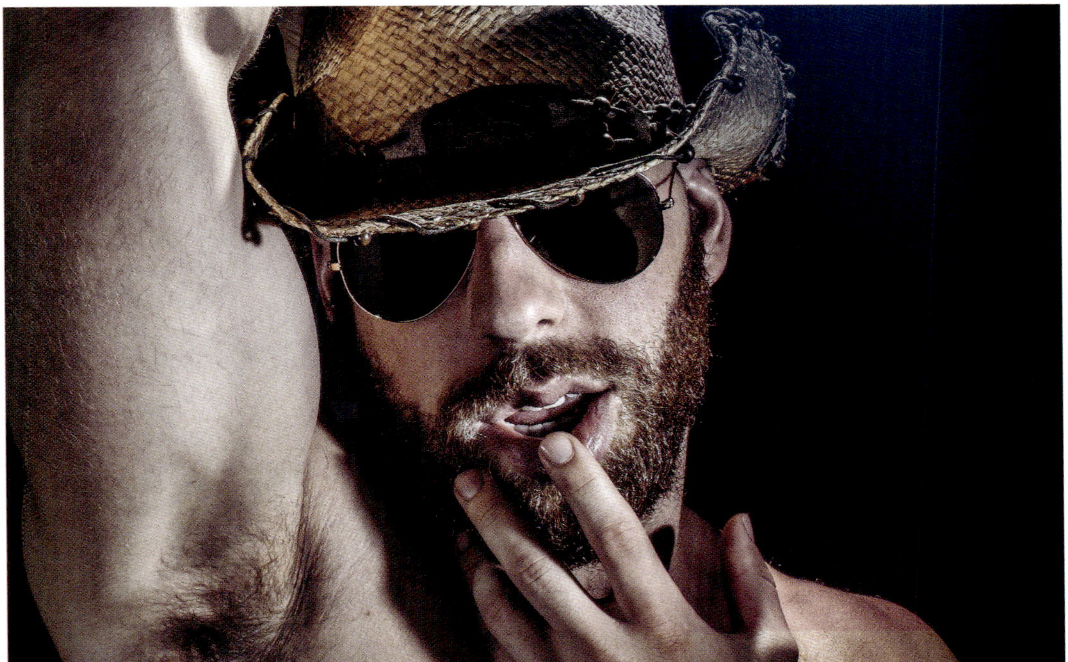

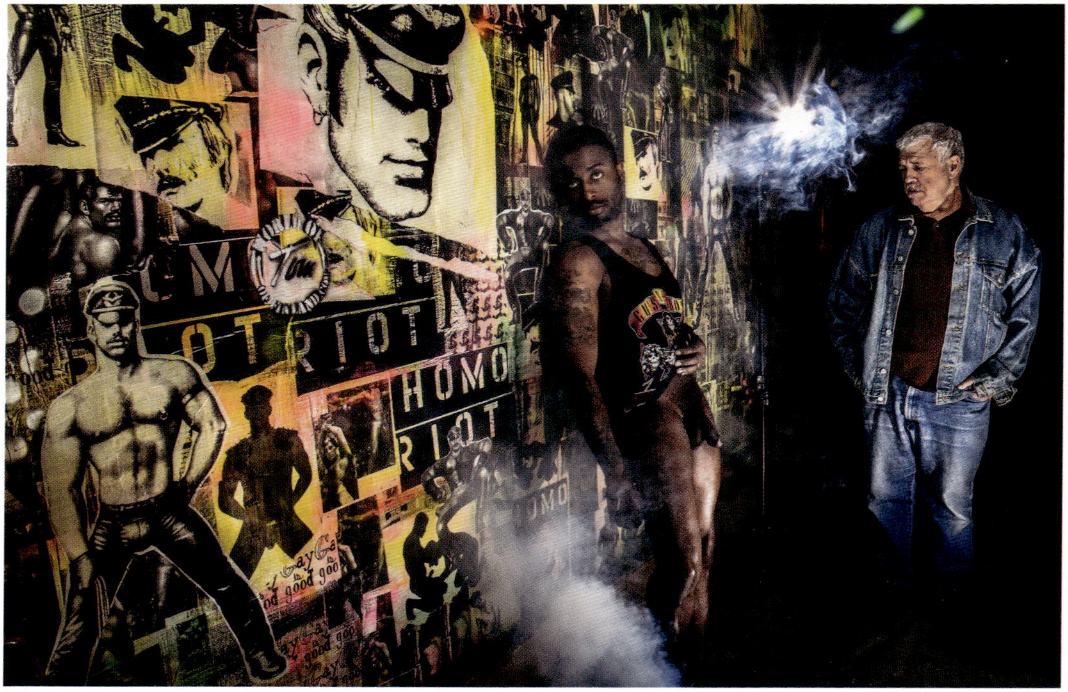

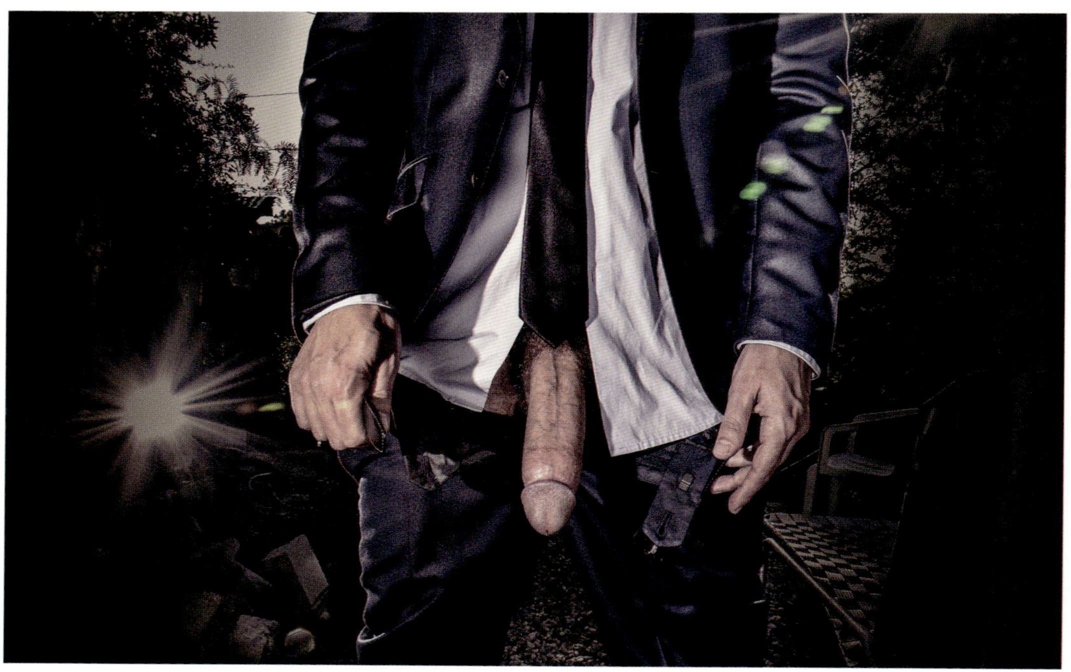

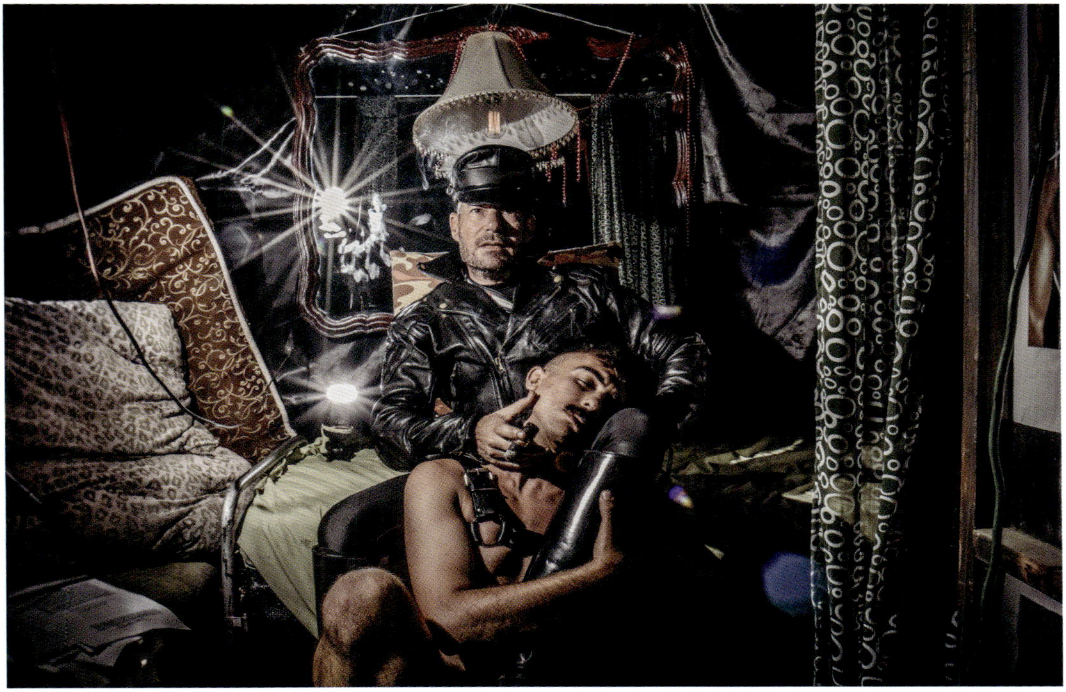

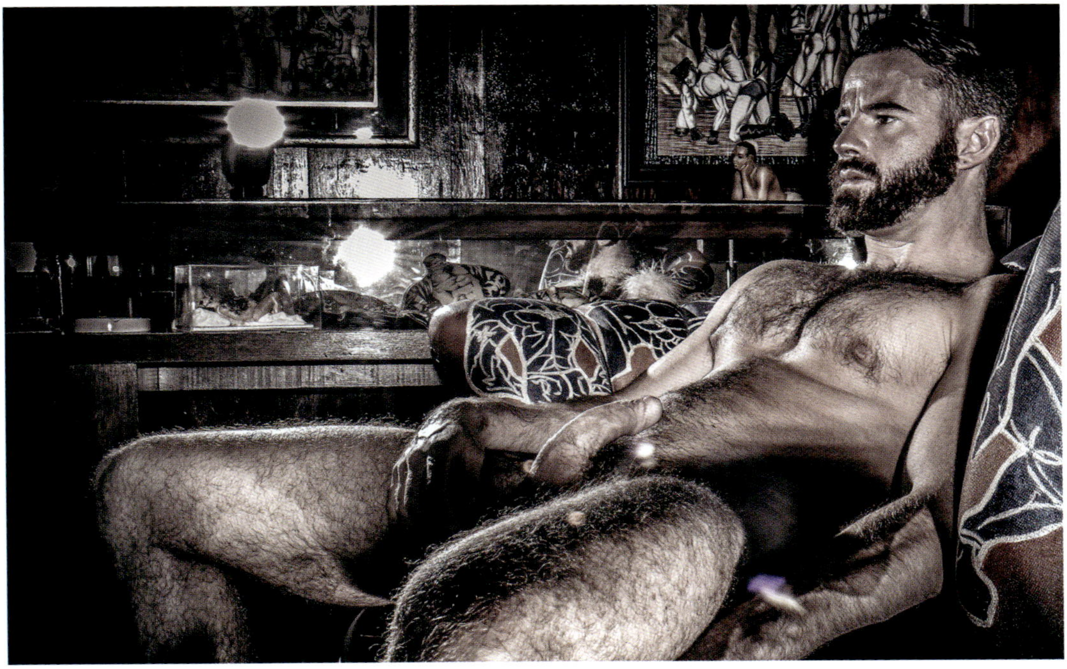

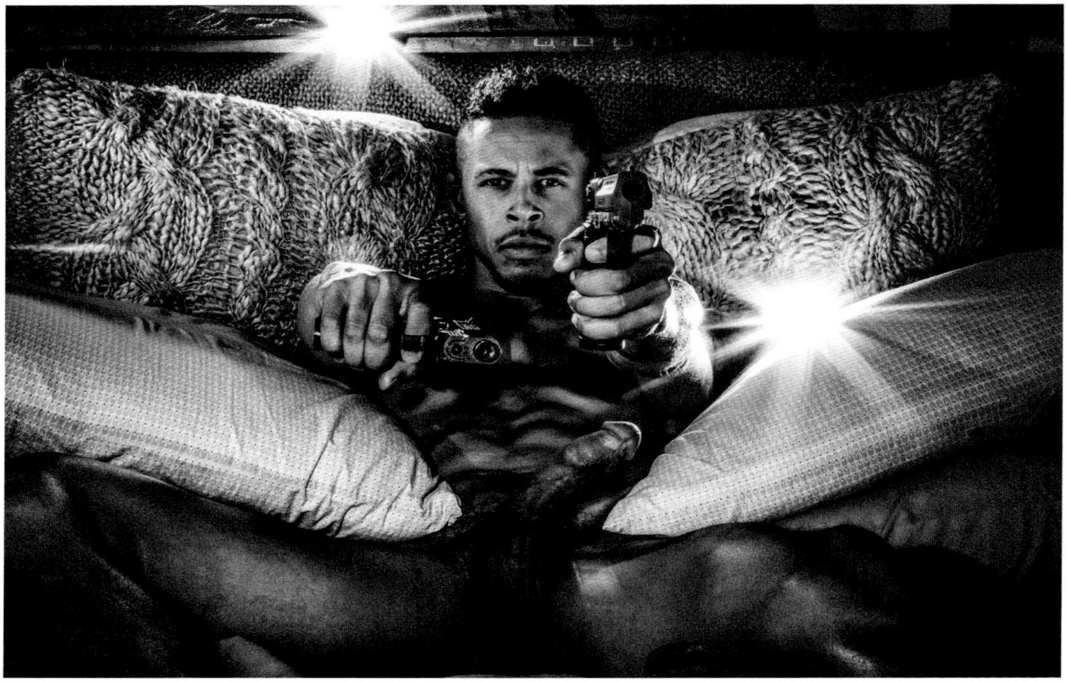

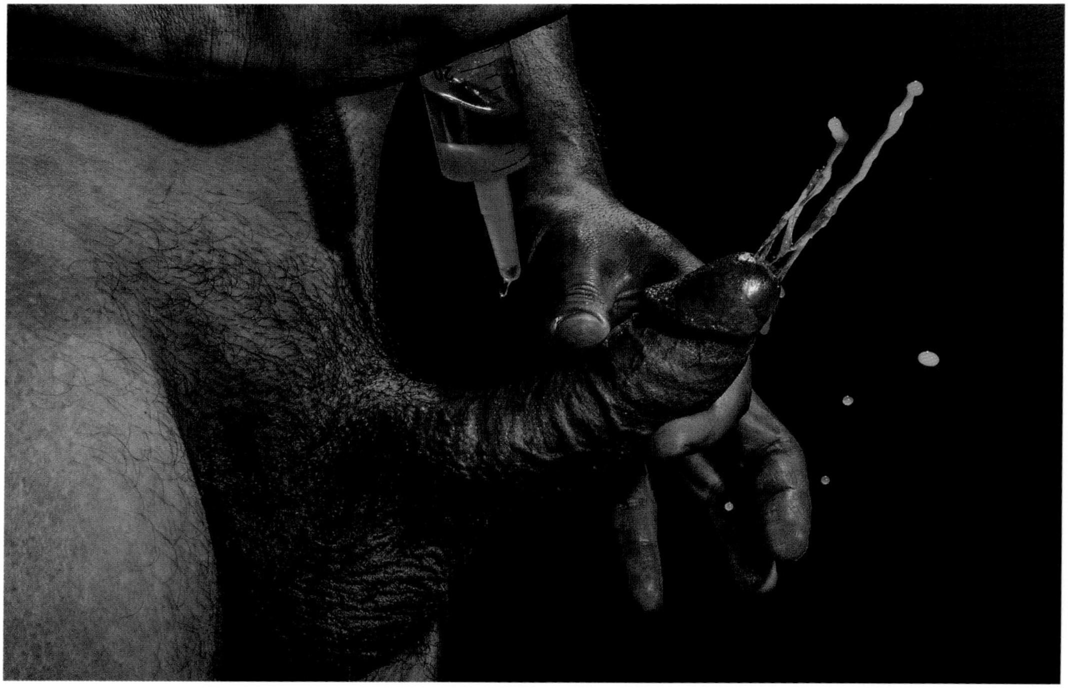

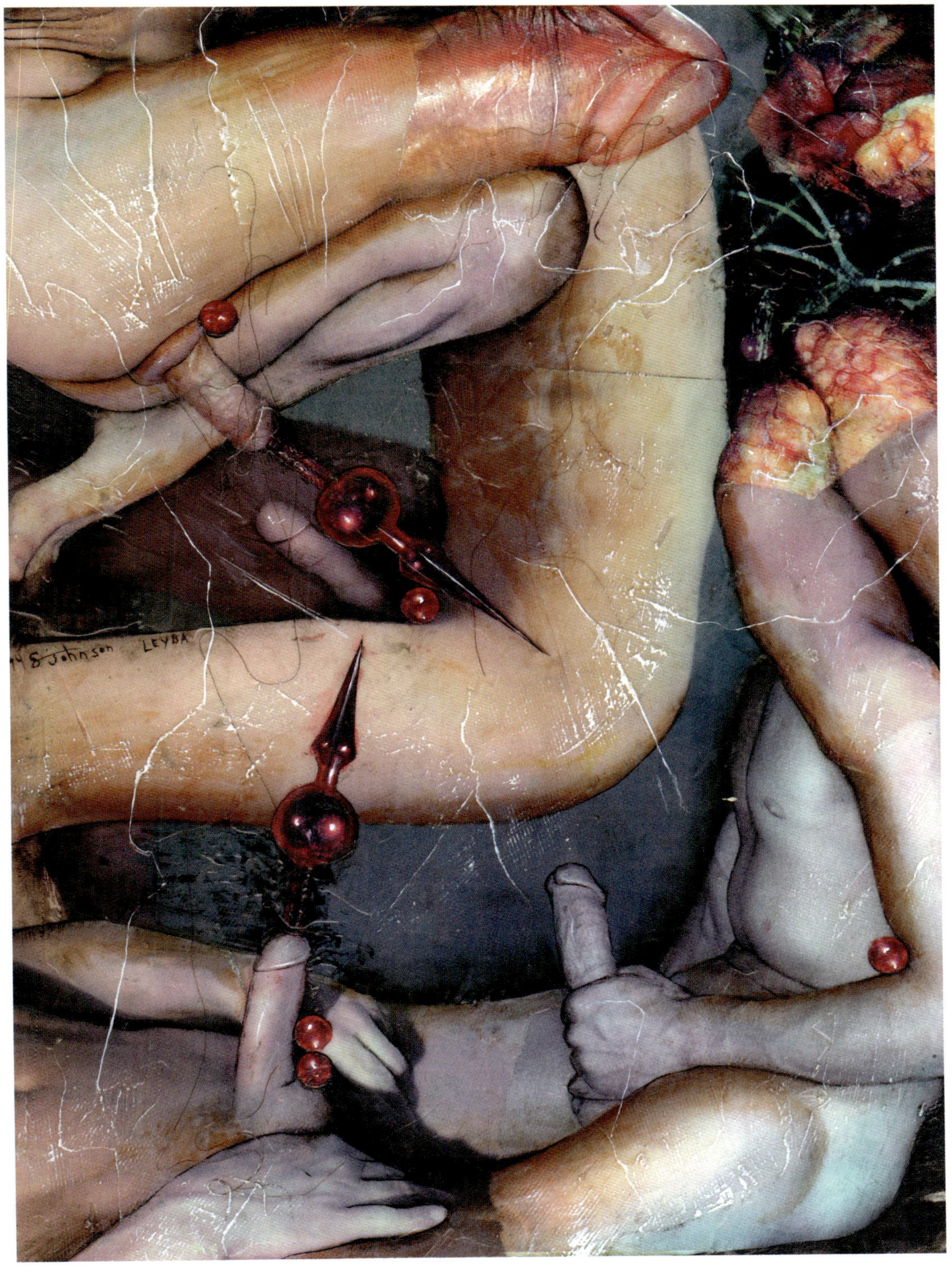

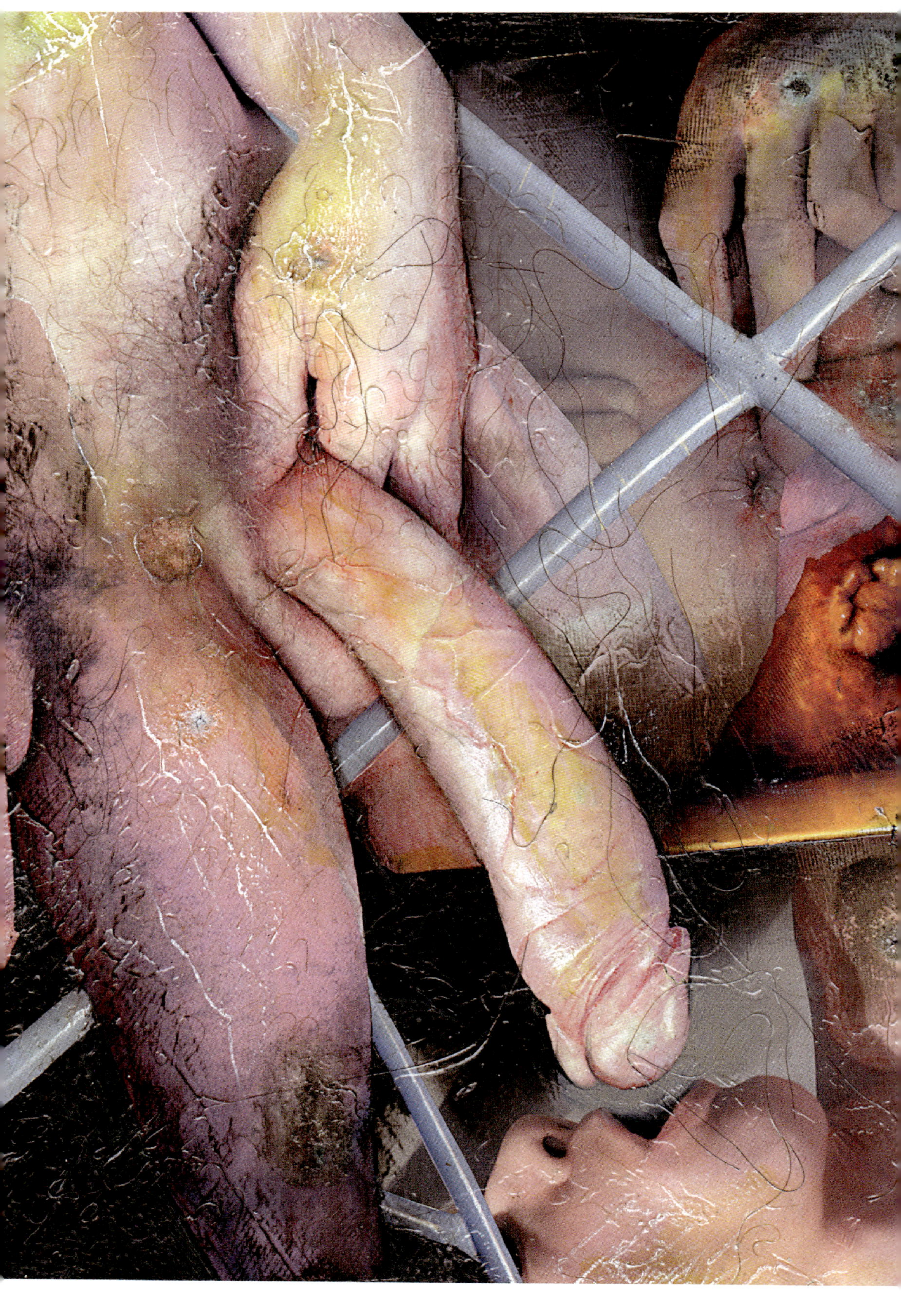

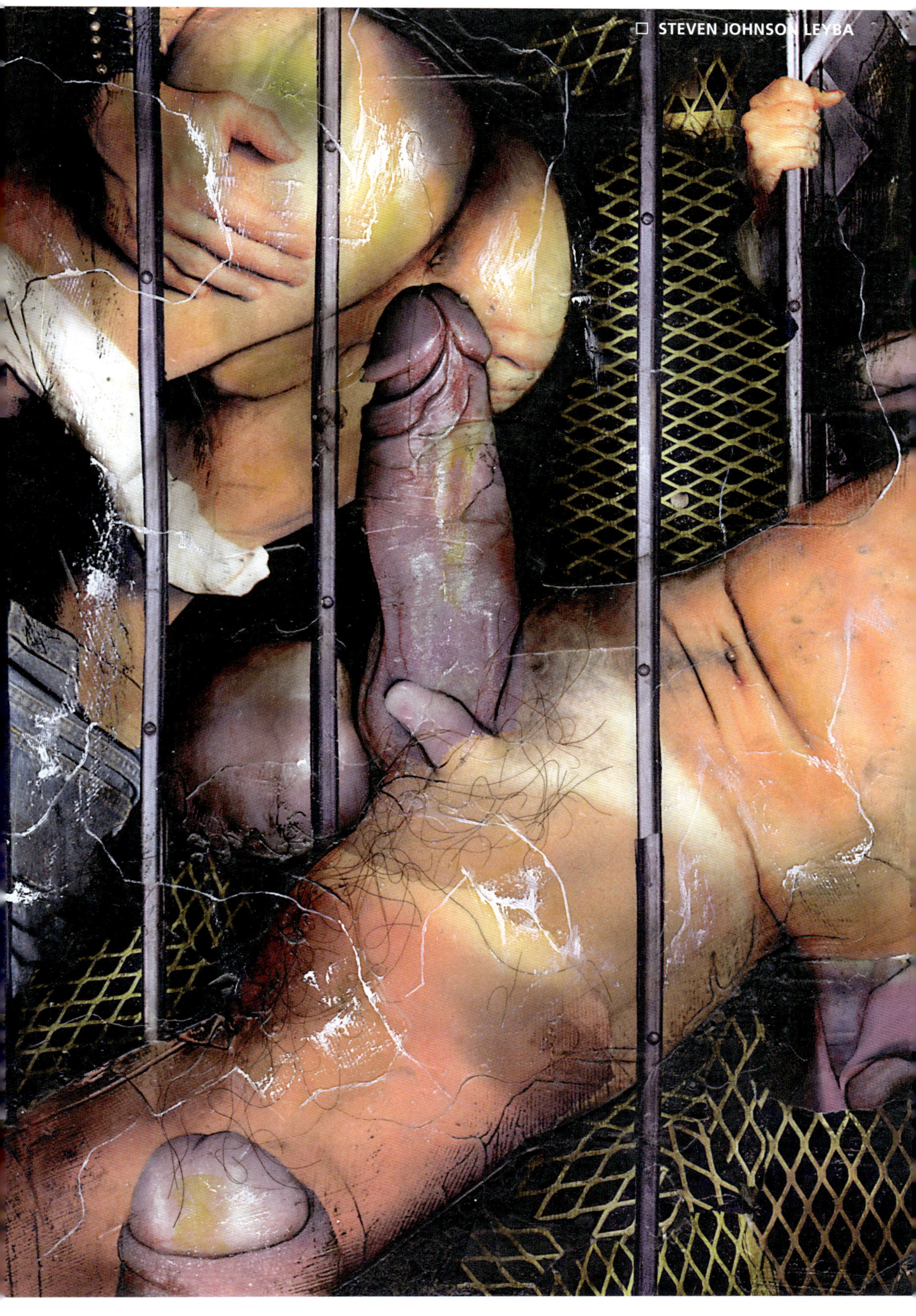

STEVEN JOHNSON LEYBA

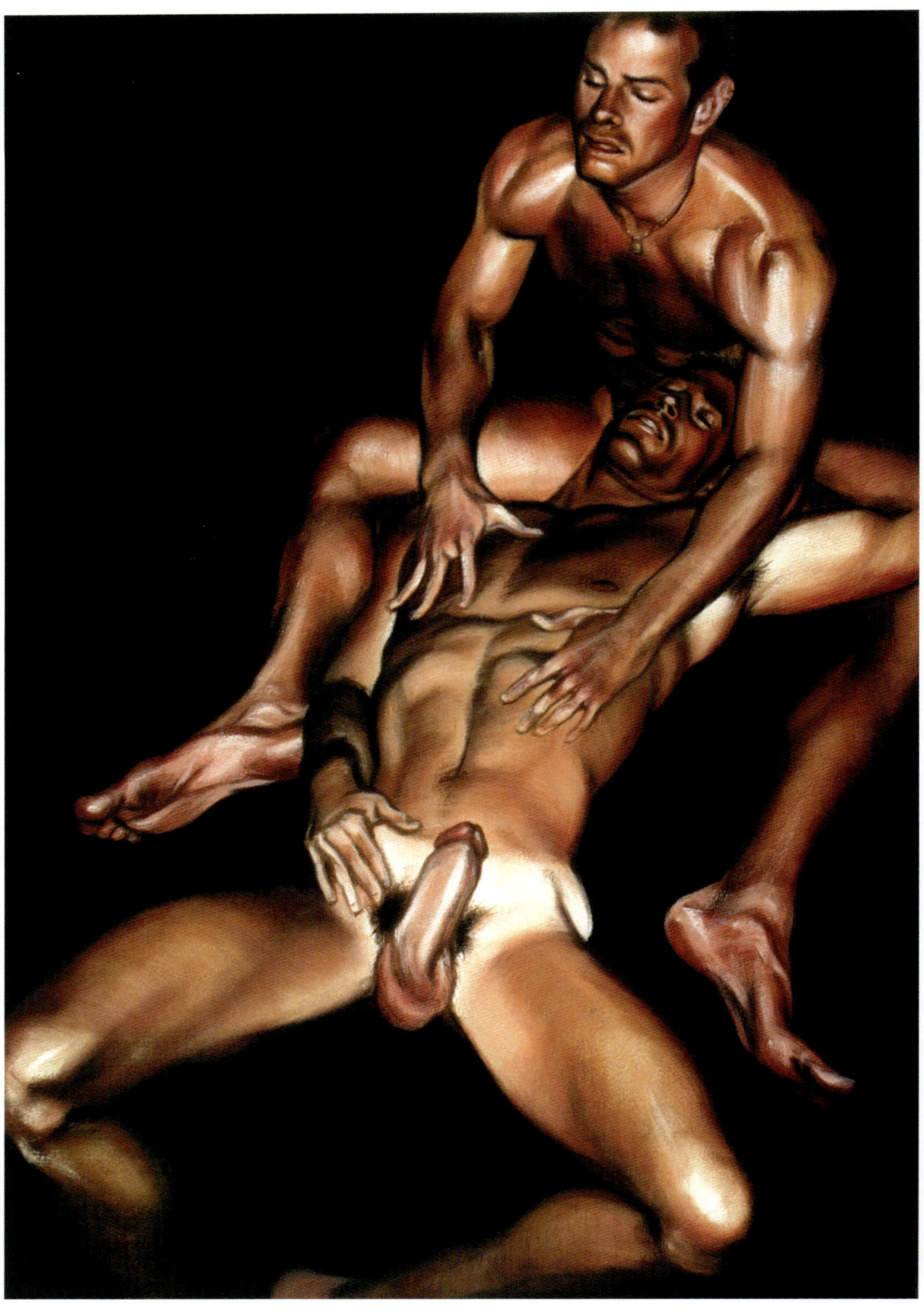

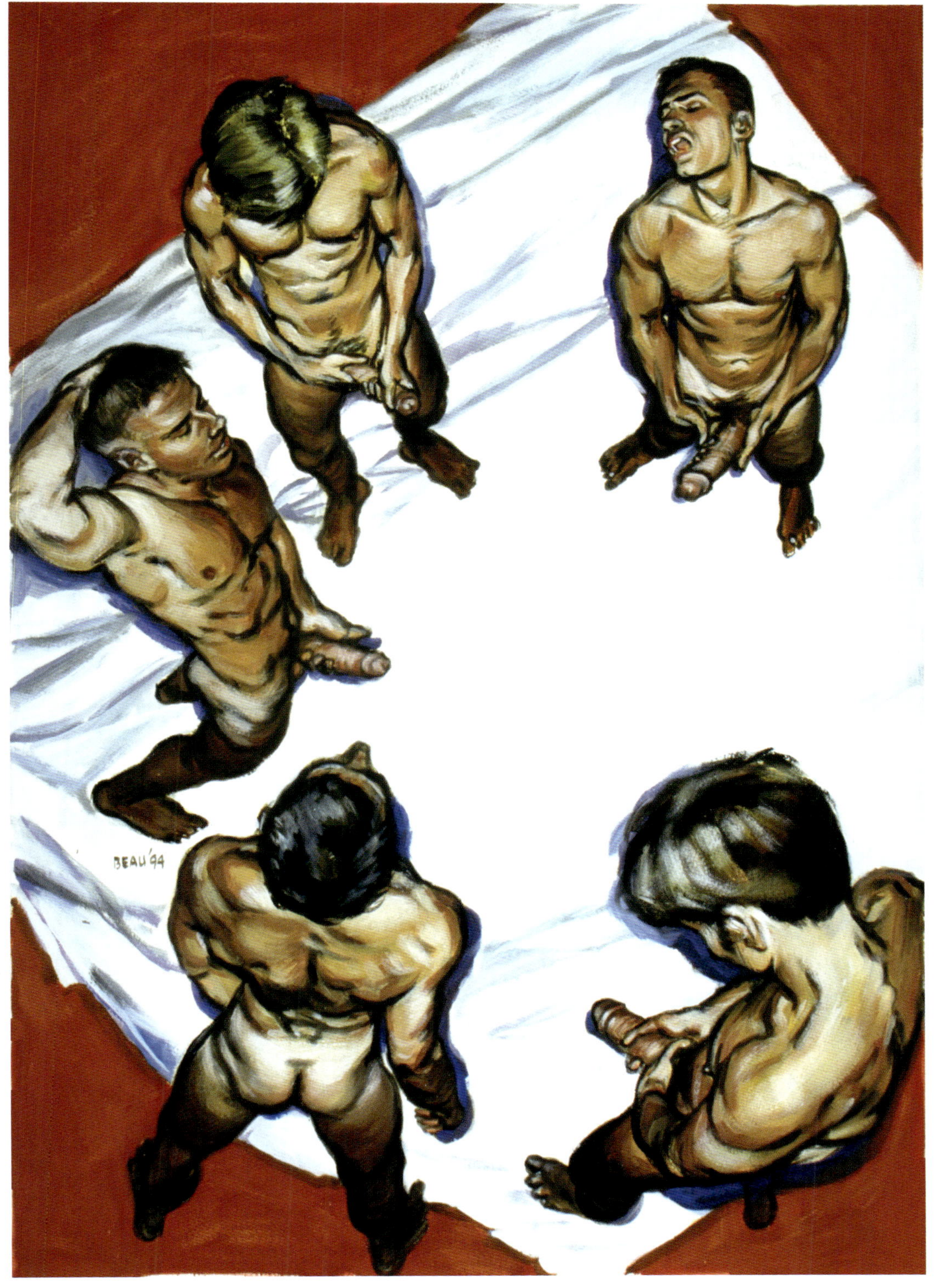

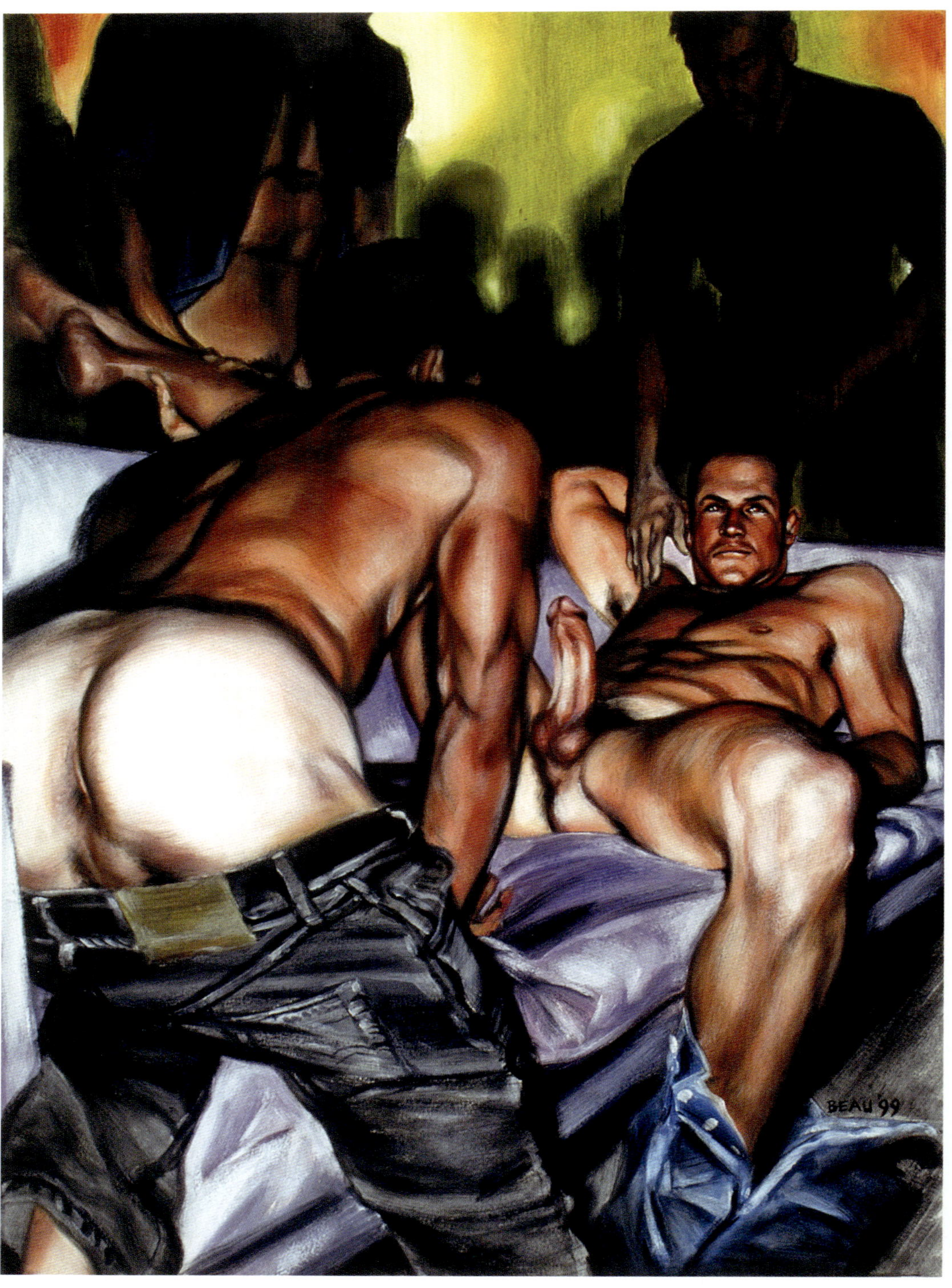

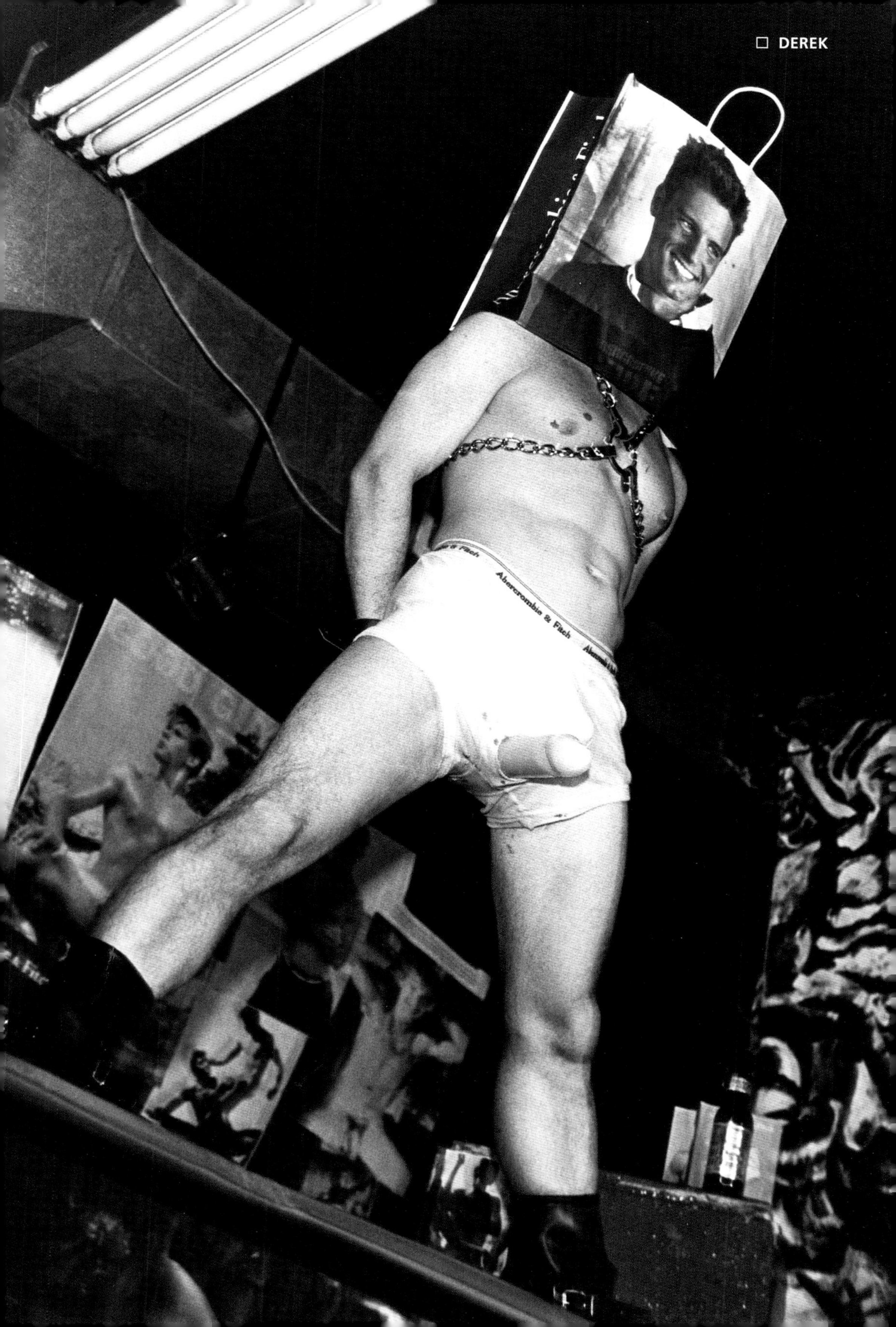

□ DEREK

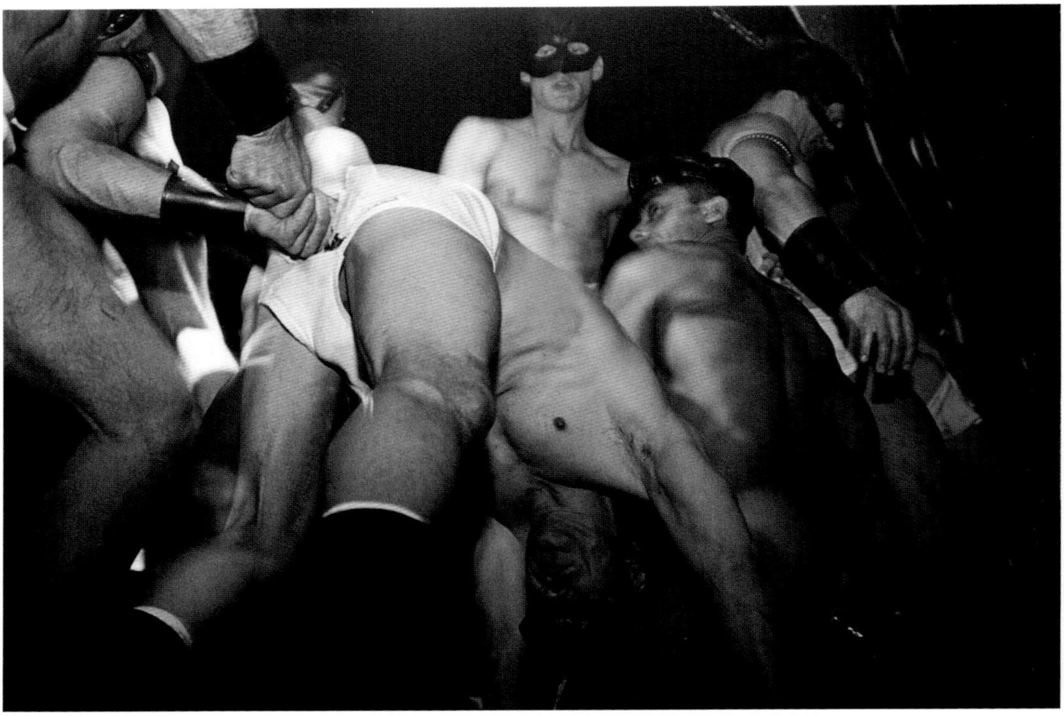

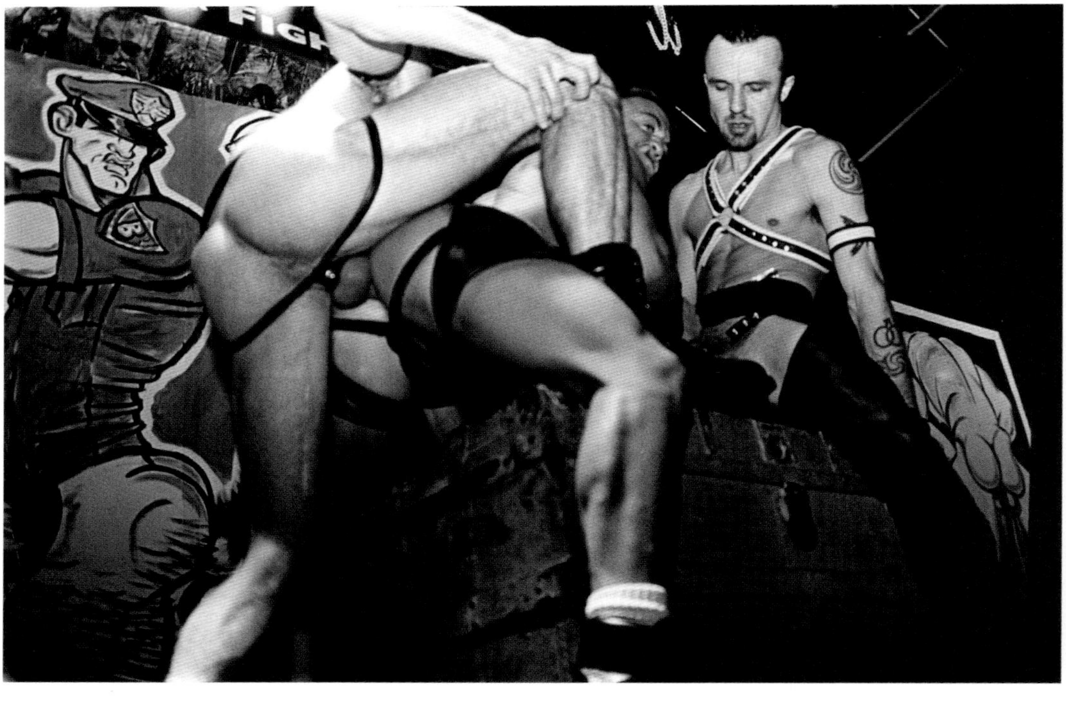

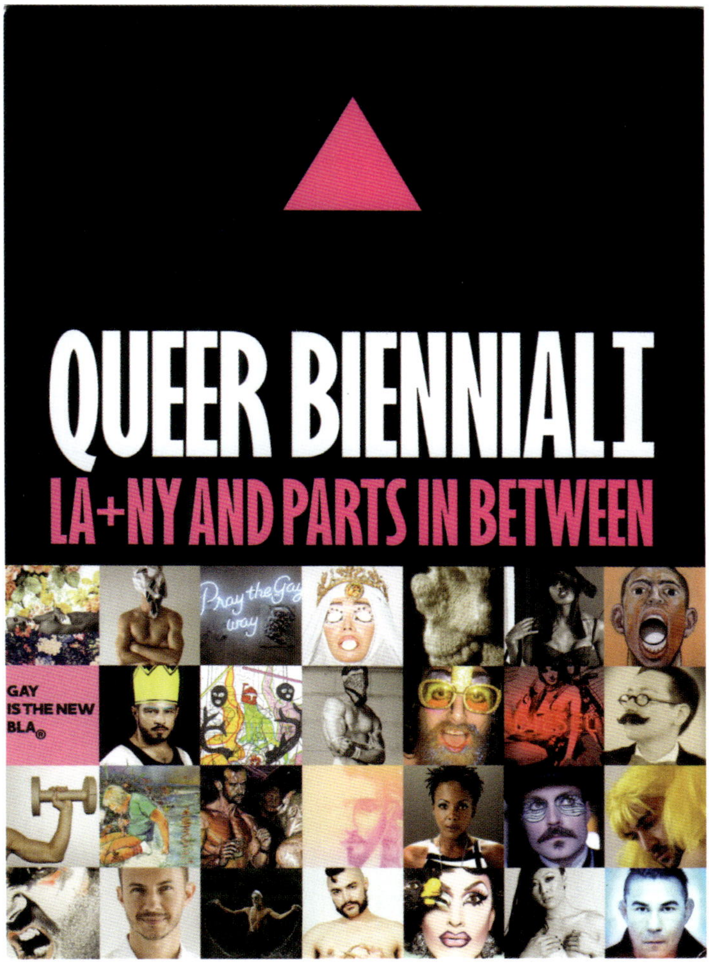

Queer Biennial

The Queer Biennial is an international survey focusing on the current moments in out/Queer/LGBT art and culture that showcases emerging, mid-career, and established artists. Featured work includes installation, film, live performance, and historical documentation. It was founded by Rubén Esparza, artist and curator, based in Los Angeles. The Queer Biennial began in 2014 and is firmly planted in Los Angeles and New York, with satellite happenings around the world. It is connected with Tom of Finland Foundation on many levels.

Die Queer Biennale ist ein internationales Festival, das sich mit aktuellen Strömungen der queeren/LGBT Kunst und Kultur beschäftigt und junge wie etablierte Künstler präsentiert. Zum Programm gehören auch Installationen, Filme, Live-Performances und geschichtliche Dokumentationen. Sie wurde vom Künstler und Kurator Rubén Esparza, Los Angeles, gegründet. Die Queer Biennale fand erstmals 2014 statt und ist fest in Los Angeles und New York verankert mit Satellitenveranstaltungen rund um die Welt. Sie ist auf vielen Ebenen mit der Tom of Finland Foundation verbunden.

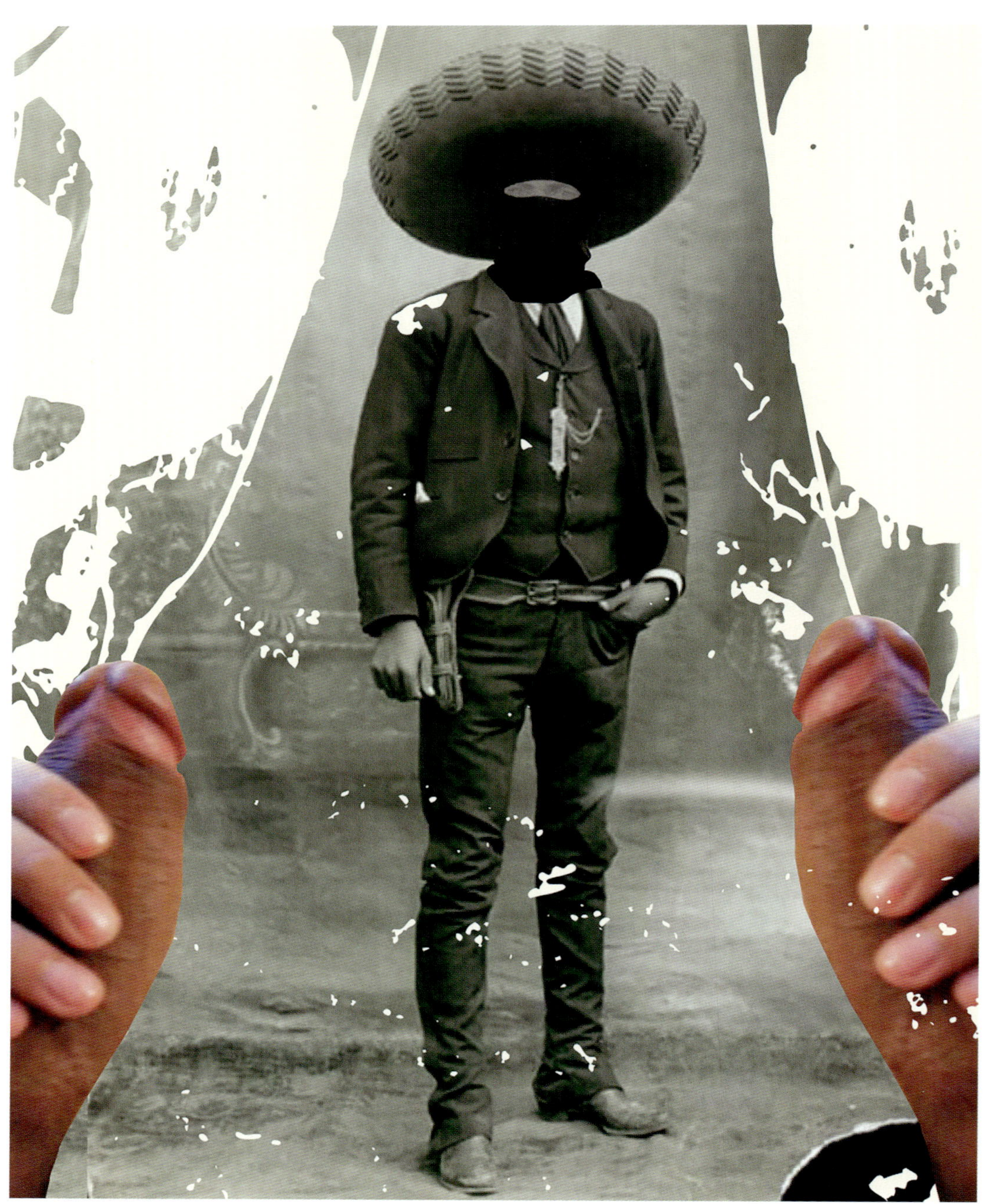

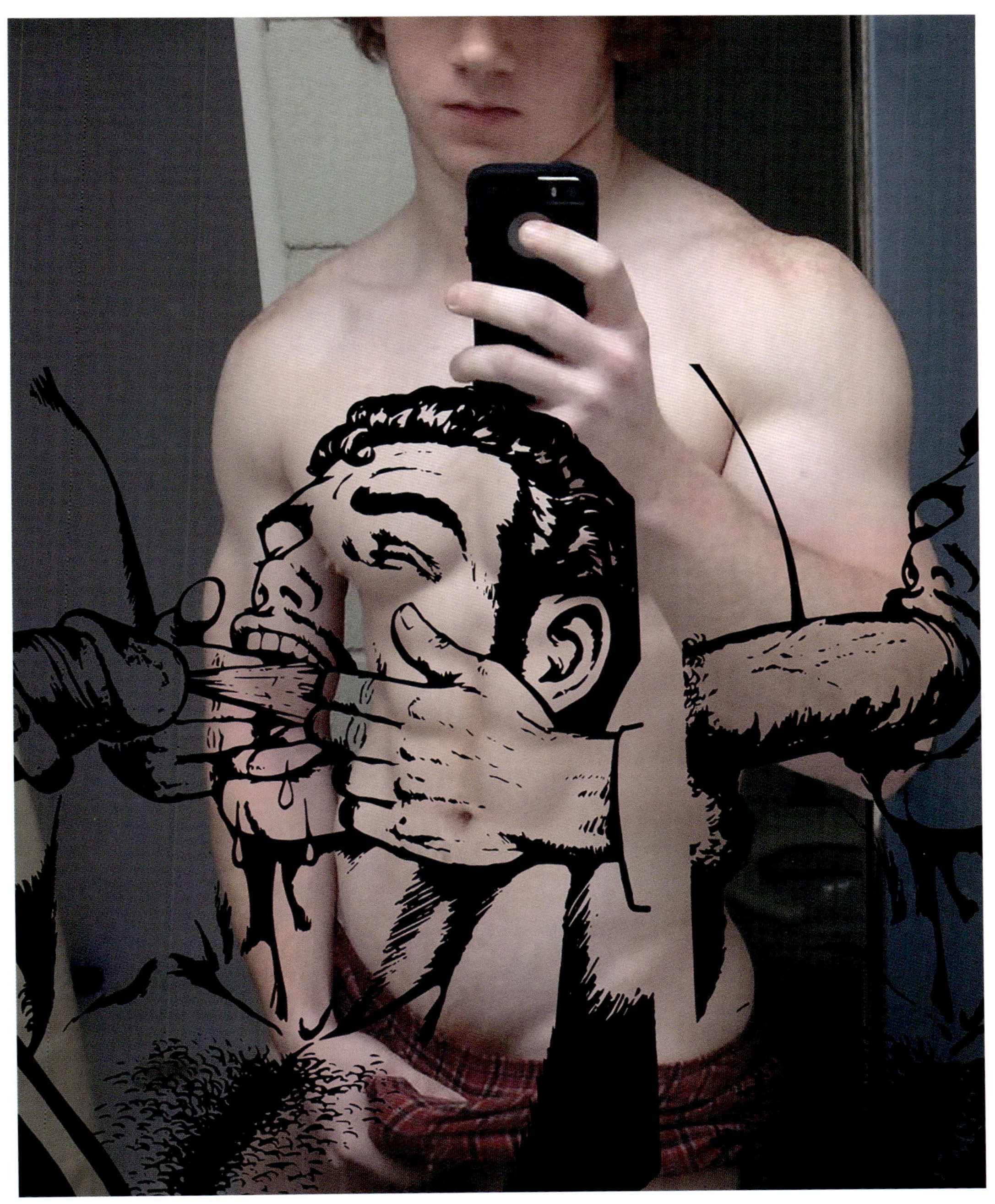

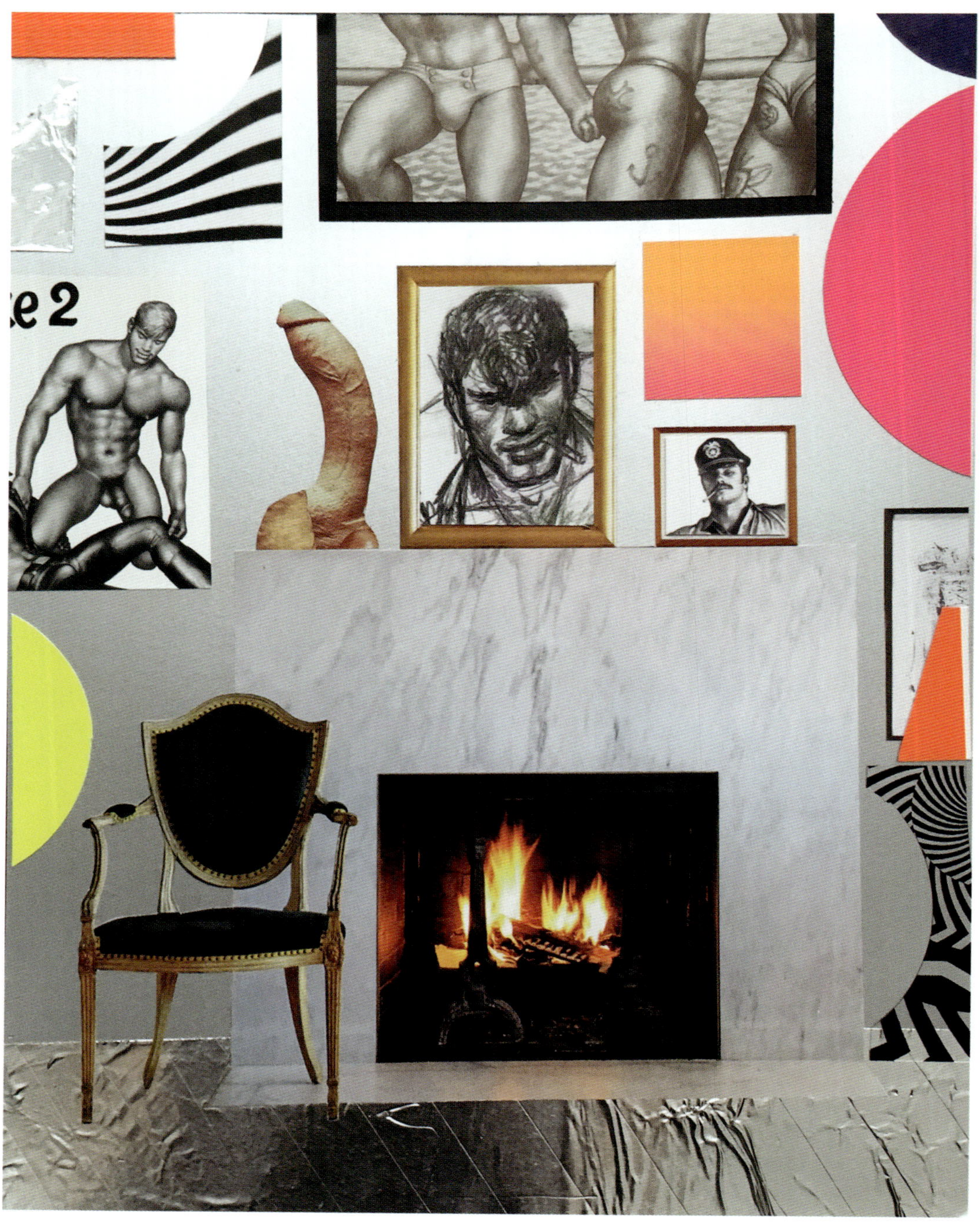

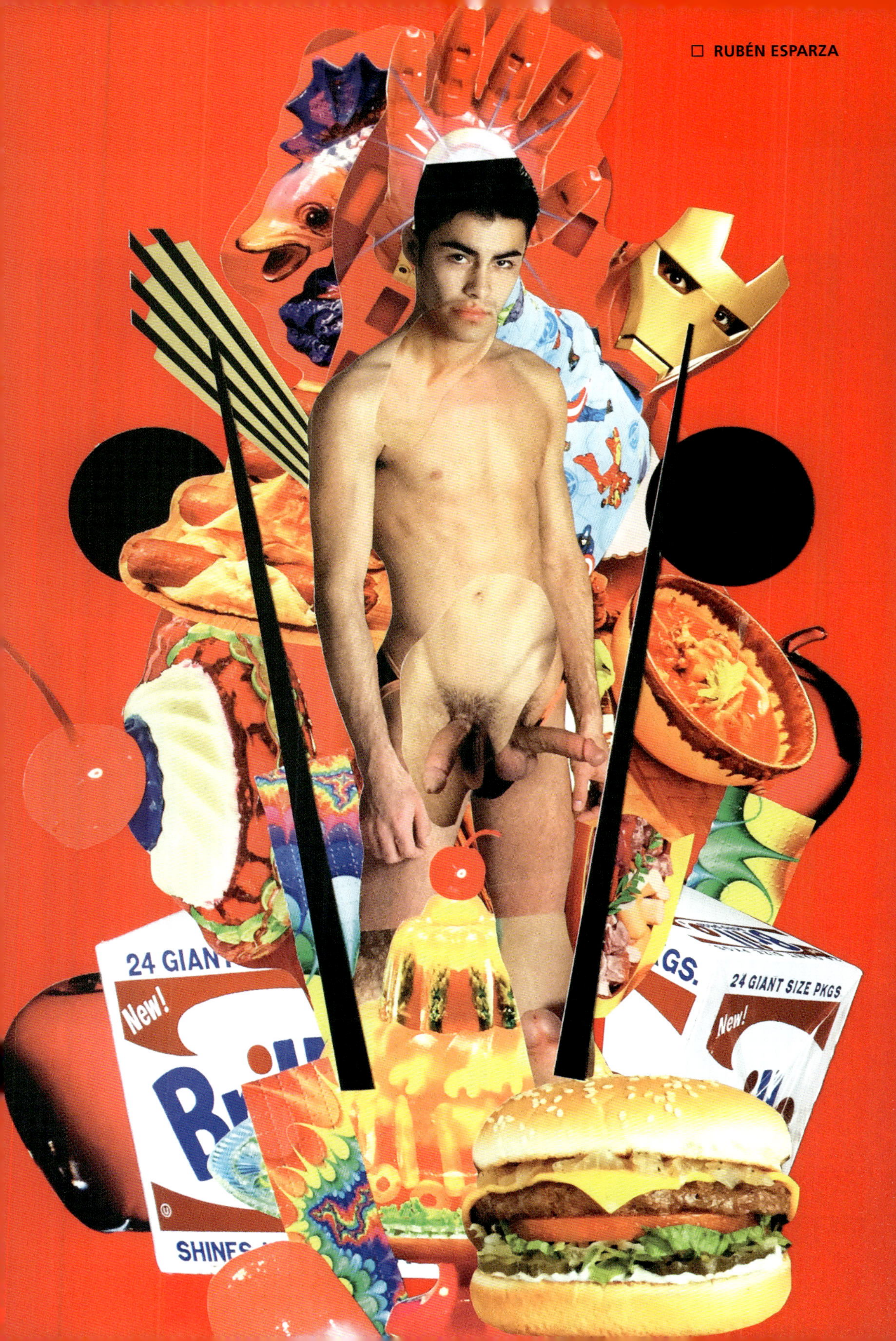

RUBÉN ESPARZA
24 GIANT
New!
SHINES
GS.
24 GIANT SIZE PKGS
New!

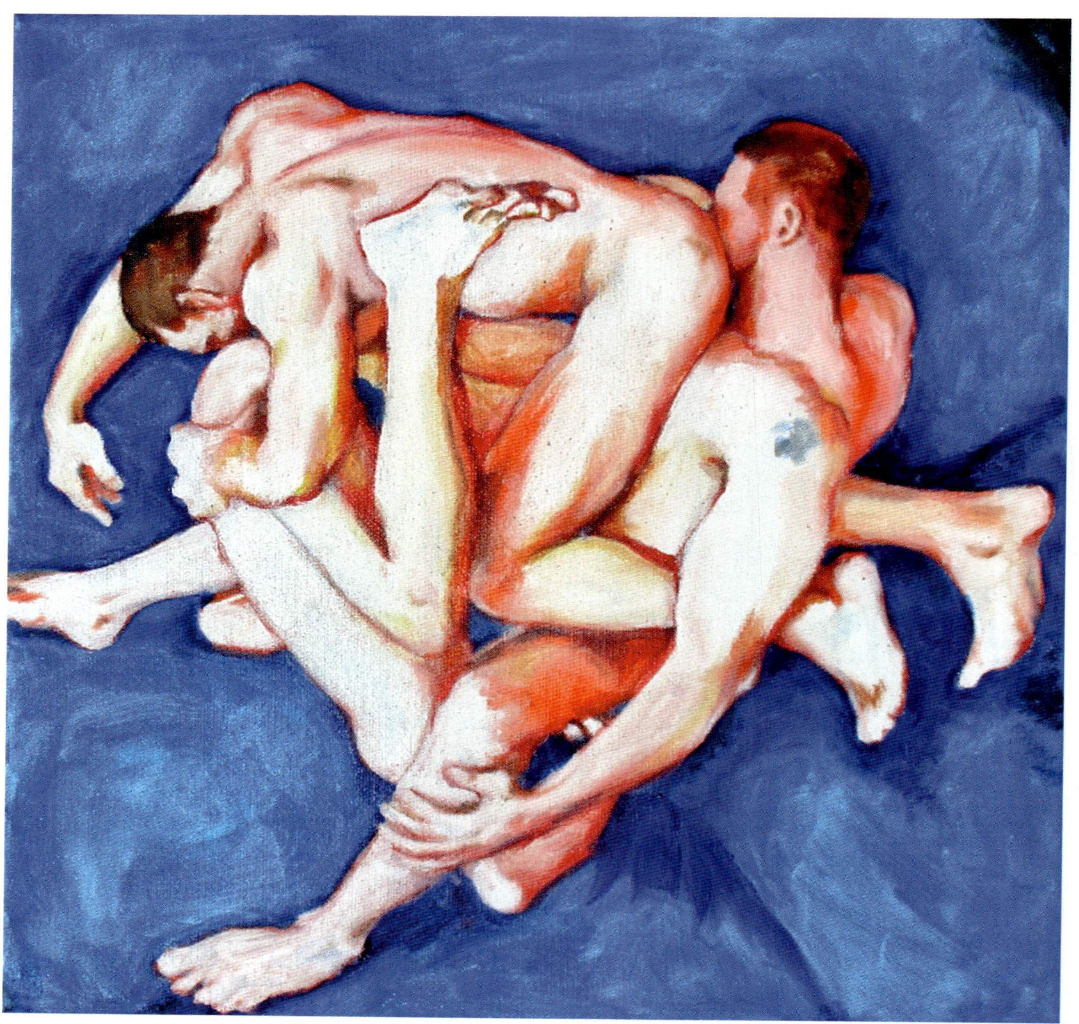

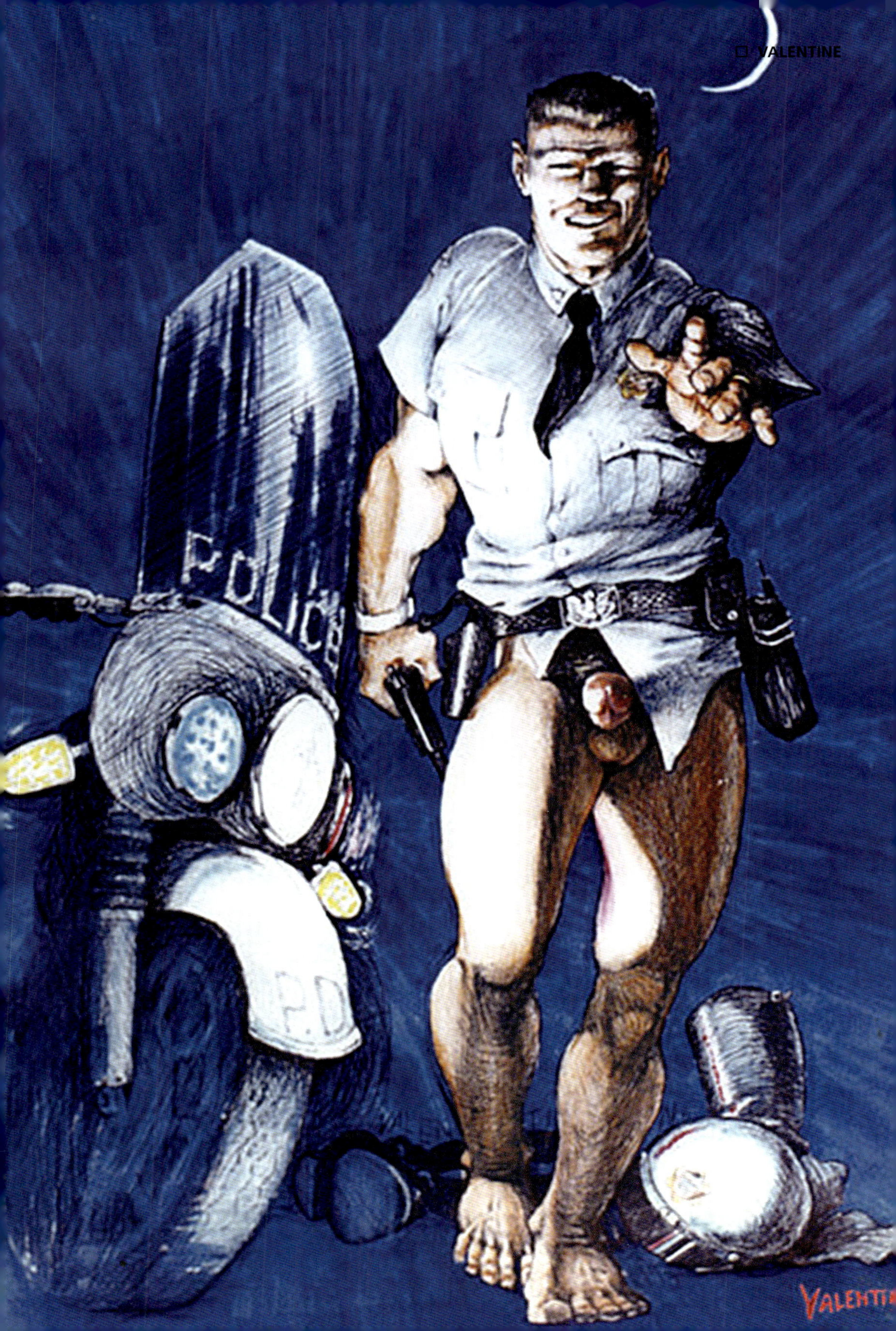
VALENTINE
POLICE
P.D.
P.D
VALENTINE

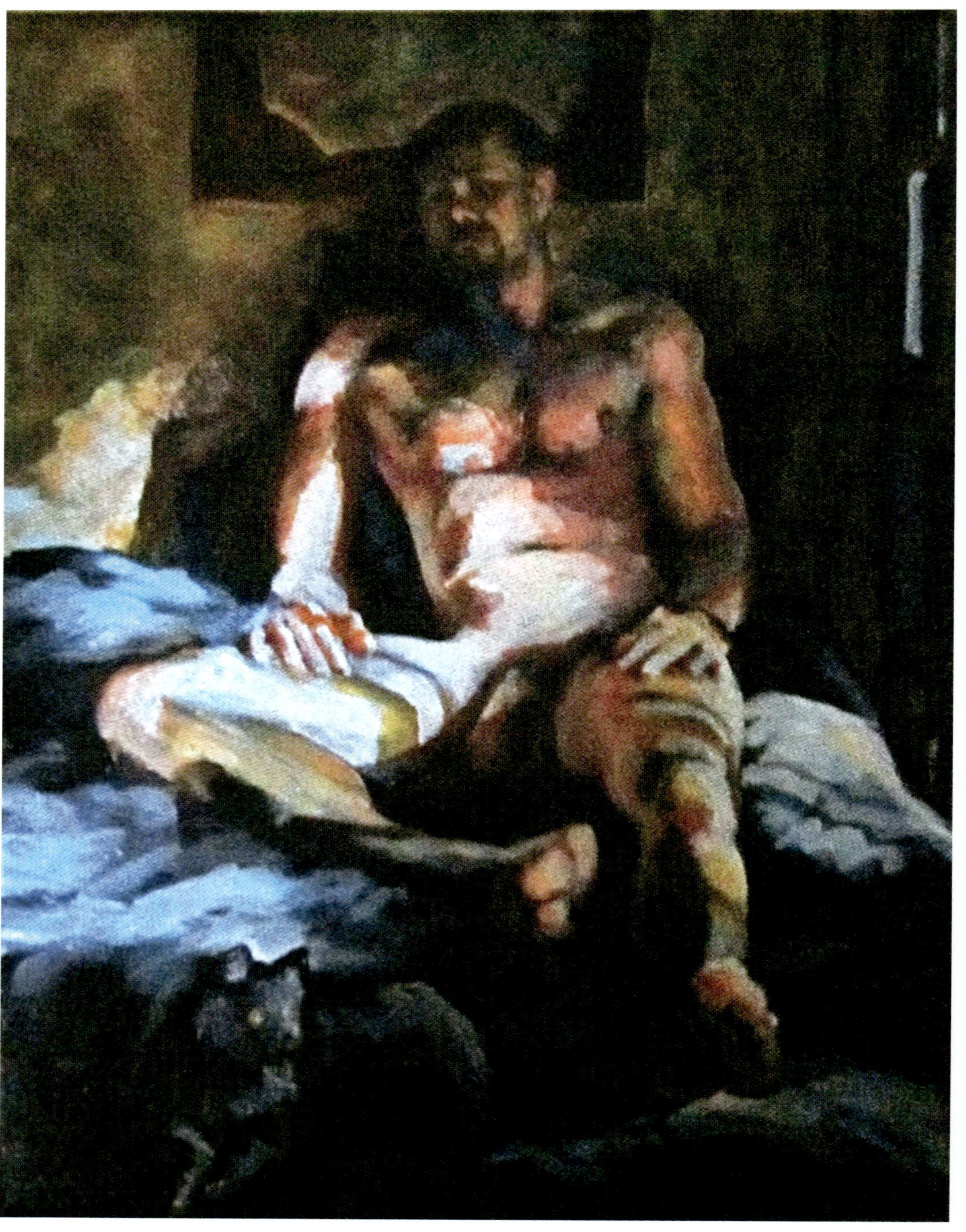

RAINER HÖRMANN

„A Love That Will Never Grow Old" – Über die Männer Tom of Finlands • The men of Tom of Finland

Seltsam, aber ich kann mich gar nicht daran erinnern, wann ich den Männern meiner Träume das erste Mal begegnet bin. Sicher, es muss Mitte der achtziger Jahre gewesen sein, als ich mein Coming-out hatte. Aber verliebte ich mich vor meinem ersten Besuch einer schwulen Jeans-Leder-Kneipe oder erst danach? Oder war es im schwulen Buchladen in meiner Heimatstadt, wo ich beim Durchblättern der Magazine für Männer einer meiner ersten Lieben, dem Buchhändler, sogleich untreu wurde? Die Traummänner waren treuer und zogen mit mir nach Berlin. Ich hängte die Bilder im Schlafzimmer und im Badezimmer nur gelegentlich ab, meist um heterosexuelle Besucher, die in die Wunder schwuler Fetischwelten nicht eingeweiht waren, von allzu neugierigen Nachfragen abzuhalten. Und doch blieb unsere Liebe auch immer ein wenig unerfüllt, trieb mich eine Sehnsucht – nach was eigentlich? – in die Lederkneipen. Die Männer meiner Träume erwiesen sich oft als eifersüchtig und machten mir das Spiel mit anderen Männern schwer. So dominant waren die Kerle meiner Träume in all ihren unzähligen Erscheinungen, ihren Uniformen. Wir teilten so viele Geheimnisse und manche geile Nacht miteinander – damals.

Vor den Zeichnungen von Touko Laaksonen waren definitiv die Superhelden-Comics meiner Kindheit und Jugend. Schon damals galt meine Sympathie nicht nur den Guten, sondern heimlich auch den Bösewichtern, hatten sie doch neben dem muskulösen Körper auch den schwarz-geheimnisvollen Schnauzbart. Natürlich ahnte ich damals schon – ohne Worte dafür zu haben – die homoerotische Anziehung, die der dargestellten Gegnerschaft zugrunde lag. Die Männer von Tom of Finland überwanden die Grenze. Highway-Patrol versus Biker, Gefängniswärter versus Insasse, Meister versus Sklave – alles Trennungen, Machtverhältnisse, die dazu da waren, im gemeinsamen, enthemmten Sex aufgehoben zu werden. Lustvoll und nicht ohne Heiterkeit. Oder Höflichkeit? Wenn etwa zwei Cops nach

Strange, I really can't remember when I first met the men of my dreams. It must have been in the mid-eighties, during my coming-out. Did I fall in love before I went to my first leather bar or afterwards? Or did it happened at the gay bookstore in my hometown while leafing through some of the men's magazines, causing me immediately to become unfaithful to my other first love, the bookseller? The men of my dreams proved more loyal and even came along when I moved to Berlin. Now and then, I took the pictures of them down from my bedroom wall and from the bathroom just to keep heterosexual guests – most of them unaccustomed to the wonders of the gay fetish world – from asking questions. But yet our love still remained somewhat unrequited, which perhaps nurtured my desire to go out to the leather bars. The men of my dreams were quite jealous which often made it difficult for me to play with other men. The men of my dreams were so dominant with all their posing, their uniforms. We shared so many secrets and many a horny night – back in the day.

Before I discovered the drawings of Tom of Finland (born Touko Laaksonen), there were the comic book superheroes of my childhood. Even then I empathized not only for the good guys but also, secretly, for the villains with their muscular bodies and their sinister black moustaches. Of course, I was aware of the homoerotic attraction that lay beneath the rivalry shown – although I had no words for these feelings. The men of Tom of Finland bridged that gap. Highway Patrol vs. biker, prison guard vs. inmate, master vs. slave – subtle distinctions, and yet these hierarchies were negated in a lust-filled no-holds-barred orgy. Lewd, and yet not without a hint of joviality. Or was it merely good manners? When two cops part ways, after a rollicking threesome, with a nonchalant salute while the third, his

dem Dreier zum Abschied freundlich salutieren und ihnen der erschöpfte, aber glückliche Kerl, die Lederhose noch offen, zurückwinkt? In der überstilisierten Welt von Tom of Finland paarte sich Dominanz mit Zärtlichkeit, wurde die Zumutung der männlichen Gewalt, die im gesellschaftlichen Alltag als Bedrohung für Schwule durchaus real war, in einer vielleicht absurden, aber geilen Fantasie handhabbar. In gewisser Weise erlaubten die Zeichnungen eine Transformation, so wie das Tragen des Leders gleichsam als zweite Haut den Träger transformiert und es ihm ermöglicht, wenn auch nur für kurze Zeit und nur ästhetisch, ein anderer zu sein.

Für einen Moment ließ sich das Paradox, dass man eine Hypermaskulinität verklärte, die im realen Leben für weibische Schwule nur Verachtung übrighatte, auf lustvolle Weise aufheben. Das Ringen um eine Rolle, um eine Identität, hier war es noch ein Spiel. Eine meiner Lieblingszeichnungen hat es mittlerweile zum Motiv einer Briefmarke der finnischen Post geschafft. Ein nackter Mann sitzt zwischen den Beinen eines dominanten Lederkerls.

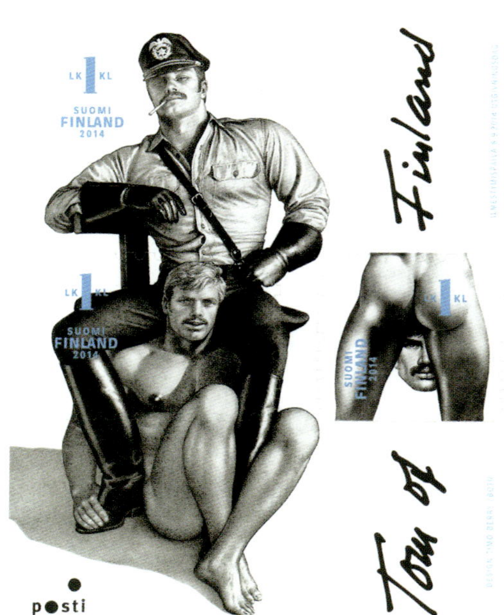

Noch immer schwelge ich gern in der wohligen Geborgenheit dieser inszenierten Hierarchie. Aber die stille Sehnsucht nach dem Lekken der Stiefel findet keine Entsprechung im Lecken der Briefmarke. Sie ist selbstklebend. Moderne Bequemlichkeit!

Es hat lange gedauert, bis ich erstmals eine Zeichnung von Touko Laaksonen im Original sehen konnte. Welch ein Erlebnis. Die dominante Eindeutigkeit des Dargestellten löste sich auf in der Zärtlichkeit des Bleistiftstrichs. In gewisser Weise sind Laaksonens Bilder auch Vexierbilder. Man muss zwei, drei Schritte Abstand halten zu einem Original, um das Ganze wahrzunehmen, die Muskeln, das glänzende

leather pants still down around his ankles, cheerfully waves back in response.

In the stylish world of Tom of Finland, dominance went hand-in-hand with tenderness; the dark side of male aggression – in actual life a real threat to gay men – became tolerable, albeit in a crude yet horny fantasy. In a certain way, the drawings supported a mode of transformation just as wearing leather as a second skin transforms you and allows you to become someone else even if for a short time and in a mere aesthetic way. Just for a moment, the paradox of worshipping hyper-masculinity, which in real life despises the "effeminate" gay man, could be overcome in a lustful manner. The struggle for a role, for an identity, in his world it was just a game.

One of my favorite drawings has just recently been made into a postage stamp in Finland. A naked guy is sitting between the legs of a dominant man clad in leather. Till this day, I dwell in the comfortable coziness of that staged hierarchy. Alas, the mute desire to lick those boots cannot be sublimated by licking the stamp. It's self-adhesive. That's what I call modern convenience!

When I finally had the chance to look at an original drawing by Tom, it was a drastic experience for me. The dominant directness of the scene dissolved amidst the tenderness of his pencil strokes. In a certain way, the drawings are optical illusions. You need to take a couple of steps back in order to appreciate the entire image, the muscles, the shiny leather ... if you come close enough that your nose almost touches the surface, the figures are transformed into a symphony of poetically thin lines, one beside the next, executed so patiently

Leder ... Wer näher kommt und mit der Nase fast auf das Papier stößt, dem verschwimmen die Gestalten und lösen sich auf in die Feinheit der Linien, geduldig eine an die andere gefügt, liebevoll gezogen. Aber diese Entdeckung birgt eine Gefahr, wie sie in jeder Liebe liegt: Kommt man sich zu nah, kann auch das sexuelle Begehren schwinden. In einer Kunstausstellung haben mich die Zeichnungen nie geil gemacht. Geil gemacht haben mich die billigen Reproduktionen, die ich in Heftchenform mit ins Bett nehmen konnte. Schlechte Drucke, in denen das feine Geflecht der Linien zu einem satten schwarzen Klecks verschmolz. Erregend war das Grobe, das Derbe, das die filigrane Mühe seiner Entstehung verbarg. Vielleicht hätte die Kunst Touko Laaksonens niemals Kunst werden dürfen, hätte es niemals ins Museum of Modern Art in New York und andere Tempel schaffen dürfen. Bitte nicht falsch verstehen – es geht nicht darum, dem Künstler seine posthume Anerkennung nicht zu gönnen. Es ist mehr die Trauer um den Verlust einer Intimität, um den Verlust der Geheimnisse, die ich einst mit den Männern von Tom of Finland teilte. Es geht etwas verloren, wenn ich die Zeichnungen gerahmt an einer weißen Wand sehe ... der fest gebundene, prachtvoll gestaltete Ausstellungskatalog ist nicht der abgegriffene Nachdruck, nicht das dünne *Kake*-Heftchen, das man so leicht mit unter die Bettdecke nehmen konnte.

Aber auch der gesellschaftliche Kontext, in dem Tom of Finlands Männerwelten betrachtet werden können, hat sich verändert. Fragen nach der Affirmation heteronormativer Verhältnisse, nach Frauenunfreundlichkeit, nach Ausschluss bzw. Darstellung von People of Color können und müssen heute in einer kritischen Würdigung gestellt werden können. Gleichwohl unbestreitbar ist der Einfluss, die stilprägende Wirkung des Werks von Touko Laaksonen auf die schwule (Sub-)Kultur im Allgemeinen und die Leder- und Fetischszene im Besonderen, einschließlich all der unzähligen Epigonen in der schwulen erotischen wie pornografischen Kunst. Der Versuch, gleichsam wie ein Cosplayer die Manga- und Superhelden, die Kerle Tom of Finlands lebendig werden zu lassen, war freilich damals wie heute peinlich. Andererseits: Sehen heute nicht längst alle (Leder-)Männer

and passionately. But there's a danger in this experience as with every love: If you get too close, the sexual desire is lost. In an art exhibition, the drawings of Touko Laaksonen never made me horny. I was sexually aroused when I looked at cheap reproductions, lousy reprints in which the mesh of fine lines is smudged into one dark spot. It was the roughness, the coarseness that was exciting, that hid the meticulous and delicate efforts of its origin. Perhaps the art of Tom of Finland should never have become art. Should never have made it to the Museum of Modern Art in New York or elsewhere. Don't get me wrong – it's not that I begrudge Touko Laaksonen the posthumous recognition he deserves as an artist. It's more about sacrificing the intimate atmosphere, the secret realm the men of Tom of Finland and I once shared to a public space. Something is lost when I see them framed against a white wall in an empty room ... the most stylish and most expensive exhibition catalogue will never match the cheap reprints, the pulp Kake comic rags, that fit so well under the covers at night.

The social context that enables us to study the all-male world of Tom of Finland changed. We should critically evaluate how heteronormative structures are enhanced, how misogynistic gay fantasies can be, how for example people of color were depicted, were included or rather excluded. But without a doubt, there's no ignoring the massive iconic influence of Touko Laaksonen's art on gay male (sub-) culture in general and on the leather and fetish scene in specific, including the innumerable vignettes in the field of gay erotic and pornographic art.

The effort to mimic the men of Tom of Finland – just as cosplayers try to imitate their manga favorites and comic book superheroes – was pathetic in the old days and still is today; however, leather men have long assumed the guise of characters from Tom of Finland's world – their bodies trained and pumped at the gym, with their Langlitz jackets, their Wesco boots. All this is now celebrated as the new minimal standard.

so aus wie die Kerle von Tom of Finland – der Körper im Fitnessstudio muskulös getrimmt, mit der Langlitz-Jacke, die zum Minimalstandard geworden ist? Selbstoptimierung ist eine unwidersprochene Norm, teure Fetischklamotten wie eh und je ein Mittel der sozialen wie wirtschaftlichen Abgrenzung. Wo bei Tom of Finland die Verherrlichung der Macht und ihrer Insignien noch mit deren Auflösung und Sublimierung in der lustvoll kreativen Fantasie einherging, sind der Fetisch und die maskuline Selbstwahrnehmung nun den Regeln einer ökonomisierten, auf Effizienz und Funktionalität bedachten Gesellschaft unterworfen. Die lebensbejahende Homosexualität scheint mir heute nicht mehr die spontane Lust zwischen Männern, wie sie den quasi selbstverständlich hypermaskulinen Männern Tom of Finlands noch eigen ist, sondern das Produkt von Arbeit am eigenen, optimierten Körper. Das lässt das Werk von Tom of Finland anachronistisch, vielleicht altmodisch, erscheinen und macht es zugleich aktuell und wichtig in seinem anarchistischen Potenzial.

Ich muss lächeln, wenn ich darüber nachdenke, wie eng einst meine Liebe zu den Männern war. Ist sie verblasst, bevor oder erst nachdem ich mich der Leder- und Fetischszene entfremdet habe? Es lag eine gehörige Portion Naivität darin, eine Leidenschaft, die nach Ausdruck suchte. Ich möchte diese Liebe nicht missen. Sie war, wie es Thomas Mann wohl ausgedrückt hätte, gut und fruchtbar. Es ist immer noch viel Sehnsucht darin, ein klein wenig Verachtung und eine geile Seligkeit.

Self-optimization has become a norm unopposed. Expensive fetish gear has, and can, create social and economic distinctions. While in the world of Tom of Finland, the worship of power and its insignias once led to the extinction of lustfully creative fantasies, today fetish and masculine self-awareness follow the rules of a highly capitalistic society in terms of efficiency and functionality. Life-affirmative homosexuality seems to me to no longer equate with the spontaneous lust among two or more men so typical for the hypermasculine figures of Tom of Finland; moreover, it is the result of diligent work on each individual optimized body. That makes the oeuvre of Tom of Finland anachronistic, perhaps even old-fashioned and yet proves valid today and even more important because of its anarchic potential.

I smile when I think about how close we were, me and the men of Tom of Finland. Did our love affair wear thin before or after I became estranged from the leather and fetish scene? There was so much naivety there, a passion and desire that longed for expression. I don't regret these bygone feelings. They were in their time, as Thomas Mann might have said, good and fruitful. And there is still an inherent longing, a gentle envy, and just a wee touch of horny bliss.

Translation: Jim Baker

In those days, a gay man was made to feel nothing but shame about his feelings and his sexuality. I wanted my drawings to counteract that, to show gay men being happy and positive about who they were. Oh, I didn't sit down to think this all out carefully. But I knew - right from the start - that my men were going to be proud and happy men!

In jener Zeit wurde ein schwuler Mann dazu gebracht, nichts als Scham wegen seiner Gefühle und seiner Sexualität zu empfinden. Ich wollte dem mit meinen Zeichnungen entgegenwirken und glückliche schwule Männer mit einem positiven Selbstbild zeigen. Ich habe mich nicht hingesetzt und mir das alles ausgedacht. Aber ich wusste von Anfang an, dass meine Männer stolz und glücklich sein sollten!
– Tom of Finland

Gallery by Mail

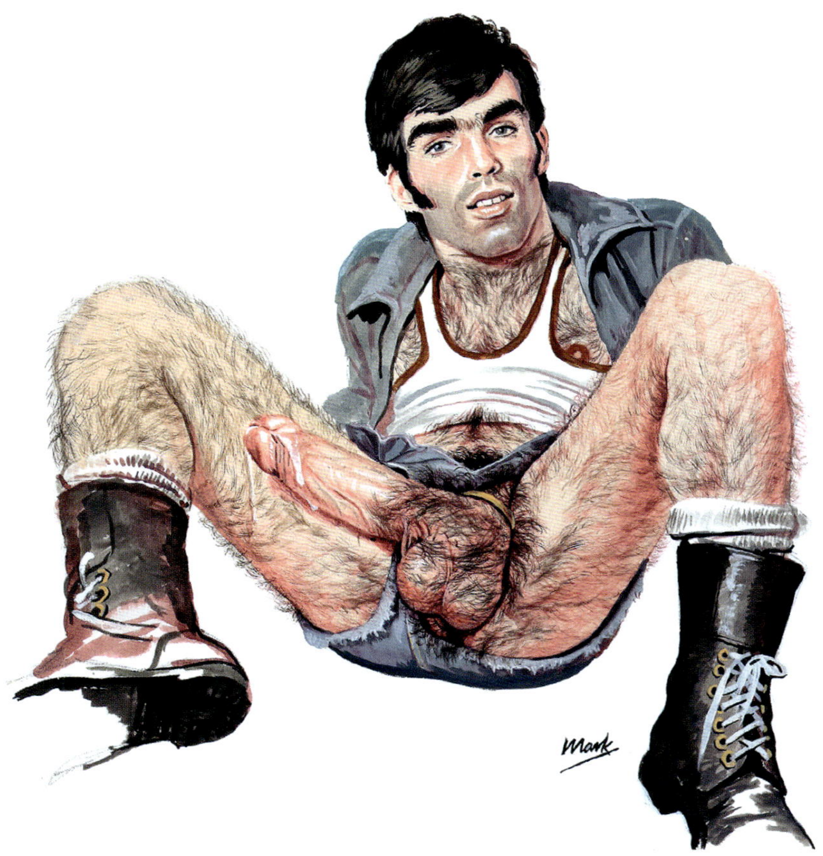

MARK AKA ROGER PAYNE

This program was originally put into place prior to the Internet with the mailing of catalogues of works-for-sale by many artists that were a part of the Foundation, a service ToFF provided for both artists and collectors. This evolved into online galleries and eventually included links to artists' websites as they were developing them, thus providing a service of bringing artists together with potential collectors internationally.

Versandgalerie: Dieses Programm wurde bereits vor dem Internetzeitalter entwickelt. Ursprünglich haben wir Kataloge mit käuflichen Werken der Künstler versandt, die mit der Stiftung verbunden waren; ein Service, den wir sowohl Künstlern als auch Sammlern anboten. Diese Kataloge haben sich mittlerweile zu einer Online-Galerie entwickelt (mit Links zu den jeweiligen Künstler-Webseiten), um so Künstlern und Sammlern die Möglichkeit zu eröffnen, auf internationaler Ebene zusammenzukommen.

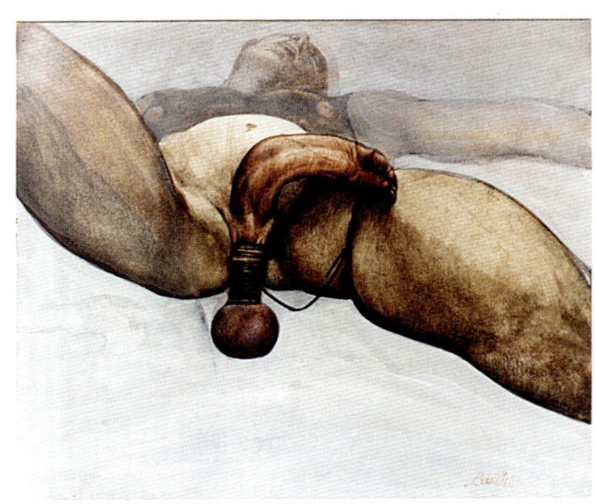

175.
BASTILLE
"BROUILLARD"
1983
7.75 X 9 "
GOUACHE
ON BOARD

176.
BASTILLE
"SCHWEINE-
BRÜDER II"
1980
13 X 6.5 "
GOUACHE
ON BOARD

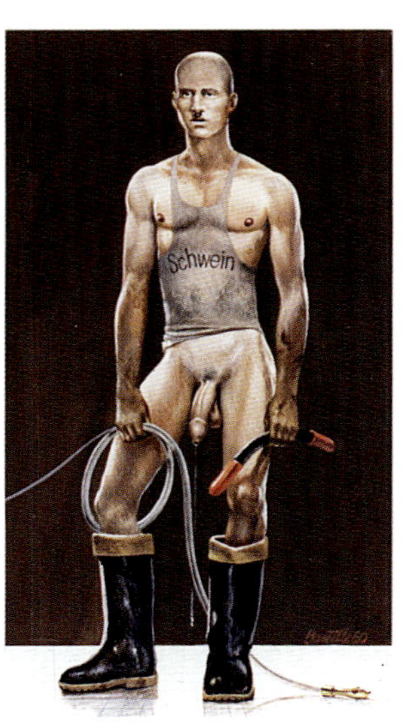

177.
TOM OF
FINLAND
(NO TITLE)
1987
11.75 X 8.5 "
PENCIL ON
PAPER

178.
TOM OF
FINLAND
(NO TITLE)
1985
11.75 X 8.5 "
PENCIL ON
PAPER

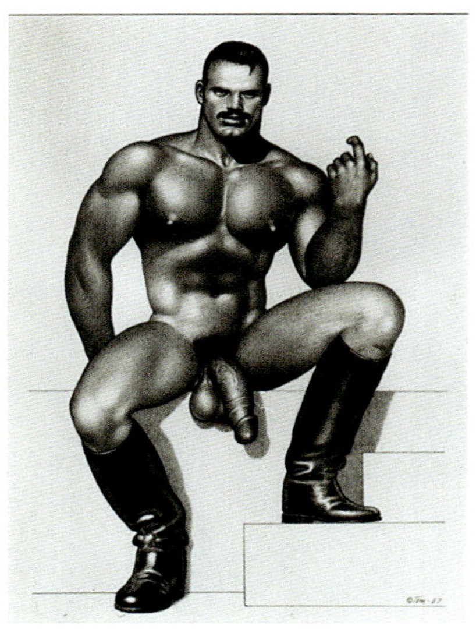

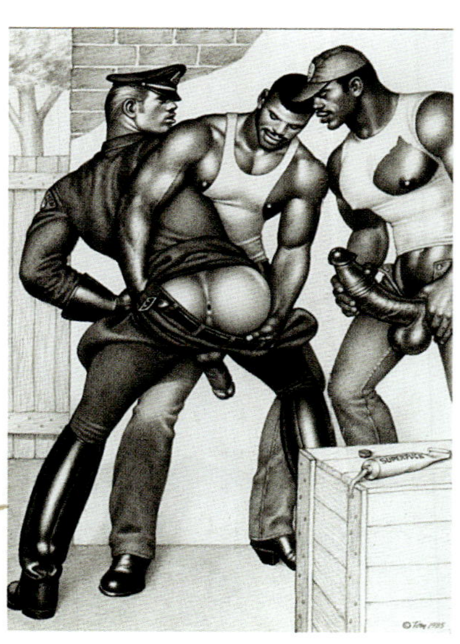

179.
MARC
DeBAUCH
"MERMENS
KISS"
1996
14 X 10.5 "
GOUACHE
ON PAPER

180.
MARC
DeBAUCH
"EDÚARDO'S
EJACULATION"
1995
15 X 10 "
GOUACHE
ON PAPER

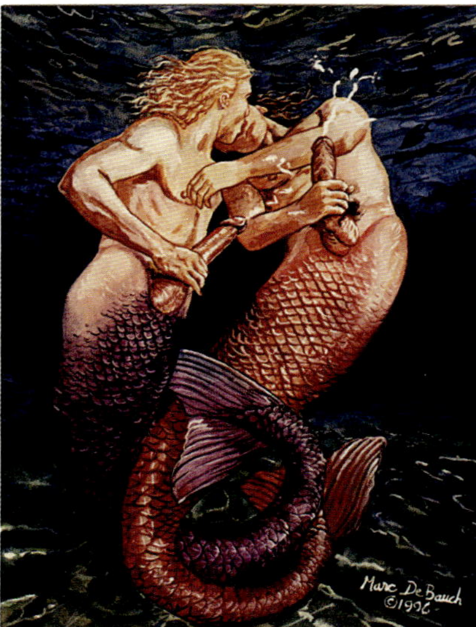

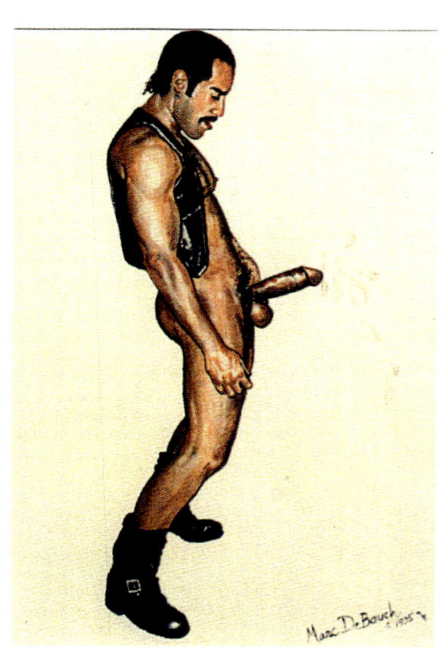

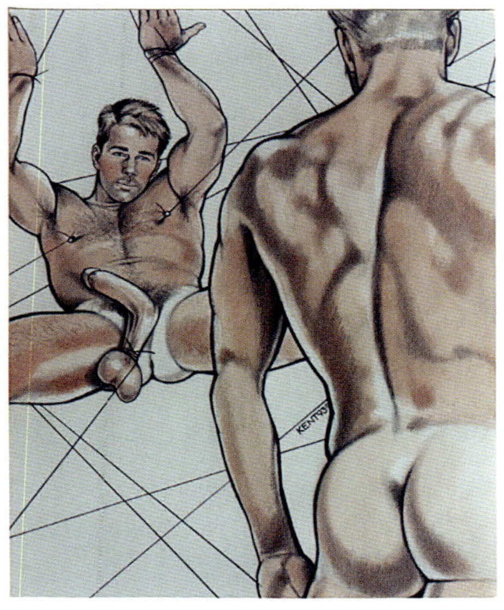

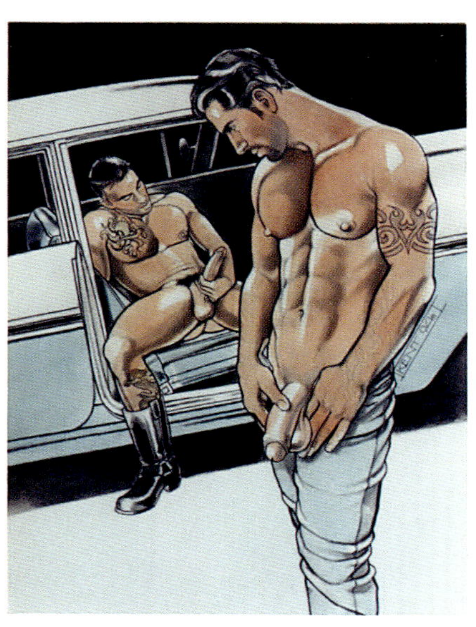

181.
KENT
"SPIDER"
1993
13 X 10 "
GOUACHE
/PENCIL ON
PAPER

182.
KENT
"REST STOP"
1994
14 X 11 "
GOUACHE
/PENCIL ON
PAPER

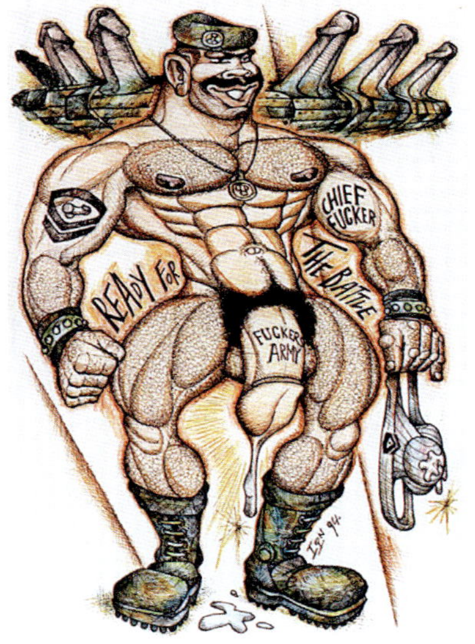

183.
IΩN
"READY FOR
THE BATTLE"
1994
11.75 X 8.25 "
COLORED
PENCIL/INK
ON PAPER

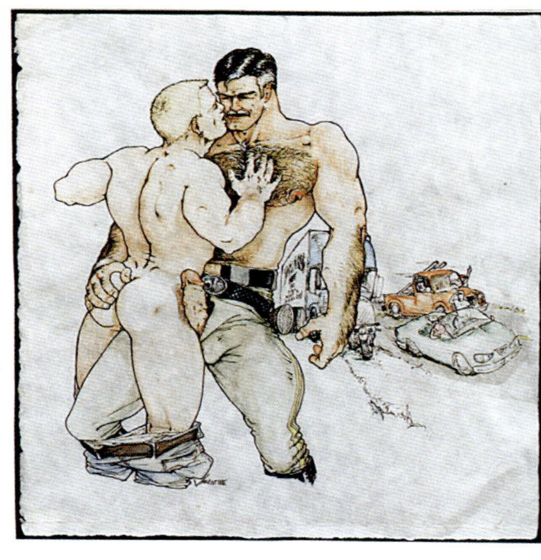

184.
VALENTINE
"BUTTFUCK
RADAR"
1996
14 X 14 "
WATERCOLOR
/INK ON
ANTIQUED
PARCHMENT
PAPER

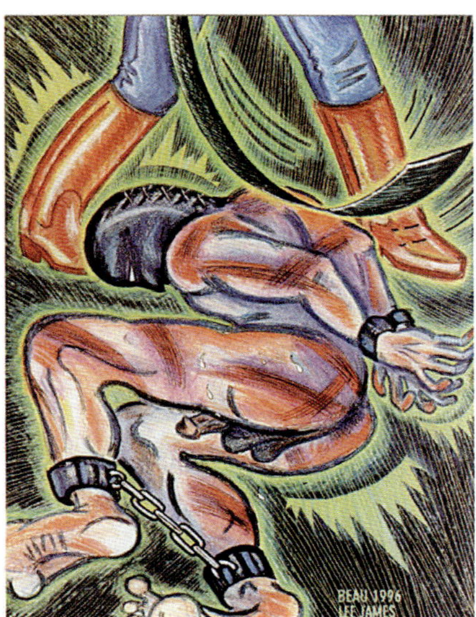

185.
BEAU LEE
JAMES
"THE
ROUNDUP"
1996
10 X 7.5 "
INK/CRAYON
ON PAPER

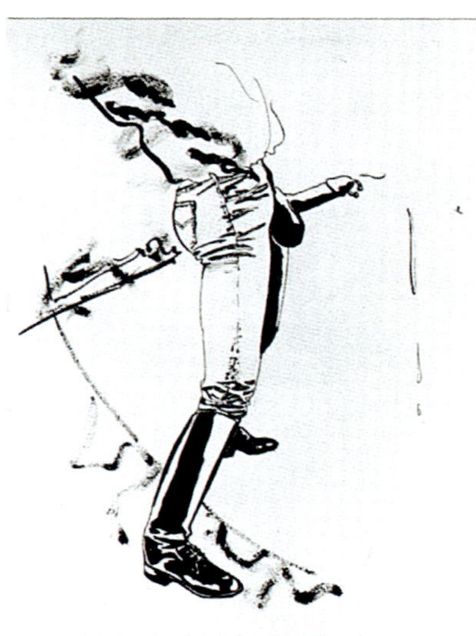

186.
DARRAGH
PARK
"P. A.: FIRST
COME"
1996
16.25 X 12.25 "
INK ON PAPER

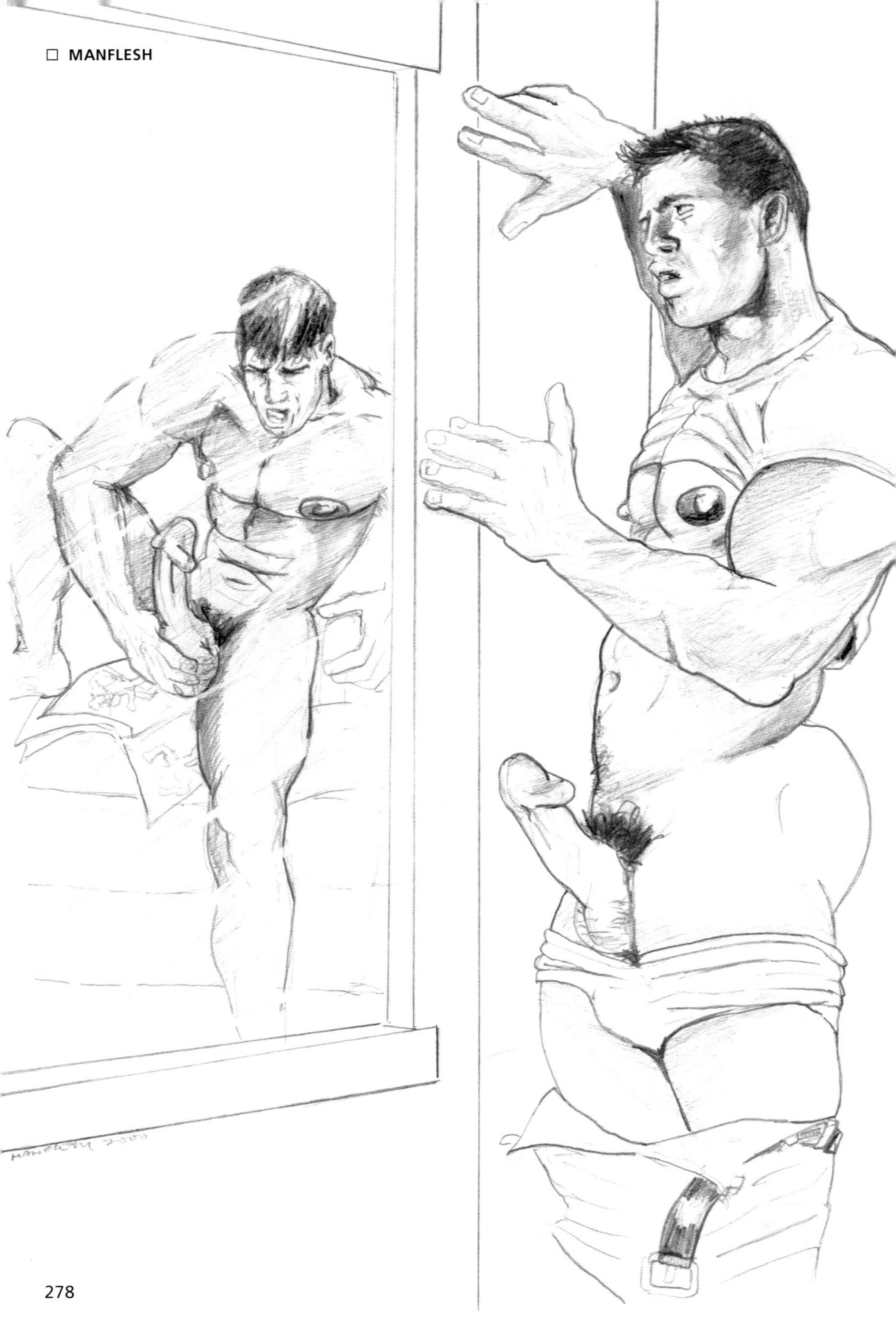

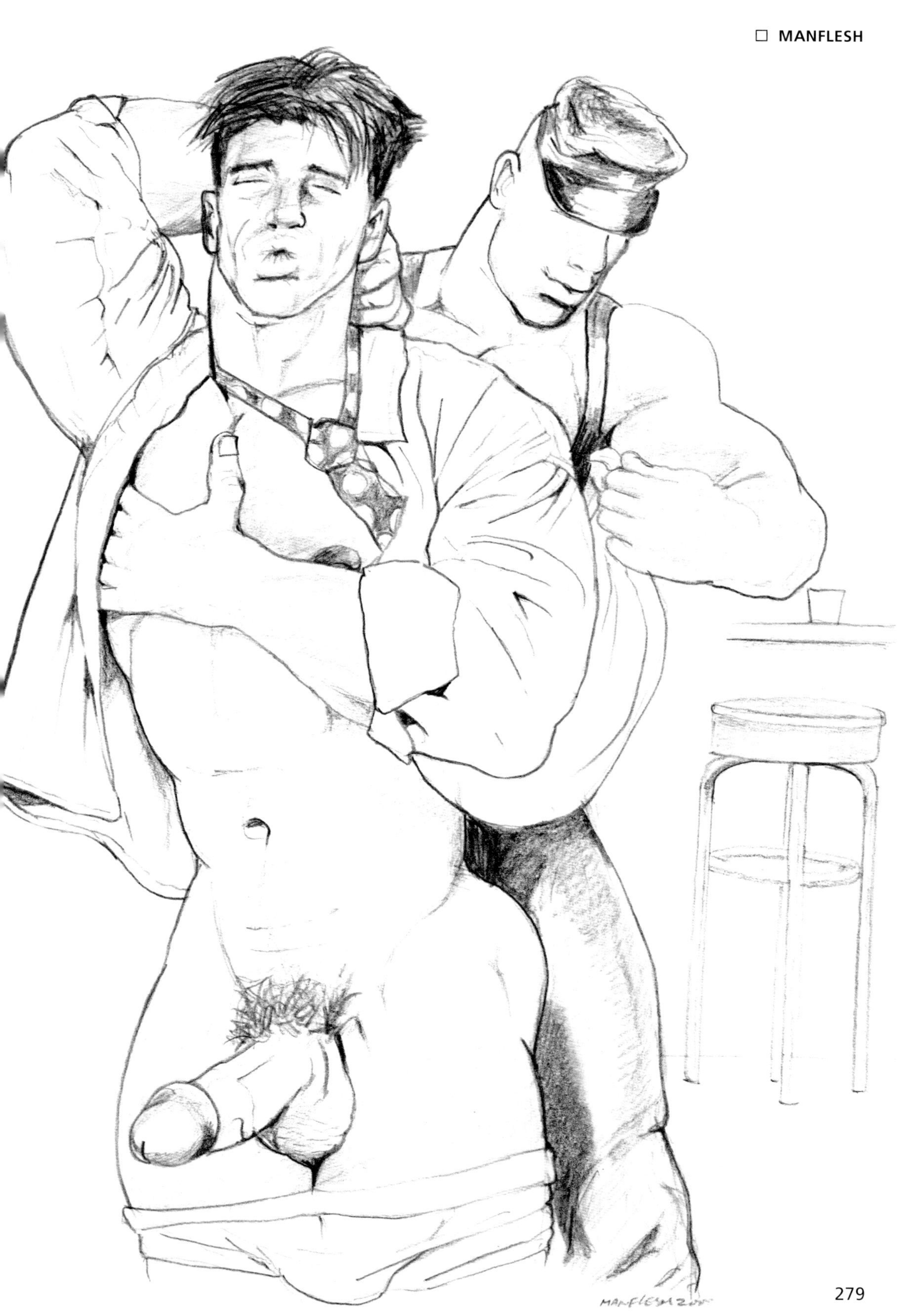

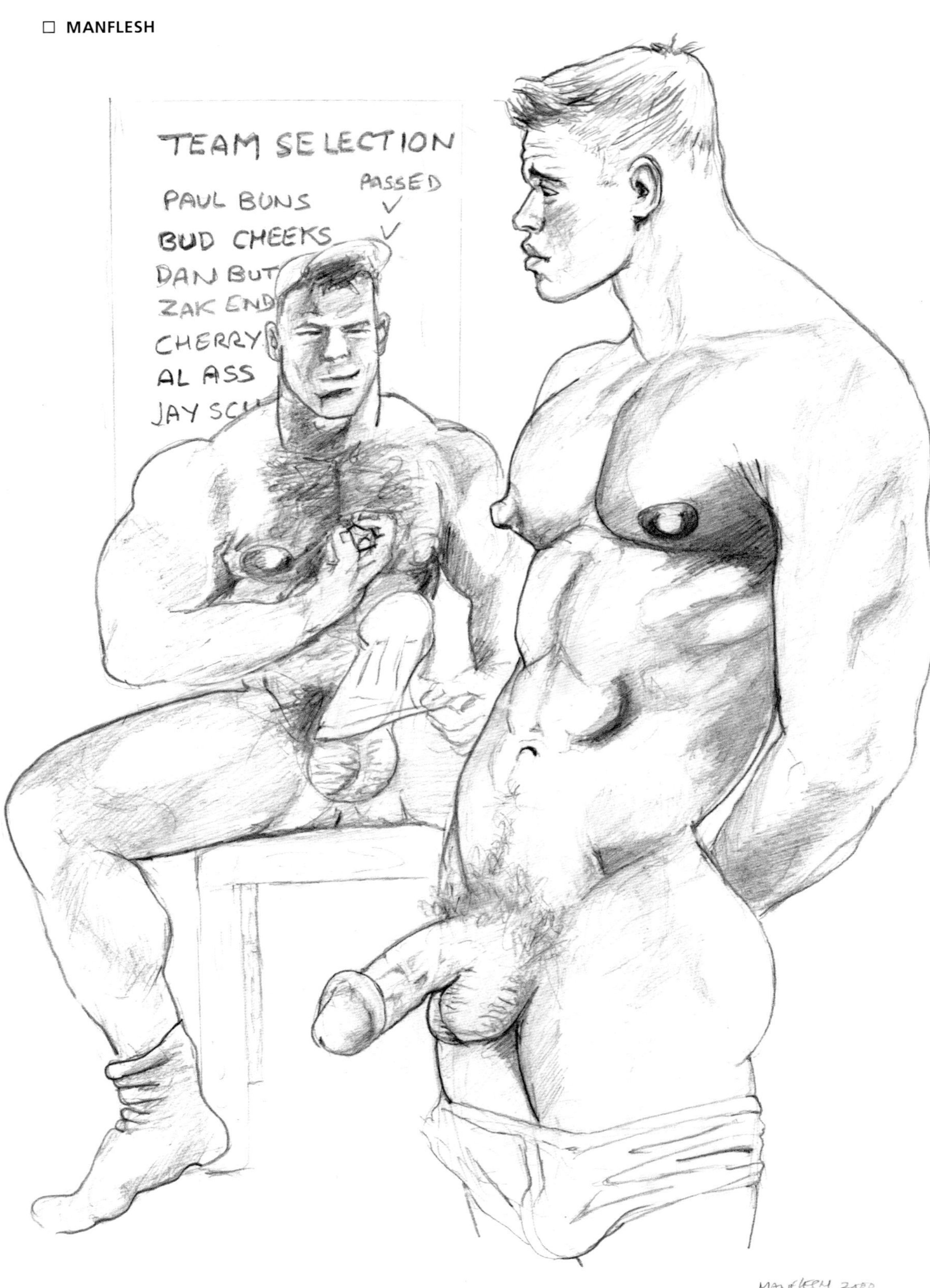
TEAM SELECTION
PASSED
PAUL BUNS ✓
BUD CHEEKS ✓
DAN BUT
ZAK END
CHERRY
AL ASS
JAY SC
MANFLESH 2000

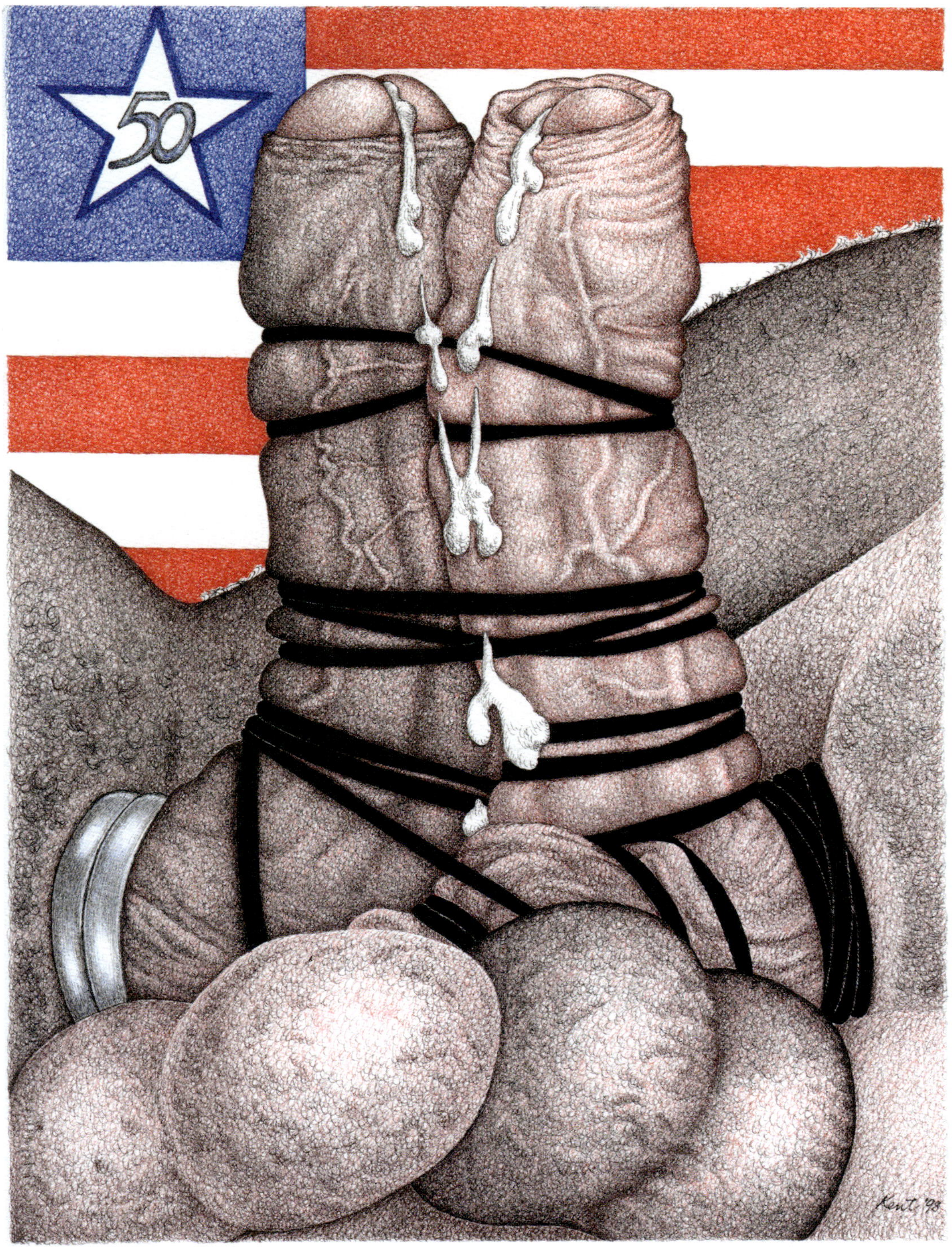

NIGEL KENT

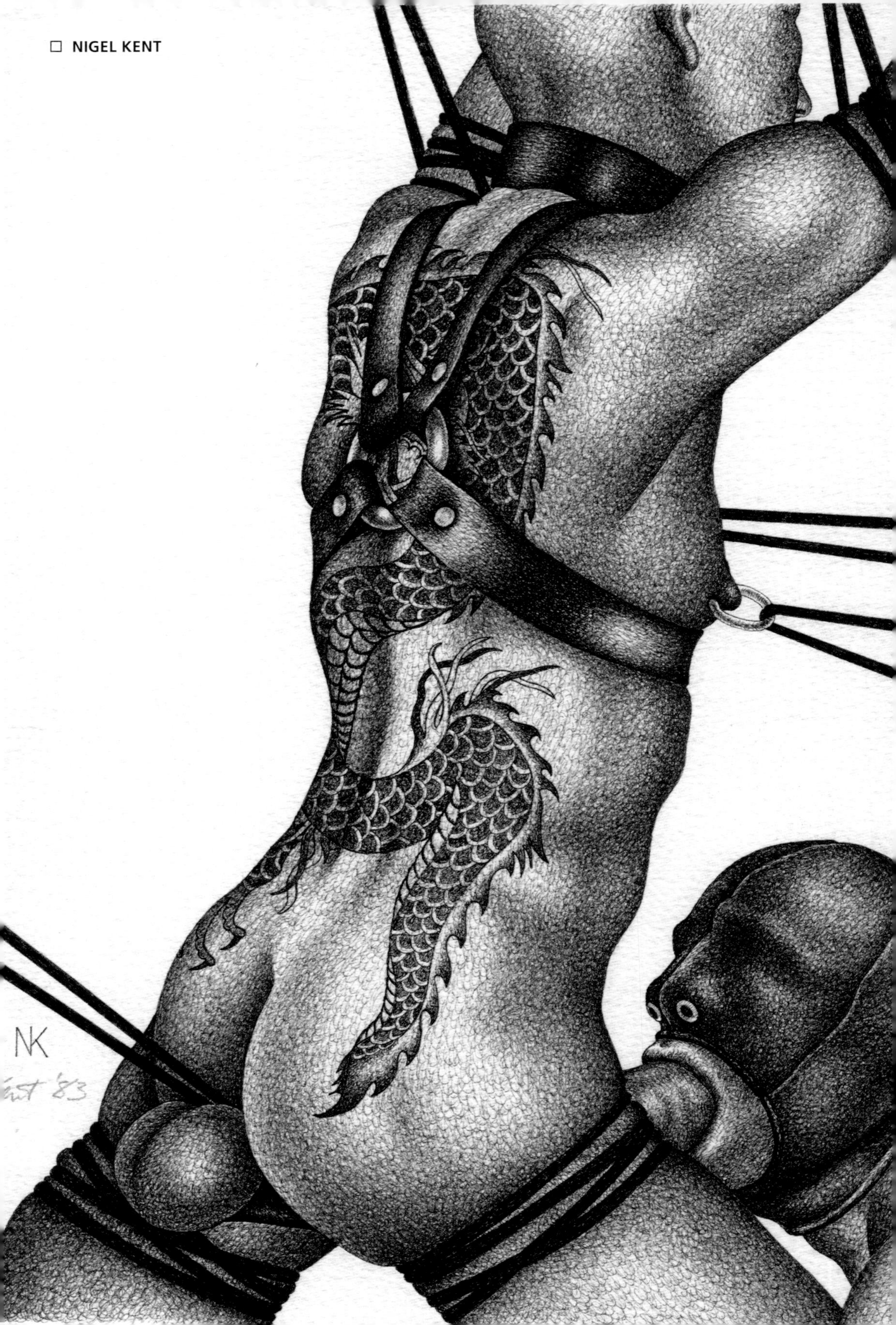

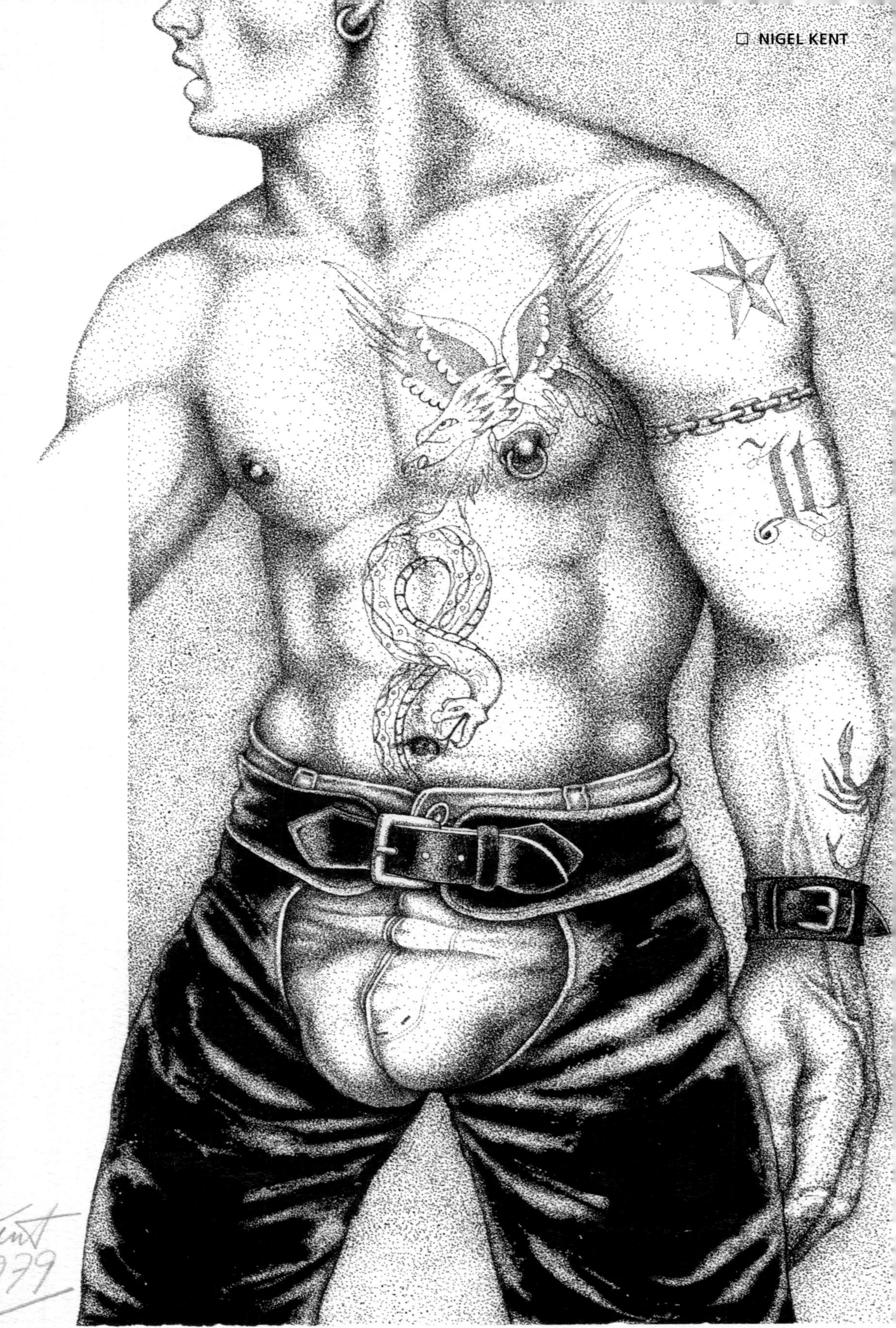

"DAD'S EARLY MORNING BIRTHDAY SURPRISE!"

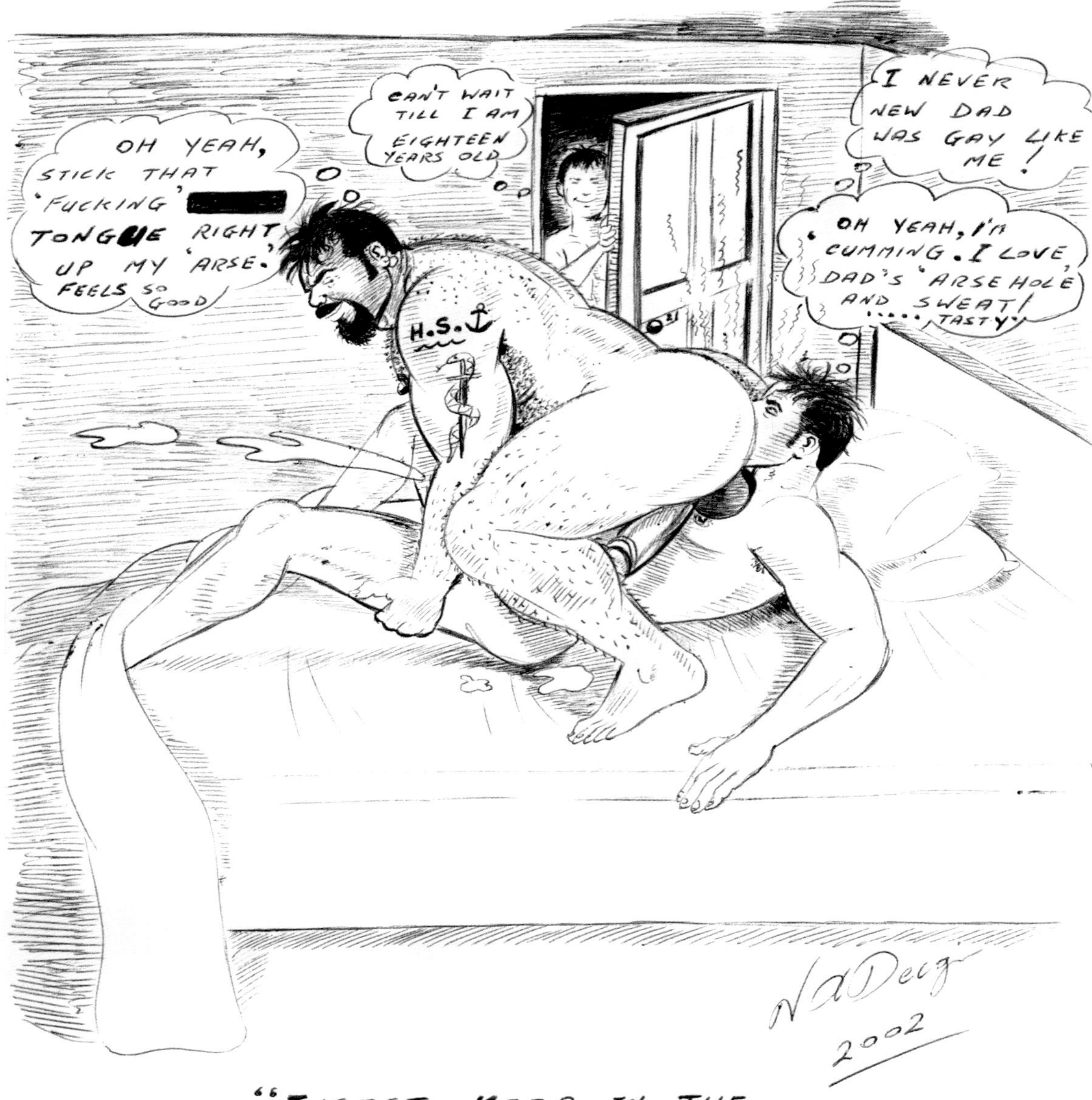

"INCEST, KEEP IN THE FAMILY!"

ORAL LUST AT THE HIGHLAND GAME.

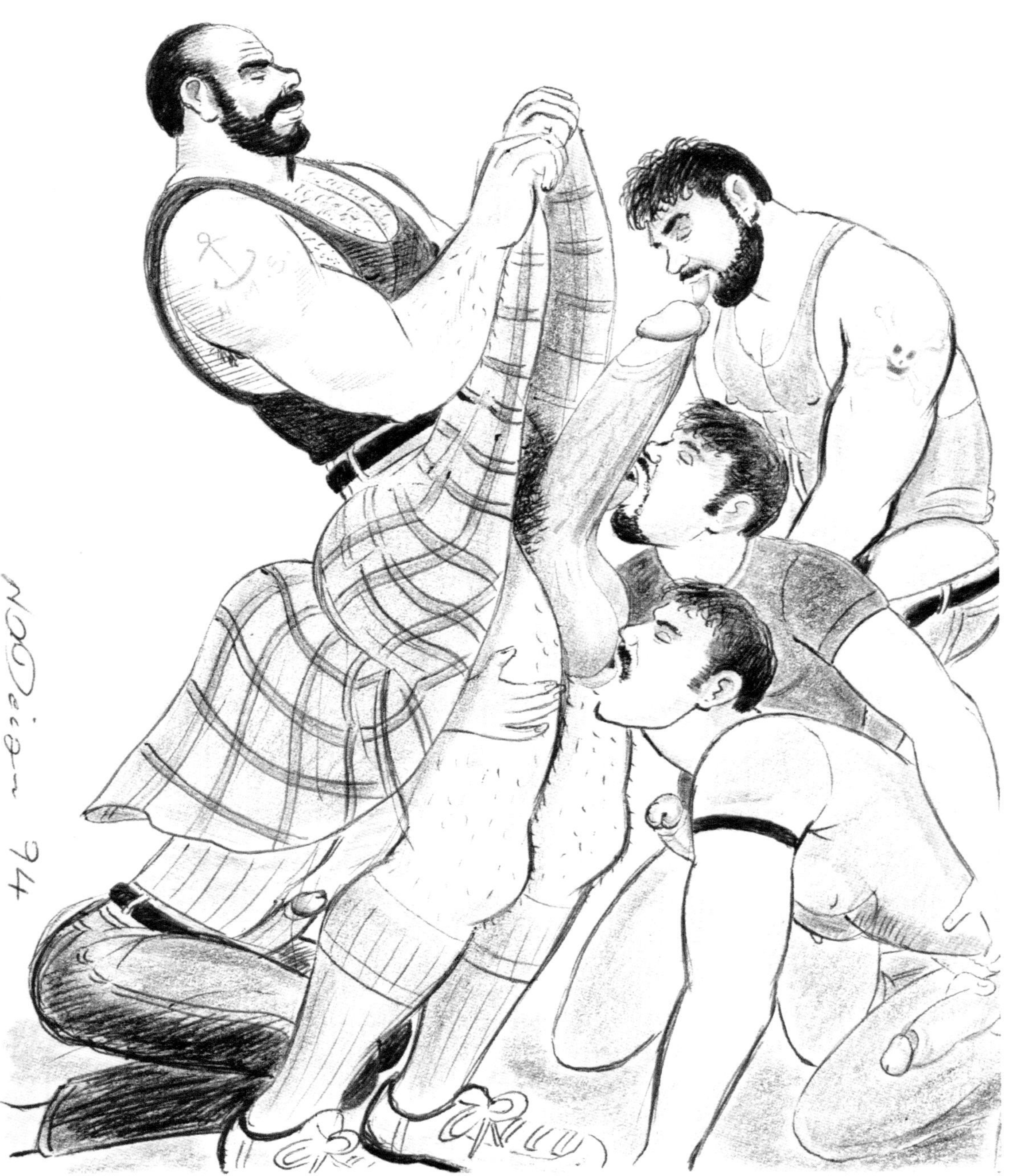

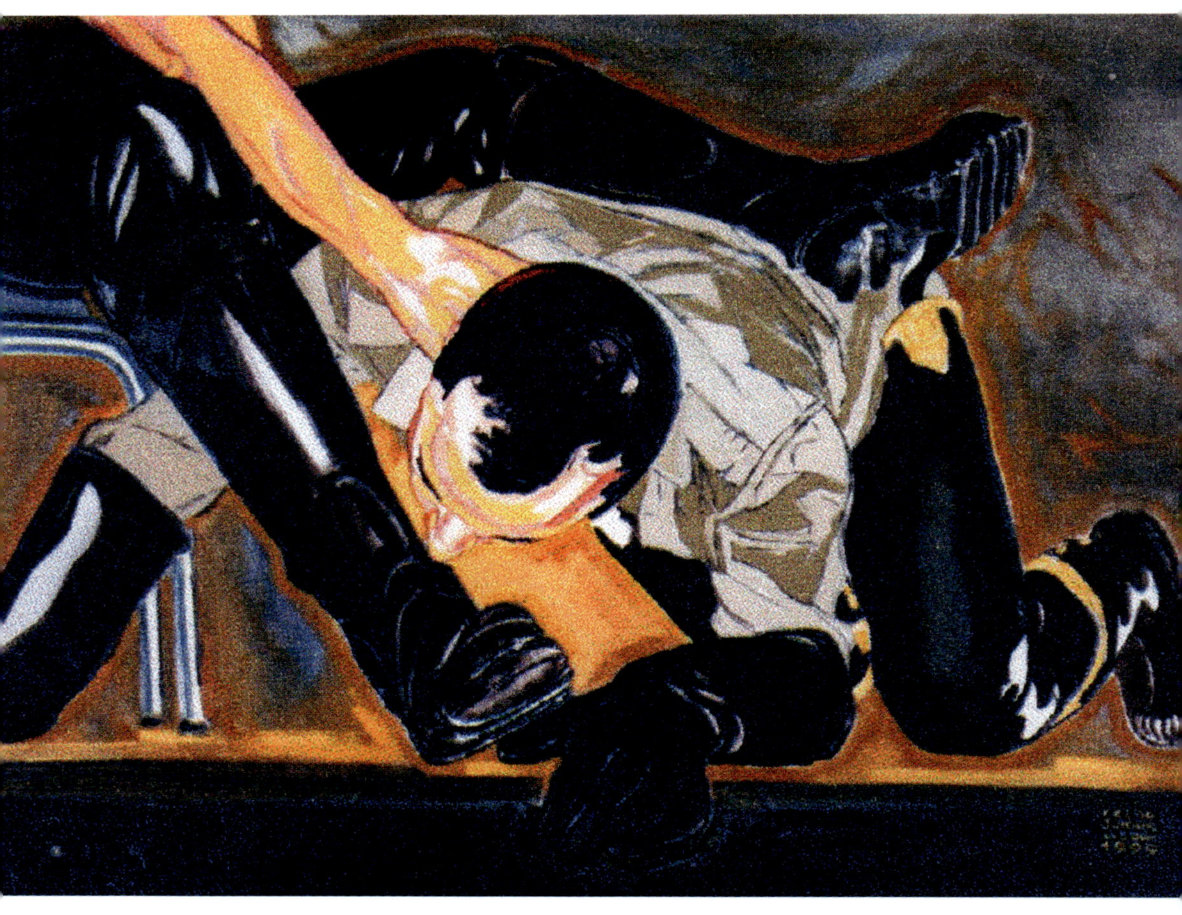

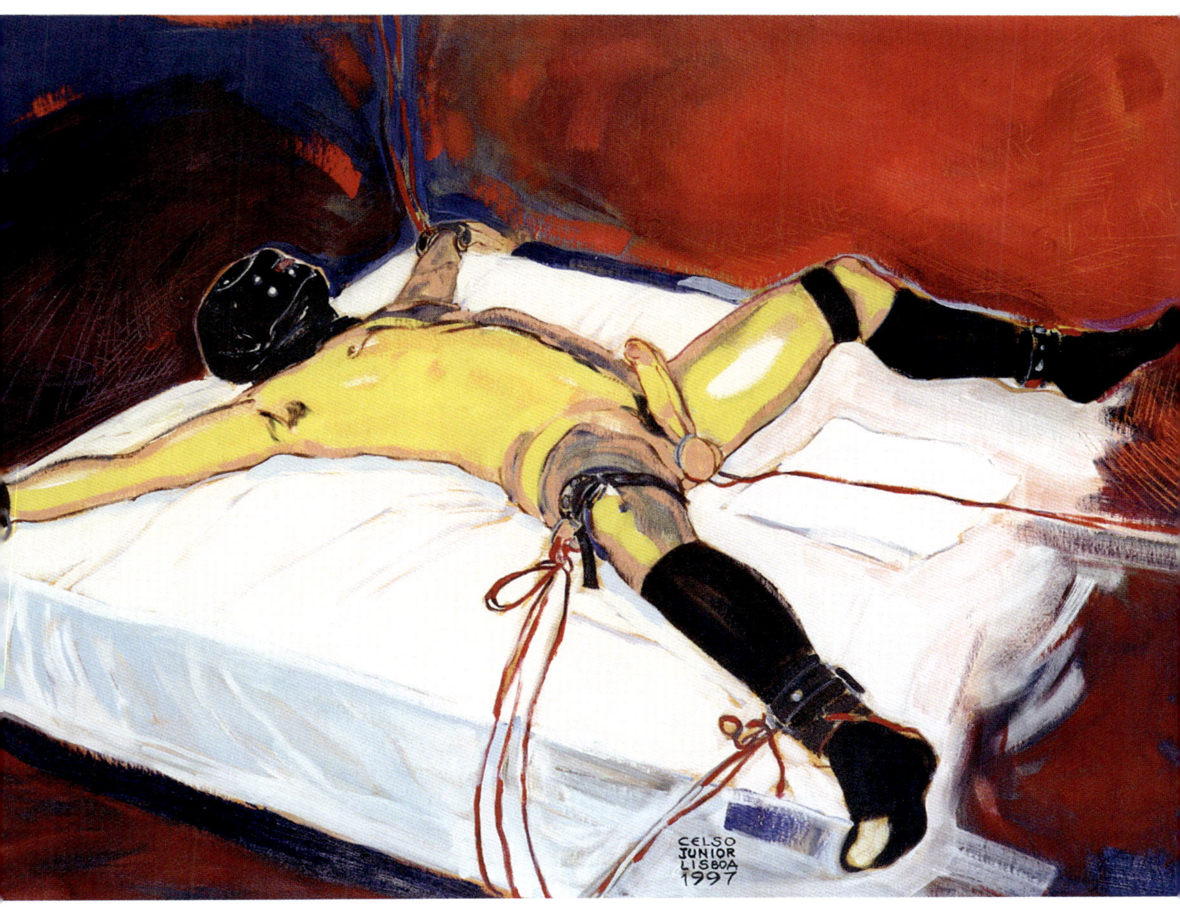

CELSO
JUNIOR
LISBOA
1997

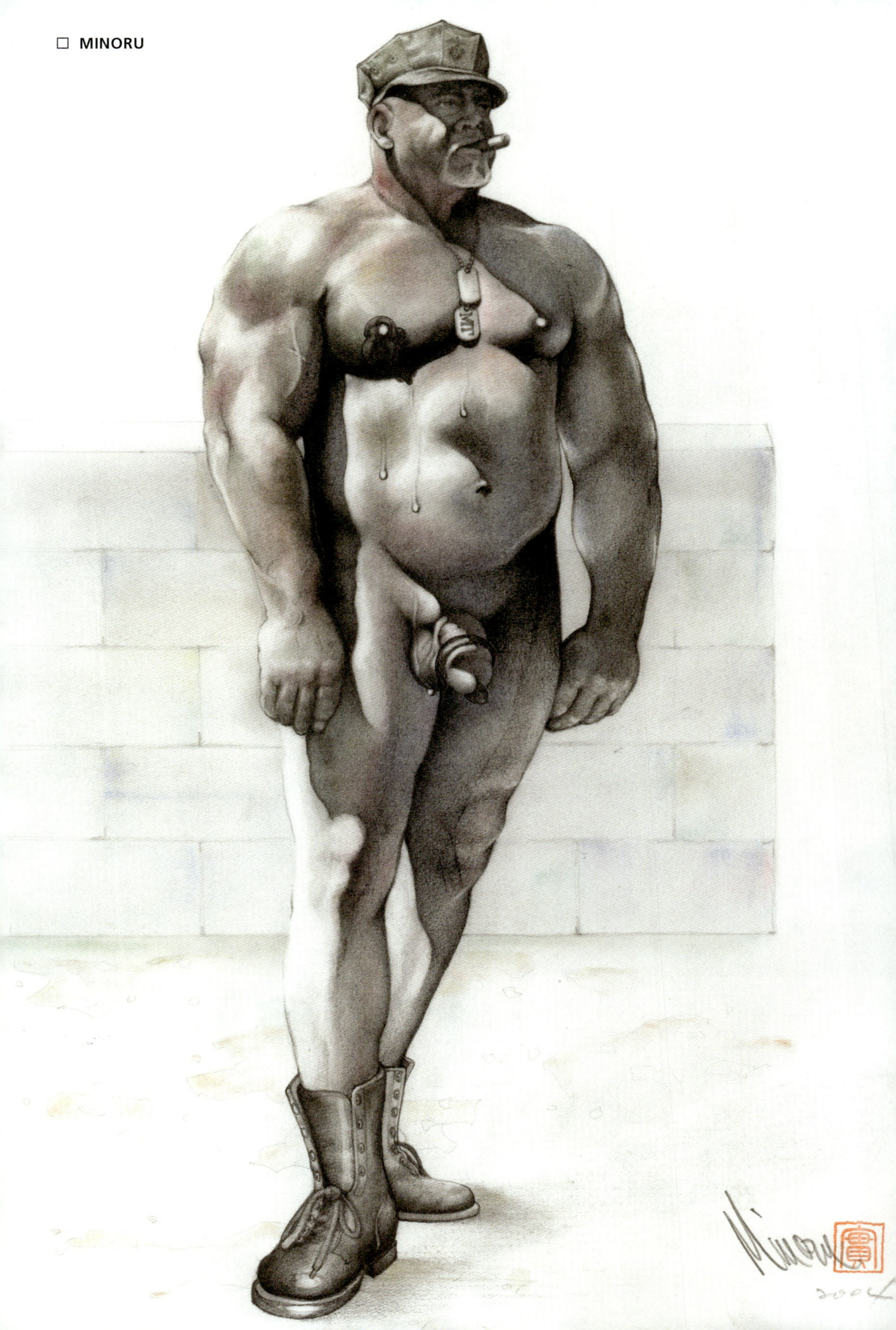

MINORU

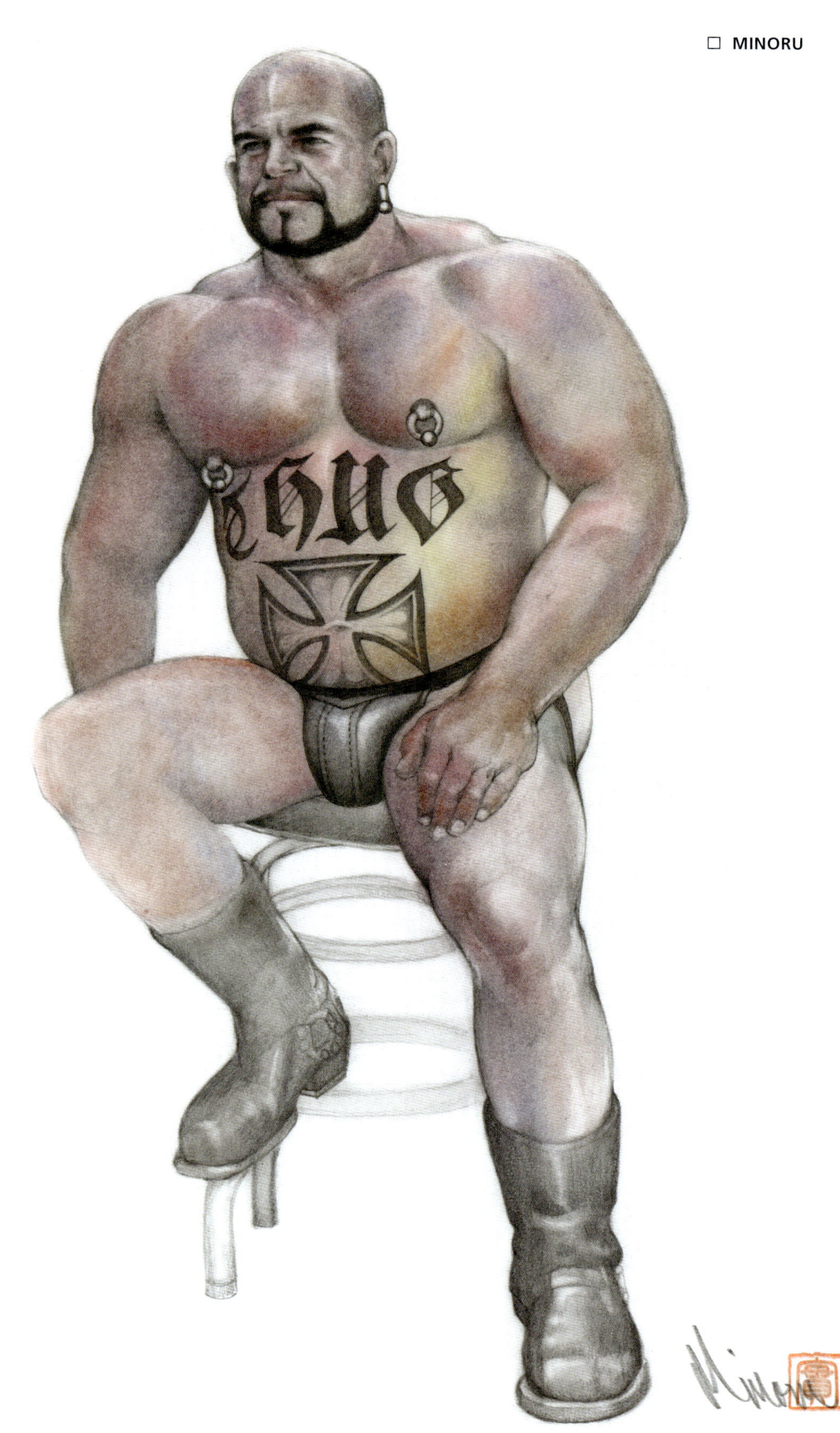

THUG

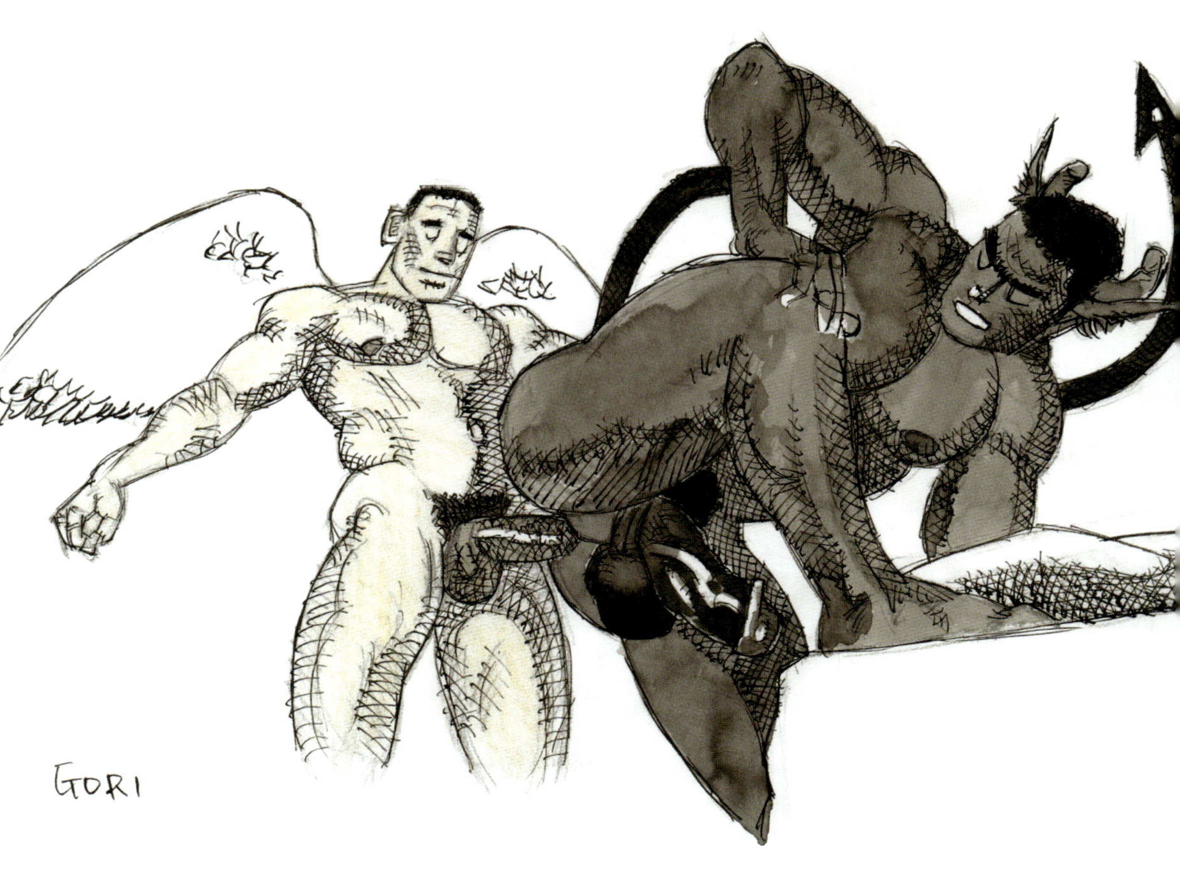

GORI

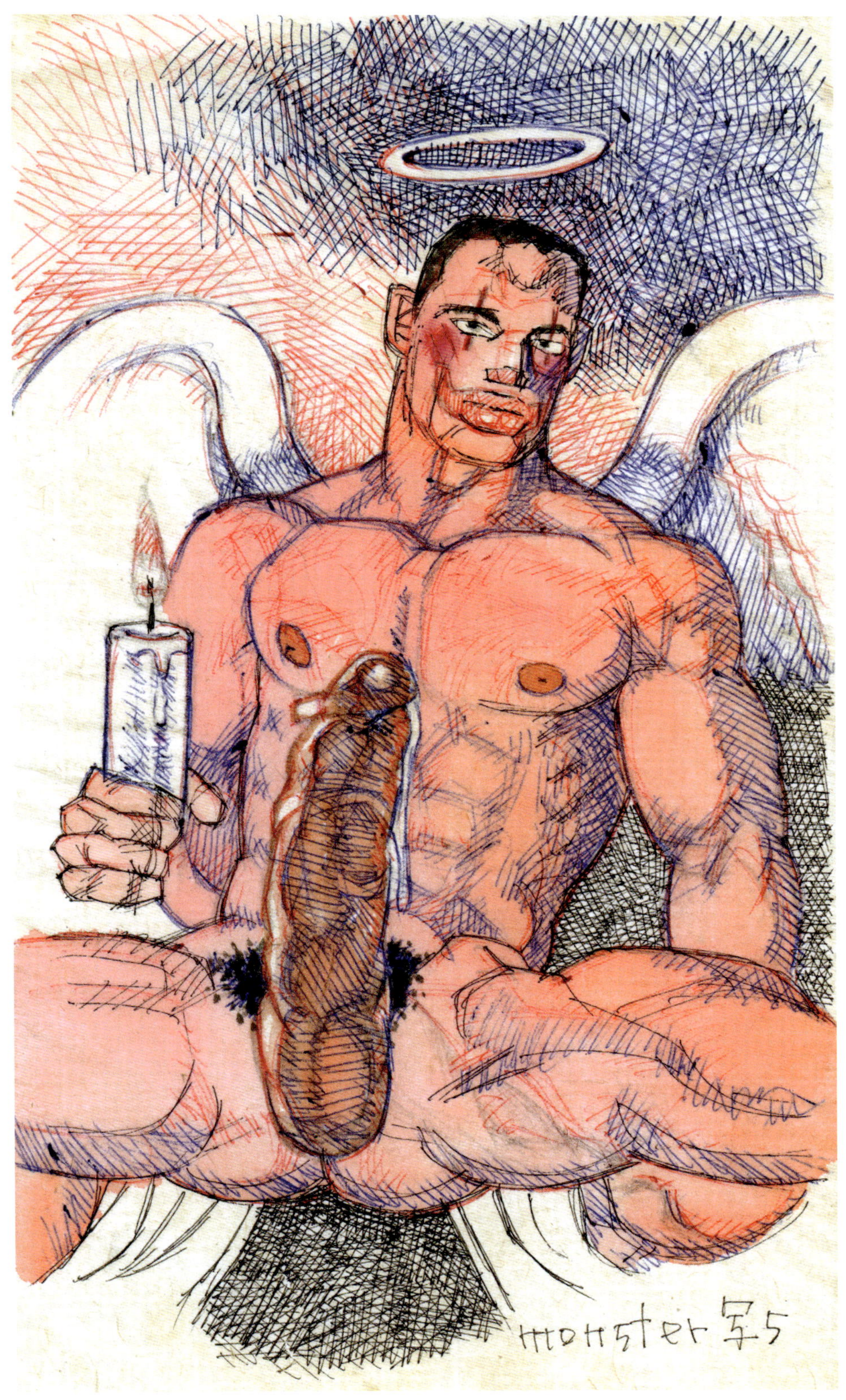

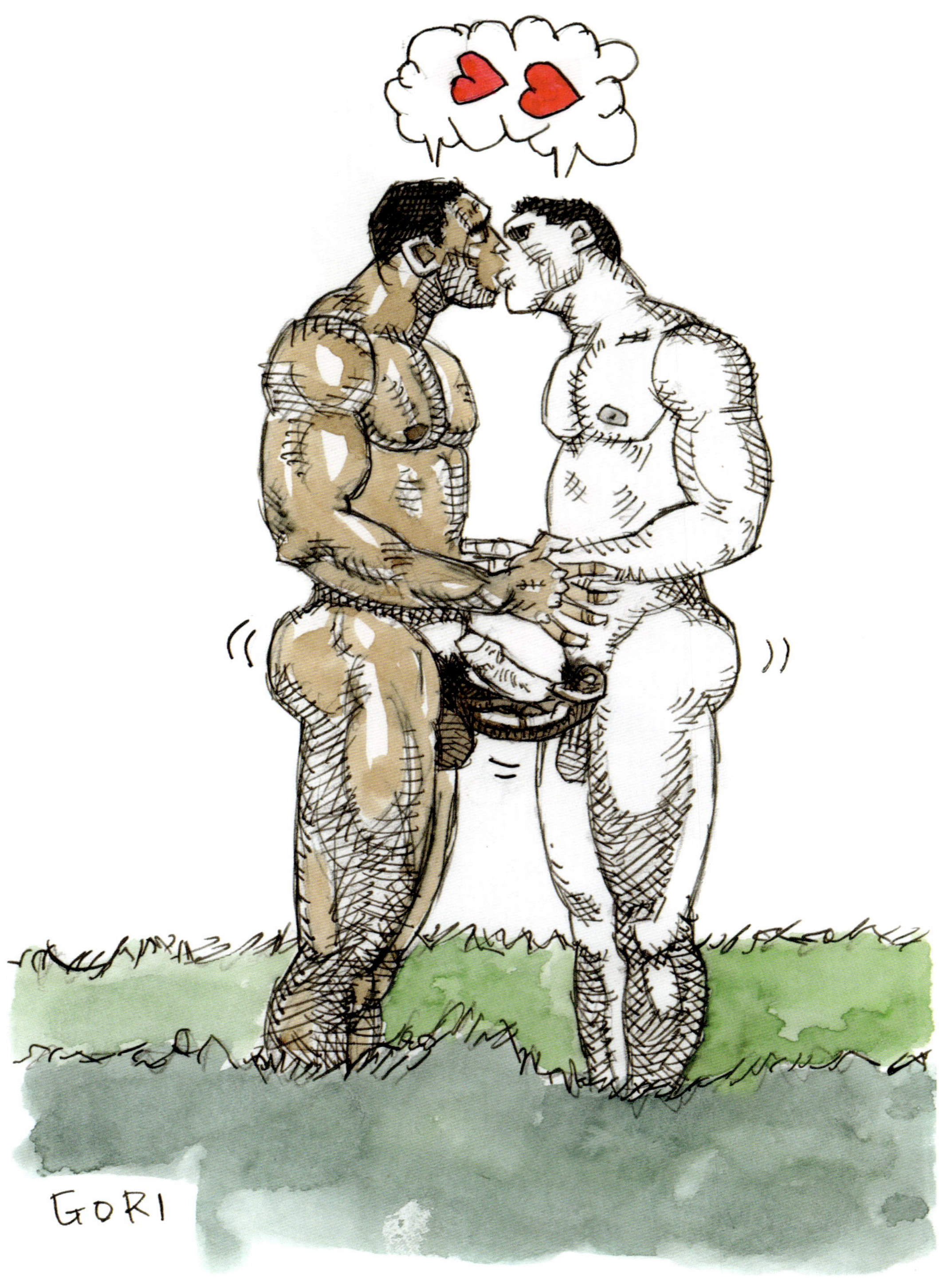

GORI

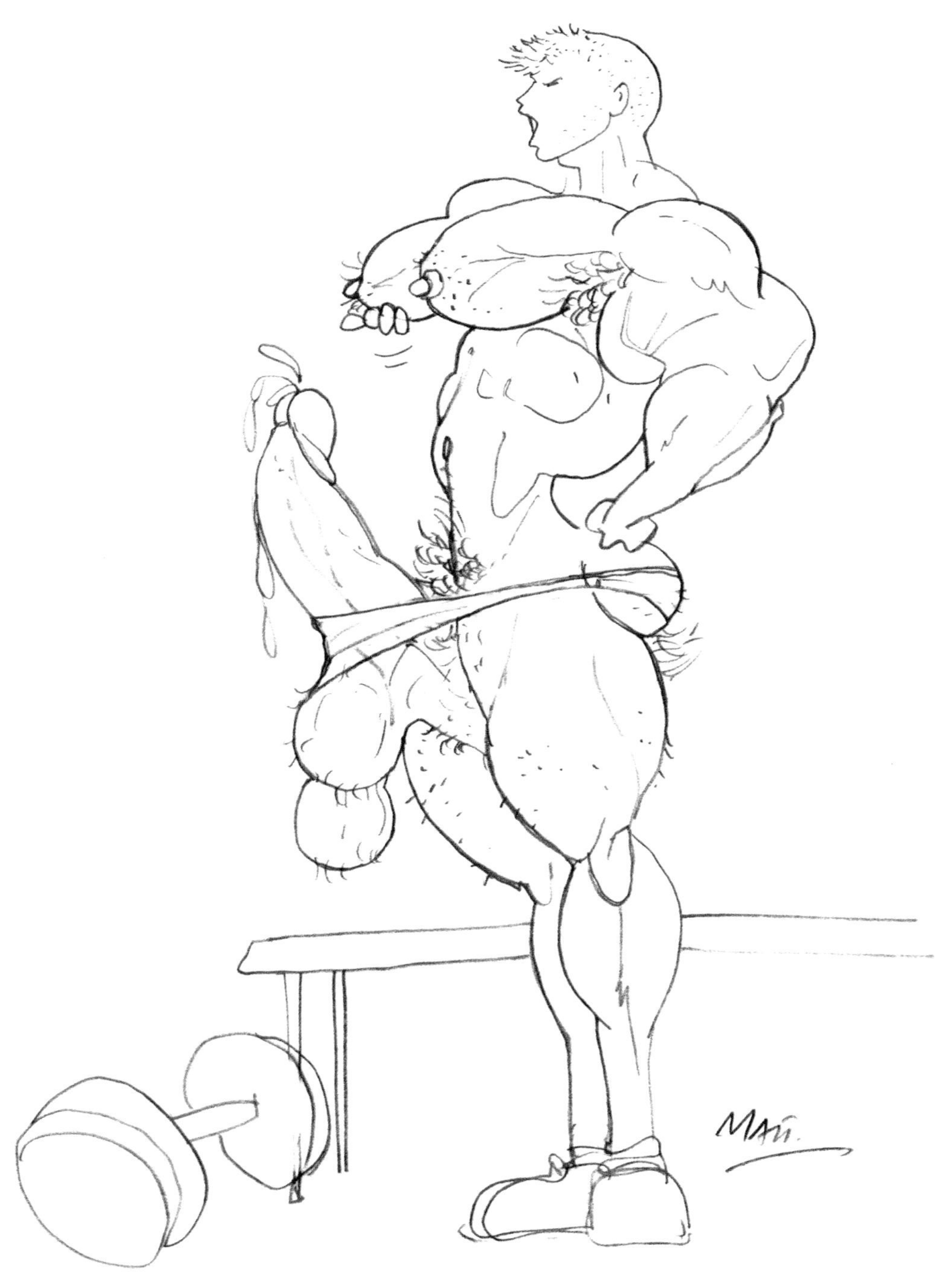

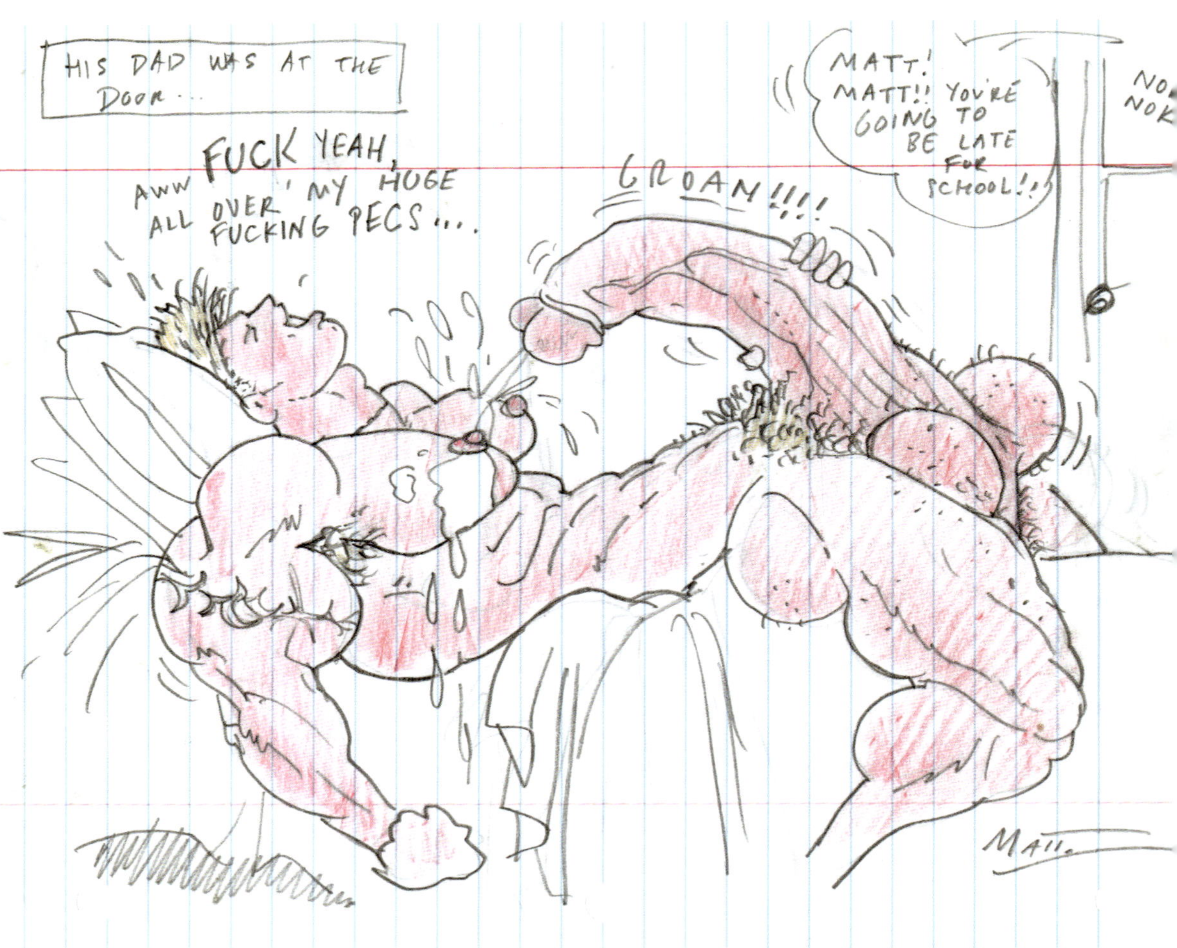
HIS DAD WAS AT THE DOOR...
AWW FUCK YEAH, ALL OVER MY HUGE FUCKING PECS...
GROAN!!!!
MATT! MATT!! YOU'RE GOING TO BE LATE FOR SCHOOL!!
NOK NOK

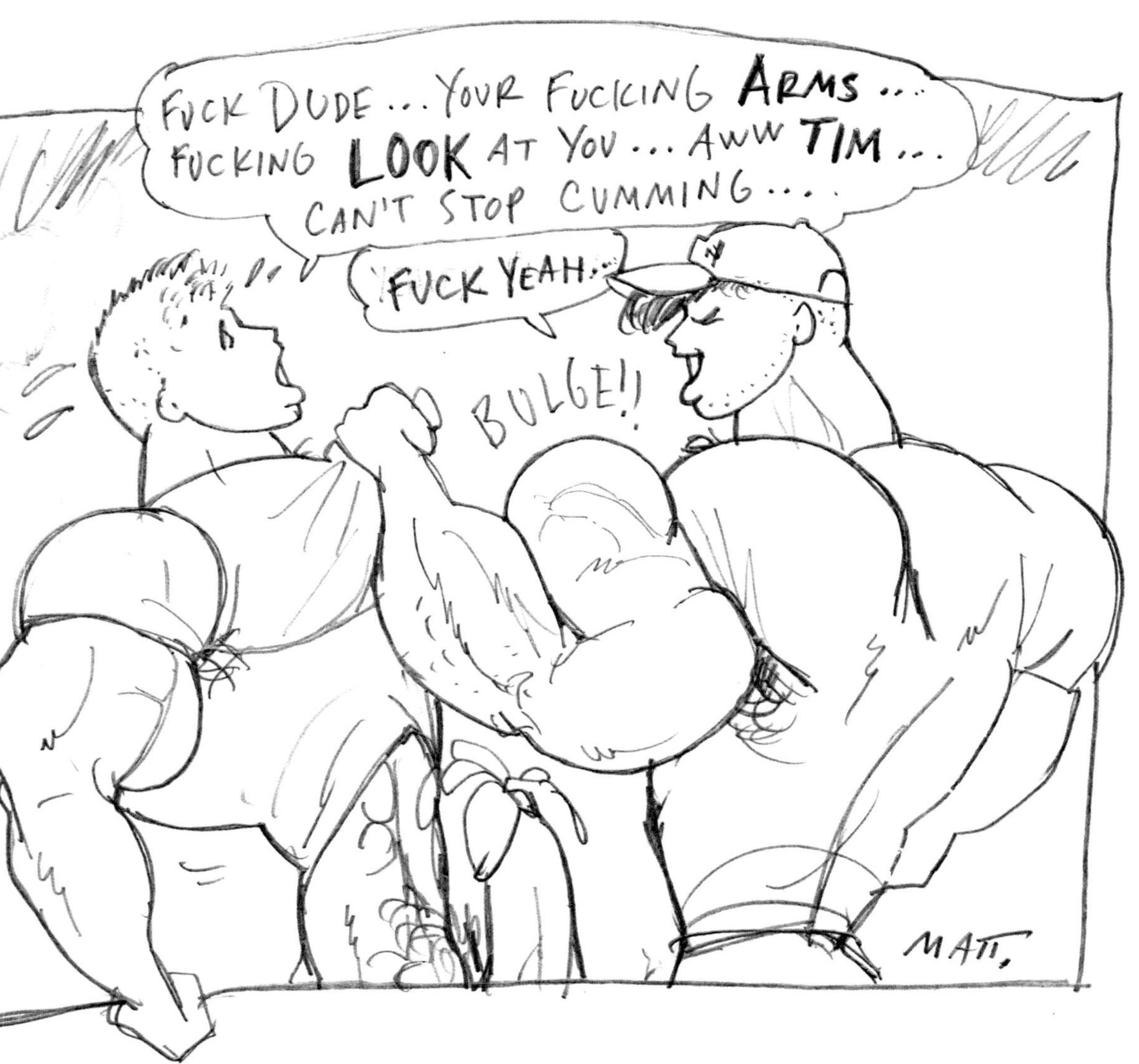
FUCK DUDE... YOUR FUCKING ARMS... FUCKING LOOK AT YOU... AWW TIM... CAN'T STOP CUMMING...
FUCK YEAH...
BULGE!!
MATT.

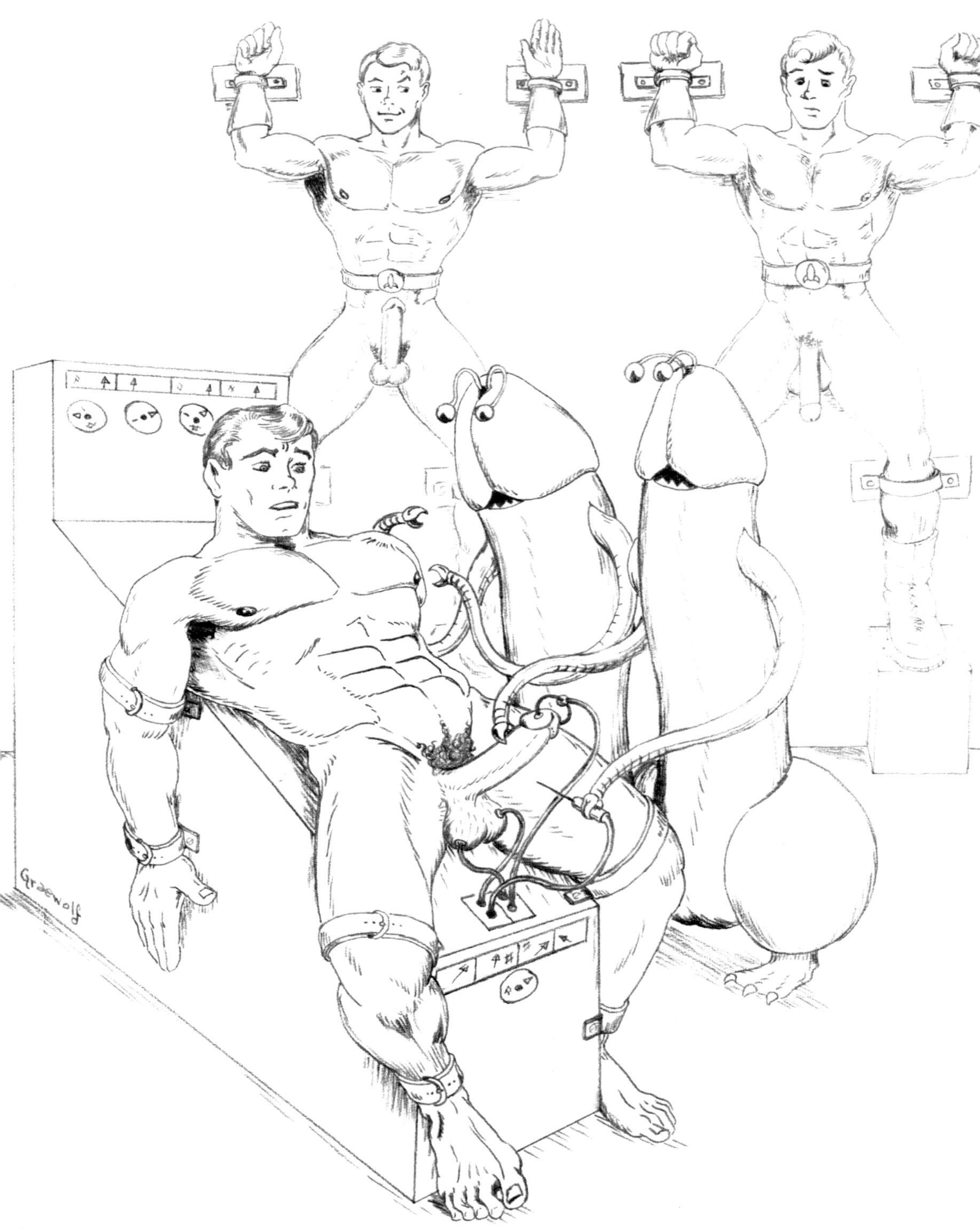

Emerging Artist Competition

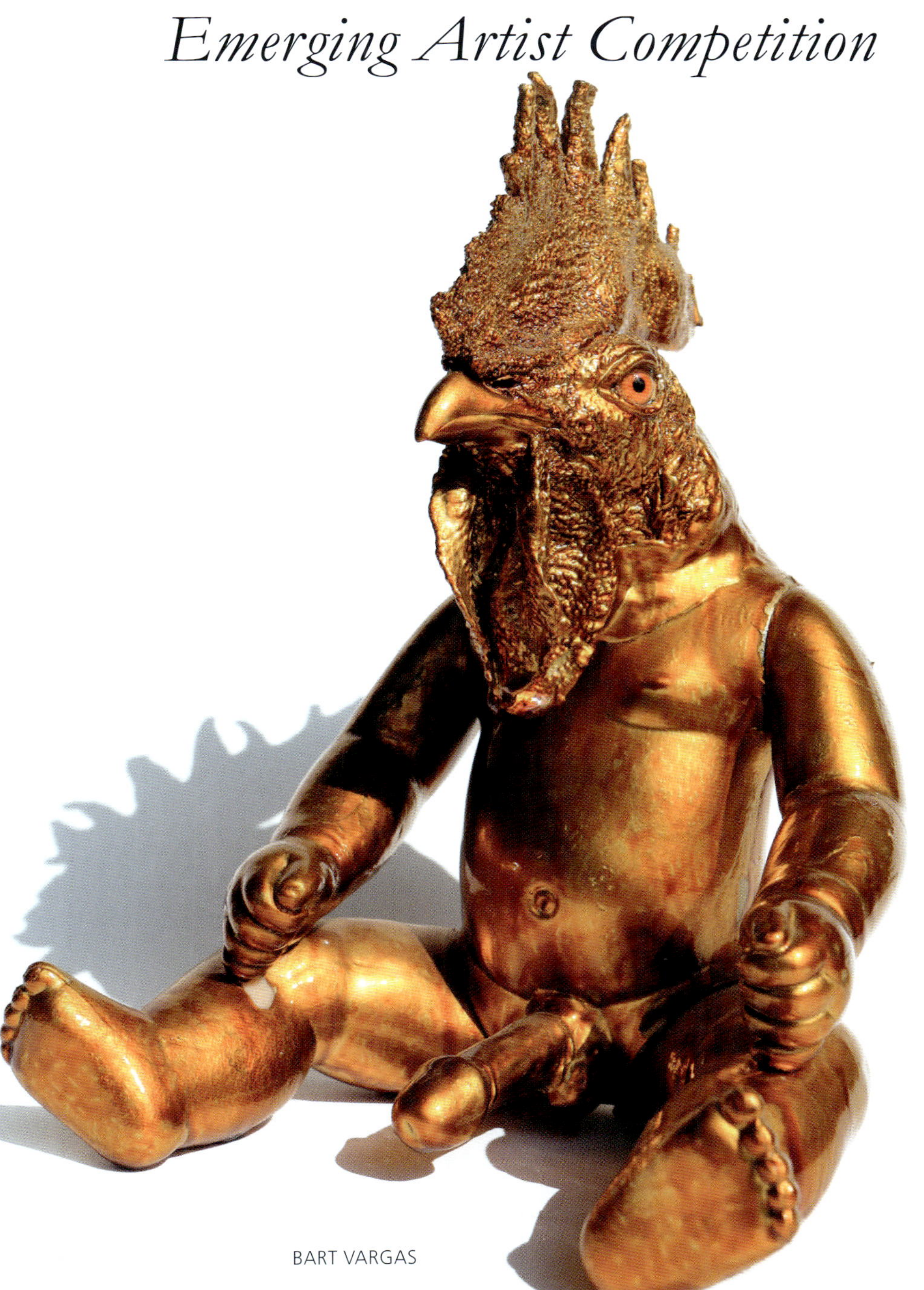

BART VARGAS

The purpose of this contest is to encourage artists to share their work by rewarding the best examples. The competition is open to any artist with the exception of previous winners of this competition, or artists who are already commercially selling work that portrays sexuality.

Der Zweck dieses Wettbewerbs ist es, Künstler zu ermutigen, ihr Werk zu zeigen. Die besten Beispiele werden prämiert. Der Wettbewerb ist offen für alle Künstler mit Ausnahme der früheren Gewinner dieses Wettbewerbs oder von Künstlern, die bereits gewerblich Werke verkaufen, die Sexualität darstellen.

TOMBOY

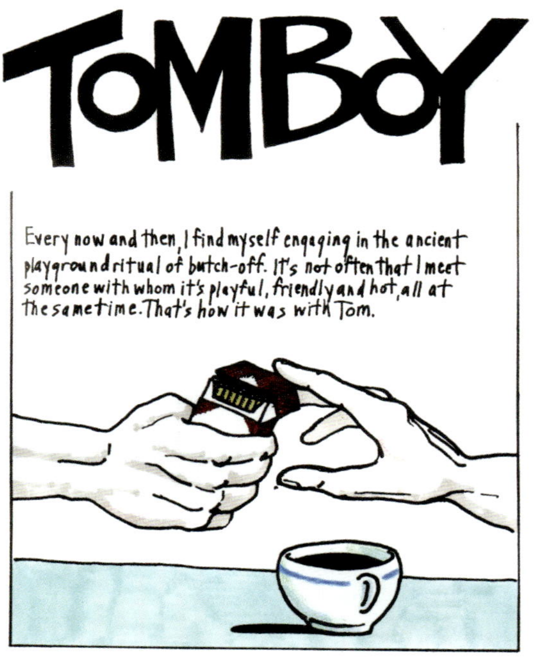

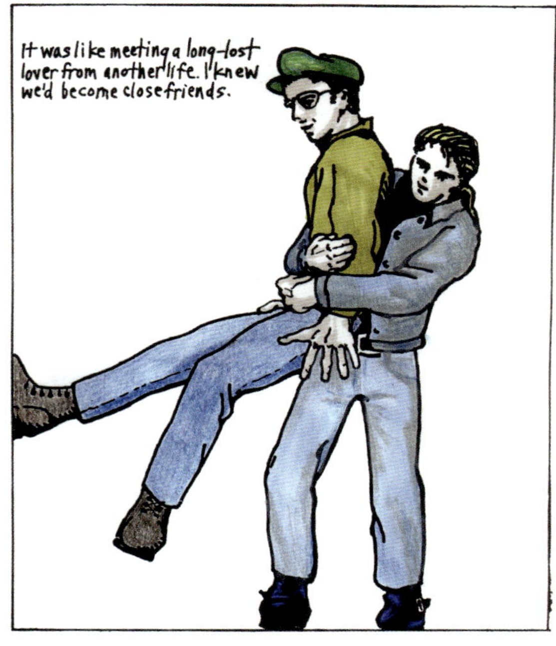

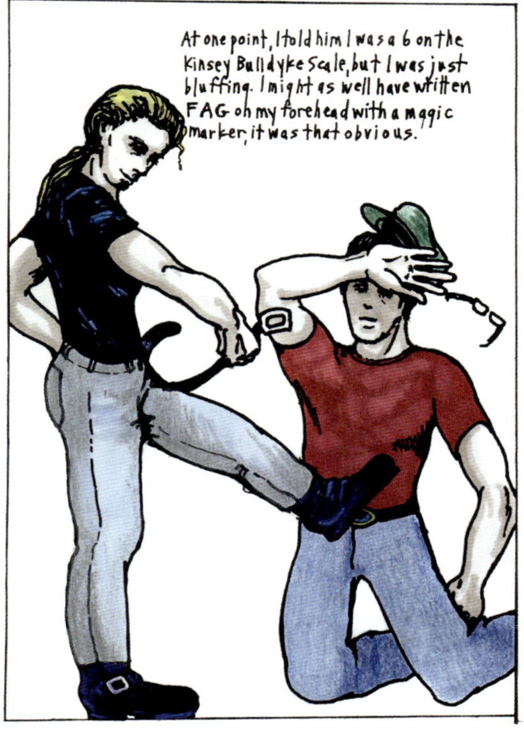

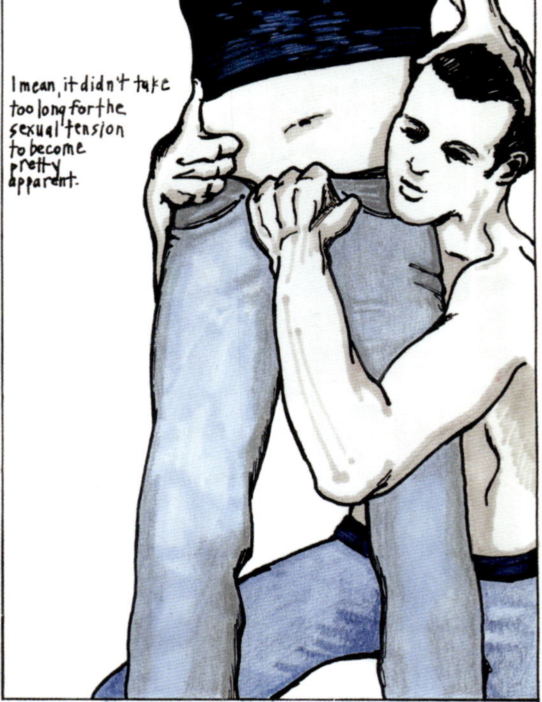

callaghan

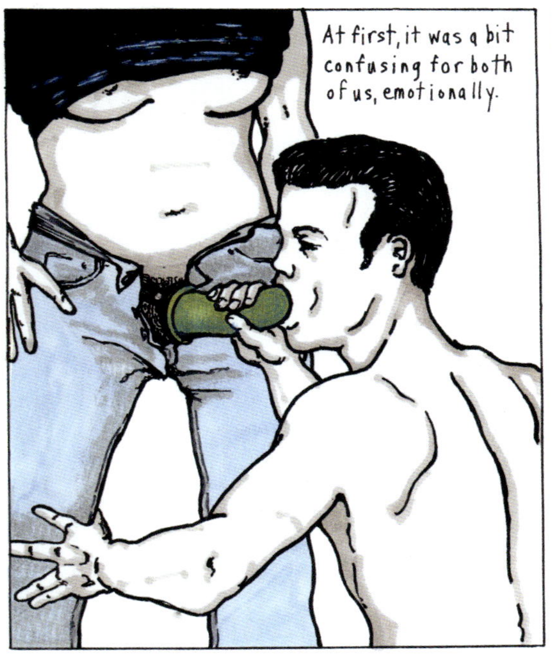

At first, it was a bit confusing for both of us, emotionally.

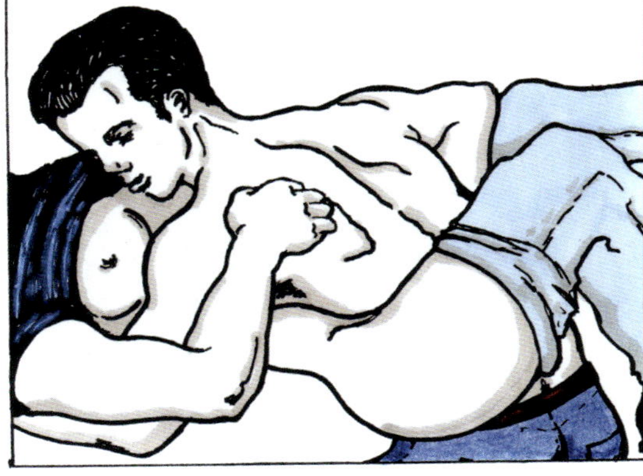

Not the part about him being a boy and me being a dyke, really. I used to think that being attracted to boys disqualified me as a dyke, but I don't worry about it anymore. A certain kind of energy turns me on, regardless of the source. It was more that we seemed to be walking the line between friendship and sex that, given the circumstances, would have had to be casual. Neither one of us was too anxious to fuck up our friendship.

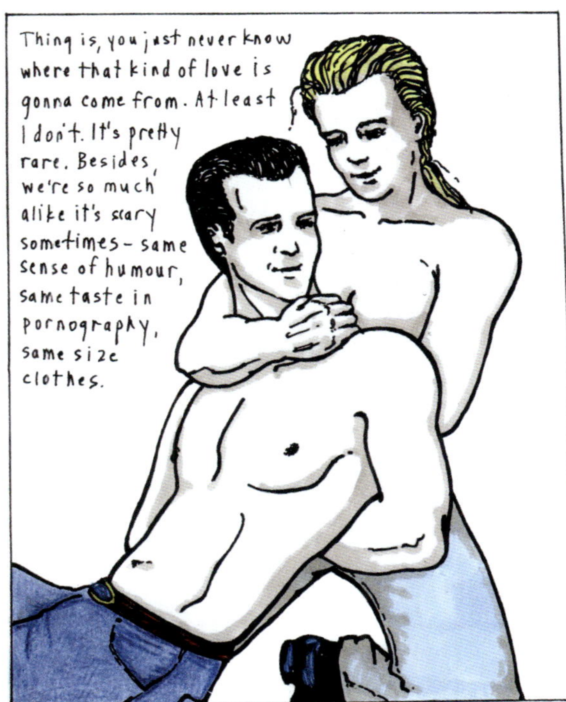

Thing is, you just never know where that kind of love is gonna come from. At least I don't. It's pretty rare. Besides, we're so much alike it's scary sometimes — same sense of humour, same taste in pornography, same size clothes.

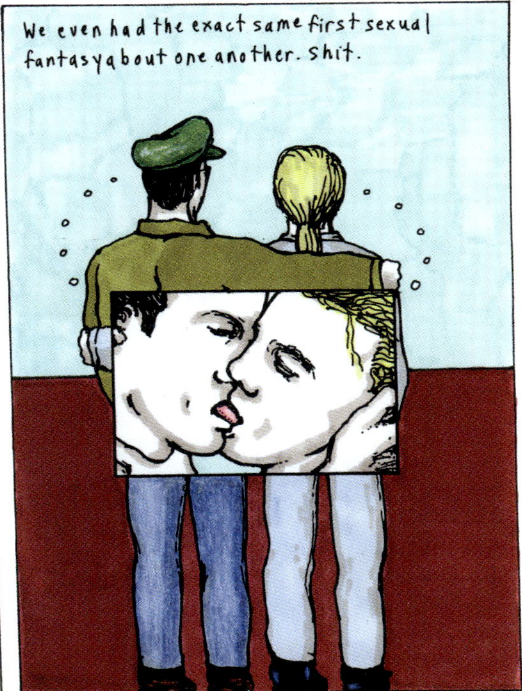

We even had the exact same first sexual fantasy about one another. Shit.

callaghan

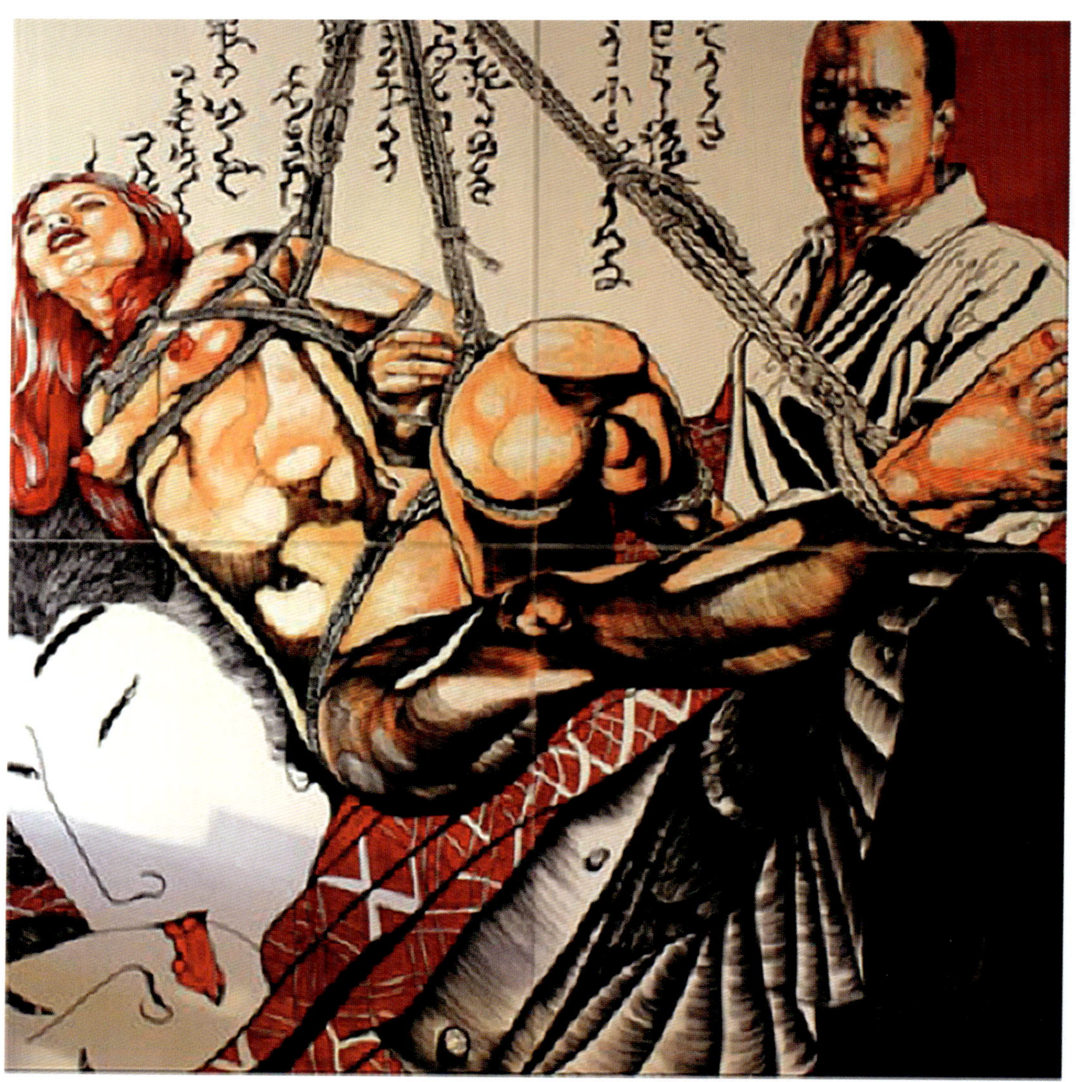

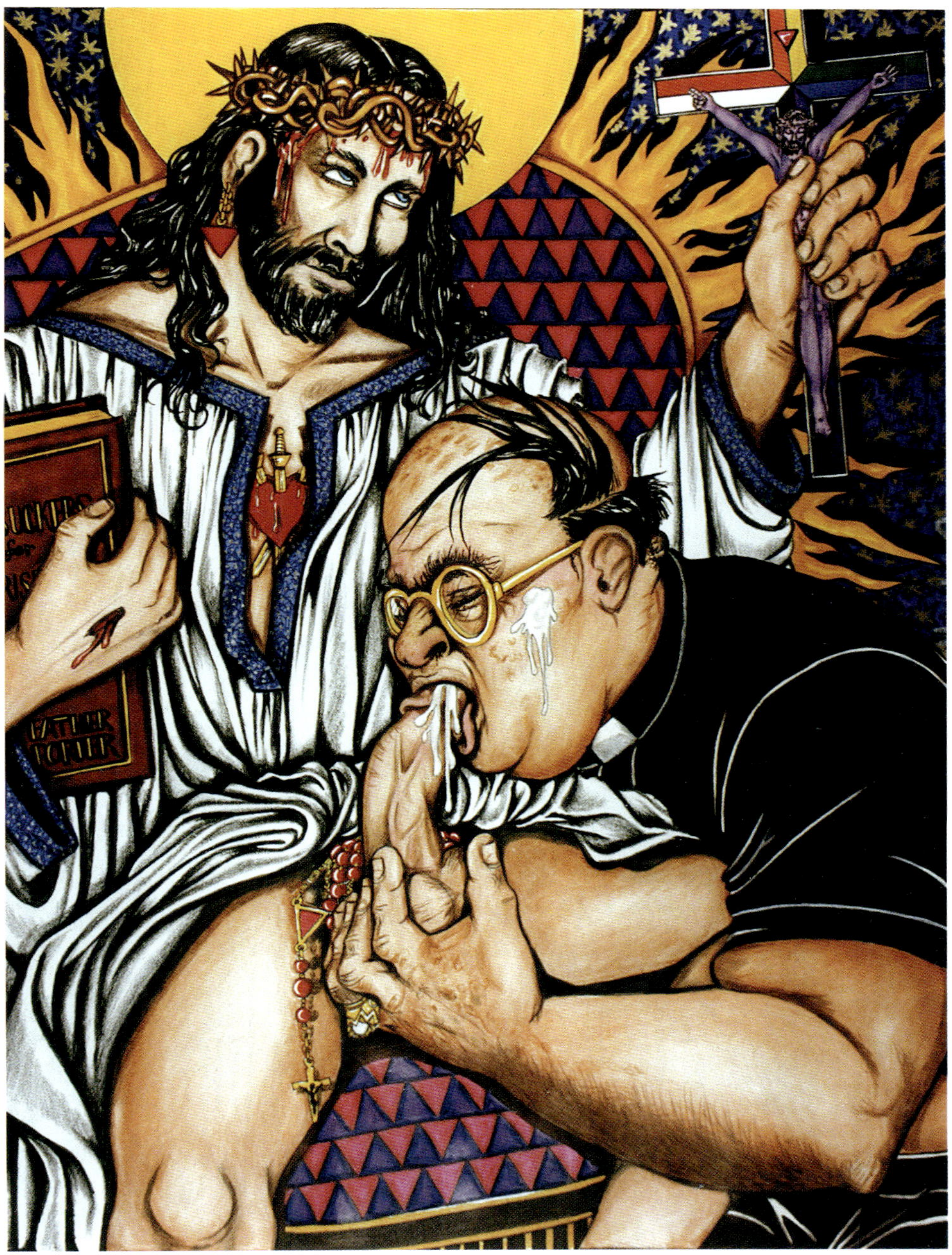

In 1995, the Grand Prize winner of the Tom of Finland Emerging Artist Competition was *Cocksuckers for Christ* by Garilyn Brune. We rallied, and gave it the same level of press exposure as all of our winners receive – and let's say it rained letters for the next year. You gotta love those pink triangles…

Im Jahr 1995 gewann *Cocksuckers for Christ* von Garilyn Brune den Tom of Finland Emerging Artist Wettbewerb. Wir haben dieses Gemälde genauso promoted wie alle anderen Gewinnerbilder auch. Und sagen wir es mal so: im darauffolgenden Jahr wurden wir von Bewerbungen überflutet. Man muss diese rosa Winkel einfach lieben …
  – Durk Dehner

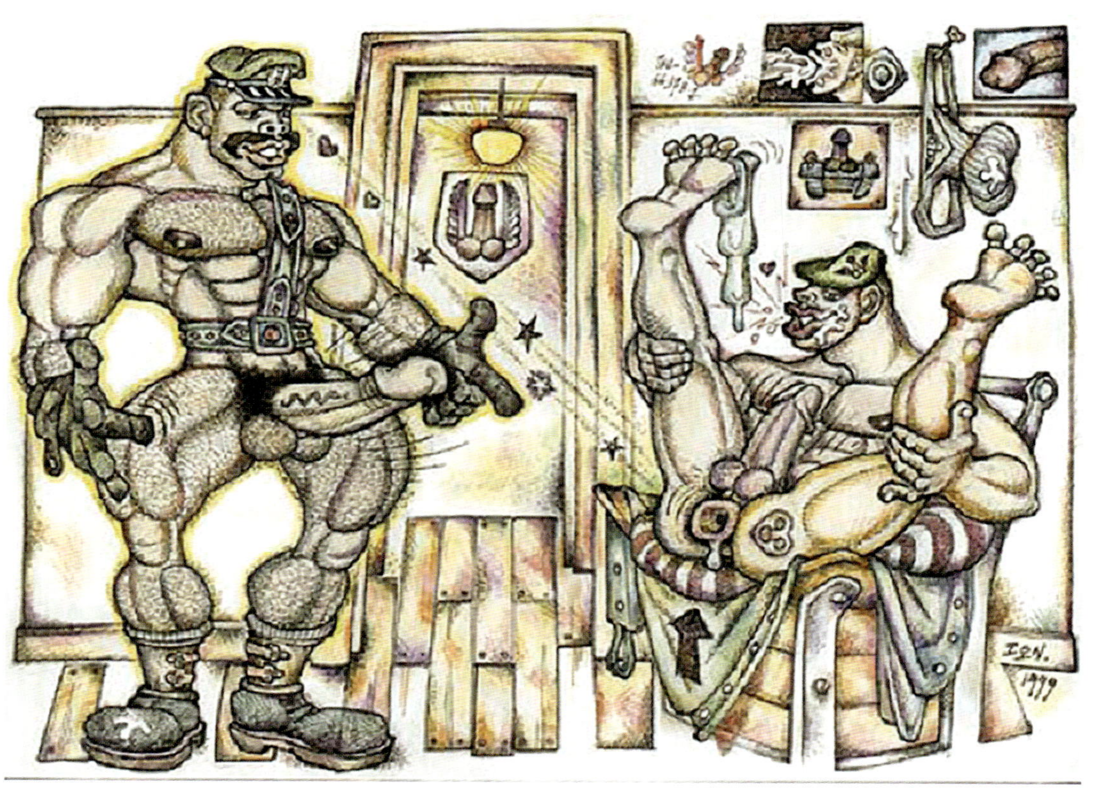

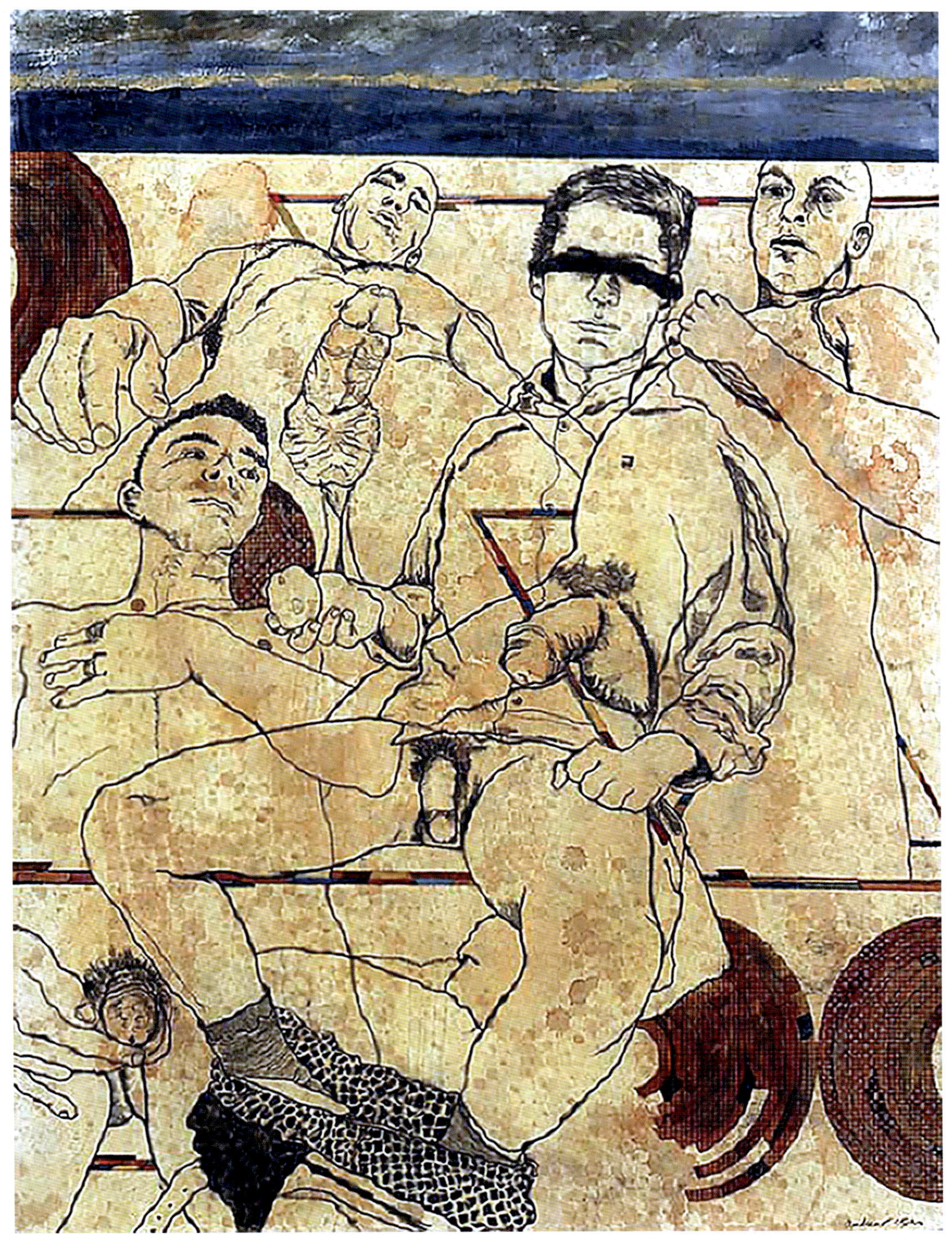

☐ PAUL BUIJS

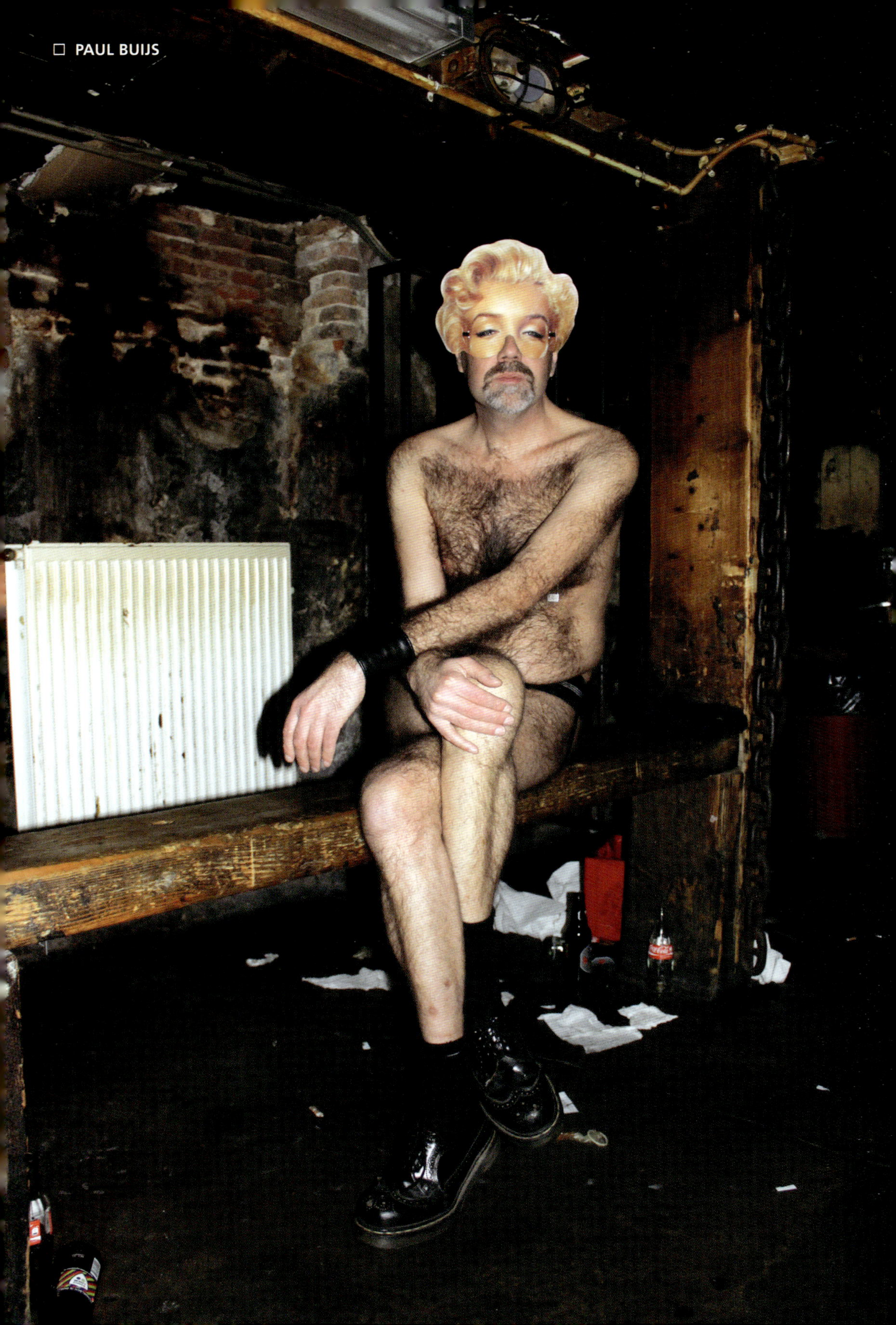

MICHAEL BULLOCK

Tom of Finland, Feminist?! Silvia Prada, Gay Fan Boy?!
Tom of Finland, ein Feminist? Silvia Prada, ein lesbischer Fanboy?

The concept of manhood in most societies is defined (and measured) by the ability to dominate, whether it's in sports, business, or sex. To be born with a penis but give up one's status as a dominator is to be a traitor against one's gender and against nature itself. For this ideology to resonate, one would have already bought into the idea that women hold a secondary status. By that standard homophobia is the anxiety-ridden stepchild of misogyny, centered on the fear men have of their potential to be feminized. The derogatory meaning of passivity in our society is continually present in our language today. It's seen in the way we praise men who penetrate multiple women as "studs" but shame women who get penetrated by multiple men as "sluts." Or in the negative ways we use the word *fuck*. "He fucked you over", "I'm going to fuck you up" in these aggressions to be fucked is presented as a punishment, to be taken advantage of, and ultimately to be weaker than the fucker. So, the ultimate treason against masculinity is for a man to participate in sex as a passive partner.

"The Bottom" spits in the face of society's contempt and finds joy, pleasure and satisfaction in his so-called domination. On the flip side, the active partner, "The Top" should be revered. As the dominator of dominators his rightful place is at the top of this macho hierarchy but instead he evokes fear because he has the power to rob a man of his status by subjecting him to a woman's sexual role. The male homophobe's psychology is a two-part condition made up of disdain and anxiety: disdain for all receptive partners (be it women or men) as less-than, and anxiety caused by the active partner because they present the threat of being dominated, or worse, confront them with the prospect that they could enjoy that domination.

In den meisten Gesellschaften wird das Konzept von Männlichkeit durch die Fähigkeit zu dominieren definiert (und gemessen) – sei es im Sportbereich, in der Arbeitswelt oder beim Sex. Mit einem Penis geboren zu werden, aber den Status des Beherrschenden aufzugeben, kommt dem Verrat des eigenen Geschlechts und der Natur gleich. Um mit dieser Ideologie im Einklang zu sein, muss man die Vorstellung, dass Frauen einen sekundären Status innehaben, verinnerlicht haben. Daran gemessen ist Homophobie das angstbesetzte Stiefkind der Misogynie, das aus der Angst von Männern entspringt, feminisiert zu werden.

Die abwertende Bedeutung von Passivität in unserer Gesellschaft ist in unserer heutigen Sprache ständig präsent. Es zeigt sich in der Art, wie wir Männer, die viele Frauen penetrieren, als „Hengste" preisen, aber Frauen, die von vielen Männern penetriert werden, als „Schlampe" beschimpfen. Oder in der negativen Art, wie wir das Wort Fuck benutzen: "He fucked me over", "I'm going to fuck you up" (Im Deutschen: „Fick dich ins Knie", „Die gehört gefickt" etc.). Bei diesen Aggressionen wird „gefickt werden" als Bestrafung präsentiert, um ausgenutzt zu werden und letztendlich schwächer zu sein als der „Ficker". Ergo ist für einen Mann der ultimative Verrat an der Maskulinität, Sex als passiver Partner zu haben.

„Der Bottom" spuckt in das Gesicht der ihn verachtenden Gesellschaft und findet Genuss und Befriedigung in seiner so genannten Unterwerfung. Auf der anderen Seite sollte der aktive Partner, „der Top", verehrt werden. Der Dominante hat seinen rechtmäßigen Platz an der Spitze dieser Machohierarchie, aber stattdessen ruft er Angst hervor, weil er die Macht hat, einen Mann seines Status zu berauben, indem er ihn in die sexuelle Rolle einer Frau zwingt. Die männliche, homophobe Psychologie basiert auf zwei Säulen, auf Verachtung und Angst: Die Verachtung aller passiven Partner (seien es Frauen oder Männer), die als weniger wert angesehen werden, und die Angst vor den aktiven Partnern, weil sie eine Gefahr darstellen, einen Mann zu dominieren, oder schlimmer noch: Sie könnten einen damit konfrontieren, dass man diese Dominanz genießen könnte.

I have laid out the basics of homophobia and its roots in misogyny to think about Tom of Finland's project in different terms. While the initial impulse for his work was a need to satiate his own sexual fantasy, it was immediately intertwined with a political mission: to deconstruct the negative clichés society associates with gay men, by making imagery that aimed to eradicate homophobia's horrific impact on their self-esteem. By doing so he could liberate himself and his gay peers from what he called "the pathetic plight of the homosexual." Taking a step back to the beginning of his career, there was Touko Laaksonen, the young advertising man in post-war Finland. I had never given much thought to Tom's day job. At best, I had considered it an inconvenience, a source of income for his work as an artist. But looking through the source material [also seen on the pages of *My Gay Eye*], I began to understand how meticulous he was in finding the perfect character, expression, smile and pose to communicate the desired effect. He was considered a master draftsman but this obvious talent may have blinded us to equal areas of his genius: as a curator of human expression. It's clear that his advertising career deeply informed his personal work giving him years of practice at composing images in service of selling ideas and products to the mass market. Tom adopted the strategies of image making from advertising to create his own work. By day Touko created campaigns that sold soft drinks, appliances and candy to the Finnish people. By night Tom of Finland worked on his lifelong advertising campaign, rebranding homosexuality to sell a joyful vision of gay sex to gay men.

If his campaign were to have received a client brief, its objective would have been to dismantle homophobia. Not to change the minds of the homophobes but to ensure that their options to make gay men feel shame for what they desired would no longer be effective. His campaign would need to destroy the idea that gay men were weak by depict-

Ich habe die Grundlagen der Homophobie und deren Wurzeln in der Frauenfeindlichkeit hier dargestellt, um in anderer Weise über das Werk von Tom of Finland nachzudenken. Während der anfängliche Impuls für seine Arbeit ein Bedürfnis war, seine eigene sexuelle Phantasie zu befriedigen, wurde das sehr bald mit einer politischen Mission verflochten: die negativen Klischees, die in der Gesellschaft mit schwulen Männern assoziiert werden, zu dekonstruieren, indem er Bilder erschuf, die die schrecklichen Auswirkungen, die die Homophobie auf das schwule Selbstbewusstsein hatte, aus der Welt schaffen sollten. Auf diese Weise konnte er sich selbst und seine homosexuellen Altersgenossen von dem befreien, was er „die erbärmliche Notlage des Homosexuellen" nannte. Schauen wir zurück zum Anfang seiner Karriere, als Touko Laaksonen noch ein junger Werbegrafiker im Nachkriegs-Finnland war. Ich hatte nie viel über Toms Job nachgedacht. Im besten Fall hatte ich es für eine Unannehmlichkeit gehalten, eine Einkommensquelle, um seine eigentliche Arbeit als Künstler finanzieren zu können. Doch als ich seine Bildvorlagen sah (die auch in diesem Band zu sehen sind), begann ich zu verstehen, wie akribisch er darin war, den perfekten Charakter und Ausdruck, das perfekte Lächeln und die ideale Pose zu finden, um einen gewünschten Effekt zu erzielen. Er galt als ein Meister der Zeichenkunst, aber dieses offensichtliche Talent hat uns möglicherweise die Augen verschlossen vor einem anderen, gleichwertigen Teil seiner Begabung: als Kurator des menschlichen Ausdrucks. Klar ist, dass seine Karriere in der Werbebranche seine persönliche Arbeit stark geprägt hat und ihm ermöglichte, jahrelang zu üben, Bilder für den Verkauf von Ideen und Produkten im Massenmarkt zu komponieren. Tom hat Strategien der Bildproduktion aus der Werbung übernommen, um seine eigene Arbeit zu schaffen. Tagsüber kreierte Touko Kampagnen, mit denen Erfrischungsgetränke, Haushaltsgeräte und Süßigkeiten an die Finnen verkauft wurden. In der Nacht arbeitete Tom an seiner lebenslangen Werbekampagne, an der „Umfirmierung" von Homosexualität, um schwulen Männern eine freudvolle Vision von schwulem Sex zu verkaufen.

Wenn seine Kampagne ein Kundenbriefing erhalten hätte, wäre darin das Ziel festgelegt worden, Homophobie abzubauen. Es ginge weniger darum, die Meinung von Homophoben zu ändern, als sicherzustellen, dass deren Möglichkeiten, schwule Männer dazu zu bringen, sich für ihr Verlangen zu

ing more honestly the fulfilling roles that both passive and dominant partners enjoy during sex. Tom's strategies to solve these conceptual problems were deceptively simple and extremely consistent. They could be broken down in four simple points:

1. Show naked men in nature, in daylight (refusing to hide in darkness), thus making the link that they are part of nature and that their acts are natural.
2. Depict the men as physically strong, so their muscular bodies are the embodiment of masculine pride.
3. Depict sex partners as equals by pioneering a clone look, so both dominant and submissive roles are indistinguishable and interchangeable. Tom's men (with very little exception) are confident grown adults that are always both at once object and objectifier.
4. Reintroduce the authority figure, so whether it's police or military officers, the men in charge of keeping the moral authority are now encouraging in and participating in the fun.

The rest, as they say, is history, or gay history. Tom's art gave his community a road map to his vision of utopia, and once exposed to it, it would be much harder for gay men to go back to living in fear, darkness or shame. His imagery is so real, so abundant and so widely distributed, that his powerful vision of homosexual sex dominated reality, making it submit to his vision. His campaign succeeded in demonstrating sexual equality and elevating passive sexuality from a place of disdain to a place of envy. It may be unnecessary to ask my title question, is Tom of Finland a feminist? But by showcasing pride in all forms of sexual desire, by showing equality and partnership and balance within sexual relationships, he demonstrated a model of pleasure that could be consumed, learned and appropriated no matter who is participating in the sex.

schämen, nicht mehr länger wirksam wären. Seine Kampagne sollte die Idee, dass schwule Männer schwach sind, zerstören, indem sie die erfüllenden sexuellen Rollen, die der passive und der aktive Partner beim Sex genießen, ehrlicher darstellen. Toms Strategien, diese konzeptionellen Probleme zu lösen, waren täuschend einfach und extrem konsistent. Sie könnten in vier Punkte unterteilt werden:

1. Zeige nackte Männer in der Natur, bei Tageslicht (die Weigerung, sich in der Dunkelheit zu verstecken), um so die Verbindung herzustellen, dass sie Teil der Natur sind und dass ihre Handlungen „natürlich" sind.
2. Stelle Männer als körperlich stark dar, sodass ihre muskulösen Körper die Verkörperung des männlichen Stolzes sind.
3. Stelle Sexpartner auf gleicher Augenhöhe dar, indem ein Klon-Look entwickelt wird, sodass die aktiven und die passiven Rollen nicht mehr zu unterscheiden sind und damit austauschbar werden. Toms Männer (mit wenigen Ausnahmen) sind selbstbewusste Erwachsene, die immer zugleich Objekt und Objektivierende sind.
4. Führe Autoritätsfiguren ein, seien es Polizisten oder Soldaten. Jene Männer, die für die Aufrechterhaltung der moralischen Autorität verantwortlich sind, ermutigen nun zum Spaß und beteiligen sich daran.

Der Rest ist Geschichte oder schwule Geschichte. Toms Kunst gab seiner Gemeinde einen Leitfaden für seine Vision von Utopia, und von da an war es schwieriger für schwule Männer, in ein Leben voller Angst, Dunkelheit oder Scham zurückzukehren. Seine Bilder sind so real, so zahlreich und so weit verbreitet, dass seine kraftvolle Vision von homosexuellem Sex die Realität dominierte und sie seiner Vision unterwarf. Seiner Kampagne gelang es, sexuelle Gleichheit darzustellen und passive Sexualität von einem Ort der Verachtung zu einem beneidenswerten Ort, zu erheben. Es mag unnötig erscheinen danach zu fragen, ob Tom of Finland ein Feminist ist. Indem er aber Stolz in allen Formen sexuellen Verlangens zeigte, indem er Gleichheit, Partnerschaft und Ausgewogenheit in sexuellen Beziehungen zeigte, zeigte er ein Modell der Lust, das konsumiert, erlernt und angewendet werden kann – unabhängig davon, wer am Sex beteiligt ist.

In northern Spain, teenage Silvia Prada's identity was beginning to take form in the most unlikely place: her father's salon for men. There she received an education in men's style that developed into a fetishistic obsession with male beauty. "My dad wasn't gay himself but through the salon I was exposed to gay culture." That could all seem normal enough, but parallel to this, Silvia was coming to terms with her attraction to women. This complicated configuration —her position as an outsider with neither a place in the straight world, nor the traditional lesbian community— could have been lonely and traumatic, but it forced the resourceful budding artist to take the opportunity to forge her own path. Through exposure to the hair salon's waiting room magazines, Silvia Prada became an obsessive super-fan of pop culture imagery. She studied all the identities popular culture offered and made collages of the stars and styles that she felt best connected to her own sensibilities. Like many of her generation, Silvia Prada became obsessed with George Michael and Madonna but was seduced mostly by their ability to utilize the full spectrum of gender expression Like her heroes before her, her definition of sex appeal came to be defined as someone who embodies the full range of masculine and feminine energies: an ability that she found most present in gay men.

"I have never gone to lesbian bars. I met all my girlfriends at either university or male gay bars, I'm a different kind of girl, I was socialized as a fag." So when the 17-year-old came across a Tom of Finland article in *Interview* magazine she was primed for an immediate, deep connection. Even though Tom's imagery would seem to be far from the aesthetics of a teenage Lesbian she saw no boundary between the world he presented and her own. "I thought it was so pretty, for me it was beautiful, I was attracted to how the men present themselves more than the specifics of the sex acts, which I also enjoyed. Even though the characters' body types in Tom's drawings are depicted as hyper-masculine, the facial expressions

Wir kommen nun zu Silvia Prada. Als Teenager begann sie sich an einem unwahrscheinlichen Ort zu entwickeln: im Herrenfrisörsalon ihres Vaters. Dort erhielt sie eine Ausbildung als Herrnfrisörin, die sich zu einer fetischistischen Obsession für männliche Schönheit entwickelte. „Mein Vater war selbst nicht schwul, aber durch den Salon kam ich mit schwuler Kultur in Berührung." Das könnte alles relativ normal erscheinen, aber parallel musste sich Silvia Prada damit auseinandersetzen, dass sie Frauen begehrte. Diese komplizierte Konfiguration – ihre Position als Außenseiterin, die weder einen Platz in der heterosexuellen Welt noch in der traditionellen, lesbischen Gemeinschaft hatte – hätte einsam und traumatisch sein können, aber sie zwang die angehende Künstlerin, diese Gelegenheit zu nutzen, ihren eigenen Weg zu gehen.

Durch die Magazine im Friseursalon wurde Silvia Prada zu einem obsessiven Superfan von Bildern der Popkultur. Sie beschäftige sich mit all den Promis und erstellte Collagen jener Stars, mit denen sie sich am meisten verbunden fühlte. Wie viele andere ihrer Generation war Silvia besessen von George Michael und Madonna, und wurde besonders von deren Fähigkeit in den Bann gezogen, das komplette Spektrum von Geschlechtsidentitäten auszunutzen. Wie ihre Helden begann auch sie selbst, Sexappeal als etwas zu definieren, das die ganze Bandbreite von männlichen und weiblichen Eigenschaften verkörpert: eine Fähigkeit, die sie am ehesten bei schwulen Männern fand.

„Ich bin nie in Lesbenbars gegangen. Ich habe alle meine Freundinnen an der Uni oder in Schwulenbars getroffen. Ich bin eine andere Art Mädchen, denn ich wurde als Schwuchtel sozialisiert." Als die 17-Jährige einen Tom of Finland-Artikel im Magazin *Interview* sah, war dies der Beginn einer unmittelbaren und tiefen Verbindung. Obwohl Toms Bildsprache weit entfernt von der Ästhetik eines lesbischen Teenagers zu sein schien, sah sie keine Grenzen zwischen der Welt, die er repräsentierte und ihrer eigenen. „Ich fand das alles so hinreißend. Ich fühlte mich von der Art, wie sich diese Männer präsentieren, noch mehr angezogen als von den eigentlichen sexuellen Handlungen, die ich aber ebenfalls genoss." Obwohl der Körpertypus der Figuren in Toms Zeichnungen hypermaskulin dargestellt wird, sind die Mimik und Reaktionen der Männer aufeinander sehr frei. Silvia Prada erklärt: „Toms

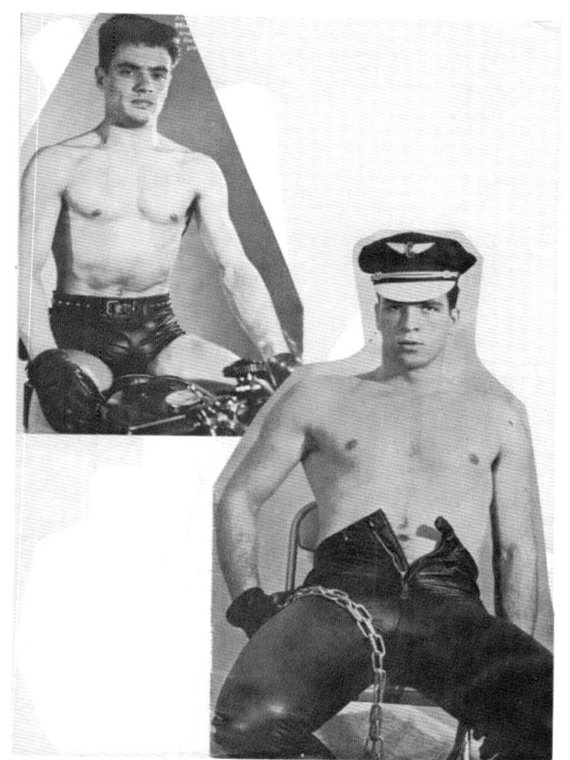

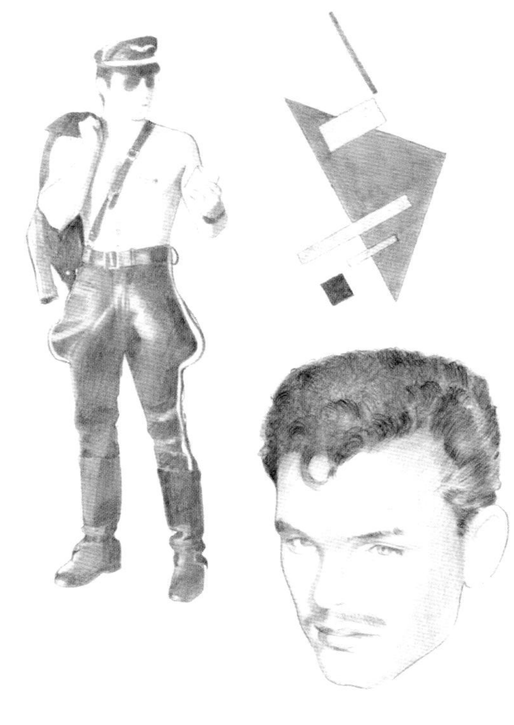

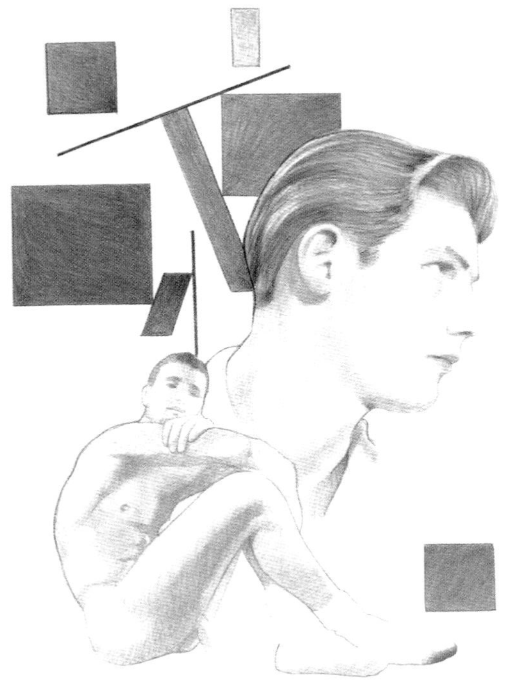

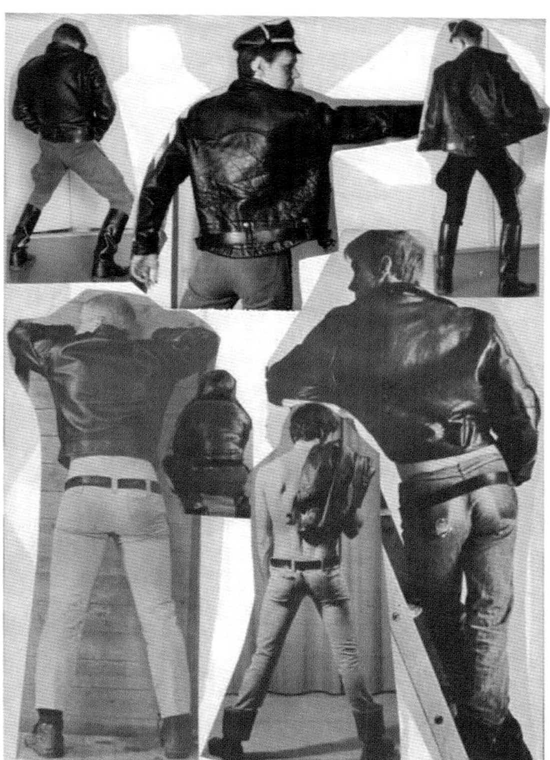

and reactions the men have to each other have no restriction. Prada explains: "Tom's men are flirtatious, coy, humble, happy, embarrassed, confrontational, shy, courageous, joyous, proud, aggressive, and affectionate. They move between hard and soft aspects of personality that are typically prescribed to one gender or the other."

The impact Tom had on Silvia Prada's life choices and artistic practice are profound. In Tom she saw aspects of herself, an alienated artist who used their work to create an acceptable place in the world for an unacceptable identity. This empowered her to never conform her own identity to be accepted by any group. Artistically, she also followed in Tom's footsteps. She chose the pencil as her tool of expression, and like him her process involved obsessively cataloging magazine clippings, collaging them and re-rendering them.

Working with Tom of Finland Foundation, Silvia Prada was given access to Tom's archive of source material, a combination of photos from *Physique Pictorial* photo shoots, porn magazines, and mass media. Looking through the thousands of images he amassed she chose pictures of the men that spoke to her own sense of beauty, sexuality, and empowerment. This is an exploration of types, styles, expression and identities. Prada meditates on and brings attention to the characters we have lost in the march towards acceptance. The models showcased and redrawn here examine the outlaw rebel spirit and celebrate the balanced energy that is created by men that are at once the object and objectifier. The porn models in Tom's archive are radical sexual renegades; despite all of society's backlash, these men acted as honest witnesses to their desires, allowing their faces and bodies to be photographed in a time where that could have cost them their jobs, their families and their place in society. "I connect with their defiant attitudes. For me to be gay is not just a sexual option, it's an energy. It's a shared culture."

Männer sind kokett, scheu, demütig, glücklich, peinlich, streitlustig, schüchtern, mutig, freudvoll, stolz, aggressiv und zärtlich. Sie bewegen sich zwischen harten und weichen Aspekten der Persönlichkeit, die typischerweise entweder dem einem oder dem anderen Geschlecht zugeordnet werden."

Der Einfluss, den Tom auf Silvia Pradas Lebensentscheidungen und ihre künstlerische Arbeit hatte, ist tiefgreifend. In Tom sah sie Aspekte ihrer selbst, einer entfremdeten Künstlerin, die sich mit ihrer Arbeit einen akzeptierten Platz für eine inakzeptable Identität in der Welt schuf. Dies ermöglichte es ihr, ihre eigene Identität niemals anpassen zu müssen, um von irgendeiner Gruppe akzeptiert zu werden. Künstlerisch folgte sie auch Toms Fußstapfen. Sie wählte den Stift als ihr Ausdrucksmittel, und genau wie er, begann sie Zeitungsausschnitte zu sammeln, sie zu collagieren und neu anzuordnen.

Durch die Zusammenarbeit mit der Tom of Finland Foundation erhielt Silvia Prada Zugang zu Toms Quellenmaterial: Fotos aus *Physique Pictorial*, von Fotoshootings, aus Pornomagazinen und aus den Massenmedien. Aus den Tausenden von Bildern, die er sammelte, wählte sie die Bilder jener Männer aus, die ihrem eigenen Sinn für Schönheit, Sexualität und Ermächtigung entsprachen. Sie untersucht Typen, Stile, Ausdruck und Identitäten, setzt sich damit auseinander und erinnert an Menschen, die wir auf dem Marsch zur Akzeptanz verloren haben. Ihre hier präsentierten und neu gezeichneten Modelle zeigen den rebellischen Geist der Außenseiter und feiern die gesunde Energie, die von Männern ausgeht, die zugleich das Objekt und der Objektivierende sind. Die Pornomodels in Toms Archiv sind radikale sexuelle Rebellen. Trotz all der gesellschaftlichen Gegenreaktionen handelten diese Männer als wahre Zeugen ihrer Lust und ließen ihre Gesichter und Körper in einer Zeit fotografieren, als sie noch damit rechnen mussten, dadurch ihre Arbeit, ihre Familien und ihren Platz in der Gesellschaft verlieren zu können. „Ich kann diese trotzige Einstellung verstehen. Für mich ist Homosexualität nicht nur eine sexuelle Option, sondern eine Energie. Es ist eine gemeinsame Kultur."

Übersetzung: Florian Hetz

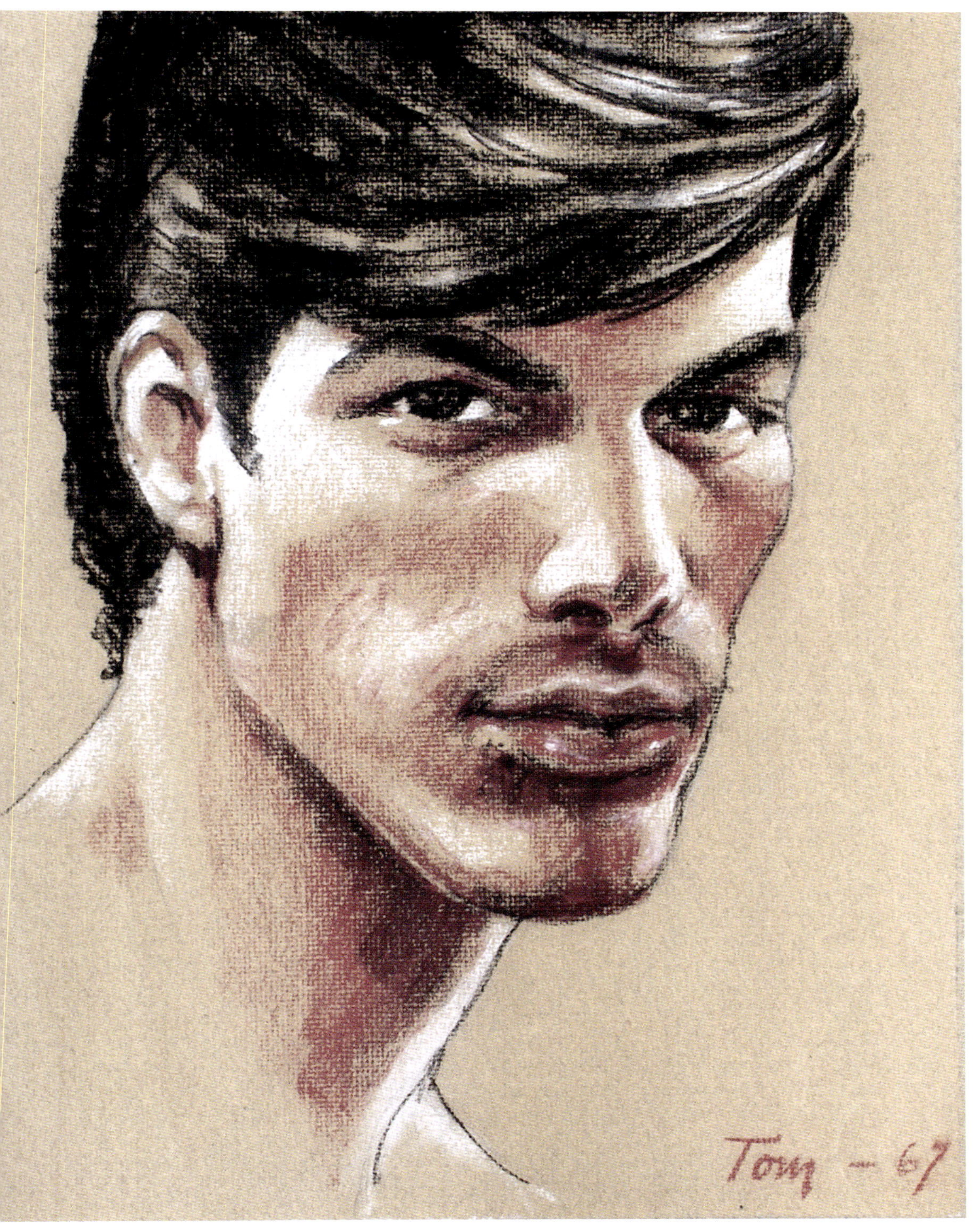

PETER REHBERG

Versatility

Tom of Finlands Superhelden und die Erfindung der schwulen Männlichkeit •
Tom of Finland's superheroes and the invention of gay masculinity

Darstellungen schwuler Sexualität waren aufgrund strafrechtlicher Bestimmungen in den 1950er-Jahren lediglich in Form keuscher Magazine wie etwa dem US-amerikanischen *Physique Pictoral* zugänglich. Hier wurden Amateur-Modelle in Szenen sportlichen Wettkampfs oder in historischem Kontext präsentiert und auch der in Kalifornien damals bereits populäre Body-Building-Kult fand in diesen Heften sein zentrales Forum. Sportliche Posen dienten den Magazinen als Vorwand für die Präsentation fast vollständiger männlicher Nacktheit.

Auch frühe Zeichnungen Tom of Finlands erschienen in den *Physique Pictoral* [1]. In einem von der Zensur bestimmten Klima boten Zeichnungen ein paar strategische Vorteile gegenüber fotografischen Bildproduktionen, indem sie nicht unbedingt auf reale Modelle angewiesen waren und ohne großen technischen Aufwand sexuelle Fantasien visualisieren konnten. Das Medium Zeichnung setzte damit auch die Tradition der obszönen Kritzeleien fort, die die Kontaktanzeigen auf den Wänden öffentlicher Toiletten illustrieren: Gay Sex Graffiti – oder wie sie der US-amerikanische Schriftsteller Armistead Maupin bezeichnet: „homoerotische Höhlenzeichnungen in den Schwulenbars." [2]

In seiner über fünfzigjährigen Karriere hat Tom of Finland neben Porträts und anderen Einzelmotiven bereits in den 1950ern Comics von schwulen Männern gezeichnet. Später entstanden dann die legendären und offensiveren „Kake-Comics", benannt nach dem Helden der sexuellen Abenteuer.

Auch viele Motive Tom of Finlands, die nicht eigentlich Comics im Sinne narrativ organisierter Bilderfolgen sind, bedienen sich einer Comic-Erzählweise:

In the 1950s, because of criminal laws, representations of gay sexuality were only accessible through chaste magazines like the American *Physique Pictorial*. Here, amateur models were presented in historical and athletic scenes and the burgeoning California bodybuilding cult was edified within its pages. These tableaux served as a pretext to display the nearly nude male form.

Early drawings by Tom of Finland also appeared in *Physique Pictorial*. [1] Within a cultural climate generally marked by censorship, in contrast to photographs, drawings offered some strategic advantages: They didn't necessarily require real models and could visualize sexual fantasies completely. Tom of Finland's drawings elevated the tradition of crude doodles, which illustrated the "personal ads" on the walls of public bathrooms: gay sex graffiti – or as the American writer Armistead Maupin called it: "homoerotic cave drawings in gay bars." [2]

In his more than 50-year-long career, Tom of Finland drew, apart from single and dual portraits, also "comics" – in the sense of narrative sequences – of gay men. He already started with this in the 1950s. Later, his legendary and sexually explicit *Kake* series, named after the hero of the stories, were published.

Even those illustrations of Tom of Finland, that aren't actually comics in the sense of temporally organized sequences of drawings, use their narrative style: Often they bring several consecutive layers of time

---

[1] Ein anderer Weg, schwule Erotik oder Pornografie zu zeigen, waren in den 1950ern neben dem Sport- der Kunstkontext: die Bücher und Filme von Jean Genet und Kenneth Anger. Schwule Erotik wurde auf diesem Wege zwar keinem Massenpublikum zugänglich, bekam aber gerade durch die Skandale, die diese Werke nicht zuletzt wegen der Darstellung nackter männlicher Körper noch auslösen konnten, öffentliche Aufmerksamkeit.

[2] Maupin, Armistead (2009): „Toms Titten". In: Hanson, Dian (Hg.), *Tom of Finland XXL*, Köln: Taschen, S. 95

[1] Another way of showing gay eroticism and pornography in the 50s was, apart from the sports context, the art context with the books and movies of Jean Genet and Kenneth Anger. Even if in this way gay eroticism didn't become accessible to a mass audience, it gained public attention, especially through the scandals which could still be produced by the presentation of naked male bodies.

[2] Maupin, Armistead (2009): "Toms Titten". In: Hanson, Dian (ed.), *Tom of Finland XXL*, Köln: Taschen, p. 95

Oft holen sie mehrere aufeinander folgende Zeitebenen ins Bild und fangen damit die narrative Abfolge in einer einzelnen Zeichnung ein.

Die Bildsequenzen Tom of Finlands reichen von Verführungsszenen bis hin zu sexueller Action. Die Narration ist in der Regel ziemlich schematisch und erstreckt sich vom ersten Blickkontakt bis zum romantischen Nachspiel. In dieser Hinsicht ließen sich Toms Bilder mit den professionellen, seit den späten 1970ern entstandenen schwulen Pornofilmen vergleichen,

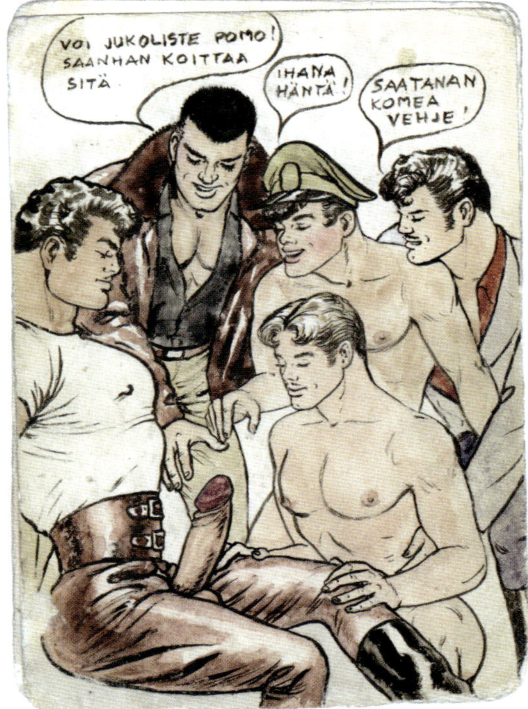

Frühe Zeichnung mit Text • *Drawing with lettering*

die oft einem ähnlichen Muster folgen. Während die früheren Comics aus den 1950ern noch von Texten begleitet sind, findet man diese bei den späteren Kake-Geschichten und auch danach immer seltener.

Das Fehlen von Worten und die Konzentration auf visuelle Codes spiegeln dabei auch die Kommunikationsformen einer schwulen Subkultur wieder, in der schneller und anonymer Sex oft sprachlos abläuft und zum Beispiel über den Zeichencharakter von Fetischen organisiert wird; oder über den mittlerweile aus der Mode gekommenen *Hanky-Code* – farbigen Taschentüchern, die abhängig davon, wo sie getragen werden, signalisieren, worauf man beim Sex steht.

Seine Sexgeschichten – und genau das ist charakteristisch für sein Werk – setzten dabei auf den immer gleichen Typus Mann: Ein schwuler sexueller Superheld mit unwahrscheinlichen Körpermaßen. Deshalb bietet es sich auch jenseits einzelner Zeichnungen an, den Tom-of-Finland-*Typ* zu analysieren. Er hat auch in der realen schwulen Welt der zurückliegenden vier Jahrzehnte unter der Bezeichnung „Clone" Karriere gemacht. Der Clone lässt sich ungefähr

into one picture and capture through this the temporality of the narrative in a single drawing. These sequences range from seduction scenes to hard core action. The narration is usually pretty schematic and proceeds from the first eye contact to the romantic afterplay. In this regard, Tom's drawings could be compared with professional gay porn, which originated in the late seventies and often follows a similar pattern. While the earlier comics from the '50s were still accompanied by texts, they became rarer in the *Kake* stories and his later career.

The lack of words and the concentration on visual codes in Tom's work also mirror the forms of communication of a gay subculture, in which fast and anonymous sex often happens speechlessly. It is organized for example, through the symbols of fetishes, as well as through the *Hanky Code*: bandanas that signal a guy's sexual preferences depending on the color and the side on which they are worn (a practice which by now is somewhat out of fashion).

His sex stories – and this is a signature of his work – feature the same type of man: A gay, sexual superhero with improbable anatomy. That's why, even beyond the individual drawings, the Tom of Finland type can be analyzed more generally. In the real gay world of the last four decades he also made a career under the label "clone". The "clone" can be described as follows: short hair; strongly structured

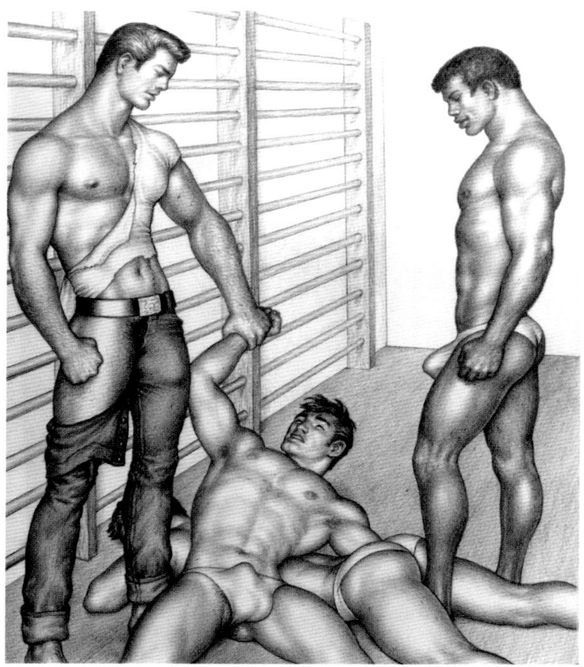

Tom drew Interracial scenes early and until the end of his carreer, if fact the last story on which he was working before he died was titled Black Magic.

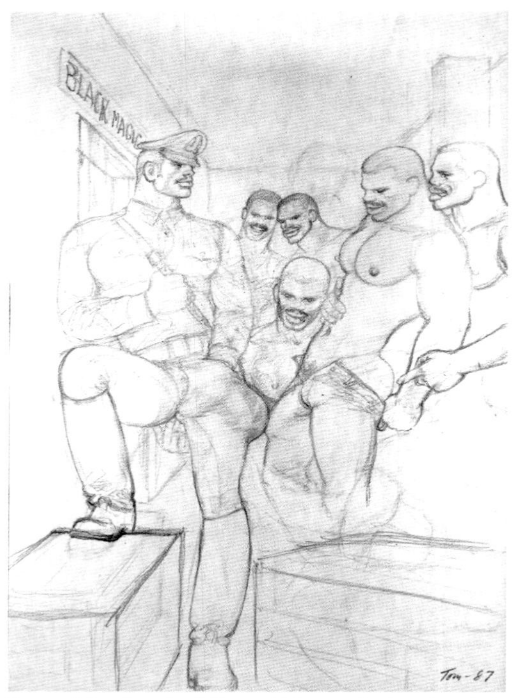

Tom zeichnete sehr früh und bis zum Ende seines Lebens auch Szenen mit farbigen Männern. Eines seiner letzten Projekte vor seinem Tod hieß Black Magic.

so beschreiben: Kurze Haare, kantig-maskuline Gesichtsformen, manchmal ein Bart, breite Schultern, trainierte Brustmuskulatur, schmale Taille, kräftige Beine, große Geschlechtsteile und ein knackiger Hintern, die von engen Hosen betont werden.

Tom of Finlands Zeichnungen hatten nicht nur die Funktion, sexuelle Erregung zu provozieren, sondern prägten auch gleichzeitig einen schwulen Lebensentwurf (ähnlich wie die Pornofilme der späten 1970er). Männer, die er im wirklichen Leben traf, inspirierten ihn zu seinen Fantasien, die wiederum zum Vorbild einer schwulen Subkultur und Community wurden. Von den US-Schwulenmetropolen San Francisco und New York ausgehend, eroberte der Clone-Look – sozusagen eine Nachinszenierung der Tom-of-Finland-Motive – die westliche Homokultur. Der US-amerikanische Queer-Theoretiker Tim Dean schreibt: „Before Stonewall, being openly gay usually meant being flamboyant (conforming to the model of gender inversion), whereas sexual liberation ostensibly distengled gender from sexuality, such that one could conform to normative gender expectations while

facial features; sometimes a beard; broad shoulders; developed chest muscles; slim waist, sturdy legs; big genitals; and a luscious butt, which is frequently accentuated by tight pants.

Tom of Finland's drawings didn't only have the function to provoke sexual arousal but they also shaped a gay lifestyle (as did the porn movies of the late seventies).
Men he met in "real life" inspired him to his fantasies, which in return became a model for a gay subculture and community.
Starting from the gay capitals of the US, San Francisco and New York, the "clone look" – a kind of restaging of Tom's pictures, so to speak – conquered the western homo culture. The American queer theorist Tim Dean writes: "Before Stonewall, being openly gay usually meant being flamboyant (conforming to the model of gender inversion), whereas sexual liberation ostensibly disentangled gender from sexuality, such that one could conform to normative gender expectations while nevertheless acknowledging one's non-normative sexual identity." [3]

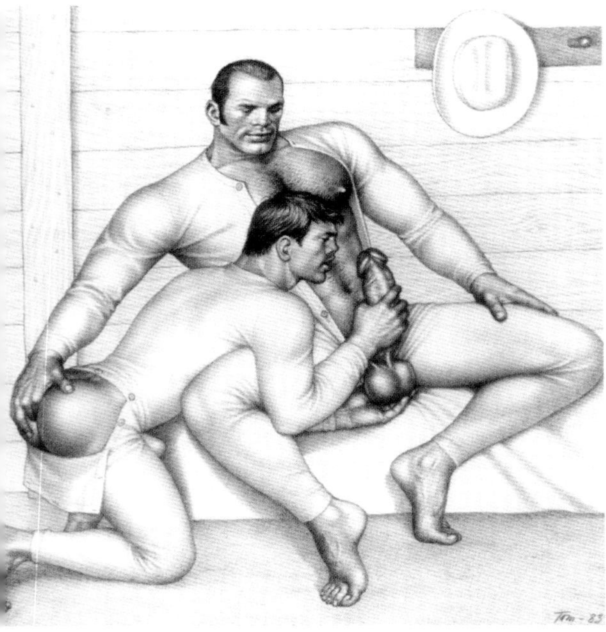

It appears that as Tom matured, so did his subjects •
Es schien, als würden die Männer seiner Zeichnungen
mit ihm reifer und älter werden.

Preparatory drawing • Rohskizze
"I consistently represent masculine beauty. Of course
I do exaggerate the muscles and genitals, for this
is what makes it a dream." • „Ich zeige immer die
männliche Schönheit. Natürlich übertreibe ich dabei
Muskeln und Genitalien, denn das macht es zu
einem Traum." – Tom of Finland

nevertheless acknowledging one's non-normative sexual identity."[3]
Eine Variante des emanzipatorischen Gestus nach
Stonewall war es also, sich als Schwuler seine
Männlichkeit nicht länger absprechen zu lassen,
sondern sie stolz zu feiern. Ohne das Bedürfnis
nach weiterer Problematisierung schreibt Tom of
Finlands Partner Durk Dehner in der Einleitung
zum voluminösen Foto- und Essayband „Tom of
Finland XXL" dementsprechend, dass Toms Zeichnungen „eine vollwertige, gleichberechtigte und
authentische Männlichkeit"[4] repräsentierten.
„Stolz" auf schwule Männlichkeit war in diesem
historischen Kontext der Gegenbegriff zu einer
schamhaften schwulen Position, die sich ihrer
Männlichkeit nicht sicher war. Die Begriffspaare
Stolz und Scham, Sicherheit und Unsicherheit
waren mit einer Reihe weiterer Oppositionen verknüpft, wie *in the closet/out* und privat/politisch.
Bezieht man den euphorischen Befreiungsmoment
der Schwulenbewegung auf die Bilder Tom of
Finlands, lässt sich dieser zunächst so fassen: Die
Aneignung einer „toughen Männlichkeit" erlaub-

One version of the emancipatory gesture after
Stonewall was to protest against the fact that
gay men were denied their masculinity. Now,
they would proudly celebrate it. Accordingly,
without feeling the need to further prob-
lematize this move, Tom of Finland's partner
Durk Dehner writes in the introduction to the
voluminous photo and essay collection *Tom of
Finland XXL*, that Tom's drawings represent "a
full-fledged, equal and authentic masculinity."[4]
"Pride" for one's gay masculinity was in this
historic context the opposite of a shameful
gay position which wasn't confident in its
masculinity. The conceptual pairs of pride and
shame, confidence and insecurity were connected to a series of other oppositions, like in
the closet/out and private/political.

[3] Dean, Tim (2002): „Sameness without Identity". In: *Umbra* 2002, S. 32
[4] Dehner, Durk (2009): „Versuch, den Finnen zu verstehen." In: In:
Hanson, Dian (Hg.), *Tom of Finland XXL*, Köln: Taschen, S. 13

[3] Dean, Tim (2002): "Sameness without Identity". In: *Umbra* 2002, p. 32
[4] Dehner, Durk (2009): "Versuch, den Finnen zu verstehen." In:
Hanson, Dian (ed.), *Tom of Finland XXL*, Köln: Taschen, p. 13

te eine Form der Selbstvergewisserung durch ein stabiles Geschlechterbild. Wie bis heute innerhalb des sozialen Kosmos vieler Schwulenbars und -clubs kommen auch hier Alter und Krankheit nicht vor; gibt es in Toms Universum nur „pure Energie und ewige Jugend".[5] Das schwule Begehren wird in diesem Kontext durch eine rigide Zulassungspolitik bestimmt: Wer in die von Tom visualisierten Männerclubs aufgenommen werden will, muss einiges zu bieten haben.
Bewertet man die Erfindung des Schwulen in den Sex-Zeichnungen Tom of Finlands politisch, lauert hier natürlich der Vorwurf der Kollaboration: Im Feiern normativer Männlichkeiten machen Homos gemeinsame Sache mit Heteros, anstatt die queeren Potentiale ihres Andersseins auch durch alternative Bilder von Männlichkeit – mit denen zum Beispiel die Tunte experimentiert – zu verwirklichen. So gesehen handelt es sich bei den Bildern Tom of Finlands auf den ersten Blick um eine Form von Genderkonformismus, in dem sich auch der Wunsch nach Teilhabe an patriarchaler Macht ausdrückt.

Es gibt aber auch einen guten Grund dafür, zu bezweifeln, dass Tom of Finlands Bilder trotz ihrer aufdringlichen Virilität lediglich Vorgaben von Heteromännlichkeit imitieren und bestätigen. Denn was es zu sehen gibt, ist ja weniger eine „natürliche", sondern eben eine unwahrscheinliche Männlichkeit. Tom of Finland bietet dem Blick nicht nur überproportionierte Schwänze, sondern seine übertriebene Darstellung sämtlicher sekundärer Geschlechtsmerkmale lässt den männlichen Körper insgesamt zu einer Art Schwellkörper werden. Eine solche Art der Inszenierung von Hypermaskulinität ist von queeren Theoretikern oft als eine Form von Parodie interpretiert worden: Ein Körper, der im allzu plakativen Ausstellen seiner Geschlechtsmerkmale auch seinen Inszenierungscharakter zugibt und damit die „Unnatürlichkeit" seines Genders. Ein „echter" Mann zu sein ist harte Arbeit wie jeder Besucher eines Fitness-Studios weiß.
Das Problem einer solchen queerthoretischen Betrachtungsweise von Tom of Finlands Bildern ist nur: gerade sexuelle Szenarien sind nun eben jene Anlässe, bei denen man die Mühen der eigenen Geschlechtsaneignung, und damit die Machbarkeit von Geschlecht, eben gerade nicht zugeben

If you relate the euphoric moment of liberation of the gay movement to the work of Tom of Finland, this moment can be described as follows: Assuming a "tough masculinity" allows a kind of self-assurance through a stable gender image. Just like today within the social cosmos of many gay bars and clubs, in Tom's universe there's nothing but "pure energy and infinite youth" [5]. Here too, aging and illness make no appearance. Gay desire is framed in this context through a rigid admissions policy: Those who want to be accepted to the men's clubs that Tom visualized must have plenty to offer.
If you evaluate the invention of the gay man in the sexual drawings of Tom of Finland politically, an accusation of collaboration lurks beneath the surface: In celebrating normative masculinity, gays connive with the straights, instead of realizing the queer potential of their otherness through alternative images – like the ones that drag queens experiment with, for example. At first glance, Tom of Finland's pictures seem to be about gender conformity, in which the desire to participate in patriarchal power is expressed.

But there's also a good reason to doubt that Tom of Finland's drawings only imitate and confirm guidelines of heterosexual masculinity regardless of their pushy virility, because what is shown is less a "natural" but rather an improbable masculinity. Tom of Finland doesn't only offer humongous dicks to the viewer but his exaggerated presentation of all secondary sexual characteristics turns the whole male body into a kind of Corpus Cavernosum. Such a display of hyper-masculinity has often been read as parody by queer theorists: A body which admits its staged nature and with it the "unnaturalness" of its gender through a striking display of its sexual characteristics. To be a "real" man is hard work as every visitor of a gym knows!
The only problem of such a queer-theoretical approach to Tom of Finland's pictures is that sexual scenarios in particular are exactly those occasions at which you're not allowed to admit the struggle of your own acquisition of gender and its general feasibility. So

5, 6 Paglia, Camille (2009): „Die Suche nach Sex bei Tom of Finland." In: Hanson, Dian (Hg.), *Tom of Finland XXL*, Köln: Taschen, S. 85

5,6 Paglia, Camille (2009): "Die Suche nach Sex bei Tom of Finland." In: Hanson, Dian (ed.), *Tom of Finland XXL*, Köln: Taschen, p. 85

darf! Von wegen Parodie – hier gibt es nichts zu lachen! So hat der US-amerikanische Queer-Theoretiker Leo Bersani darauf hingewiesen, dass die offensichtlich erkennbare Imitation sexueller Attraktivität unter schwulen Männern ein totaler Turn-off ist. Während die Maskerade die Attraktivität von Frauen erhöht und ein Spiel der Verführung einleiten kann, muss die männliche Maske eine Form der Ernsthaftigkeit und Echtheit behaupten, um sexuell zu funktionieren. Wegen dieser erotisch-ernsthaften Behauptung von Männlichkeit kann man bei schwulen Sexszenen, wie Tom of Finland sie zeichnet, eigentlich nicht von einer Parodie im Sinne eines permanenten Zitierens und Verfehlens von Geschlecht sprechen, wie Judith Butler es analysiert hat. Die Männer bei Tom of Finland beherrschen ihre Rollen perfekt, in ihrer maskulinen Eleganz unterlaufen ihnen keine Patzer. Fehlzitieren im Sinne einer Verfehlung von Geschlechtsidentität, wie sie etwa Drag Queens kultivieren – als „falsche" Frauen – und dadurch ihren Ruhm vermehren, kommt hier nicht vor.

Und dennoch hat Bersani mit dem Hinweis auf die Notwendigkeit sexueller Ernsthaftigkeit unter Männern in Bezug auf Tom of Finland nicht ganz recht. Denn anders als die sexuellen Fantasien bei Jean Genet und Kenneth Anger finden Toms Männer ihre Ermächtigung auch nicht in einem Kult des Bösen. So finster sie in ihren Fetisch-klamotten auch wirken mögen: Ihre Drohgebärden stehen erkennbar im Dienste des Sexuellen. In Tom of Finlands Kosmos wird schwule Existenz fast ausschließlich auf sexuelle Existenz reduziert. Seine potenten Kerle können und wollen immer, von „Erschöpfung und Zögern keine Spur"[6]. Das Leben ist eine nicht endende Orgie. Eine Welt, die ausschließlich von sexuell zur Verfügung stehenden *Clones* mit ihren übertrieben männlichen Körperformen bevölkert wird. Die Idealisierung kanonischer Männlichkeit ist gepaart mit permanenter sexueller Bereitschaft.
Im Kontext eines andauernden homosexuellen Begehrens kollabieren hier Verlangen und Identität im Bild des *Clone*: Über strenge Dresscodes und Bodybuilding machten Schwule sich zu den Männern, die sie begehrten.
Und das ist ein entscheidender Punkt, denn gegenüber der Darstellung von Heterosex hat die Darstellung schwuler Sexualität wie in den Finland-Zeichnungen damit einen strategischen Vorteil: Auch wenn es naiv wäre zu glauben,

much for parody – gender is no laughing matter! That's why the American queer theorist Leo Bersani pointed out that an obvious attempt at performing sexual attractiveness is a huge turn-off for gay men. While the confession of gender as a masquerade can increase the attractiveness of women and can initiate a game of seduction, the mask of masculinity has to claim a kind of seriousness and realness in order to work sexually. Because of this serious statement of masculinity, you can't actually talk about a parody in the sense of a permanent citing and missing of gender in regard to the gay sex scenes Tom of Finland draws, the way that Judith Butler analyzed it in *Gender Trouble*. Tom of Finland's men play their roles perfectly, no sexual blunders occur to them in their masculine elegance. Falsely citing in the sense of a missing of one's gender, like drag queens cultivate it – as "fake" women – and through which they increase their fame, doesn't happen here.

And still, Bersani wasn't quite right when he talked about the importance of sexual sincerity in regard to Tom of Finland. After all, his men were also different from those that inhabit the sexual fantasies of Jean Genet and Kenneth Anger. For Tom's men didn't find their power in a cult of evil. As sinister as they might appear in their fetish clothes, their intimidating postures are obviously performed in the service of sexual pleasure. In Tom of Finland's world, gay existence is almost exclusively defined by sexual existence. His potent men are always hot and horny, "without a trace of exhaustion or hesitation." (Paglia 2009: 85)[6] Life is nothing but a never-ending orgy. A world populated by clones, brimming with muscles and masculinity, in a constant state of sexual willingness. The idealization of canonical masculinity is paired with permanent readiness for the next sexual experience.
In the context of this perpetual homosexual lust, identity and desire collapse in the picture of the clone: homosexuals, through rigid dress codes and bodybuilding, have sculpted themselves to be the men that they are longing for. And that's important because compared with the representation of straight sex the representation of gay sexuality in Tom of Finland's

soziale Machtgefälle spielten z.B. in der pornografischen Darstellungen unter Männern keine Rolle,[7] liefert das Genre des Schwulenpornos auf den ersten Blick eben keine direkte Analogie zwischen sexuellen und sozialen Positionen, die im Heteroporno über anatomische Unterschiede – Männlichkeit und Weiblichkeit – naturalisiert werden: In der Darstellung von schwulem Sex sind die Rollen potenziell austauschbar, jeder kann beim Sex aktiv oder passiv sein. Daraus beziehen Toms sexuelle Zeichnungen ihr Potenzial: Die Bottoms können kurz darauf als Tops auftreten und umgekehrt. „In seinen Zeichnungen wechselten dominante und unterwürfige Partner vorbehaltlos ihre Rollen und lebten damit vor, dass auf der Spielwiese der Sexualität jeder frei nach seiner Lust und Laune alle Rollen einnehmen kann."[8]

Toms lüsterne Power-Bottoms können es gar nicht erwarten, dass sie rangenommen werden, ihre Libido ist der phallischen in keiner Weise untergeordnet. Die Sexzeichnungen folgen einer doppelten Perspektive: Sie zeigen die Lust, beim Sex aktiv zu sein genauso offensiv wie die Lust, passiv zu sein. Der schwule Blick ist anders als der heterosexuell-männliche nicht nur auf die phallische Aufgabe der Penetration fokussiert. Das heißt aber, dass die Sexualisierung des Körpers, der sich doch so sehr bemüht, seine Stabilität unter Beweis zu stellen, durch die Austauschbarkeit der Positionen beim schwulen Sex eine spezifisch schwule Art von schwuler Männlichkeit hervorbringt. Der subtile Humor in den Bildern Tom of Finlands scheint weniger einem Bewusstsein über die Theatralität der sexuellen Rollen geschuldet zu sein, als vielmehr einer unbekümmerten Darstellung wilder Obszönitäten, die auf dem sexuellen Rollenwechsel basiert.[9] Ist es nicht diese exhibitionistische Verschwörung, die sich im Grinsen der Tom-of-Finland-Männer zeigt? Und den Betrachter einlädt, es ihnen gleich zu tun?

drawings has a strategic advantage: Though it would be naive to think that social imbalances of power don't matter in the presentation of sexuality amongst men,[7] obviously gay sex images do not offer a direct analogy between sexual and social positions which are naturalized in straight porn through anatomical differences – masculinity and femininity. In the representation of gay sex, the roles have become potentially interchangeable, every man can be active or passive during sex. From this Tom's drawings derive their power: The bottoms of Tom of Finland can shortly after appear as tops as well as the other way round. "In his drawings dominant and submissive partners unreservedly changed roles and with this they proved that on the playground of sexuality everyone can take on all roles when they feel like it."[8]

Tom's libidinous power-bottoms can't wait to be taken; their libido is in no way inferior to the phallic one. The drawings follow a double perspective: They show the pleasure of being active during sex as relentlessly as the pleasure of being passive. The gay glance, in contrast to the straight glance, is not only focused on the phallic penetration. But this also means that the sexual charging of the body, which makes a great effort to prove its own stability, produces a specifically gay form of masculinity through the interchangeability of positions. The subtle humor in Tom of Finland's work is less due to an awareness of the theatricality of sexual roles than to the easygoing presentation of obscenity based on the sexual change of roles.[9] Isn't it this exhibitionistic conspiracy which is obvious in the grin of Tom of Finland's men? And an invitation to do the same?

---

[7] Dieser Aspekt kommt beispielsweise im Kontext osteuropäischer Jungs zum Tragen, deren Fetischisierung unter anderem das schwule Porno-Label *Bel Ami* forciert.

[8] Dehner, Durk (2009), S. 13

[9] Der Humor von Tom of Finlands Comic-Strips hat auch eine erzählerische Dimension. Zum Beispiel lässt Tom in den „Kake"-Comics einen „Einbrecher" durchs Fenster steigen, der erst den Jungen rannimmt. Die beiden werden dann vom Vater überrascht und dieser hat nichts Besseres zu tun, als den Einbrecher zu ficken, während sein Sohn dazu masturbiert.

[7] This aspect takes effect in the context of Eastern European boys whose fetishizing accelerates among others the gay porn label *Bel Ami*.

[8] Dehner, Durk (2009), p. 13

[9] The humor of Tom of Finland's comic strips also has a narrative dimension. For example, Tom lets a "burglar" climb through a window in the "Kake" comics who then first screws the boy, before they're surprised by the father who has nothing better to do than to fuck the burglar while his son masturbates to it.

Translation: Sunita Sukhana

Artist Residencies

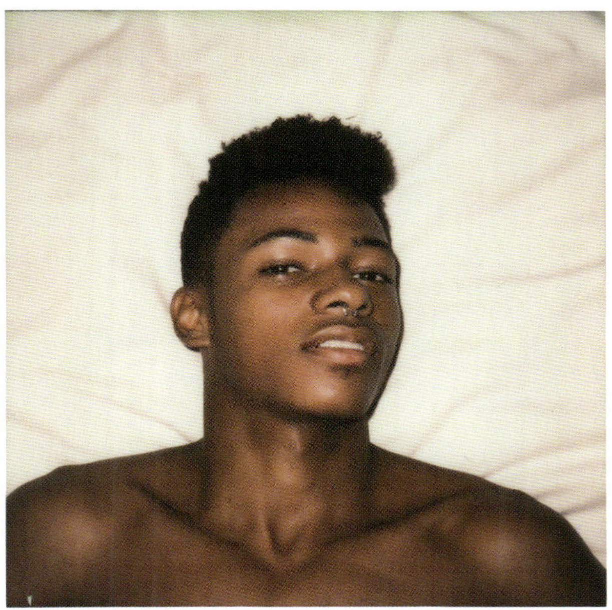

STUART SANDFORD

The artist-in-residence program has developed in a very organic way. The Tom of Finland Foundation recognized that young artists and others, who are established, were making profound discoveries in their exploration of ToFF's museum, archives and library. It took place on its own with the simple act of making the past accessible to the present through exposure. It was something of which the Foundation was always aware and wanted to make the experience more intensive. The Foundation started inviting artists to come and spend several months at TOM House.

Künstlerresidenzen

Das Artist-in-Residence-Programm hat sich sehr organisch entwickelt. Die Tom of Finland Foundation hat immer wieder erlebt, dass sowohl junge als auch etablierte Künstler für sie wichtige Entdeckungen machen konnten, wenn sie ToFF's Museum, das Archiv und die Bibliothek erkundeten. Das geschieht quasi ganz von selbst, einfach, indem ihnen die Vergangenheit zugänglich gemacht wird. Das war der Foundation immer bewusst, und sie wollte dieses Erlebnis intensiver gestalten. Sie hat deshalb damit begonnen, Künstler einzuladen, jeweils einige Monate im TOM House zu verbringen.

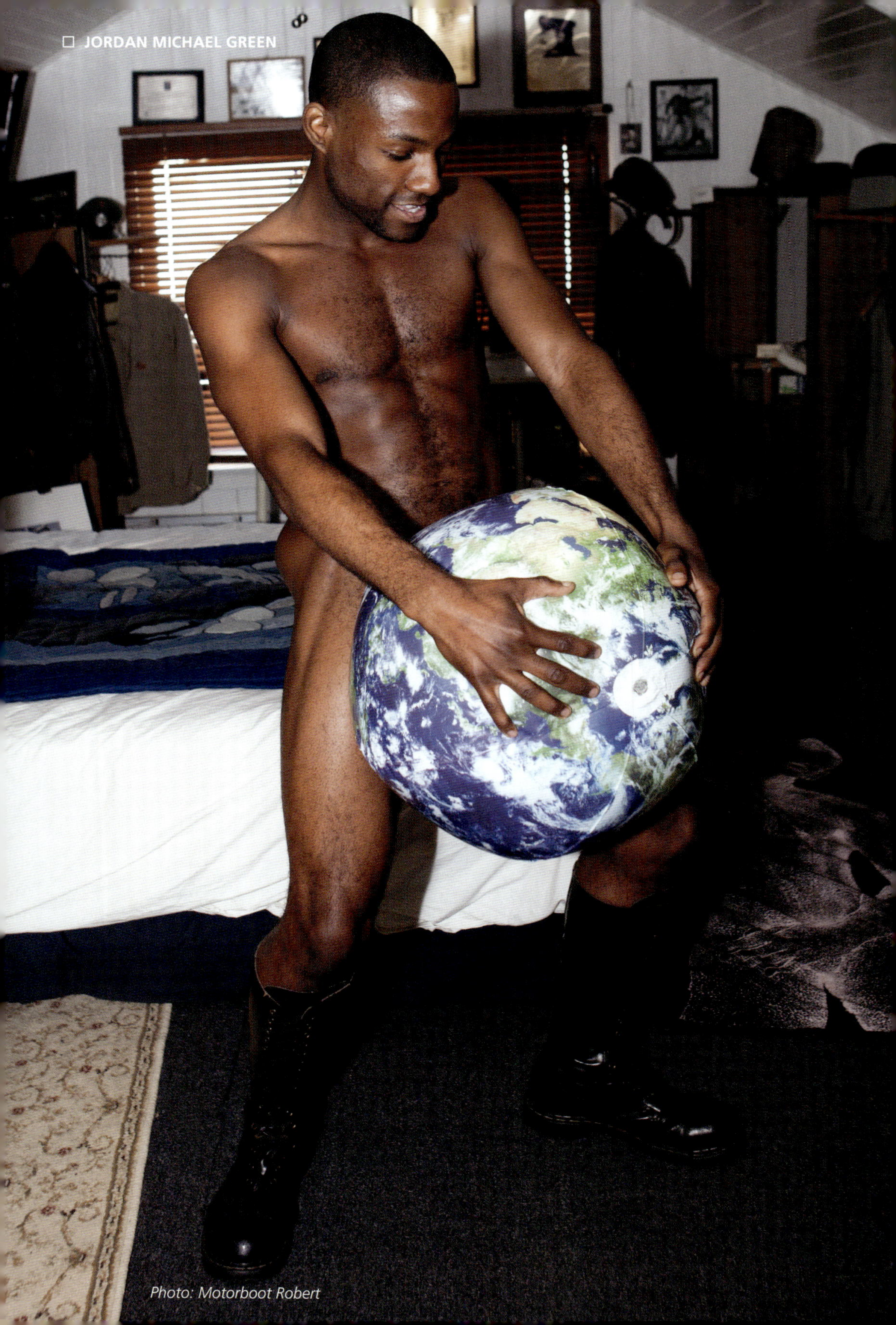

JORDAN MICHAEL GREEN
Photo: Motorboot Robert

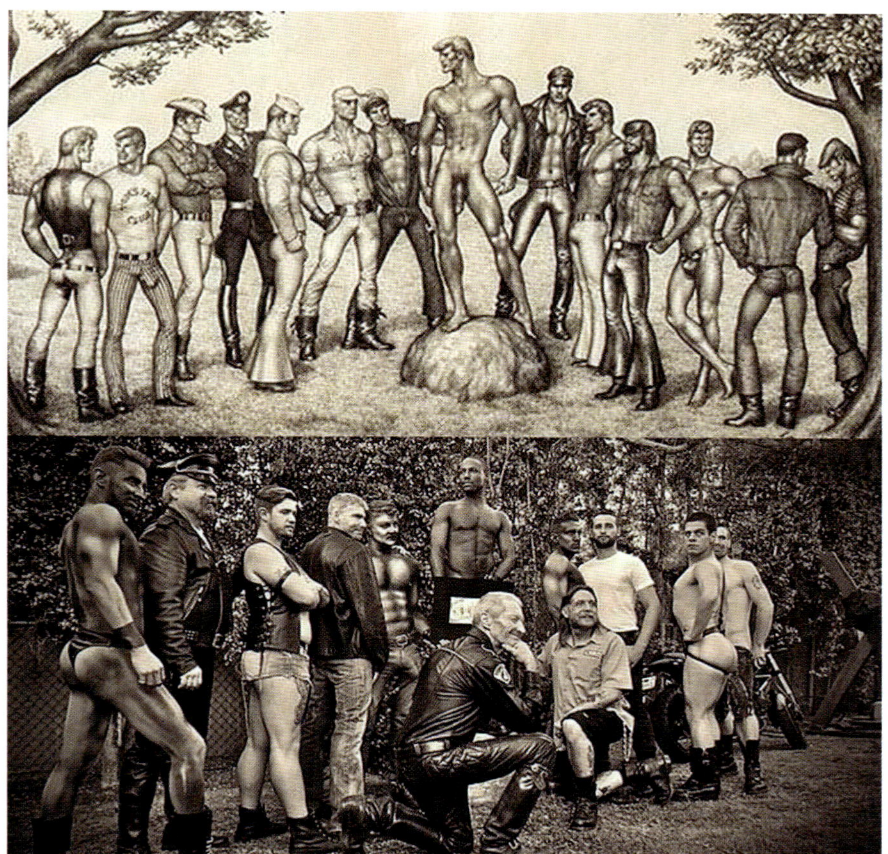

Drawing: Tom of Finland. Photo: Luis Paul Canales. Jordan coordinated Tableaux Vivant Deux in 2014

Time flies when you're having fun. During my artist-in-residency, I aimed not only to focus on the cocks that passed the welcome mat, but the creativity I knew that would influence my artistry, and help build a clear, decisive point of view. I wanted to add color – literally and figuratively. I wanted to eat, sleep and breathe art. I gorged myself on talent from all over the world, and made people smile. Whether hosting the yearly awards ceremony, entertaining at the holiday party, or conceiving live performances, I wanted to expand and allow us to think about where we have come from and where we can go. I felt involved and a part of something I'll always know as my family. My home is TOM House.

Wie die Zeit vergeht, wenn man Spaß hat! Ich hatte mir vorgenommen, mich während meiner Künstlerresidenz nicht nur auf die Schwänze der Männer zu konzentrieren, die das TOM House besuchten, sondern auch auf die Kunst. Sie sollte meine Kreativität anregen und mich dabei unterstützen, einen eigenen künstlerischen Standpunkt zu entwickeln. Ich wollte Farbe hinzufügen – im wörtlichen und im übertragenen Sinne. Ich wollte essen, schlafen und Kunst atmen. Ich habe mich von den Künstlern aus der ganzen Welt inspirieren lassen und die Leute zum Lächeln gebracht – sei es als Gastgeber der jährlichen Preisverleihung, als Unterhalter auf der Weihnachtsfeier oder bei der Konzeption von Live-Auftritten. Ich wollte dazu anregen, darüber nachzudenken, woher wir kommen und wohin wir gehen. Ich wurde Teil einer Gruppe, die ich immer als meine Familie ansehen werde. Das TOM House ist zu meinem Zuhause geworden.
– Jordan Michael Green

Jordan's residency had a focus on Tom's evolving relationship with his Black men. Jordan created public, engaging events and is still working on Tom's unfinished story Black Magic. *It is in the plans to develop it into a book, or maybe a short film.*

Jordans Künstlerresidenz konzentrierte sich auf die Beziehung von Tom zu seinen schwarzen Männern. Jordan kreierte öffentliche, mitreißende Events und arbeitet immer noch an Toms unvollendeter Geschichte Black Magic. *Es ist geplant, ein Buch oder vielleicht sogar einen Kurzfilm aus diesem Material zu erstellen.*
– Durk Dehner

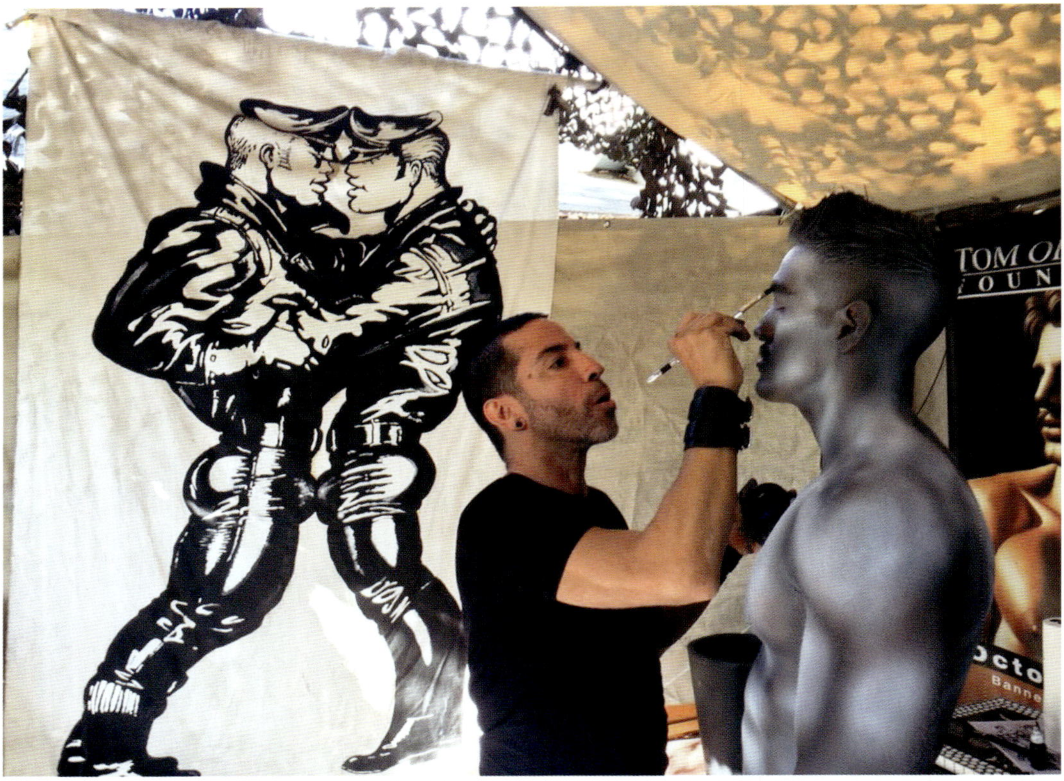

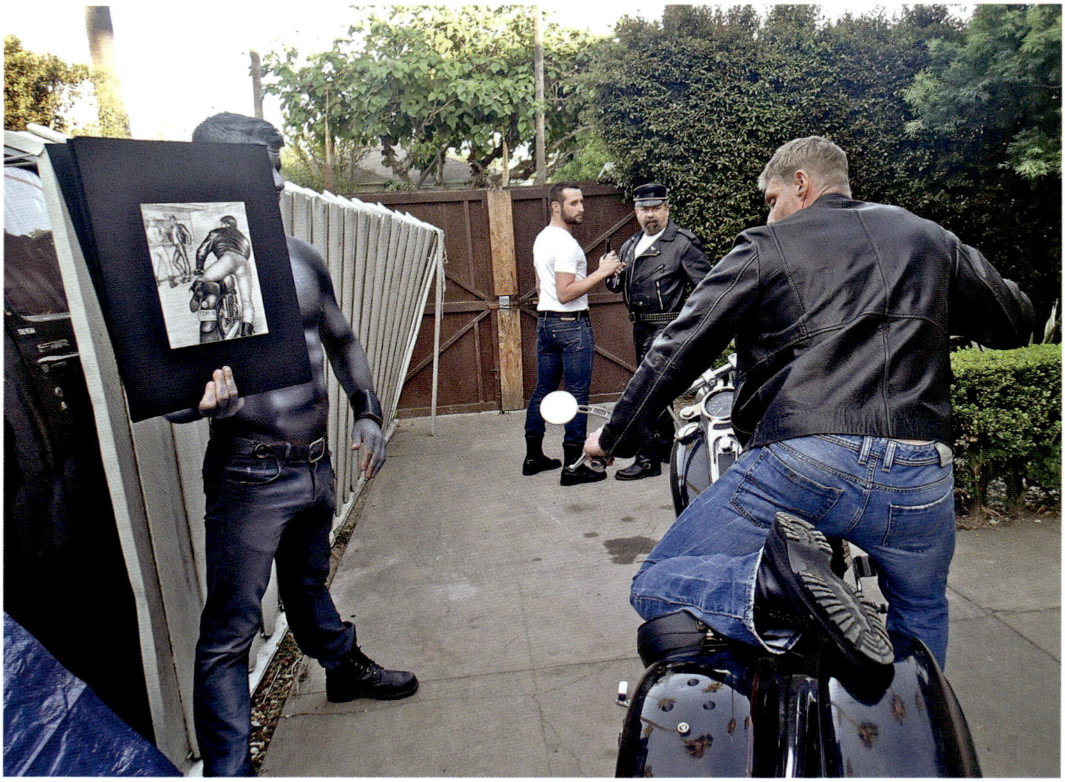

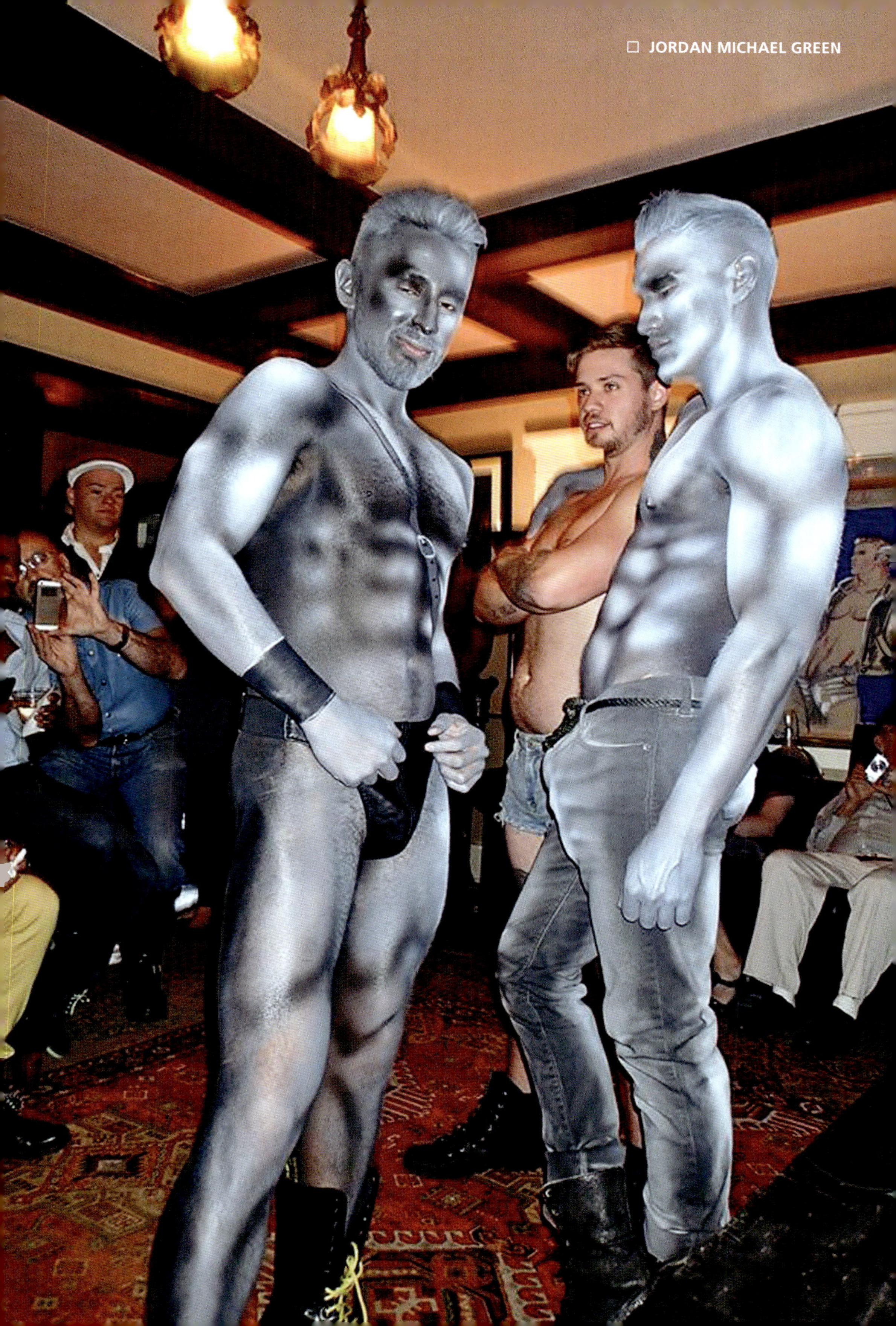

JORDAN MICHAEL GREEN

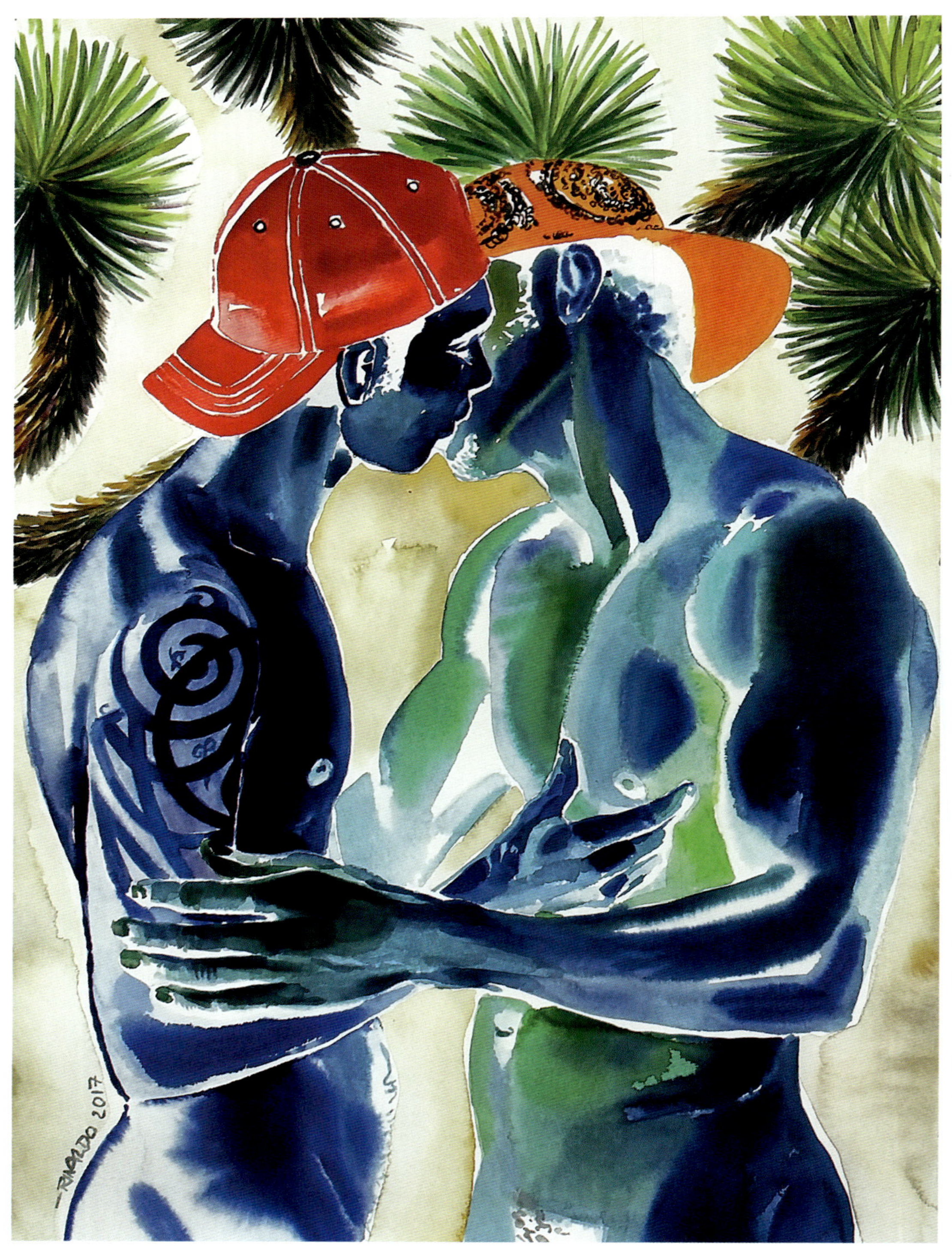

RINALDO 2017

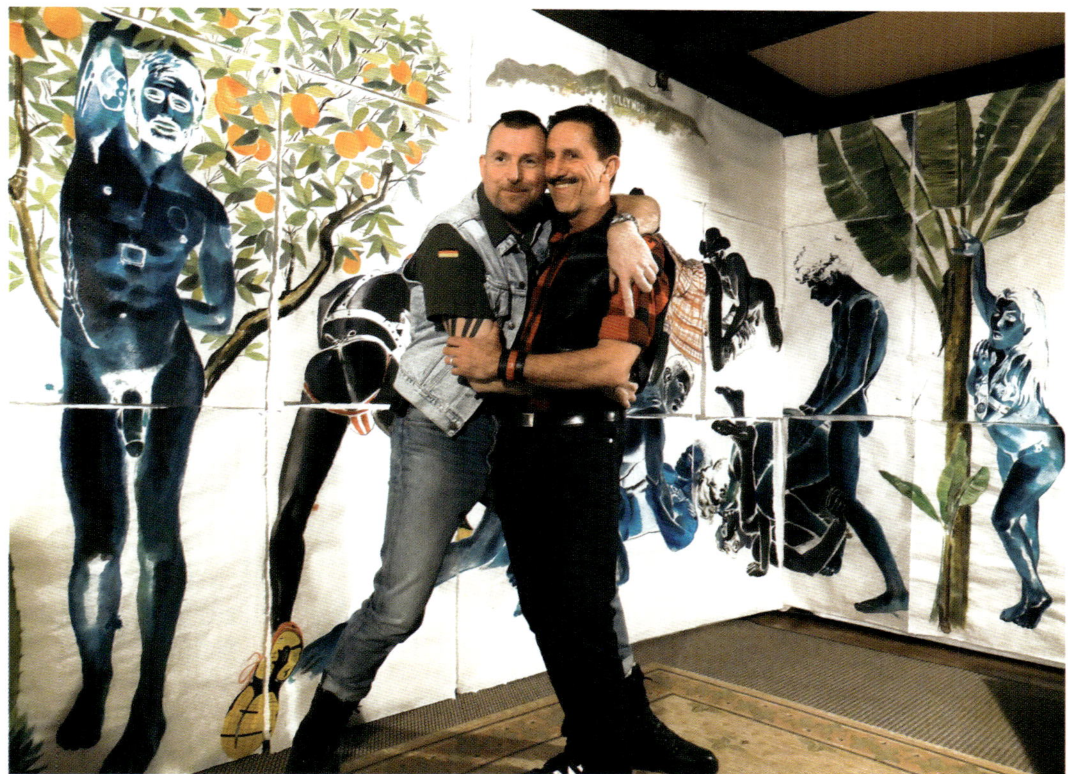

Frank Tepel and Rinaldo Hopf, TOM House 2017. Photo: Mark Timothy Hayward

Pleasure Park

Als ich die Einladung erhielt, für einige Monate im TOM House zu arbeiten, beschloss ich, als Hommage an Tom eine Orgien-Szene zu malen. TOM House ist ein Tempel für Gott Phallus, dem hier ohne jede Scheu und Scham lustvoll gehuldigt wird, ein Kult, dem man sich kaum entziehen kann. Auch der große subtropische Garten mit seinen Orangenbäumen und Bananenstauden ist ein schwuler Lustgarten mit allem Drum und Dran. Inspiriert von Toms Werken, dem Haus und Garten und den außergewöhnlichen Bewohnern, sowie der unmittelbaren Nachbarschaft Hollywoods schuf ich ein Orgien-Panorama im Cinemascope-Format auf Dutzenden handgeschöpften chinesischen Papieren. Unter den Bewohnern und Gästen fand ich attraktive Modelle, daneben benutzte ich Bildmaterial aus dem Internet. Da ich meistens im Garten malte, hatte ich die passende Flora und den Hollywood-Schriftzug (in der Ferne) direkt vor Augen.

When I received an invitation to work at TOM House for a few months, I decided to paint an orgy scene as a tribute to Tom. TOM House is a temple dedicated to the god Phallus, who is relished without any shyness or shame, a cult that you can hardly escape. Even the large subtropical garden with its orange and banana trees is a gay pleasure park with everything included. Inspired by Tom's works, the house with its subtropical garden and the extraordinary inhabitants, as well as the immediate neighborhood of Hollywood, I created an orgy panorama in cinemascope format on dozens of hand-crafted Chinese papers. Among the residents and guests I found attractive models, additionally I used images from the Internet. Since I mostly painted in the garden, I had the right flora and the Hollywood sign (in the distance) right in front of my eyes.

– Rinaldo Hopf

MARK TIMOTHY HAYWARD
David of the Oranges

For RH

What Goliath did you slay
to initiate the ritual?
This hero-magic soaks through me;
sumi ink bleeds beyond Mulberry paper
to absorbent blotters underneath.
I am indelible
joining the fibrous apostle orgy;
glancing over my shoulder
straight in your eye.

That's a sweet ass.
You should fuck it.
You like that cock in your ass?
Oh yeah, fuck it!
Take that big cock!
Yeah --fuck my ass!

Our pleasure is a nation
and this is our national park;
not an untouched landscape,
but one embracing of lovers
so set aside in service
of future generations' sense of awe.

Our economy needs no money.
There is nothing I wouldn't give
you if you asked.
It is my honor to know you.
The six panel Japanese screen
has five pairs of hinges.
The road to the studio winds
down Nichols Canyon.
But when there is no studio,
the painter must improvise.

The painter needs coffee before yoga.
The painter sets the easel aside working directly
on the door to the office full of keys.
Painting on the door ensures the work has a destination.
Waterproof ink thinned by water is still waterproof.

And then there is the matter of the orange trees
defying the coldest wettest winter;
sinking roots deep in the frigid hillside.
Despite our best efforts
the hill migrates west.
For all its upheaval
it just wants is to be low and flat,
primed for the next geologic event
that launches ancient beaches
back to the tops of hills double lined
with Mexican Fan Palms weeping fronds in high winds.

Viewers must piece it together by themselves.
They study the projections one by one
and trace meridians and parallels
that do not describe a spherical world
but one flatter than our ancestors
could have imagined;
quite the opposite of unrequited love.

We are the offering of ass,
butt, sphincter, rectum, rump.
We fuck you while you are fucking.
We double penetrate dick, cock, dong and balls.
We cum on our own stomachs and socks.
These balls produce the sweetest juice
and jealousy in the orange trees of
Southern California

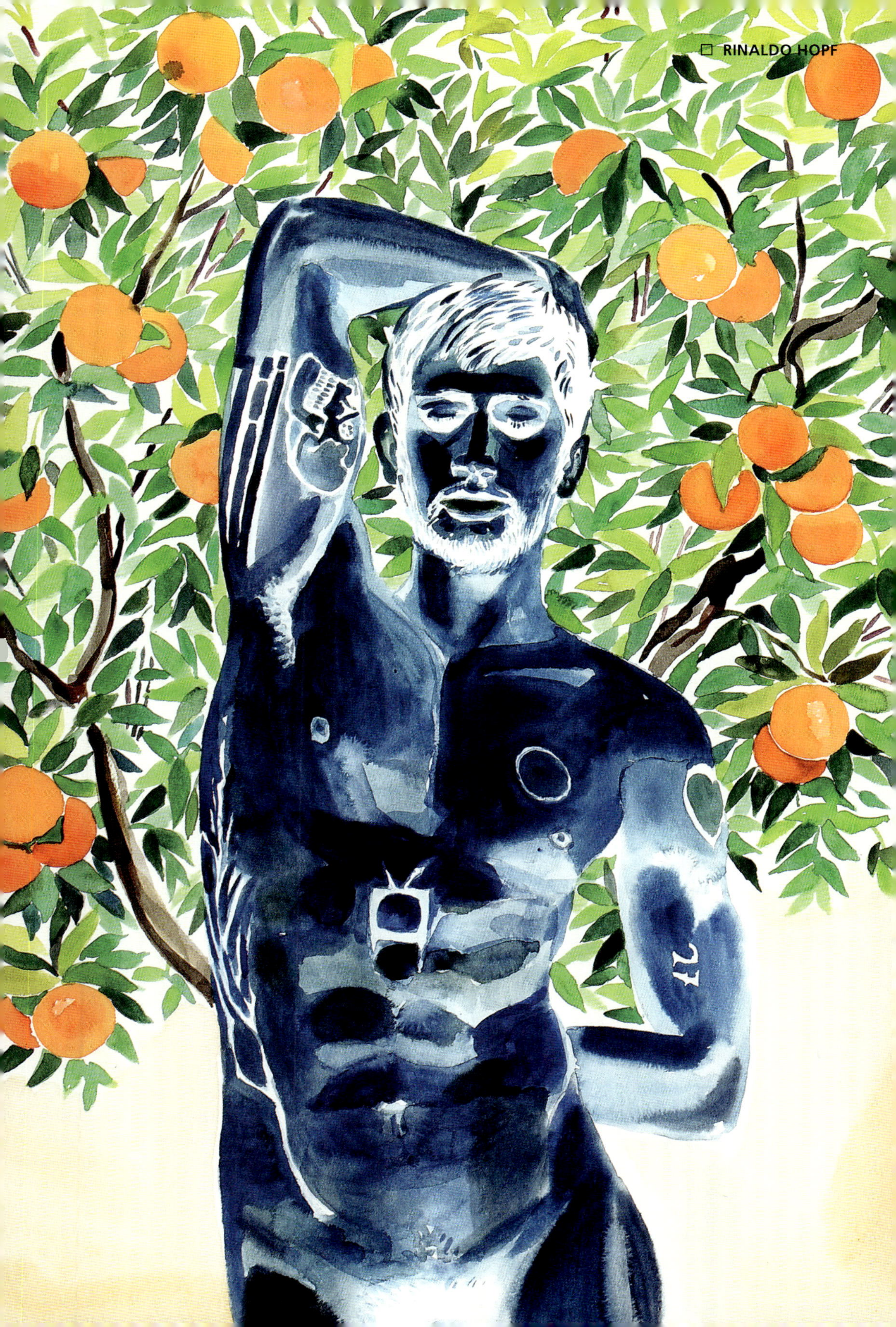
□ RINALDO HOPF

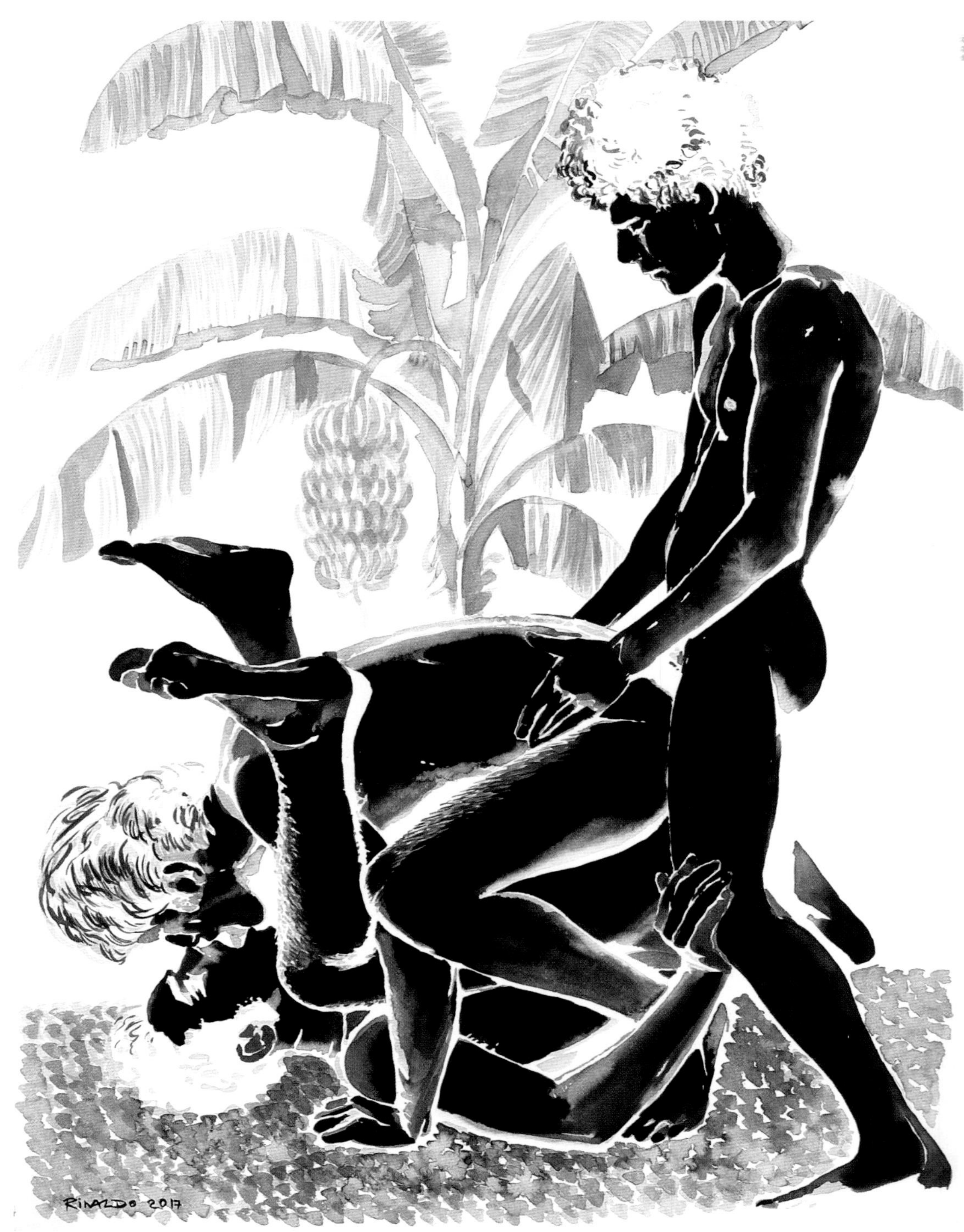
RINALDO 2017

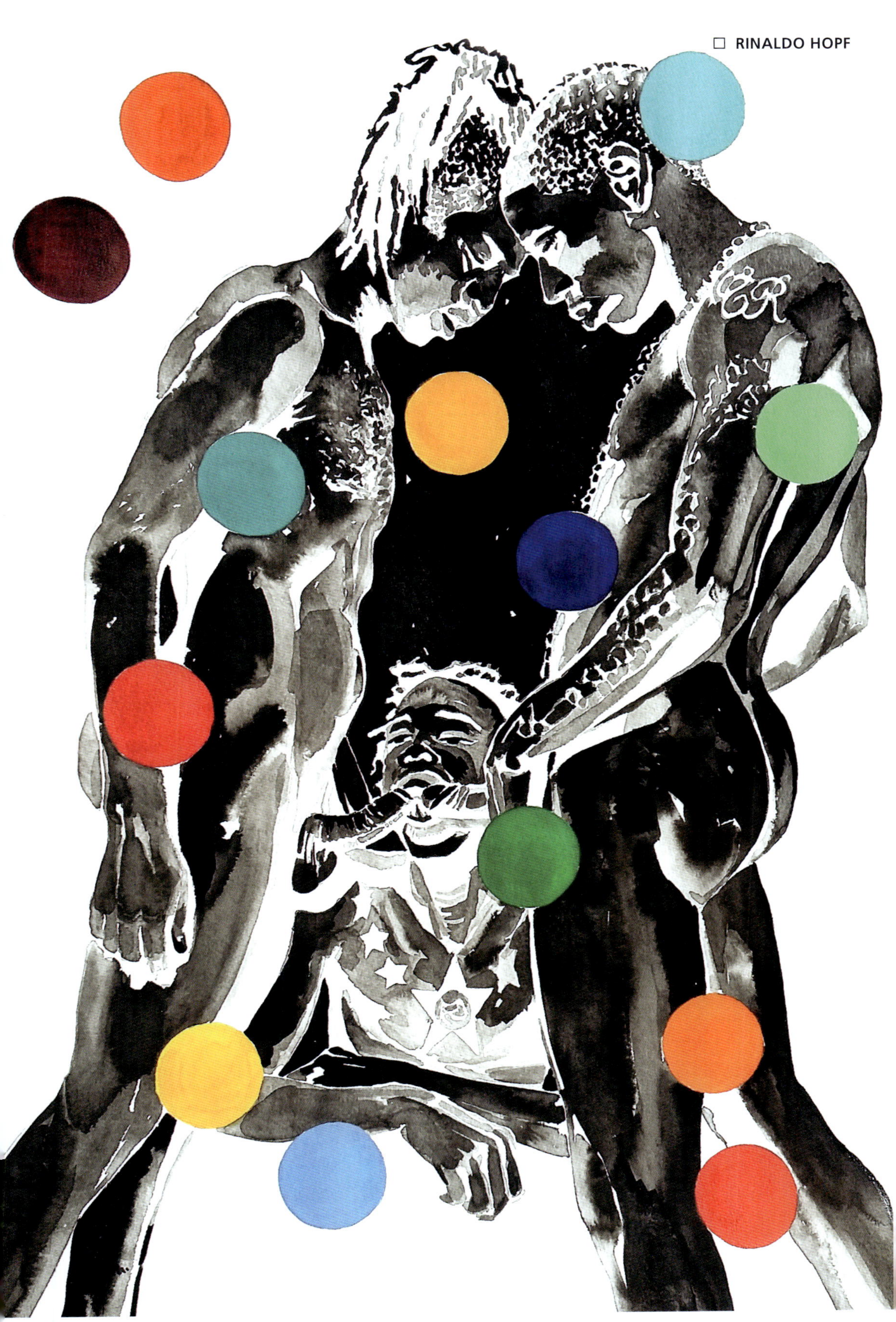

☐ RINALDO HOPF

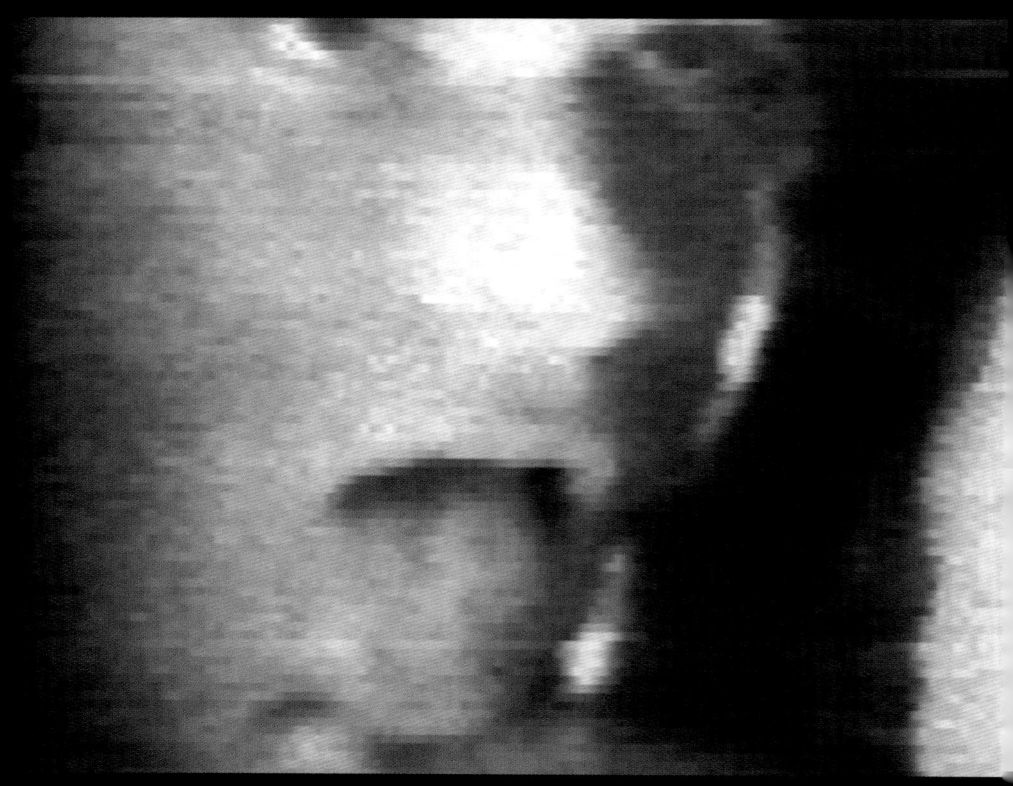

Tom's Flickering Cinerama

A Hallucinatory Tribute to Tom of Finland Foundation

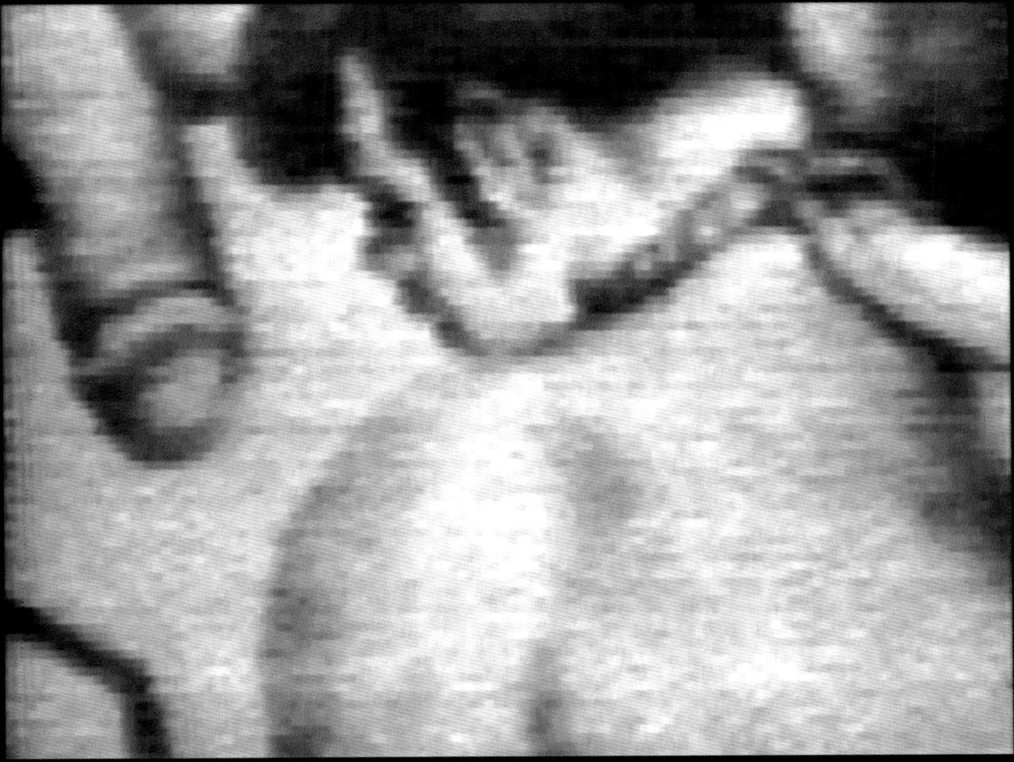

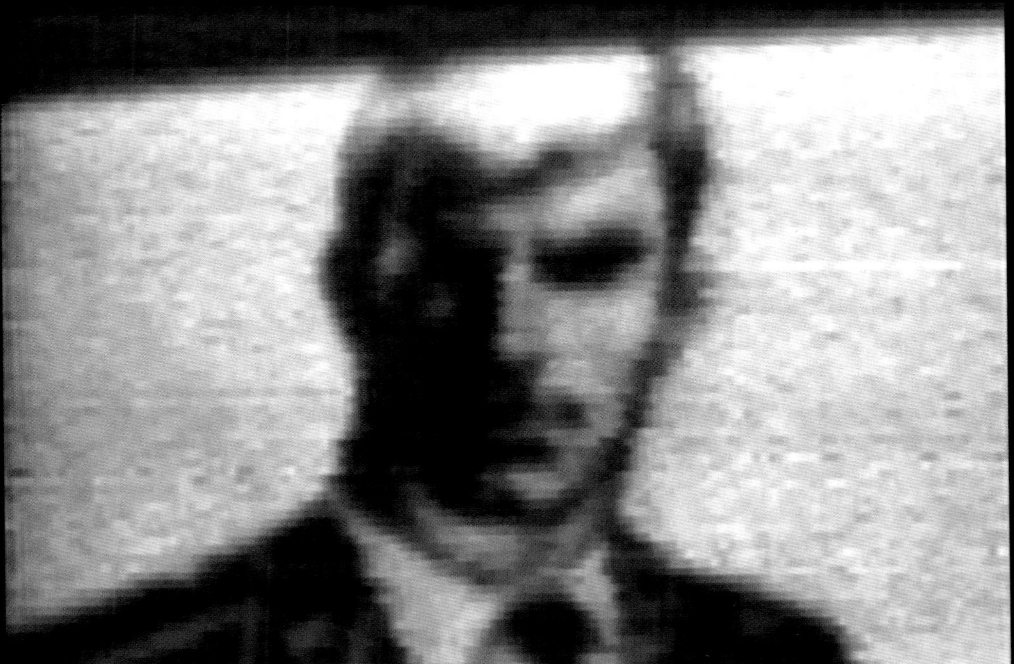

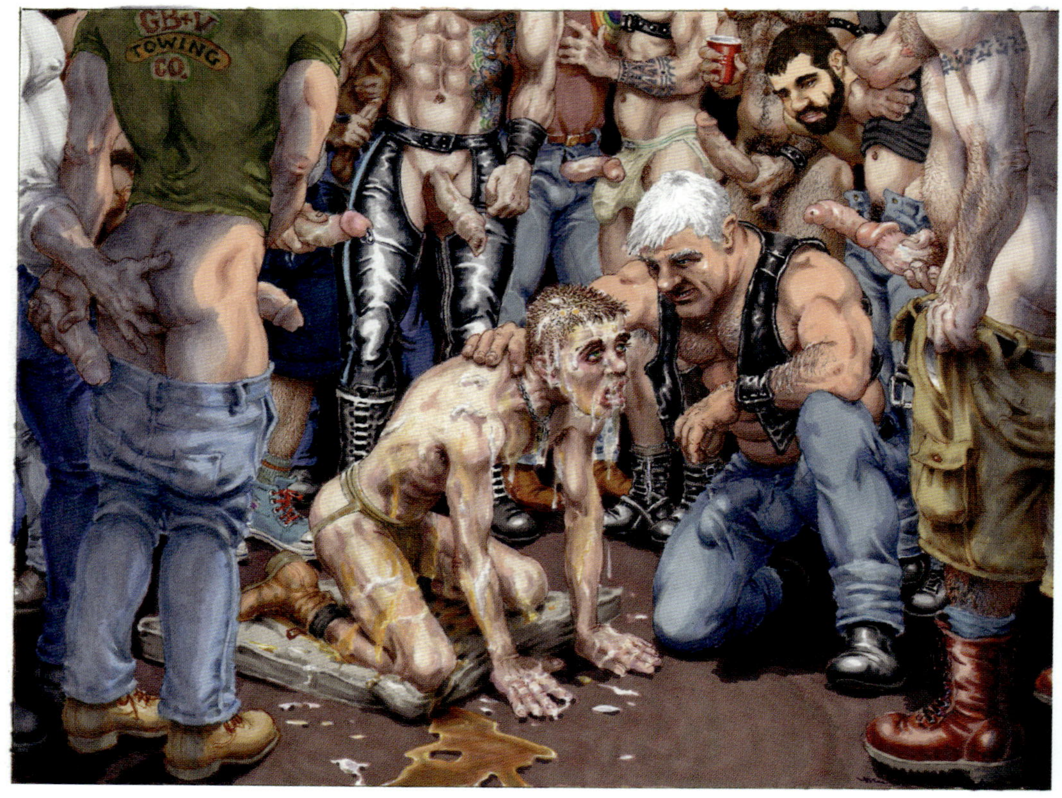

MICHAEL KIRWAN

He was the first artist-in-residence at the Tom of Finland Foundation, and the room he inhabited at TOM House is now officially named "The Kirwan Solarium". In his work, his "everyman" characters are perfect specimens of lust. Everything the artist attempts is far, far from average. He has weathered many storms, always staying true to his trade.

Er war der erste Künstler, der als Artist-in-Residence von der Tom of Finland Foundation eingeladen wurde. Der Raum, den er damals bewohnte, heißt nun offiziell „The Kirwan Solarium". Die Durchschnittstypen in seinen Arbeiten sind mustergültige Beispiele von Begierde. Dabei ist alles, was dieser Künstler macht, weit davon entfernt, nur Durchschnitt zu sein. Er hat viele Stürme überstanden und ist dabei immer seiner Berufung treu geblieben.
– Durk Dehner

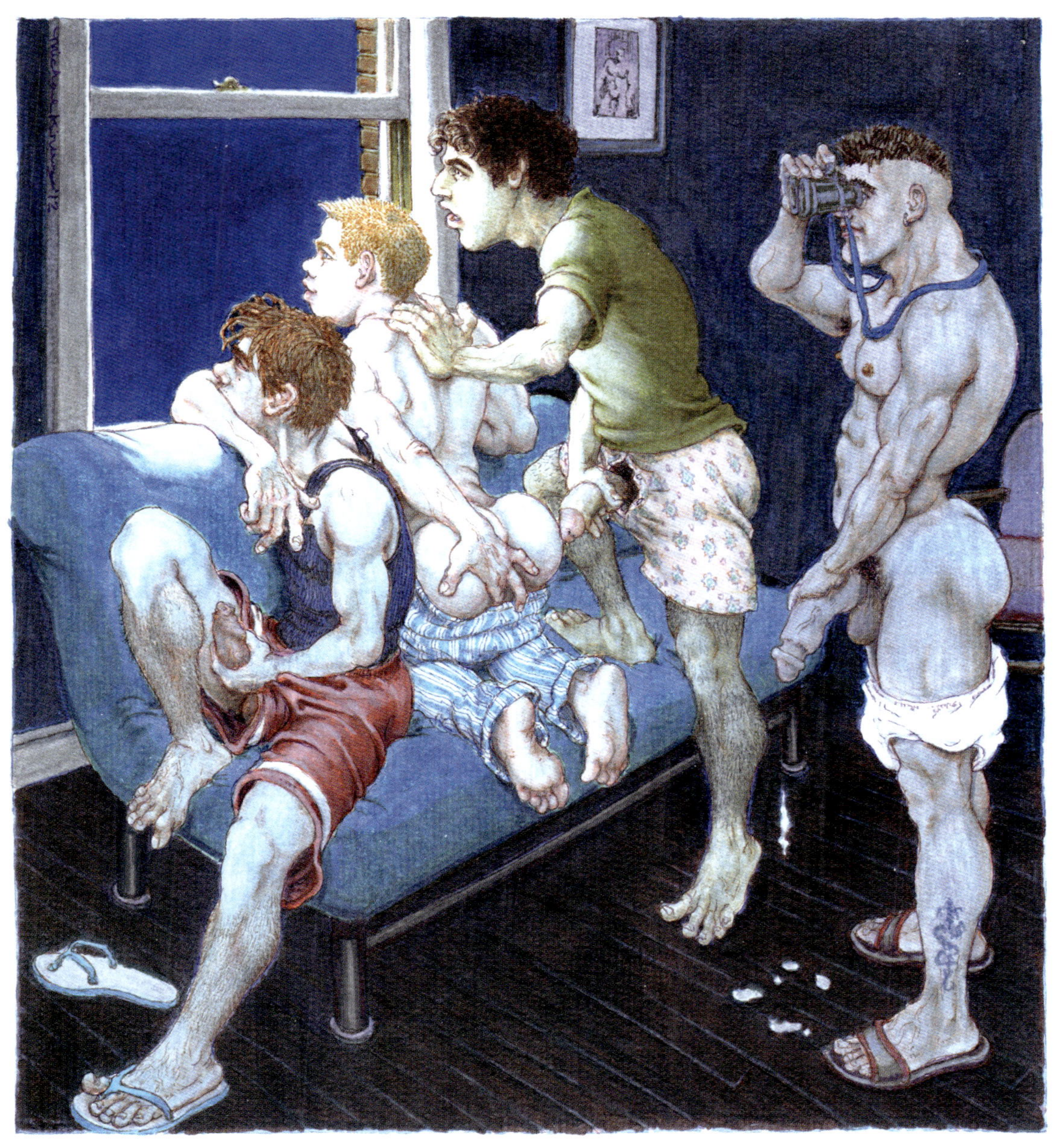

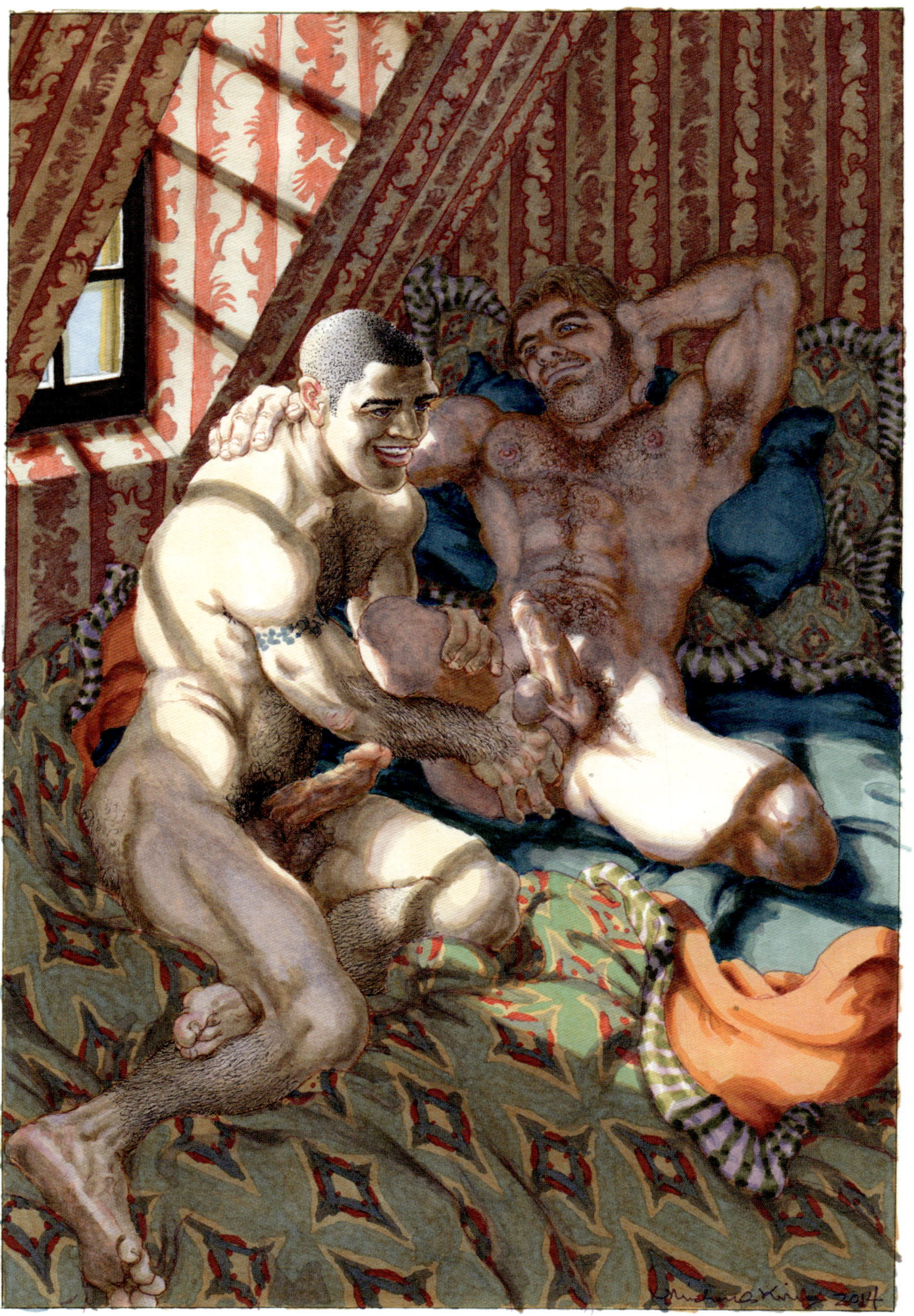

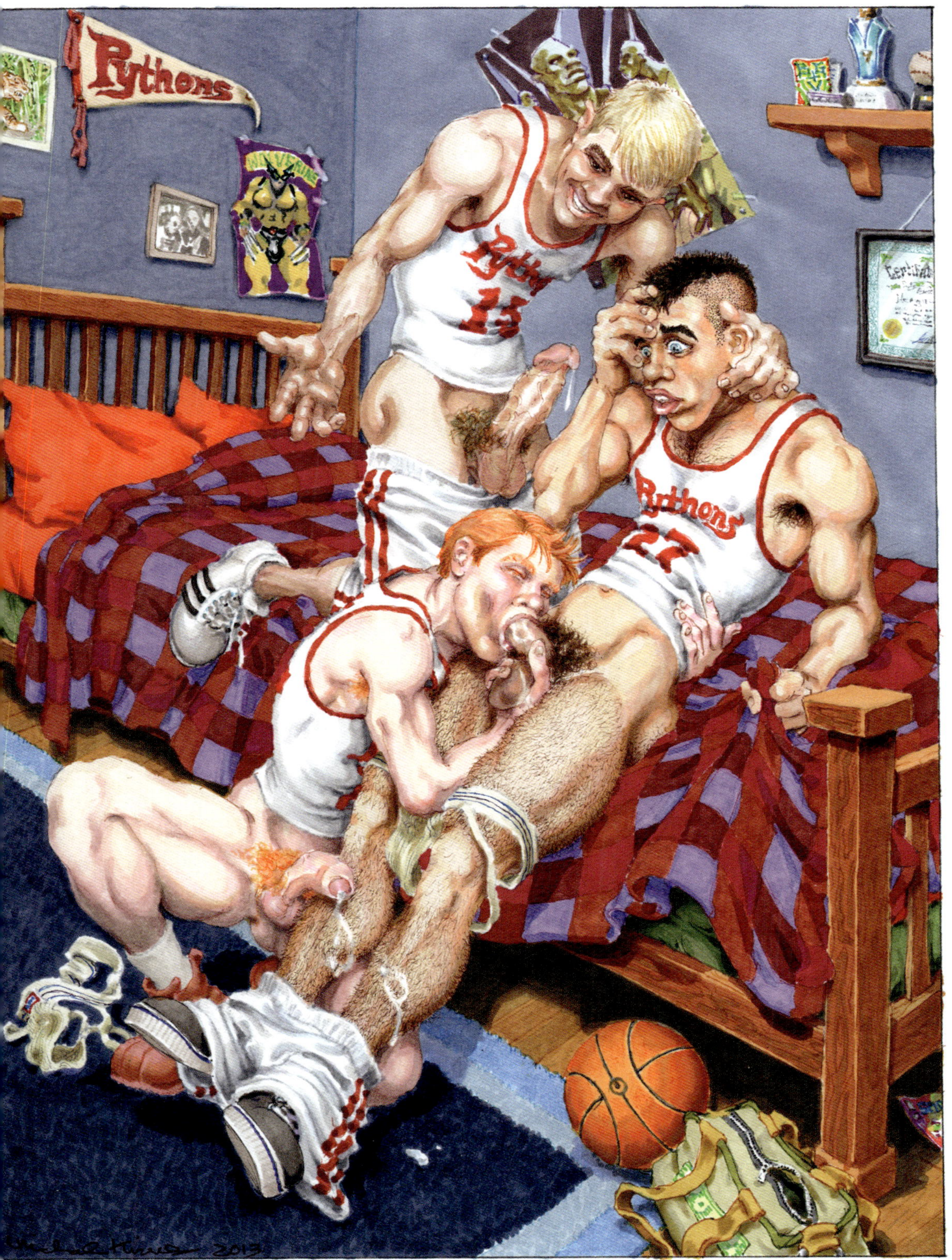
Pythons
WOLVERINE
Pythons
Pythons

□ MICHAEL KIRWAN

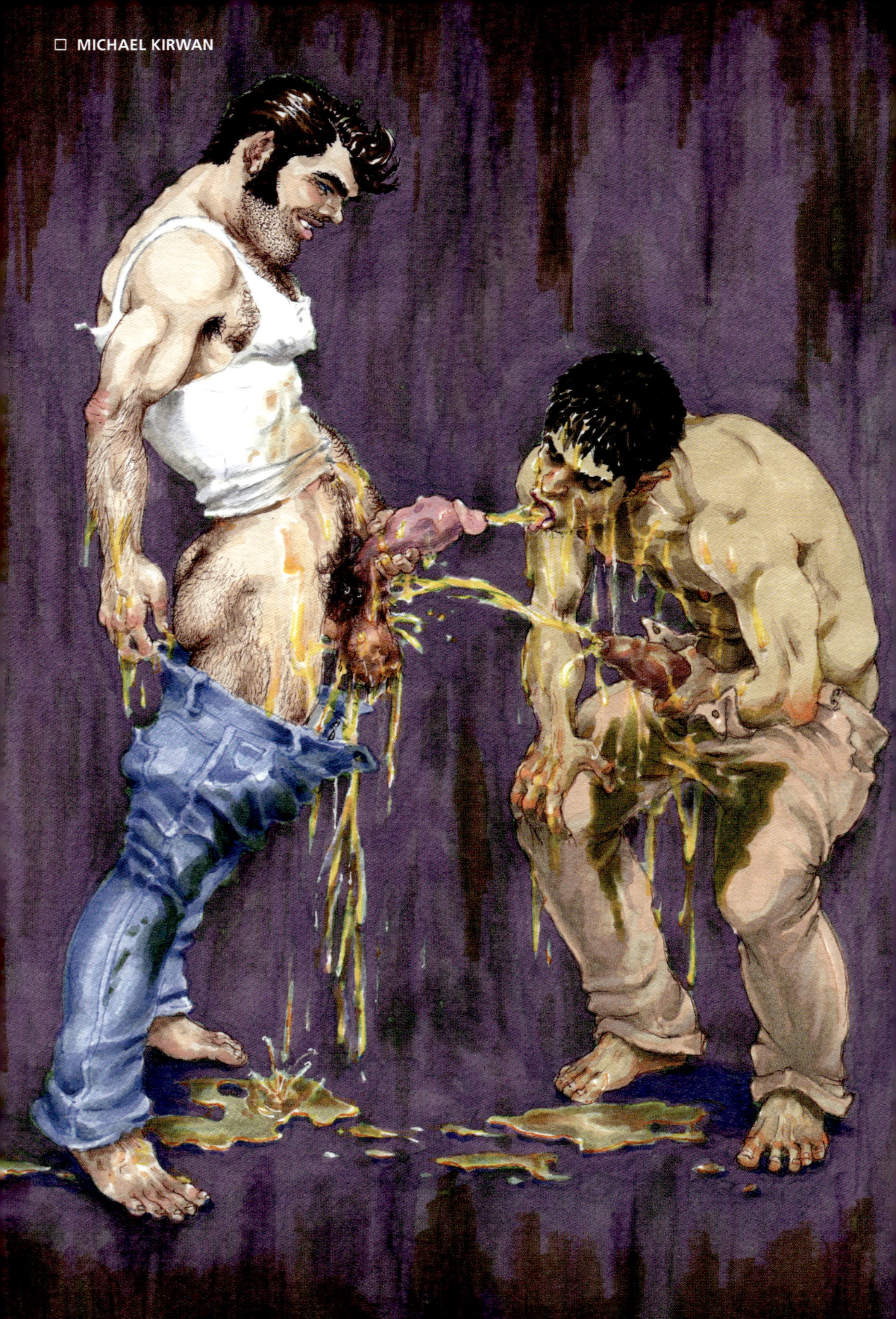

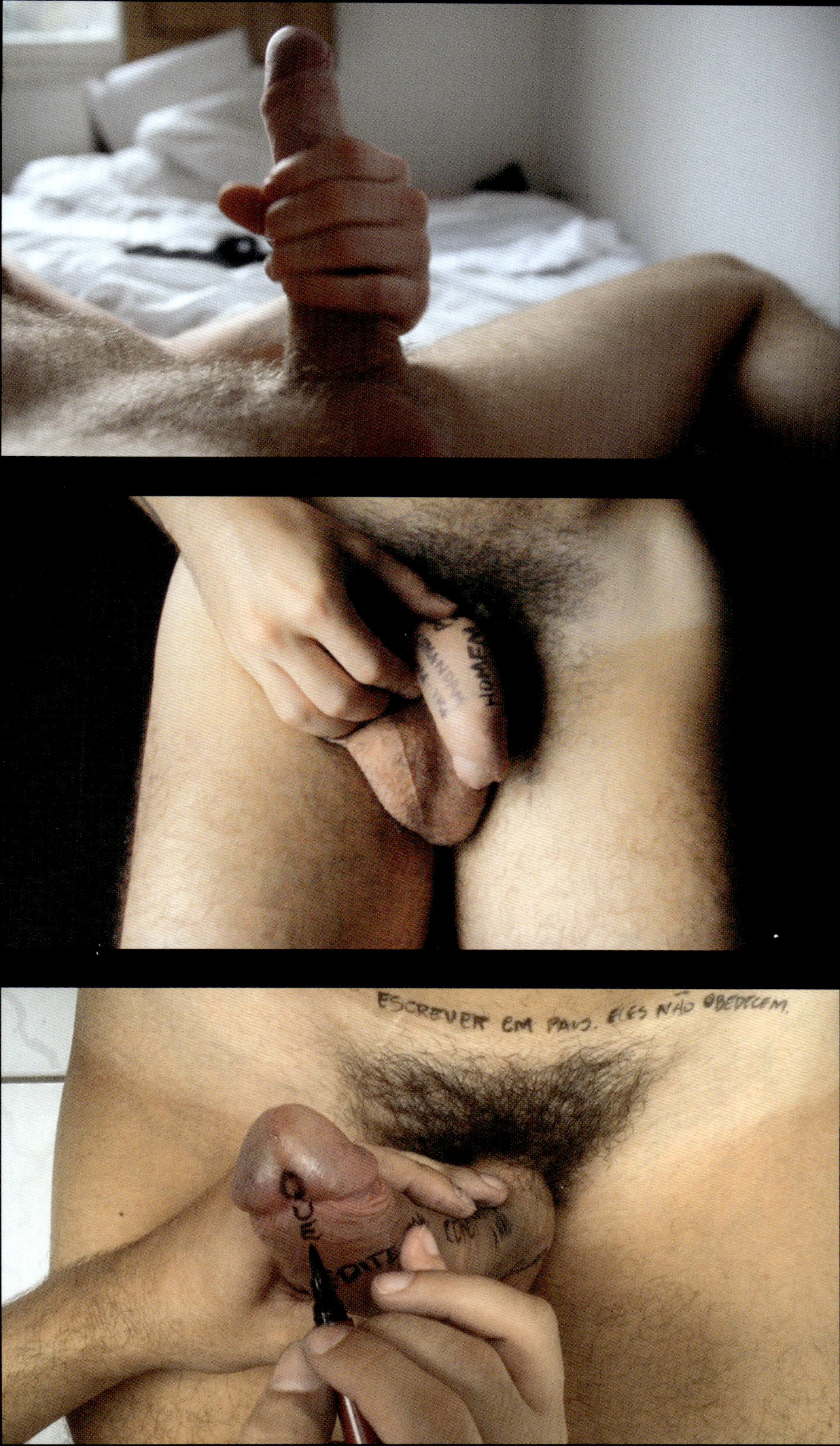

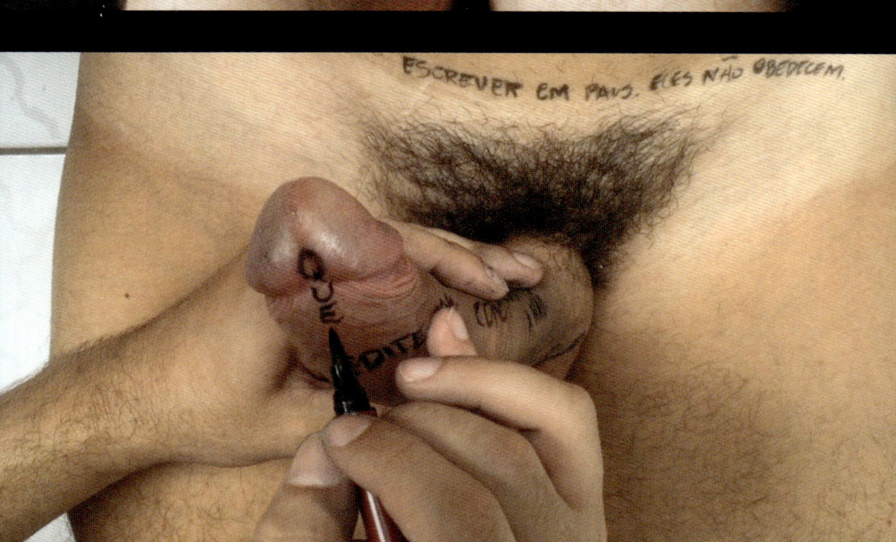

Penis Poetry. Film 2016

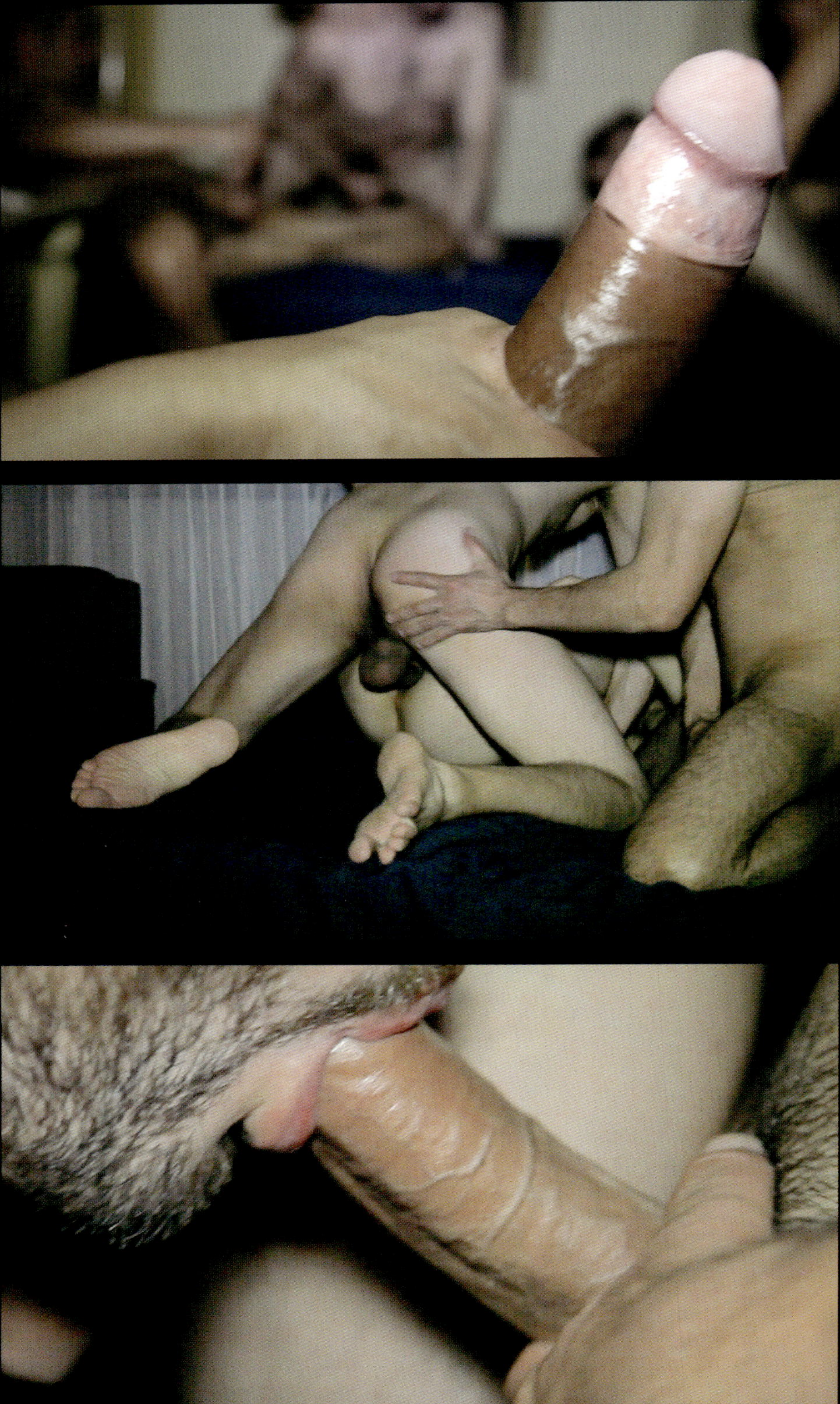

Machos. Film 2017

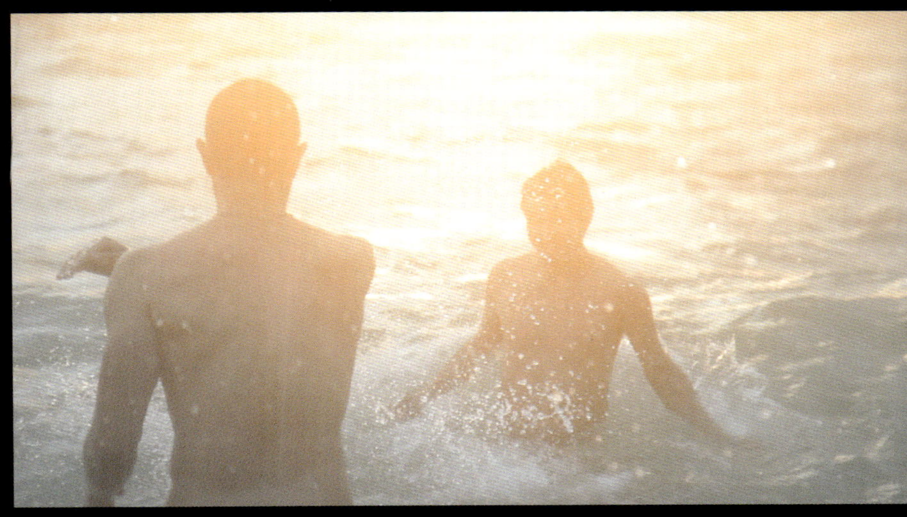
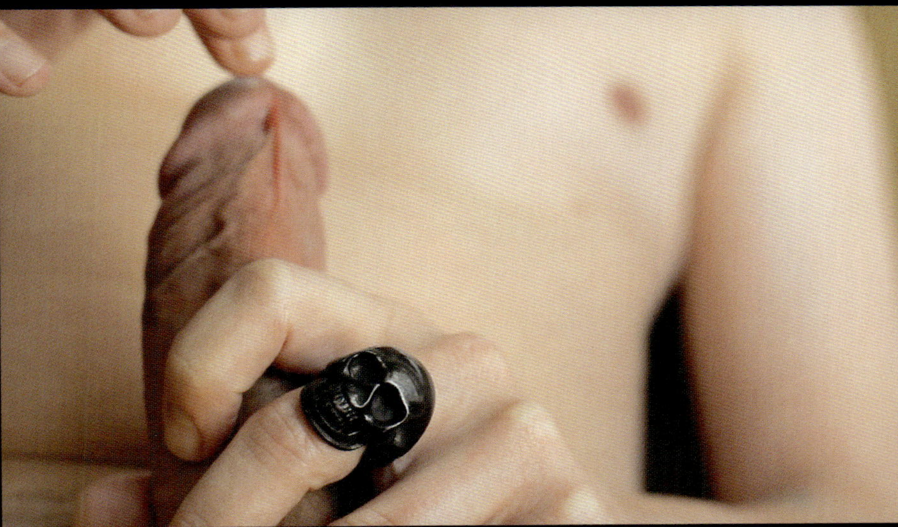
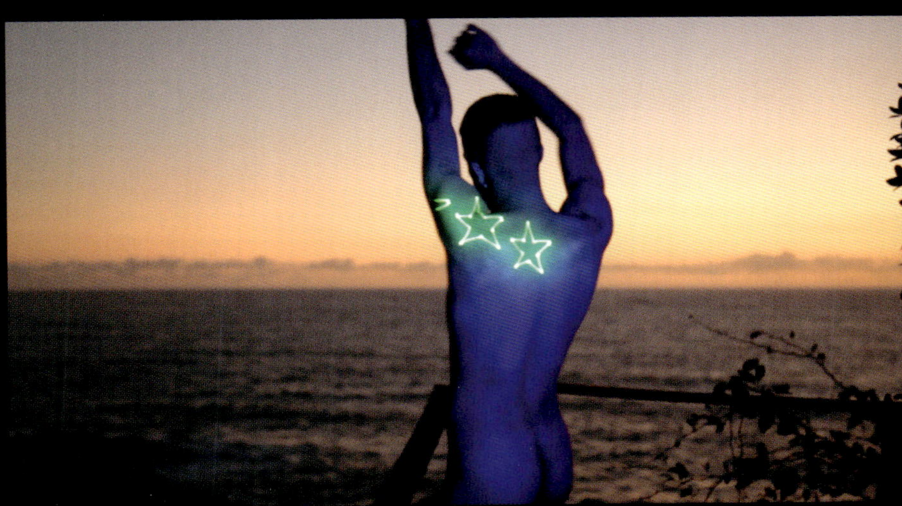

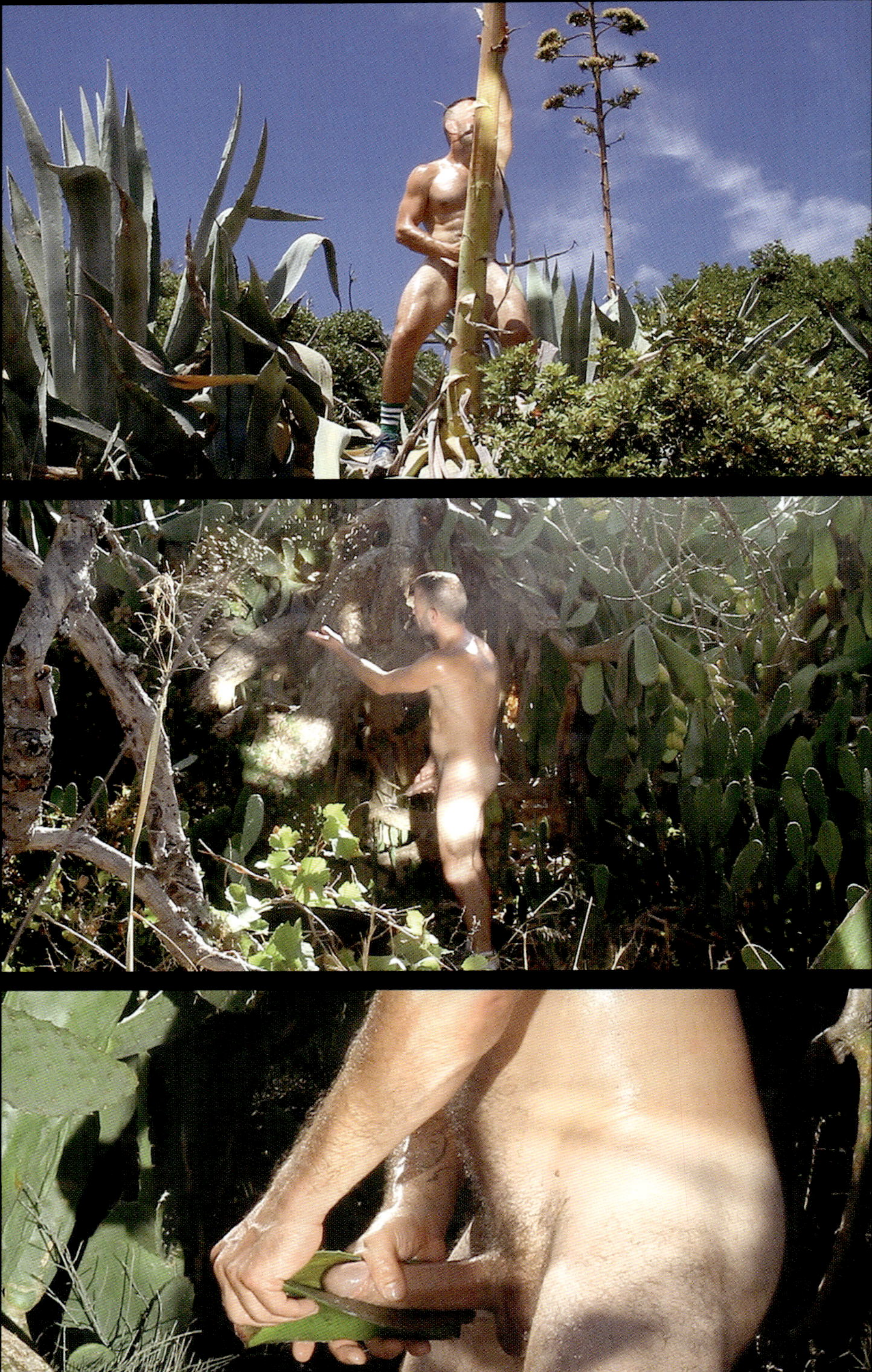

Ecosexual. Film 2017 with Rowland Byass

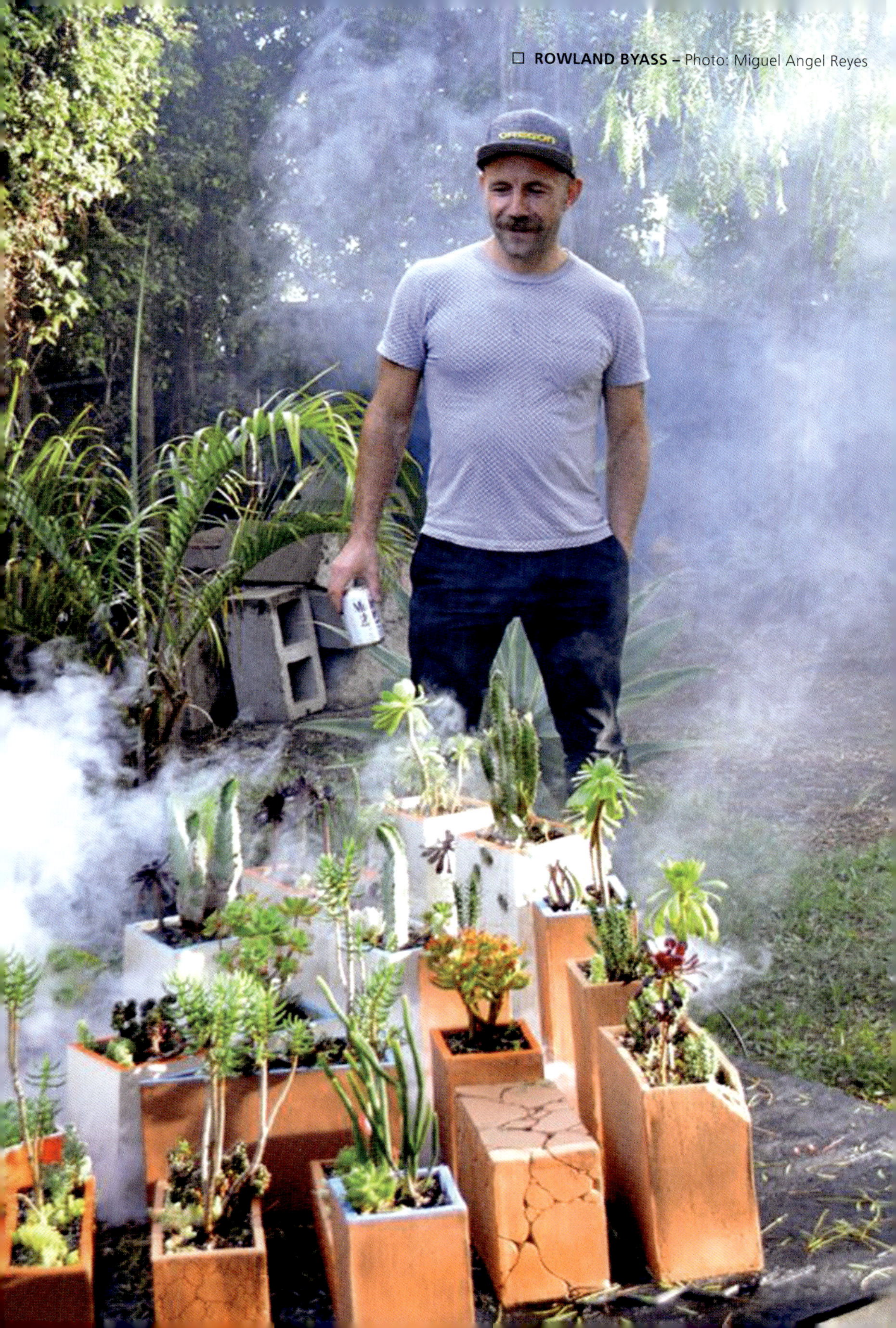

ROWLAND BYASS – Photo: Miguel Angel Reyes

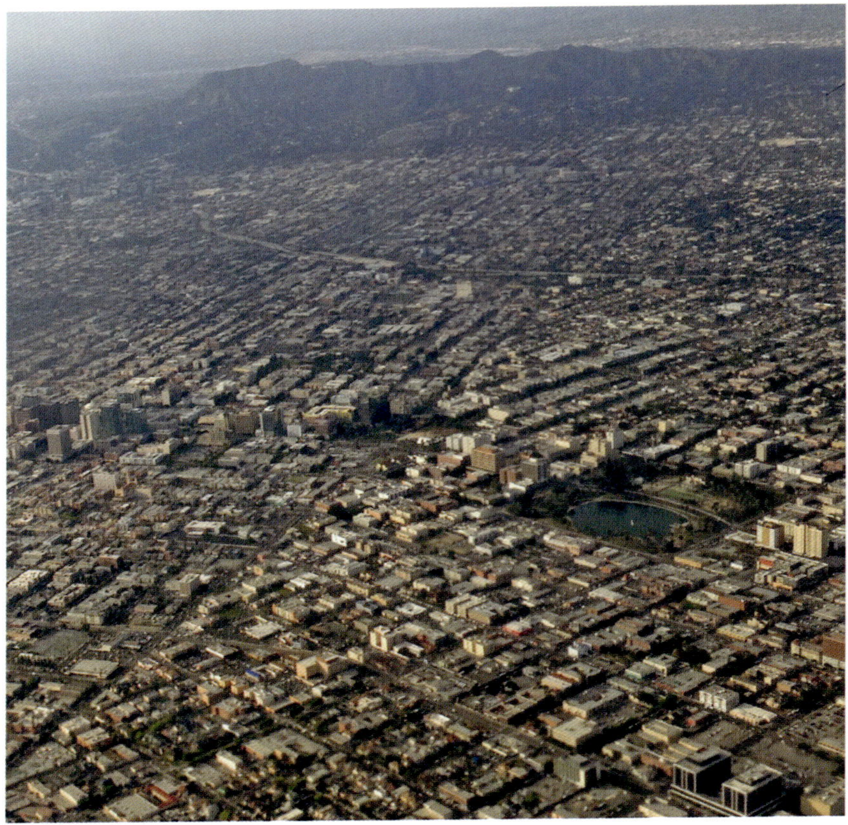

I came to TOM House in late February 2017. The house and garden are steeped in the spirit of Tom and the place possesses a certain queer creative magic that I will always associate with Los Angeles.
Working in the garden, I made an array of sculptural ceramic planters which represented the urban landscape of Los Angeles. It was a wonderful, enriching time and I feel bound to the place and its people after it. I owe TOM House a return trip, to make a ceramic shrine for the garden which will house its resident spirit.

Ich kam Ende Februar 2017 in das TOM House. Das Haus und der Garten sind von Toms Geist beseelt und der Ort besitzt eine gewisse queere kreative Magie, die ich immer mit Los Angeles verbinden werde. Ich arbeitete im Garten an einer Reihe von plastischen Blumenkübeln aus Keramik, die die Stadtlandschaft von L.A. darstellten. Es war eine wunderbare, bereichernde Zeit und ich fühle mich dem Ort und seinen Menschen weiterhin eng verbunden. Ich schulde dem TOM House noch einen Besuch, um einen Keramikschrein für den Garten zu bauen, in dem der Geist des Hauses wohnen wird.
– Rowland Byass

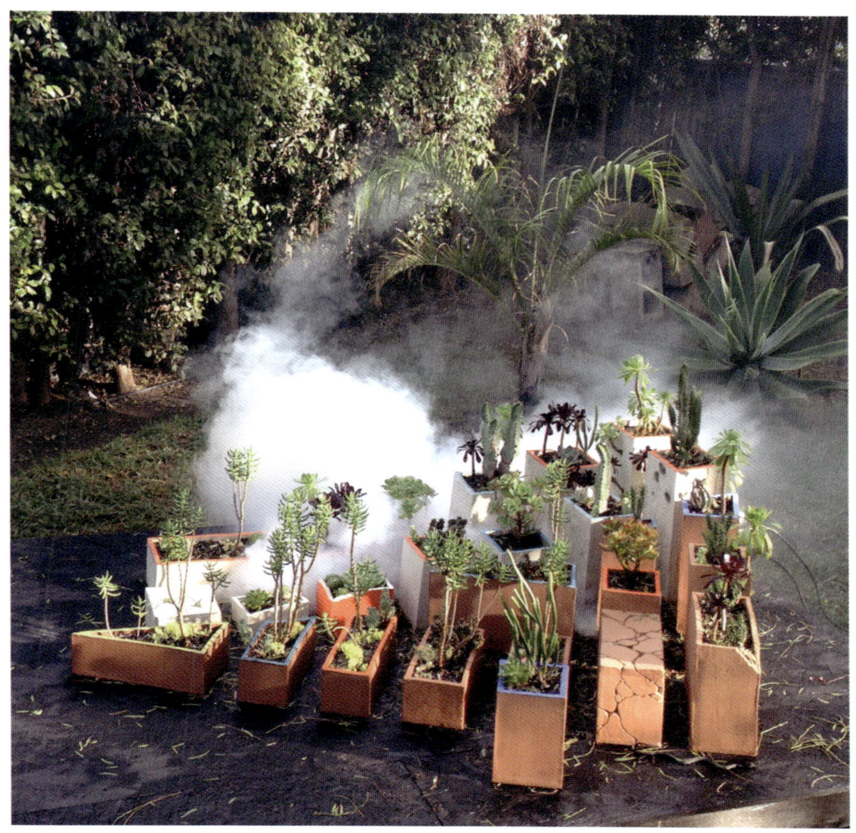

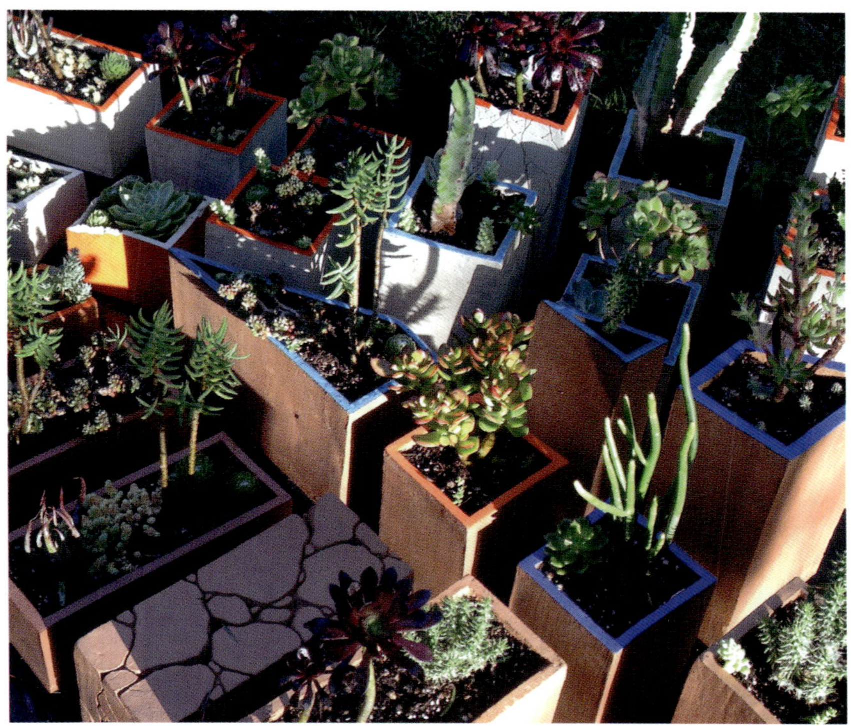

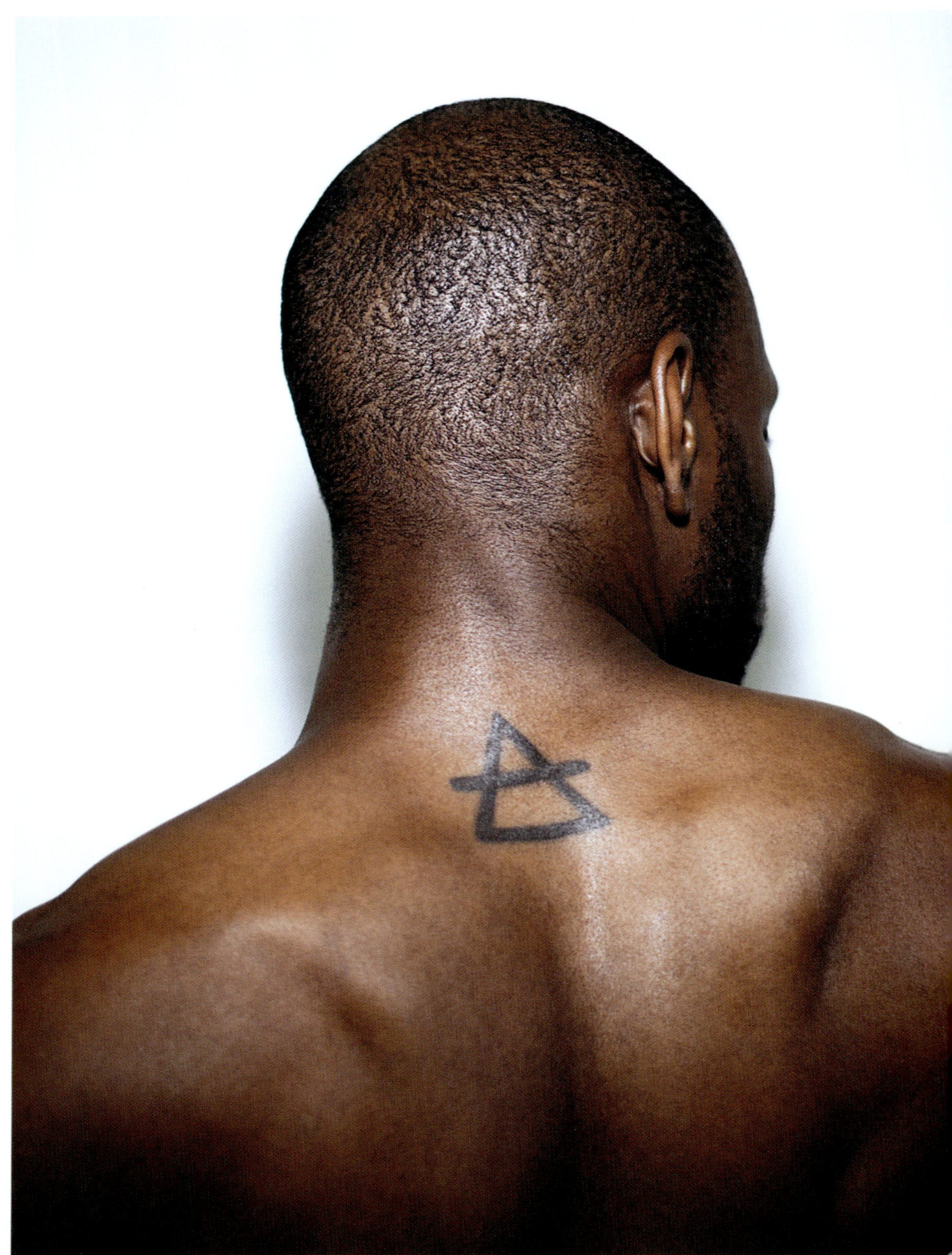

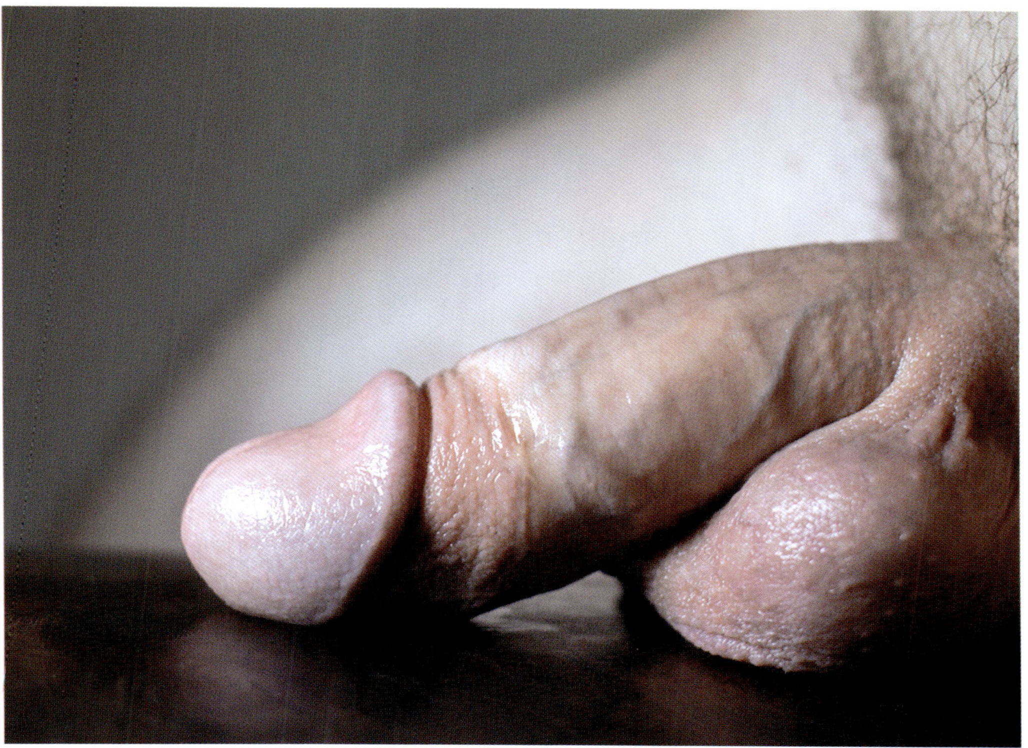

In the spring of 2017, on the day of the opening of a group show in which my friend Matt Lambert and I were showing work, Matt brought me to TOM House for the first time and introduced me to Durk, Sharp and Stuart. We had a couple of beers and I got a personal guided tour through the House and got to see a first glimpse of the archive. When we left that afternoon, I was in awe. I discovered Tom of Finland when I was 17 through a thin Taschen paperback book, and with this book a whole new world opened up for me. Tom's world helped me to develop a healthy way of dealing with sexuality. Little did I know back then that Tom of Finland Foundation would invite me to stay with them in Los Angeles as an artist-in-residence. It´s 26 years now since the death of Touko Laaksonen, but because of the relentless work of all the wonderful people of the Foundation, Tom of Finland is still alive more than ever, and a new generation is discovering the work of this master. While I'm writing these lines I am staying in Tom's room on the 3rd floor, surrounded by his personal belongings and artwork. I feel honoured to be here.

Im Frühling 2017, am Tag der Eröffnung einer Gruppenausstellung, in der mein Freund Matt Lambert und ich neue Arbeiten zeigten, hat mich Matt zum ersten Mal zum Tom of Finland Haus gebracht und mich Durk, Sharp und Stuart vorgestellt. Wir tranken Bier, bekamen eine private Führung durch das Haus und ich habe einen kurzen Blick auf das Archiv werfen können. Als wir nach diesem Nachmittag das Haus verließen, war ich beeindruckt.
Mit 17 habe ich Tom of Finland durch ein dünnes Paperback-Buch von Taschen entdeckt, und das Buch eröffnete mir eine komplett neue Welt. Damals half mir Toms Welt, eine gesunde Einstellung zu meiner Sexualität zu entwickeln. Ich hätte mir damals nicht vorstellen könne, dass die Tom of Finland Foundation mich eines Tages einladen würde, im Toms Haus zu leben und Artist in Residence zu sein. Seit dem Tod von Touko Laaksonen sind 26 Jahre vergangen, aber durch die unermüdliche Arbeit der wundervollen Menschen der Foundation ist Tom of Finland lebendiger denn je. Und eine neue Generation entdeckt gerade wieder die Arbeiten dieses Meisters. Während ich diese Zeilen schreibe, wohne ich in Toms Zimmer im 3. Stock, umgeben von seinen persönlichen Gegenständen und seinen Kunstwerken. Ich fühle mich geehrt, hier zu sein.
– Florian Hetz

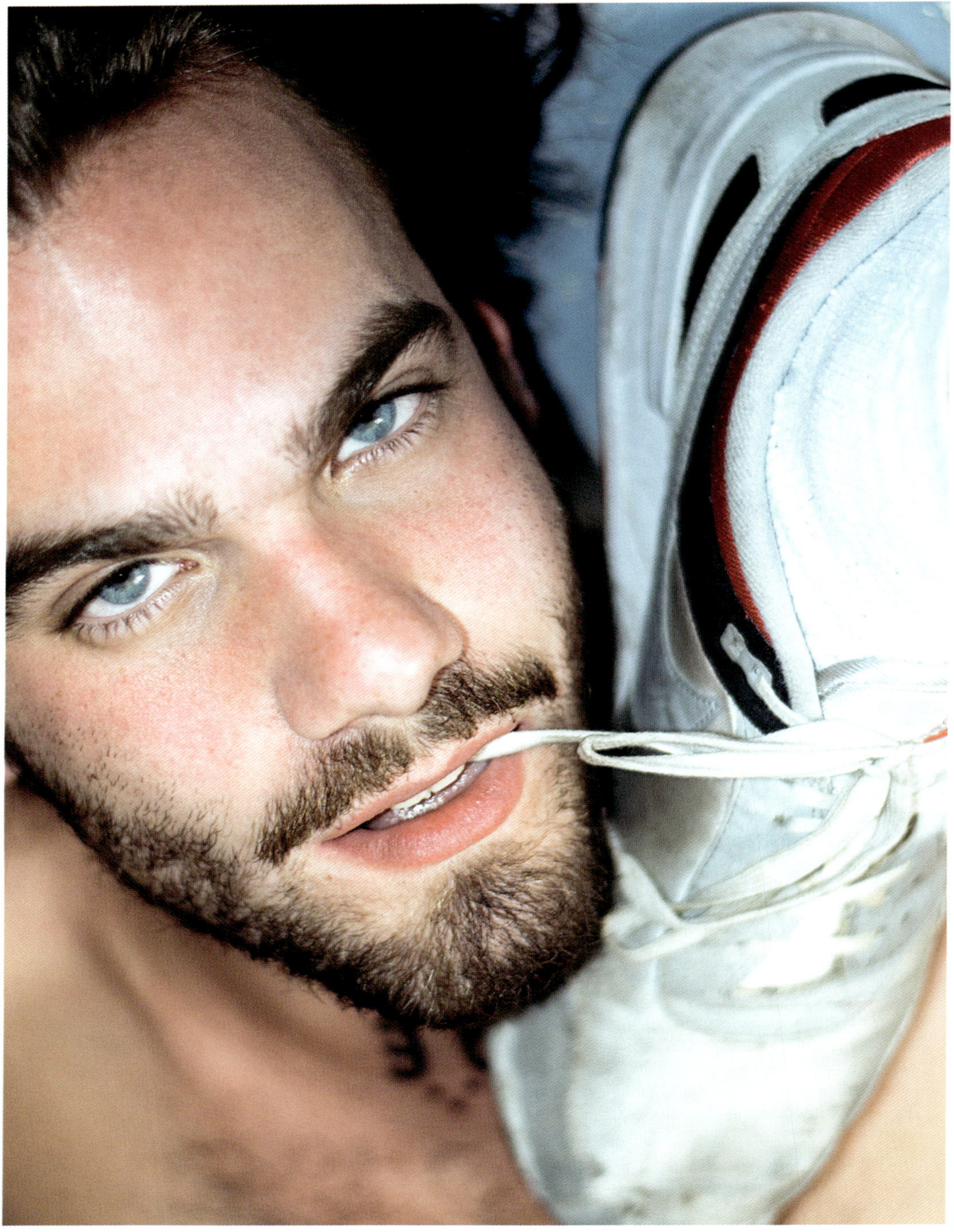

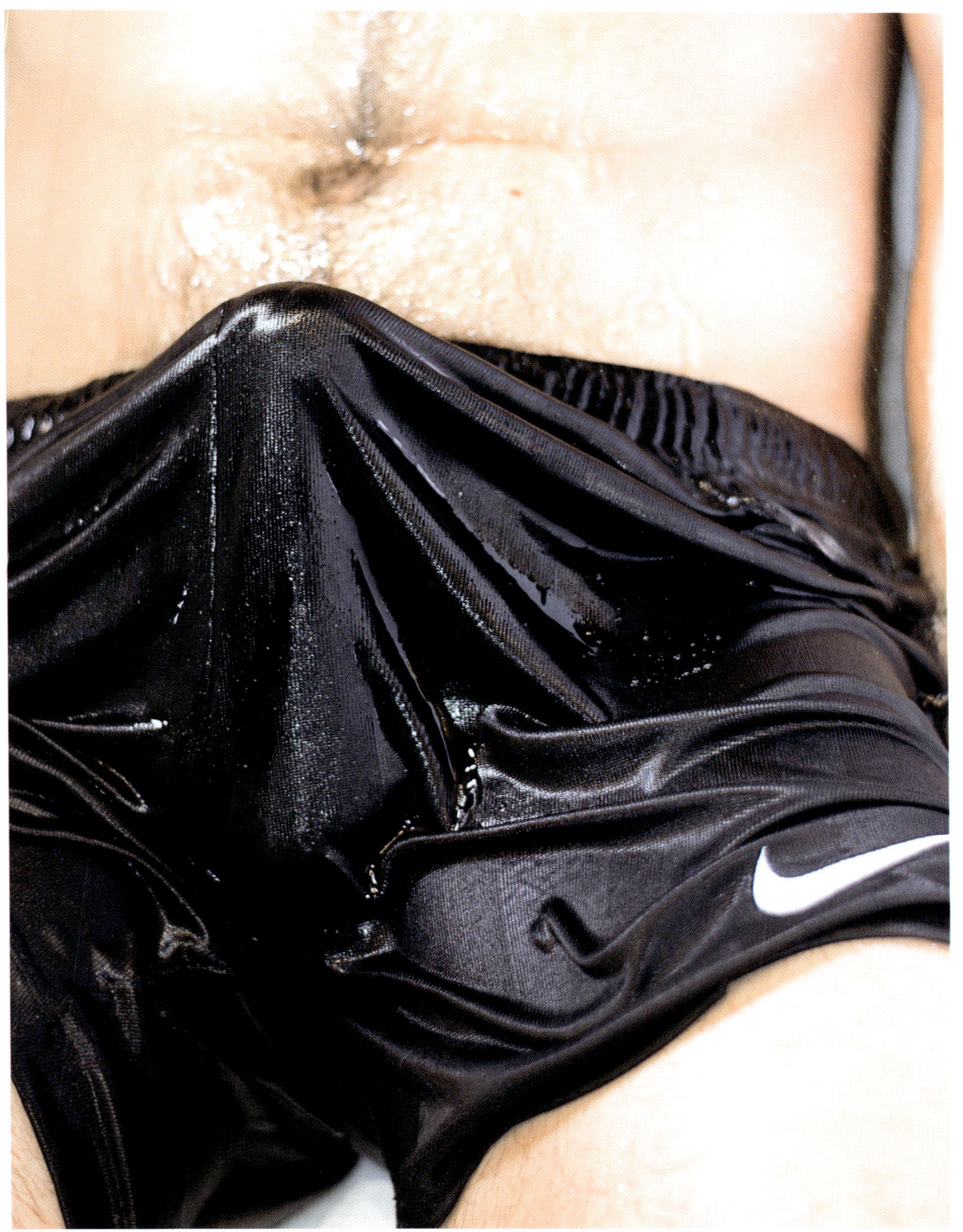

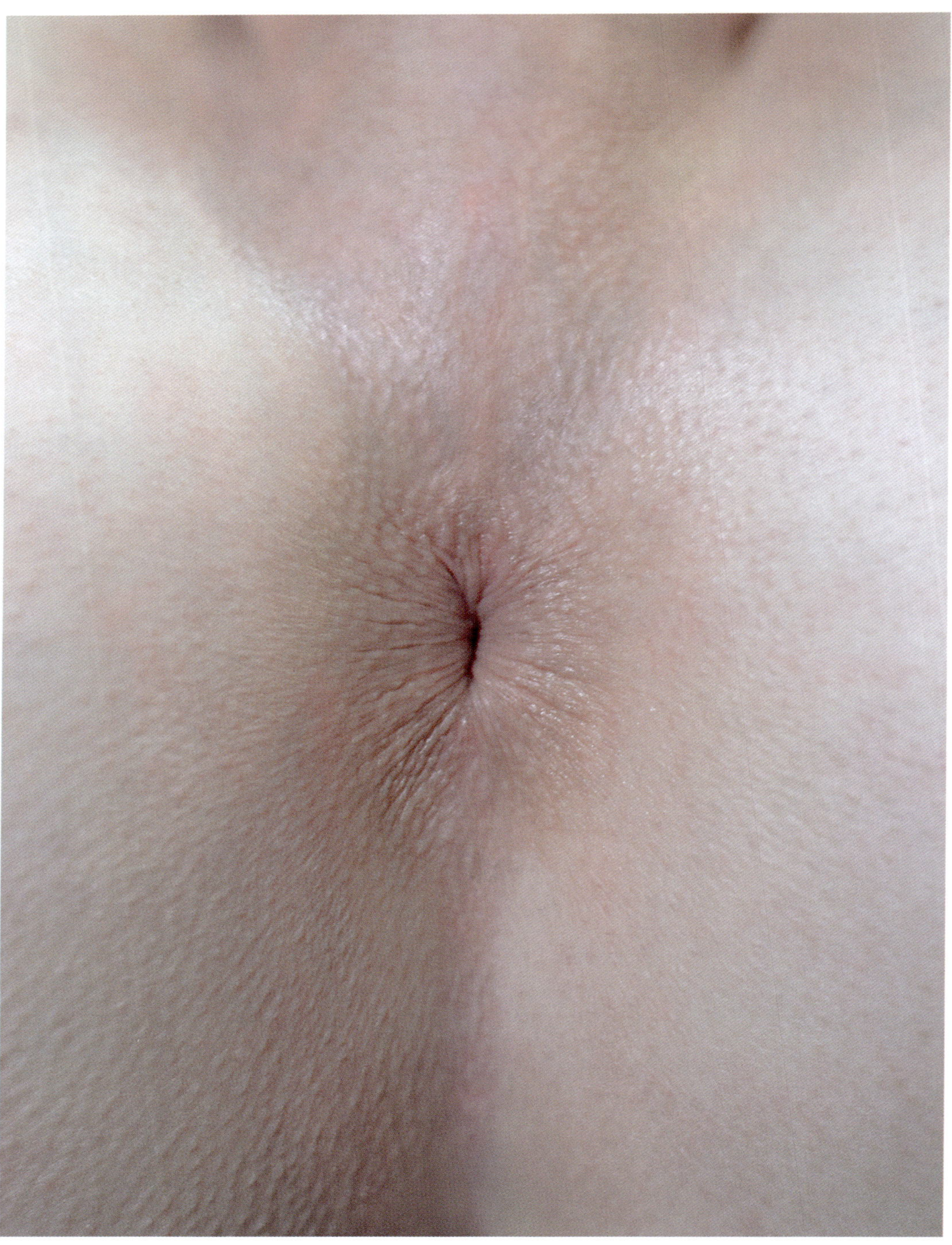

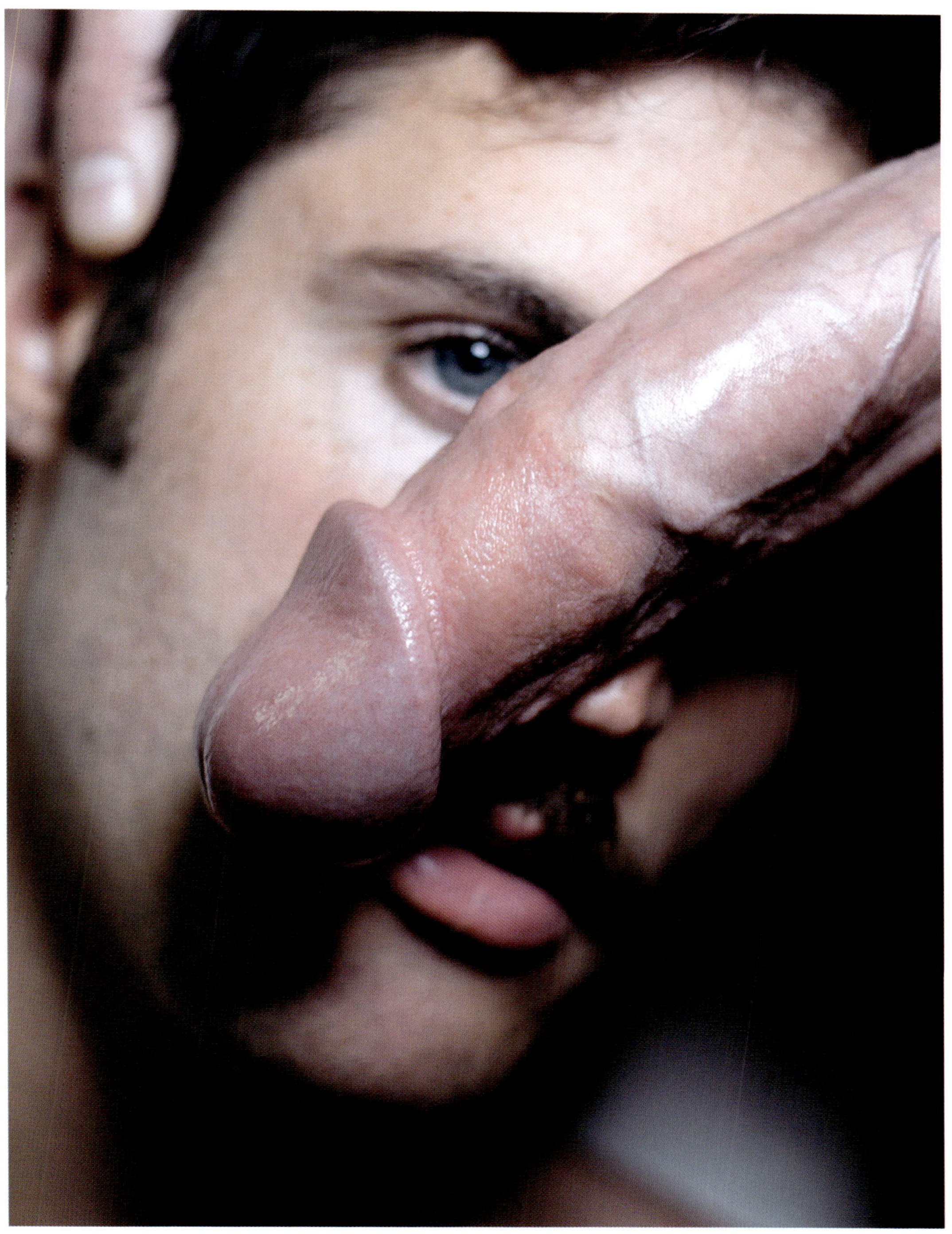

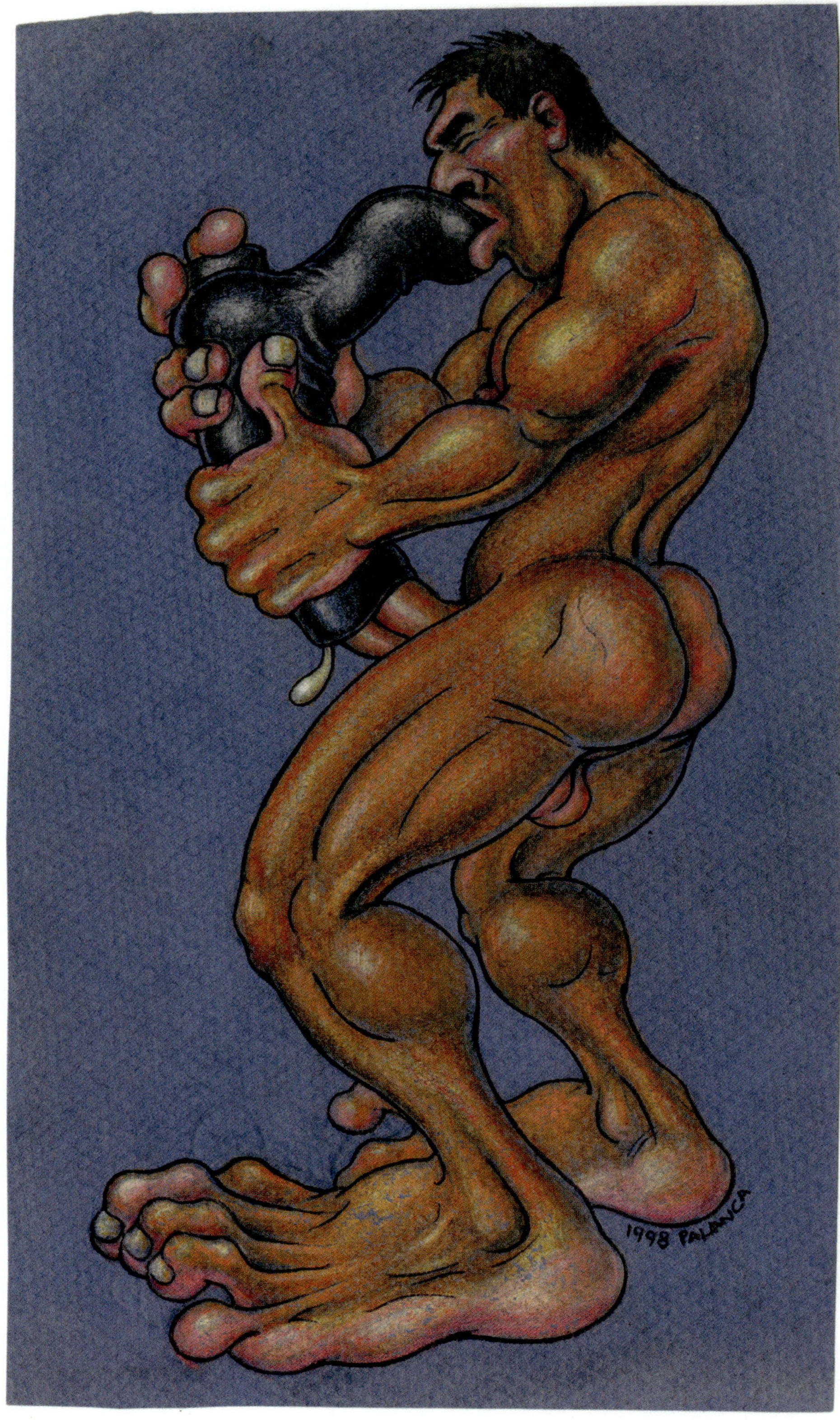
1998 PALANCA

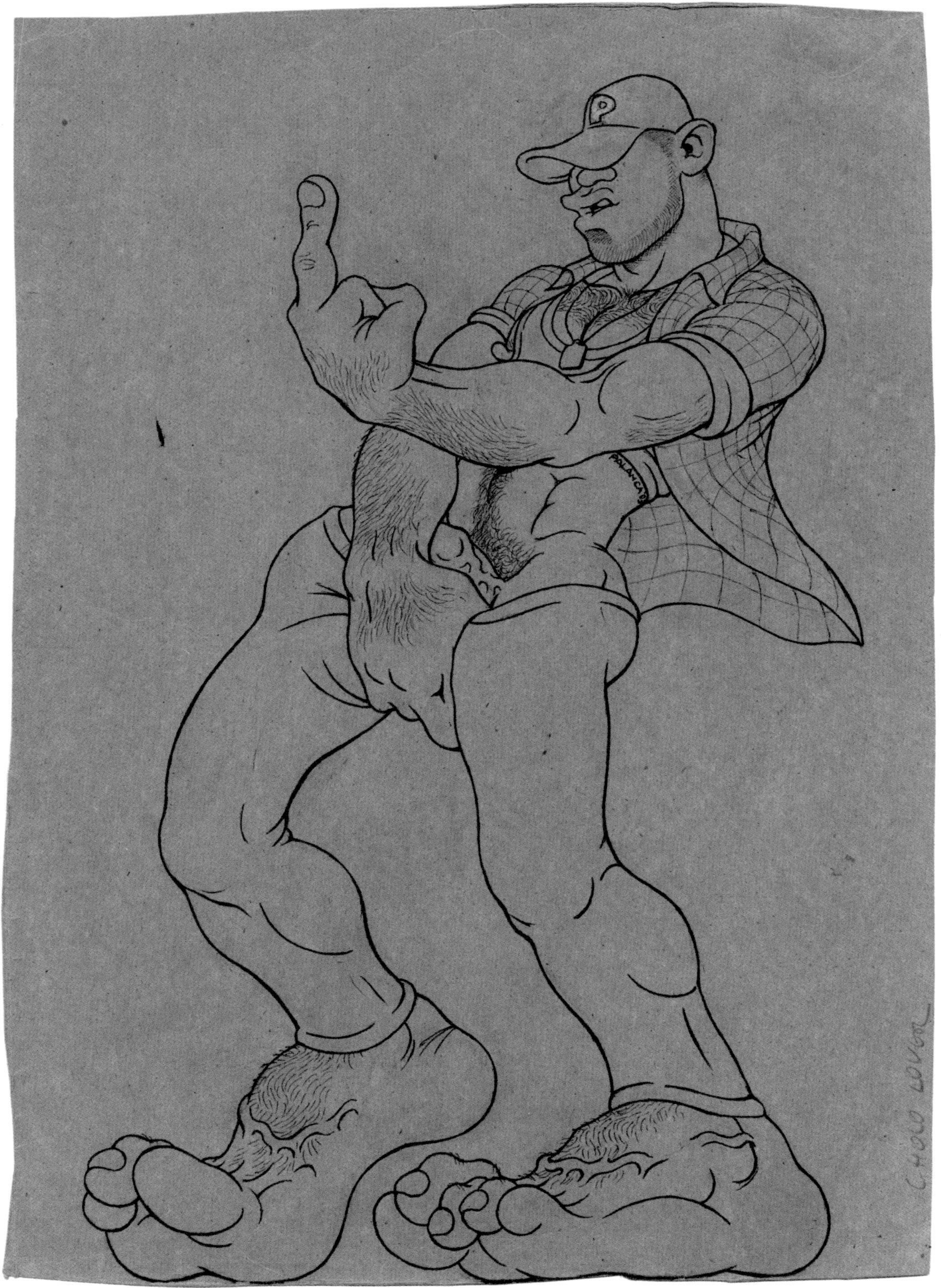

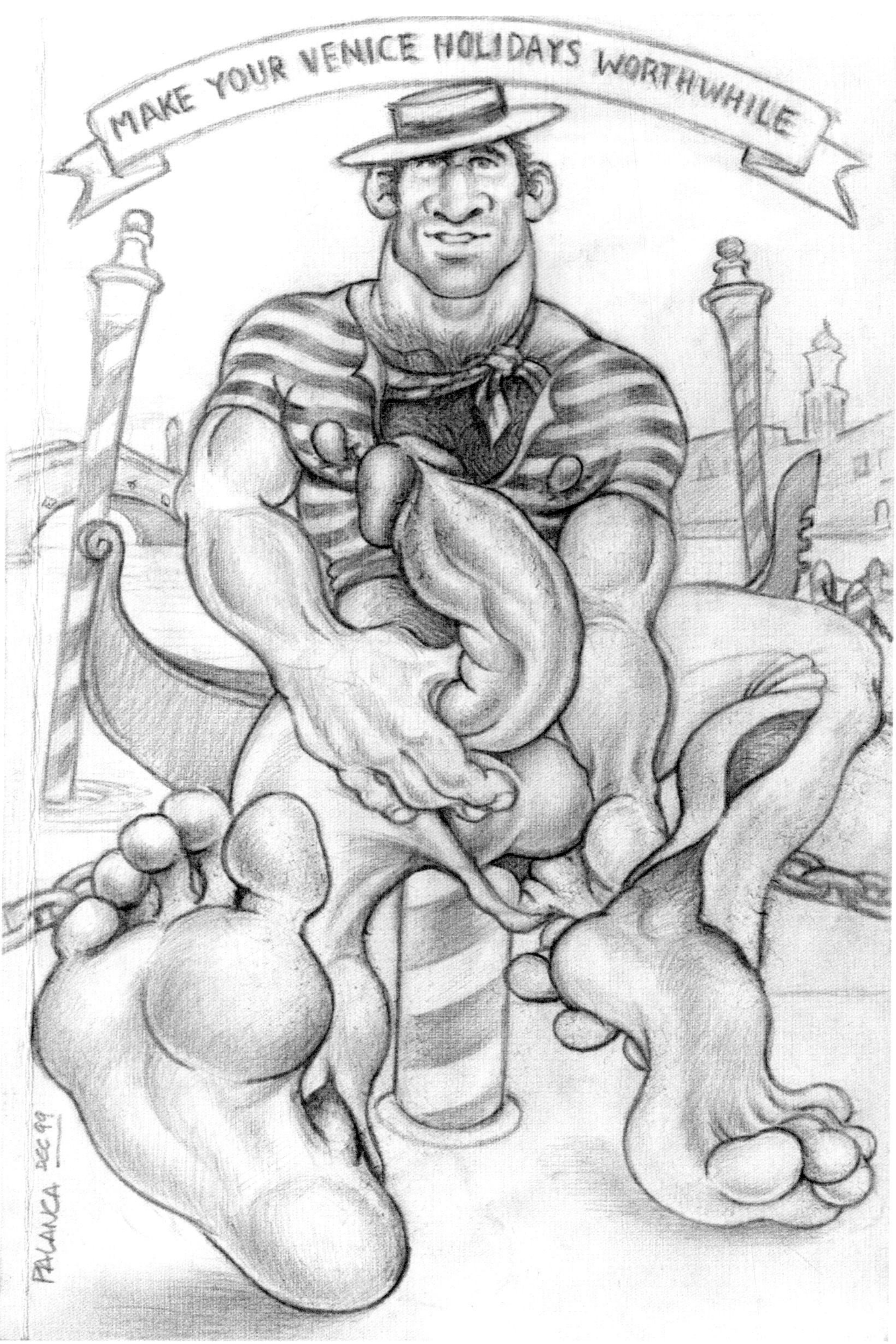
MAKE YOUR VENICE HOLIDAYS WORTHWHILE
PALANCA DEC 99

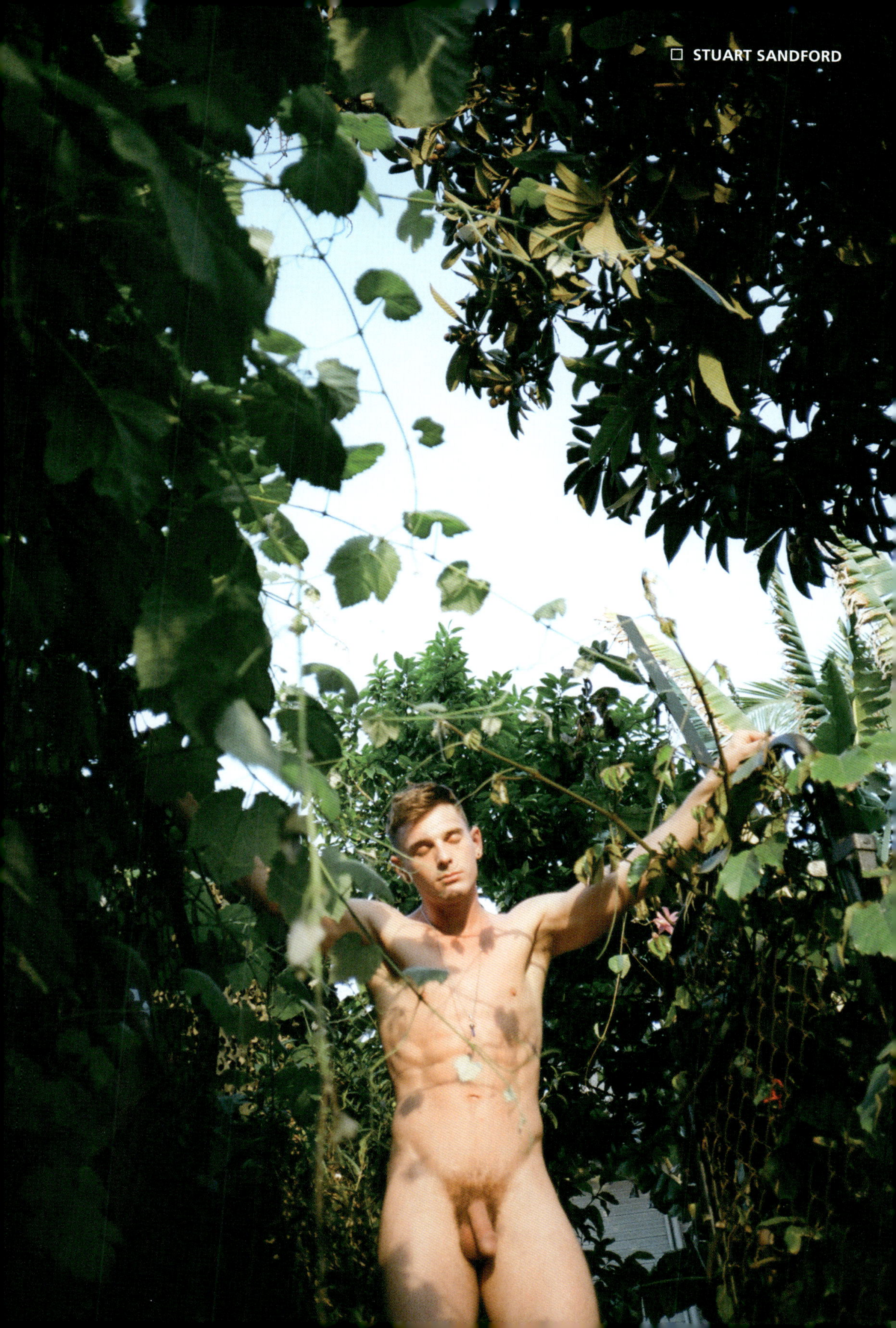
STUART SANDFORD

My name is Kelly, and you can call me Kelly

I will fucking never say thank you to them. They are robbers and self-righteous thugs. They took from me what wasn't theirs to take. They have never had the right to give me my rights. Negotiations are unpalatable. My freedom, my liberty is mine. Why would I be content with begrudged "equality" when (moral) superiority is attainable? Seriously, who wants to be "tolerated"? After all the shit they've put me through, I want to be *venerated*.

I do, and will, say thank you to the artist Tom, from Finland. And god, if I'm depicted as a Greek/Nordic/Venice Beach god, kudos and kiitos. What will they think of me now? That I might throw sand in *their* faces? Tom's realm takes on new validities as our culture changes. Tom told me I didn't have to be what they told me to be, or worse, what they *let* me be. I didn't have to be lesser-ed, like woman-lesser-than. When did they get to say females are not-as-great-as < or not-equal-to ≠?

Tom rendered the world as a square deal. He slammed the whole I'm-a-top-I-don't-suck-dick thing – what a fucked up rule we somehow self imposed. Christ, Tom's like the torchbearer of *reciprocation*. He said I can "be all that I can be". I can be a play soldier, I can play soldier, get into uniform play. I can do a soldier. I can *be* a friggin' soldier.

I can order a sex sub around like a drill sergeant. I can squeal like a sweet-sixteenager getting her first sort of lite-to-medium-blue gift box. I can be butch with the best of them. I can whip the ass of a masochist and can whip up some fierce crêpes fourrées à la crème au citron. Avec Château Rieussec Sauternes, merci. You may think I was in the closet for a long time – but there's a lot in there to try on. There's not enough colors in the rainbow (flag) for me. Hell, there's not enough minutes in an hour for me to be me. I am your buffest bitch, your nelliest dyke. I can do macho for a minute; prissy for a couple. I didn't navigate this process to be a *Transgender* – I did 'cause it's me. My definitions, my identity, my rules.

I love calling you what you want to be called: Mistress, scum, Sir, dollface. Ne, ve, ze, xe. But I love love calling you Chris. Can I say on my Grindr profile that I'm "not into redheads"? But not say, I'm "not into Redskins"? Like Truth, Political Correctness must be measured cautiously. Personal Ethics must be dispensed liberally, consistently, universally. They say my "lifestyle" makes them "uncomfortable". Am I supposed to feel sorry? Uncomfortable is a new pair of Ferragamos. Or when the dry-cleaners shrinks your St. John's cardigan. Didn't they persecute us *painfully*? For like, Two. Thousand. Years.?

I like my Tom of Finland unfiltered. I hate the insidious censorship of FacebookInstagram – we're all susceptible. I'm publically for privacy. No one should be able to tell me what I can put in, and take out of, my holes. No individual, group, organization or state can dictate what's in my head. Or heart. I don't need to explain myself. Or my fetishes – like Magik, it might explain them away. It's more than likely I won't be going to their heaven, odds have it, – hell, who cares? There's no footwear in the kingdom come! Yet, I'm joyful; I've found my bliss in Tom's utopia of subversion.

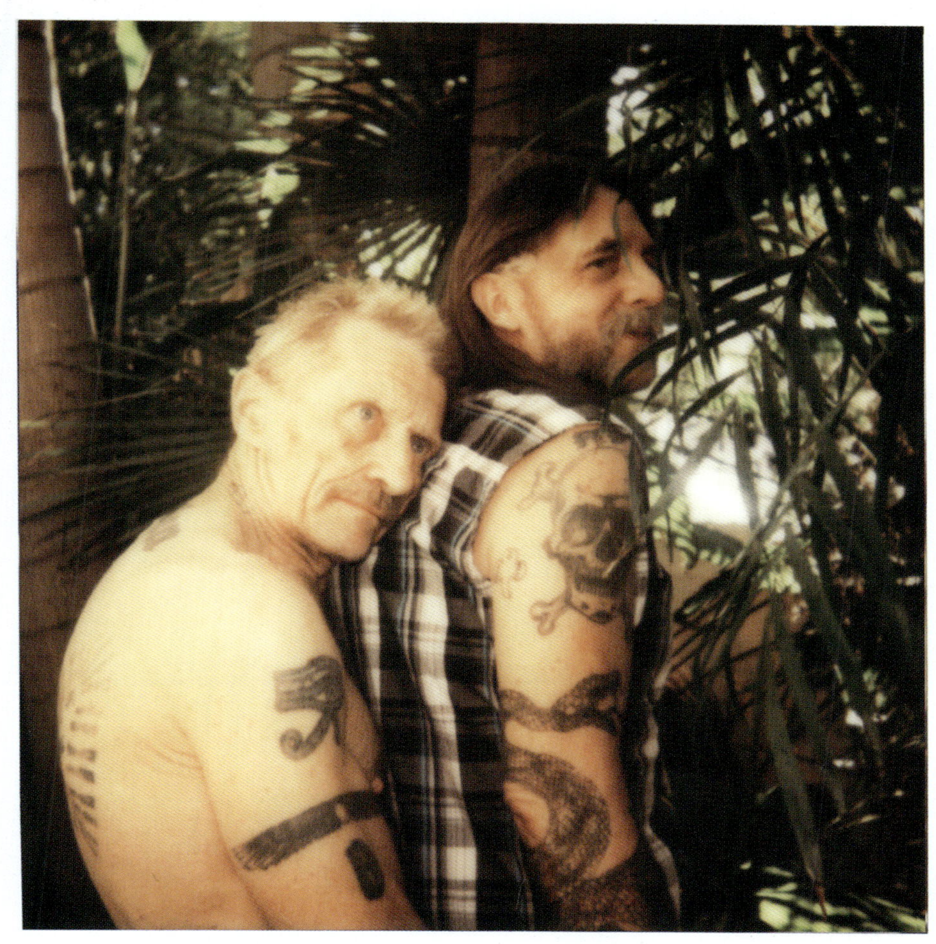

Durk and Sharp

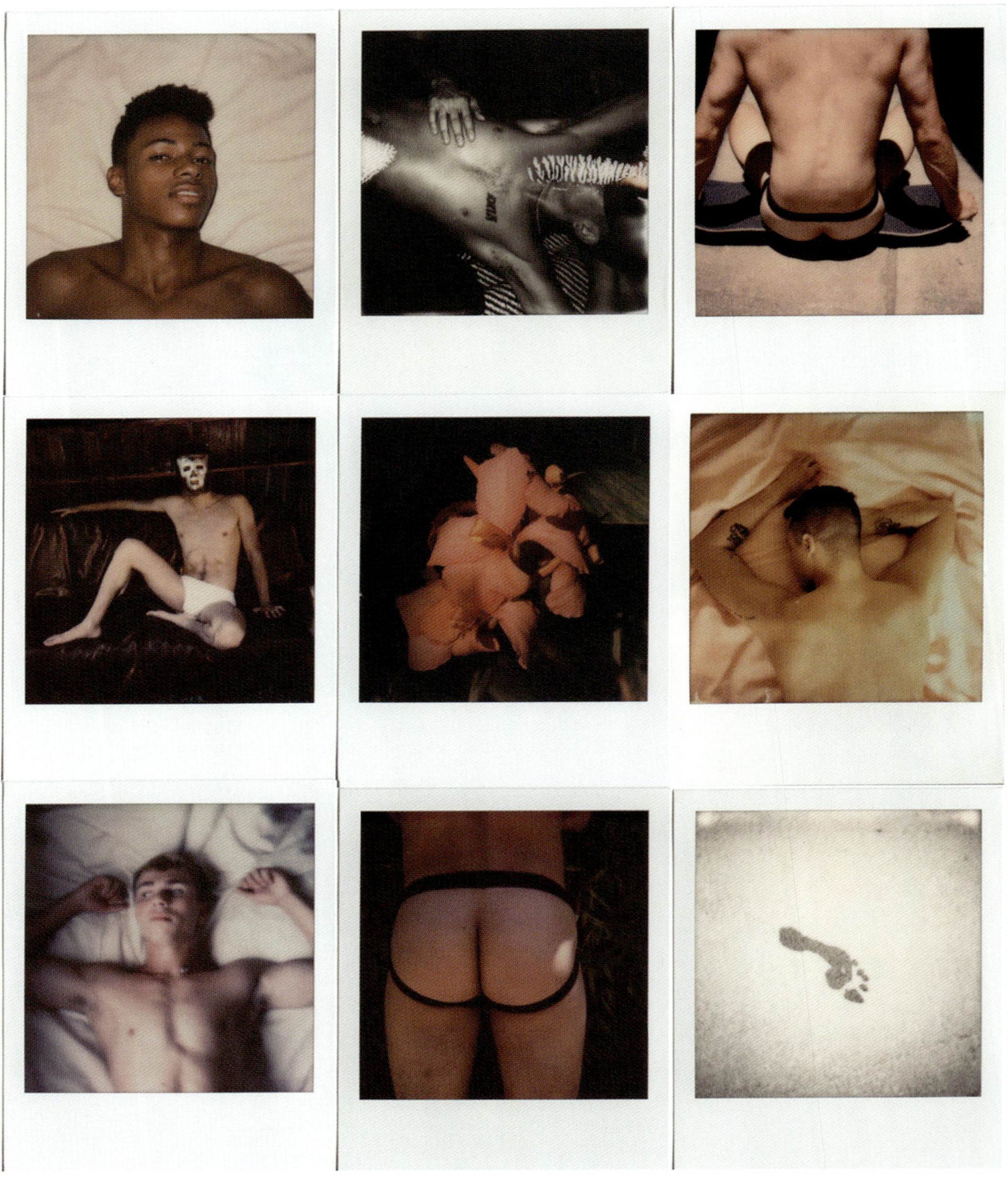

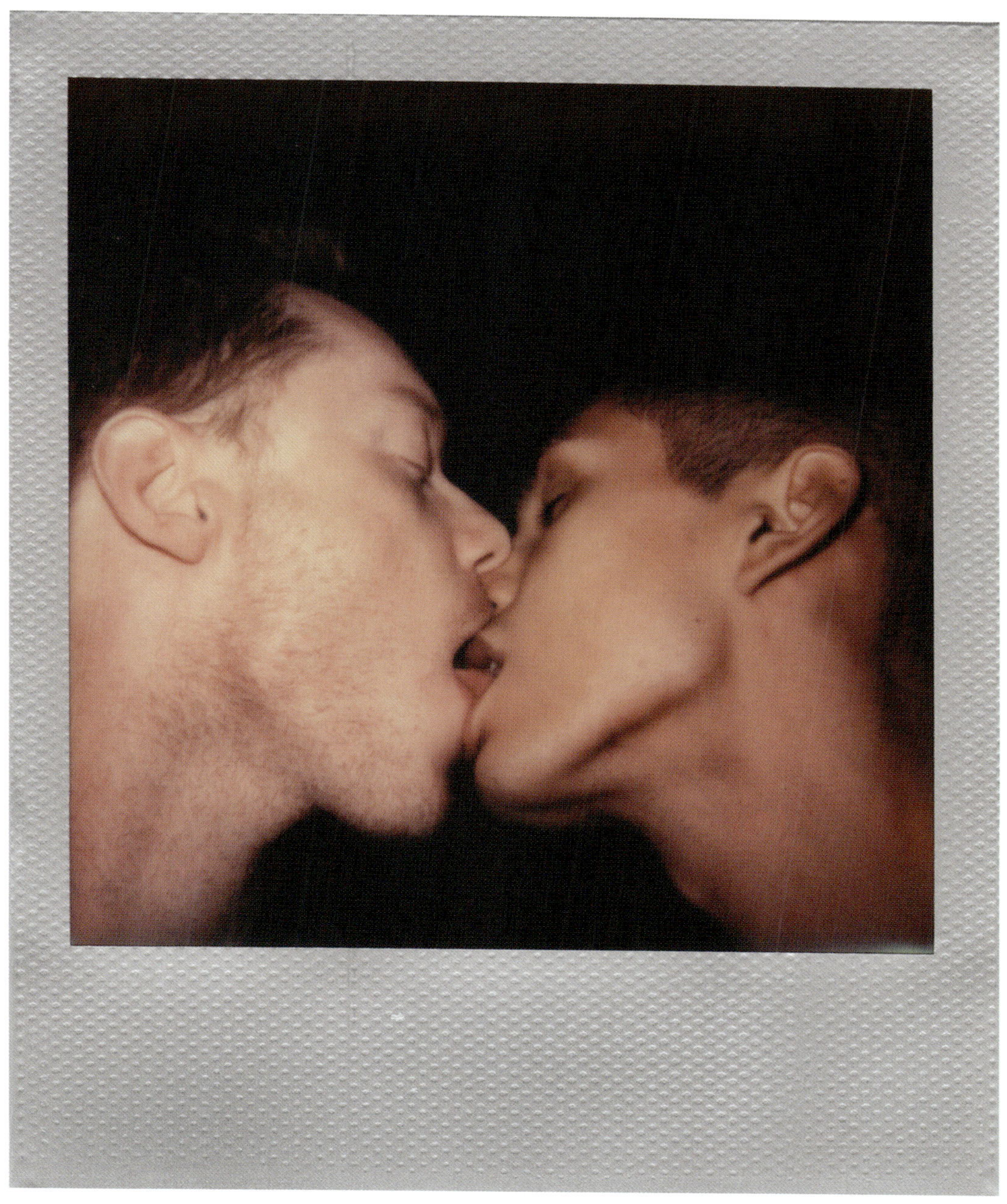

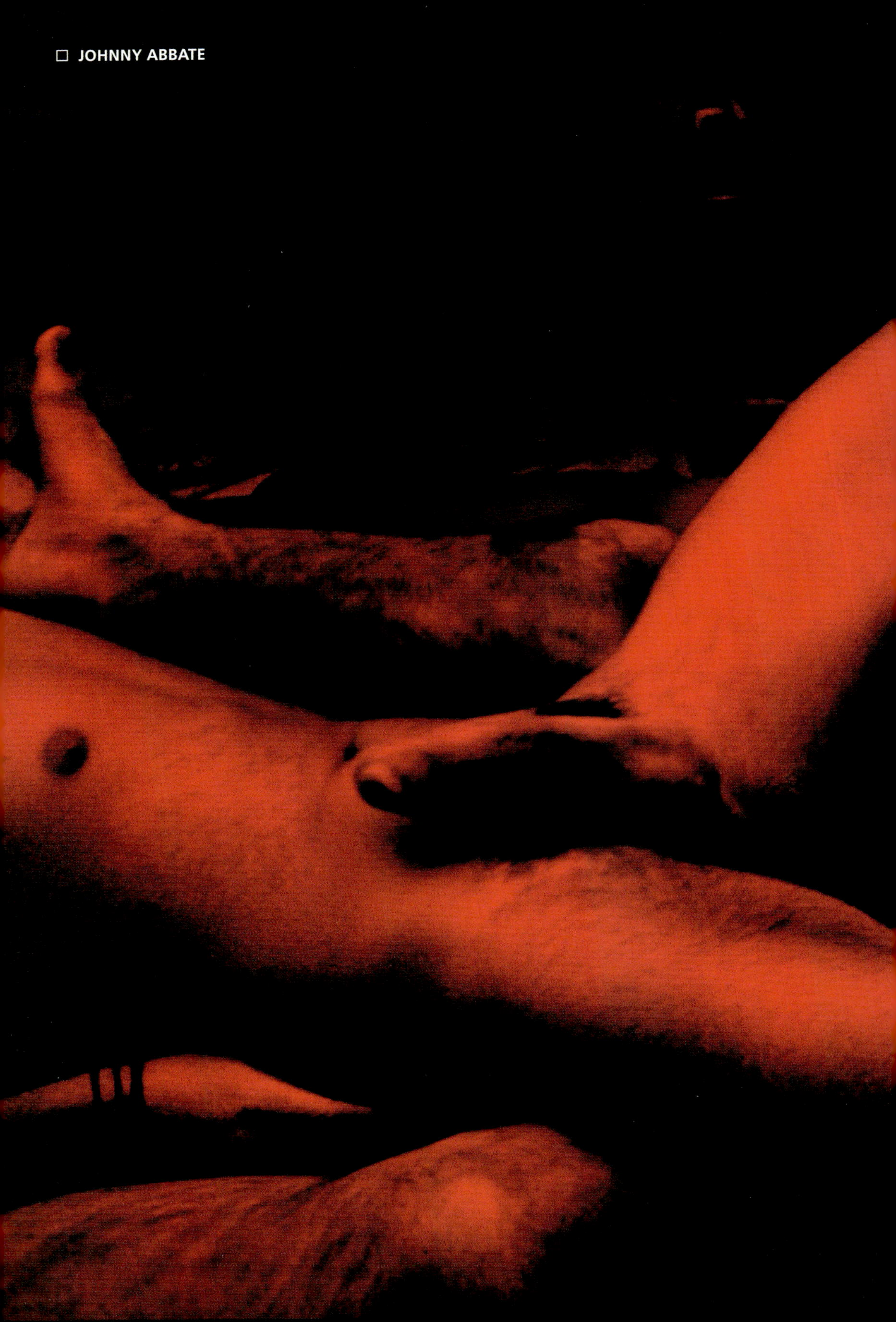

☐ JOHNNY ABBATE

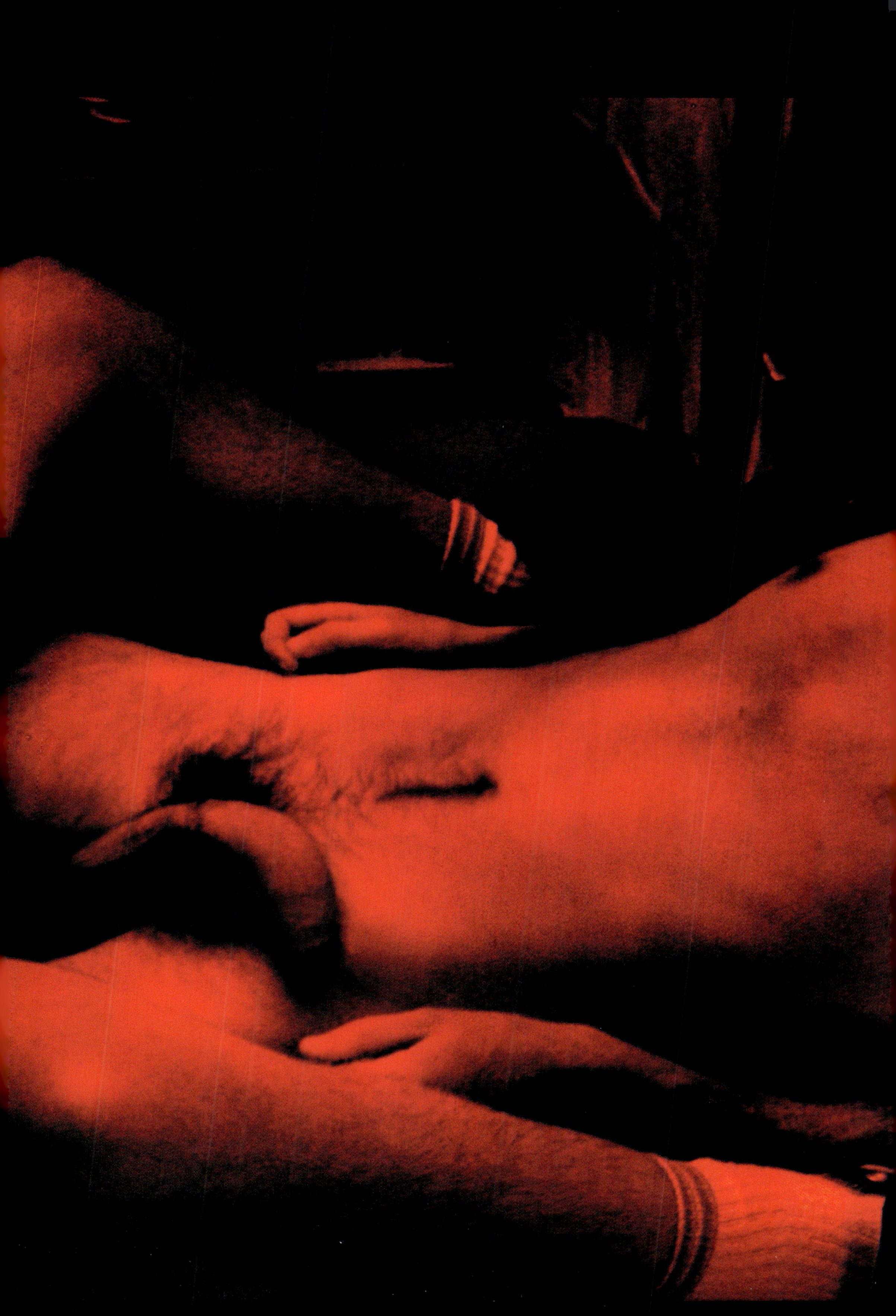

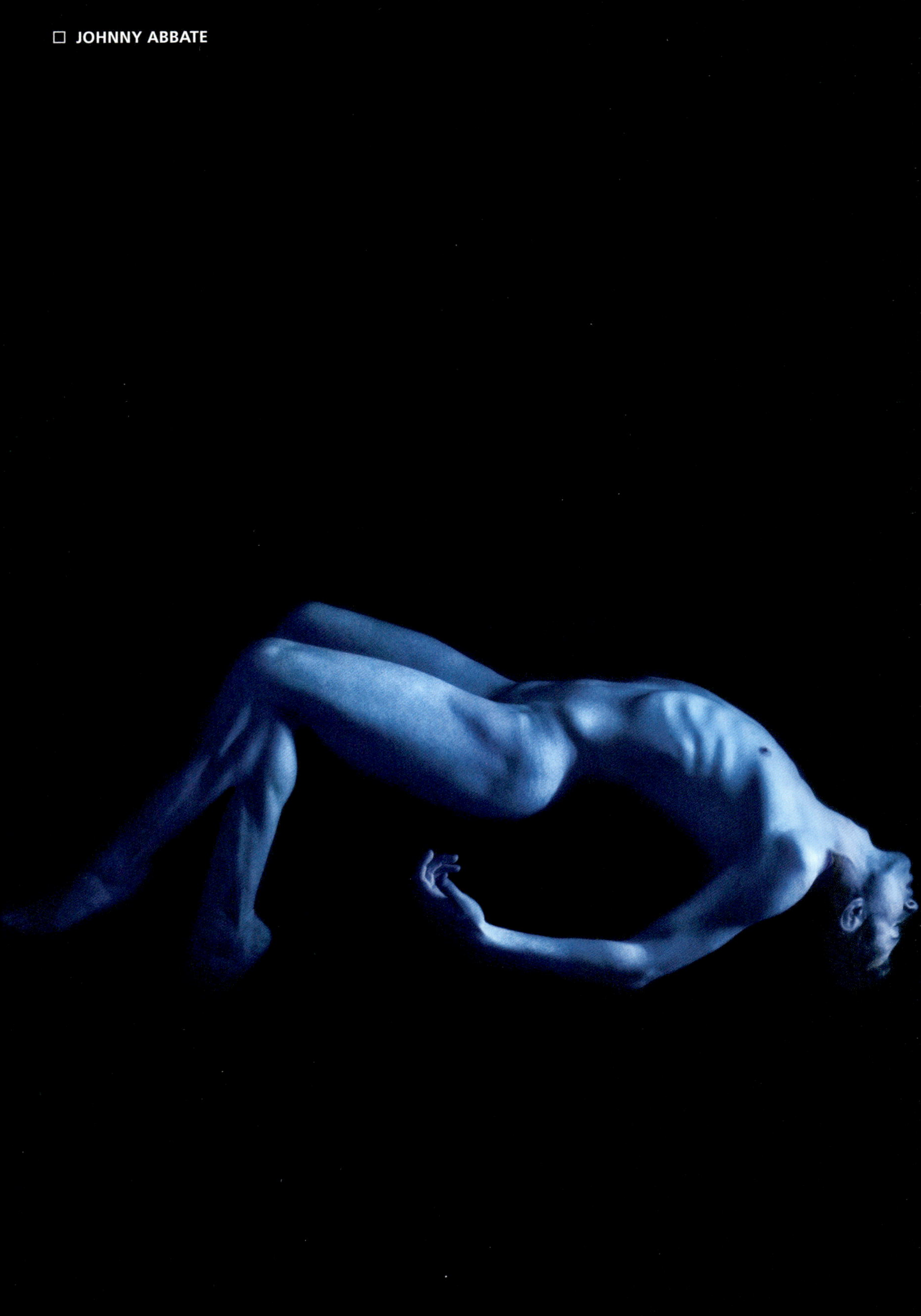
JOHNNY ABBATE

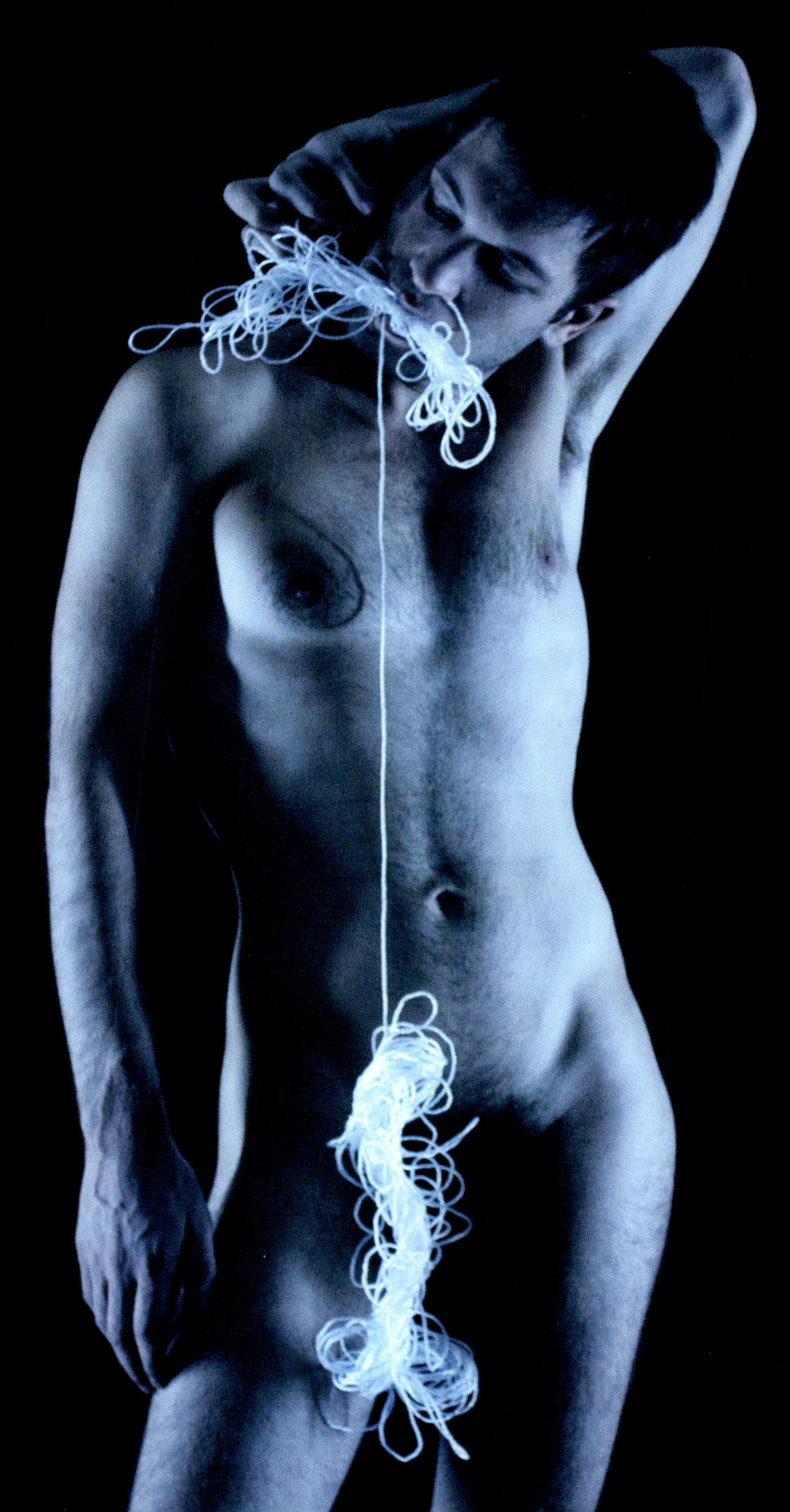

RALPH J. POOLE

Schöne Finnen im Wilden Westen •
Beautiful Finns in the Wild West

Können Finnen schön sein? Mir wurde gesagt, finnische Männer zählen nicht zu den schönsten. Doch man muss nicht alles glauben, was einem suggeriert wird, auch nicht von sogenannten Experten, seien es Finnougristen, also Wissenschaftler, die den finno-ugrischen Kulturraum beforschen, oder seien es Touristen, die diesen Kulturraum bereisen auf der Suche nach amourösen Abenteuern. Schönheit liegt im Auge des Betrachters, wie es so redlich heißt, und wenn das Auge ein schwules ist, mag mann auch Schönheit dort entdecken, wo andere sie nicht sehen. Ich habe mich auf die Spurensuche gemacht, nicht nur den schönen Finnen zu finden, sondern herauszufinden, wohin die Spuren des schönen Finnen führen. Und sie führen mich in den Wilden Westen Amerikas.

Finnen zählten zu den frühen Einwanderergruppen des kolonialen Amerikas und literarisch schlägt sich diese Präsenz in einem der ersten amerikanischen Romane nieder, der sich dieser frühen Besiedlungsgeschichte widmet. *Koningsmarke, the Long Finne, A Story of the New World* heißt der Roman von James Kirke Paulding von 1823, und der Held ist ein schöner Finne. Von diesem Prototyp des Mannes am Rande der Zivilisation, der schöne finnische und im Laufe der Handlung amerikanisierte Naturbursche, führt ein direkter Weg zu den späteren Cowboys des Wilden Westens, deren Erfolgsgeschichte sich als hypermaskuliner und hypersexualisierte Heldenmythos von Hollywood bis in die schwule Subkultur fortschreibt und dort in den Zeichnungen von Tom of Finland als erotisches Leitbild einer neuen schwulen Männlichkeit einen weiteren Höhepunkt erreicht.

Pauldings pikaresker historischer Roman spielt im 16. Jahrhundert in jenem Grenzbereich zwischen Zivilisation und Wildnis, der als ‚frontier' bezeichnet wird. Der junge finnische Hüne namens Koningsmarke begibt sich auf Abenteuersuche in die Neue Welt, und Abenteuer findet er doch auch reichliche. Er wird von den schwedischen Siedlern ins Gefängnis geworfen, von Indianern entführt, von Engländern des Hochverrats bezichtigt und kann

Can Finns be beautiful? I'm told that Finnish men are not counted among the most beautiful in the world. But we don't have to believe everything we are told, not even from so-called experts, no matter if they are Finno-Ugrists—scholars who research the Finno-Ugrian cultural area—or tourists traveling to this region in search of amorous adventures. Beauty is in the eye of the beholder, as they say, and if the eye is gay, men can also discover beauty where others don't see it. I went on a quest not only to track down the beautiful Finn, but to learn where the traces of the beautiful Finn lead. And they have led me to America's Wild West.

Finns were one of the first immigrant groups to colonial America and their presence is represented literarily in one of the first American novels about the early settlement period. The 1823 novel by James Kirke Paulding is called Koningsmarke, the Long Finne, A Story of the New World and its hero is a beautiful Finn. There's a direct link from this prototype of a man at the edge of civilization. A beautiful Finnish male who over the course of the tale becomes an American outdoorsman, to the later cowboys of the Wild West, whose success story as a hyper-masculine and hyper-sexualized hero myth is upheld everywhere from Hollywood to the Gay subculture, reaching a further climax in the latter through the drawings of Tom of Finland as an erotic model for a new gay masculinity.

Paulding's picaresque historical novel is set in the 16th century in the borderland between civilization and wilderness also known as the American Frontier. A young, tall and burly Finn named Koningsmarke sets out in search of adventure in the New World – and adventure he finds. He is thrown into jail by Swedish settlers, kidnaped by Indians, accused of treason by Englishmen and only barely escapes branding and slavery in the end. Koningsmarke

am Ende nur knapp der Brandmarkung und Versklavung entkommen. Koningsmarke ist ein Grenzgänger, zwischen Alter und Neuer Welt, zwischen verschiedenen Lagern und Parteien in den Kolonien, und letztlich auch zwischen den Geschlechtern. Seine ungewöhnliche Schönheit ist paradox, zum einen unterdeterminiert, weil seine Männlichkeit nicht der Norm entspricht: er wird beschrieben als "too fair", "too light", "somewhat effeminate". Zum anderen aber ist sie überdeterminiert, seine Muskeln und Furchtlosigkeit sind deutlich prononciert: "Koningsmarke was, in truth, a figure that might have drawn the particular attention of a lady whose eyes were accustomed to the finest forms of mankind. He was nearly, or quite six feet high, straight, and well proportioned, with a complexion almost too fair for a man, and eyes of a light blue. His hair was somewhat too light to suit the taste of the present day, but which, to an eye accustomed to associate it with ideas of manly beauty, was rather attractive than otherwise.

With these features, he might have been thought somewhat effeminate in his appearance, were it not that a vigorous, muscular form, and a certain singular expression of his eye, which partook somewhat of a fierce violence, threw around him the port of a hardy and fearless being." (*Koningsmarke* 19)

War Koningsmarkes androgyne Schönheit noch etwas dubios, "rather attractive than otherwise" laut Erzählerkommentar, so ist ein später Nachfahre dieser Figur "more than beautiful". Touko Laaksonen alias Tom of Finland schwärmt von seinen aufreizenden, halbnackten Modellen: "I almost never draw a completely naked man. He has to have at least a pair of boots or something on. To me a fully dressed man is more erotic than a naked one. A naked man is, of course, beautiful, but dress him in black leather or a uniform – ah, then he is more than beautiful, then he is sexy!" (zitiert in Hooven 62)

Toms Statement, dass ein nur teilweise entblößter Mann viel sexier sei als ein völlig nackter, entspricht Roland Barthes' rhetorischer Frage: "Ist die erotischste Stelle eines Körpers nicht da, *wo die Kleidung auseinanderklafft*?" (16, Hervorhebung im Original). Es sind die Unterbrechungen, die erotisch wirken, "die Haut, die zwischen zwei Kleidungsstücken glänzt [...]; das Glänzen selbst verführt, oder besser noch: die In-

is a border crosser between the Old and New World, between different factions and parties in the Colonies, and lastly between genders. His unusual beauty is a paradox. On one hand it's unresolved because his masculinity doesn't fit the norm, he's "too fair," "too light," and "somewhat effeminate." On the other hand his beauty is validated, as his muscles and dauntlessness are explicitly pronounced:

"Koningsmarke was, in truth, a figure that might have drawn the particular attention of a lady whose eyes were accustomed to the finest forms of mankind. He was nearly, or quite six feet high, straight, and well proportioned, with a complexion almost too fair for a man, and eyes of a light blue. His hair was somewhat too light to suit the taste of the present day, but which, to an eye accustomed to associate it with ideas of manly beauty, was rather attractive than otherwise.

With these features, he might have been thought somewhat effeminate in his appearance, were it not that a vigorous, muscular form, and a certain singular expression of his eye, which partook somewhat of a fierce violence, threw around him the port of a hardy and fearless being. (*Koningsmarke* 19)

While Koningsmarke's androgynous beauty was still something dubious, "rather attractive than otherwise," according to the narrator's comment, a descendent of him is "more than beautiful." Touko Laaksonen, aka Tom of Finland, raves about his saucy, demi-nude models: "I almost never draw a completely naked man. He has to have at least a pair of boots or something on. To me a fully dressed man is more erotic than a naked one. A naked man is, of course, beautiful, but dress him in black leather or a uniform – ah, then he is more than beautiful, then he is sexy!" (quoted in Hooven 62) Tom's statement, according to which a seminude man is even sexier than a completely naked one, matches Roland Barthes' rhetorical question: Isn't the most erotic part of a body that part *where the clothes are gaping open?* (16, cursive in the original) It's the disruptions which appear erotic, "the skin which shines between two

szenierung eines Auf- und Abblendes" (Barthes 17). Die Erregung kommt durch die Phantasie der fortschreitenden Enthüllung, dass am Ende das vollständig entblößte Geschlecht zu sehen ist. Barthes koppelt das körperliche Ablegen der Kleidung – das Spiel um Abwesendes und Verborgenes – an eine Erzählung, in der Wahrheit allmählich entschleiert wird. In beiden Inszenierungen wird das Publikum ‚verführt' durch das gekonnte Spiel mit Entblößen und Verdecken (Auf- und Abblenden). Daher sind in den Bildern Tom of Finlands Männer selten völlig nackt. Im Gegensatz zum männlichen Akt, der nach Tom eher de-erotisierend auf den Betrachter wirken kann, ist ein schöner Mann gerade erst durch seine vestimentäre Inszenierung aufreizend. Tom of Finland treibt dieses Spiel allerdings auf die Spitze. Bei seinen Bildern kommt es dabei in der spezifischen Kombination von Realismus und Übertreibung zu einem "homophile hyperrealism" (Ramakers 39) und infolgedessen gerät die Distanz zwischen betrachtendem Subjekt und dargestelltem Objekt ins Wanken. Durch die Geschichten, die die Bilder suggerieren, wird dem Betrachter das Gefühl vermittelt, er sei Teil einer utopischen, bruderschaftlichen Welt von "Tomland". Denn die Bilder haben eine narrative Qualität, die auf einer mythischen Ikonographie beruhen. Die utopische Welt von "Tomland" ist angesiedelt jenseits zivilisierter und technologisierter Urbanität und entwirft stattdessen alternative Gemeinschaften, die in halbzivilisierten oder gänzlich unzivilisierten Landschaftsräumen situiert sind. Mit seinen Holzfäller-Helden wie Kake und Pekka verknüpft Tom of Finland damit archetypische Männlichkeitsentwürfe, die aus Finnland stammen, mit jener traditionslastigen Ikonographie des amerikanischen Cowboys. Beiden wird aufgrund ihrer Naturverbundenheit und ihres durch schwere körperliche Arbeit gestählten muskulären Körpers eine Hypermaskulinität zugeschrieben.

Die Verknüpfung funktioniert deshalb so gut, weil sich in Amerika die Figur des Cowboys noch bis in die Gegenwart im kulturellen Mainstream wie in der Subkultur anhaltend großer Beliebtheit erfreut, man denke an den Hype um die traurige Liebesgeschichte zweier schöner ‚Cowboys' (in Wahrheit sind sie Schafhirten) in *Brokeback Mountain* (2005). Die Popularität des Cowboys in Amerika entstand zu einer

pieces of clothing [...]; the shining in itself seduces, or rather: the staging of fading in and out." (Barthes 17) Arousal occurs because of the fantasy of the undressing yet to come which will leave the genitals completely exposed in the end. Barthes connects the physical act of undressing – the game of the absent and the hidden – with a tale about slowly unveiling the truth. In both cases the audience is seduced by the skillful game of exposing and concealing (fading in and out). That's why Tom of Finland's pictures are rarely completely nude. In contrary to the male nude, which according to the artist can be rather deeroticizing for the viewer, a beautiful man is tantalizing only through his vestimentary staging. Tom of Finland carries this game to extremes. His pictures produce through a combination of realism and exaggeration a "homophile hyper-realism" (Ramakers 39) and therefore the distance between the viewed subject and the presented object unravels. The stories which seemingly lie behind the images, convey a feeling to viewers of belonging to the brotherly world of "Tomland." The pictures have a narrative quality which is based on a mythical iconography. The utopian world of "Tomland" is placed beyond civilized and technologized urbanity and instead creates alternative communities which are situated in demi-civilized or uncivilized landforms. With his lumberjack heroes like Kake and Pekka, Tom of Finland links archetypical beauty standards from Finland to an iconography rich in tradition of the American cowboy. Both are ascribed a hyper-masculinity because of their muscular bodies which were steeled through hard physical labor.

The link works so well because, even in present America, the character of the cowboy remains very popular within the cultural mainstream, as well as, the subculture – one thinks of the hype surrounding the sad love story of two "cowboys" (shepherds actually) in Brokeback Mountain (2005). The popularity of the cowboy in America emerged in a time when the Wild West wasn't really wild anymore. Around 1900 the western expansion had

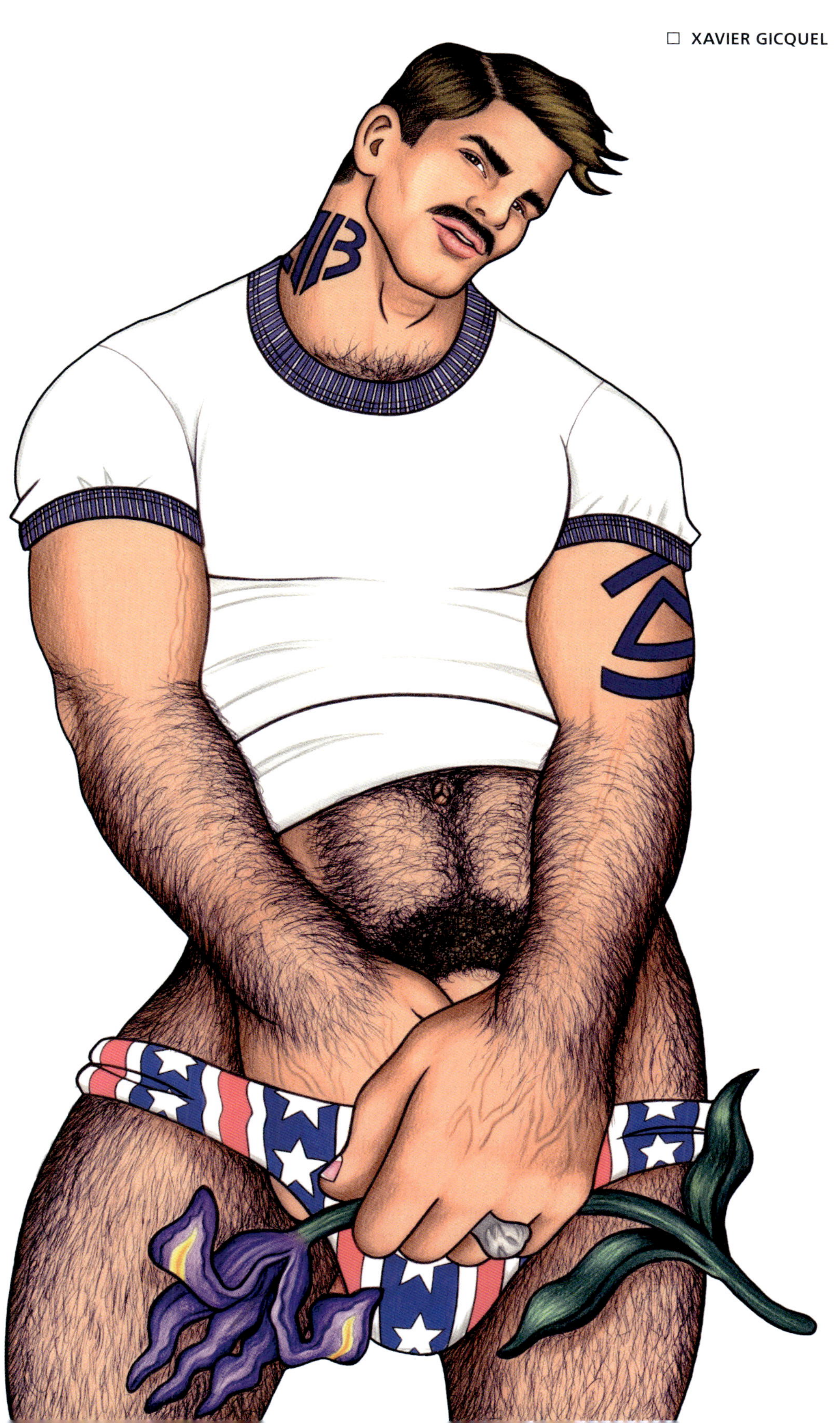

Zeit, als der Wilde Westen bereits kein wilder mehr war. Um 1900 hatte die Westexpansion ihr Ende erreicht, die Westküste war besiedelt und damit war offiziell auch die *frontier* verschwunden. Um diese Zeit wurde die Figur des Cowboys mit Wildwest-Romanen wie Owen Wisters *The Virginian* (1902) und Zane Greys *Riders of the Purple Sage* (1912) als retrospektiv installierter Mythos ‚geboren' und damit der Pioniergeist wachgehalten. Die Figur des Cowboys hält gewaltige sexuelle Implikationen bereit, die sich nicht zuletzt über den Lebens- und Kleidungsstil kommunizieren. Der Cowboy lebt unter seinesgleichen in naturverbundener Gemeinschaft, fern der Zivilisation, Stadt und Frauen. Was bei Western in Literatur und Film als archetypisches Bild einer männerdominierten Gesellschaft kursierte (man denke an die Cowboyrollen von John Wayne), florierte ab den 1960er Jahren im schwulen, subkulturellen Kontext als idealisierte mann-männliche Phantasie. Und der ikonische Look des Cowboys (Stiefel, Sporen, Jeans, Chaps, Flanellhemd, Hut) sind zur fetischbesetzten Uniform eines bestimmten schwulen erotischen Männerarchetyps geworden.

Dabei sind die Tom-of-Finland-Cowboys allerdings Hybride, denn sie bedienen sich zwar einer etablierten Tradition, geben dieser aber eine zeitgenössische Gestalt. Vor allem über Kleidung und Handlung wird ein Szenario entworfen, das sich schwerlich historisch begründen lässt. Die Bilder mischen zum Beispiel Cowboys in traditioneller Aufmachung mit Figuren, die sich über deren Kleidungscodes dem zeitgenössischen Bikermilieu zuordnen lassen. Ebenso wird das Lasso eines Cowboys nun nicht mehr zum Einfangen von Kälbern eingesetzt, sondern um Gespielen für Sex ‚einzufangen'. Zerrissene T-Shirts und halbentblößte Brust zeugen zwar vom Kampf, sind jedoch Teil des Narrativs sexueller Eroberung im Sinne Barthes'. Vor allem aber wird der ohnehin strapazierte Realismus noch weiter überhöht durch die unverhohlen hypertrophe Körperlichkeit der Männer: extrem schmale Hüften betonen den massiven Oberkörper und der zum Bersten pralle Schritt suggeriert einen monströsen Schwanz. Die Holzfäller und Cowboys in seinen Bildern rekurrieren – und subvertieren – damit die Vorstellung einer ‚natürlichen' Männlichkeit. Teil dieser ‚Natür-

reached its end, the west coast was populated and the "frontier" ceased to exist. In this time the character of the cowboy was born as a retrospectively installed myth through Wild West novels like Owen Wister's The Virginian (1902) and Zane Grey's Riders of the Purple Sage (1912) and with it the pioneer spirit was kept alive. The character of the cowboy has important sexual implications which are communicated largely through his lifestyle and clothing. The cowboy lives among his fellows in close touch to nature, far away from civilization, cities and women. What circulated as an archetypical picture of a society dominated by men in movie and book Westerns (just think about the cowboy characters played by John Wayne), flourished on from the 1960s in a gay subcultural context as an idealized manly fantasy. The iconic look of cowboys (boots, spurs, jeans, chaps, flannel shirt, hat) has become a fetish uniform of a certain erotic gay archetype of men.

And yet Tom of Finland's cowboys are hybrids, using established traditions in a contemporary form. Through clothing and plot, scenarios are created which are hard to explain historically. For example, pictures mix traditional cowboy styles with characters, who because of their way of dressing, can be placed within the contemporary biker milieu. In the same way, the lasso of a cowboy isn't used for catching calves anymore but for "catching" a playmate for sex. Torn t-shirts and semi-exposed chests bear witness to a fight, but they're also a part of the narrative of sexual conquest in the sense of Barthes. Most notably though, the already stressed realism is being elevated further through the blatantly hypertrophic physicality of the men: extremely slim hips emphasize the massive upper body and the firm bulge between their legs suggests a monstrous dick. The lumberjacks and cowboys in his pictures refer back to – and with that endowment – the idea of a "natural" masculinity. Part of this "naturalness" would be a heterosexual desire of such a man. The nature-boy, no matter if in the form of the Finnish lumberjack or the American cowboy, can't be a real man – a natural man – if he desires another man. In this regard, Connell talks of a draft

lichkeit' wäre das heterosexuelle Begehren eines solchen Mannes. Der Naturbursche, ob als finnischer Holzfäller oder amerikanischer Cowboy, kann kein echter Mann sein – kein natürlicher Mann – wenn er einen anderen Mann begehrt. Connell spricht hierbei vom Entwurf einer hegemonialen Männlichkeit als Strategie moderner Geschlechterideologie:
"True masculinity is almost always thought to proceed from men's bodies – to be inherent in a male body or to express something about a male body. Either the body drives and directs action (e.g., men are naturally more aggressive than women; rape results from uncontrollable lust or an innate urge to violence), or the body sets limits to action (e.g., men naturally do not take care of infants; homosexuality is unnatural and therefore confined to a perverse minority)." (Connell 45)
Die Bilder von Tom of Finland greifen diese Merkmale hegemonialer Männlichkeit auf und bringen sie in eine dezidiert und unmissverständlich schwule Begehrensökonomie. Dadurch installiert er genau jene ‚Perversität' des Homosexuellen als zentrales – und somit nicht mehr marginales – Kennzeichen in seiner Repräsentation von Männlichkeit. Die unnatürliche, unreine, ‚hybride' Rasse der Homosexuellen, über die Owen Wister, Schöpfer ikonischer Cowboyfiguren, schreibt, ist bei Tom zur einzig natürlich geworden:
"No rood of modern ground is more debased and mongrel with its hordes of encroaching alien vermin, that turn cities to Babels and our citizenship to a hybrid farce, who degrade our commonwealth from a nation into something half pawn-shop, half broker's office. But to survive in the clean cattle country requires spirit of adventure, courage, and self-sufficiency; you will not find many Poles or Huns or Russian Jews in that district; but the Anglo-Saxon is still forever homesick for out-of-doors. (Wister zitiert in Davis 37)
Wister bedient sich hier rassistischer Stereotype, die zwar zeitgebunden, deshalb aber nicht weniger pejorativ gemeint sind. Zu diesen um 1900 kursierenden Rassismen gehörte auch der als orientalisch kategorisierte – und damit als effeminiert wahrgenommene – Finne, denn in der Tat galten Finnen im Unterschied zu anderen Nordeuropäern als "Nicht-Weiße" und waren aufgrund der *Oriental Exclusion Acts* bis

of hegemonic masculinity as a strategy of modern gender ideology:
"True masculinity is almost always thought to proceed from men's bodies – to be inherent in a male body or to express something about a male body. Either the body drives and directs action (e.g., men are naturally more aggressive than women; rape results from uncontrollable lust or an innate urge to violence), or the body sets limits to action (e.g., men naturally do not take care of infants; homosexuality is unnatural and therefore confined to a perverse minority)." (Connell 45)
The pictures of Tom of Finland take up these traits of hegemonic masculinity and bring them into a decidedly and unmistakably gay economy of desire. Through this he installs exactly this "perversity" of the homosexual as a central – and therefore not anymore marginal – indicator in his representation of masculinity. The unnatural, impure, "hybrid" race of homosexuals, about whom Owen Wister, creator of iconic cowboy characters, writes, has turned into the only natural one for Tom:
"No rood of modern ground is more debased and mongrel with its hordes of encroaching alien vermin, that turn cities to Babels and our citizenship to a hybrid farce, who degrade our commonwealth from a nation into something half pawn-shop, half broker's office. But to survive in the clean cattle country requires spirit of adventure, courage, and self-sufficiency; you will not find many Poles or Huns or Russian Jews in that district; but the Anglo-Saxon is still forever homesick for out-of-doors. (Wister quoted in Davis 37)
Here Wister uses racist stereotypes which are meant temporarily but not any less pejoratively. One of these racisms circulating around 1900 is that of the Finn categorized as oriental – and with this perceived as ef- feminate – because in fact the Finns, in contrary to other northern Europeans, were classified as "Non-Whites" and were not allowed to acquire the American citizenship until 1908 because of the *Oriental Exclusion Acts.* Now the cowboy of the 19th century, who Wister praised as ideal-typical, was precisely not the independent, adventurous

1908 vom Erwerb der amerikanischen Staatsbürgerschaft ausgeschlossen. Der Cowboy des 19. Jahrhunderts, wie ihn Wister als idealtypisch pries, war nun aber gerade nicht der unabhängige, unternehmungslustige Angelsachse, sondern ein junger unterbezahlter und unterernährter Arbeiter, der sich oftmals lange Zeit ohne Anstellung durchschlagen musste. Damit verkörperte der Cowboy keineswegs eine erstrebenswerte Männerleitfigur; er galt vielmehr als streitbarer Trunkenbold und mittelloser Tagelöhner, ein *outlaw* unspezifischer Herkunft. Um 1900 war der reale Cowboy zu einer gänzlich obsoleten Figur geworden. Durch Autoren wie Wister und dem einsetzenden Wildwest-Literatur-Boom allerdings wurde er zu einem Mythos stilisiert, der in allen Sparten der Populärkultur reüssierte.

Die Bilder Tom of Finlands nehmen in paradoxer Weise teil an der Mythisierung und Ikonographie hegemonialer Männlichkeit, indem sie diese in der Repräsentation homosexueller Lustszenarien zitieren – freilich mit einer signifikanten Umschreibung. Im Vernetzen heterosexueller Männlichkeitssymbole (der kerlige Naturbursche) mit Konzepten homoerotischen Begehrens (Riesenpenisse in S/M-Aktionen) entsteht nicht nur eine gezielte Irritation in den gewohnten Seh- und Lesegewohnheiten der Mainstreamkultur. Die Holzfäller und Cowboys bei Tom of Finland sind hypermaskuline Helden aus den unteren Bevölkerungsschichten, die einerseits den Typus des ‚natürlichen' männlichen Körpers glorifizieren und zum Fetisch erheben, andererseits traditionelle Bilder von Männlichkeit destabilisieren und homoerotisieren. Der Finne ist nun endgültig zum Inbegriff eines Schönheitsideals natürlicher Männlichkeit geworden und damit hat die hypertrophe Ästhetik Tom of Finlands ein untrügliches Zeichen im Bilderarsenal der amerikanischen Populärkultur gesetzt.

Anglo-Saxon but the young underpaid and malnourished worker who often had to get by for long periods of time without employment. In this sense the cowboy did not embody a male role model worth striving for; instead he was regarded as a strident drunk and penniless day laborer, an outlaw of unspecific origin. By 1900 the real cowboy has become a totally obsolete character. But through the Wild West literature boom, authors like Wister stylized the cowboy myth which succeeded in all sectors of pop culture.

Paradoxically, the pictures of Tom of Finland take part in the mystification and iconography of hegemonic masculinity, through citing them in the representation of homosexual pleasure scenarios – of course with a significant Alteration. By linking straight symbols of masculinity (the nature boy) to concepts of homoerotic desire (gigantic dicks in S&M acts), viewing and reading habits of the mainstream straight culture are being questioned and even assaulted. Tom of Finland's lumberjacks and cowboys are hyper-masculine heroes from low social classes who, on the one hand glorify the "natural" manly body raising it to a fetish, while on the other hand, destabilizing and homoeroticizing traditional pictures of masculinity. The Finn has finally become the epitome of ideal of beauty, natural masculinity and the hypertrophic aesthetic of Tom of Finland has left an unmistakable mark in the arsenal of pictures of the American pop culture.

Translation: Sunita Sukhana,
Mark Timothy Hayward

Verweise;
Barthes, Roland: *Die Lust am Text*. Übers. Traugott König. Frankfurt/M.: Suhrkamp 1974.
Connell, R. W.: *Masculinities*. Berkeley: University of California Press 1995.
Davis, Robert Murray (Hg.): *Owen Wister's West: Selected Articles*. Albuquerque: University of New Mexico Press 1987.
Hooven, F. Valentine III: *Tom of Finland: His Life and Times*. New York: St. Martin's Press 1993.
Paulding, James Kirke: *Koningsmarke, the Long Finne* [1823]. Schenectady: Union College Press 1988.
Ramakers, Micha. *Dirty Pictures: Tom of Finland, Masculinity, and Homosexuality*. New York: St. Martin's Press 2000.

Referrals:
Barthes, Roland: Die Lust am Text. Übers. Traugott König. Frankfurt/M.: Suhrkamp 1974.
Connell, R. W.: Masculinities. Berkeley: University of California Press 1995.
Davis, Robert Murray (Hg.): Owen Wister's West: Selected Articles. Albuquerque: University of New Mexico Press 1987.
Hooven, F. Valentine III: Tom of Finland: His Life and Times. New York: St. Martin's Press 1993.
Paulding, James Kirke: Koningsmarke, the Long Finne [1823]. Schenectady: Union College Press 1988.
Ramakers, Micha. Dirty Pictures: Tom of Finland, Masculinity, and Homosexuality. New York: St. Martin's Press 2000.

TOM House Events

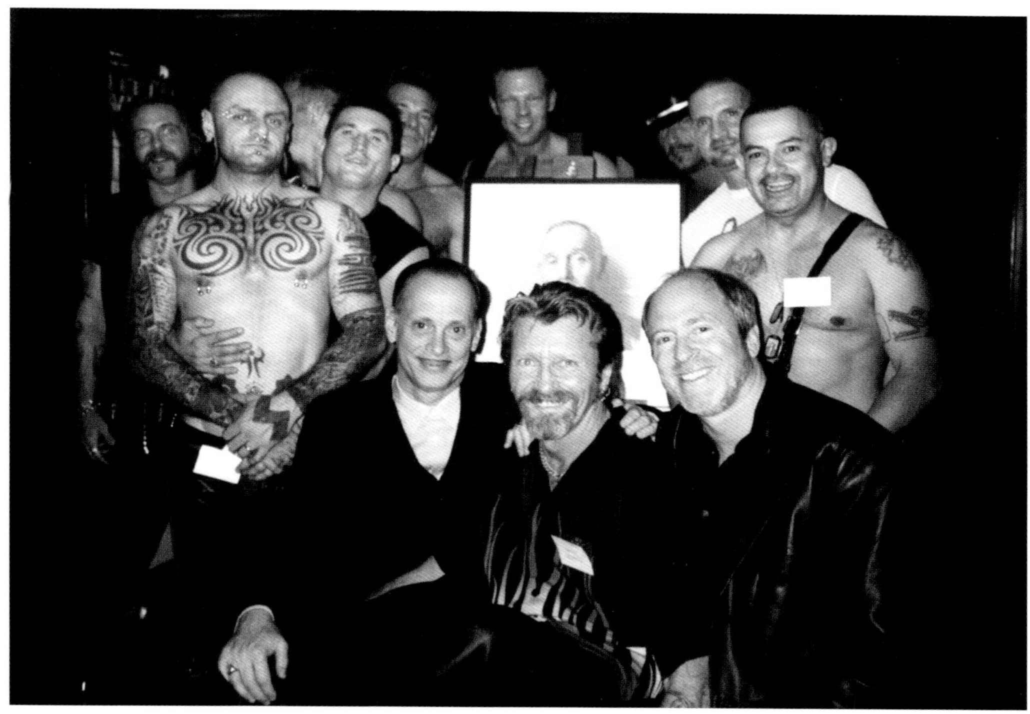

John Waters, Durk Dehner, Greg Gorman and Foundation volunteers / ehrenamtliche Helfer der Foundation

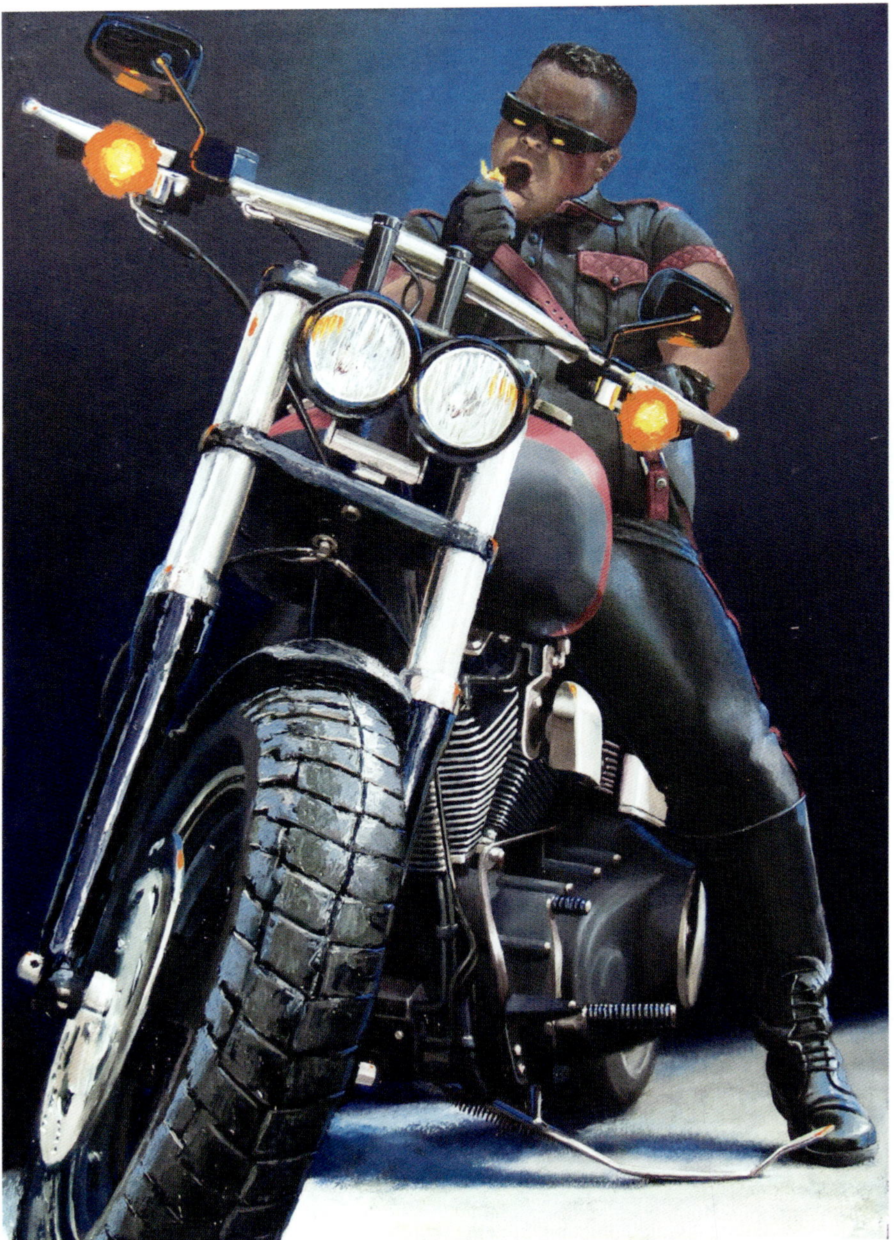

Exhibitions at TOM House

The Foundation has always exhibited artwork on its walls, always revolving its permanent collection. It also provides space for emerging and established artists, giving them a platform to present their works to the public.

Ausstellungen im TOM House

Die Foundation hat schon immer Kunstwerke in ihren Räumen ausgestellt und dabei ihre Dauerausstellung ständig verändert. Sie bietet sowohl neuen als auch etablierten Künstlern ein Forum, um ihre Werke der Öffentlichkeit zu präsentieren.

SUZANNE SHIFFLETT

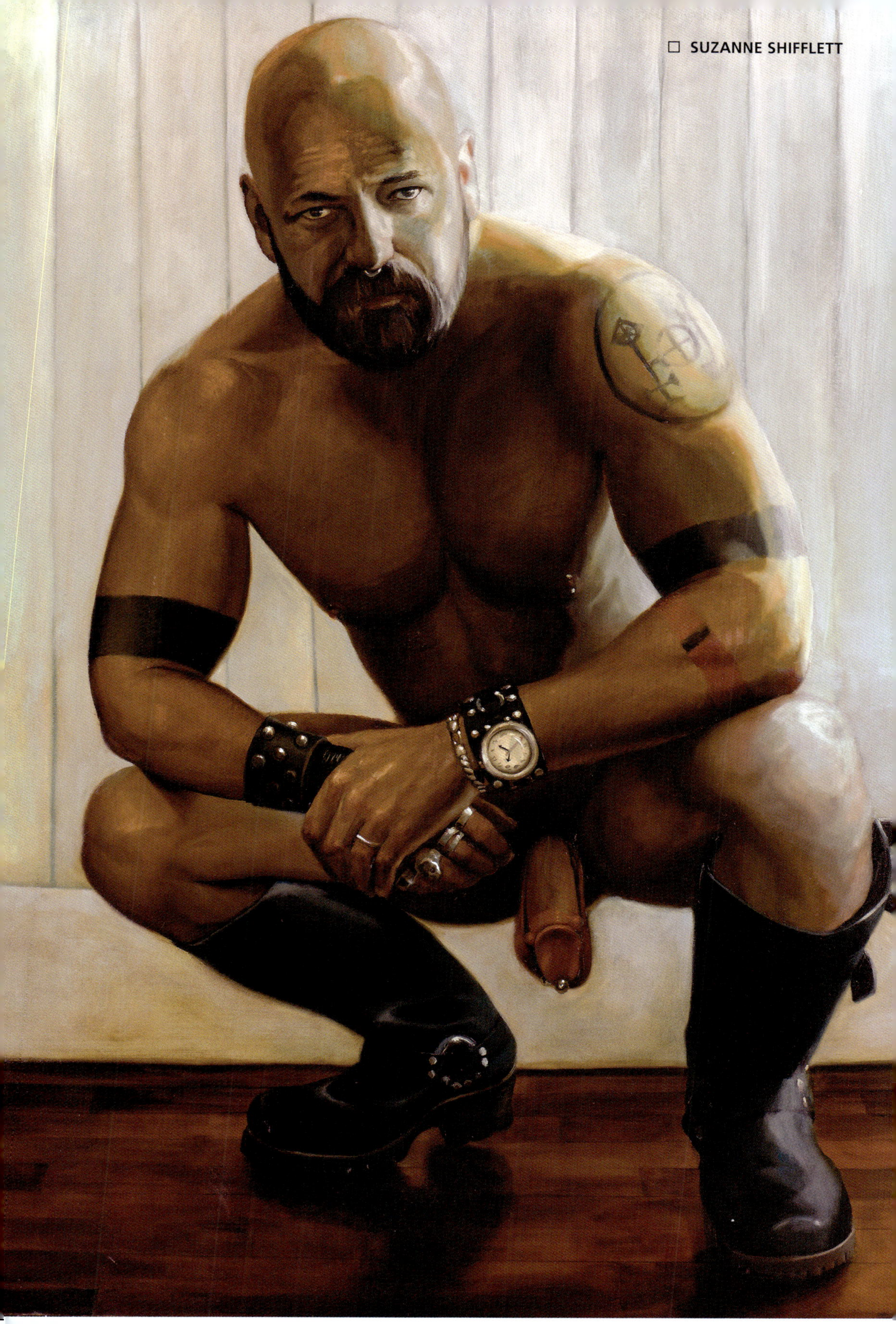

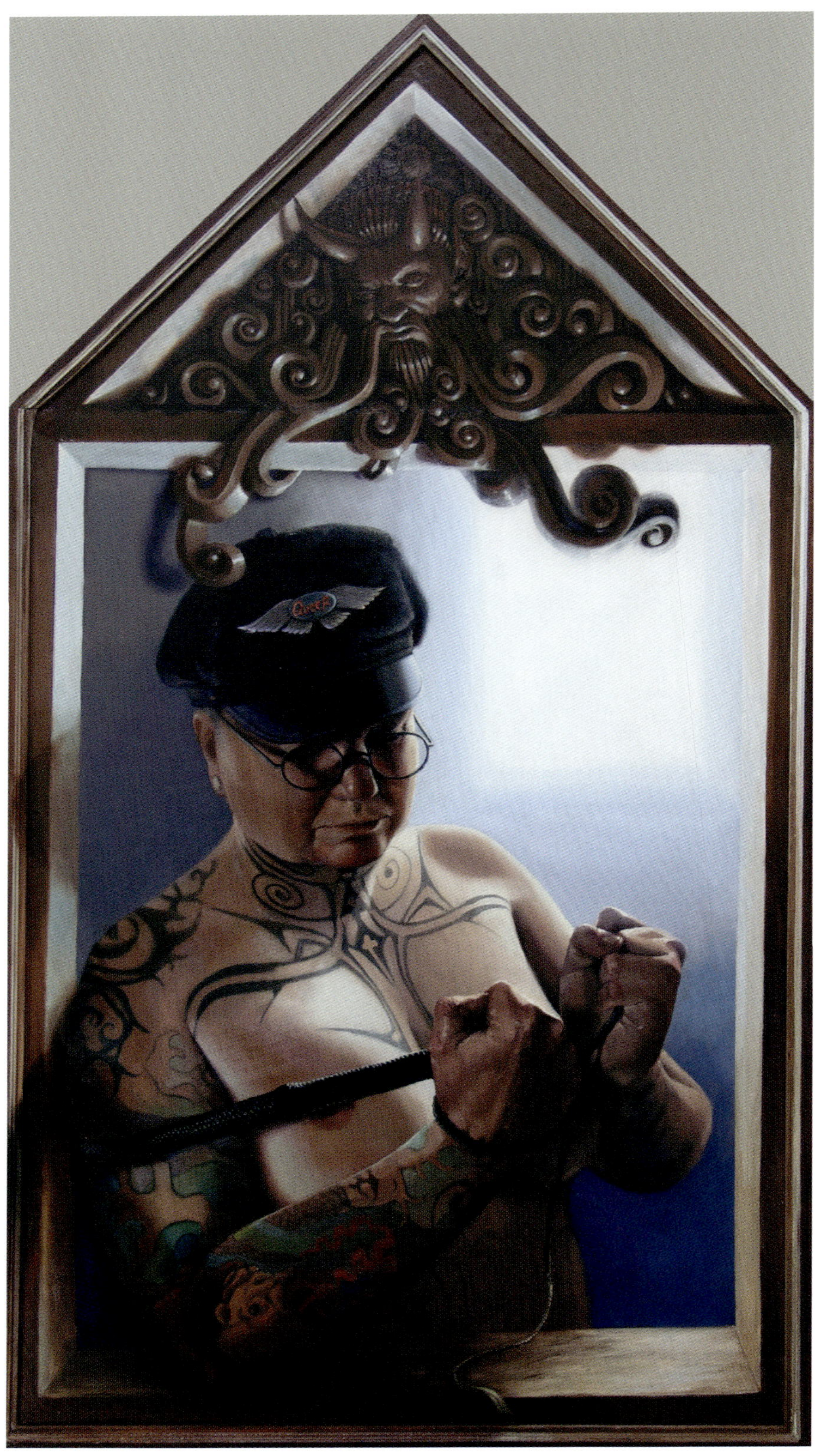

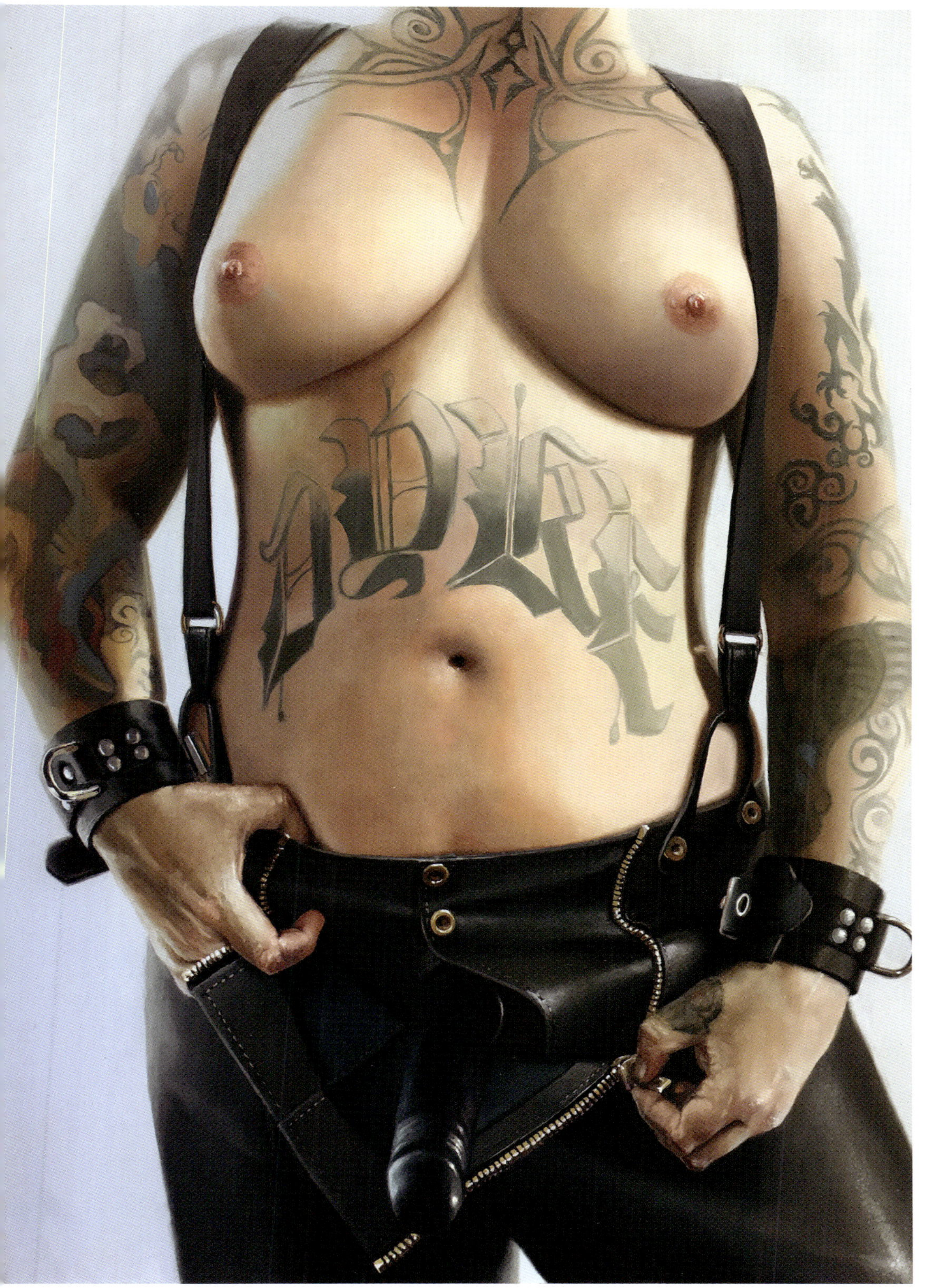

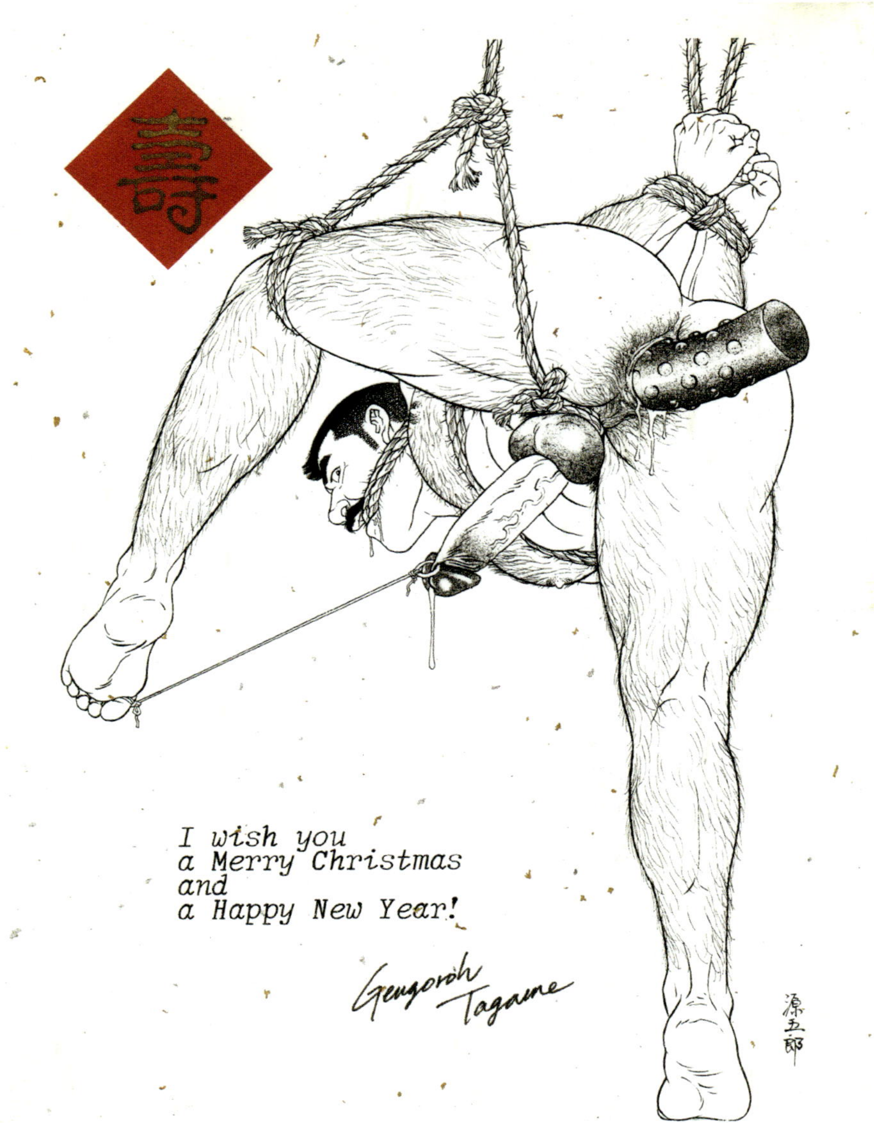

GENGOROH TAGAME

The Japanese manga artist has told me, that as it was with Tom's imagery having an effect of young men starting to appear on the streets like a Tom's drawing come to life, so did his burly men manifest in Japanese cities. Gengoroh Tagame is still very much a working artist and makes trips to Europe and the United States every few years to meet his collectors and fans.

Welche nachhaltiige Wirkung Toms Bilder haben, hat mir der japanische Manga-Zeichner einmal so geschildert: Junge Männer auf den Straßen sehen mit einem Mal so aus, als wäre eine Zeichnung Toms zum Leben erwacht. Und Ähnliches lässt sich mittlerweile in japanischen Städten auch von Gengoroh Tagames stämmigen Männern sagen. Der Künstler ist immer sehr produktiv und unternimmt alle paar Jahre Reisen nach Europa und in die Vereinigten Staaten, um dort seine Fans und Sammler zu treffen.

– Durk Dehner

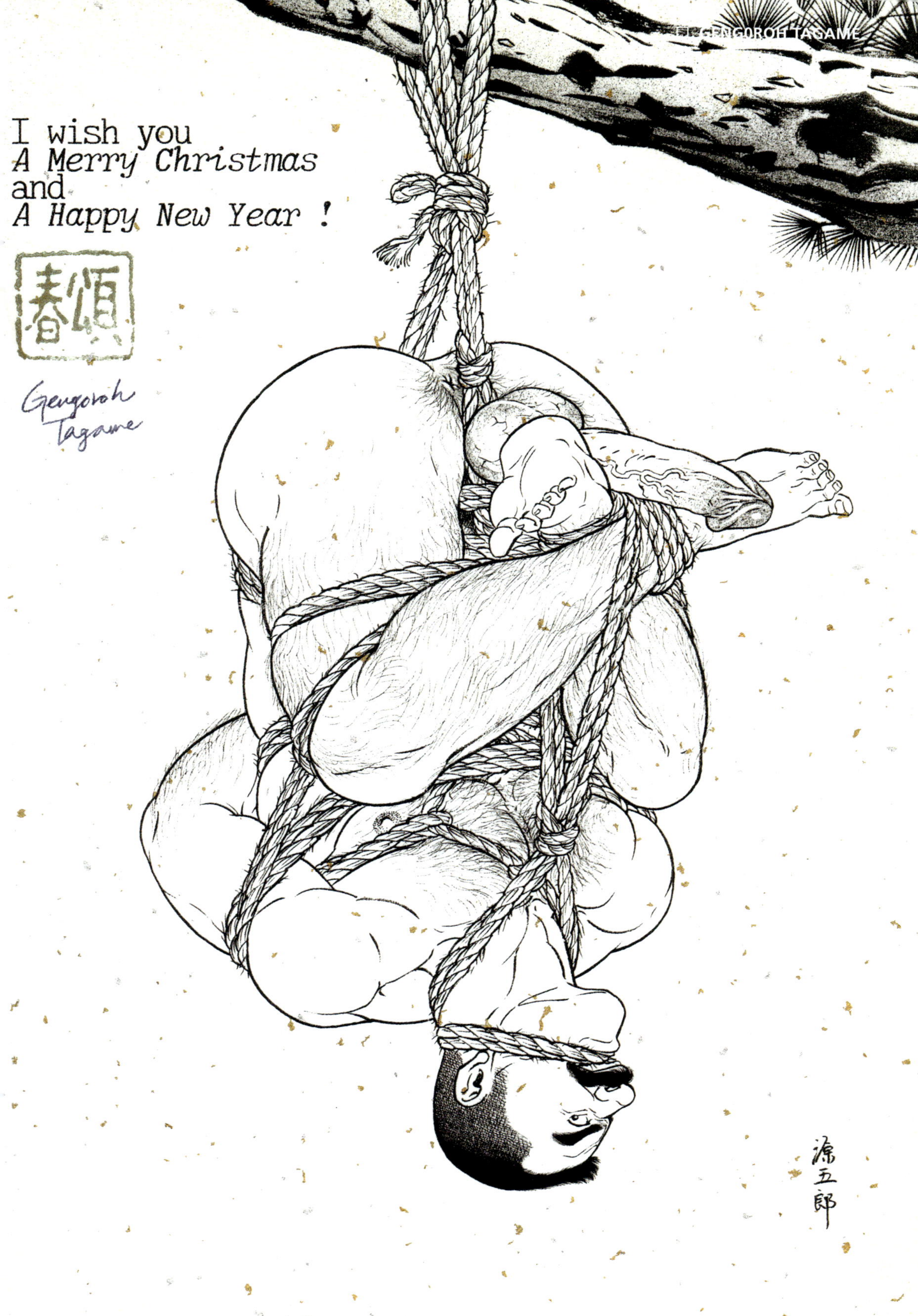
I wish you
A Merry Christmas
and
A Happy New Year !
Gengoroh Tagame

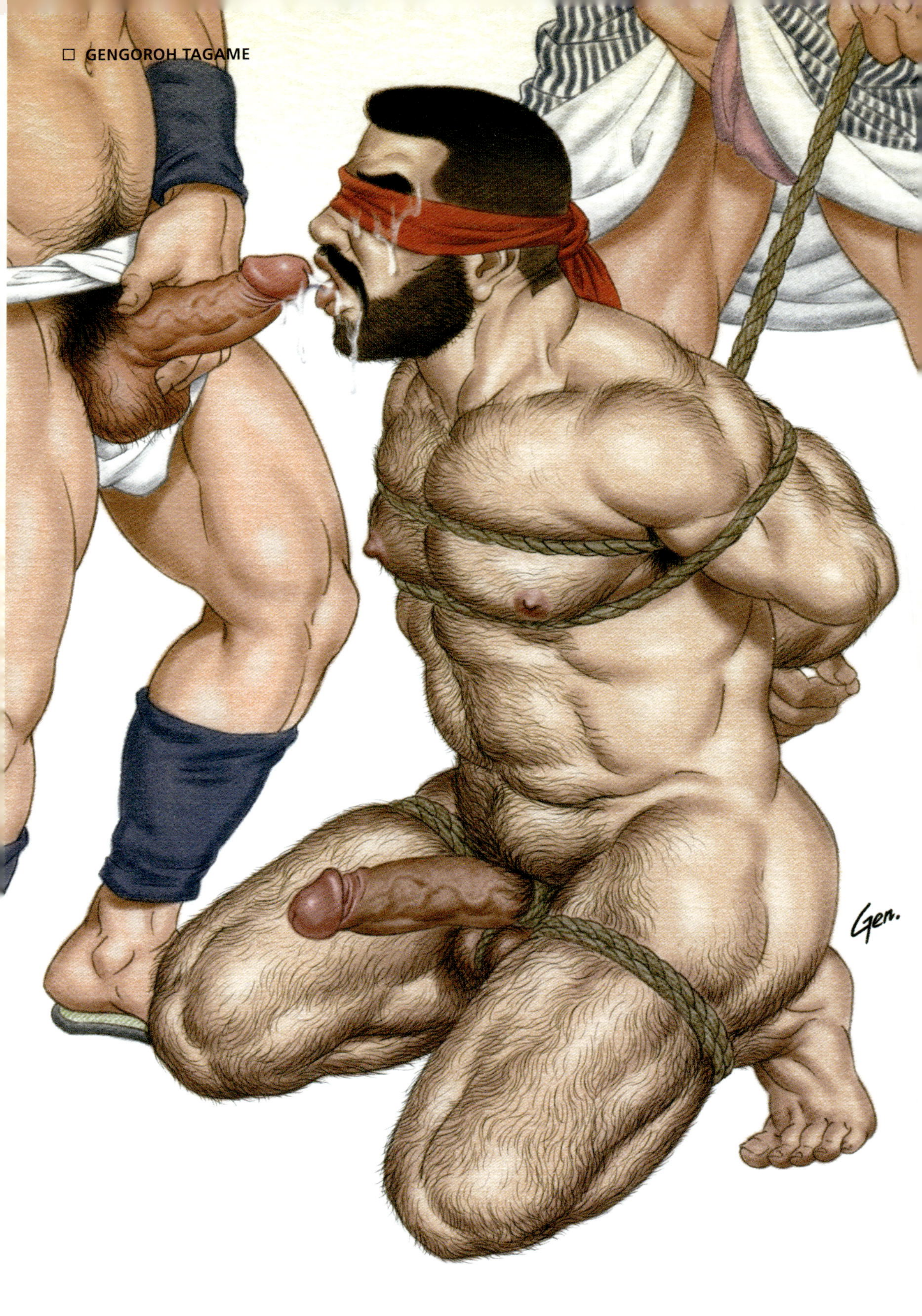

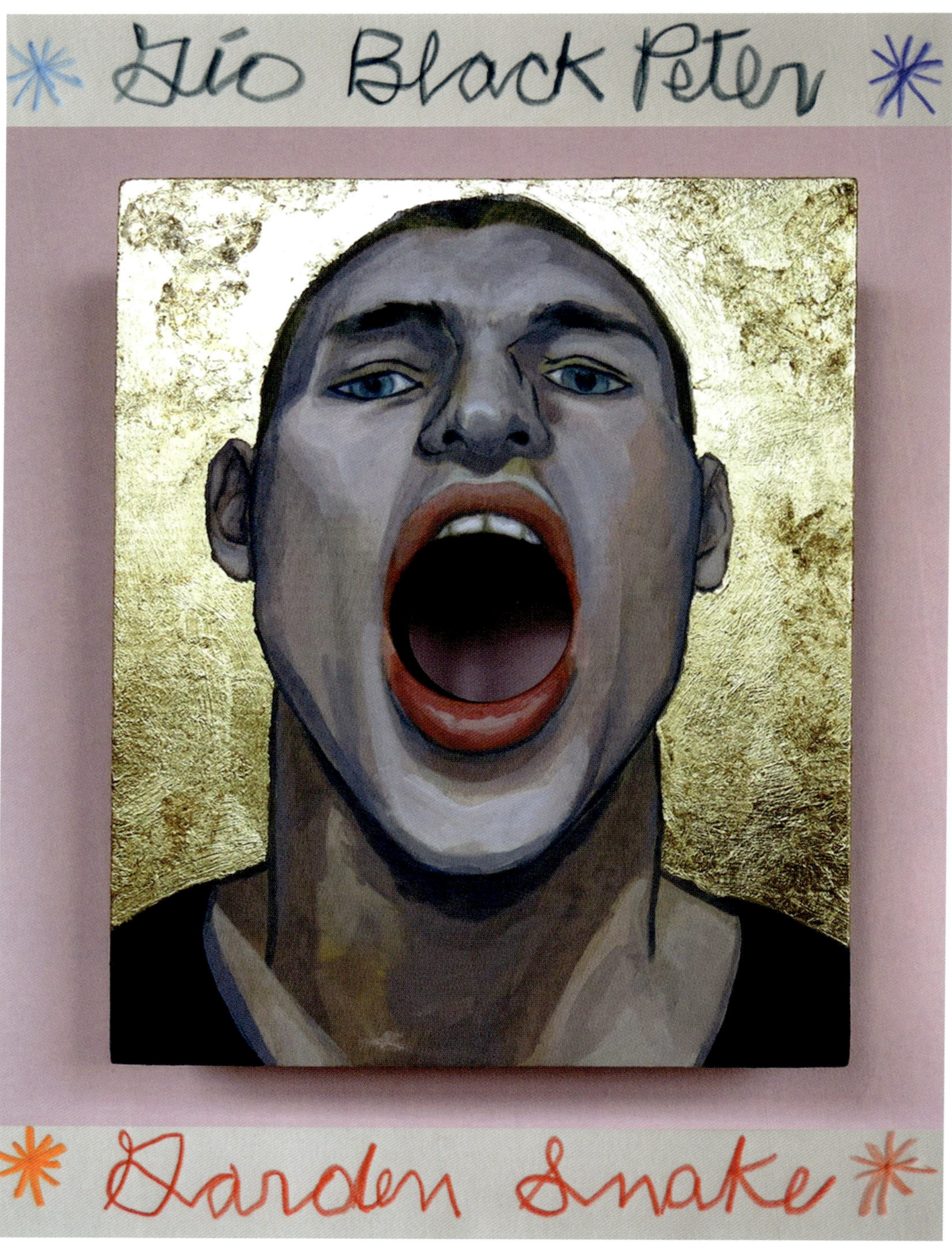

Gio Black Peter
Garden Snake

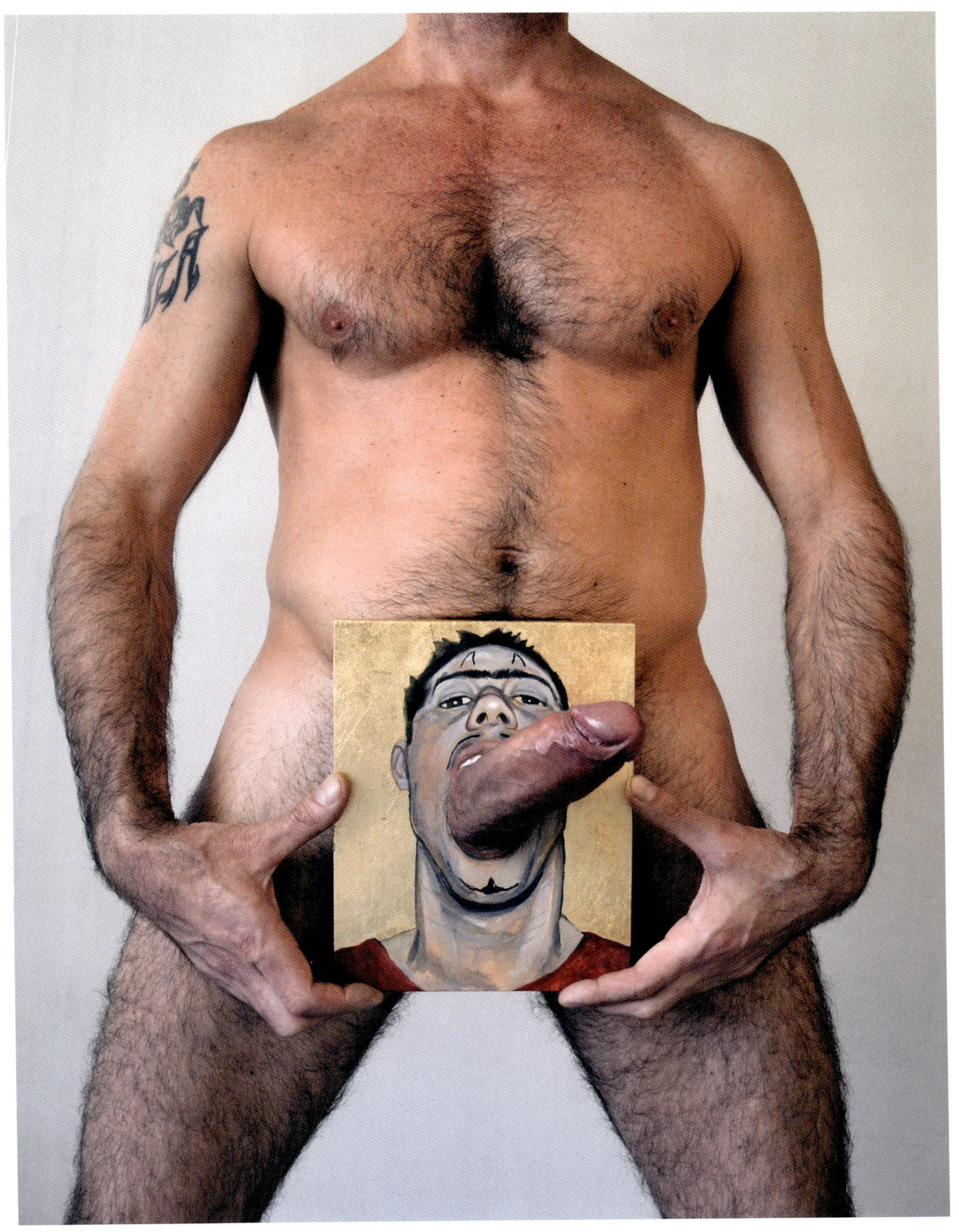

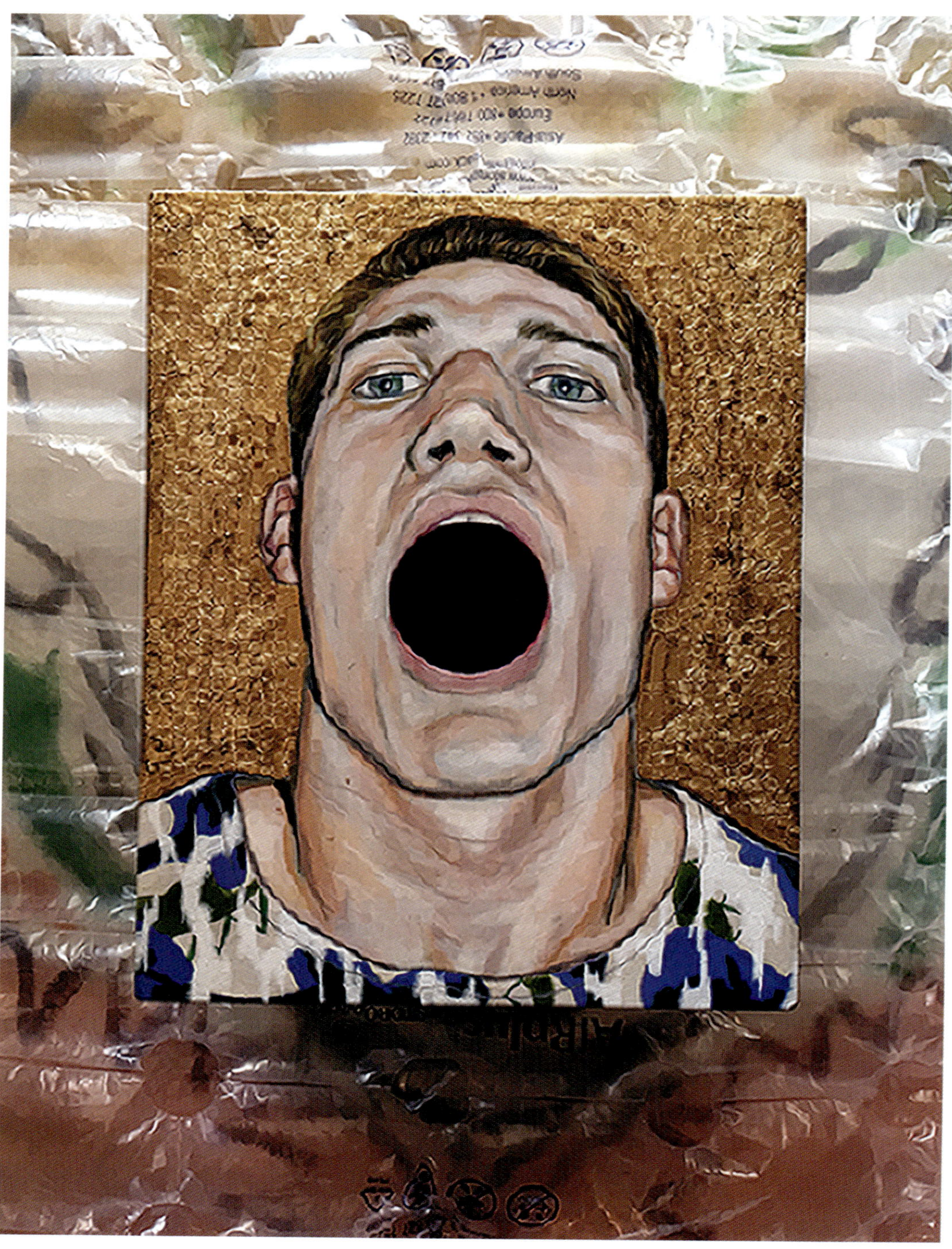

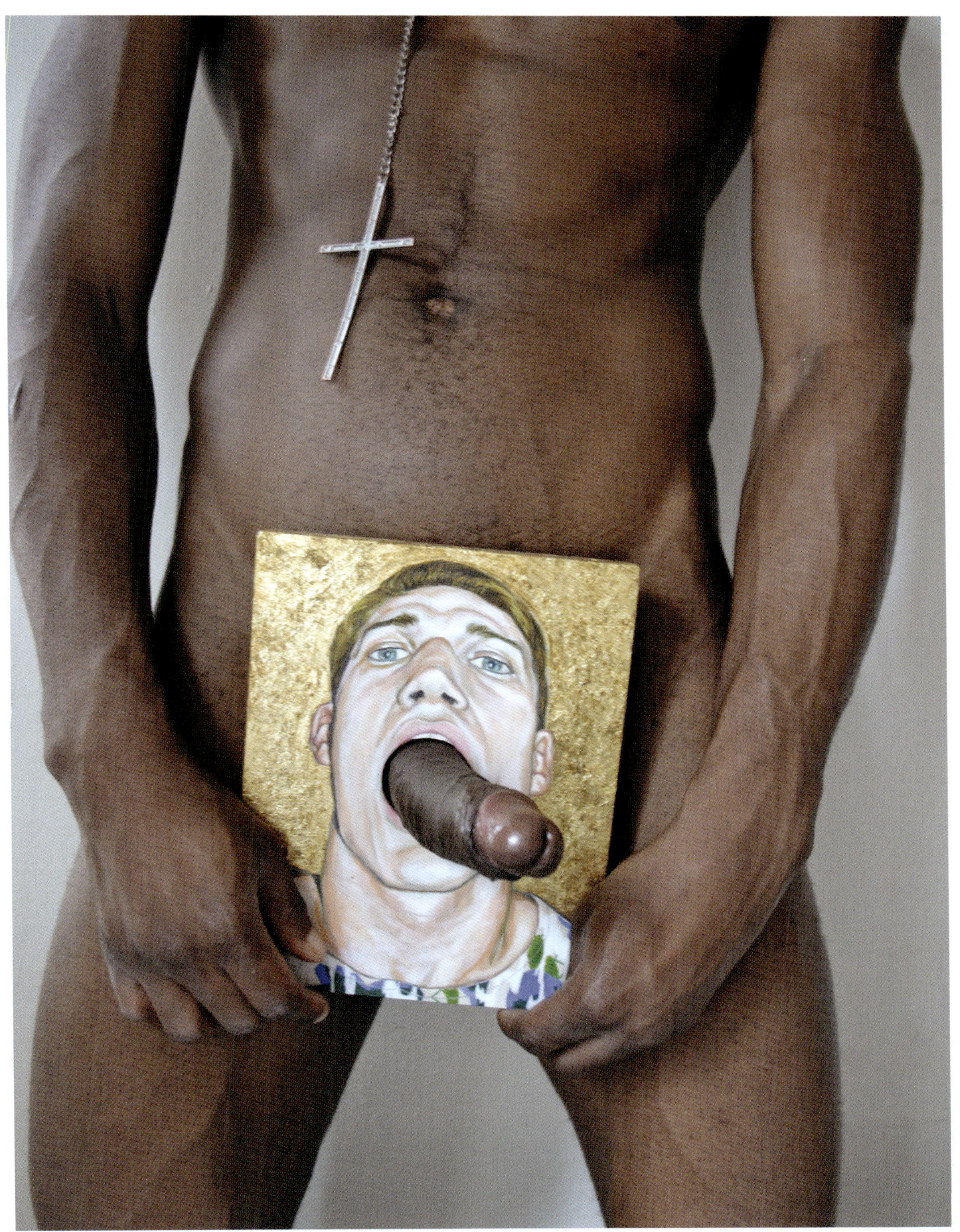

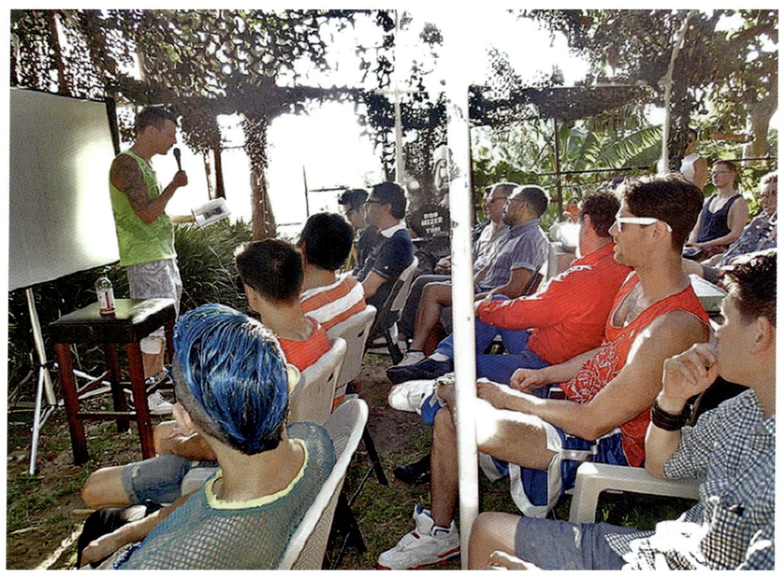

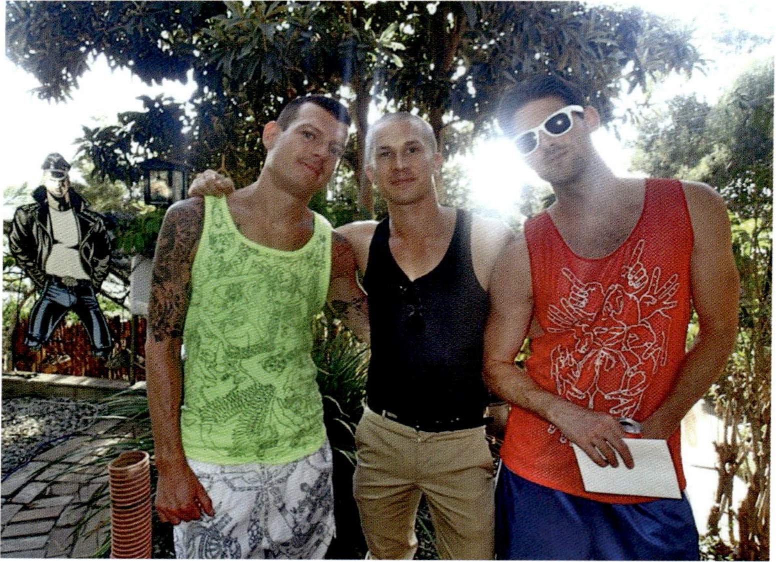

Slava Mogutin, Joakim Andreasson, Brian Kenny

Artists Receptions

The Foundation provides a program for visiting artists, guests and the public.
These are often evenings where artists give talks, readings, screenings, exhibit their
works, and meet with fans and followers. Recent guests for example have been
Gengoroh Tagame, Jiraiya, Slava Mogutin, Antonio da Silva and Bruce LaBruce.

Künstler-Empfänge

Bei diesen Künstler-Vorträgen, Lesungen, Filmvorführungen und Ausstellungen
bietet sich für die Fans die Möglichkeit, mit den Künstlern persönlich ins Gespräch
zu kommen, wie z.B. mit Gengoroh Tagame, Jiraiya, Slava Mogutin, Antonio da
Silva und Bruce LaBruce.

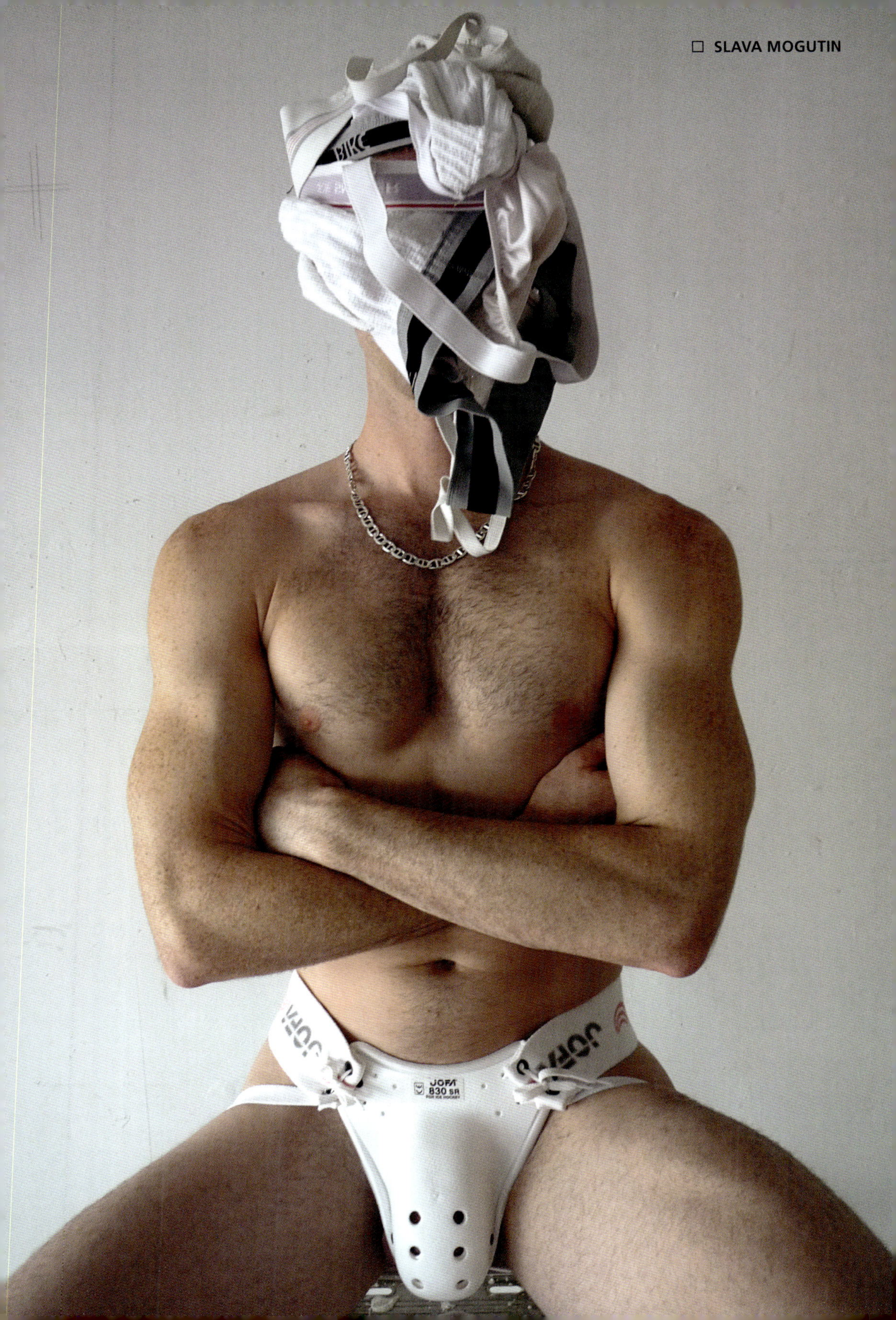

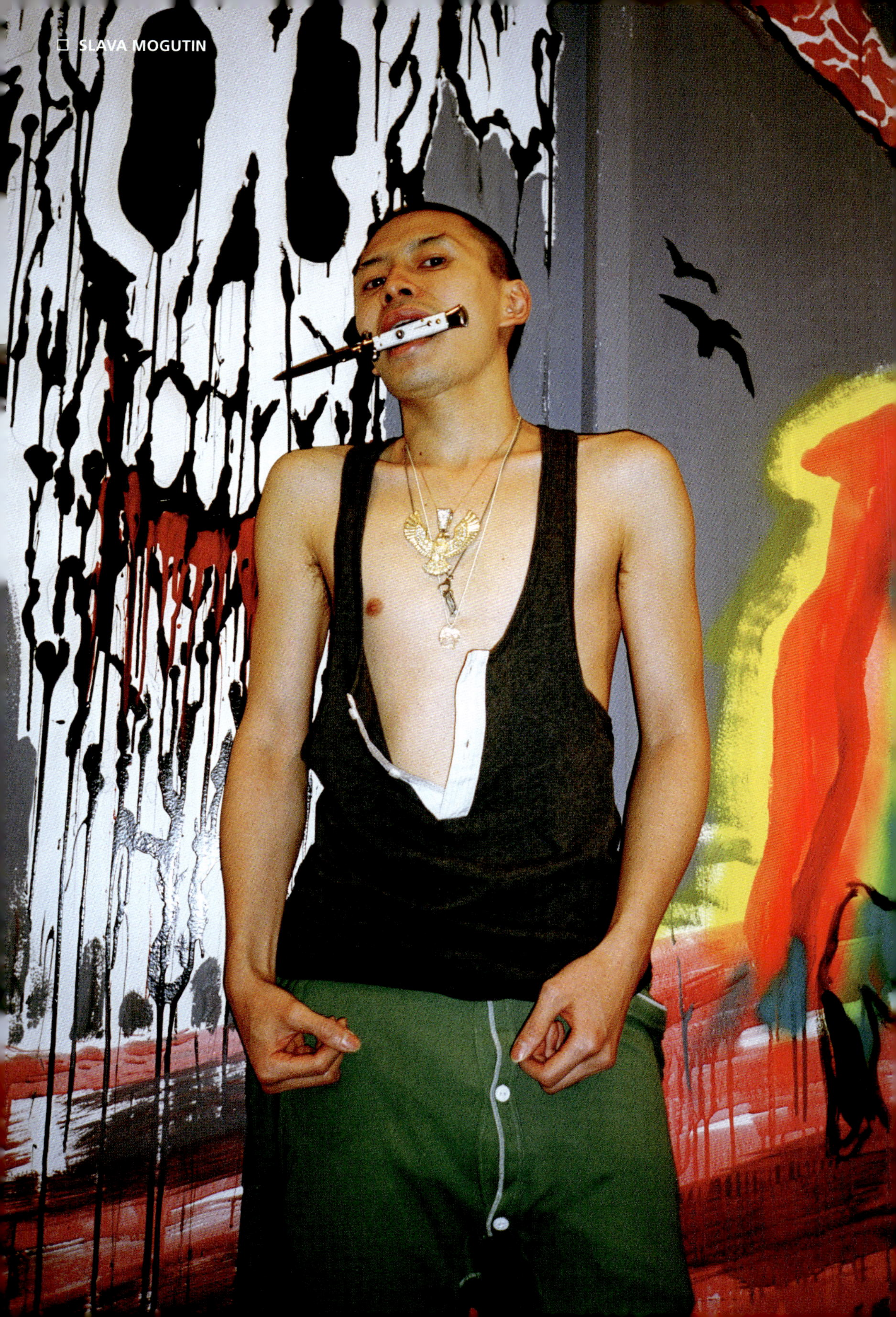

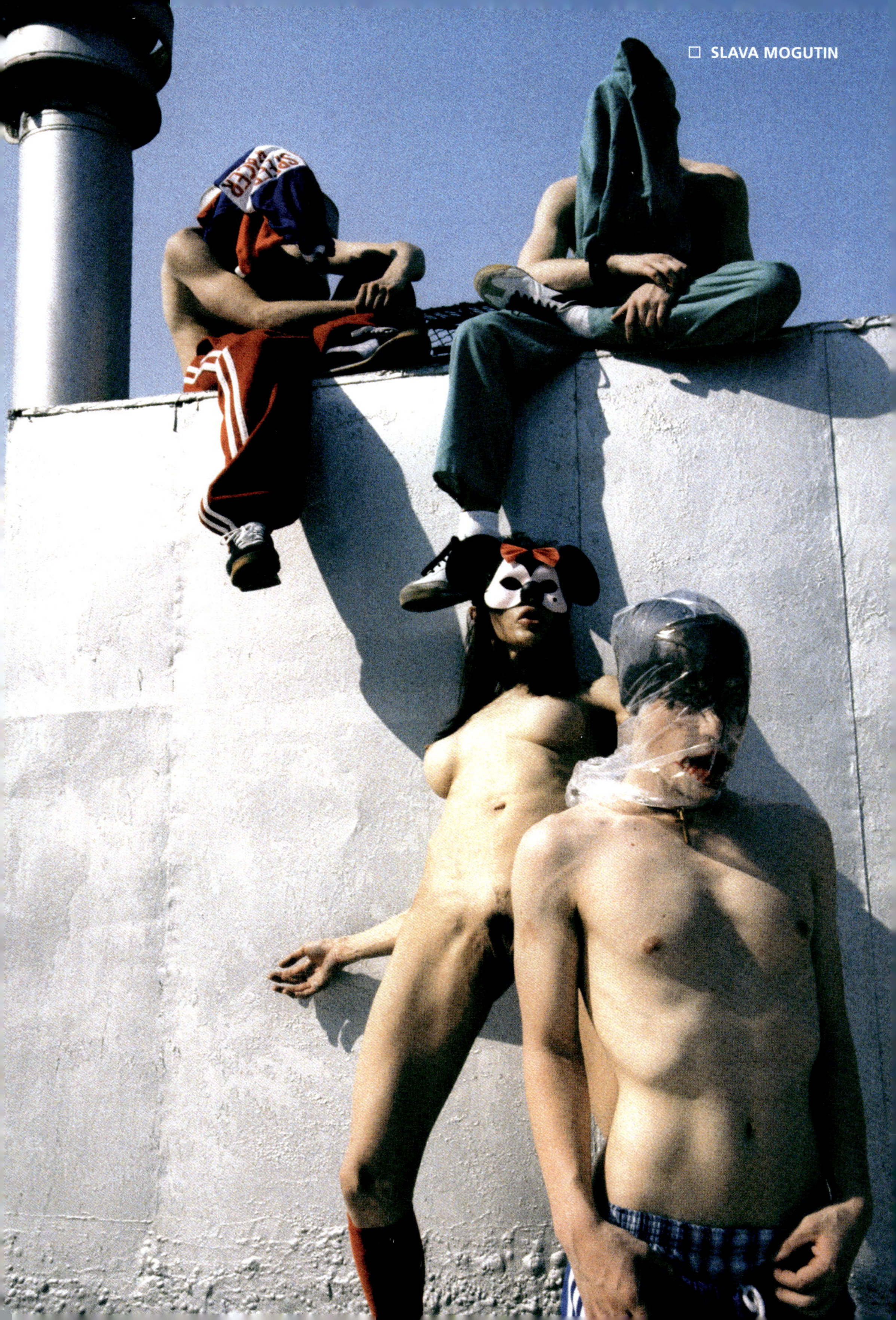

SLAVA MOGUTIN

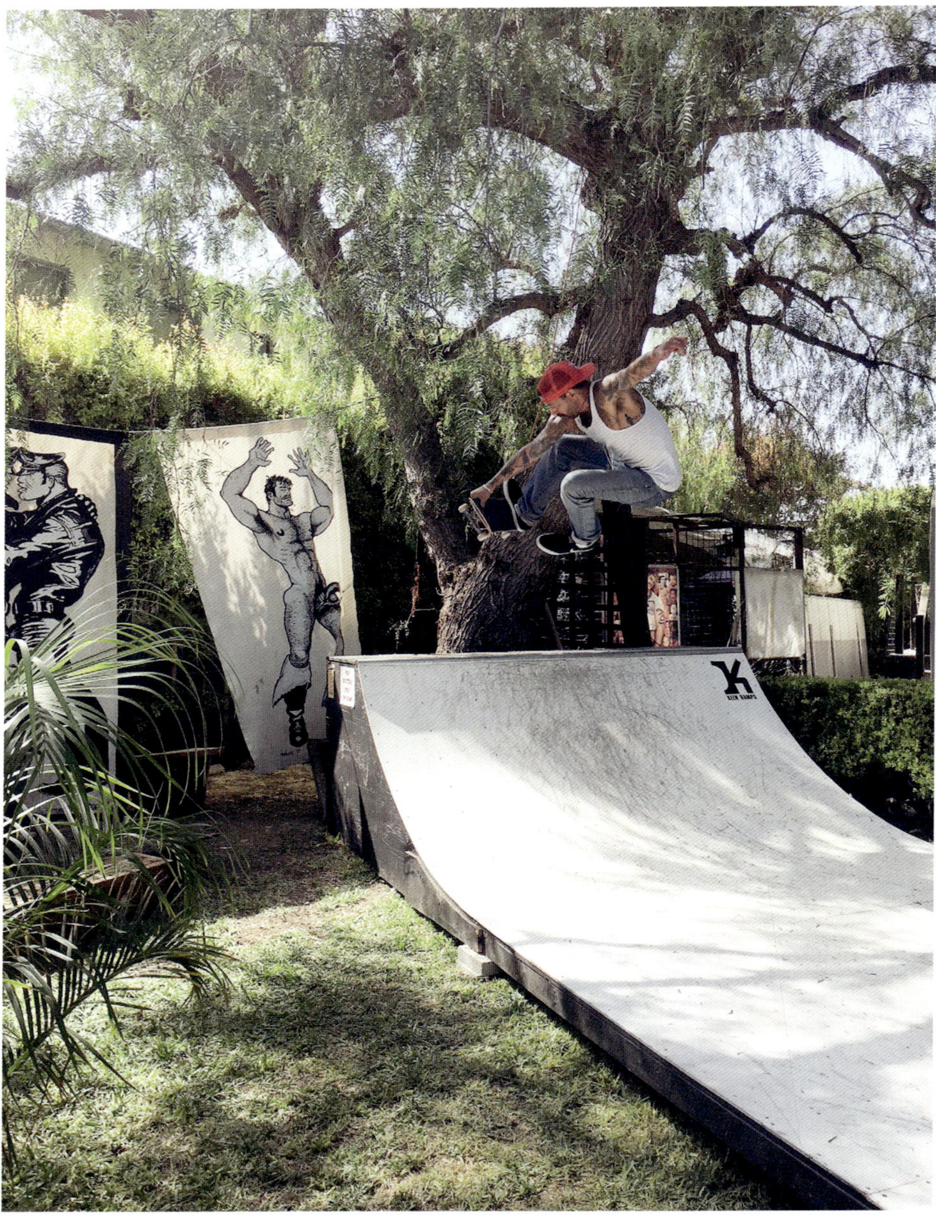

Brian Anderson

Brian Anderson is known for his international success becoming *Thrasher's* Skater of the Year in 1999 and winning the World Cup of Skateboarding in Münster, Germany the same year, he has since become one of the most iconic and respected professional skateboarders worldwide. His publicly coming out in 2016 was a big media topic.

Brian Anderson erlangte seinen internationale Durchbruch 1999, als ihn das Magazin *Thrasher* zum *Skater of the Year* ernannte. Im selben Jahr gewann er den World Cup of Skateboarding in Münster und ist seitdem einer der berühmtesten und angesehensten Skateboarder weltweit. Sein öffentliches Coming Out 2016 fand ein großes Medienecho.

☐ BRIAN ANDERSON

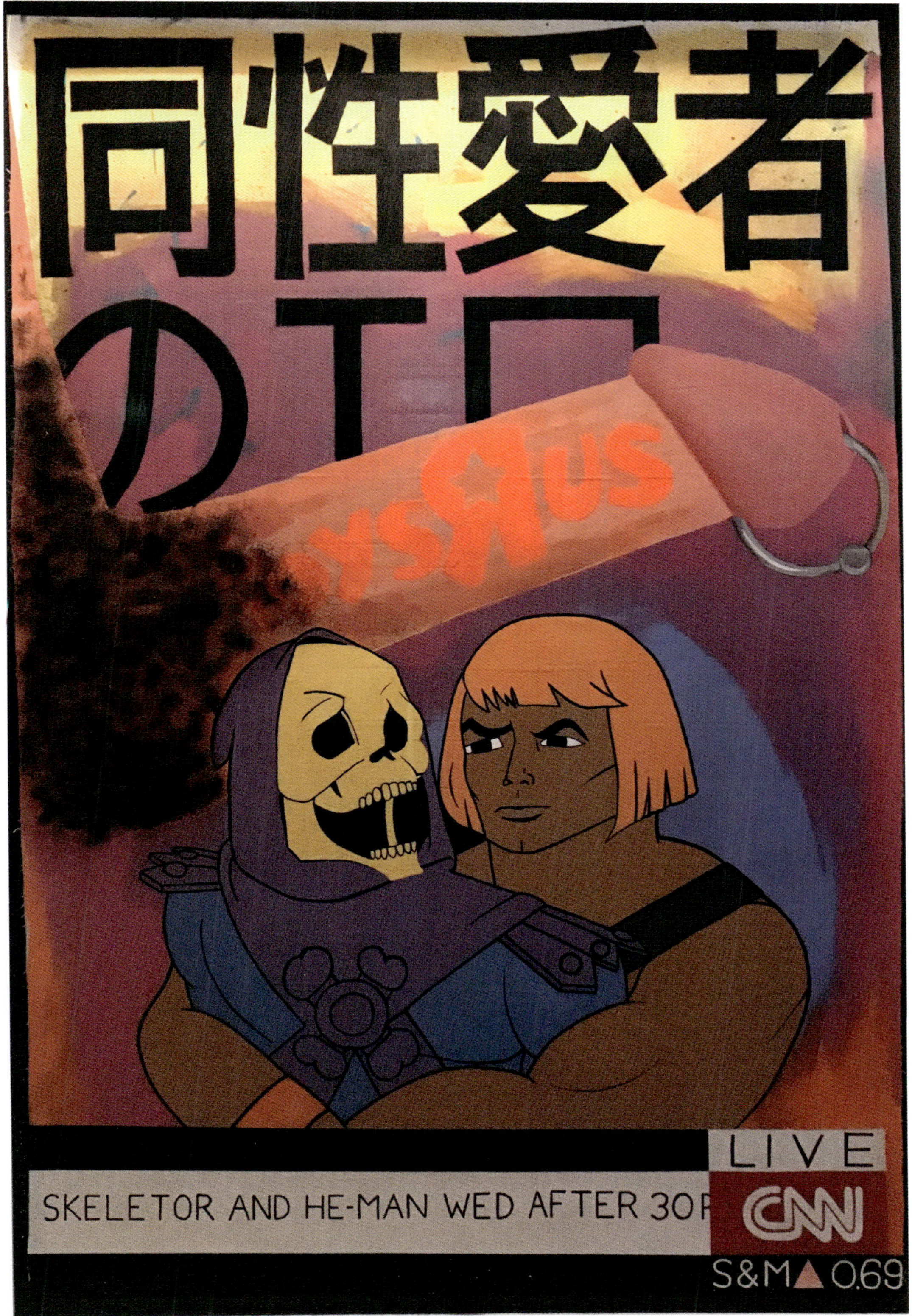

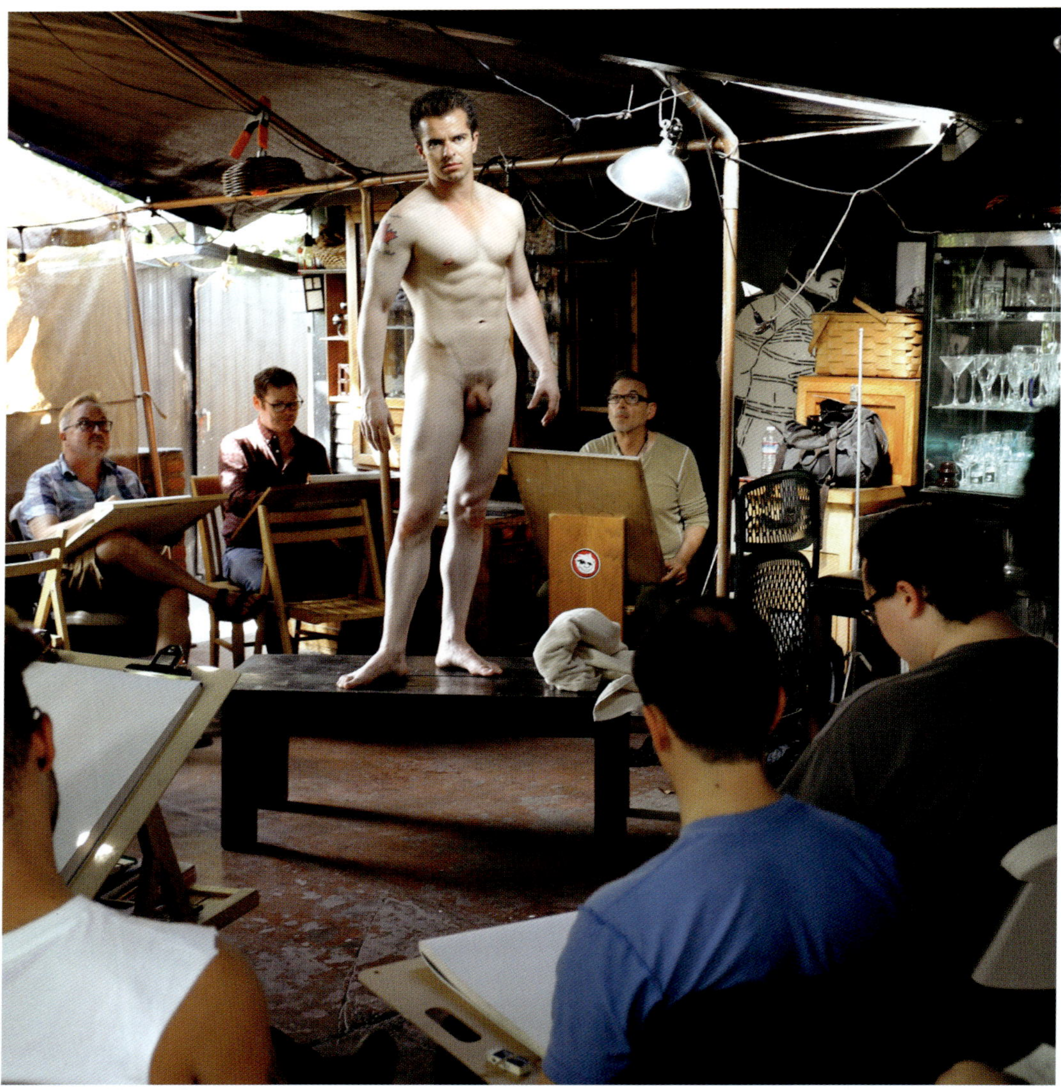

Photo: Rinaldo Hopf

Life Drawing Sessions

Figure drawing sessions have been part of the Foundation's programming almost since its inception. Over the past decade, the coordinator has been Miguel Angel Reyes. A renowned artist, having received acclaims from multiple organizations and publications, also teaches illustration professionally. Reyes oversees these monthly sessions where beginners to master artists can hone their skills in a relaxed environment. Each session is free from judgments and the models give it their own kind of excitement. Friendships are fostered among the new attendees and session regulars.

Aktzeichnen

Aktzeichnen war quasi von Anfang an Teil des Programms der Foundation. In den letzten zehn Jahren wurden die Sitzungen vom renommierten Künstler Miguel Angel Reyes organisiert, der u.a. auch Dozent für Modezeichnen ist. Reyes leitet diese monatlichen Treffen, bei denen vom Anfänger bis zum Meisterzeichner jeder seine Fähigkeiten in einer entspannten Umgebung entwickeln kann. Die attraktiven Modelle sorgen dabei ganz automatisch für die entsprechende Spannung. Dabei entstehen öfter Freundschaften zwischen Neulingen und Stammgästen.

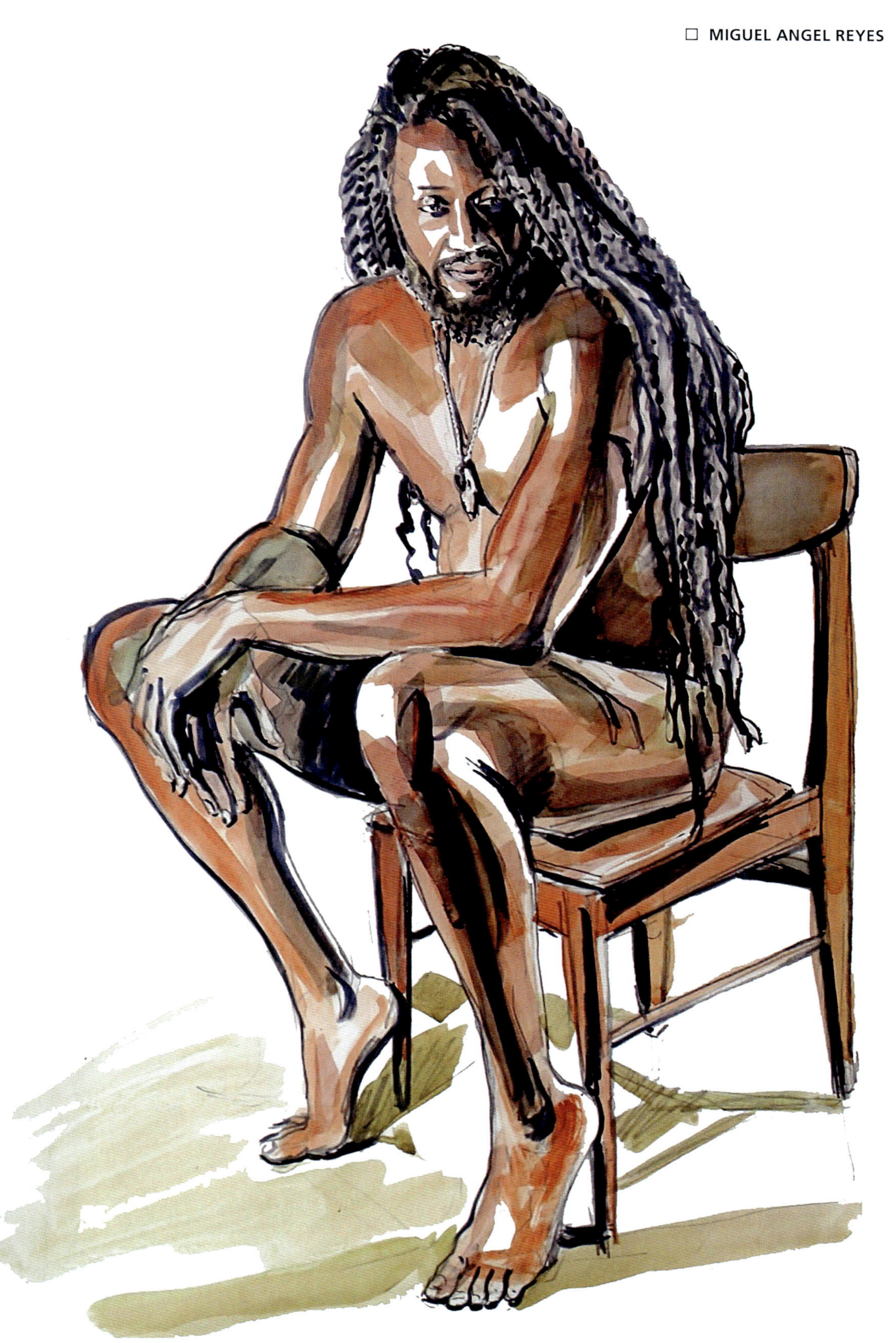
MIGUEL ANGEL REYES

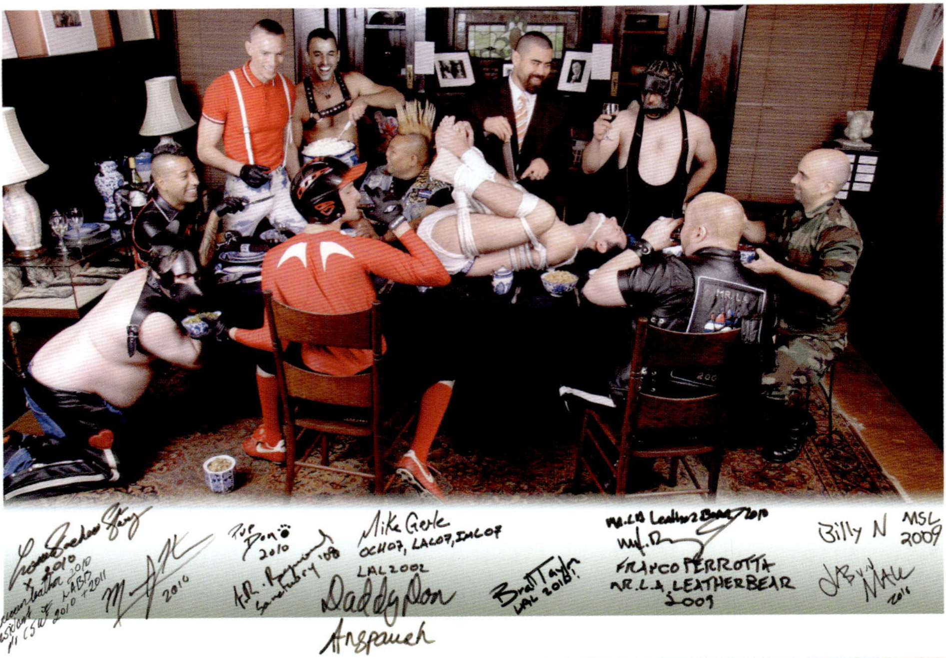

Los Angeles Band of Brothers Thanksgiving at TOM House • Thanksgiving-Party der L.A.-Leder-Organisation Bands of Brothers

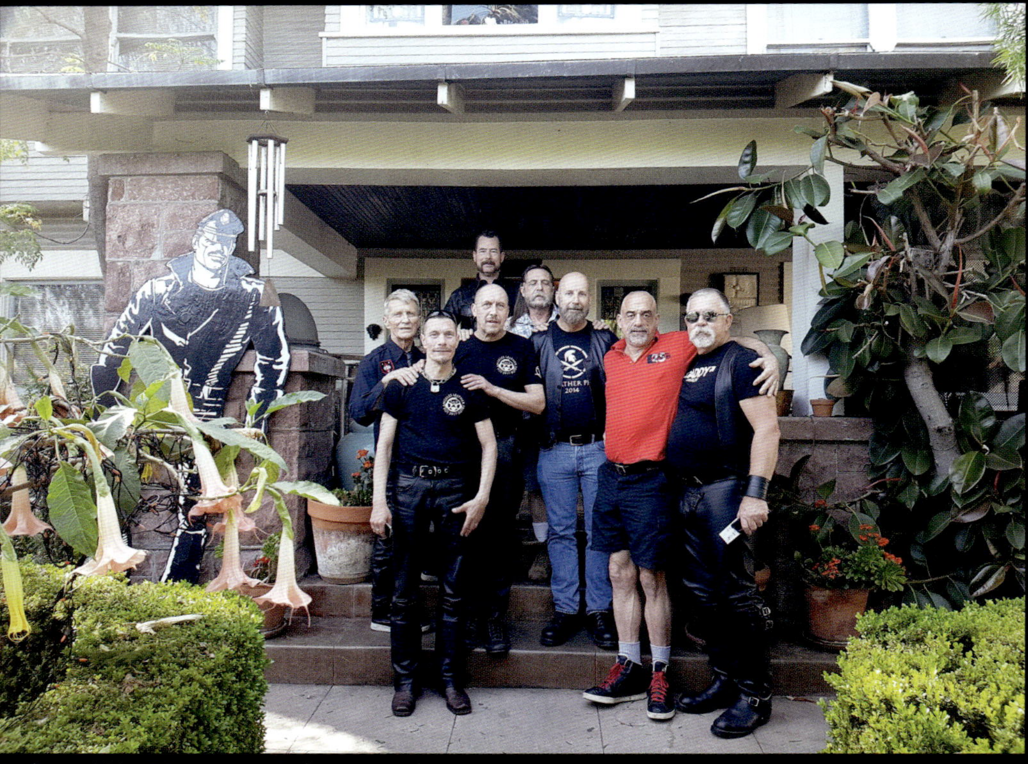

Berliners visiting TOM House • Berliner zu Besuch

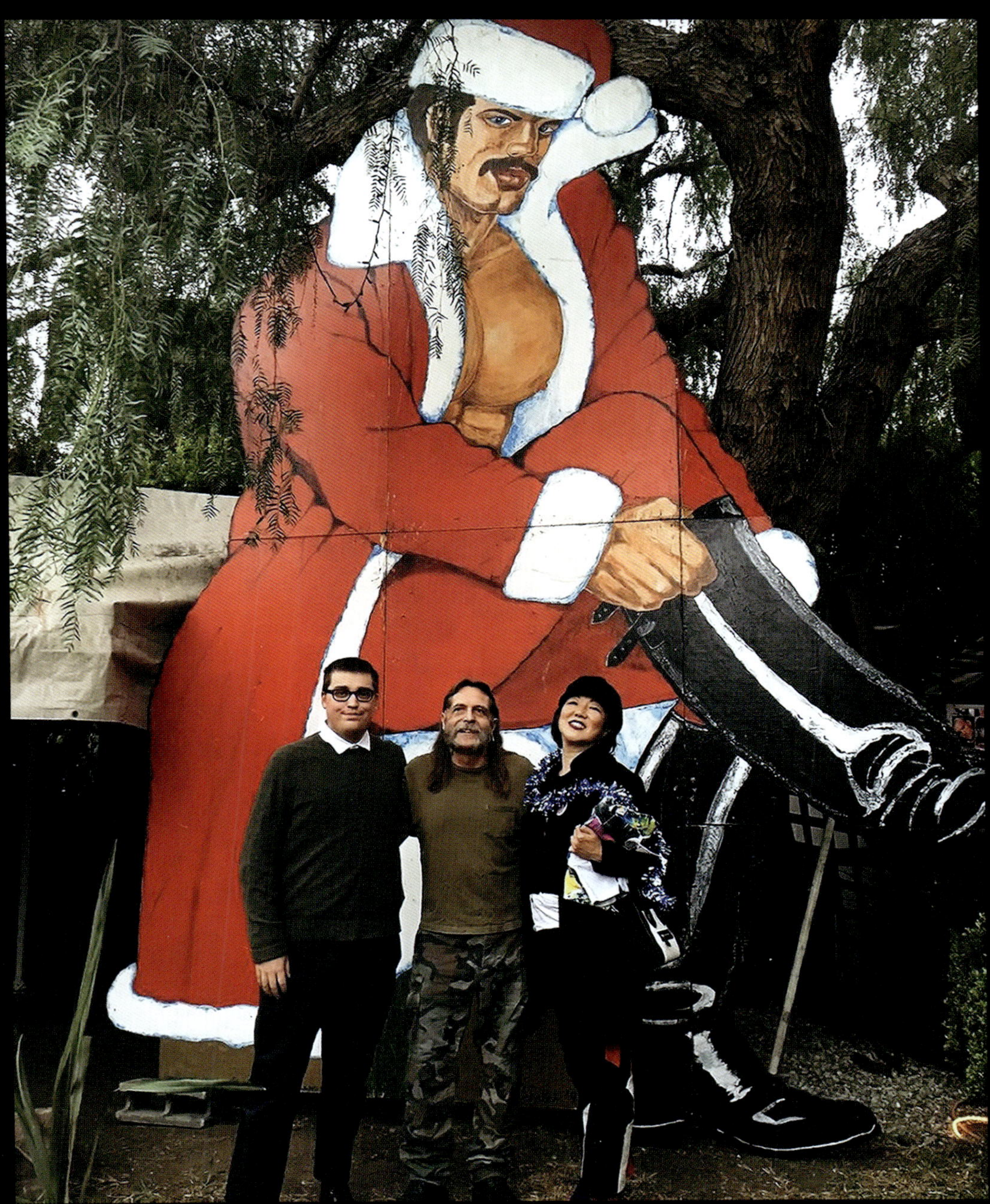

Graeme Flegenheimer, Sharp, Margaret Cho at TOM House

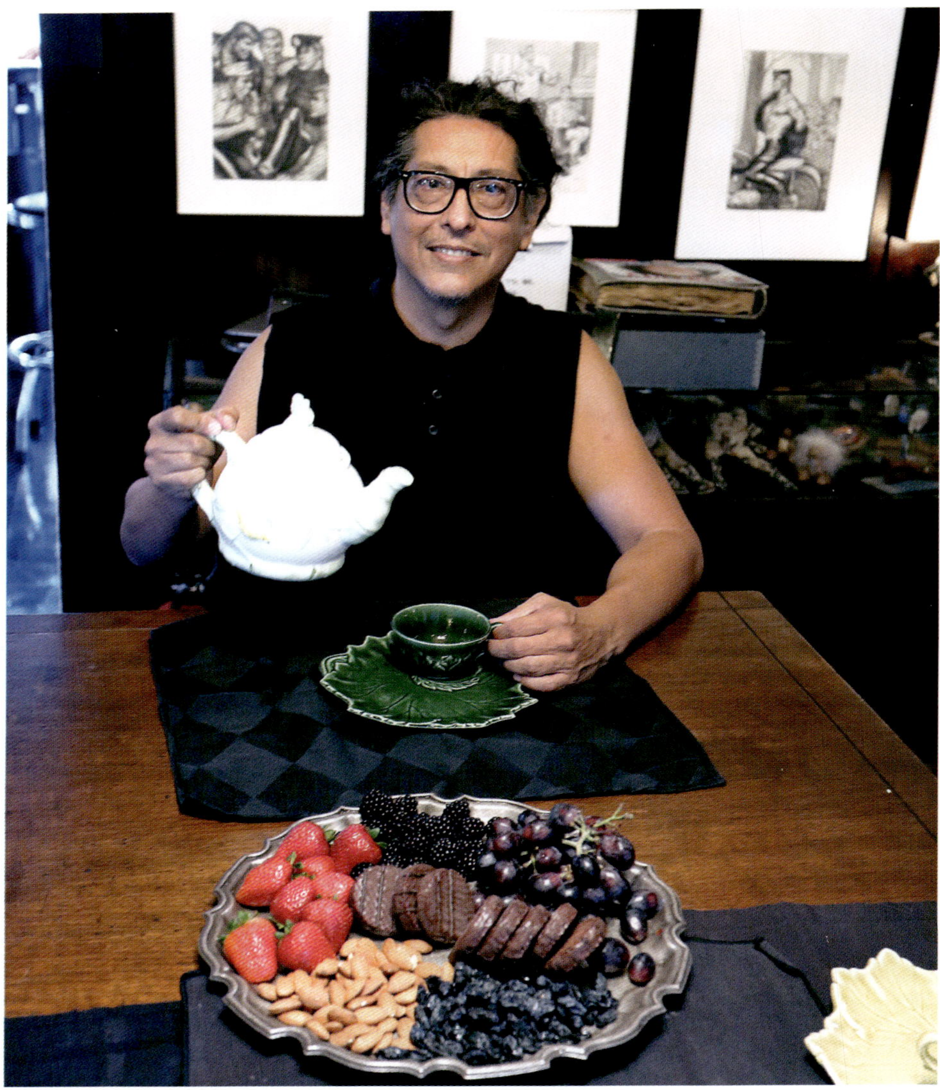

Rick Castro, TOM House. Photo: Rinaldo Hopf

Wednesday Tea Salon at TOM House Hosted by Rick Castro

When Rick Castro first showed his photos to Durk Dehner back in the mid '80s, Durk took his own money and financed the publishing of Rick's first hard cover book, simply titled *Castro*. Ever since, there has been an alliance with Tom of Finland Foundation and Rick, with the Foundation promoting and participating in exhibitions at his gallery, Antebellum. When Rick was forced out of his space with the gentrification of Hollywood, ToFF invited him to continue some of his events at TOM House. Thus, every week he hosts Salons, where discussions are wide and varied, and always fascinating.

Als Rick Castro Mitte der 80er Jahre erstmals Durk Dehner seine Fotos zeigte, finanzierte dieser persönlich die Veröffentlichung seines ersten Hardcover-Buchs mit dem schlichten Titel *Castro*. Seit dieser Zeit besteht eine enge Verbindung zwischen Rick Castro und der Foundation, die zahlreiche Ausstellungen in Castros Galerie Antebellum veranstaltet oder gefördert hat. Als Rick Castro im Zuge der Gentrifizierung Hollywoods aus diesen Räumen vertrieben wurde, lud die Foundation ihn ein, einige seiner Veranstaltungen im TOM House fortzusetzen. So ist er nun Gastgeber eines eigenen wöchentlichen Salons mit stets faszinierenden Diskussionen über die unterschiedlichsten Themen.

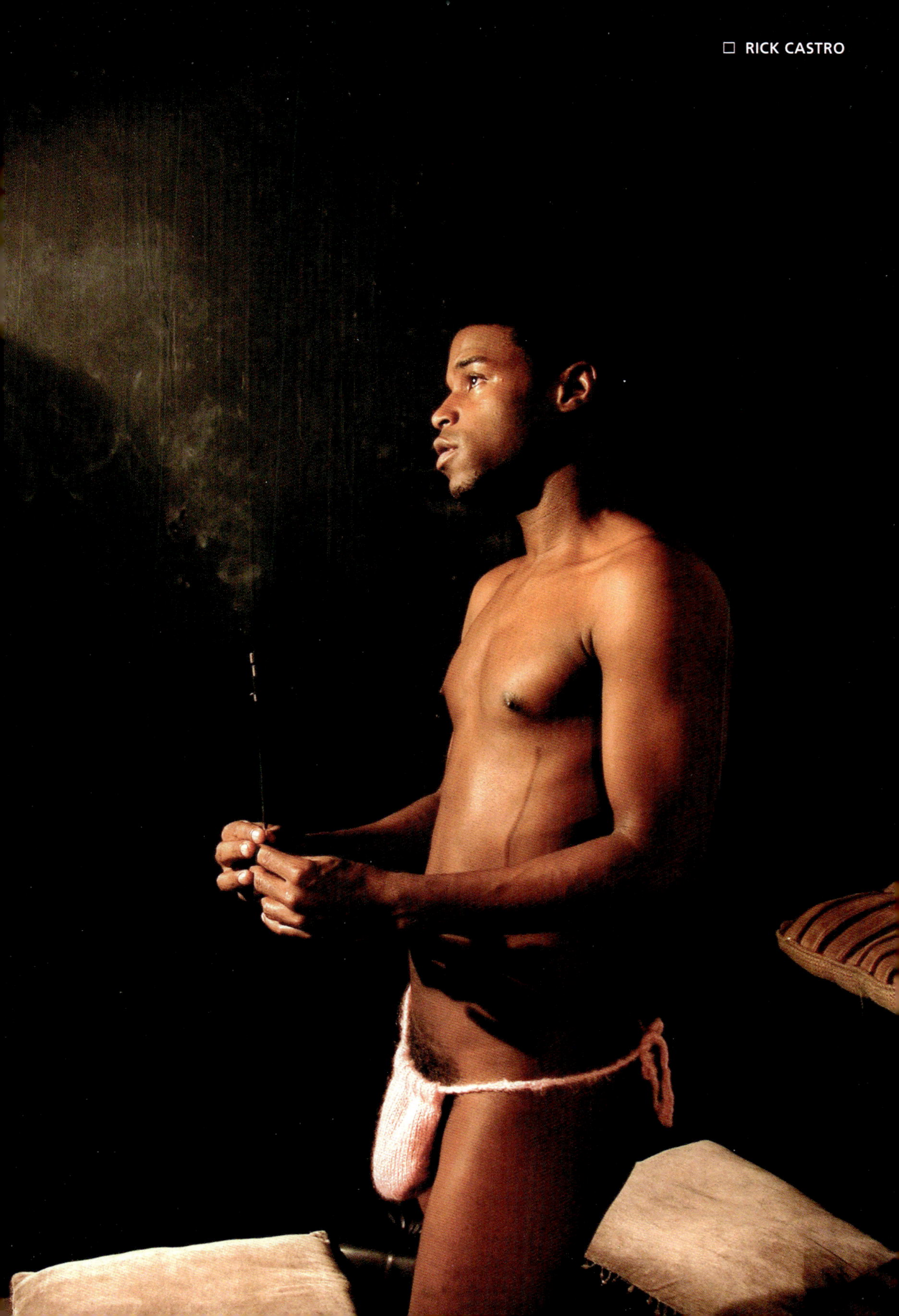
RICK CASTRO

Künstlerregister/*Artists' Directory*

Abbate, Johnny – Seite/*page* 358 ff.
*1982 (Italien/*Italy*); Anwärter auf das TOM House Artist-in-Residence-Programm • *Applicant for the TOM House Artist-in-Residence program. johnnyalexabbate@gmail.com*

Anderson, Brian Thurston – 386 f.
*1976 (USA); Aussteller/*exhibitor* Tom of Finland Art and Culture Festivals, Tom of Finland Foundation Cultural Icon 2017.

Art Daddy (A. J. Epstein) – 155
*1949 (USA); Aussteller/*exhibitor* Tom of Finland Art and Culture Festivals. aj@Epsteindesigns.com

Anonym/*Anonymous* – 99

assume vivid astro focus – 37
Künstlerkollektiv bestehend aus/*artists' collective, consisting of* Eli Sudbrack (Brazil) und/*and* Christophe Hamaide-Pierson (France). astrofocus@mac.com

Bastille – 124 f.
bürgerlicher Name/*civic name* Frank Webber, 1929-1990 (USA).

Beau – 258 ff.
*1959 (USA); Aussteller/*exhibitor* Tom of Finland Culture Festivals, Gewinner/*winner* Tom of Finland Emerging Artist Competition, Tom of Finland Foundation Honorary Membership Award 2005. kevinking915@yahoo.com

Belle – 45
(Kanada/*Canada*)

Berlin, Peter – 175 ff.
*1942 (Deutschland/*Germany*); Aussteller/*exhibitor* Tom of Finland Art and Culture Festivals, Tom of Finland Foundation Cultural Icon Award, 2015. info@peter-berlin.com

Bois – 44
(Frankreich/*France*). Post@kundodesign.de

Bruce of Los Angeles (Bruce Bellas) – 96, 203, 205, 208
1909-1974 (Kanada/*Canada*)

Brune, Garilyn – 301
1951-2014 (USA); Gewinnerin/ Grand Prize *winner* Tom of Finland Emerging Artist Competition 1995.

Buijs, Paul – 304
*1982 (Niederlande/*Netherlands*); Gewinner/*winner* Tom of Finland Emerging Artist Competition 2014. info@experienced-bypaul.com

Byass, Rowland – 341
*1967 (UK), TOM House Artist-in-Residence 2017.

Callaghan, Beth –298 f.
Tom of Finland Emerging Artist Competition 1993.

Castro, Rick – 101, 392, 395, 397, 400
1958 (USA); Aussteller/*exhibitor* Tom of Finland Art and Culture Festivals, Tom of Finland Foundation Artist Hall of Fame 2015. antebellum@earthlink.net

Celso – 286 f.
*1961 (Brasilien/*Brazil*). celso.de.oliveira@gmx.ch

Copper – 70
(USA).

Courbet, Gustave – 200
1819 -1877 (Frankreich/*France*).

Da Silva, Antonio – 337 ff.
*1977 (Portugal); TOM House Artist-in-Residence, 2016. contact@antoniodasilvafilms.com

Day, Greg – 237 ff.
(USA); Aussteller/exhibitor Tom of Finland Art and Culture Festivals. gregday1@mac.com

DeBauch, Marc – 3, 244 ff.
*1956 (USA); Aussteller/*exhibitor* Tom of Finland Art and Culture Festivals, Gewinner/*winner* Tom of Finland Emerging Artist Competition 1995. marc@marcdebauch.com

Derek – 261 f.
Aussteller/*exhibitor* Tom of Finland Art and Culture Festivals.

Deigan, Norman – 284 f.
(UK)

Domino – 132 ff.
1929-1990 (USA).

Donelan – 153
*1949 (USA).

E.M.A. Studio –190 ff.
bürgerlicher Name/*civic name* Edward S. McAndrews, 1950-2009 (USA); Aussteller/*exhibitor* Tom of Finland Art and Culture Festivals, Gewinner/*winner* Tom of Finland Emerging Artist Competition 1998.

Esparza, Rubén – 263 ff.
*1962 (USA); Aussteller/*exhibitor* Tom of Finland Art and Culture Festivals, Tom of Finland Foundation Achievement Award, 2016. Leiter/*director* Queer Biennial seit/*since* 2014. ruben@rubenesparza.com

Etienne – 105 ff.
aka Stephen, bürgerlicher Name/*civic name* Domingo Orejudos, 1933-1991 (USA). Leather Archives & Museum, Chicago, IL USA.

French, Jim – 103, 126 ff., 130 f.
aka Colt, Rip Colt, Luger, Arion; 1932-2017 (USA); Mitbegründer/*Cofounder* Colt Studio Group, Tom of Finland Foundation Artist Hall of Fame 2017.

Galen, Carrington – 2
1975-2016 (USA); Aussteller/*exhibitor* Tom of Finland Art and Culture Festivals, Tom of Finland Foundation Inspiration Award 2015.

Galrão, João – 90
*1975 (Portugal).

Gicquel, Xavier – 365
*1965 (Frankreich/*France*); Aussteller/*exhibitor* Tom of Finland Art and Culture Festivals.

Gio Black Peter – 378 ff.
*1979 (Guatemala); Aussteller/*exhibitor* Tom of Finland Art and Culture Festivals. gioblackpeter@gmail.com

Goh Mishima – 145 ff.
bürgerlicher Name/*civic name* Tsuyoshi Yoshida, 1924-1989 (Japan).

Graewolf – 296

Green, Jordan Michael – 320 ff.
*1985 (USA); Aussteller/*exhibitor* Tom of Finland Art and Culture Festivals, TOM House Artist-in-Residence 2016. jordan@jordanmichaelgreen.com

Hasegawa, Sadao – 148
1945-1995 (Japan).

Hayward, Mark Timothy – 325
siehe Autorenregister/see under Authors' Directory

Hetz, Florian – 344 ff.
*1975 (Deutschland/*Germany*); TOM House Artist-in-Residence 2018. digitalaidsss@gmail.com

HOMO RIOT – 216 ff., Rückumschlag/*back cover*
Aussteller/*exhibitor* Tom of Finland Art and Culture Festivals. homoriot@gmail.com

Hopf, Rinaldo – 4, 53, 93, 212 ff., 324 f., 327 ff., 388, 392
siehe Autorenregister/*see under Authors' Directory*

Hurles, David – 141 ff.
*1944 (USA); Tom of Finland Foundation Artist Hall of Fame 2016.

IΩN – 302
(Griechenland/*Greece*): Tom of Finland Emerging Artist Competition 1993.

Jakal – 193 ff.

Jazmin, Van – 221, 223 ff.
*1991 (USA). Exhibitor Tom of Finland Art and Culture Festivals. jazmin.van@gmail.com

Jones, G. B. – 54 ff.
1965 (Kanada/Canada). gbjonestown@yahoo.com

Kent, Nigel – 281 ff.
*1993 (Australien/Australia).

Kirwan, Michael – 332 ff.
*1953 (USA); Aussteller/*exhibitor* Tom of Finland Art and Culture Festivals, TOM House Artist-in-Residence 2006, Tom of Finland Foundation Artist Hall of Fame 2004.

König, Ralf – 83. 85 f.
siehe Autorenregister/*see under Authors' Directory*

Lanuit, Eric – 66 ff.
*1965 (Frankreich/France); ericlanuit@me.com

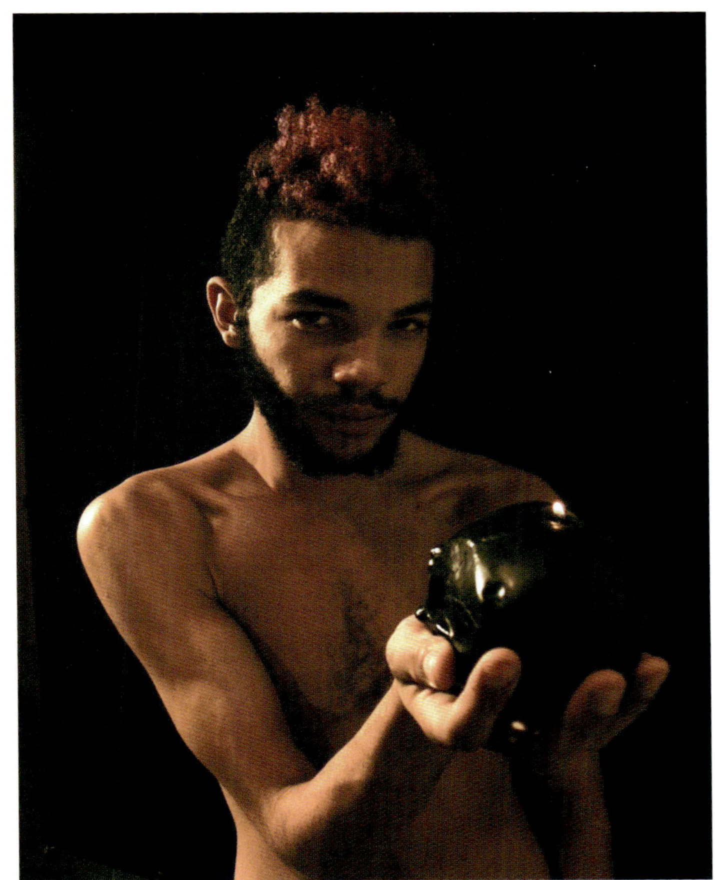

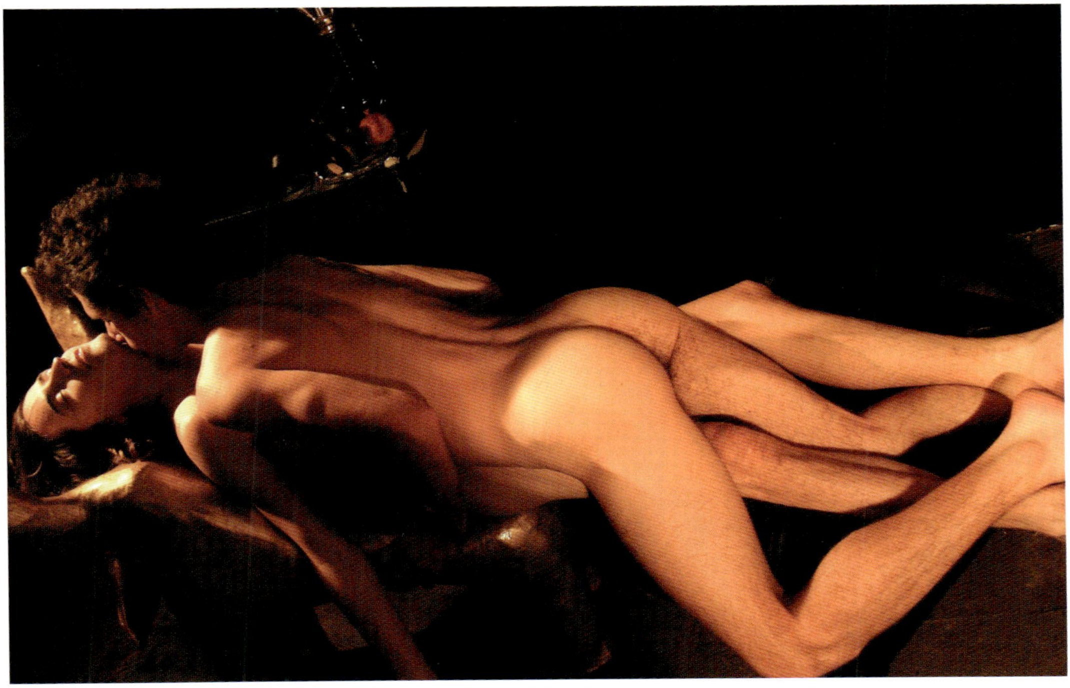

Lee, Patrick – 184 f.
*1969 (USA); Aussteller/*exhibitor* Tom of Finland Art and Culture Festivals, Gewinner/*Winner* Tom of Finland Emerging Artist Competition 1993.

Leyba, Steven Johnson – 255 ff.
*1966 (USA). leybaart@gmail.com

Link – 169 ff.
(USA)

Liu, Yu-Liang – 46 ff.
*1988 (Taiwan); yuliangliuphoto@gmail.com

Lukacs, Attila Richard – 186 ff.
*1962 (Kanada/Canada); arl@telus.net

Manflesh – 278 ff.
 (UK); Tom of Finland Emerging Artist Competition 1993. phillipgassor@yahoo.co.uk

Mark aka Roger Payne – 275 ff.
*1934 (UK). rogermarksmen@blueyonder.co.uk

Mikkonen, Mies – 330 f.
* 1984 (Finland); TOM House Artist-in-Residence 2011; Regisseur des Kurzdokumentarfilms "Tom of Finland" (2011) • *Director of the short documentary film "Tom of Finland" (2011).*

Minoru (Minoru Terada) – 288 f.
*1948 (Japan); Tom of Finland Art and Culture Festival exhibitor. Tom of Finland Emerging Artist Competition 2003. www.facebook.com/minoru.terada.338

Mizer, Bob – 95
1922-1992 (USA). Gründer/*founder* Athletic Model Guild. Bob Mizer Foundation, El Cerrito, CA USA.

Mogutin, Slava – 382 ff.
*1974 (Russland/*Russia*). slava@slavamogutin.com

Motorboot Robert – 320
motorboot@gmail.com

Muscle Boy Matt – 293 ff.
(USA).

Ogus, Andrew – 303
1948 (USA); Gewinner/*winner* Emerging Artist Competition 2014. andrewogus@gmail.com

Olaf – 115 ff.
bürgerlicher Name/*civic name* Olaf Odegaard 1938-1997 (USA).

Oppedisano, Joe – 58 f.
*1967 (USA); Aussteller/*exhibito*r Tom of Finland Art and Culture Festivals. jopped@aol.com

Palanca – 350 ff.
1968-2014 (Peru); Aussteller/*exhibitor* Tom of Finland Art and Culture Festivals, Tom of Finland Foundation Special Recognition for Commitment and Perseverance in Their Art, 2007

Peach, Nancy – 300
Aussteller/*exhibitor* Tom of Finland Art and Culture Festivals, Gewinner/*winner* Tom of Finland Emerging Artist Competition 2009.

Prada, Silvia – 309
*1969 (Spanien/*Spain*). Aus / *from*: Silvia Prada *TOM* (Capricious LLC, 2017). silviaprada@silviaprada.com.

Pinto, Stefan – 251 ff.
*1980 (Trinidad und Tobago); Aussteller/*exhibitor* Tom of Finland Art and Culture Festivals. stefanpinto@mac.com

Prévot, Benoît – 181
*1968 (Frankreich/*France*); Aussteller/*exhibitor* Tom of Finland Art and Culture Festivals, Tom of Finland Foundation Special Recognition for Commitment and Perseverance in Their Art 2007. lifegallerynyc.com

Quaintance, George – 92, 182 f.
1902-1957 (USA).

REX – 136 ff.
(USA); Aussteller/*exhibitor* Tom of Finland Art and Culture Festivals, Tom of Finland Foundation Artist Hall of Fame 2016. rexwerk.com

Reyes, Miguel Angel – 228 ff., 341, 389
*1964 (USA); Aussteller/*exhibitor* Tom of Finland Art and Culture Festivals, First Tom of Finland Foundation Special Recognition for Volunteers: Leiter der Aktzeichnen-Workshops im TOM House/*Life Drawing Session Coordinator.* miguelreyesart@att.net

Richards, Robert – 232
*1941 (USA); Aussteller/*exhibitor* Tom of Finland Art and Culture Festivals. robertwrichardsartist.com

Sandford, Stuart – 319, 353, 355 ff.
*1978 (UK); Aussteller/*exhibitor* Tom of Finland Art and Culture Festivals, TOM House Artist-in-residence 2014; seitdem Mitbewohner im TOM House/*Since then resident at TOM House.* stuart@stuartsandford.co.uk

Shifflett, Suzanne – 370 ff.
*1965 (USA); Ausstellerin/*exhibitor* Tom of Finland Art and Culture Festivals. smshifflett@yahoo.com

Shimo Hiro/Gorilla, Monster – 290 ff.
(Japan).

Silva, Hector – 231, 247 ff.
(Mexico); Aussteller/*exhibitor* Tom of Finland Art and Culture Festivals, Grand Prize Tom of Finland Emerging Artist Competition 1997. artbyhector@gmail.com

Splayer – 196 f.
*1965 (UK). player@playermen.com

Sven Oliver – 88 f.
*1974 (Deutschland/*Germany*). me@svenoliver.com

Tagame, Gengoroh – 374 ff.
*1964 (Japan). tagame.org

Tank – 160 ff.
bürgerlicher Name/*civic name* Paul Tankersley, 1949-1992 (USA).

Teddy of Paris – 240 ff.
(Frankreich/*France*); Aussteller/*exhibitor* Tom of Finland Art and Culture Festivals.

Tepel, Frank – 212 ff., 325
*1969 (Germany). kinofux@t-online.de

The Hun – 91, 119 ff.
bürgerlicher Name/*civic name* Bill Schmeling, *1938 (USA). Aussteller/*exhibitor* Tom of Finland Art and Culture Festivals, Tom of Finland Foundation Artist Hall of Fame 2002.

Thomas, Josh Paul – 79, 81, Cover
*1985 (USA). joshpaulthomas@me.com

Thor of Sweden – 164 f.

Tom of Finland – 1,5, 9, 13, 17, 19 ff., 33 ff., 51, 61, 73, 78, 80, 127, 129, 272, 309, 311, 313 ff., 321
bürgerlicher Name/*civic name* Touko Laaksonen 1920-1991 (Finnland).

Townsend, Larry – 149 ff.
1930-2008 (USA). Der Autor mit Schwerpunkt BDSM errang mit „Das Lederhandbuch" (1972) internationalen Kultstatus. • *The author, with a focus on BDSM, achieved international cult status with "The Leatherman's Handbook" (1972).*

Tress, Arthur – 156 ff.
*1949 (USA); Tom of Finland Foundation Lifetime Achievement Award 2017. bigsurguy@netscape.net

Urban, Al Jr. – 166 ff.
1917-1992 (USA).

Valentine – 268 ff.
*1943 (USA); bürgerlicher Name/*civic name* F. Valentine Hooven III. Aussteller/*exhibitor* Tom of Finland Art and Culture Festivals, Tom of Finland Foundation Lifetime Achievement Award, 2015. Autor der Biografie *Tom of Finland: Sein Leben – seine Kunst* (1992) sowie Herausgeber u.a. von *Tom of Finland - Life and Work of a Gay Hero* (2012). • *Author of the biography* Tom of Finland: His Life and Times *(1994) and* Tom of Finland – Life and Work of a Gay Hero *(2012).* valentinehooven@rocketmail.com

van Batenburg, Ok – 87
*1930 (Niederlande/*Netherlands*). Vertreten von/*represented by* Galerie Mooi Man, Groningen NL, www.mooi-man.nl

Vargas, Bart – 297
*1973 (USA) Gewinner/*winner* Tom of Finland Emerging Artist Competition 2009.

Volcano, Del LaGrace – 198 f.
*1957 (USA). Fotobücher/*photobooks Sublime Mutations* and *Sex Works*, konkursbuch. dellagracevolcano@mac.com

von Berg, Henning – 233 ff.
*1961(Deutschland/*Germany*). Aussteller/*exhibitor* Tom of Finland Art and Culture Festivals. Henning@henning-von-berg.com

Wigler, Jim – 111 ff.
*1944 (USA). jimwigler@yahoo.com

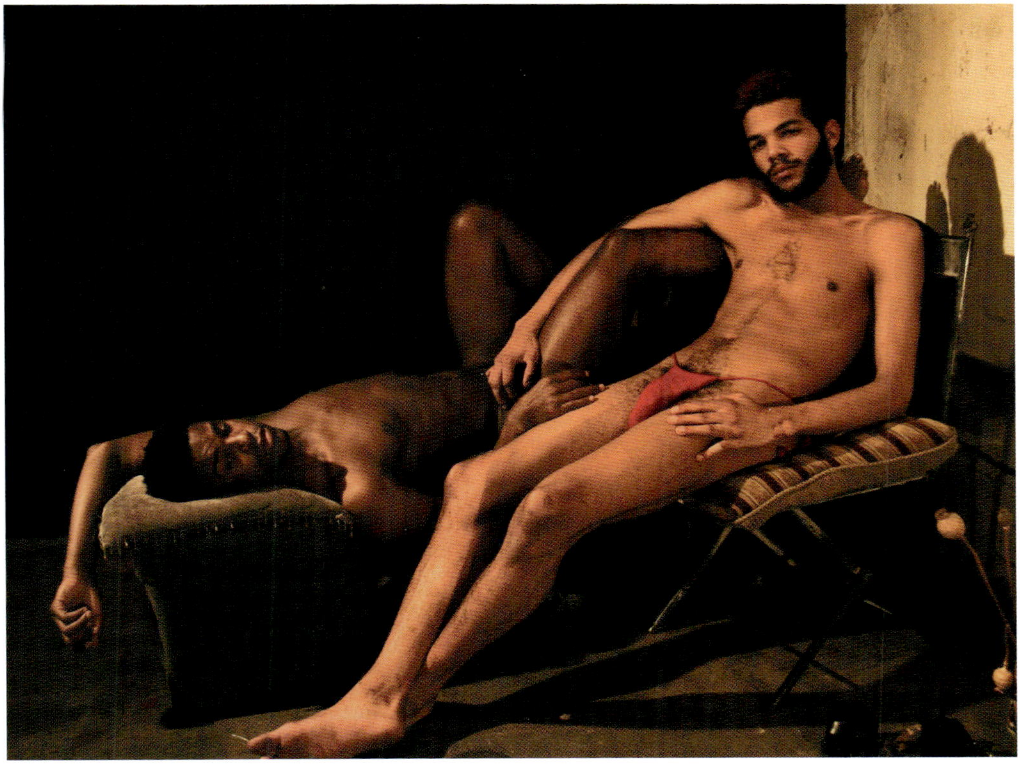

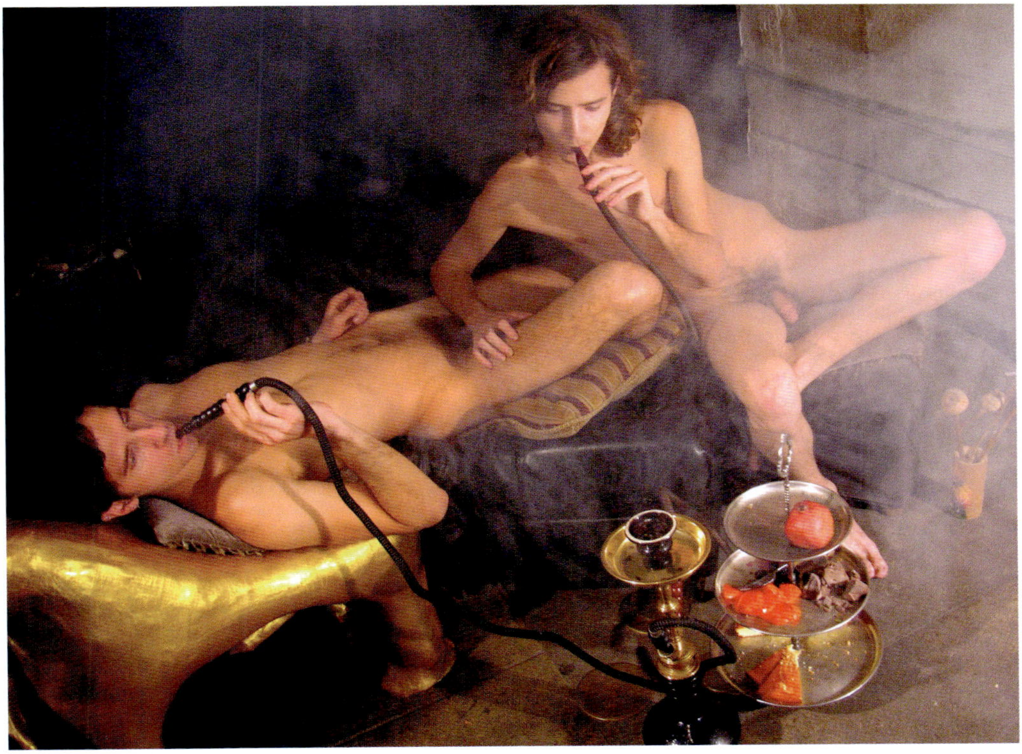

Autorenregister/*Authors' Directory*

Baker, Jim – Seite/*page* 174
*1963 (USA). Nach dem Germanistikstudium an der University of Pennsylvania/Philadelphia und an der Freien Universität in Berlin Ausbildung zum Verlagsbuchhändler. Nach Stationen in diversen schwulen Verlagen (Bruno Gmünder Verlag, Verlag rosa Winkel, Magnus Buchverlag) gründete er 1995 zusammen mit Ilona Bubeck den Querverlag, Deutschlands ersten lesbisch-schwulen Buchverlag, den er noch heute leitet. Er lebt in Berlin. • *Jim Baker was born in 1963 in North Carolina/ USA, MA degree in German Literature at the University of Pennsylvania in Philadelphia and at Freie Universität in Berlin. After working at several gay publishing houses (Bruno Gmünder Verlag, Verlag rosa Winkel, Magnus Buchverlag), he joined forces with Ilona Bubeck and together they founded Germany's first and only lesbian and gay book publishing company, Querverlag, where he is still working. He lives in Berlin.*

Balducci, Sam – 38
*1960 (Deutschland/*Germany*). Als freier Autor erzählt er aus der schwulen Welt der Lederkerle, aber auch von großen Gefühlen und unserem ganz „normalen" Alltag. Veröffentlichungen u.a.: *Sieben von hundert* (autobiografischer Roman) *Reds 1, Reds 2, Wolfsbisse* (erotische Erzählungen und erotischer Krimi), Konkursbuch Verlag, diverse Kurzgeschichten in Anthologien (*Mein schwules Auge*, Konkursbuch Verlag und *Hiebe und Triebe*, Querverlag). • *As a freelance author Balducci writes about the world of gay leather men and also about grand emotions and our ordinary everyday life. Publications: Reds 1, Reds 2, Wolfsbisse, various short stories in anthologies (My Gay Eye, Konkursbuch Verlag and Hiebe und Triebe, Querverlag).*

Bullock, Michael – 305
(USA), Journalist, Buchautor (*Roman Catholic Jacuzzi*, 2012), Mitherausgeber des Magazins *PIN-UP* und Herausgeber des *Apartamento Magazin* sowie von 2002 bis 2011 US-Herausgeber des Magazins *BUTT*. • *Journalist, author (Roman Catholic Jacuzzi, 2012), associate editor of PIN-UP magazine, contributing editor of Apartamento magazine and from 2002-2011 he was the American publisher of BUTT magazine. Eine längere Fassung des Textes / A longer version of this text was published in: Silvia Prada, TOM, Capricious LLC (November 2017).* michael@fantasticman.com

Clarke, Kevin – 200
*1967 (Deutschland/*Germany*), studierte in Berlin und Mailand Musikwissenschaft und Literaturgeschichte. Er ist Autor der Bücher *Glitter and be Gay: Homosexualität und Operette* (2007), *Porn: From Andy Warhol to X-Tube* (2013) sowie *The Art of Looking: The Life and Treasures of Collector Charles Leslie* (2015). Von 2011 bis 2012 war er Chefredakteur des Magazins *MÄNNER*. An der Uni Wien und an anderen Institutionen hat er Vorlesungen zu schwuler (Musik- und Kultur-) Geschichte abgehalten. Er ist außerdem gefragter Interviewpartner für Medienbeiträge zu LGBT-Themen und kuratiert Ausstellungen für das Schwule* Museum Berlin. • *Clarke studied musicology and history of literature in Berlin and Milan. He's the author of the books* Glitter and be Gay: Homosexualität und Operette *(2007),* Porn: From Andy Warhol to X-Tube *(2013) and* The Art of Looking: The Life and Treasures of Collector Charles Leslie *(2015). From 2011 to 2012 he was the editor in chief of the magazine* MÄNNER. *Clarke curated several exhibitions for Schwules* Museum in Berlin and lectured about gay (musical and cultural) history at the University of Vienna and other institutions and is a popular interview partner on LGBT topics.*

Dehner, Durk – 8, 100, 105, 111, 115, 119, 124, 132, 136, 178, 216, 301, 321, 332, 374
*1949 (Kanada/*Canada*). Dehner hat seit 1979 im Unternehmen Tom of Finland das Ruder in der Hand und ist Mitbegründer und Präsident der Tom of Finland Foundation. Er war daneben u.a. Pornoregisseur, Model für Bruce Weber und die Target Studios und Drummer sowie Gewinner des ersten internationalen Mr. Leather-Wettbewerbs. Er brach so viele Regeln wie möglich und veranstaltete in Los Angeles die berüchtigten Underground-Partys *Butt Boys*. • *He has been at the helm of Tom of Finland endeavors since 1979, a video porn director, a guy who was a model for Bruce Weber and for Target Studios and* Drummer *magazine, and he tied for 1ˢᵗ place in the first International Mr. Leather. He broke as many rules as he could get away with and put on the notorious underground parties in Los Angeles called* Butt Boys. *He's cofounder and president of Tom of Finland Foundation.*

Epstein, David Parke – 154
(USA); Teilnehmer/*participant* Tom of Finland Art and Culture Festival. Der ehemalige Autor und Redakteur des Magazins *Esquire* lebt zusammen mit seiner Katze Compton am Sunset Junction in Los Angeles. • *Participant of the Tom of Finland Art and Culture Festival. The former author and writer for the magazine* Esquire *lives with his cat Compton at the Sunset Junction in Los Angeles.* davidepstein107@gmail.com

Gympel, Jan – 60
*1966 (Deutschland/*Germany*); Berliner Eingeborener, Journalist, Buchautor und manches mehr. Kann mit einer Schlagbohrmaschine umgehen. • *A Berlin native, journalist, book author and more. Can handle an impact drilling machine.*

Hayward, Mark Timothy – 326
*1970 (USA); Bachelor of Fine Arts an der School of the Art Institute of Chicago. Kurator, Autor, Illustrator und Storyboard-Zeichner • *Bachelor of Fine Arts at the School of the Art Institute of Chicago. Curator, author, illustrator, storyboard-artist.* markhayw@gmail.com

Hörmann, Rainer – 271
*1964 (Deutschland/*Germany*); Publizist und Lektor, lebt und arbeitet seit 1989 in Berlin. Autor zweier Bücher über die schwule Community in Deutschland (*Samstag ist ein guter Tag zum Schwulsein* und *Immer wieder samstags – Was die schwule Welt zusammenhält*, beides im Querverlag erschienen). • *He has been a publicist and lector in Berlin since 1989. He is the author of two books about the gay community (*Samstag ist ein guter Tag zum Schwulsein *and* Immer wieder samstags – Was die schwule Welt zusammenhält, *published by Querverlag).*

Hopf, Rinaldo – 6, 324ff
*1955 (Deutschland/*Germany*); Studium der Malerei, Ethnologie und Religionswissenschaften in Freiburg und San Francisco. Er lebt hauptsächlich in Berlin als Maler, Fotograf, Herausgeber und Kurator. 2017 war er Artist-in-Residence bei der Tom of Finland Foundation. Zahlreiche internationale Ausstellungen in Museen und Galerien. Buchveröffentlichungen: die Fotobände *Subversiv* (2004) und *Amore* (2006) sowie das Kunstbuch *Trickster* (2013), alle im Konkursbuch Verlag. Mitherausgeber *Mein schwules Auge*, Band 3-14/15 zus. mit Axel Schock, ab Band 16 zus. mit Fedya Ili. • *He studied painting, ethnology and religious studies and is based in Berlin as a painter, photographer, editor and curator. He was a TOM House Artist-in-Residence in 2017 and has had many international exhibitions in museums and galleries. Two books of his on photography:* Subversiv *(2004) and* Amore *(2006), and the art book* Trickster *(2013) were published by konkursbuch. He is co-editor of* My Gay Eye, *edition 3-14/15 with Axel Schock, volume 16 and further with Fedya Ili.* info@rinaldohopf.com; www.rinaldohopf.com

Karon, Jamison – 219
(USA); Schriftsteller und Filmemacher aus Los Angeles. Bachelor of Fine Arts in Theater an der University of Arizona. Nach seinem Abschluss arbeitete er drei Jahre in New York City an eigenen queeren Stoffen und trieb seine sexpositive Stimme in den amerikanischen Zeitgeist. Jamison ist Autor, Regisseur und Produzent der Web-Serie und des Kurzfilms *Sorry You're Sad* sowie des Kunstfilms *Last Night*. 2016 war er Artist-in-Residence bei der Tom of Finland Foundation, wo er ein erotisches Sachbuch, *How to Be a Fagot*, veröffentlichte. Jamison studiert derzeit Drehbuchschreiben am American Film Institute, wo er 2019 seinen Abschluss machen wird. • *Los Angeles based writer and filmmaker. He received a BFA in Theatre from the University of Arizona in 2012. For three years following graduation, Jamison worked on original queer content in New York City, propelling his sex-positive voice into the American zeitgeist. Jamison is the writer, director, and producer of the narrative web-series and short film* Sorry You're Sad, *as well as the art film* Last Night. *In 2016, Jamison was an artist-in-residence at Tom of Finland Foundation in Los Angeles, where he published a book of erotic non-fiction,* How to Be a Faggot. *Jamison is currently a*

screenwriting fellow at the American Film Institute, and will graduate in 2019. jamisonkaron@gmail.com

König, Ralf – 82
*1960 (Deutschland/*Germany*); Comiczeichner und Autor. Seit 1979 rund 60 Buchveröffentlichungen sowie Übersetzungen in 15 Sprachen. Zuletzt erschienen *Herbst in der Hose* und *Santa Claus Junior,* beides 2017. Zahlreiche Auszeichnungen, u.a. mit dem Mejor Obra Extranjera publicada en España, dem Max-und-Moritz Sonderpreis für ein herausragendes Lebenswerk und dem Wilhelm-Busch-Preis 2017. Lebt und zeichnet in Köln. Die Veröffentlichung der Zeichnung auf S. 83 (entnommen aus der Neuausgabe *Safere Zeiten + Macho Comix,* 1997) geschieht mit freundlicher Genehmigung des Männerschwarm Verlag Hamburg. • *Comic-strip artist and author. Since 1979, he has published 60 books with translations in 15 languages. Most recently released were* Herbst in der Hose *and* Santa Claus Junior *(both 2017). He received many awards, including the Mejor Obra Extranjera publicada en España, the Max-und-Moritz special award for an outstanding oeuvre and the Wilhelm-Busch-Award 2017. Lives and works in Cologne.*

Poole, Ralph J. – 362
(Deutschland/*Germany*); Professor für Amerikanistische Literatur- und Kulturwissenschaft an der Universität Salzburg. Davor war er u.a. Associate Professor of English an der Fatih University in Istanbul und Teilnehmer des Graduiertenkollegs „Geschlechterdifferenz & Literatur" in München. Derzeit leitet er ein Forschungsprojekt zu „Geschlechterkomödien der Amerikanischen Revolution". Seine Forschungsschwerpunkte liegen im Bereich der transkulturellen und transatlantischen Amerikanistik, des Films, Fernsehens und Theaters, der *Gender/Queer Studies* und der Populärkultur. • *Ralph J. Poole is professor for American Literature and Culture Studies at the University of Salzburg. Before that he was Associate Professor of English at the Fatih University in Istanbul and participant of the post graduate program "Gender Difference and Literature" in Munich. He leads a research project about "Gender Comedies of the American Revolution". His research focuses on transcultural and transatlantic American studies, movies, television and theatre, gender/queer studies and pop culture.* ralph.poole@sbg.ac.at; www.uni-salzburg.at/ang/poole

Ransdell-Bellenger, Marc – 92
*1968 (USA); seit 2009 Kurator der Tom of Finland Foundation. Zuvor übte er diese Tätigkeit unter anderem für Walt Disney Imagineering und die MGM Studios in Orlando sowie für die Sammlung des Art Museum der Florida International University aus. Er war zudem als Sammlungsarchivar für das Boca Raton Museum of Art und das Palm Beach Community College Museum of Art tätig. Er hatte darüber hinaus eine umfangreiche Karriere als Kunsthändler und fungierte während der Clinton-Administration im Auftrag des American Craft Council als Kurator für das Weiße Haus. • *Since 2009, Curator and Community Development at Tom of Finland Foundation. Prior to his time at TOM House he was curator for Walt Disney Imagineering at Walt Disney World and MGM Orlando Studios; Curator of Collections with The Art Museum at Florida International University; Collections Registrar for the Boca Raton Museum of Art; and Registrar for the Palm Beach Community College Museum of Art, The J. Patrick Lannan Gallery. He also has had an extensive career as a private art dealer and served on the American Craft Council as a special curator to the White House under the Clinton administration.* marcb@TomOfFinlandFoundation.org

Redlin, Rolf – 72
*1958 (Deutschland/*Germany*); als Sohn eines Hafenarbeiters in Hamburg geboren. Nach einem naturwissenschaftlichen Studium veröffentlichte er mehrere Sachbücher, darunter fünf Motorradbücher. Redlin lebt in Hamburg und Nordwestmecklenburg. Seine Romane *Bullenbeißer (2010), Bärensommer* (2011), *Bodycheck (2013),* und *Sprachlos* (2014) sind im Verlag Männerschwarm erschienen. • *Born as the son of a dock worker in Hamburg and after studying natural sciences, he published several nonfiction books, among them five motorcycle books. Redlin lives in Hamburg and North-West-Mecklenburg. His novels* Bullenbeißer (2010), Bärensommer (2011), Bodycheck (2013) *and* Sprachlos (2014) *were published by*

Männerschwarm Verlag Hamburg. www.rolf-redlin.de

Rehberg, Peter – 312
Kulturwissenschaftler und Publizist mit den Schwerpunkten Queer Theory, Masculinity Studies und Media Studies. Nachdem er von 2011 bis 2016 DAAD Associate Professor an der University of Texas at Austin war, forschte er am ICI Berlin – Institute for Cultural Inquiry über die Darstellung arabischer Männlichkeiten in der Kunst und in digitalen Medien. 2018 Max-Kade-Professor an der University of Illinois Chicago. 2018 erscheint sein Buch *Hipster Porn: Queere Männlichkeiten, affektive Sexualitäten und neue Medien* bei b_books. Darüber hinaus veröffentlichte er die Romane *Play, Fag Love, Boymen* (alle Männerschwarm Verlag) • *Peter Rehberg received his PhD from New York University in Germanic Languages and Literatures. He worked predominantly in the fields of queer theory, popular culture, and media studies. 2011-2016 DAAD Associate Professor at the University of Texas at Austin, 2018 Max-Kade-Professor at the University of Illinois in Chicago. In addition to his academic work, he also published three novels (*Play, Fag Love, Boymen*), worked as an editor for queer magazines, and is a regular contributor to the weekly* Der Freitag.

Reigns, Steven – 50
(USA); Schriftsteller und Pädagoge aus Los Angeles, der zum ersten Poet Laureate von West Hollywood gekürt wurde. Er ist Herausgeber des Bandes *My Life is Poetry* mit den Arbeiten seiner Schüler aus dem ersten autobiographischen Poesie-Workshop für LGBT-Oberstufenschüler. Er hat Schreibworkshops für LGBT-Jugendliche und Menschen, die mit HIV leben, durchgeführt. Derzeit fördert er den monatlichen Lambda Lit Book Club und arbeitet an einer neuen Gedichtsammlung. Lesungen im Rahmen der Tom of Finland Art and Culture Festivals. • *Los Angeles-based poet and educator who was appointed the first Poet Laureate of West Hollywood. He edited* My Life is Poetry, *showcasing his students' work from the first-ever autobiographical poetry workshop for LGBT seniors. Reigns has lectured and taught writing workshops around the country to LGBT youth and people living with HIV. Currently he facilitates the monthly Lambda Lit Book Club and is at work on a new collection of poetry. Tom of Finland Art and Culture Festival poet.* www.stevenreigns.com

Schock, Axel – 6, 82, 94
*1965 (Deutschland/*Germany*); Redakteur, Herausgeber, Buchautor und Journalist. Diverse Buchveröffentlichungen, u.a. *Die Bibliothek von Sodom. Das Buch der schwulen Bücher *(Eichborn Verlag), *Absolut Berlin. Das Berlin-Sammelsurium *(Hirschkäfer Verlag) und *Schwule Orte. 150 berühmt-berüchtigte Schauplätze.* (Querverlag). Mitherausgeber von *Mein schwules Auge,* Band 3-14. Seit 2013 Organisator des internationalen poesiefestival berlin. • *Journalist, editor and author of over a dozen books, mostly on LGBT subjects. Co-editor of* My Gay Eye, *editions 3-14. Since 2013 organizer of the International Poetry Festival in Berlin.* Axel.Schock@web.de

Sharp – 354
(USA); studierte Bildende Kunst, Kunstgeschichte und Design an verschiedenen Schulen des Mittleren Westens und leitete das Contemporary Arts Center in Cincinnati, Ohio. Er arbeitete 30 Jahre als Designer für Film und Fernsehen und verliebte sich vor mehr als zehn Jahren Hals über Kopf in die Tom of Finland Foundation. Herausgeber des Foundation-Newsletters *The Dispatch* und Chef-Kurator der Dauerausstellung der Foundation. Über die Kunst sagt Sharp: „Mich beeindrucken Anstand, Verrücktheit, strahlende Aufrichtigkeit und all die Dinge, du wiedersehen willst, wenn du nachts deine Augen schließt, bevor du einschläfst." • *Sharp studied Fine Arts, Art History and Design at several Midwest schools and managed the Contemporary Arts Center in Cincinnati, Ohio. He worked in design for film and television for 30 years and fell head-over-heels for Tom of Finland Foundation more than a decade ago. He has acted as the editor of its newsletter,* The Dispatch, *and is the Head Curator of its Permanent Collection. Says Sharp of art, "I'm impressed by integrity, wackiness, resplendent candor and all those things you want to revisit when you close your eyes at night before you* fall asleep."

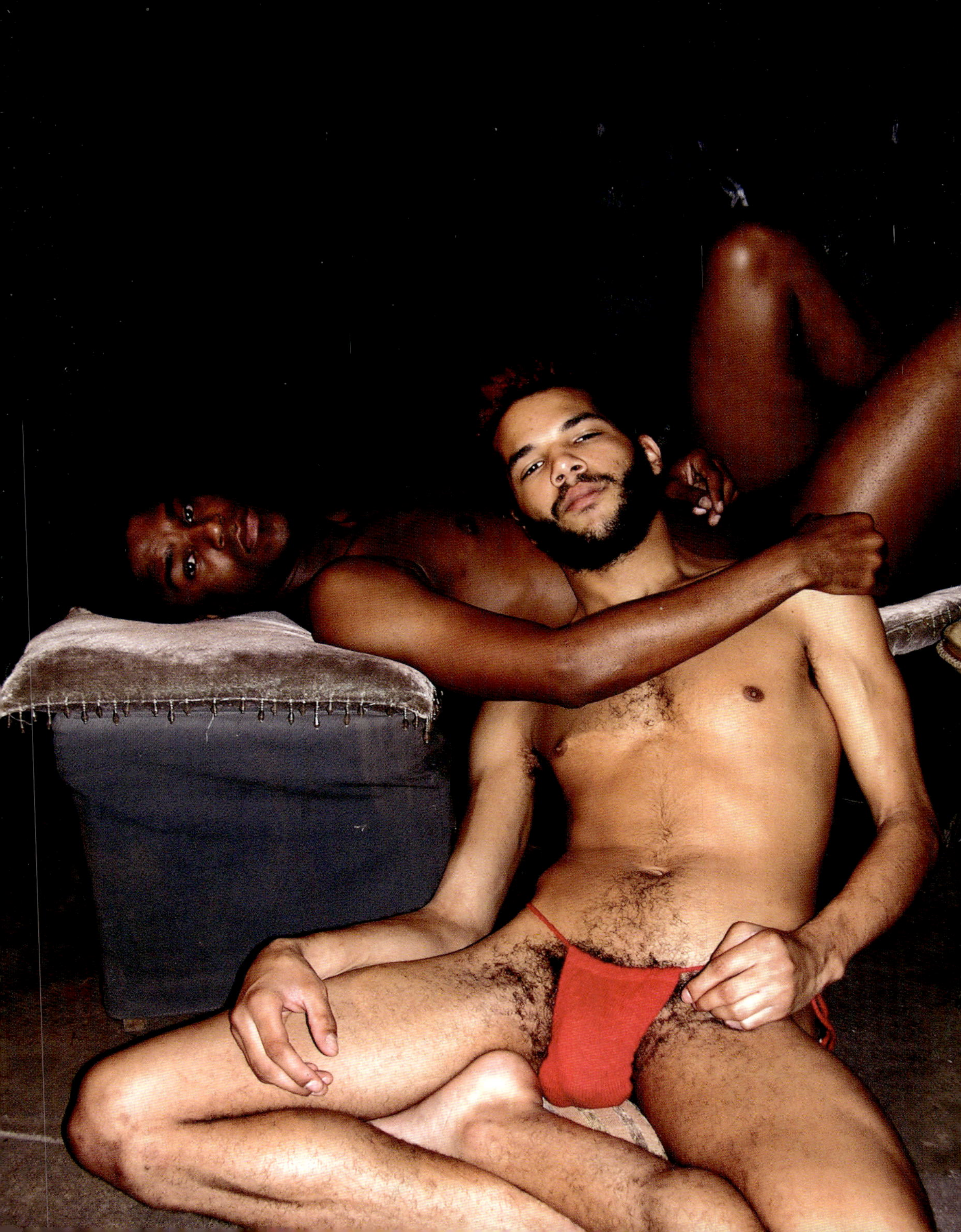